PRINCIPLES
OF
PHYSICAL
CHEMISTRY

William H. Hamill
University of Notre Dame

Russell R. Williams, Jr.
formerly of Haverford College

Colin MacKay
Haverford College

PRINCIPLES

OF

PHYSICAL

CHEMISTRY

second edition

PRENTICE-HALL, INC.
englewood cliffs, new jersey

Current printing (last digit):
10   9   8   7   6   5   4   3   2   1

Library of Congress Catalogue Card Number 65—27310

Printed in the United States of America
C—70964

PRENTICE-HALL INTERNATIONAL, INC. *London*
PRENTICE-HALL OF AUSTRALIA, PTY. LTD. *Sydney*
PRENTICE-HALL OF CANADA, LTD. *Toronto*
PRENTICE-HALL OF INDIA (PRIVATE) LTD. *New Delhi*
PRENTICE-HALL OF JAPAN, INC. *Tokyo*

PREFACE

In this revision we have tried to remain true to the original philosophy of the text. Our aim is at the average student of physical chemistry. We do not try to provide him with an encyclopedic overview of all of physical chemistry. Instead we strive for an examination in some detail of the basic areas of physical chemistry, and we try to conduct this examination with as much rigor as his preparation will permit. We hope that from this he will learn how physical chemists think about and attack chemical problems.

Thermodynamics is the core of introductory physical chemistry, and it is presented first to leave no doubts that it is self-contained. A minimum of non-thermodynamic explanation has been interpolated because it obscures the monolithic simplicity of thermodynamics and implies a fatal deficiency. The presentation of atomic and molecular structure has been treated more extensively, in both depth and scope. The final chapter on chemical statistics synthesizes these separate disciplines, but this order of presentation can be modified, and even inverted.

The chapter on Nuclear Chemistry has been eliminated, with regrets, because it is becoming more nearly identified with inorganic chemistry. We recommend to those who prefer to retain this topic the recent text by Bernard Harvey, *Introduction to Nuclear Physics and Chemistry* (Englewood Cliffs, N.J.: Prentice-Hall, Inc., 1962).

A mathematical appendix has been added to provide a handy review of some basic mathematical techniques. These include partial differentiation, series expansion, and some material required for specific developments in the later chapters.

We are indebted to many and acknowledge particularly the students of the University of Notre Dame and of Haverford College who have also taught and tested us. We solicit their continued cooperation. Professor George Strauss of Rutgers University and Professor Richard Fink of Amherst College read much of the text and made invaluable comments. The treatment of X-ray crystallography benefits from the good advice of Professor Alexander Tulinsky of Michigan State University. Professor Richard Wolfgang of Yale University contributed the problem sets he uses in his course there.

CONTENTS

12 Surface Chemistry   319

13 Atomic Structure   345

PRINCIPLES
OF
PHYSICAL
CHEMISTRY

1

INTRODUCTION AND DESCRIPTION OF THE PROPERTIES OF MATTER

1.1 Physical Chemistry

Physical chemistry is concerned with the measurement, description, and prediction of the characteristics of chemical systems and their interactions with each other with respect to the transfer of mass and energy. Some of the principal subdivisions of physical chemistry which will be introduced in this book are: (1) *chemical thermodynamics*, which deals with the transfer of energy in chemical changes and seeks to characterize the equilibrium state of chemical systems; (2) *chemical kinetics*, which deals with the rates and mechanisms of chemical changes; (3) *structure of matter*, a broad area of experimental and theoretical description of the properties of matter at the atomic and molecular level.

All considerations in the physical sciences begin with experimental measurement, and all theory must ultimately agree with experiment. Physical chemistry, in common with all physical sciences, depends heavily on theory for "understanding." Crudely, a *theory* is an integrated body of concepts which successfully correlates the behavior of a material system with an imagined system or *model* whose behavior is considered to be understood. For example, the kinetic theory of gases describes the behavior of an imagined system of point masses by the methods of classical mechanics and yields a moderately accurate description of the behavior of real gases. However, in at least one important instance, the wave mechanical theory of the electronic structure of atoms and molecules (see Chapters 13 and 14), the literal significance of the original models has been abandoned although the vocabulary of the theory

1

still employs such terms as *spin, angular momentum,* and *orbit* in referring to electrons. The "model" of this theory is now taken to be the Schrödinger wave equation, and insofar as it yields accurate descriptions of the behavior of matter in terms of measurable quantities such as mass, charge, time, and energy, it may be regarded as a satisfactory model. The thermodynamic approach to the correlation of chemical and physical phenomena is quite different from that of wave mechanics.

1.2 Thermodynamics

Thermodynamics is empirical, not speculative. It is based firmly upon experiment and observation, summarized and generalized in three abstractions known as the *laws of thermodynamics.* They are, in fact, unprovable, and therefore postulates or assumptions. They have not been arbitrarily invented and do not involve any assumptions about atomic and molecular structure but are founded upon observation about the universe as it is, in terms of instrumental operations. As such, the laws of thermodynamics provide a basis for a completely rigorous science for correlating such observations. The systems suitable for examination and thermodynamic treatment comprise bulk matter, that is, gases, liquids, and solids. Suitable input data include temperature, pressure, volume, composition, heat, and work. Any problem is solved first in generalized symbolic form by thermodynamic operations in terms of experimentally established, general relationships such as (pressure) × (volume) = const. × (temperature). Proceeding in this manner one can obtain formulas involving only experimentally measurable quantities, and therefore verifiable. From such prosaic raw material and the three laws of thermodynamics scientists have achieved generalizations of the greatest importance.

The conceptual approach of thermodynamics will be unfamiliar, and perhaps less congenial than others which use models. It is nonpictorial and altogether abstract. Its language is mathematics, but of no great difficulty. In fact, the most striking characteristic of thermodynamics is the essential simplicity of its approach. This simplicity cannot be perceived readily by the beginner unless all facts and ideas which are superfluous and extraneous to the subject are excluded. For this reason, the early chapters of this book deal only with thermodynamics, while kinetics and the structure of matter appear later. It seems preferable not to try to "explain" thermodynamics by invoking the methods and conclusions of other disciplines.

Before proceeding to thermodynamics we need some facts and empirical generalizations which have been found useful in describing the behavior of bulk matter. The rest of this chapter is devoted to these thermodynamic preliminaries.

The subject of any investigation is a *system,* whether the study consists of experimental observations or pencil-and-paper operations. In experimental work the system is necessarily *real,* but in pencil-and-paper work the system treated is often *ideal*, so that the problem can be treated more simply. An ideal system is always partly but not completely imaginary, since it is intended to serve as a simplified but still realistic substitute for the actual system. This simplification invariably introduces some inaccuracies and the equations which result are often valid only under special "limiting conditions," as, for example, Boyle's law, which is valid only in the limit of vanishingly small pressures. (See section 1.4.)

Other systems in the immediate environment which interact by exchange of matter or energy with the system of primary interest are treated collectively as the *surroundings*. A *closed system* does not exchange matter with the surroundings and an *isolated system* exchanges neither matter nor energy.

A system is characterized by describing its *state*, specifying a sufficient number of its properties, such as mass, volume, temperature, or pressure, so that another investigator can construct a duplicate. Such properties are of two types: (1) *extensive* properties, which vary with the size of the system, such as mass, volume, heat capacity, or electric charge; and (2) *intensive* properties, which do not depend on the size of the system, such as density, temperature, or refractive index.

It is not necessary to specify every possible property of a system in order to characterize its state. For a given mass of a known pure substance it suffices to specify any two independent variables, usually pressure and temperature. Once these are known, other properties, such as volume, refractive index, and heat capacity, are automatically fixed. In a system of n components it is necessary to specify, in addition to three properties such as mass, pressure, and temperature, $n - 1$ additional properties, that is, quantities describing the composition of the system. The total number of properties to be specified is therefore $n + 2$.

The preceding statement requires some qualification since it is only for "well behaved" systems of n components that the specification of $n + 2$ independent properties is sufficient to characterize the state of the system. Except when rate phenomena are of primary interest, it is to be understood that the system is stable and that its properties are reproducible and independent of its history. Some systems may attain a given state very rapidly, as, for example, the system: one gram of oxygen gas at 50° and one atmosphere pressure. However, the properties of a system such as one gram of acetic acid plus one gram of ethanol at 25° and one atmosphere may change with time until a final equilibrium state has been reached in which acetic acid, ethanol, ethyl acetate, and water are all present. This final state can be characterized with precision and can be reproduced indefinitely. Both of the preceding types of systems can be said to be "well behaved." On the other hand, a solution of egg albumin is more difficult to characterize, and some types of measurements on it give results depending on its previous history. The stress-strain relation of rubber depends on the degree and duration of prior elongations, and this system behaves reproducibly only within a restricted range of conditions.

A *change in state* consists of any change in one or more properties of a system. Any experimentally detectable change is a change in state. Such changes are most conveniently described in the form of chemical equations, as for example:

(i) $$H_2O(c, 1 \text{ atm.}, 0°) = H_2O(1, 1 \text{ atm.}, 0°)$$
(ii) $$O_2(g, 10 \text{ atm.}, 50°) = O_2(g, 1 \text{ atm.}, 50°)$$
(iii) $$Zn(c, 1 \text{ atm.}, 25°) + 2HCl(1 \text{ } M \text{ aq.}, 1 \text{ atm.}, 25°)$$
$$= ZnCl_2(1 \text{ } M \text{ aq.}, 1 \text{ atm.}, 25°) + H_2(g, 1 \text{ atm.}, 25°)$$

State of aggregation is indicated by c for crystalline (sometimes s for solid), l for liquid, g for gaseous.

Such statements of change in state are not to be confused with thermo-dynamic *processes* for which a detailed knowledge of the actual path is required. To describe a process it is necessary to specify every intermediate state; to describe a change in state it is sufficient to specify only the *initial state* and the *final state*. Thus the change in state (ii) above may be attended by absorp-tion of heat from the surroundings in any amount from zero to 1470 cal. per mole of oxygen, depending on the path of expansion. If it is specified that the gas is subjected to a constant pressure of 1 atm. during expansion, and that the temperature is maintained at 50° throughout, then the process has been adequately specified and the heat absorbed will amount to 575 cal. per mole.

Processes which occur at constant temperature are called *isothermal;* at constant pressure, *isobaric;* and at constant volume, *isochoric*, although the last term is rarely used. Whenever, by choice or by necessity, there is no ex-change of heat between system and surroundings, the process is called *adiabatic*. A calorimetric measurement may be conducted in an adiabatic manner for reasons of experimental convenience. Flames and explosions are nearly ad-iabatic by nature because the chemical change is fast and the system reaches its final temperature before heat loss is appreciable. Meteorological changes may be nearly adiabatic, though slow, because the surface to volume ratio is small.

If the state of a system does not change with time while the surroundings are unaltered or while it is isolated, it is in a state of *equilibrium*. If the different parts of a system are at rest with reference to each other (mechanical equi-librium), and if it is not spontaneously changing in chemical composition, it is in a state of *chemical equilibrium*. When it is also in thermal equilibrium, both in respect to its parts and its surroundings, it is in a state of *thermodynamic equilibrium*.

1.3 Temperature

Before discussing chemical phenomena, in which the reactants and products are gases, liquids, solids, and solutions, we must examine some of the major physical properties of these states of matter.

One of the most important of the fundamental properties of matter is tem-perature, and yet this property and its measurement are much more subtle than such properties as mass, length, or time. In the case of the latter properties a standard is adopted and assigned a value for the property, e.g., the standard kilogram. The value of the property for other bodies or events is measured by direct or indirect comparison and given in multiple or submultiple units. In the case of temperature this method of comparison with a single standard is not possible.

We usually say that temperature is measured with a thermometer but in actual fact the observation which we make is one of change in volume, that is, the change in the length of a column of fluid in a capillary tube. We presume that this measurement of volume bears some unique relation to the temperature of the system, such as

$$t = kV + c$$

where t is temperature, V is volume, k and c are constants. The thermometer scale is defined by calibration at fixed points, i.e., systems of reproducible temperature, such as ice-water at 1 atm. (the ice point), and boiling water at 1 atm. (the steam point). These points are defined as $0°$ and $100°$ on the centigrade scale. Unless otherwise specified, all temperatures in this text are given in the centigrade scale, and the symbol C is omitted.

The choice of fixed points in the centigrade scale implies that the temperature interval between them is to be divided into one hundred equal parts and that temperatures above and below the fixed points may be measured by suitable extrapolation. However, it must be kept in mind that such a scale is divided into units of volume rather than temperature. This shortcoming may be illustrated by comparing the measurements obtained with two different thermometric fluids: mercury, the fluid used in most common thermometers, and amyl alcohol. Suppose that the mercury thermometer and the alcohol thermometer are each marked at the ice point and the steam point. Then on each thermometer the space between these marks is divided into one hundred equal intervals of volume called *degrees*. While the two thermometers necessarily agree in their readings at $0°$ and $100°$, if they are placed in a bath of such a temperature that the mercury thermometer reads $50°$ it will be found that the amyl alcohol thermometer reads $42.4°$. Its volume has increased by less than half the change observed between the fixed points. In general, two thermometers using different fluids cannot be expected to agree except at common points of calibration, although in some instances the disagreements are small. It is apparent that the temperature scale may depend on the choice of thermometric fluid as well as upon the choice of fixed points. In a later section a method of avoiding this limitation of temperature measurement will be discussed.

1.4 Isothermal Gas Expansion

Gases are distinguished by their ability to expand without limit to fill the space available, and to exert pressure uniformly on all walls of a container. Over a moderate range of pressures many gases show, at constant temperature, the simple relationship between pressure and volume known as *Boyle's law: For a given mass of gas at a constant temperature, the volume is inversely proportional to the pressure.*

$$P_1 V_1 = P_2 V_2 = const. \text{ at const. temp.} \tag{1.1}$$

Boyle's law may be expressed in graphical form as shown in Fig. 1.1, in which the data for a sample of gas at a given temperature lie on a rectangular hyperbola called an isotherm. The curves in the figure refer to several temperatures for the same sample.

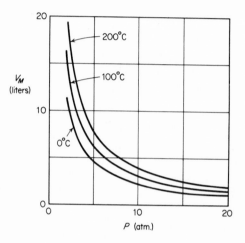

V_M (liters)

200°C

100°C

0°C

P (atm.)

FIG. 1.1. Gas isotherms (sample = 1 mole).

EXERCISE 1.1

A cylinder of compressed gas at 145 atm. and 20° when opened liberates 194 cubic feet of gas at 1 atm. and 20°. What is the volume of the tank?   *Ans.* 1.34 cu. ft.

EXERCISE 1.2

Two gas samples at a common temperature occupy volumes V_a at P_a and V_b at P_b. When a connecting valve is opened, what will be the common pressure?

Ans. $(P_a V_a + P_b V_b)/(V_a + V_b)$.

The value of the constant in equation (1.1) depends on the size of the sample. At any given pressure and temperature the volume of the sample is proportional to its weight. One gram of carbon dioxide occupies 0.506 l. at 1 atm. and 0°, and therefore 10 g. of this gas at the same pressure and temperature will occupy 5.06 l.

An important regularity appears if the volumes occupied by 1 gram-molecular weight (V_M) of various gases are compared: *The gram-molecular volumes of all gases are approximately the same when measured at the same temperature and at the same low pressure.* For example, at 0° and 1 atm.

	Density (g./l.)	V_M (l.)
H_2	0.0899	22.25
O_2	1.429	22.40
N_2	1.2506	22.35
CO_2	1.977	22.25

This regularity was first stated by Avogadro as a hypothesis (now given the status of a law) that *equal volumes of gases under the same conditions of temperature and pressure contain the same number of molecules.*

EXERCISE 1.3

A bulb filled with oxygen at $t°$ and p atm. weighs 220.400 g. Evacuated it weighs 219.850 g. Filled with an unknown gas, also at $t°$ and p atm., the bulb weighs 221.005 g. Find the molecular weight of the gas.   *Ans.* 67.

Since the volume of a gas sample at constant pressure and temperature is proportional to the number of moles of gas in the sample, equation (1.1) may be written

$$PV = nk \qquad (1.2)$$

where n is the number of moles of gas in the sample and the proportionality constant k is very nearly the same for all gases at the same temperature, but varies with temperature. Its value is 22.4 l. atm. at 0° and 30.6 l. atm. at 100°.

EXERCISE 1.4

A sample of gas at 100° and 0.80 atm. has a density 1.15 g/l. What is the molecular weight?   *Ans.* 44.

Boyle's law is only an approximate description of the behavior of real gases, and this approximation becomes less satisfactory as the pressure increases and as the temperature decreases. This is shown in Fig. 1.2 where observed values of PV_M are plotted versus pressure for several gases at 0° and 100°.

While the curves for PV_M vs. P for various gases at a given temperature behave differently with increasing pressure, they all have precisely the same intercept on the PV_M axis, that is, *the limiting value $(PV_M)^0$ of the pressure-volume product as P approaches zero is independent of the nature of the gas and depends only on the temperature.* The value of $(PV_M)^0$ at 0° is 22.4136 l. atm. and at 100° the value is 30.6192 l. atm.

In the precise description of real gases Boyle's law and Avogadro's law may be regarded as limiting relations approached at infinitely small pressures. The behavior of real gases at small pressure may be described approximately by these relations, but accurate description will require more complicated formulas.

As a first step in developing a more accurate description of real gases we note that for some substances the plot of PV_M versus P is an approximately straight line. An equation of the type

$$PV_M = (PV_M)^0 + bP \qquad (1.3)$$

will evidently describe hydrogen up to 1000 atm. The parameter b is an empirical constant adjusted to best describe the data.

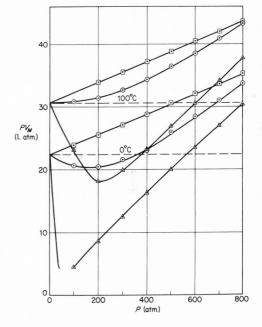

FIG. 1.2. Deviations from Boyle's law. □ hydrogen; ⊙ oxygen; △ carbon dioxide.

EXERCISE 1.5

Evaluate the constant b of equation (1.3) from the slope of the curve for hydrogen at 100° in Fig. 1.2. From this measurement find the % difference between $(PV_M)^0$ and PV_M at 1 atm.   *Ans.* $b = 0.0164$ l./mole; 0.073 %.

1.5 Thermal Expansion of Gases

When a gas confined at a constant pressure is heated, its volume increases. From Fig. 1.2 it appears that PV_M at large pressures depends on the nature of the gas and the pressure as well as the temperature. However, as the pressure approaches zero, individual characteristics vanish, and all substances in the gaseous state approach a limiting universal law. *The value of* $(PV_M)^0$ *depends only on the temperature.*

Values of $(PV_M)^0$ are very nearly a linear function of the centigrade temperature (measured by a mercury thermometer) as shown in Fig. 1.3. That is,

$$(PV_M)^0 = a + bt \tag{1.4}$$

where t is the centigrade temperature. This relation is a form of Charles' law.

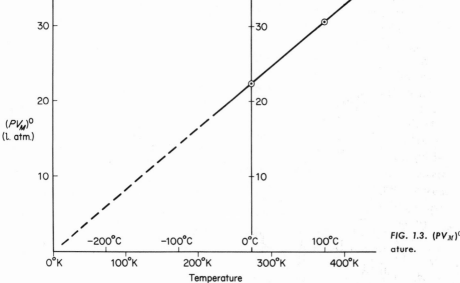

FIG. 1.3. $(PV_M)^0$ vs. temperature.

In order to avoid the arbitrariness involved in the choice of mercury (or any other particular fluid) as a measure of temperature, it is better to define a *gas temperature scale* such that $(PV_M)^0$ is a *precisely* linear function of temperature. (On this scale, the thermal expansion coefficient of mercury is almost, but not precisely, constant.) It is convenient, but completely arbitrary, to retain the centigrade definition of the size of the degree, dividing the interval between the ice point and the steam point into 100 degrees.

Since a variety of substances (gases) show precisely the same relation between $(PV_M)^0$ and t given in Fig. 1.3 and equation (1.4), it would appear that there is a natural lower limit on the gas temperature scale, namely, the intercept with the horizontal axis. This can be found by evaluating the constants a and b in equation (1.4) as follows: Since $(PV_M)^0 = 30.6192$ l. atm. at $100°C$ and 22.4136 l. atm. at $0°C$, solution of the simultaneous equations

$$30.6192 = a + 100b, \qquad 22.4136 = a$$

yields $\qquad\qquad\qquad b = 0.082056$ l. atm. deg.$^{-1}$

Therefore the temperature at which $(PV_M)^0 = 0$ is given by

$$0 = 22.4136 + 0.082056\, t$$

$$t = -273.15°C$$

We shall provisionally adopt this natural zero on the gas temperature scale as an *absolute zero*. This zero defines an absolute temperature scale, that is,

$$(PV_M)^0 = bT(\text{abs.}) \qquad\qquad (1.5)$$

$$T_{\text{steam}} - T_{\text{ice}} = 100° \qquad\qquad (1.6)$$

This choice will necessarily be well suited to describing thermal expansion of gases. Fortunately, this way of measuring temperature proves to be equally satisfactory in other applications as well; the ideal gas temperature scale is identical with another independent measure of temperature, the thermodynamic or Kelvin scale. Therefore we shall use T and $°K$ to designate absolute temperature.

Since we have retained the centigrade definition of the size of the degree, the relation between the centigrade and Kelvin temperature scales is one of simple translation along the temperature axis as indicated in Fig. 1.3. The slope of $(PV_M)^0$ versus T is unchanged, $b = 0.082056$ l. atm deg.$^{-1}$, while the new intercept is zero.

The fact that $(PV_M)^0$ versus absolute temperature passes through the origin of the graph does not imply anything regarding the volume of samples at the absolute zero, but is simply a mathematical consequence of their behavior at higher temperatures. On the absolute temperature scale

$$T_{\text{ice}} = 22.4136/0.082056 = 273.15°K$$

and all other centigrade temperatures (t) are related to the Kelvin temperature (T) by

$$T = t + 273.15°$$

While the simple relation in equation (1.5) applies only to $(PV_M)^0$, it is a good approximation to the behavior of real gases at moderate pressures. Considering thermal expansion at constant pressure, it states that *the volume of a gas is directly proportional to its absolute temperature*, a more common form of *Charles' law*.

$$V = kT \text{ at const. } P$$

$$V_1/T_1 = V_2/T_2 = V_3/T_3 \qquad\qquad (1.7)$$

EXERCISE 1.6

Charles' law defines a method of measuring temperature. A sample of gas occupies 100 cc. at 0° and 1 atm. What is the value of t when the gas volume is 80 cc. at 1 atm? *Ans.* −55°.

1.6 The Ideal Gas Law

An equation of state is a mathematical expression of the observed relationship between the various properties of a sample of matter, particularly the pressure, volume, temperature, and amount of sample. It has been shown that Boyle's law ($PV = nk$) is an approximate description of the isothermal behavior of real gases at low pressures. It has been further shown that $(PV)^0$ is a linear function of temperature and that this property may be used to define an absolute temperature scale such that $(PV)^0$ is proportional to the absolute temperature. For real gases at low pressures, this relation

$$PV = nRT \qquad (1.8)$$

is an approximate equation of state known as the *ideal gas law*. The quantity R is known as the *gas constant*.

EXERCISE 1.7

Four 1. of gas at 25° and 1 atm. is heated to 150° and expanded to 6 l. What will be the final pressure? *Ans.* 0.95 atm.

The value of R, the gas constant, has been obtained from previous data on the value of $(PV_M)^0$ at various temperatures.

$$R = (PV_M)^0/T = 22.4136/273.15 = 0.082056 \text{ 1. atm. mole}^{-1} \text{ deg.}^{-1}$$

It is useful to note that the liter-atmosphere has the dimension of energy and therefore, in general, the dimensions of the gas constant must be energy mole^{-1} deg.$^{-1}$

EXERCISE 1.8

Compute the volume of 1 mole of hydrogen at 200 atm. and 100°, using the ideal gas law. Compare the measured volume indicated by the value of PV_M at 100° and 200 atm. in Fig. 1.2. *Ans.* Ideal = 0.153 1.; real = 0.168 1.

Equation (1.8) may be readily modified to show the connection between gas density and molecular weight. The mole number n can be expressed in terms of sample weight W and molecular weight M, to give

$$PV = (W/M)RT$$

Solving for gas density ρ gives

$$\rho = W/V = PM/RT \qquad (1.9)$$

Although this relation is only approximate for real gases at finite pressures, it sometimes supplies adequate information, since chemical analysis can give the precise empirical formula of a compound and an approximate value of M suffices to determine the molecular formula.

EXERCISE 1.9

A compound analyzes 24.5% C, 4.1% H, 71.4% Cl. Find the empirical formula. The gas density is approximately 2.8 g./l. at 700 mm. and 100°. Find the molecular formula.   *Ans.* $C_2H_4Cl_2$.

Equation (1.9) can be used to obtain accurate molecular weights as follows: Densities are measured at several low pressures and the function ρ/P is plotted versus pressure, as in Fig. 1.4. The points usually lie on a very nearly straight line. That is

$$\frac{\rho}{P} = \left(\frac{\rho}{P}\right)^0 + aP \tag{1.10}$$

where a is a constant. Since real gases approach ideal behavior at low pressures (see Fig. 1.2), the intercept of the curve should give an accurate value of the molecular weight.

$$\left(\frac{\rho}{P}\right)^0 = \frac{M}{RT}, \qquad M = \left(\frac{\rho}{P}\right)^0 RT \tag{1.11}$$

In Fig. 1.4, a straight line drawn through the data gives an intercept corresponding to $M = 64.06$ for sulfur dioxide.

Gas mixtures can be treated by application of *Dalton's law*, which states that *in a mixture of gases the total pressure is equal to the sum of the partial pressures of the separate components.* The partial pressure of a component is defined as the pressure that it would exert if present alone in the system, and for the ith component of an ideal gas,

$$P_i = n_i \frac{RT}{V} \tag{1.12}$$

where V is the volume of the system. Dalton's law is

$$P_t = P_1 + P_2 + P_3 + \cdots = \sum_i P_i \tag{1.13}$$

where P_t is the total pressure. Taking each component to be ideal,

$$P_t = \frac{RT}{V} \sum_i n_i = n_t \frac{RT}{V} \tag{1.14}$$

where $n_t = n_1 + n_2 + n_3 + \cdots = \sum_i n_i$

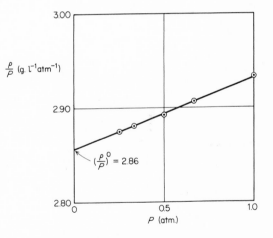

FIG. 1.4. Molecular weight of sulfur dioxide from gas density measurements at 0°C [after E. Moles, T. Toral, and A. Escribano, *Trans. Far. Soc.*, **35**, 1451 (1939)].

EXERCISE 1.10

An equimolar mixture of hydrogen and oxygen occupies 80 cc. at 0.24 atm. and 100°. What will be the pressure of the gaseous mixture after ignition at 100°?   *Ans.* 0.18 atm.

Another useful form of this relation is obtained by stating the composition in terms of mole fractions. The mole fraction X_i of the ith component is the number of moles of that component divided by the total number of moles of all components.

$$X_i = n_i/n_t$$

Dividing equation (1.12) by $P_t = n_t RT/V$ we have

$$P_i/P_t = n_i/n_t = X_i$$

or

$$P_i = X_i P_t \tag{1.15}$$

Dalton's law of partial pressures can be used to determine the composition of a two-component gas mixture from gas density measurements. For example, if a mixture of methane ($M = 16$) and ethane ($M = 30$) has a gas density of 1.00 g./l. at 1 atm, and 0°, its composition is computed as follows:

$$P_t V/RT = n_t = n_{CH_4} + n_{C_2H_6}$$

$$P_t V/RT = W_{CH_4}/M_{CH_4} + W_{C_2H_6}/M_{C_2H_6}$$

We also have the relation

$$W_{CH_4} + W_{C_2H_6} = 1.00 \text{ g./l. of mixture}$$

Substituting, we have

$$\frac{1 \times 1}{0.082 \times 273} = \frac{W_{CH_4}}{16} + \frac{1 - W_{CH_4}}{30}$$

$$W_{CH_4} = 0.39 \text{ g.}$$

in the sample of total weight 1.00 g.

1.7 Equations of State for Real Gases

Gas imperfections, or deviations from the ideal gas law, may be stated in terms of the compressibility factor z, which is defined by

$$z = PV/nRT \tag{1.16}$$

A compressibility factor close to unity means nearly ideal behavior, and a compressibility factor significantly different from unity attests to the inadequacy of the ideal gas law.

Figure 1.2 illustrates the pressure dependence of the compressibility factor of three typical gases at two temperatures. We may recall that the intercept of the curves on the PV axis defines the value of $nRT = PV$. A horizontal line drawn from this intercept at any temperature corresponds to $z = 1$. Values of (PV) greater than $(PV)^0$ correspond to $z > 1$ and, conversely, values of (PV) less than $(PV)^0$ correspond to $z < 1$. It appears from the figure that the compressibility factor depends upon temperature, and that the minimum exhibited by the more condensable gases tends to disappear at higher temperatures.

There are several equations of state which attempt to describe the behavior of real gases more accurately than does the ideal gas law. Some of these are entirely empirical, obtained by simply fitting an equation with adjustable parameters to the observed data, with no implication of any physical significance to the various terms. On the other hand, some equations of state have been used in which correction terms are based on a concept of the causes of deviation from ideality. These may properly be called semi-theoretical; a simple example of this type is the van der Waals equation:

$$(P + an^2/V^2)(V - nb) = nRT \qquad (1.17)$$

The origin of the correction terms can be seen from a qualitative consideration of the behavior of gases at high densities (small molar volumes). The term nb arises from the fact that gases are not infinitely compressible, due to the finite volume of the gas molecules. A correction for this effect is made by subtracting from the observed volume a quantity proportional to the number of moles of gas in the system. The constant b is sometimes referred to as the molecular volume (per mole) and its value depends primarily on the nature of the gas.

The term an^2/V^2 allows for the fact that molecules attract each other. These forces are responsible for condensation of vapor to liquid, an effect expected to be proportional to the square of the density of the gas and to the nature of the gas. The attractive forces act in the same sense as an externally applied pressure; the effective pressure on the gas is determined by the combined internal and external forces.

The van der Waals constants, a and b, are adjustable parameters characteristic of the individual gas and also dependent on the temperature of the system. They are chosen to fit the observed gas isotherm over a range of pressures and volumes. Table 1.1 gives values of the van der Waals constants for some common gases.

TABLE 1.1

PROPERTIES OF GASES

Substance	van der Waals Constants a (l.^{2} atm. mole^{-2})	b (l. mole^{-1})	Critical Constants T_c (°K)	P_c (atm.)
He	0.0341	0.0237	5.3	2.26
H$_2$	0.2444	0.0266	33.3	12.8
N$_2$	1.390	0.0391	126.1	33.5
CO	1.485	0.0399	134.2	35.0
O$_2$	1.360	0.0318	154.4	49.7
CH$_4$	2.253	0.0428	190.7	45.8
C$_2$H$_4$	4.471	0.0571	282.9	50.9
CO$_2$	3.592	0.0427	304.3	73.0
NH$_3$	4.170	0.0371	405.6	111.5
SO$_2$	6.714	0.0564	430.4	77.7
H$_2$O	5.464	0.0305	647.2	217.7

The van der Waals equation can describe pressure-volume data more accurately than the ideal gas law since it allows for variation of PV with pressure.

The information most readily obtained from the van der Waals equation is the pressure of a gas sample at a given volume and temperature. Solving equation (1.17) for the pressure, we have

$$P = nRT/(V - nb) - an^2/V^2 \tag{1.18}$$

or for comparison with the data in Fig. 1.2, we may compute PV_M by taking $n = 1$ and multiplying by V_M

$$PV_M = \frac{RT}{1 - b/V_M} - \frac{a}{V_M} \tag{1.19}$$

With increasing pressure (decreasing V_M) the first term on the right hand side of equation (1.19) leads to increasing values of PV_M, while the second term tends to diminish PV_M. Therefore it should be possible to describe, at least qualitatively, a curve such as that for oxygen at $0°$ in Fig. 1.2.

EXERCISE 1.11

From the data in Table 1.1 and equation (1.19), evaluate PV_M for oxygen at $0°$ and 800 atm. by successive approximations. Compare this result with the fact that $z = 1.50$.

EXERCISE 1.12

At 200 atm. and $0°$ the ideal gas law predicts the molar volume of oxygen to be 0.1120 l. Use the van der Waals equation (1.18) to predict the pressure of 1 mole of oxygen in this volume.   *Ans.* 171 atm.

For comparison with the result obtained in the preceding exercise, we find from Fig. 1.2 that in this region of pressure $PV_M = 20.5$ l. atm. ($z = 0.915$) for oxygen and therefore the observed pressure of 1 mole in 0.1120 l. is 184 atm. The results of similar computations at other volumes are given in Table 1.2. It is evident from these values that the van der Waals equation is of some use in describing deviations of a few per cent, but that it is quite inadequate at high pressures.

Several more complex and more nearly accurate equations of state are available. One of the most useful of these is the virial equation, which may be regarded as an extended form of equation (1.3). It contains a series of correction terms in increasing powers of $1/V$ or P which take account of the change in PV with increasing gas density. Written in a form for computation of the pressure of n moles of gas in volume V, the equation is

$$P = nRT/V + \beta n^2/V^2 + \gamma n^3/V^3 + \delta n^4/V^4 \tag{1.20}$$

The coefficients β, γ, and δ depend on the nature of the gas and on the temperature. J. A. Beattie [*Chem. Rev.*, **44,** 144 (1949)] has developed the following relations for the temperature dependence of the virial coefficients.

$$\beta = RTB_0 - A_0 - Rc/T^2$$
$$\gamma = -RTB_0 + A_0 a - RB_0 c/T^2 \tag{1.21}$$
$$\delta = RB_0 bc/T^2$$

The several constants have the following values for oxygen: $A_0 = 1.4911$ l.^{2} atm., $a = 0.02562$ l., $B_0 = 0.04624$ l., $b = 0.004208$ l., and $c = 4.80 \times 10^4$ l. deg.^{3}. Inserting these values in equation (1.21) we may compute the virial coefficients per mole of oxygen at 0°.

$$\beta = -0.4300 \text{ l.}^2 \text{ atm.}$$

$$\gamma = 0.03270 \text{ l.}^3 \text{ atm.}$$

$$\delta = 4.797 \times 10^{-6} \text{ l.}^4 \text{ atm.}$$

EXCERCISE 1.13

Show that equation (1.20) and the values of β, γ, and δ for oxygen at 0° permit one to locate a minimum in PV vs. P (cf. Fig. 1.2).

Values of the pressures given by the virial equation for several other volumes are given in Table 1.2 for comparison with the observed pressure and with the predictions of other equations of state. It is evident that the virial equation is useful over a much greater range of pressure than the van der Waals equation. This improvement follows from the increased number of adjustable parameters.

TABLE 1.2

TEST OF EQUATIONS OF STATE; OXYGEN AT 0°

Molar vol.	Ideal P	v.d.W. P	Virial P	Real P
0.224 l.	100 atm.	89 atm.	94 atm.	94 atm.
0.112	200	171	190	184
0.0560	400	492	446	440
0.0448	500	1040	650	675

1.8 Liquefaction of Gases

Any gas can be liquefied if subjected to sufficiently high pressure and low temperature, but there exists for each gas a certain temperature above which it cannot be liquefied, no matter how great the pressure. This temperature is the *critical temperature T_c*. At this temperature there will also be a minimum *critical pressure P_c* required for liquefaction and a corresponding *critical volume V_c*. The critical constants for several substances are given in Table 1.1.

The isotherms of a gas which is near its critical temperature are badly distorted from the hyperbolic shape corresponding to Boyle's law. Isotherms for isopentane near the critical point are shown in Fig. 1.5. The isotherms corresponding to temperatures below the critical temperature have a discontinuity due to the difference in molar volume of the liquid and gas. This difference decreases as the critical temperature is approached and above it disappears entirely. That is, the density of the liquid and of the vapor in equilibrium with it approach each other with increasing temperature and become equal at the critical temperature.

The critical properties of various gases may be quite different from one an-

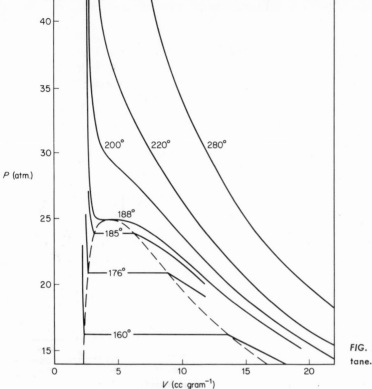

FIG. 1.5. Isotherms of isopentane.

other; a qualitative comparison of the critical constants in Table 1.1 with the compressibility factors of Fig. 1.2 shows that the degree of deviation from ideality is greatest when the pressure and temperature of the gas are near the critical pressure and temperature of that substance. This suggests that for the purpose of considering deviations from ideality, the relation of the temperature and pressure of the system to the critical temperature and pressure are more important than their absolute values. To assist in this correlation we define the *reduced temperature* T_r and *reduced pressure* P_r by

$$T_r = T/T_c, \qquad P_r = P/P_c \qquad (1.22)$$

When the compressibility factors are plotted as a function of the reduced pressure at a given reduced temperature, as in Fig. 1.6, the points for various substances fall on the same curve. This regularity permits the prediction of the compressibility factor over a wide range of temperature and pressure from a knowledge of the critical constants of the substance concerned. For example, to find the compressibility factor for carbon dioxide at 122° and 300 atm., we obtain the critical properties of this substance from Table 1.1 and find

$$T_r = 395/304.3 = 1.30, \qquad P_r = 300/73.0 = 4.11$$

Since the curve for $T_r = 1.3$ is not given in Fig. 1.6, the value of z is estimated by interpolation, yielding $z = 0.70$, that is,

$$PV/nRT = 0.70 \text{ for } CO_2 \text{ at } 122° \text{ and } 300 \text{ atm.}$$

EXERCISE 1.14

From the data given in Fig. 1.6 and Table 1.1 compute the molar volume of ammonia at 172° and 167 atm.   *Ans.* 0.11 1.

1.9 Properties of Liquids and Solids

The liquid state is usually distinguished from the gaseous state by higher density and smaller compressibility. At any given temperature below the critical temperature there will be a characteristic pressure at which the liquid and vapor can coexist. In Fig. 1.5, the isotherms referring to temperatures less than the critical temperature show a discontinuity. At the pressure corresponding to this discontinuity, both phases are present; the total volume of the system varies with the relative amount of each phase. At any given temperature there is only one pressure at which both phases can exist in equilibrium. This pressure is the *equilibrium vapor pressure* of the liquid at that temperature. From Fig. 1.5 it is evident that the equilibrium vapor pressure increases with increasing temperature, a behavior characteristic of all liquids.

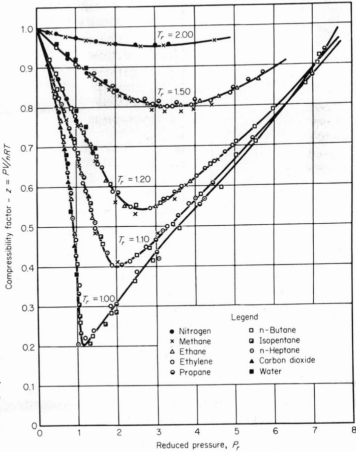

FIG. 1.6. Compressibility factor as function of reduced state variables [from Gouq-Jen Su, *Ind. Eng. Chem.*, **38**, 803 (1946)].

The vapor pressure of a liquid is usually observed in a more direct fashion than by examination of PV isotherms. Figure 1.7 illustrates an apparatus, the isoteniscope, used for measurement of the vapor pressure of pure liquids. A sample in the chamber A is boiled to remove air from the space between A and B. Then with the thermostat held at the desired temperature, pressure on the system is adjusted until the liquid levels at B and C are equal. This pressure is measured on the manometer and is equal to the pressure of vapor in the space AB.

Figure 1.8 describes the vapor pressure of several liquids as a function of temperature. When a liquid is heated in an open vessel the temperature rises until the vapor pressure of the liquid equals the pressure of the atmosphere above it, at which point the phenomenon of boiling sets in and continues with no further increase in temperature until the liquid has completely evaporated. Since the atmospheric pressure varies with weather and geographic location, the boiling temperature varies correspondingly, increasing with increasing atmospheric pressure and vice versa. In order to avoid ambiguity it is necessary to specify the pressure at which a boiling point is measured. The *normal boiling point* of a liquid is the temperature at which the vapor pressure equals 1 atm. (760 mm. Hg).

For most pure liquids solidification occurs at a well-defined temperature. The temperature at which liquid and solid can exist together indefinitely is the *freezing point*. At higher temperatures solid will eventually melt to form liquid, and at lower temperatures liquid will eventually solidify. The freezing point is only very slightly affected by the pressure on the system and its change with atmospheric pressure is neglected in all except the most precise measurements.

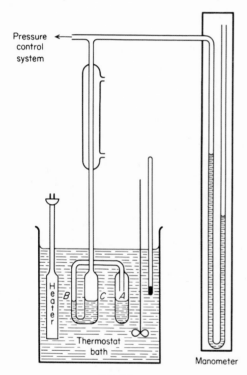

FIG. 1.7. Isoteniscope.

Solids are distinguished from liquids by their rigidity, their lack of tendency to flow and assume the shape of the container. Solids have compressibilities and densities approximately the same as the corresponding liquids.

At a given temperature each pure solid has a characteristic vapor pressure (sublimation pressure) which increases with increasing temperature. The vapor pressure of ice as a function of temperature is indicated in Fig. 1.9. At the freezing point the vapor pressures of liquid and solid forms of a substance are identical, while at temperatures above the freezing point the vapor pressure of the solid exceeds that of the liquid and the solid is metastable. At temperatures below the freezing point the vapor pressure of the liquid exceeds that of

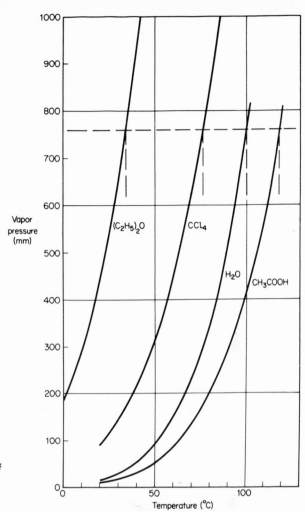

FIG. 1.8. Vapor pressure as a function of temperature for several liquids.

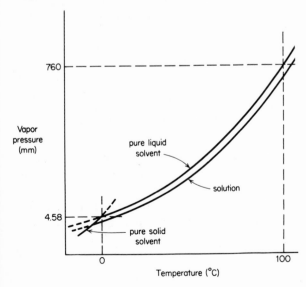

FIG. 1.9. Vapor pressure lowering (schematic, not drawn to scale).

the solid and the liquid is metastable. If the vapor pressure of the solid exceeds that of the atmosphere at a temperature which is less than the melting point, then the solid sublimes rather than melts. This is the case with solid carbon dioxide (Dry Ice), which has a vapor pressure of 1 atm. (760 mm.) at $-78°$, while the melting point is $-56°$. At the latter temperature the vapor pressure is 5.25 atm.

1.10 Solutions

When two or more substances can be physically combined to form a homogeneous mixture, a sample which exhibits the same properties throughout and in its smallest subdivision, the mixture is called a solution. Mixtures of gases are always homogeneous, barring chemical reaction.

In the most common type of solution, one of the components is a liquid. The other components may be gases, liquids, or solids. The most abundant component in a solution is usually referred to as the *solvent*, while the less abundant components are referred to as the *solutes*, but the distinction is arbitrary.

The proportions in which the two components of a solution can be mixed to yield a homogeneous sample are sometimes limited. For example, at 15° 100 ml. of alcohol will dissolve any quantity of iodine up to 20 g., forming a homogeneous solution. If more than this proportion of iodine is used, the resulting mixture is heterogeneous, containing undissolved crystals of iodine. This limit of miscibility is called the *solubility* of iodine in alcohol, and the solution containing the maximum amount of dissolved solute is said to be *saturated*. The solubility of a substance depends on the nature of both solute and solvent, and on the temperature of the system (also on pressure for gases—see below). The solubility tends to be large when the components closely resemble each other in chemical properties; water and ethyl alcohol are completely miscible, but water and *n*-butyl alcohol are partly miscible, while ethyl alcohol and *n*-butyl alcohol are completely miscible.

The solubility of gases in liquids is a function of the partial pressure P_i of the gas above the solution, as well as the variables mentioned above. A simple empirical relation known as *Henry's law* states that *the solubility of a gas is proportional to its partial pressure above the solution* and describes gas solubilities with good accuracy when the solutions are dilute.

$$X_i = kP_i \tag{1.23}$$

X_i is the mole fraction of dissolved gas, and in the dilute solutions to which Henry's law applies it may be considered to be proportional to the molarity.

A simple consequence of Henry's law is that the volume solubility of a gas is independent of pressure. For example, in dilute solution the number of moles of solute dissolved in 1 mole of solvent is nearly equal to the mole fraction of solute. Therefore the number of moles dissolved is given by

$$n = kP \text{ per mole of solvent}$$

In terms of volume of gas (ideal) dissolved, this becomes

$$PV/RT = kP, \qquad V = kRT$$

which is a constant at constant temperature. This relation gives no clue as to the variation of solubility with temperature, since k, the Henry's law constant, is temperature dependent. Some gas solubilities are given in Table 1.3.

TABLE 1.3

SOLUBILITIES OF GASES IN WATER

(Values given are solubility coefficients, i.e., volume of gas, measured at 273°K, absorbed by 1 volume of water when the partial pressure of gas is 1 atm.)

Substance	Temperature		
	0°	25°	50°
N_2	0.02354	0.01434	0.01088
O_2	0.04889	0.02831	0.02090
H_2	0.02148	0.01754	0.01608
CO	0.03537	0.02142	0.01615
CO_2*	1.713	0.759	0.436
H_2S*	4.670	2.282	1.392

* Solubility increased by chemical interaction with solvent.

EXERCISE 1.15

Nitrogen at 1 atm. is bubbled through 0.02 M aqueous carbon dioxide at 0°. What is the initial composition of the effluent gas?   *Ans.* $X_{CO_2} = 0.26$.

A solute in a liquid has a significant effect upon the properties of the liquid, particularly its vapor pressure and related properties. The vapor pressure of the solvent is lowered by the addition of a solute; in dilute solutions the lowering is proportional to the concentration of solute.

This effect may be represented qualitatively as shown in Fig. 1.9, where the lower curve represents the pressure of solvent vapor over a liquid phase containing a small concentration of nonvolatile solute. This representation indicates that the boiling point of the solution (T_b) is higher than that of the pure solvent (T_b^0) and that the freezing point of the solution (T_f) is lower than that of the pure solvent (T_f^0). The generalizations assume that the solute is present only in the solution and not in the second phase (solid or vapor).

For so-called *ideal solutions* the vapor pressure of a volatile component is described by the relation

$$P_A = P_A^0 X_A \tag{1.24}$$

where P_A is the vapor pressure of the substance over the solution in which its mole fraction is X_A. P_A^0 is the vapor pressure of the pure substance at the temperature of interest. Equation (1.24) is *Raoult's law* and defines an ideal solution.

Equation (1.24) can be rearranged to show that the vapor pressure lowering of a solvent is proportional to the concentration of solute. In a two-component system

$$X_A + X_B = 1$$

and therefore

$$P_A = P_A^0(1 - X_B)$$

Rearranging, we have

$$\frac{P_A^0 - P_A}{P_A^0} = 1 - \frac{P_A}{P_A^0} = X_B \tag{1.25}$$

For example, the vapor pressure of toluene ($C_6H_5CH_3$) at $50°$ is 92.6 mm. If sufficient naphthalene is added to make a solution containing 10 mole per cent naphthalene the vapor pressure of toluene over the solution will be lowered to

$$P = 92.6 \times 0.9 = 83.3 \text{ mm.}$$

EXERCISE 1.16

How many moles of anthracene ($C_{14}H_{10}$) should be added to 1 mole of toluene at $50°$ in order to produce a vapor pressure lowering from 92.6 mm. to 90.75 mm.

Ans. 0.02 mole.

The ideal solution law, equation (1.24), also includes Henry's law, equation (1.23). In an ideal solution the Henry's law constant is $1/P_A^0$.

The vapor pressure of a solvent over an ideal solution as a function of composition is shown in Fig. 1.10. When the solute is also volatile, its vapor pressure over an ideal solution may also be represented by a straight line corresponding to Raoult's law, as indicated in Fig. 1.10. The total vapor pressure over such solutions

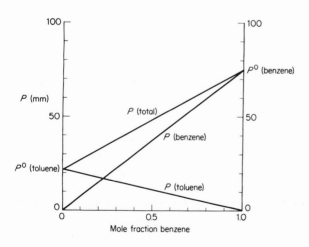

FIG. 1.10. Vapor pressure of toluene-benzene solutions at $20°$.

$$P_t = P_A + P_B$$

will be given by a straight line joining P_A^0 and P_B^0.

$$P_t = P_A^0 X_A + P_B^0 X_B$$
$$= P_A^0 X_A + P_B^0(1 - X_A)$$
$$= (P_A^0 - P_B^0) X_A + P_B^0 \qquad (1.26)$$

Since P_A^0 and P_B^0 are fixed for a given system at a given temperature, equation (1.26) describes a straight line having intercept P_B^0 and slope $(P_A^0 - P_B^0)$.

For example, a solution containing 10 mole per cent of heptane (C_7H_{16}) in toluene will have a partial pressure of toluene vapor of 83.3 mm. at 50°, as before. However, the heptane, which in the pure state has a vapor pressure of 140.9 mm. at 50°, will also contribute to the total vapor pressure by an amount given by

$$P_{\text{heptane}} = 140.9 \times 0.1 = 14.1 \text{ mm.}$$

and the total vapor pressure will be

$$P_t = 83.3 + 14.1 = 97.4 \text{ mm.}$$

EXERCISE 1.17

Find the composition at which $P_{\text{heptane}} = P_{\text{toluene}}$ (cf. Fig. 1.10).

Many real solutions show rather marked deviations from the simple behavior predicted by Raoult's law. The measured total vapor pressure may be either greater than or less than that predicted by equation (1.26), as is illustrated in Fig. 1.11. It is found, however, that Raoult's law is still a good approximation to the observed behavior of the major component when the mole fraction of that component is near unity. In the region labelled A in Fig.

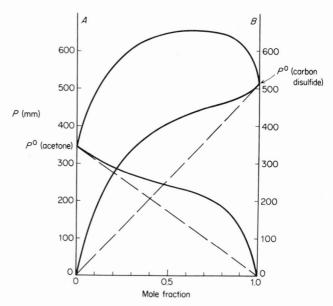

FIG. 1.11. Vapor pressure of acetone-carbon disulfide solutions at 35.2°.

1.11, the observed curve for vapor pressure of acetone approaches asymptotically the Raoult's law line; the same is true for carbon disulfide in region B.

It is also found in real solutions that the minor component obeys Henry's law as its mole fraction approaches zero. In region A of Fig. 1.11, the curve representing the observed vapor pressure of carbon disulfide becomes nearly a straight line, as predicted by equation (1.23), although the value of the constant k in that equation is not $1/P°$, as would be the case if the solution were ideal.

There is a large class of solutions which conduct electric current, the electrolyte solutions, which will be given special consideration in a later chapter.

SUMMARY, CHAPTER 1

1. Temperature: $t = kV + c$

    Fixed points: ice point, $0°$; steam point, $100°$

2. Isothermal gas expansion

    Boyle's law

    $$PV = const. \text{ at const. temp.}$$

    Avogadro's law

    $$PV = nk(k = 22.4 \text{ l. atm. at } 0°)$$

    Real gases

    $$PV_M = f(P)$$

    $(PV_M)^0$ depends only on temperature

3. Thermal expansion of gases

    $$(PV_M)^0 = 0.082056 \; T \; (°K)$$

    Charles' law

    $$V = kT \; (°K) \text{ at const. pressure}$$

4. Ideal gas law: $PV = nRT$

    $$R = 0.082056 \text{ l. atm. deg.}^{-1} \text{ mole}^{-1}$$

    Ideal gas density

    $$\rho = PM/RT$$

    Real gas density

    $$\rho/P = (M/RT)^0 + aP$$

    Dalton's law

    $$P_i = X_i P_t$$

    where $X_i = n_i/(n_1 + n_2 + \ldots)$

5. Equations of state

    Compressibility factor

    $$z = PV/nRT$$

    van der Waals equation

    $$(P + an^2/V^2)(V - nb) = nRT$$

    Virial equation

    $$P = nRT/V + \beta n^2/V^2 + \gamma n^3/V^3 + \delta n^4/V^4$$

6. Liquefaction of gases
   Critical properties

$$T_c \text{ and } P_c$$

   Reduced properties

$$T_r = T/T_c \text{ and } P_r = P/P_c$$

   Compressibility factor

$$z = f(T_r, P_r)$$

7. Properties of liquids and solids
   Vapor pressure
   Normal boiling point
   Freezing point

8. Solutions
   Henry's law

$$X_i = kP_i$$

   Raoult's law

$$P_i = P_i^0 X_i$$

PROBLEMS, CHAPTER 1

1. The tank of a pressure type van der Graaf generator has a volume of 2400 l. and it is filled with nitrogen to a pressure of 8 atm. at 25°. Use the ideal gas law to estimate the weight of nitrogen required. *Ans.* 22.0 kg.

2. By means of a gas density balance it was found that oxygen at 419 mm. produces the same buoyancy as an unknown gas at 304 mm. What is the molecular weight of the unknown? *Ans.* 44.

3. A glass bulb connected to a mercury manometer of negligible volume contains helium at 350 mm. and 0°. When it is used as a thermometer to measure the temperature of a system the pressure becomes 280 mm. What is the temperature of the system in °C.? *Ans.* −54.7°

4. A glass bulb was evacuated and weighed, then filled with oxygen and re-weighed. The difference in weights was 0.250 g. The operation was repeated under the same conditions of temperature and pressure with an unknown gas and it weighed 0.375 g. Find the molecular weight of the unknown gas. *Ans.* 48.

5. Suppose that a hot air balloon is constructed with a volume of 100,000 l. and that the contained air is maintained at a temperature of 200°. If the exterior air has a temperature of 20° and a density of 1.2 g./l., what mass could the balloon lift? *Ans.* 46 kg.

6. A mixture of carbon monoxide and carbon dioxide is found to have a density of 1.50 g./l. at 30° and 730 mm. What is the composition of the mixture? *Ans.* $X_{CO} = 0.322$.

7. A gas cylinder with a volume of 690 cc. contains ethylene at a pressure of 51 atm. at a temperature of 38°. How many grams of ethylene does the cylinder contain? Use (a) the compressibility factor from Fig. 1.6 and (b) compare with the ideal gas law. *Ans.* (a) 57g. (b) 39g.

8. One hundred 1. of dry air at 1 atm. is passed through an equilibrator containing water maintained at $0°$. The gas mixture is then passed through a drying tube, the weight of which increases by 0.487 g. Find the vapor pressure of water at $0°$. *Ans.* 4.6 mm.

9. From the data in Table 1.3 compute (a) the solubility of air and (b) the mole fraction of dissolved gas in water at $0°$ and 10 atm.

Ans. (a) 0.286 cc./cc.

(b) 2.3×10^{-3}.

10. The vapor pressure of toluene at $50°$ is 92.60 mm. and at the same temperature the vapor pressure of a toluene solution containing 1.00 weight per cent of nonvolatile solute is 92.10 mm. What is the molecular weight of the solute?

Ans. 170.

11. The composition of the vapor in equilibrium with a solution of heptane-toluene at $50°$ was found to be 30 mole per cent toluene. The vapor pressure of heptane at $50°$ is 140.9 mm. while that of toluene is 92.6 mm. What is the composition of the solution? *Ans.* 39.3 mole % toluene

---

12. How many 36 l. cylinders of nitrogen at 147 atm. and $-25°$ would be required to fill an evacuated tank of 10^4 l. capacity to 5.5 atm. at $-25°$? Obtain z from Fig. 1.6.

13. A sealed one-liter glass bulb weighs 245.60 g. when suspended in an atmosphere of pure oxygen and 245.10 g. in an atmosphere of an unknown, both at $20°$ and $P = 1$ atm. What is the gram-molecular weight of the unknown?

14. A glass bulb connected to a mercury manometer of negligible volume contains helium at P mm. and $0°$. When it is used as a thermometer it is desirable that the pressure become 323 mm. at $50°$. Specify the value of P at $0°$.

15. Referring to the balloon in problem 5, what mass could be lifted if the balloon were filled with hydrogen at 1 atm. and $20°$?

16. A sample of unknown liquid weighing 0.180 g. is volatilized to displace an equal volume of air which is collected over water at $25°$ and 740 mm. total pressure. The observed volume is 60 cc. and the vapor pressure of water at $25°$ is 24 mm. Find the molecular weight of the unknown.

17. A mixture of water vapor, carbon dioxide, and excess oxygen resulting from combustion of a hydrocarbon occupies 85.0 cc. at $100°$ and 760 mm. At $-20°$ (negligible water vapor pressure) and constant volume the pressure becomes 296 mm. At $-130°$ (negligible carbon dioxide vapor pressure) the pressure becomes 105 mm. What is the empirical formula of the compound?

18. A soft drink bottle with a total volume of 200 cc. is $\frac{9}{10}$ filled with a water solution saturated with carbon dioxide at 2 atm. and $25°$. The solubility of gases in ice is negligible. Using the ideal gas law, estimate the gas pressure developed when the contents are frozen at $-10°$. The density of ice at $-10°$ is 0.917 g. cc.$^{-1}$.

19. The total vapor pressure over a solution of heptane-toluene at $50°$ is found to be 110 mm. What is the composition of the solution?

20. Use Raoult's law to predict the volume solubility of CH_3F in benzene at 25° and 1 atm. The vapor pressure of CH_3F at 25° is 40 atm. The density of liquid benzene at this temperature is 0.875 g./cc.

21. To 24.00 cc. of gas, known to contain only hydrogen, nitrogen, and excess water, is added 15.50 cc. of oxygen, both measured at 250 mm. and 0°. Following ignition the residual gases occupy 39.50 cc. at 22.3 mm. and 0° C. Find % H_2 in the original gas mixture.

22. The apparent molecular weight of a gas mixture is defined by $M_{ap.} = WRT/PV$. Find $M_{ap.}$ for air (20% O_2, 80% N_2).

23. A mixture of H_2 and CH_4 has a density 0.25 as great as the density of O_2 at the same temperature and pressure. Find the % CH_4 in the mixture.

24. An oil diffusion vacuum pump has a speed of 50 l./sec. at 10^{-4} mm. (a) How long would it take at this rate to remove 1 cc. of gas originally measured at 1 atm. and at the same temperature?

In order to operate the diffusion pump described above, its exhaust pressure must be maintained at 10^{-1} mm. or better by a mechanical fore pump. (b) What is the required speed of the fore pump?

25. A sealed glass bulb terminates in a capillary tube of uniform diameter and length L. It contains gas at an unknown pressure P and a liquid of density d. The bulb is rotated to a vertical position in a constant temperature bath with the capillary tube down. The confined column of gas has length l_1, the liquid l_2. Solve for P, ignoring the effect of surface tension.

26. A capillary glass tube of uniform diameter and temperature contains gas samples A and B, separated by a short column of mercury, L mm. in length. The ends are sealed. In horizontal position the confined gases occupy volumes a mm. and b mm. in length at the common unknown pressure P. In vertical position the lengths become a' and b'. Solve for P.

27. The dependence of barometric pressure upon altitude is described by the barometric formula. It can be derived by considering a vertical column of unit cross-section area containing an ideal gas of molecular weight M at uniform temperature T. The weight of gas above compresses the gas below. Representing gas density at altitude h by ρ, $dP = \rho g dh$. Find P as a function of h.

2

FIRST LAW
OF THERMODYNAMICS

2.1 Conservation of Energy

Processes of interest to the chemist almost invariably give evidence of transfer of energy between the system under study and its surroundings. Reaction between an acid and a base liberates heat. Combustion of coal produces light and heat. Exploding a gasoline-air mixture produces light, heat and work. The discharge of a storage battery produces electrical energy. The nature and quantity of these energy effects are not only of interest in themselves, but also furnish important insights into the nature of the process which is taking place. The science of chemical thermodynamics gives a quantitative accounting of the energy effects of chemical processes, and also uses such information in the prediction of chemical behavior.

The results of many careful measurements of a variety of processes lead to the conclusion that when a given process is performed repeatedly in the same way, it always results in producing heat and work effects which are also the same from one trial to another. To illustrate, whenever 17,480 joules of electric energy is degraded to heat in a well-insulated body of water weighing 1 kilogram (kg.) and initially at 25.00°, its temperature rises to 29.18°; whenever 10^5 kg. cm. of mechanical work is degraded to heat by friction in such a body of water, its temperature rises from 25.00° to 27.34°.

Energy may be manifested in several forms: light, heat, work, and electric energy are some examples. Unless the energy is produced as heat, it is experimentally convenient to convert it to heat in order to permit quantitative comparisons, since other forms of energy can be converted, easily and quan-

28

titatively, into heat. One can then compare the heat liberated when a given amount of gasoline burns in an open vessel with the combined heat + light + work when the same net change occurs in an internal combustion engine. Or one can conduct the process

$$Zn + Cu^{++} (aq.) = Zn^{++} (aq.) + Cu$$

in a beaker, measuring the heat liberated, and compare this with the total energy liberated when the same process occurs in a galvanic cell. *In any such comparison of two or more processes which bring about exactly the same change in state, it is always found that the total energy produced or consumed is precisely the same.*

In the study of any process, the energy term is measured by the effects produced in the immediate surroundings. In a calorimetric process such as

$$12 \text{ g. C } (25°) + 32 \text{ g. O}_2 \text{ (1 atm., } 25°) + 10 \text{ kg. water } (25°)$$
$$= 44 \text{ g. CO}_2 \text{ (34.6°, 1 atm.)} + 10 \text{ kg. water } (34.6°)$$

"12 g. C and 32 g. O_2" is the system and "10 kg. water" the immediate surroundings. Our repeated experience is consistent with the interpretation that when a system is in effective contact with its immediate surroundings, so that energy can be interchanged, and when these are isolated from the rest of the laboratory and universe, then for any process

$$(\text{system})_{\text{state I}} = (\text{system})_{\text{state II}}$$
$$\text{energy change} = \Delta E$$

there is a concomitant process

$$(\text{imm. surr.})_{\text{state 1}} = (\text{imm. surr.})_{\text{state 2}}$$
$$\text{energy change} = -\Delta E$$

That is, the total energy change is equal in magnitude and opposite in sign to the total energy change in the immediate surroundings. The isolated region "system + immediate surroundings" behaves as though an entity, *total energy*, is conserved. Not only is the effect of a given process on the immediate surroundings precisely reproducible, but any process which brings about the same change in state will produce the same total energy effect on the immediate surroundings, although the form of the energy may vary. Thus a given chemical change may produce only heat, or it may also produce electrical energy.

Within the experience of man, all machines run down. Many devices produce work, but all must be supplied energy in some way, for example through a fuel, or electrically, or by a waterfall, or by the wind. No known device generates work or heat continuously without consuming either work or heat. We say that *perpetual motion of the first kind is impossible.* (Another type of perpetual motion is related to the second law, and will be considered later.) Experience leads to the conclusion that work and heat may only be interconverted, and this limitation can be accounted for in terms of the concept of an entity, *total energy*, which is conserved in the universe. A common statement of the *principle of conservation of energy* is that *energy can be neither created nor destroyed.*[1]

The conceptual difficulties of thermodynamics arise at this point. It is essential for the student to understand that we have not explained energy. We have invented it. Later, we shall define it.

2.2 Heat and Heat Capacity

Heat as such cannot be measured at all, but the effects which it produces are measurable. When a system absorbs energy as heat, its temperature increases. On this basis, heat was formerly measured by the increased temperature of a body of water. The amount of heat required to raise the temperature of 1 g. of water from 14.5° to 15.5° became a unit of heat, the calorie (cal.). Since we shall demonstrate later by rigorous thermodynamic development that temperature is fundamentally defined and measured in terms of heat, the 15° cal. is no longer suitable. There are also experimental difficulties which arise from using the 15° cal. Another definition, which avoids circular logic, is that heat is that form of energy which melts ice. This definition has an experimental advantage, since quantity of heat can be related to quantity of ice melted in an ice calorimeter (to be described in section 2. 3). In turn, the amount of electric energy required to melt a given amount of ice can be accurately measured. The *defined calorie* equals 4.1840 joules.[2]

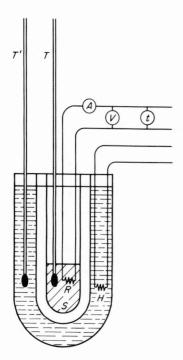

FIG. 2.1. Adiabatic calorimeter (schematic). *T*, sample thermometer; *T'*, jacket thermometer; *S*, sample; *R*, sample heating resistance; *H*, jacket heating resistance; *A*, ammeter; *V*, voltmeter; *t*, timer.

Measurements of temperature change vs. energy input are often carried out in a calorimeter of the type indicated in Fig. 2.1. Heat is delivered by dissipation of electric energy in a resistance heater at a measured voltage and current for a measured time. The temperature of the outer jacket is manually or automatically adjusted so that it is as close as possible to that of the sample. This minimizes heat transfer between the sample and its surroundings; a process carried out under such conditions is said to be *adiabatic*. For reasons of experimental convenience, such measurements are often made with the sample subjected to a constant pressure, usually that of the atmosphere.

----

[1]Modern physical theory regards mass as a form of energy, quantitatively related through the equation due to Albert Einstein, energy = mass × (velocity of light)[2], and the conservation law is broadened to include mass as well as energy.

[2]The magnitude chosen for the defined calorie is such that this amount of energy will raise the temperature of 1 g. of water from 14.5° to 15.5° within the precision of ordinary measurements.

EXERCISE 2.1

An electric timer t, an ammeter A, a voltmeter V, a resistance heater R, and an adiabatic calorimeter are arranged as shown in Fig. 2.1. Express in defined calories the heat generated within the calorimeter system when a current of 2.250 amp. at 1.500 v. is passed through the heater for 1000 sec.   *Ans.* 806 cal.

The change in temperature of the sample resulting from the input of a measured quantity of energy is observed and the nature of the results obtained is indicated for an idealized case in Fig. 2.2. The ratio of energy input as heat to temperature increase depends strongly on the nature of the substance and its

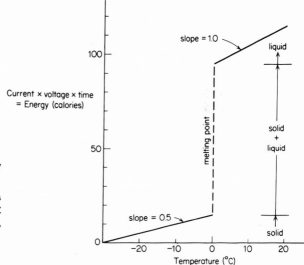

Current × voltage × time = Energy (calories)

FIG. 2.2. (*Right*) Temperature vs. energy input as heat. Sample: 1 gram H_2O.

FIG. 2.3. (*Below*) Molar heat capacities as a function of temperature ⊙ CH_4(g); ▫ C (graphite); △ H_2O: 0-273(s), 273-373(1), 373- (g).

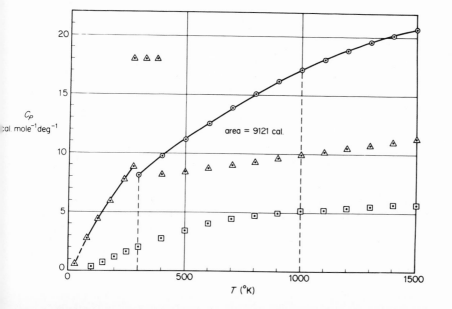

C_P cal. mole^{-1}deg^{-1}

area = 9121 cal.

T (°K)

physical state. It is described by the property called the heat capacity, C, which is defined by

$$\frac{dq}{dT} = C \tag{2.1}$$

where q is the quantity of heat. The heat capacity is given by the slope of the curve in Fig. 2.2. The observation of q versus T may be made either at constant pressure or at constant volume. The heat capacity of one phase varies smoothly with temperature, as shown in Fig. 2.3.

A mean value of the heat capacity, $\bar{C}$, for a finite temperature interval may be computed from the temperature increase resulting from a finite heat input.

$$\bar{C} = \frac{q}{\Delta T} \tag{2.2}$$

If the temperature interval is small, the value of $\bar{C}$ thus obtained is a useful approximation to the value of C at the mean temperature of the interval covered.

$$C_T \approx \frac{q}{T_2 - T_1} \quad \text{at} \quad T = \frac{T_2 + T_1}{2} \tag{2.3}$$

For instance, we observe that the quantity of energy required to raise the temperature of the specimen described in Fig. 2.2 from $-15°$ to $0°$ is 7.5 cal. By equation (2.3) we obtain

$$\bar{C} = 0.5 \text{ cal. deg.}^{-1}$$

for the temperature interval $-15°$ to $0°$. This may also be taken as the approximate value of C at the mean temperature $-7.5°$.

EXERCISE 2.2

In Exercise 2.1 if the calorimeter consists of a block of metallic lead weighing 1000 g. and its temperature rose from $0.0°$ to $26.3°$, what is the atomic heat capacity of lead in defined calories? *Ans.* 6.36 cal. deg.$^{-1}$ (g. atom.)$^{-1}$.

Values of the molar heat capacities of several substances are displayed in Fig. 2.3. The values given are for C_P, the molar heat capacity at constant pressure. If samples are heated in a rigid container, so that volume rather than pressure is constant, different values of the heat capacities are obtained.

Experimental information may often be represented with considerable precision by empirical equations. With some substances, such as H_2O (g) as shown in Fig. 2.3, the value of C_P is a nearly linear function of temperature and therefore may be represented by the equation

$$C_P = a + bT \tag{2.4}$$

One must be cautious in assigning physical meaning to the parameters of empirical equations. It might appear that $C_{T=0} = a$, but this inference is not supported by the experimental evidence which extends only from $100°$ to higher temperatures. An empirical equation is valid only for the range of experimental conditions for which its parameters have been evaluated.

EXERCISE 2.3

Evaluate the constants a and b in equation (2.4) for the case of H_2O (g) from the data in Fig. 2.3 over the temperature range 373–1500°K.

Ans. $a = 7.0$; $b = 3.0 \times 10^{-3}$.

In order to represent the data for other substances, such as CH_4 (g) shown in Fig. 2.3, it may be necessary to add a third term to equation (2.4), yielding

$$C_P = a + bT + cT^2$$

or

$$C_P = a + bT + cT^{-2}$$

or

$$C_P = a + bT + cT^{-1} \tag{2.5}$$

and again the constants a, b, and c are chosen for best fit to the experimental values of C_P. The curve drawn through the data for methane in Fig. 2.3 corresponds to the equation

$$C_P = 3.381 + 18.044 \times 10^{-3}T - 43.00 \times 10^{-7}T^2$$

Table 2.1 contains a representative selection of heat capacity data given in terms of the constants in equation (2.5).

TABLE 2.1

MOLAR HEAT CAPACITIES AT CONSTANT PRESSURE*

$C_P = a + bT + cT^2$ (300–1500°K)

Substance	a	$b \times 10^3$	$c \times 10^7$	C_P at 25°
H_2 (g)	6.947	−0.200	4.808	6.89
O_2 (g)	6.148	3.102	−9.23	7.02
N_2 (g)	6.524	1.250	−0.01	6.90
H_2O (g)	7.256	2.298	2.83	8.03
CO_2 (g)	6.214	10.396	−35.45	8.87
CO (g)	6.420	1.665	−1.96	6.97
CH_4 (g)	3.381	18.044	−43.00	8.54
C_2H_4 (g)	2.830	28.601	−87.26	10.41
C_2H_6 (g)	2.247	38.201	−110.49	12.59
NH_3 (g)†	6.189	7.887	−7.28	8.52

*From H. M. Spencer and J. L. Justice, *J. Am. Chem. Soc.*, **56**, 2311 (1934), H. M. Spencer and G. N. Flannagan, *ibid.*, **64**, 2511 (1942), H. M. Spencer, *ibid.*, **67**, 1859 (1945), H. M. Spencer, *Ind. Eng. Chem.*, **40**, 2152 (1948).

†300–1000°K.

From tabulated data on heat capacities one may reverse the operations described above to compute the heat required to increase the temperature of a substance over any interval within the range of validity of the data. Equation (2.1) integrated over a finite interval of temperature becomes

$$q = \int_{T_1}^{T_2} C \, dT \tag{2.6}$$

If values of C are available over the temperature interval of interest, q may be obtained graphically. Values of C_P are plotted against T as in Fig. 2.3, and the area under the curve between the temperature limits is measured as indicated in the case of heating methane from 300°K to 1000°K. For this process $q_P = 9121$ cal. mole^{-1}.

When the heat capacity is known as a function of temperature, the integral in equation (2.6) becomes, e.g.,

$$q = \int_{T_1}^{T_2} (a + bT + cT^2)\, dT$$
$$= a(T_2 - T_1) + \frac{b}{2}(T_2^2 - T_1^2) + \frac{c}{3}(T_2^3 - T_1^3) \tag{2.7}$$

EXERCISE 2.4

Using the empirical equation for the heat capacity of methane, compute the energy required to raise the temperature of one mole of this substance from 300°K to 1000°K. Compare with the result of the graphical integration indicated in Fig. 2.3.

2.3 Latent Heat Effects

The heat effects associated with changes in physical state such as fusion, vaporization, and modification of crystal structure (often called *phase changes*) are known as *latent heat* effects. The curve of energy input vs. temperature in Fig. 2.2 shows the effect of a transition (fusion of ice) at 0°.

At temperatures below 0° the energy input increases the temperature of the sample, which is a solid. When the temperature of the sample reaches 0°, further energy input does not increase the temperature, but results in conversion of solid into liquid. When this conversion is complete, energy input again increases the temperature of the sample, which is now completely liquid.

Heat capacities computed from the slopes of the curve in Fig. 2.2 would show a discontinuity at 0° as is indicated in Fig. 2.3. This behavior is one of the best indications of a phase change. The heat capacities of the various phases of a substance bear no simple relationship to each other, and the curve for the heat capacity of water vs. temperature in Fig. 2.3 should be regarded as discontinuous at 0° and 100°. The figure gives data only for the phase which is stable at 1 atm., but values can be measured for metastable phases, and the values lie on a continuous curve with those of the stable phases.

The amount of energy required to convert a substance from one phase to another, at constant temperature, is the latent heat of transition. In general, graphs of energy vs. temperature for various types of phase change resemble that for fusion in Fig. 2.2. In each case, the discontinuity occurs at the characteristic transition temperature. Latent heats can be obtained from the ΔE given by the discontinuity. Thus, from Fig. 2.2 the heat of fusion of ice is 79.71 cal./g. at 0° and 1 atm. Similarly, the latent heat of vaporization of water is 539.55 cal./g. at 100° and 1 atm.

EXERCISE 2.5

Using the heat capacities and latent heats given above, compute the energy required to carry out the following process with 10 g. of H_2O: H_2O (s, 263°K, 1 atm.) = H_2O (g, 383°K, 1 atm.).   *Ans.* 7290 cal.

The latent heat of fusion of ice can be measured precisely, and then used as a calorimetric standard. The ice calorimeter, illustrated in Fig. 2.4, utilizes this method. The process to be measured occurs in chamber D, in good thermal contact with an ice-water mixture. Ice melts in the well-insulated vessel A by absorbing heat from the isothermal reaction system. Since the densities of ice and water at 0° are 0.917 g./cc. and 1.000 g./cc., respectively, the volume of the ice-water mixture decreases by 0.01 cc. for each 0.12 g. of ice melted by absorbing 9.5 cal.

EXERCISE 2.6

In the apparatus of Fig. 2.4, 138 g. of 66.1% by weight of H_2SO_4 and 200 g. of H_2O, both at 0°, were mixed. The decrease in volume observed was 6.05 cc. How much heat was liberated?   *Ans.* 5.75 kcal.

2.4 Expansion Work

A system under study may exchange energy with its surroundings not only as heat but also as work, w. In the terminology of thermodynamics, all energy transfer which is not heat is work. *The work done by a system equals the increase in potential energy of the surroundings, both in respect to magnitude and sign.* In the context of thermodynamics, (force) × (distance) does not necessarily equal work. When a system expends energy only to overcome friction in an isothermal process, that energy appears in the surroundings as heat. Regardless of the changes occurring within the system, unless there is an increase in the potential energy of the surroundings, no work has been performed. For our purpose it will be sufficient to consider only electrical work and expansion work.

Expansion work can be measured as the product of the change in volume, V, of the system, and the opposing pressure exerted by the surroundings, P_{surr}.

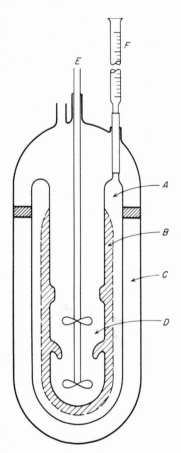

FIG. 2.4. Ice calorimeter [from T. L. Smith, J. Phys. Chem., **59**, 385 (1955)]. A, ice-water chamber; B, ice mantle; C, insulating jacket; D, sample chamber; E, stirrer; F, microburet.

That is

$$\text{work} = \text{force} \times \text{distance}$$
$$\text{pressure} = \text{force} \times \text{area}^{-1}$$
$$\text{work} = \text{pressure} \times \text{area} \times \text{distance}$$
$$= \text{pressure} \times \text{volume}$$

Then

$$dw = P_{\text{surr.}}\, dV \qquad (2.8)$$

and in a finite process of expansion the work will be given by the definite integral of equation (2.8).

$$w = \int_{V_1}^{V_2} P_{\text{surr.}}\, dV \qquad (2.9)$$

If no change in volume occurs, that is, if the process of heating, chemical reaction, or other change is carried out in a rigid container, then the work of expansion is zero, regardless of any change in pressure which may occur in the system. On the other hand, if the pressure exerted by the surroundings on the system is zero, then w is zero, regardless of any change in volume. Thus a gas, in expanding and pushing back a piston which generates heat through friction, does no work (in the terminology of thermodynamics) unless it also stores potential energy in the surroundings, for example by compressing a spring or another sample of gas, or by lifting a weight.

Since the volume of a system is a function of temperature, pressure, and state of physical or chemical combination, it is convenient to consider separately the work of expansion arising from changes in each one of these variables.

2.5 Thermal Expansion

Work of expansion is always given by equation (2.9). For expansion at constant pressure that equation integrates to

$$w = P_{\text{surr.}}(V_2 - V_1) \qquad (2.10)$$

EXERCISE 2.7

The density of liquid water at 1 atm. and 0° is 0.99984 g. cc.$^{-1}$; and at 1 atm. and 100°, 0.95835 g. cc.$^{-1}$ Evaluate the work of expansion when 18 g. of water is heated from 0° to 100° at a constant pressure of 1 atm.   *Ans.* 7.85×10^{-4} l. atm.

When only the initial and final temperatures are known, the coefficient of thermal expansion is needed. This may be obtainable from an equation of state, as in the case of an ideal gas where, at constant pressure, $PdV = nRdT$. When P_{gas} and $P_{\text{surr.}}$ are actually the same, and they often are not, equation (2.8) becomes $dw = P_{\text{gas}}\, dV_{\text{gas}}$, or simply PdV. Since V and T are the variables and are related by $PV = nRT$, it follows that $dw = nRdT$, or

$$w = \int_{T_1}^{T_2} nR\, dT = nR(T_2 - T_1) \qquad (2.11)$$

EXERCISE 2.8

Calculate the expansion work done when 1 mole of ideal gas is heated at a constant pressure of 1 atm. from 0° to 100°.   *Ans.* 8.2 l. atm.

It is often desirable to express expansion work in units of calories rather than liter-atmospheres. The conversion factor is 1 l. atm. = 24.217 cal. When the gas constant R appears in the expression for work done or heat absorbed, its value in calories per degree per mole may be conveniently employed. $R = 1.9872$ cal. deg.$^{-1}$ mole^{-1}. In this system of units, the answer to exercise 2.8 is evidently 199 cal.

2.6 Isothermal Gas Expansion

The second type of expansion work, that done in isothermal pressure-volume changes, will be examined in detail for gases. Consider a gas confined in a cylinder by a frictionless piston upon which weights can be placed; the device is surrounded by a large constant temperature bath. The piston will assume a position such that the pressure of the gas, P, is equal to the pressure exerted by the piston with its weights, $P_{surr.}$. For a gas sample of 1 mole, at 0° and 10 atm., the volume will be 2.24 l.

If the weights on the piston are suddenly reduced so that $P_{surr.} = 1$ atm., the gas will force the piston to a new position where $P_{gas} = 1$ atm., and the volume becomes 22.4 l. The expansion has occurred against the constant pressure of the surroundings and equation (2.9) may be integrated thus:

$$w = P_{surr.} \int_{V_1}^{V_2} dV = P_{surr.}(V_2 - V_1) \tag{2.12}$$

The result in the example given is

$$w = 1 \times (22.4 - 2.24) = 20.2 \text{ l. atm. mole}^{-1}$$

The same overall change from an initial volume of 2.24 l. to a final volume of 22.4 l. may, however, be accomplished in an infinite variety of ways, each yielding a different amount of work by the system. For example, reduce the pressure of the surroundings to 5 atm.; this will result in an increase in volume to 4.48 l. Next reduce $P_{surr.}$ to 1 atm.; the volume now increases to the desired final value of 22.4 l. The total work done in this two-stage process is given by the sum of two terms corresponding to equation (2.12).

$$w = 5 \times (4.48 - 2.24) + 1 \times (22.4 - 4.48)$$
$$= 29.1 \text{ l. atm. mole}^{-1}$$

The same total change in volume may be carried out in a many-stage process, in which the pressure of the surroundings is decreased in small steps until the final value is reached. The course of such a process is indicated by path 3 in Fig. 2.5, along with the course of the two processes described above. The third path would obviously result in a larger value of w than either path 1 or 2. This is most easily seen if we observe that the value of w is given by the area under each of the paths described, since

$$w = \int_{V_1}^{V_2} P \, dV$$

We see that paths 1, 2, and 3 enclose successively larger areas between the fixed initial and final volumes.

Since the gas will not expand unless the pressure of the surroundings is less than that of the gas, there is evidently a limit to the work which can be obtained in expansion between these fixed initial and final states. This limiting or *maximum work* is obtained when the pressure of the surroundings is only infinitesimally less than the pressure of the gas at all times during the expansion from V_1 to V_2. Substituting P_{gas} for $P_{surr.}$ in equation (2.9) we have

$$w_{max.} = \int_{V_1}^{V_2} P_{gas} \, dV \qquad (2.13)$$

and if the gas is assumed to be ideal the substitution $P = nRT/V$ may be made.

$$w_{max.} = nRT \int_{V_1}^{V_2} \frac{dV}{V} = nRT \ln \frac{V_2}{V_1} \qquad (2.14)$$

The maximum work in an isothermal expansion is also measured by the area under the smooth curve, whose equation is $PV = $ const., in Fig. 2.5. Since $P_1 V_1 = P_2 V_2$ for isothermal expansion of an ideal gas, equation (2.14) may also be written in the form

$$w_{max.} = nRT \ln \frac{P_1}{P_2} \qquad (2.15)$$

EXERCISE 2.9

Calculate the maximum work for the expansion of 1 mole of ideal gas from 2.24 l. to 22.4 l. at 0°; repeat at 100°.

Ans. 51.5 and 70.4 l. atm.; 1247 and 1705 cal.

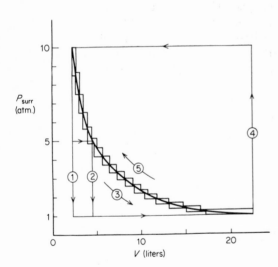

FIG. 2.5. Isothermal gas expansion, one mole ideal gas at 273 °K.

Isothermal compression of a gas may also be carried out in a variety of ways. If the gas sample, maintained at 0° and initially at a volume of 22.4 l., is suddenly subjected to an external pressure of 10 atm., the volume will rapidly decrease to the final value of 2.24 l. and the work done *by the gas* will be obtained by substitution in equation (2.12).

$$w = 10(2.24 - 22.4) = -202 \text{ l. atm. mole}^{-1}$$

This process is described by path 4 in Fig. 2.5, and the work is measured by the area under this curve generated from right to left. This area has a negative value, indicating that work is done *on the gas* in compression. The work done by the surroundings would be less than that computed above if a path such as 5, consisting of a series of small pressure increments, were followed. The work done *on the gas* would evidently be minimized if the pressure of the surroundings were only infinitesimally greater than the pressure of the gas, and the work done *by the gas* in compression (which is negative) would be the maximum. This limiting case is obviously described by equations (2.13), (2.14), and (2.15), but in compression the value of V_2 is less than that of V_1 and the value of $w_{max.}$ is negative.

It has been shown that there is a maximum amount of work which a gas can do on its surroundings in an isothermal expansion. The value of the maximum work is determined by the initial and final volumes, by the temperature, and of course by the amount of gas involved. The maximum work done by the gas in compression is given by the same relation. The process which yields maximum work in expansion may also be described as *reversible*, since each infinitesimal state of the system can be traversed in reverse order in a subsequent compression which utilizes only the potential energy stored in the surroundings during the first half of the cycle. *The system and its surroundings can both be restored to their initial states*, and therein lies the test of reversibility. On the other hand, a process such as that described by path 1 in Fig 2.5 is an *irreversible* expansion, since a succeeding compression cannot retrace that path. Furthermore, although the system can be restored to its initial state by utilizing potential energy from the surroundings, over and above that stored during expansion, the surroundings do not regain the initial state.

The maximum work of isothermal expansion can be computed for real gases by returning to equation (2.13) and substituting the appropriate relation for P as a function of V. If the equation of state (see Chapter 1) is

$$PV = nRT + nbP$$

the integrated equation is

$$w_{max.} = \int_{V_1}^{V_2} \left(\frac{nRT}{V - nb} \right) dV = nRT \ln \frac{V_2 - nb}{V_1 - nb} \tag{2.16}$$

If experimental values of P vs. V for a gas are available these may be graphed and the value of

$$\int_{V_1}^{V_2} P \, dV$$

obtained from the area under the curve between the limits V_1 and V_2.

EXERCISE 2.10

From data given in Fig. 1.2 plot P vs. V_M for oxygen and find, by graphical integration, $w_{max.}$ for the expansion of 1 mole of oxygen from a pressure of 500 atm. to a pressure of 200 atm at 0°. Compare with the result of application of equation (2.15).   *Ans.* Real $w_{max.} = 15$ l. atm.; ideal $w_{max.} = 20.6$ l. atm.

2.7 Volume Change at Constant *P, T*

Expansion work resulting from a change in constitution of a system at constant temperature and pressure is exemplified by such processes of phase change as fusion and vaporization. In the former case the work is quite small, as may be seen from data given previously on the densities of liquid and solid water at 0° and 1 atm. In that instance we find that a decrease in volume of 1.49 cc. accompanies the fusion of 1 mole of ice to form 1 mole of liquid water. Since $P_{surr.}$ is constant, equation (2.9) may be integrated

$$w = P_{surr.} \int_{V_1}^{V_2} dV = P_{surr.}(V_2 - V_1) \tag{2.17}$$

and *w* evaluated.

$$w = 1 \text{ atm.} \times (-1.49 \times 10^{-3}) \text{ l. mole}^{-1}$$
$$= -1.49 \times 10^{-3} \text{ l. atm. mole}^{-1}$$

The work of expansion in vaporization is much larger, since a gas is formed. For example, the molar volume of liquid water at 100° is 18.8 cc., while the molar volume of water vapor at 100° and 1 atm. is 30.2 l. Thus the change in molar volume on vaporization under these conditions is practically equal to the molar volume of the vapor, 30.2 l., and the work of vaporization obtained from equation (2.17) is

$$w = 1 \times 30.2 \text{ l. atm. mole}^{-1}$$

In any phase change involving vapor, it is usually an excellent approximation to evaluate the change in volume from the change in the quantity of gas, neglecting the volume of the liquid. The gas volume may be approximated from the ideal gas law. In such cases we differentiate $PV = nRT$ with V and n as variables to give

$$dw = PdV = RTdn$$

At constant temperature and pressure

$$w = RT \, \Delta n \tag{2.18}$$

where Δn is the number of moles of *gas or vapor* formed or condensed, with due regard to sign.

EXERCISE 2.11

Evaluate approximately *w* per mole at 50° and 1 atm. for the process $H_2O(l) \longrightarrow H_2O(g)$. (This is not a process which occurs in nature, but that does not prevent calculation of *w*.)   *Ans.* 26.5 l. atm. mole^{-1}.

Expansion work due to changes in volume resulting from chemical reaction at constant temperature and pressure is also computed as described above. Again the volumes of liquid and solid phases are usually neglected when gases are involved. The computation thus reduces to a determination of the number of moles of gas produced or consumed in the process.

EXERCISE 2.12

Evaluate w approximately at 25° and 1 atm. for the process $CaCO_3(s) = CaO(s) + CO_2(g)$ *Ans.* 24.4 l. atm. mole^{-1}.

2.8 Electric Work

Exchange of energy between a system and its surroundings may take the form of electrical phenomena. It is possible to employ electric energy to bring about chemical change, and thus to convert electric energy into chemical potential energy, as in charging a storage battery. It is also possible to devise processes in which chemical potential energy is converted into electric energy, as in the discharge of a dry cell. This type of device is called a galvanic cell and in Fig. 2.6 a simple form, the Daniell cell, is illustrated. If an electrical connection is made from the zinc electrode to the copper electrode, electrons will flow in the direction indicated in the diagram. The negative electrode, at which electrons are released to the external circuit, is called the *anode*, and at this electrode zinc metal is oxidized to zinc ion.

$$Zn = Zn^{++} + 2e$$

The positive electrode, at which electrons from the external circuit are consumed, is called the *cathode*, and at this electrode copper ions are reduced to copper metal.

$$2e + Cu^{++} = Cu$$

The net chemical process which accompanies the discharge of the Daniell cell is

$$CuSO_4 \text{ (aq.)} + Zn \text{ (s)} = ZnSO_4 \text{ (aq.)} + Cu \text{ (s)}$$

(Ions also migrate through the porous barrier in amount corresponding to the flow of electrons in the external circuit.)

The amount of electric work which can be obtained from an electrochemical process is proportional to the extent of reaction (Faraday's law, see Chapter 10) and is therefore conveniently stated for 1 gram-equivalent of reaction. This corresponds to the passage of 6.0225×10^{23} electrons through the external circuit. Each electron carries a charge of 1.6021×10^{-19} coulombs; the total charge is 96,487 coulombs (1 faraday, $\mathscr{F}$) per gram-equivalent. The electric work done is the product of charge times potential difference $\mathscr{E}$, and therefore the electric work done is given by

$$w = n \times \mathscr{E} \times \mathscr{F}$$

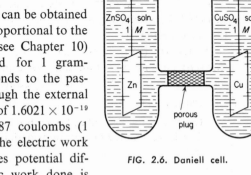

FIG. 2.6. Daniell cell.

where n is the number of gram-equivalents of reaction. Thus a cell which develops a potential difference of 1 v. can do $1 \times 96{,}487$ volt-coulombs (joules) of electric work per gram-equivalent of reaction.

Because such a cell has a finite internal resistance, the magnitude of the potential difference indicated by an external measuring instrument will depend on the current drawn during the measurement. A simple voltmeter may have a resistance as small as 100 ohms, thus drawing a current of 10^{-2} amp. when indicating a potential difference of 1 v. The current, I, passing through a cell with internal resistance R_{cell}, causes an internal voltage drop of $R_{cell} \times I$, which decreases the potential available for work in the external circuit, an effect often observed in lead storage batteries and dry cells. The external potential difference of a cell approaches a maximum as the current drain is reduced toward zero, thus minimizing the potential drop in the cell. The limiting value of the potential difference is observed by opposing the potential of the cell with a known potential difference of opposite polarity, which is adjusted so that no current can be detected by a galvanometer in the circuit. This arrangement is known as a *potentiometer*.

The zero current potential or *electromotive force* (emf) of a galvanic cell is its maximum potential, and therefore the electric work per unit chemical change is a maximum under this condition. This maximum work is analogous to the maximum work of expansion discussed in the preceding section, in that it is obtained when the restraining force of the surroundings is only infinitesimally different from the driving force of the system. Just as in gas expansion, this kind of electrochemical process may be described as *reversible*, since it is possible to retrace in reverse sequence each of the successive states that the system occupies in the course of the process and to return both system and surroundings to their initial states. Discharge of a galvanic cell through a small resistance is analogous to expansion of a gas against a low pressure. In both cases the system does less than the maximum work, and the process is *irreversible* in the sense that the rundown cell cannot be recharged utilizing only energy which it has stored in the surroundings. The cell, of course, can be restored to its initial state, but only at the expense of uncompensated potential energy from the surroundings.

Unless the contrary is specified, the emf of a system is understood to mean the zero current potential, that corresponding to the reversible process producing maximum work. It will be designated by $\mathscr{E}$, in volts.

EXERCISE 2.13

The emf of the Daniell cell described in Fig. 2.6 is 1.1 v. Calculate the maximum electric work in the process of oxidation of 1 g. at. wt. of zinc (2 gram-equivalent weights). *Ans.* 212,000 joules.

2.9 Formulation of the First Law

Any type of energy exchange between a system and its surroundings involves either heat or work. When a system absorbs heat, q, this energy is not lost; it is stored, and can be recovered. Absorption of heat increases the internal energy, or the energy content, E, of the system. When a system performs work, w, this is done at the expense of the total energy of the system. These two ideas can be combined in a single equation, applicable to any change in state of any system.

$$E_2 - E_1 = \Delta E = q - w \qquad (2.19)$$

E_1 and E_2 represent the values of the internal energy of the system in the initial and final states, whether for reversible or irreversible processes. Equation (2.19) is our most useful statement of the first law of thermodynamics. Only q and w can be measured. The internal energy is an idea, or concept, which cannot be measured, as such. Nor can changes in the internal energy, ΔE, be measured, as such. But measurement of $q - w$ establishes ΔE, by definition. The concept of internal energy cannot be explained within the framework of thermodynamics, and it does not lend itself to representation by models or pictures. It is an abstraction, but it has operational significance, namely $E_2 - E_1 = q - w$. When a weight is lifted, the internal energy of the system increases. To say that this represents an increase in potential energy does not explain it, since potential energy is only another aspect of the same concept.

EXERCISE 2.14

Evaluate ΔE per mole at 100° and 1 atm. for the process

$$H_2O(l) = H_2O(g)$$

(Values of q and w have been given in preceding sections.)　　　*Ans.* 8975 cal.

The absolute value of E cannot be found, since energy is measurable in transit, but not *in situ*. All forms of energy can be expressed as

energy = intensity factor × capacity factor

or

energy = generalized force × generalized displacement

Pressure is the generalized force and volume the generalized displacement in expansion work. Potential difference and electric charge transferred are the corresponding terms in electric work. In every instance, the generalized displacement vanishes unless a process occurs with a corresponding change in state. Consequently, the energy is always describable in terms of the initial and final states as $\Delta E = E_2 - E_1$. The impossibility of measuring an absolute value of E does not impair the value of the concept. Another statement of the first law is implicit in equation (2.19): *the energy content of a system in a given state has a fixed and finite value.*

There may well be several processes by which a specified change in state can be brought about, each with its characteristic value of q and w; but if the initial and final states are fixed, equation (2.19) and the first law indicate that the difference $q - w$ is fixed. To demonstrate this principle, reconsider the various processes of gas expansion described in Fig. 2.5. It was shown there that the change in state

$$\text{gas } (2.24 \text{ l.}, \ 10 \text{ atm.}, \ 0°) = \text{gas } (22.4 \text{ l.}, \ 1 \text{ atm.}, \ 0°)$$

can be carried out by a variety of paths with various values of w. The first law tells us that ΔE is the same for all these processes, and therefore equation (2.19) tells us that q must increase or decrease as w decreases or increases.

The statement that ΔE, *the change in internal energy, depends only on the initial and final state and not on the path* applies to all kinds of processes, both physical and chemical. A characteristic of a system such as the internal energy E, whose value depends only on the state of the system and not on its history, is known as a *thermodynamic property of state*. Other useful properties which meet this requirement will be introduced later. The change in internal energy, ΔE, may be called a function of state. As indicated above q and w are not, in general, functions of state, since their values depend on the path described by the process.

Many processes of interest occur cyclically. In a simple cycle, the final state of the system is identical with the initial state, regardless of the path, while the initial and final states of the surroundings may or may not be the same. The restoring process need not retrace the forward process. A cyclic process which produces maximum work is also said to be reversible. It must not be supposed that this necessarily entails retracing the forward process, but only that

$$\Delta E_{\text{forward}} = -\Delta E_{\text{reverse}}$$

$$w_{\text{forward}} = -w_{\text{reverse}}$$

$$q_{\text{forward}} = -q_{\text{reverse}}$$

From the first law we conclude that for the system

$$\Delta E_{\text{cycle}} = E_{\text{final}} - E_{\text{initial}} = 0$$

and therefore

$$q_{\text{cycle}} = w_{\text{cycle}} \tag{2.20}$$

This places no restriction on the values of q and w except that they must be equal. Referring again to Fig. 2.5, consider the expansion-compression cycle which is described by paths 1 plus 4. The total work done by the gas in this cycle is $20.2 - 202.0 = -181.8$ l. atm. The sign indicates that the net result is work done *on* the gas. Since ΔE for the cycle is zero, equation (2.19) indicates that the heat absorbed by the gas would be -181.8 l. atm. $= -4400$ cal., and again the sign indicates that heat flows from the system to the surroundings.

The device of a cycle is useful to evaluate ΔE and other functions of state for a variety of noncyclic physical and chemical processes. Imagine a completely generalized process of interest for which the initial state is A and the final state is B, as indicated in Fig. 2.7. No restrictions as to the nature of the process are implied. It may not be possible to measure q_{AB} and w_{AB}, and thus compute ΔE_{AB}, for the particular process of interest. However, it is often possible to measure or compute q's and w's for another process which produces the same

net change in state, such as by the route ACB. Suppose
that it is possible to obtain values of ΔE_{AC} and ΔE_{CB},
then since $\Delta E_{\text{cycle}} = 0$, $\Delta E_{AB} = \Delta E_{AC} + \Delta E_{CB}$. No limitations are placed on the nature of the state C, but it
should be chosen so that $q_{AC} - w_{AC} = \Delta E_{AC}$ and
$q_{CB} - w_{CB} = \Delta E_{CB}$ are convenient to evaluate. The
relation between the several values of ΔE is a direct
consequence of the first law, but no conclusions can be
drawn regarding relationships between the q's alone or
the w's alone. Numerous applications of this method
will be given in the next chapter.

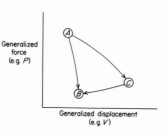

FIG. 2.7. Indicator dia-
gram for a generalized
process.

2.10 ΔE at Constant Volume

For any process in which no work is done, equation (2.19) indicates
that the change in internal energy is directly measured by the heat absorbed.
In section 2.4 it was pointed out that no work of expansion is done in constant
volume processes. If, further, no provision is made to obtain electric or other
work, then $w = 0$ and

$$\Delta E_V = q_V \qquad (2.21)$$

where q_V denotes heat absorbed in the constant volume process. This condition is encountered in chemical reactions when the process is carried out
in a rigid container, as in the "bomb" of a calorimeter. Examples of this method
of evaluating ΔE will be given in the next chapter.

In many processes carried out at constant pressure, the magnitude of the
expansion work term is so small as to be practically negligible and the heat
absorbed in the process is a very good measure of ΔE. For instance, in the
process

$$H_2O \text{ (s, 1 atm. } 0°) = H_2O \text{ (1, 1 atm., } 0°)$$

q is 1435 cal. mole^{-1} and w is 1.5 cc. atm. mole$^{-1} = 0.036$ cal. mole^{-1}, and
therefore w is negligible compared to q. A similar approximation may be made
in chemical processes involving only condensed phases (liquids, solids, no
gases) and the heat of reaction may be taken as a measure of ΔE. When gases
are produced or consumed in the process, or when a gas is heated, the volume
change at constant pressure may be appreciable, and the heat absorbed is not
a measure of ΔE.

The change of internal energy accompanying the change in temperature of
a substance is measured by the heat absorbed when the process is carried out
at constant volume, so that $w = 0$. The heat capacity at constant volume, C_V,
should then be used.

$$\Delta E_V = q_V = \int_{T_1}^{T_2} C_V \, dT \qquad (2.22)$$

If experimental values of C_V as a function of T are available, graphical integration may be employed, or an empirical equation for C_V may be inserted in equa-

tion (2.22) and integrated (see section 2.2). For approximate results or for small temperature change, C_V may be considered constant and

$$\Delta E_V \approx C_V \, \Delta T \tag{2.23}$$

2.11 Enthalpy or Heat Content

Many chemical and physical processes of practical interest are conducted at constant pressure. In such cases, expansion work, $w = P \, \Delta V$, may occur. Thus for a process at constant pressure (and no provision for electric work) the integral of $dw = P \, dV$ becomes $P \, \Delta V$ and equation (2.19) can be written

$$q_P = \Delta E_P + P \, \Delta V \tag{2.24}$$

From this relation it is seen that the heat absorbed in a process at constant pressure measures the change in internal energy plus the work of expansion. This combination of energy terms makes it convenient to define a new thermodynamic property, the *enthalpy* or *heat content H*, by the relation

$$H = E + PV \tag{2.25}$$

Since H is defined in terms of properties of state, H is also a property of state; that is, its value depends only on the state of the system and not on its history. It follows that ΔH is zero for any cyclic path in any system.

For any process, the change in enthalpy is given by

$$H_2 - H_1 = E_2 - E_1 + (P_2 V_2 - P_1 V_1)$$
$$\Delta H = \Delta E + \Delta PV \tag{2.26}$$

and the value of ΔH depends only on the initial and final states of the system, not the path.

For a process at constant pressure

$$\Delta H_P = \Delta E_P + P \, \Delta V \tag{2.27}$$

and substituting by equation (2.24),

$$\Delta H_P = q_P \tag{2.28}$$

It is seen that the heat absorbed in a process at constant pressure is a direct measure of the change in heat content. For a process at constant volume, ΔE_V is a more useful thermodynamic property than ΔH_V. Since H is a function of state, ΔH_V can be determined by equations (2.21) and (2.26).

EXERCISE 2.15

Express ΔH_V in terms of q, P, and V.

The heat of vaporization of water given in a preceding section refers to the process carried out at the constant pressure of 1 atm. and 100°. Therefore ΔH for this process is equal to the heat absorbed.

$$H_2O \text{ (l, 1 atm., 100°)} = H_2O \text{ (g, 1 atm., 100°)}$$
$$\Delta H = 9700 \text{ cal. mole}^{-1}$$

ΔE for this process may be obtained by use of equation (2.27) since

$$P \, \Delta V = 1 \text{ atm.} \times 30.2 \text{ l. mole}^{-1} = 730 \text{ cal. mole}^{-1}$$

and therefore

$$\Delta E = 9700 - 730 = 8970 \text{ cal. mole}^{-1}$$

The change in enthalpy accompanying a change in the temperature of a substance can be measured by the heat absorbed when the process is carried out at constant pressure.

$$\Delta H_P = q_P = \int_{T_1}^{T_2} C_P \, dT \qquad (2.29)$$

where C_P is the heat capacity at constant pressure. Several instances of this computation are discussed in section 2.2.

2.12 Thermodynamic Properties

Two new and useful properties of physical chemical systems have been introduced: the internal energy E, and the enthalpy H. It has been shown that the experience embodied in the principle of conservation of energy requires that E and H are properties of state, whose values depend only on the state of the system and not on its history. Such properties are called *thermodynamic properties*, and others in this category will be introduced in later chapters.

Since we observe only the results of changes in E and H, that is, values of ΔE and ΔH, the corresponding definition of a thermodynamic property is of more direct interest. *For any given change in state, the change in the value of a thermodynamic property depends only on the initial and final state and not on the path.*

Consider the nature of q and w, which do not in general represent changes in a thermodynamic property. Their values depend on the path which the system follows from the initial to the final state as shown in section 2.6. However, if it is specified that the process of interest is carried out at constant pressure or constant volume, then by equations (2.28) and (2.21) we see that q_P and q_V are functions of state only in these special cases.

In dealing with thermodynamic properties of state, subscripts V, P, T, etc., specify that the property noted is the same for the final state of the system as for the initial state, but this implies nothing about the volume, pressure, temperature, etc., for any intermediate states. Thus in the change in state

$$H_2O \text{ (l, 1 atm., } 100°) = H_2O \text{ (g, 1 atm., } 100°)$$

$$\Delta H_{373} = 9700 \text{ cal. mole}^{-1}$$

the amount of heat required is unaffected by whether or not the system assumes intermediate temperatures other than $100°$, as in superheating. In specifying q_P and q_V, however, the subscripts refer to *constancy* of pressure (or of volume) along the entire path, and not only for initial and final states. The reason for this difference is that values of changes in thermodynamic properties are independent of path, whereas values of q and w depend on path. This behavior is indicated by the notation. Definite integrals of dE and dH are $E_2 - E_1$ and $H_2 - H_1$. The differentials are said to be exact. Integrals of dw and dq have been written as w and q. These differentials are inexact.

2.13 Applications of the First Law to Ideal Gases

In this section we shall explore in more detail some of the applications of the first law to gases. The development will be limited to gases which obey the equation $PV = nRT$ within acceptable limits of error. The derived equations will, of course, be rigorously correct for systems which obey the ideal gas law. In any given application of the derived equations, numerical results will be more or less in error because a mathematically simple but not quite adequate description of experimental reality has been chosen. In subsequent chapters we will illustrate the use of other equations of state.

A further description of the ideal gas is furnished by consideration of the classic experiments of Joule and Thomson, who studied the heat effects of gas expansion. Early experiments by Joule consisted of allowing a gas to expand into a vacuum while observing the temperature of a water bath surrounding the vessels. The sensitivity of the method was not great, and no temperature change was noted. (This is not surprising since we now know that for expanding a typical real gas from 0.5 l. and 2 atm. to 1 l. and 1 atm. the internal energy changes by approximately 0.1 cal. Temperature measuring devices of that time would not respond to so small a quantity of energy.)

Since no work was done and no heat absorption was observed, ΔE was zero within the precision of the experiment. We may therefore state as an approximation for a real gas, and as a correct description of an ideal gas,

$$\left(\frac{\partial E}{\partial V}\right)_T = 0 \tag{2.30}$$

In other words, the internal energy of an ideal gas is a function of the temperature alone, given by

$$dE = C_V \, dT \qquad \text{[see equation (2.22)]}$$

For a change in state of an ideal gas,

$$\text{gas } (P_1, V_1, T_1) = \text{gas } (P_2, V_2, T_2); \; \Delta E_{\text{total}}$$

we can devise two partial processes:

$$\text{gas } (P_1, V_1, T_1) = \text{gas } (P_2', V_2', T_1); \; \Delta E_{T_1} = 0$$

$$\text{gas } (P_2', V_2', T_1) = \text{gas } (P_2, V_2, T_2); \; \Delta E = \int C_V \, dT$$

Since ΔE_{total} depends only on the initial and final states, it follows that $\Delta E_{\text{total}} = \int C_V \, dT$.

A simple relation between C_P and C_V for an ideal gas can be obtained by combining $dH = C_P \, dT$ and $dE = C_V \, dT$. Since, at constant pressure for any ideal gas

$$dH_P = dE + PdV \qquad \text{[see equation (2.25)]}$$

$$dH_P = C_V \, dT + PdV$$

For one mole of gas at constant pressure, with V and T as variables, the work of thermal expansion is $PdV = RdT$. Substituting into the preceding equation gives

$$dH_P = C_V \, dT + RdT = (C_V + R) \, dT$$

and we see that

$$C_P = C_V + R \qquad (2.31)$$

That is, C_P and C_V differ by the amount of work performed during thermal expansion. This expression is often useful for estimating values of C_V from C_P, and vice versa. Although it is derived for an ideal gas, and therefore subject to the limitations of that equation of state, it does not depend upon molecular complexity, which exerts a great effect upon C_V.

EXERCISE 2.16

From the expression for C_P in Table 2.1 and the relation between C_P and C_V in equation (2.31), calculate the ΔE for increasing the temperature of methane from 300°K to 1000°K.   *Ans.* 7736 cal. mole^{-1}.

The work of isothermal gas expansion was considered in section 2.6. Since E is invariant at constant T

$$q = w = \int P_{\text{surr.}} \, dV$$

For the reversible process, producing maximum work

$$q_{\text{rev.}} = w_{\text{max.}} = nRT \ln V_2/V_1 \qquad (2.32)$$

Boyle's law applies and equation (2.32) may also be written

$$q_{\text{rev.}} = w_{\text{max.}} = nRT \ln (P_1/P_2) \qquad (2.33)$$

EXERCISE 2.17

One mole of gas is allowed to expand from a pressure of 10 atm. to a pressure of 0.1 atm. at a temperature of 100°. Assuming the gas to be ideal, what is the maximum amount of heat which can be absorbed? What is the minimum amount?
                                           Ans. Max. $= 3400$ cal.

A second type of gas expansion of some practical interest is that in which no heat transfer occurs between the system and its surroundings. This condition may be met by use of thermal insulating material or by consideration of processes which, by virtue of their speed or magnitude, do not permit appreciable heat exchange during the period of measurement. Such processes are called *adiabatic* and by definition $q = 0$. If the expansion takes place against a restraining pressure greater than zero, so that w is greater than zero, the internal energy of the gas and therefore its temperature must decrease. We will now show

how the final temperature may be computed. This relation may be formulated from the first law, with $q = 0$, thus

$$w = -\Delta E$$

$$\int_{T_1}^{T_2} C_V \, dT = -\int_{V_1}^{V_2} P_{\text{surr.}} \, dV \tag{2.34}$$

If the expansion is an irreversible one against some constant restraining pressure, and if we assume for simplicity that C_V is constant over the temperature range involved, the relation in integrated form becomes

$$C_V(T_2 - T_1) = -P_{\text{surr.}}(V_2 - V_1) \tag{2.35}$$

To illustrate the application of this equation, let us compute the final temperature attained in the following expansion: An ideal gas with $C_V = 8.0$ cal. mole^{-1} is initially confined at a pressure of 10 atm. and a temperature of 0°. The pressure of the surroundings is suddenly decreased to 1 atm. and the gas expands adiabatically against this pressure until $P_{\text{gas}} = P_{\text{surr.}}$. What is the final temperature of the gas? Substituting in equation (2.35), we have

$$8.0(T_2 - 273) = -1 \times (V_2 - 2.24) \times 24.2 \text{ cal. (l. atm.)}^{-1}$$

To evaluate T_2 and V_2 we require a second equation, viz.

$$P_1 V_1 / T_1 = P_2 V_2 / T_2$$

or

$$\frac{10 \times 2.24}{273} = \frac{1 \times V_2}{T_2}$$

Solution of these simultaneous equations gives $T_2 = 218°K$ and $V_2 = 17.9 \text{ l.}$ Comparison of this result with that of the isothermal expansion from 10 to 1 atm. indicated in Fig. 2.5 shows that the final volume in the adiabatic expansion is smaller, corresponding to the decrease in temperature. Also, since the volume increase is less, the work of expansion is less.

$$w = P_{\text{surr.}}(V_2 - V_1)$$
$$= 1(17.9 - 2.24) = 15.7 \text{ l. atm.}$$

The reversible adiabatic expansion producing maximum work is of particular interest. Again

$$\Delta E = -w$$

and

$$\int_{T_1}^{T_2} C_V \, dT = -w_{\text{max}} = -\int_{V_1}^{V_2} \frac{RT}{V} \, dV$$

Collecting variables T and V and integrating gives

$$C_V \int_{T_1}^{T_2} \frac{dT}{T} = -R \int_{V_1}^{V_2} \frac{dV}{V}$$

$$C_V \ln \frac{T_2}{T_1} = -R \ln \frac{V_2}{V_1} \tag{2.36}$$

To express T in terms of P, substitute V by RT/P in equation (2.36).

$$C_V \ln \frac{T_2}{T_1} = -R \ln \frac{P_1}{P_2} - R \ln \frac{T_2}{T_1}$$

and since for an ideal gas $C_P = C_V + R$

$$C_P \ln \frac{T_2}{T_1} = R \ln \frac{P_2}{P_1} \tag{2.37}$$

EXERCISE 2.18

Apply equation (2.37) to determine the final temperature in the adiabatic, reversible expansion of an ideal gas with $C_V = 8.0$ cal. mole^{-1} from 10 atm. and 0° to 1 atm.

Ans. 173°K.

SUMMARY, CHAPTER 2

1. First law of thermodynamics: The internal energy content E of a system has a fixed and finite value depending only on its state and not on its history.

2. Heat
   Definition of heat capacity, C

$$\frac{dq}{dT} = C, \qquad q = \int_{T_1}^{T_2} C \, dT$$

   Empirical equations for heat capacity

$$C = a + bT + cT^2$$

3. Work: $w = \int P_{surr.} \, dV$
   Thermal expansion of an ideal gas

$$w = nR(T_2 - T_1)$$

   Isothermal expansion of an ideal gas

$$w = P_{surr.} \, \Delta V \text{ (const. } P_{surr.})$$

$$w_{max.} = nRT \ln (V_2/V_1)$$

   Expansion work in physical and chemical changes, constant P, T.

$$w = \Delta n_{gas} RT$$

4. Electric work

$$w = n\mathscr{E}\mathscr{F}$$

5. Applications of first law

$$\Delta E_{cycle} = 0; \qquad q_{cycle} = w_{cycle}$$

$$\Delta E_{AB} = \Delta E_{AC} + \Delta E_{CB}$$

$$\Delta E_V = q_V$$

   Definition of the heat content

$$H = E + PV$$

$$\Delta H_P = \Delta E_P + P\Delta V$$

$$\Delta H_P = q_P$$

6. Thermodynamic properties of gases
   Ideal gas $(\partial E/\partial V)_T = 0$

$$C_P - C_V = R$$

Isothermal reversible expansion

$$q_{max.} = w_{max.} = nRT \ln (V_2/V_1) = nRT \ln (P_1/P_2)$$

Adiabatic reversible expansion

$$C_V \ln (T_2/T_1) = -R \ln (V_2/V_1)$$

PROBLEMS, CHAPTER 2

1. Evaluate C_P for one mole of nitrogen at 125° using the parameters of Table 2.1. Find the corresponding value of C_V.
   Ans. $C_P = 7.02$ cal. mole^{-1} deg^{-1}, $C_V = 5.03$ cal. mole^{-1} deg^{-1}.

2. The average C_P of carbon dioxide from 0–100° is 8.90 cal. deg.$^{-1}$ mole^{-1}. For heating 10 moles of this gas from 0° to 100° at constant pressure, find q, w, ΔH, ΔE.   *Ans.* $q = \Delta H = 8.90$ kcal., $w = 1.99$ kcal., $\Delta E = 6.91$ kcal.

3. Use the data of the preceding problem to find q, w, ΔH, ΔE for heating 10 moles of carbon dioxide at constant volume from 0° to 100°.
   Ans. $q = \Delta E = 6.91$ kcal., $w = 0$, $\Delta H = 8.90$ kcal.

4. How many grams of ice at 0° would have to be added to 100 g. of water at 50° to bring the final temperature of the system to 10°?   *Ans.* 44.5 g.

5. Benzene melts at 5.48° and its heat of fusion at this temperature is 30.3 cal. g.$^{-1}$. C_P for the solid is 0.30 cal. g.$^{-1}$ deg.$^{-1}$ and C_P for the liquid is 0.40 cal. g.$^{-1}$ deg.$^{-1}$. Find ΔH for the process

$$C_6H_6(s, 0°, 1 \text{ atm.}) = C_6H_6(l, 50°, 1 \text{ atm.})$$

                                                   Ans. 3.94 kcal.

6. The heat of vaporization of benzene at 80.2° (n.b.p.) and 1 atm. is 94.3 cal. g.$^{-1}$ For the process

$$C_6H_6(l, 80.2°, 1 \text{ atm.}) = C_6H_6(g, 80.2°, 1 \text{ atm.})$$

compute $w_{max.}$, ΔH, and ΔE.   *Ans.* $w = 695$ cal.

7. A 10 g. sample of helium initially at 50 atm. and 25° is allowed to expand isothermally against a constant external pressure of 1 atm. Assume that the gas is ideal and compute q, w, $w_{max.}$, ΔH and ΔE.
   Ans. $q = w = 1.45$ kcal., $w_{max.} = 5.79$ kcal.
   $\Delta H = \Delta E = 0$

8. One hundred g. of nitrogen gas ($C_P = 6.96$ cal. mole^{-1} deg.$^{-1}$) initially at 25° and 10 atm. is allowed to expand adiabatically against a constant pressure of 1 atm. Assume that the gas is ideal and compute the final temperature, ΔE and ΔH.
   Ans. $T = 222°K$, $\Delta E = -1349$ cal., $\Delta H = -1889$ cal.

9. One mole of helium gas ($C_V = 3$ cal. deg.$^{-1}$ mole^{-1}) is confined in a cylinder and piston at 25°. The area of the piston is 100 cm.^{2} and the gas is subjected to a total external force of 10 kg. acted upon by the acceleration of gravity. (The acceleration of gravity $= 980$ cm. sec.$^{-2}$) To what extent must the gas be heated

in order to raise the piston 5 cm.? How much heat will be absorbed in the process?

Ans. 0.59°, 2.95 cal.

10. For the constant pressure process

$$C_2H_6(g) + \tfrac{7}{2}O_2(g) = 2CO_2(g) + 3H_2O(l)$$

$$\Delta H_{298} = q_P = -372.800 \text{ kcal. mole}^{-1}$$

(a) Find w and ΔE for the process.

(b) The heat of vaporization of water at 25° and 1 atm. is 10.519 kcal. mole^{-1}. Find ΔH_{298} and ΔE_{298} for the process

$$C_2H_6(g) + \tfrac{7}{2}O_2(g) = 2CO_2(g) + 3H_2O(g)$$

Ans. (a) -1.48 kcal., $\Delta E = -371.325$ kcal.

(b) $\Delta H = -341.240$ kcal., $\Delta E = -341.535$ kcal.

11. When the process

$$H_2(g) + 2AgCl(s) = 2HCl \text{ (1 molar sol.)} + 2Ag(s)$$

occurs at 25° in a galvanic cell a zero current e.m.f. of 0.2329 v. is observed. When the same change in state is carried out in such a way that no electric work is done, $q = -17,400$ cal. per mole of hydrogen consumed. Evaluate $w_{max.}$ and the corresponding $q_{rev.}$ for operation of the galvanic cell.

Ans. $w_{max.} = 10.74$ kcal.

$q_{rev.} = -6.67$ kcal.

---

12. From the empirical equation given in Table 2.1 compute the heat capacity at constant pressure of carbon dioxide at 50°. Compute the heat capacity at constant volume at this temperature, assuming that the gas is ideal.

13. Use the values of the heat capacities computed above as constants over the temperature range 0–100° in the following calculations: A 10 g. sample of carbon dioxide initially at 1 atm. and 0° is heated to 100°. Assume that the gas is ideal.

(a) For the case that pressure is constant, compute the final volume, q, w, ΔE, and ΔH.

(b) For the case that volume is constant, compute the final pressure, q, w, ΔE, and ΔH.

14. Insert the empirical equation for the heat capacity of carbon dioxide as a function of temperature in the expression for q, integrate and repeat the computation of q, w, ΔE, and ΔH for the process described in problem 13 (a).

15. To determine the heat capacity of methanol vapor, a steady flow of vapor is maintained over an electric heater at constant voltage and constant current. In an experiment at 76.5° the heater dissipated 0.04674 cal. sec.$^{-1}$; 94.45 g. of CH_3OH passed through the calorimeter during 45 min. at an average temperature rise of 2.464°. Find the specific heat of methanol.

16. (a) One mole of an ideal gas at 1 atm. and 0° is to be compressed isothermally until its volume is 1 l. What is the minimum work which must be done on the gas?

(b) If the initial state is 1 atm. and 100°, what is the minimum work to compress the gas sample to 1 l. at 100°?

17. What is the lowest temperature that can be attained by adiabatic expansion of nitrogen initially at 25° and 10 atm. expanding to a pressure of 1 atm.? (Use data from problem 8 assuming that C_P is independent of temperature.)

18. When crystallization is induced in supercooled water it returns rapidly to 0°, producing some ice. How much ice is produced per gram of water per degree of supercooling?

19. 2,2,3-trimethylbutane melts at 247.7°K. Given the following values of its specific heat, construct an empirical equation describing the heat capacity over the temperature range covered and determine the amount of heat required to raise the temperature of 1 mole of this substance from 247.7°K to 298.2°K.

T (°K)	253.2	258.5	275.3	281.6	293.9
C_P (cal. g.$^{-1}$)	0.459	0.463	0.479	0.485	0.497

20. One mole of an ideal gas at 0° and 1 atm. is expanded isothermally and reversibly to a volume of 100 l. and then heated at constant volume until the pressure is again 1 atm. Compute q, w, ΔE, and ΔH for the total process, taking $C_P = 4.96$ cal. mole^{-1} deg.$^{-1}$

21. One mole of an ideal gas at 0° and 1 atm. pressure is expanded isothermally against a constant external pressure of 0.1 atm. and then cooled at constant pressure until the volume is again 22.4 l. Compute q, w, ΔE, and ΔH for the total process, taking $C_P = 5$ cal. mole^{-1} deg.$^{-1}$

22. A system undergoes a certain change in state by path x for which $w_x = 0$, $q_x = 10,000$ cal. For the same change in state by path y, $w_y = 0.5 \, w_{max.}$ and $q_y = 11,000$ cal. Find $q_{max.}$.

23. An ideal gas at P_1, V_1, T_1 expands adiabatically against zero pressure to V_2. Find P_2, T_2, w, ΔE, ΔH.

24. For gases which obey an equation of the type $PV = RT + bP$
(a) does Boyle's law apply?
(b) does Charles' law apply? Explain.

25. For isothermal expansion of ideal gases, ΔH and ΔE are equal. Show why this is so.

26. When one mole of A (l) and one mole of B (l) at a common temperature T_1 are mixed rapidly and adiabatically the temperature of the resulting solution falls to T_2. By analogy with Fig. 2.7 describe a simple procedure for measuring the enthalpy change for

$$A(l, T_1) + B(l, T_1) = \text{solution}(l, T_1)$$

27. For gases which obey equations of the type $PV = RT + aP + bP^2$, find an expression for the difference between ΔH and ΔE in the isothermal process

$$aA(g) + bB(g) = mM(g) + nN(g)$$

28. For the decomposition $O_3 \longrightarrow 1.5 O_2$, $\Delta H = -34$ kcal. at 25°. A mixture of 10% O_3 in O_2 at 25° and 1 atm. is exploded, expanding against a constant external pressure of 1 atm. What is the final temperature of gas before heat exchange with the surrounding occurs? Take $\bar{C}_P$ for oxygen as approximately 8 cal. mole^{-1} deg.$^{-1}$.

29. In a calorimetric measurement the system liberates heat Q which is entirely absorbed by the surroundings, of unknown heat capacity $\bar{C}_{surr.}$, producing a temperature rise $T_2 - T_1$. Work effects are negligible. The same combination of system and surroundings is raised from T_1 to T_2 by a measured input of electrical energy, $n \mathcal{F} \mathcal{E}$.

(a) Find a relation expressing Q in measured quantities.

(b) Show explicitly how the first law has been invoked.

30. For a gas which obeys the equation of state $PV = RT + bP$ find a relation between T and V for adiabatic reversible expansion.

31. In gas mixtures, each constituent contributes to the total heat capacity as though it were present alone. Find the empirical equation for the heat capacity at constant pressure of a mixture containing 0.5 mole CH_4, 1.0 mole C_2H_4, and 2 moles C_2H_6.

32. A 20 l. vessel contains dry gas at 20° and 785 mm. A large quick-acting valve opens briefly, establishing equalization of pressure with the atmosphere at 745 mm. The residual confined gas, after adiabatic expansion, recovers its original temperature. The final pressure is 723 mm. What is the value of C_P?

33. The equation $PV = RT + bP$ describes the behavior of hydrogen at 100° over a range of 10^3 atm. when $b = 0.0164$ l. Evaluate $w_{max.}$ for the isothermal expansion of 1 mole of hydrogen from 10^3 atm. to 1 atm.

34. With reference to the preceding problem, evaluate $C_P - C_V$ for one mole of hydrogen at 100° and 10^3 atm.

35. Water vapor at 100° and 500 mm. is expanded reversibly and adiabatically. The vapor pressure of water can be expressed by $\log P_{mm.} = -2120/T + 8.63$ and the mean molar heat capacity taken as 8.0 cal. mole^{-1} deg^{-1}. At what pressure will condensation begin?

36. A very large mass of dry air (take $\bar{C}_P$ as 7 cal. mole^{-1} deg^{-1}) at 20° and 750 mm. is pushed by steady winds over the top of a mountain range where the pressure is 550 mm. Estimate the air temperature on the mountain top.

37. Real gases at high pressures are non-ideal and both H and E become functions of P (or V) at constant T. For the free, adiabatic expansion ($\Delta H = 0$) of oxygen from $P_1 = 200$ atm. and $T_1 = 298°$ to $P_2 = 0.1$ atm., the final temperature is $T_2 = 248°$. Devise a simple cycle from which ΔH_{T_2} for the isothermal expansion O_2 (200 atm., 248°K) = O_2 (0.1 atm., 248°K) can be evaluated. Find ΔH_{T_2}.

38. Two gases are confined in a long cylinder and separated by a membrane at a uniform temperature and unequal pressures. Their mean heat capacities are $\bar{C}_A$ and $\bar{C}_B$. The membrane is broken and A expands, compressing B. Find an expression relating ΔT_A and ΔT_B.

39. Derive a relation between C_P and T for adiabatic reversible expansion of an ideal gas starting with the equation $dH = dE + d(PV)$.

3

THERMOCHEMISTRY

3.1 Heats of Reaction

Thermochemistry is the study of the heat effects accompanying chemical and associated physical changes. Processes which are accompanied by the evolution of heat by the system are called *exothermic* and those which are accompanied by the absorption of heat are called *endothermic*. In the former case the value of q, the heat absorbed by the system, is negative, and in the latter case q is positive. For example, complete combustion of 12 g. of carbon (graphite) to form 44 g. of carbon dioxide gas at 25° and 1 atm. liberates 94.05 kcal. This quantity

$$C\,(\text{graph.}) + O_2(g) = CO_2(g); \qquad q = -94.05 \text{ kcal.}$$

is called the heat of combustion of graphite. The combustion process is exothermic and the value of q, the heat absorbed, is negative. The value of q is often given in kilogram-calories (kcal), a unit of heat equal to 1000 cal.

The first law of thermodynamics is applied to the measurement and computation of heat effects in chemical and physical processes through the thermodynamic properties E and H. For processes carried out at constant volume the heat absorbed q_V is a direct measure of the change in internal energy of the system ΔE; for processes carried out at constant pressure the heat absorbed q_P is a direct measure of the change in heat content of the system ΔH.

$$q_V = \Delta E \tag{3.1}$$
$$q_P = \Delta H \tag{3.2}$$

Therefore, under these two specific conditions the heats of reaction are thermodynamic functions whose values depend only on the initial and final states of the systems under study. This important application of the first law of thermodynamics will enable us to develop several useful relationships among heats of reaction.

3.2 Calorimetry

The measurement of heats of reaction is known as *calorimetry*. Processes of combustion are among the most readily studied since in general they can be initiated at will and take place rapidly and completely. Heats of combustion are often measured in an adiabatic bomb calorimeter, illustrated in Fig. 3.1.

A weighed sample of the material to be burned is introduced into the heavy-walled inner chamber or "bomb." This chamber is charged to a high pressure with oxygen, so that an excess is present. A weighed quantity of water is placed in the bucket in which the charged bomb is immersed. Reaction is initiated by passing an electric current through a fuse wire in contact with the sample, and the heat evolved in the process is absorbed by the material of the bomb and by the water in contact with it. The heat evolved is measured by noting the change in temperature of the bomb and water (the total heat capacity of the bomb plus the water must be known) or by subsequently measuring the amount of electric energy required to produce the same temperature increment as the process of interest.

Throughout the operations the outer jacket is kept at a temperature as close as possible to that of the bomb and its surrounding water in order to minimize heat losses. Minor corrections for heat input during ignition of the sample and heat input by stirring devices are necessary.

By proper choice of the sample size, the net temperature increment is usually limited to a few degrees, so that for practical purposes the isothermal heat of reaction has been measured. In a fast reaction local temperatures inside the bomb may be much higher than either the initial or final temperatures of the whole system, but the quantity of heat absorbed or evolved in the process depends only on the initial and final states of the system in this constant volume process.

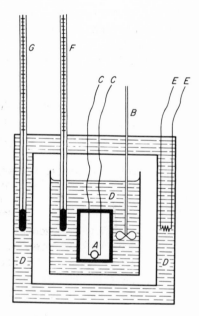

FIG. 3.1. Adiabatic bomb calorimeter.

EXERCISE 3.1

In a typical measurement of the heat of combustion of solid benzoic acid, $C_7H_6O_2$, to form carbon dioxide and liquid water the following data were obtained: Weight of benzoic acid, 0.9350 g.; weight of water in contact with the bomb, 1235 g.; heat capacity of bomb, 535 cal. deg.$^{-1}$; observed temperature increment, 3.340°; average temperature, 25°. Ignore minor corrections and compute the molar heat of combustion of benzoic acid at constant volume.

$Ans. q_V = -771.5$ kcal. mole^{-1}.

Since the work done by the system in bomb calorimetry is zero, the heats of reaction observed in such a device are to be equated to ΔE for the process, as in equation (3.1). For example, the combustion of a gram of liquid methanol in a bomb calorimeter at 25° liberates 5410 cal. Therefore, for the constant volume, constant temperature process

$$CH_3OH \text{ (l)} + \tfrac{3}{2}O_2 \text{ (g)} = CO_2 \text{ (g)} + 2 H_2O \text{ (l)}$$

$$q_V = \Delta E_{298} = -173.34 \text{ kcal. mole}^{-1}$$

Many processes are carried out under constant pressure, often that of the atmosphere, and the heat effect is given by ΔH rather than ΔE, as shown in equation (3.2). For a constant pressure process, the relation between ΔH and ΔE is given by equation (2.27).

$$q_P = \Delta H_P = \Delta E + P \Delta V \qquad (3.3)$$

The initial and final volumes of the system will be largely determined by the volumes of gases present in the initial and final states, and

$$\Delta V = \Delta nRT/P, \qquad \Delta n = n_f - n_i$$

where n_f and n_i denote the final and initial numbers of moles of gas in the system. Substitution in equation (3.3) yields

$$q_P = \Delta H_P = \Delta E + \Delta nRT \qquad (3.4)$$

While the processes which take place in a bomb calorimeter are not constant pressure processes, the internal energies of the products and reactants are practically independent of pressure. For the gases this is equivalent to saying that they are approximately ideal. Therefore we may state as a good approximation that for the constant *pressure*, constant temperature process

$$CH_3OH \text{ (l)} + \tfrac{3}{2} O_2 \text{ (g)} = CO_2 \text{ (g)} + 2 H_2O \text{ (l)}$$

$$\Delta E_{298} = -173.34 \text{ kcal.}$$

In this process $\Delta n = -\tfrac{1}{2}$ mole of gas and

$$q_P = \Delta H_{298} = -173.34 - (\tfrac{1}{2} \times 1.99 \times 298 \times 10^{-3}) = -173.64 \text{ kcal.}$$

When $\Delta n = 0$, that is, when the number of moles of gaseous products is the same as the number of moles of gaseous reactants, ΔE and ΔH become identical in this approximation.

A brief list of heats of combustion at constant pressure can be found in Table 3.1.

TABLE 3.1

HEATS OF COMBUSTION AT 25°*

(to form liquid water and carbon dioxide)

Substance	ΔH_{298} (combustion) (kcal. mole^{-1})
H_2 (g)	-68.317
C (s) (graphite)	-94.05
CO (g)	-67.64
CH_4 (g)	-212.798
C_2H_6 (g)	-372.820
C_2H_4 (g)	-337.234
C_2H_2 (g)	-310.615
C_6H_6 (l)	-780.98

* From *Selected Values of the Properties of Hydrocarbons*, Circular C461, National Bureau of Standards, 1947.

EXERCISE 3.2

From the data given in Table 3.1 find ΔE_{298} for the constant pressure combustion of ethylene.   *Ans.* -336.054 kcal. mole^{-1}.

3.3 Thermochemical Equations; Hess's Law

In the preceding chapter it was shown that E and H are thermodynamic properties. Their values depend only on the state of the system, not on its history. Then, for any process

$$aA + bB + \ldots = mM + nN + \ldots$$

the change in heat content (or internal energy) for the process is always given by the total heat content (internal energy) of the products less the total heat content (internal energy) of the reactants, regardless of how the process is carried out.

$$\Delta H = mH(M) + nH(N) - aH(A) - bH(B)$$
$$\Delta E = mE(M) + nE(N) - aE(A) - bE(B)$$

$$(3.5)$$

where $H(M)$, $E(M)$, etc., represent the absolute values of the molar heat contents and internal energy contents of the reactants and products. These quantities have fixed, although unknown, values for any specified state of the substance concerned.

Equation (3.5) is to be regarded as a limited statement of the first law of thermodynamics in its application to a chemical process and, as such, constitutes the basis for thermochemistry. Equation (3.5) contains no restriction as to temperature but for the sake of simplicity we will be largely concerned with its application to isothermal processes.

As a specific example of the applicability of equation (3.5), consider again the combustion of liquid methanol at a constant total pressure of 1 atm. and 25°. For this process,

$$CH_3OH \text{ (l)} + \tfrac{3}{2}O_2(g) = CO_2(g) + 2H_2O \text{ (l)}$$

$$\Delta H_{298} = H \text{ (CO}_2\text{, g)} + 2H \text{ (H}_2\text{O, l)} - H \text{ (CH}_3\text{OH, l)} - \tfrac{3}{2}H \text{ (O}_2\text{, g)}$$

and although it is not possible to measure H (CO_2, g), etc., we can measure ΔH_{298}. Not only can this value be measured, but it is always the same for the change from the specified initial state [CH_3OH (l) $+ \tfrac{3}{2}O_2(g)$ at 25°, 1 atm.] to the specified final state [$CO_2(g) + 2H_2O$ (l) at 25°, 1 atm.] regardless of what path is taken.

Equation (3.5) applies with equal validity to the "reverse" process as well as the "forward" process, since the direction of the process is arbitrary. That is, every member of equation (3.5) may be multiplied by (-1) and one obtains ΔH_R for the "reverse" process. For the generalized process given at the beginning of this section,

$$\Delta H_R = aH(A) + bH(B) - mH(M) - nH(N)$$
$$\Delta H_R = -\Delta H_F \tag{3.6}$$

where ΔH_F refers to the forward reaction.

Equation (3.5) also illustrates the fact that E and H are extensive properties, with values proportional to the amounts of substance. If every member of the equation is multiplied by any common factor α, the value of ΔH is multiplied by the same factor. For the process

$$\alpha aA + \alpha bB + \cdots = \alpha mM + \alpha nN + \cdots$$
$$\Delta H' = \alpha mH(M) + \alpha nH(N) - \alpha aH(A) - \alpha bH(B)$$
$$\Delta H' = \alpha \Delta H \tag{3.7}$$

EXERCISE 3.3

For the constant pressure process

$$CO \text{ (g)} + H_2 \text{ (g)} = H_2O \text{ (g)} + C \text{ (s)}$$
$$\Delta H_{298} = -31.38 \text{ kcal.}$$

What is the heat of reaction at constant pressure and 25° when 1 g. of carbon reacts completely with water vapor to form carbon monoxide and hydrogen? What is the heat of reaction at constant volume?

Ans. $q_P = \Delta H = 2615$ cal., $q_V = \Delta E = 2565$ cal.

Since each substance involved in a chemical or physical process has unique values of E and H depending only on its state, it follows that the values of ΔE and ΔH for a specified process are independent of the number and nature of intermediate states. If the generalized process takes place through an intermediate state represented by $jJ + kK + \ldots$, relations equivalent to equation (3.5) may be written for each step.

$$\Delta H(A - J) = jH(J) + kH(K) - aH(A) - bH(B)$$
$$\Delta H(J - M) = mH(M) + nH(N) - jH(J) - kH(K)$$

The change in heat content for the over-all process, $\Delta H(A - M)$, is simply the sum of the two described above, as illustrated in the following diagram.

$$aA + bB + \cdots \xrightarrow{\Delta H(A-M)} mM + nN + \cdots$$

$$\Delta H(A-J) \searrow \quad \nearrow \Delta H(J-M)$$

$$jJ + kK + \cdots$$

$$mH(M) + nH(N) - aH(A) - bH(B) = j\!\!\!/H(J) + k\!\!\!/H(K) - aH(A)$$
$$- bH(B) + mH(M)$$
$$+ nH(N) - j\!\!\!/H(J) - k\!\!\!/H(K)$$
$$\Delta H(A - M) = \Delta H(A - J) + \Delta H(J - M) \qquad (3.8)$$

Since the values of $H(J)$ and $H(K)$ are unique for those substances in specified states, the cancellation indicated in equation (3.8) is always permitted, provided the values of the stoichiometric coefficients j and k are the same in $\Delta H(A - J)$ and in $\Delta H(J - M)$. This can always be arranged by multiplying one or the other by a constant factor.

As an example of the application of equation (3.8), consider the combustion of hydrogen to form water vapor, which may be regarded as the net result of two processes,

$$H_2(g) + \tfrac{1}{2}O_2(g) = H_2O \text{ (l)}$$
$$\Delta H_{298} = -68.32 \text{ kcal.}$$

and
$$H_2O \text{ (l)} = H_2O(g)$$
$$\Delta H_{298} = 10.52 \text{ kcal.}$$

Therefore,

$$H_2(g) + \tfrac{1}{2}O_2(g) = H_2O(g)$$
$$\Delta H_{298} = -68.32 + 10.52 = -57.80 \text{ kcal.}$$

As a second example, let us find ΔH for the formation of carbon monoxide from graphite and oxygen from the following information:

(i)
$$C(\text{graph.}) + O_2(g) = CO_2(g)$$
$$\Delta H_{298}(i) = -94.05 \text{ kcal.}$$

(ii)
$$CO(g) + \tfrac{1}{2}O_2(g) = CO_2(g)$$
$$\Delta H_{298}(ii) = -67.64 \text{ kcal.}$$

The process for which we wish to compute ΔH is

(iii)
$$C(\text{graph.}) + \tfrac{1}{2}O_2(g) = CO(g)$$

This is evidently equivalent to formation of one mole of CO_2, followed by the reverse of process (ii). This relationship is illustrated in Fig. 3.2, where the heat content of the system in various states is represented by a vertical displacement.

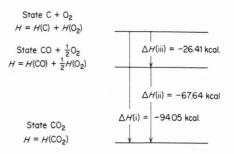

FIG. 3.2. Heat content of the system C + O₂.

State C + O₂
$H = H(C) + H(O_2)$

State CO + $\tfrac{1}{2}O_2$
$H = H(CO) + \tfrac{1}{2}H(O_2)$

State CO₂
$H = H(CO_2)$

$\Delta H(iii) = -26.41$ kcal.

$\Delta H(ii) = -67.64$ kcal

$\Delta H(i) = -94.05$ kcal.

It is evident that

$$\Delta H_{298} \text{ (iii)} = \Delta H \text{ (i)} - \Delta H \text{ (ii)}$$
$$= -94.05 + 67.64$$
$$\Delta H_{298} \text{ (iii)} = -26.41 \text{ kcal.}$$

EXERCISE 3.4

Using data given above compute the value of ΔH_{298} for

$$CO \text{ (g)} + H_2 \text{ (g)} = H_2O \text{ (g)} + C \text{ (graph.)}$$

Ans. −31.38 kcal.

The addition and subtraction of thermochemical data specified in equation (3.8) and illustrated above is an application of the first law of thermodynamics, known as *Hess's Law of Constant Heat Summation*, which states that *the heat of reaction* (ΔH or ΔE) *is independent of path and depends only on initial and final states of the system.* This principle permits the computation of the heat effects of many processes for which direct measurements are not available. For example, we may compute ΔH_{298} for

(i) $$2 C \text{ (graph.)} + 3 H_2(g) = C_2H_6(g)$$

from the observed heats of combustion of graphite, hydrogen, and ethane given in Table 3.1. The values given there refer to the processes

(ii) $$C \text{ (graph.)} + O_2(g) = CO_2(g)$$
$$\Delta H_{298} \text{ (ii)} = -94.05 \text{ kcal.}$$

(iii) $$H_2 \text{ (g)} + \tfrac{1}{2} O_2(g) = H_2O \text{ (l)}$$
$$\Delta H_{298}\text{(iii)} = -68.32 \text{ kcal.}$$

(iv) $$C_2H_6(g) + \tfrac{7}{2} O_2(g) = 2 CO_2(g) + 3 H_2O \text{ (l)}$$
$$\Delta H_{298} \text{ (iv)} = -372.82 \text{ kcal.}$$

Treating these relations as algebraic equations, we see that the combination

$$2\text{(ii)} + 3\text{(iii)} - \text{(iv)} = \text{(i)}$$

corresponds to

$$
\begin{aligned}
2 C &+ 2 O_2 &&= 2 CO_2 \\
3 H_2 &+ \tfrac{3}{2} O_2 &&= 3 H_2O \\
2 CO_2 &+ 3 H_2O &&= C_2H_6 + \tfrac{7}{2} O_2 \\
\hline
2 C &+ 3 H_2 &&= C_2H_6
\end{aligned}
$$

and therefore the value of ΔH_{298} for this process is given by

$$\Delta H_{298} \text{ (i)} = 2 \Delta H_{298} \text{ (ii)} + 3 \Delta H_{298} \text{ (iii)} - \Delta H_{298} \text{ (iv)}$$
$$= 2(-94.05) + 3(-68.32) - (-372.82)$$
$$= -20.24 \text{ kcal.}$$

Note that this operation consists in adding the heats of combustion of the reactants and from this sum subtracting the heats of combustion of the products. In each case the molar heat of combustion is multiplied by the appropriate stoichiometric coefficient.

EXERCISE 3.5

For the combustion of liquid ethanol to form carbon dioxide and liquid water, $\Delta H_{298} = -326.70$ kcal. mole^{-1}. Find ΔH_{298} for the process

$$2\ C\ (graph.) + 3\ H_2\ (g) + \tfrac{1}{2}O_2\ (g) = C_2H_5OH\ (l)$$

Ans. $\Delta H = -66.36$ kcal.

3.4 Heats of Formation; Standard States

The values of ΔH computed in the preceding example and exercise are for the formation of a compound from its elements. They are called heats of formation and represented by ΔH_f. They afford a convenient means of compiling thermochemical information, as in Table 3.2. From the data given

TABLE. 3.2

HEATS OF FORMATION AT 25°*

(from the elements in their standard states)

Substance	$\Delta H^0{}_{298}$ (kcal. mole^{-1})	Substance	$\Delta H^0{}_{298}$ (kcal. mole^{-1})
H_2O (g)	-57.7979	methane, CH_4 (g)	-17.889
H_2O (l)	-68.3174	ethane, C_2H_6 (g)	-20.236
HCl (g)	-22.063	propane, C_3H_8 (g)	-24.820
HBr (g)	-8.66	normal butane, C_4H_{10} (g)	-29.812
HI (g)	6.20	isobutane, C_4H_{10} (g)	-31.452
SO_2 (g)	-70.96	normal pentane, C_5H_{12} (g)	-35.00
SO_3 (g)	-94.45	normal hexane, C_6H_{14} (g)	-39.96
H_2S (g)	-4.815	benzene, C_6H_6 (g)	19.820
NO (g)	21.600	benzene, C_6H_6 (l)	11.718
NO_2 (g)	8.091	ethylene, C_2H_4 (g)	12.496
NH_3 (g)	-11.04	acetylene, C_2H_2 (g)	54.194
CO (g)	-26.415	formaldehyde, $HCHO$ (g)	27.7
CO_2 (g)	-94.0518	acetaldehyde, CH_3CHO (g)	-39.76
$AgCl$ (s)	-30.362	methanol, CH_3OH (l)	-57.02
$AgBr$ (s)	-23.78	ethanol, C_2H_5OH (l)	-66.356
Fe_2O_3 (s)	-196.5	formic acid, $HCOOH$ (l)	-97.8
Al_2O_3 (s)	-399.09	acetic acid, CH_3COOH (l)	-116.4
$NaCl$ (s)	-98.232		

*From *Selected Values of Chemical Thermodynamic Properties*, Circular 500, National Bureau of Standards, 1952; and from *Selected Values of Properties of Hydrocarbons*, Circular C461, National Bureau of Standards, 1947.

in Table 3.2, we may compute the value of ΔH_{298} for the oxidation of ethane to ethanol by application of Hess's law (equation 3.8).

(i) $$C_2H_6\ (g) + \tfrac{1}{2}\ O_2\ (g) = C_2H_5OH\ (l)$$

The formation of ethane and ethanol from the elements corresponds to the following processes:

(ii)
$$2 \text{ C (graph.)} + 3 \text{ H}_2 \text{ (g)} = \text{C}_2\text{H}_6 \text{ (g)}$$
$$\Delta H_{298} \text{ (ii)} = -20.236 \text{ kcal.}$$

(iii)
$$2 \text{ C (graph.)} + 3 \text{ H}_2 \text{ (g)} + \tfrac{1}{2} \text{O}_2 \text{ (g)} = \text{C}_2\text{H}_5\text{OH (l)}$$
$$\Delta H_{298} \text{ (iii)} = -66.356 \text{ kcal.}$$

The process of interest is equivalent to the reverse of process (ii) followed by process (iii)

$$\text{C}_2\text{H}_6 \text{ (g)} = 2 \text{ C (graph.)} + 3 \text{ H}_2 \text{ (g)}$$
$$2 \text{ C (graph.)} + 3 \text{ H}_2 \text{(g)} + \tfrac{1}{2} \text{O}_2 \text{(g)} = \text{C}_2\text{H}_5\text{OH (l)}$$

$$\overline{\text{C}_2\text{H}_6\text{(g)} + \tfrac{1}{2} \text{O}_2 \text{(g)} = \text{C}_2\text{H}_5\text{OH (l)}}$$

It follows that

$$\Delta H\text{(i)} = -\Delta H\text{(ii)} + \Delta H\text{(iii)}$$
$$= -(-20.236) + (-66.356) = -46.120 \text{ kcal.}$$

In a similar fashion, the value of ΔH may be computed for any process in which the values of ΔH of formation of all of the compounds involved are known. For the purpose of computation we may imagine that decomposition of reactants into the elements is followed by formation of products from these elements. For example, in the simple process

$$\text{HI (g)} + \text{NaCl (s)} = \text{NaI (s)} + \text{HCl (g)}$$

let

$$\text{HI(g)} + \text{NaCl(s)}$$
$$\downarrow$$
$$\tfrac{1}{2} \text{I}_2 \text{(s)} + \tfrac{1}{2} \text{H}_2 \text{(g)} + \text{Na(s)} + \tfrac{1}{2} \text{Cl}_2 \text{(g)}$$
$$\downarrow$$
$$\text{NaI(s)} + \text{HCl(g)}$$

and therefore ΔH for the process of interest is given by the sum of the ΔH's for the two steps. With rearrangement, these may be written

$$\Delta H = \begin{cases} H\,(\text{NaI, s}) & + H\,(\text{HCl, g}) - H\,(\text{NaCl, s}) - H\,(\text{HI, g}) \\ - H\,(\text{Na, s}) - \tfrac{1}{2}H\,(\text{H}_2\text{, g}) + H\,(\text{Na, s}) & + \tfrac{1}{2}H\,(\text{H}_2\text{, g}) \\ - \tfrac{1}{2}H\,(\text{I}_2\text{, s}) - \tfrac{1}{2}H\,(\text{Cl}_2\text{,g}) + \tfrac{1}{2}H\,(\text{Cl}_2\text{, g}) & + \tfrac{1}{2}H\,(\text{I}_2\text{, s}) \end{cases}$$

$$\Delta H = \quad \underset{(\text{NaI, s})}{\Delta H_f} \quad + \underset{(\text{HCl, g})}{\Delta H_f} \quad - \underset{(\text{NaCl, s})}{\Delta H_f} \quad - \underset{(\text{HI, g})}{\Delta H_f}$$

In general, for

$$a\text{A} + b\text{B} + \ldots = m\text{M} + n\text{N} + \ldots$$
$$\Delta H = m\Delta H_f(\text{M}) + n\Delta H_f(\text{N}) - a\Delta H_f(\text{A}) - \qquad (3.9)$$
$$b\Delta H_f(\text{B})$$

where $\Delta H_f(\text{M})$, etc., represent molar heats of formation of the compounds, M, etc., at the temperature of interest. This is a special form of equation (3.8).

Let us apply this method to

$$\text{C}_2\text{H}_6\text{(g)} + 7/2 \text{ O}_2\text{(g)} = 2 \text{ CO}_2\text{(g)} + 3 \text{ H}_2\text{O(l)}$$

and find ΔH_{298} for the combustion from the data of Table 3.2. From equation (3.9)

$$\Delta H_{298} = 2\,\Delta H_f(CO_2) + 3\,\Delta H_f(H_2O, 1) - \Delta H_f(C_2H_6)$$

Note that no term corresponding to the heat of formation of oxygen appears, since this is an element and therefore its heat of formation is zero. The expression above is equivalent to:

$$2\,C(\text{graph.}) + 2\,O_2(g) = 2\,CO_2(g) \qquad \Delta H = -\;188.104$$
$$3\,H_2(g) + \tfrac{3}{2}O_2(g) = 3\,H_2O\,(l) \qquad \Delta H = -\;204.951$$
$$C_2H_6(g) = 2\,C(\text{graph.}) + 3\,H_2(g) \quad \Delta H = \quad\;\; 20.236$$

$$\overline{C_2H_6(g) + \tfrac{7}{2}\,O_2(g) = 2\,CO_2(g) + 3\,H_2O(l) \quad \Delta H = -\;372.819}$$

EXERCISE 3.6

From the values of ΔH_{298} for formation of CH_4 (g), CO_2 (g), and H_2O (l) from the elements given in Table 3.2 compute ΔH_{298} for the process

$$CH_4\,(g) + 2\,O_2\,(g) = CO_2\,(g) + 2\,H_2O\,(l)$$

and compare with the heat of combustion given in Table 3.1.

EXERCISE 3.7

By analogy with the development of equation (3.9), obtain a corresponding relation in terms of ΔE.

In order for equation (3.9) to be valid, it is evident that the heats of formation of the compounds involved in a process must refer to identical states of their constituent elements. Only in this case will the heat contents of the elements disappear in the equation. In the case of

$$HI(g) + NaCl(s) = NaI(s) + HCl(g)$$

the heats of formation of both $HI(g)$ and $NaI(s)$ must refer to a single state of the element iodine. In the example given, the formation processes for $HI(g)$ and $NaI(s)$ both refer to $I_2(s)$, although one could just as well have used the values of ΔH_{298} for the formation processes from gaseous iodine. In such a case, $\Delta H_f(NaI, s)$ and $\Delta H_f(HI, g)$ would both be altered by exactly the same amount, the ΔH_{298} for sublimation of $\tfrac{1}{2}I_2$. Therefore no particular state of an element need be chosen, but the state chosen must be used consistently within any set of calculations.

In order to make the tabulated values of heats of formation consistent in this respect, it is convenient to specify *standard states* for the elements. At each temperature the standard state of the element is that physical state (g, 1, s) which is most stable, at a pressure of 1 atm. By this convention the standard state of hydrogen at 25° is the gaseous state (H_2, g) at 1 atm.;[1] the standard state of mercury is the liquid at 1 atm. With crystalline solids which exhibit

---

[1]This definition of the standard state of gases assumes that they are ideal. For greater precision in dealing with real gases, the standard state is defined as the state of unit *fugacity*, a property which may be described as the ideal pressure of a real gas.

more than one crystalline form it is also necessary to further specify the form. Thus the standard state of carbon at 25° is graphite at 1 atm.; the standard state of sulfur at 25° is the rhombic form at 1 atm., but at 100° the standard state is the monoclinic form at 1 atm.

The specification of the standard state is also extended to compounds, except that the restriction as to physical state is not used and the standard state of a compound is simply that of 1 atm. Thus water vapor at 1 atm. is the standard state of water vapor at any given temperature and liquid water at 1 atm. is the standard state of liquid water at any given temperature.

A superscript o attached to the symbol for the change in heat content thus, ΔH^o, denotes the standard states. For example, the standard change in heat content for the formation of liquid water from its elements refers to

$$H_2(g, 1 \text{ atm.}) + \tfrac{1}{2}O_2(g, 1 \text{ atm.}) = H_2O(l, 1 \text{ atm.})$$
$$\Delta H^o_{298} = -68.32 \text{ kcal.}$$

and the standard change in heat content for the formation of water vapor refers to

$$H_2(g, 1 \text{ atm.}) + \tfrac{1}{2}O_2(g, 1 \text{ atm.}) = H_2O(g, 1 \text{ atm.})$$
$$\Delta H^o_{298} = -57.80 \text{ kcal.}$$

In practice, the pressures of the reactants and products have small influence on ΔH except for pressures considerably above 1 atm. For an ideal gas the value of ΔH for isothermal compression or expansion is zero, and for real gases, liquids, and solids it is negligible for all except extreme changes. The specification of the phase or state of aggregation of the elements, however, is an important consideration in reactions of formation.

3.5 Other Applications of Hess's Law

Experimental thermochemical methods for atoms, free radicals, electronically excited species, and gaseous ions are very unlike those of classical thermochemistry. Some of these methods, involving optical spectra, electron impact and chemical kinetics, will be considered later. The corresponding thermochemical calculations are, however, entirely classical and will be considered now.

The energy required to dissociate a molecule into atoms and free radicals is known as the *bond dissociation energy*, D. Examples are:

$$H_2(g) = 2 H(g), \quad \Delta H_{298} = D_{H-H} = 103 \text{ kcal.}$$

$$I_2(g) = 2 I(g), \quad \Delta H_{298} = D_{I-I} = 36.1 \text{ kcal.}$$

$$CH_4(g) = CH_3(g) + H(g), \quad \Delta H_{298} = D_{CH_3-H} = 103 \text{ kcal.}$$

The information is completely interconvertible with standard heats of formation. For some processes it is easier to remember, and to use, values of D rather than ΔH_f. As an example, for

$$CH_4(g) + H(g) = CH_3(g) + H_2(g)$$
$$\Delta H = D_{H-H} - D_{CH_3-H} = 0 \text{ kcal.}$$

EXERCISE 3.8

For the reaction $AB + CD = AC + BD$ show that

$$\Delta H = \Delta H_f(AC) + \Delta H_f(BD) - \Delta H_f(AC) - \Delta H_f(CD)$$
$$= D_{A-B} + D_{C-D} - D_{A-C} - D_{B-D}$$

In the example above, the value of ΔH_f (H) is one-half the heat of dissociation of H_2 or 51.5 kcal./g. atom. For iodine, however, the ΔH_f (I) corresponds, by definition, to

$$\tfrac{1}{2}I_2(s) = I(g)$$

It is therefore necessary to include the heat of sublimation of iodine

$$I_2(s) = I_2(g), \Delta H_{298}^o = 14.88 \text{ kcal.}$$

EXERCISE 3.9

Show that $\Delta H_f(I)$ is 25.5 kcal./g. atom.

EXERCISE 3.10

From information given in this chapter find ΔH_{298}^o for $HI(g) = H(g) + I(g)$.
$$Ans. \ \Delta H_{298}^o = 70.8 \text{ kcal.}$$

The bond dissociation energy should not be confused with a quantity sometimes called the bond strength. A single illustration will suffice. For the complete atomization of CH_4,

$$CH_4(g) = C(g) + 4H(g)$$

the value of ΔH can be obtained from

$$C(graphite) = C(g), \Delta H_{298}^o = 171 \text{ kcal.}$$
$$C(graphite) + 2H_2(g) = CH_4(g), \Delta H_{298}^o = -18 \text{ kcal.}$$
$$H_2(g) = 2H(g), \ \Delta H_{298}^o = 103 \text{ kcal.}$$

Combining these data, for atomization of CH_4

$$\Delta H_{298}^o = 171 + (2 \times 103) - (-18) = 395 \text{ kcal.}$$

and the bond strength is $\tfrac{395}{4} = 98.7$ kcal.

EXERCISE 3.11

Show that the thermochemical quantity just found is the sum of the four individual bond dissociation energies:

$$D_{CH_3-H} + D_{CH_2-H} + D_{CH-H} + D_{C-H} = 395 \text{ kcal.}$$

For physico-chemical purposes the individual values of D are required. In the present example $D_{aver.} = 98.7$ kcal. per $C-H$ bond. To obtain D_{CH_3-H} it is necessary to proceed differently. The energy required to decompose relatively unstable compounds can be deduced from chemical kinetics, as

(i)
$$CH_3I(g) = CH_3(g) + I(g)$$
$$\Delta H_{298}^o = 54.0 \text{ kcal.}$$

This value is combined with other heats of formation and dissociation as follows:

(ii)
$$CH_4(g) + I_2(s) = CH_3I(g) + HI(g)$$
$$\Delta H^o_{298} = \Delta H_f(CH_3I, g) + \Delta H_f(HI, g) - \Delta H_f(CH_4, g)$$
$$= 29.0 \text{ kcal.}$$

(iii)
$$HI(g) = H(g) + I(g)$$
$$\Delta H^o_{298} = 70.8 \text{ kcal.}$$

(iv)
$$I_2(s) = 2 I(g)$$
$$\Delta H^o_{298} = 51.0 \text{ kcal.}$$

Combination of these equations yields for the process

$$CH_4(g) = CH_3(g) + H(g)$$
$$D_{CH_3-H} = \Delta H(i) + \Delta H(ii) + \Delta H(iii) - \Delta H(iv)$$
$$= 54.0 + 29.0 + 70.8 - 51.0$$
$$= 102.8 \text{ kcal.}$$

A table of bond dissociation energies will be found in Chapter 16.

EXERCISE 3.12

The ΔH_f for $Hg(CH_3)_2(l)$ is $+14.31$ kcal. Representing the successive bond dissociation energies for removing first one, then the second, CH_3 from CH_3-Hg-CH_3 by D_1 and D_2, show that $D_1 + D_2 = 2\Delta H_f(CH_3, g) + \Delta H_f(Hg, g) - \Delta H_f[Hg(CH_3)_2, g]$. Take the heats of vaporization of $Hg(CH_3)_2$ and $Hg(g)$ as 8.1 and 14.5 kcal., respectively, and evaluate $D_1 + D_2$. From chemical kinetics it has been found that $D_1 = 51.4$ kcal. *Ans.* $D_1 + D_2 = 58.9$ kcal.

Gaseous ions and solvated ions differ greatly in their chemistry. That will be considered later, but let us be careful to distinguish between them as, eg., $H^+(g)$ and $H^+(aq.)$. In either case, Hess's law can apply. If it could not, the first law would be invalidated.

The common ions form spontaneously in aqueous media, and often very exothermically, as with sodium. Ionization in water (and other polar media) is a complicated business. The difficulties may be glossed over by writing

$$Na(s) = Na^+(aq) + e(aq)$$

and we do not at all understand how H_2 forms. In the gaseous state the formation of ions is much simpler in principle, but invariably very endothermic. The first, and best understood ionization is

$$H(g) = H^+(g) + e$$

To avoid misconceptions arising from the symbol H^+, it should be understood that gaseous ions bear little relation to aqueous ions. Well-known gaseous ions include H_2^+, H_3^+, OH^+, CH_4^+, CH_5^+. The relevent thermochemical quantity in cases of simple electron removal is the *ionization potential*, I, for products in their lowest energy states. It can be measured from the least energetic quantum of light which just produces ions from an atom, radical, or molecule [K. Watanabe, *J. Chem. Phys.*, **26**, 542 (1957)]. It can also be identified with the minimum electron accelerating voltage required to produce ions by electron impact in a mass spectrometer. By this method it is possible to distinguish between simple electron removal.

$$CH_4(g) + e = CH_4^+(g) + 2e, \quad \Delta H = I$$

and formation of fragment ions,

$$CH_4(g) + e = CH_3^+(g) + H(g) + 2e, \quad \Delta H = A$$

The thermochemical quantity A is the *appearance potential*. For the example chosen $A(CH_3^+) = D_{CH_3-H} + I_{CH_3}$

Although the determination of appearance potentials is less precise than photo-ionization measurements, a wider variety of processes can be studied. For example, the appearance potentials[2] of $C_2H_5^+$ ions from C_2H_6 and from C_3H_8 have been determined [J.J. Mitchell and F.F. Coleman, *J. Chem. Phys.*, **17**, 44 (1949)]:

(i) $$C_2H_6 + e = C_2H_5^+ + H + 2e$$
$$A\,(i) = 12.71 \text{ e. v.}$$

(ii) $$C_3H_8 + e = C_2H_5^+ + CH_3 + 2e$$
$$A\,(ii) = 12.03 \text{ e. v.}$$

When combined, by use of Hess's law, with the process

(iii) $$C_2H_6 + CH_4 = C_3H_8 + 2\,H$$
$$\Delta H(iii) = 116.3 \text{ kcal. mole}^{-1}$$

whose heat effect is obtained from standard heats of formation, a value of D_{CH_3-H} is obtained

(iv) $$CH_4 = CH_3 + H$$
$$\Delta H = \Delta H\,(iii) + A\,(ii) - A\,(i)$$
$$= 116.3 + 277.3 - 293.0 = 100.6 \text{ kcal. mole}^{-1}$$

EXERCISE 3.13

The appearance potentials for the processes

$$CH_4 + e = CH_3^+ + H + 2e; \quad A = 14.4 \text{ e. v.}$$
$$CH_3 + e = CH_3^+ + 2e; \quad A = 10.1 \text{ e. v.}$$

have been observed as indicated. From these data find a value for D_{CH_3-H}.
Ans. 99 kcal. mole^{-1}.

3.6   Heats of Solution

When two or more substances are mixed to form a homogeneous solution it is observed that heat is usually evolved or absorbed. This heat of

---

[2]One electron volt (e. v.) per molecule = 23.061 kcal. mole^{-1}.

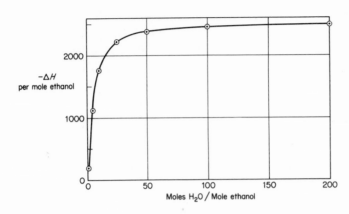

FIG. 3.3. Integral heat of solution of ethanol in water at 25°.

mixing or of solution depends of course upon the nature of the substances and also on their amounts. Figure 3.3 describes the heat effects accompanying the process

$$C_2H_5OH \text{ (l)} + nH_2O \text{ (l)} = C_2H_5OH \text{ } (nH_2O), \Delta H \text{ (sol. } nH_2O)$$

as a function of the extent of dilution of the solution formed. It is evident that the process is exothermic by an amount which increases with increasing dilution. The heat evolved in the formation of a solution of some particular concentration from the pure components is known as the *integral heat of solution*. From the figure we find for the process

$$C_2H_5OH \text{ (l)} + 5H_2O \text{ (l)} = C_2H_5OH \text{ (in } 5H_2O)$$
$$\Delta H \text{ (sol., } 5H_2O) = -1120 \text{ cal.}$$

It appears from the figure and is generally true that the integral heat of solution increases with increasing dilution, approaching a limiting value, the *heat of solution at infinite dilution*. In the case of ethanol, we find for

$$C_2H_5OH \text{ (l)} + \infty H_2O \text{ (l)} = C_2H_5OH \text{ (aq.)}$$
$$\Delta H(\text{sol., } \infty H_2O) = -2500 \text{ cal.}$$

The information given in Fig. 3.3 may also be used to compute integral *heats of dilution*, in which the initial state is a solution of some specified concentration. For example, applying Hess's law to the data quoted above,

$$C_2H_5OH(5 H_2O) + \infty H_2O \text{ (l)} = C_2H_5OH \text{ } (\infty H_2O)$$
$$\Delta H(\text{dil., } 5 H_2O) = \Delta H(\text{sol., } \infty H_2O) - \Delta H(\text{sol., } 5 H_2O)$$
$$= -2500 - (-1120)$$
$$= -1380 \text{ cal.}$$

In giving heats of dilution both the initial and final concentrations must be specified, but usually the final state is assumed to be that of infinite dilution unless otherwise noted.

EXERCISE 3.14

From the data in Fig. 3.3 compute the heat effect of adding 45 moles of water to a solution containing 1 mole of ethanol and 5 moles of water at 25° and 1 atm.   *Ans. q* $\cong$ -1300 cal.

Integral heats of solution or dilution may also be used to compute the heat effects accompanying the mixing of two solutions of different concentrations. For example, when a solution of 1 mole of ethanol in 5 moles of water is mixed with a solution of 2 moles of ethanol in 20 moles of water, the result will be a solution of 3 moles of ethanol in 25 moles of water and the process of interest is

$$C_2H_5OH\ (5H_2O) + 2[C_2H_5OH\ (10H_2O)] = 3[C_2H_5OH\ (\tfrac{25}{3}H_2O)]$$

From Fig. 3.3

$$C_2H_5OH + 5H_2O = C_2H_5OH\ (5H_2O),$$

$$\Delta H\ (\text{sol., } 5H_2O) = -1120\ \text{cal.}$$

$$C_2H_5OH + 10H_2O = C_2H_5OH\ (10H_2O),$$

$$\Delta H\ (\text{sol., } 10H_2O) = -1760\ \text{cal.}$$

$$C_2H_5OH + 8.33H_2O = C_2H_5OH\ (8.33H_2O),$$

$$\Delta H\ (\text{sol., } 8.33H_2O) = -1650\ \text{cal.}$$

The value of ΔH for the process of interest is obtained by application of Hess's law.

$$\Delta H = 3 \times \Delta H(8.33) - 2 \times \Delta H(10) - \Delta H(5)$$
$$= 3(-1650) - 2(-1760) - (-1120) = -310\ \text{cal.}$$

3.7 Thermochemistry of Ionic Solutions

Many important chemical reactions are conducted in aqueous solutions, and heat effects often accompany these processes. The simple mixing of dilute solutions of two salts, such as sodium nitrate and potassium chloride, which do not undergo mutual chemical reaction produces a negligible heat effect. This general observation is known as the *principle of thermoneutrality of salt solutions*. Only when some reaction occurs, such as precipitation, neutralization, or ionization, is there evolution or absorption of heat.

For example, when silver nitrate solution is added to sodium chloride solution, insoluble silver chloride is formed and heat is liberated. Utilizing the principle of thermoneutrality of salt solutions stated above, the heat effect is attributed entirely to the process

$$Ag^+(\text{aq.}) + Cl^-(\text{aq.}) = AgCl(s)$$
$$\Delta H_{298} = -15,650\ \text{cal. mole}^{-1}$$

Note that this process is the reverse of solution and therefore the ΔH_{298} of solution of AgCl (s) is $+15,650$ cal. mole^{-1}.

Neutralization of strong acids by strong bases in dilute aqueous solutions exhibits a remarkable regularity. The heat of neutralization, per equivalent, is approximately constant with $\Delta H_{298} = -13,500$ cal. This can be understood in terms of the common process

$$H^+(aq.) + OH^-(aq.) = H_2O\ (l)$$

for which $\Delta H_{298} = -13,360$ cal. in the limit for infinitely dilute solutions.

When a very weak acid reacts with a strong base, an additional heat effect is involved. As an example

$$HCN(aq.) + OH^-(aq.) = CN^-(aq.) + H_2O(l)$$
$$\Delta H = -2900 \text{ cal.}$$

The reaction can be resolved into steps:

$$HCN(aq.) = H^+(aq.) + CN^-(aq.), \qquad \Delta H(\text{dissoc. HCN})$$
$$H^+(aq.) + OH^-(aq.) = H_2O\ (l), \qquad \Delta H = -13,360 \text{ cal.}$$

By Hess's law, $\Delta H(\text{dissoc. HCN}) = -2900 + 13,360 = 10,460$ cal. mole^{-1}.

EXERCISE 3.15

The heat evolved in the neutralization of metaboric acid, HBO_2, with strong base is 10,000 cal. mole^{-1}. Compute the heat of dissociation of metaboric acid.
Ans. $\Delta H = 3360$ cal. mole^{-1}.

Thermochemical data on reactions of electrolytes in aqueous solution may be summarized in the form of heats of formation of the aqueous ions. These data are extrapolated to infinite dilution to remove the influence of interionic forces. The symbol (aq.) denotes this. Since the heat of formation of liquid water is known, the heat of neutralization can be used to give the heat of formation of a solution of $H^+(aq.)$ and $OH^-(aq.)$.

$$H_2(g) + \tfrac{1}{2}O_2(g) = H_2O(l)$$
$$\Delta H_{298} = -68.317 \text{ kcal. mole}^{-1}$$
$$H_2O(l) = H^+(aq.) + OH^-(aq.)$$
$$\Delta H_{298} = 13.360 \text{ kcal. mole}^{-1}$$

By Hess's law we have

$$H_2(g) + \tfrac{1}{2}O_2(g) = H^+(aq.) + OH^-(aq.)$$
$$\Delta H_{298} = -54.957 \text{ kcal. mole}^{-1}$$

EXERCISE 3.16

Compute the value of ΔH for

$$Ag\ (s) + \tfrac{1}{2}Cl_2\ (g) = Ag^+\ (aq.) + Cl^-\ (aq.)$$

by application of Hess's law to the values of the heat of formation of AgCl (s) and the heat of solution of AgCl (s). *Ans.* $\Delta H_{298} = -14.71$ kcal. mole^{-1}.

Heats of formation of ions in solution necessarily involve two or more ions, the sum of whose charge is zero. Individual heats of formation of ions cannot be obtained, but differences between the heat contents of two ions can be obtained. For example, from the heat of formation of HCl (g) and the heat of solution to form H^+(aq.) and Cl^-(aq.) we obtain

$$\tfrac{1}{2}H_2(g) + \tfrac{1}{2}Cl_2(g) = H^+(aq.) + Cl^-(aq.)$$
$$\Delta H = -40.023 \text{ kcal. mole}^{-1}$$

By comparison with

$$Ag(s) + \tfrac{1}{2}Cl_2(g) = Ag^+(aq.) + Cl^-(aq.)$$
$$\Delta H = -14.71 \text{ kcal. mole}^{-1}$$

we conclude that the difference in the values of ΔH_f of H^+(aq.) and Ag^+(aq.) is

$$\Delta H_f(Ag^+, \text{ aq.}) - \Delta H_f(H^+, \text{ aq.}) = -14.71 - (-40.02)$$
$$= 25.31 \text{ kcal. mole}^{-1}$$

In a similar fashion, the differences in ΔH_f for many other ions may be found.

As a matter of convenience, it is customary to assign a value of zero to the ΔH_f of H^+(aq.) or to say that the heat content of H^+(aq.) is zero. Values of the heat contents of other aqueous ions are then given with relation to this arbitrary standard, as in Table 3.3. For example, the heat content of Ag^+(aq.) is found from the data given above to be

$$\Delta H_f(Ag^+, \text{ aq.}) = 25.31 + \Delta H_f(H^+, \text{ aq.})$$
$$= 25.31 \text{ kcal. mole}^{-1}$$
or
$$\Delta H_f(Ag^+, \text{ aq.}) = 25.31 \text{ kcal. mole}^{-1}$$

Only the differences between the heat contents of the various ions have experimental significance and one could have chosen any value for ΔH_f (H^+, aq.), changing all others accordingly. It can be seen that each value quoted in the table is actually, in the case of cations

$$\Delta H_f(\text{cation}) - \Delta H_f(H^+, \text{ aq.})$$

and in the case of anions

$$\Delta H_f(\text{anion}) + \Delta H_f(H^+, \text{ aq.})$$

Consequently, whether these heat contents are used for reactions of the type

$$A + B = A^+ + B^-$$
or
$$A^+ + C = A + C^+$$

the terms in $\Delta H_f(H^+$, aq.) will always vanish in the sum or difference. It is therefore merely a convenience to employ these relative heats of formation as if they were absolute values.

Having chosen the value zero for the heat content of H^+(aq.), the heat content of OH^-(aq.) may be obtained from the heat of neutralization.

$$H^+(aq.) + OH^-(aq.) = H_2O \text{ (l)}$$
$$\Delta H = H(H_2O) - H(H^+, \text{ aq.}) - H(OH^-, \text{ aq.}) = -13.360 \text{ kcal. mole}^{-1}$$
$$H(OH^-, \text{ aq.}) = 13.360 - 0 - 68.317 = -54.957 \text{ kcal. mole}^{-1}$$

Taking the heat content of OH^-(aq.) to be zero, find the heat content of Ag^+(aq.)

Ans. -29.65 kcal. mole^{-1}.

Table 3.3 is a convenient source of thermochemical information concerning reactions involving aqueous electrolytic solutions. Together with the information contained in the table of heats of formation of compounds (Table 3.2), it facilitates evaluation of ΔH for processes such as

$$Zn(s) + 2H^+(aq.) = Zn^{++}(aq.) + H_2(g)$$
$$\Delta H = H(Zn^{++}) + H(H_2) - 2H(H^+) - H(Zn)$$
$$= -36.43 + 0 - 0 - 0 \text{ kcal.}$$

For the process which occurs in the Daniell cell (see Chapter 2)

$$Zn(s) + Cu^{++}(aq.) = Zn^{++}(aq.) + Cu(s)$$
$$\Delta H = H(Zn^{++}) - H(Cu^{++})$$
$$= -36.43 - (15.39) = -51.82 \text{ kcal.}$$

TABLE 3.3

ENTHALPIES OF AQUEOUS IONS AT 25°*

Cations	H_{298} (kcal. mole^{-1})	Anions	H_{298} (kcal. mole^{-1})
H^+ (aq.)	0	OH^- (aq.)	-54.957
Li^+ (aq.)	-66.554	Cl^- (aq.)	-40.023
Na^+ (aq.)	-57.279	Br^- (aq.)	-28.90
K^+ (aq.)	-60.04	I^- (aq.)	-13.37
Ag^+ (aq.)	25.31	CN^- (aq.)	36.1
Zn^{++} (aq.)	-36.43	NO_3^- (aq.)	-49.372
Cu^{++} (aq.)	15.39	SO_4^- (aq.)	-216.90

*From *Selected Values of Chemical Thermodynamic Properties*, Circular 500, National Bureau of Standards, 1952.

Compute ΔH for

$$Br^-(aq.) + AgCl(s) = AgBr(s) + Cl^-(aq.)$$

Ans. -4.54 kcal.

3.8 Temperature Dependence of Heat of Reaction

All discussion up to this point has been concerned with the value of ΔH for an isothermal process, usually at 298°K. We now examine the variation of the isothermal ΔH with temperature. For the generalized process

$$aA + bB + \ldots = mM + nN + \ldots$$
$$\Delta H_T = mH_T(M) + nH_T(N) - aH_T(A) - bH_T(B) \tag{3.10}$$

At constant pressure, $H_T(M)$, etc., represent molar heat contents of the products and reactants at some particular temperature, T. To find the variation with temperature of the isothermal heat of reaction, ΔH_T, we take its partial derivative with respect to temperature at constant pressure.[3]

$$\left(\frac{\partial(\Delta H_T)}{\partial T}\right)_P = m\left(\frac{\partial H(M)}{\partial T}\right)_P + n\left(\frac{\partial H(N)}{\partial T}\right)_P - a\left(\frac{\partial H(A)}{\partial T}\right)_P - b\left(\frac{\partial H(B)}{\partial T}\right)_P$$

(3.11)

The variation of the heat content of a substance with temperature is given by equation (2.29) *provided no phase change occurs;* such an equation can be written for each of the reactants and products.

$$(\partial H(M)/\partial T)_P = C_P(M), \text{ etc.}$$

(3.12)

Substitution of these expressions in equation (3.11) yields

$$(\partial(\Delta H_T)/\partial T)_P = mC_P(M) + nC_P(N) - aC_P(A) - bC_P(B)$$

(3.13)

The right-hand side of equation (3.13) is conveniently abbreviated[4] to ΔC_P. The change in ΔH_T over a finite temperature interval is obtained by integrating equation (3.13).

$$\Delta H_2 - \Delta H_1 = \int_{T_1}^{T_2} \Delta C_P dT$$

(3.14)

where ΔH_2 is for the isothermal process at T_2 and ΔH_1 is for the same process at T_1.

The relation specified by equation (3.14) may also be described by the diagram:

$$aA + bB + \ldots \xrightarrow[T_2]{\Delta H_2} mM + nN + \ldots$$

$$\Bigg\downarrow \Delta H \text{ (react.)} \qquad\qquad \Bigg\downarrow \Delta H \text{ (prod.)}$$

$$aA + bB + \ldots \xrightarrow[T_1]{\Delta H_1} mM + nN + \ldots$$

where

$$\Delta H \text{ (react.)} = \int_{T_2}^{T_1} [aC_P(A) + bC_P(B)]dT$$

and

$$\Delta H \text{ (prod.)} = \int_{T_1}^{T_2} [mC_P(M) + nC_P(N)]dT$$

Applying the principle that ΔH is independent of path, we obtain an expression for ΔH_2 given by the sum of three terms (note that a sign change has been made in the first term):

---

[3]The temperature derivative of an isothermal heat of reaction at temperature T and constant pressure is to be understood in the sense

$$\left(\frac{\partial(\Delta H_T)}{\partial T}\right)_P = \lim_{(T_2-T_1)\to 0}\left(\frac{\Delta H_2 - \Delta H_1}{T_2 - T_1}\right)_{P=\text{const.}}$$

[4]Note that $\Delta C_P = mC_P(M) + \ldots -aC_P(A)\ldots$ and that $\Delta H = mH(M) + \ldots -aH(A)$ ....Both C and H are properties of a system and for any process, including chemical reactions, the expression $\Delta property$ will always be used similarly as new thermodynamic properties arise.

$$\Delta H_2 = - \int_{T_1}^{T_2} [aC_P(\text{A}) + bC_P(\text{B})]\, dT + \Delta H_1$$

$$+ \int_{T_1}^{T_2} [mC_P(\text{M}) + nC_P(\text{N})]\, dT$$

$$\Delta H_2 = \Delta H_1 + \int_{T_1}^{T_2} \Delta C_P dT$$

This is equivalent to equation (3.14).

If the temperature interval of interest is not large, or if no great precision is required in the computation, ΔC_P may be taken to be independent of temperature. (Even when appreciable changes in $C_P(\text{M})$, etc., occur individually, the value of ΔC_P may vary much less.) With this approximation the right-hand side of equation (3.14) is

$$\Delta H_2 - \Delta H_1 = \Delta C_P(T_2 - T_1) \tag{3.15}$$

In section 3.3 it was shown that

$$\text{H}_2(\text{g}) + \tfrac{1}{2}\text{O}_2(\text{g}) = \text{H}_2\text{O}(\text{g})$$
$$\Delta H_{298} = -57.80 \text{ kcal. mole}^{-1}$$

Let us evaluate ΔH_{398} for this process, using the approximate relation given in equation (3.15). The molar heat capacities of the substances involved are $\text{H}_2(\text{g})$, 6.9; $\text{O}_2(\text{g})$, 7.0; $\text{H}_2\text{O}(\text{g})$, 8.0 cal. deg.$^{-1}$.

$$\Delta C_P = 8.0 - \tfrac{1}{2}(7.0) - 6.9 = -2.4 \text{ cal. deg.}^{-1}$$
$$\Delta H_{398} = \Delta H_{298} + (-2.4)(398 - 298)$$
$$= -58.04 \text{ kcal. mole}^{-1}$$

EXERCISE 3.19

Compute ΔH_{398} for

$$\tfrac{1}{2}\,\text{N}_2\,(\text{g}) + \tfrac{3}{2}\,\text{H}_2\,(\text{g}) = \text{NH}_3\,(\text{g})$$

Heat capacities are N_2, 6.9; H_2, 6.9; NH_3, 8.5 cal. deg.$^{-1}$ mole^{-1}.

Ans. -11.57 kcal. mole^{-1}.

When a greater temperature interval is to be considered, or when greater precision is desired, the variation of C_P with temperature must be taken into account. If empirical equations for C_P are available (see section 2.2) they may be used in equation (3.12).

$$(\partial H(\text{M})/\partial T)_P = C_P(\text{M}) = a(\text{M}) + b(\text{M})T + c(\text{M})T^2, \text{ etc.} \tag{3.16}$$

Substitution of these expressions in equation (3.11) yields

$$(\partial \Delta H_T/\partial T)_P = ma(\text{M}) + mb(\text{M})T + mc(\text{M})T^2$$
$$+ na(\text{N}) + nb(\text{N})T + nc(\text{N})T^2$$
$$- aa(\text{A}) - ab(\text{A})T - ac(\text{A})T^2 \tag{3.17}$$
$$- ba(\text{B}) - bb(\text{B})T - bc(\text{B})T^2$$

The meaning of ΔC_P in equation (3.16) now becomes

$$\Delta C_P = \Delta a + \Delta bT + \Delta cT^2 \tag{3.18}$$

where $\Delta a = ma(M) + na(N) - aa(A) - ba(B)$, etc. Integration yields

$$\Delta H_2 - \Delta H_1 = \int_{T_1}^{T_2}(\Delta a + \Delta bT + \Delta cT^2)\,dT$$

$$= \Delta a(T_2 - T_1) + \frac{\Delta b}{2}(T_2^2 - T_1^2) + \frac{\Delta c}{3}(T_2^3 - T_1^3)$$

(3.19)

Applying this relation to the computation of ΔH_{1000} for

$$\tfrac{1}{2}N_2(g) + \tfrac{3}{2}H_2(g) = NH_3(g)$$

we find from Table 2.1

$$\Delta a = 6.189 - \tfrac{1}{2}(6.524) - \tfrac{3}{2}(6.947) = -7.493$$
$$\Delta b = [7.887 - \tfrac{1}{2}(1.250) + \tfrac{3}{2}(0.200)] \times 10^{-3} = 7.562 \times 10^{-3}$$
$$\Delta c = [-7.28 + \tfrac{1}{2}(0.01) - \tfrac{3}{2}(4.808)] \times 10^{-7} = -14.49 \times 10^{-7}$$

Substitution in equation (3.19) yields

$$\Delta H_{1000} = \Delta H_{298} + \int_{298}^{1000}\Delta Cp\,dT$$

$$= -11.04 - 2.27 = -13.31 \text{ kcal. mole}^{-1}$$

For some purposes, it is more convenient to use

$$\Delta H_T = \Delta H_0 + \int_0^T \Delta C_P\,dT$$

$$\Delta H_T = \Delta H_0 + \Delta aT + (\Delta b/2)T^2 + (\Delta c/3)T^3$$

(3.20)

The constant of integration, ΔH_0, may be computed from a known value of ΔH at some temperature, usually 298°K. In the case of ammonia synthesis

$$\Delta H_0 = -11.04 + 7.493(298) - \frac{7.562 \times 10^{-3}}{2}(298)^2 + \frac{14.49 \times 10^{-7}}{3}(298)^3$$

$$\Delta H_0 = -9.16 \text{ kcal. mole}^{-1}$$

Since the empirical equations for heat capacity do not describe the experimental heat capacities down to absolute zero, the value of ΔH_0 obtained from equation (3.20) is not to be regarded as the change in heat content for the process at the absolute zero, but rather as a constant of integration applicable only with a particular set of empirical heat capacity equations.

EXERCISE 3.20

Substitute the value of ΔH_0 for the process

$$\tfrac{1}{2}N_2(g) + \tfrac{3}{2}H_2(g) = NH_3(g)$$

in equation (3.20), use previously given values of Δa, Δb, and Δc, and compute ΔH_{1000} for the process. *Ans.* -13.35 kcal. mole^{-1}.

The preceding relations apply to the temperature dependence of ΔH for a precisely specified process. That is, all properties of the reactants and products, except temperature, remain the same. However, it often happens that a change in the temperature produces a change in the physical state of one or more of the substances involved. For example, in the process

$$CH_4(g) + 2O_2(g) = CO_2(g) + 2H_2O \text{ (l)}$$
$$\Delta H_{298} = -212.80 \text{ kcal. mole}^{-1}$$

liquid water is the stable form at 25° and 1 atm., but at temperatures above 100° water vapor will be produced in a real combustion. This change in state of the product water may be taken into account in computing ΔH at an elevated temperature either by using the appropriate values of ΔH_{298} for formation of the substances in the hypothetical process

$$CH_4(g) + 2O_2(g) = CO_2(g) + 2H_2O(g)$$
$$\Delta H_{298} = -191.76 \text{ kcal. mole}^{-1}$$

and proceeding as before, or by including the process of vaporization at 100° in the steps leading from initial to final state as indicated in the diagram:

$$CH_4(g) + 2O_2(g) \xrightarrow{\Delta H_T} CO_2(g) + 2H_2O(g)$$

$$\Big\downarrow \Delta H(CH_4) \qquad \Big\downarrow \Delta H(O_2) \qquad \Big\uparrow \Delta H(CO_2) \qquad \begin{array}{c} \Big\uparrow \Delta H(H_2O,\,g) \\ -\Delta H_{373} \text{ (vap.)} \\ \Big\uparrow \Delta H(H_2O,\,l) \end{array}$$

$$CH_4(g) + 2O_2(g) \xrightarrow{\Delta H_{298}} CO_2(g) + 2H_2O \text{ (l)}$$

where

$$\Delta H(CH_4) = \int_T^{298} C_P(CH_4)\, dT$$

$$\Delta H(O_2) = 2 \int_T^{298} C_P(O_2)\, dT$$

$$\Delta H(CO_2) = \int_{298}^T C_P(CO_2)\, dT$$

$$\Delta H(H_2O,\,l) = 2 \int_{298}^{373} C_P(H_2O,\,l)\, dT$$

$$\Delta H(H_2O,\,g) = 2 \int_{373}^T C_P(H_2O,\,g)\, dT$$

Since the value of ΔH for a given change in state is independent of path,

$$\Delta H_T = \Delta H_{298} + \int_{298}^T [C_P(CO_2) - C_P(CH_4) - 2C_P(O_2)]\, dT$$

$$+ 2 \int_{298}^{373} C_P(H_2O,\,l)\, dT + 2 \int_{373}^T C_P(H_2O,\,g)\, dT$$

$$+ 2\Delta H_{373} \text{ (vap. } H_2O)$$

EXERCISE 3.21

From the heat of combustion of methane given in Table 3.1 and the following values of C_P compute the heat evolved in combustion of methane at 300°. C_P (cal. deg.$^{-1}$ mole^{-1}): CH$_4$ (g), 8.6; O$_2$ (g), 7.0; CO$_2$ (g), 8.9; H$_2$O (l), 18.0; H$_2$O (g), 8.1; ΔH_{373} (vap. H$_2$O) = 9.71 kcal. mole^{-1}. *Ans.* -192 kcal. mole^{-1}.

3.9 Adiabatic Processes

When a process which, when carried out isothermally would absorb or evolve heat, is instead carried out in such a fashion that heat is not exchanged with the surroundings, the final temperature will differ from the initial temperature. If the heat capacities of the products and reactants are known, the principle of conservation of energy may be applied to obtain a relation between the observed temperature change and the isothermal heat of reaction.

If the generalized process at constant pressure

$$aA + bB + \ldots = mM + nN + \ldots$$

is carried out adiabatically, $q = 0$ and we designate the initial and final temperatures of the system by T_1 and T_2. The overall process, in which the initial state is $aA + bB + \ldots$ at T_1 and the final state is $mM + nN + \ldots$ at T_2, is equivalent to either of the paths I, I or II, II in the following diagram:

$$
\begin{array}{ccc}
aA + bB + \ldots & \xrightarrow{\;\;\Delta H_2(T_2)\;\;} & mM + nN + \ldots \\
& \text{I} & \\
\text{I} \Big\uparrow & & \Big\uparrow \text{II} \\
aA + bB + \ldots & \xrightarrow[\text{II}]{\;\;\Delta H_1(T_1)\;\;} & mM + nN + \ldots
\end{array}
$$

The change in enthalpy for the process is independent of path and is zero, since

$$q_P = 0 = \Delta H$$

When the heat capacities of the products are known, a relation between the change in temperature and ΔH_1 may be obtained.

$$
\begin{aligned}
0 &= \Delta H_1 + \int_{T_1}^{T_2} C_P \,(\text{prod.})\, dT \\
\Delta H_1 &= - \int_{T_1}^{T_2} C_P \,(\text{prod.})\, dT
\end{aligned}
\tag{3.21}
$$

If the temperature interval is small, $C_P(\text{prod.})$ may be taken to be independent of temperature, and

$$\Delta H_1 = - C_P \,(\text{prod.})\, (T_2 - T_1) \tag{3.22}$$

When the heat capacities of the reactants are known, a relation between the change in temperature and ΔH_2 may be obtained.

$$0 = \Delta H_2 + \int_{T_1}^{T_2} C_P \,(\text{react.})\, dT \tag{3.23}$$

In order to use equation (3.21) for calculation of a flame temperature, the total heat capacity of the products must be known. For this purpose, the heat capacity due to unreacted substances must also be included, for they are heated to the final temperature along with the products of chemical reaction. For example, in the combustion of hydrogen in air, each volume of hydrogen consumed requires $2\frac{1}{2}$ volumes of air, since air contains only 20 per cent oxygen. The "products" of the reaction are therefore one mole of water and 2 moles of nitrogen:

$$H_2(g) + \tfrac{1}{2}O_2(g) + 2N_2(g) = H_2O(g) + 2N_2(g)$$

For an initial temperature of 25° the adiabatic flame temperature T in this case can, in principle, be found by solving the equation

$$\Delta H_{298} = - \int_{298}^{T} [C_P(H_2O, g) + 2\, C_P(N_2, g)]\, dT$$

The final temperature is above 2000°, well beyond the range of applicability of the empirical heat capacity equations given in Table 2.1, and an accurate solution is not practicable.

An approximate flame temperature may be obtained by estimating an average value for the heat capacity of the products. We will take $C_P(H_2O, g) = 12$ cal. deg.$^{-1}$ and $C_P(N_2, g) = 8$ cal. deg.$^{-1}$. Substitution in equation (3.21) yields

$$- 57{,}800 = - (12 + 2 \times 8)\, \Delta T$$

$$\Delta T = 2065°$$

or

$$T = 2.4 \times 10^3 \,°K$$

With a given fuel the adiabatic flame temperature is strongly influenced by the composition of the mixture. When air is used the maximum flame temperature is obtained when the proportions are such as to provide the exact stoichiometric requirement of oxygen. If the proportion of air is increased above this value, then additional nitrogen and unburned oxygen must be included in the products and, on the other hand, if an excess of hydrogen is present, this must be included in assessing the heat capacity of the products. The highest flame temperatures will be obtained when pure oxygen is mixed with the fuel gas in stoichiometric proportion, when the heat capacity of the products has its minimum value.

EXERCISE 3.22

Take $C_P(O_2) = 8$ cal. deg.$^{-1}$ mole^{-1} and estimate the flame temperature when hydrogen is burned with air in the volume ratio 1 : 3, i.e., a 20% excess of air.

Ans. $T = 2.1 \times 10^3 \,°K$.

SUMMARY, CHAPTER 3

1. Heats of reaction

$$q_V = \Delta E \qquad q_P = \Delta H$$
$$= \Delta E + \Delta n_{gas} RT$$

2. Hess's law

$$aA + bB + \ldots = jJ + kK + \ldots = mM + nN + \ldots$$
$$\Delta H(A - M) = \Delta H(A - J) + \Delta H(J - M)$$
$$\Delta H(A - M) = mH(M) + nH(N) - aH(A) - bH(B)$$

independent of path.

3. Heats of formation

$$aA + bB + \ldots = mM + nN + \ldots$$
$$\Delta H° = m\Delta H_f°(M) + n\Delta H_f°(N) - a\Delta H_f°(A) - b\Delta H_f°(B)$$

Standard state: pressure of 1 atm. and, for elements, physical form most stable at 1 atm. and given temperature. Heat content of an element in its standard state is taken to be zero

4. Heats of solution

solute + solvent $\quad=$ solution

$$\Delta H = \text{integral heat of solution}$$

solute + ∞ solvent $\quad=$ ∞ dilute solution

$$\Delta H = \text{heat of solution at infinite dilution}$$

solution + ∞ solvent $=$ ∞ dilute solution

$$\Delta H = \text{heat of dilution}$$

5. Ionic solutions

Heat of neutralization

$$H^+(aq.) + OH^-(aq.) = H_2O; \qquad \Delta H_{298} = -13,360 \text{ cal. mole}^{-1}$$

By convention $\quad H(H^+) = 0$

$$H(OH^-) = H(H_2O) - \Delta H(\text{neut.}), \text{ etc.}$$

6. Temperature dependence of ΔH

$$\Delta H_2 = \Delta H_1 + \int_{T_1}^{T_2} \Delta C_P \, dT$$

$$\Delta C_P = mC_P(M) + nC_P(N) - aC_P(A) - bC_P(B)$$

precise form: $\Delta H_2 = \Delta H_1 + \Delta a(T_2 - T_1) + \dfrac{\Delta b}{2}(T_2^2 - T_1^2)$

$$+ \frac{\Delta c}{3}(T_2^3 - T_1^3)$$

or: $\qquad \Delta H_T = \Delta H_0 + \Delta a T + \dfrac{\Delta b}{2} T^2 + \dfrac{\Delta c}{3} T^3$

approx. form: $\Delta H_2 = \Delta H_1 + \Delta C_P(T_2 - T_1)$

7. Adiabatic processes

$$\Delta H_1 = -\int_{T_1}^{T_2} C_P(\text{prod.}) \, dT$$

$$\Delta H_2 = -\int_{T_1}^{T_2} C_P(\text{react.}) \, dT$$

PROBLEMS, CHAPTER 3

1. When 1.000 g. of a substance is burned completely in oxygen in an adiabatic calorimeter, the temperature of the system rises from 23.67° to 26.90°. The same change in temperature of the calorimeter system is then reproduced by passing an electric current of 1.000 amp. through a heating coil in the calorimeter for 15 min. at a steady potential difference of 19.80 v. Evaluate the heat of combustion of the substance in cal. gram^{-1}. *Ans.* 4.26 kcal. g.$^{-1}$

2. Use the heats of combustion in Table 3.1 to find ΔH_{298} and ΔE_{298} for the following constant temperature, constant pressure processes:
(a) $2\,CH_4\,(g) = C_2H_2\,(g) + 3\,H_2\,(g)$ *Ans.* (a)89.97, 88.79
(b) $3\,C_2H_2\,(g) = C_6H_6\,(l)$ (b)$-150.88, -149.11$
(c) $C_6H_6\,(l) = 6\,C\,(graph.) + 3\,H_2\,(g)$ (c)$-11.72, -13.49$ kcal.

3. Use the heats of formation in Table 3.2 to find the heats of combustion *per gram* for the gaseous normal alkanes CH_4 through C_6H_{14}. Which is the best fuel in terms of weight?
Ans. $-13.3, -12.4, -12.2, -11.9, -11.7, -11.7$ kcal. g.$^{-1}$

4. If the heat content of each elementary substance in its standard state at 298°K were arbitrarily chosen to be 10,000 cal. (g. atom)$^{-1}$, what would be the value of the molar heat content of $CH_3OH(l)$, $CO_2(g)$ and $H_2O(l)$ at 298°K? Show that the use of these values yields the correct heat of combustion for CH_3OH (l).   *Ans.* $-22.02, -74.05, -53.32$ kcal. mole^{-1}.

5. In a series of experiments by C. A. Kraus and J. A. Ridderhof [*J. Am. Chem. Soc.*, **56**, 79 (1934)] the heat effects of reactions in liquid ammonia at $-33°$ were measured by observing the quantity of liquid ammonia vaporized by the process of interest. The heat of vaporization of ammonia at $-33°$ is 327 cal. g.$^{-1}$ When 0.835 g. of NH_4Br was dissolved in 20 g. of liquid ammonia 0.221 g. of ammonia was vaporized.
(a) Find the molar heat of solution of NH_4Br in NH_3 (l) at this concentration.
    When 0.948 g. of NH_4Br was dissolved in 20 g. of liquid ammonia containing an equimolar amount of KNH_2, then 0.845 g. of ammonia was vaporized.
(b) Find ΔH_{240} for the reaction
$$NH_4^+\,(NH_3) + NH_2^-\,(NH_3) = 2\,NH_3\,(l)$$
Ans. (a) -8.6 kcal. mole^{-1},
(b) -20.0 kcal. mole^{-1}.

6. Find the heat of formation of Mn_3O_4 from the following data of C. H. Shomate [*J. Am. Chem. Soc.*, **65**, 785 (1943)]:
(a) Manganese metal was dissolved in dilute aqueous sulfuric acid, potassium iodide solution:
$$Mn + 2H^+ = Mn^{++} + H_2, \quad \Delta H = -53,900 \text{ cal. (g. atom)}^{-1}.$$
(b) Solid iodine was dissolved in the solution resulting from expt. (a):
$$I_2 + I^- = I_3^-, \quad \Delta H = 1100 \text{ cal. mole}^{-1}$$
(c) Mn_3O_4 is dissolved in a solution such that the final composition was identical with that resulting from expts. (a) and (b):
$$Mn_3O_4 + 8H^+ + 3I^- = 3\,Mn^{++} + I_3^- + 4H_2O$$
$$\Delta H = -78,200 \text{ cal. mole}^{-1}$$
(d) The heat of solution of gaseous HI in the solution of interest was determined:
$$HI(g) = H^+ + I^-, \quad \Delta H = -18,700 \text{ cal. mole}^{-1}$$
Ans. $\Delta H_f(Mn_3O_4) = -330,600$ cal. mole^{-1}

7. From the appropriate heats of formation evaluate ΔH_{298} for the following processes:
(a) $Ag^+(aq.) + Br^-(aq.) = AgBr\,(s)$ *Ans.* (a)-20.19 kcal. mole^{-1}
(b) $SO_3\,(g) + H_2O\,(l) = 2H^+(aq.) + SO_4^{--}(aq.)$ (b)-54.13 kcal. mole^{-1}
(c) $2NH_3\,(g) + \frac{7}{2}O_2\,(g) = 2\,NO_2\,(g) + 3\,H_2O\,(g)$ (c)-135.14 kcal. mole^{-1}.

8. The following appearance potentials have been observed:

$$C_3H_6 = C_2H_3^+ + CH_3 + e; \qquad A_1 = 13.65 \text{ e.v.}$$
$$C_2H_4 = C_2H_3^+ + H + e; \qquad A_2 = 13.93 \text{ e.v.}$$

From these data together with the standard heats of formation from Table 3.2 find the bond dissociation energy of CH_3—H. [ΔH_{298} (form. C_3H_6) = 4.879 kcal. mole^{-1}.] *Ans.* 107 kcal. mole^{-1}.

9. Given the bond dissociation energy of CH_3—H as 103 kcal. mole^{-1}, find the standard heat of formation of the methyl radical. *Ans.* 33.6 kcal. mole^{-1}.

10. From the data in Fig. 3.3 compute the heat effect when 67 ml. of water ($\rho = 1.00$ g. ml.$^{-1}$) is added to 50 ml. of 10 mole per cent ethanol in water ($\rho = 0.97$ g. ml.$^{-1}$) at 25°. *Ans.* −150 cal.

11. From the heats of formation of liquid and gaseous water at 25° and other data in the text find the heat of vaporization of water at 75°. Assume heat capacities independent of temperature. *Ans.* 10.02 kcal. mole^{-1}.

12. Obtain an expression equivalent to equation 3.14 for the dependence of ΔE on temperature.

---

13. Thermochemical data for various reactions are listed below.
(1) $Fe(s) + 2H^+(soln) = Fe^{++}(soln) + H_2(g)$, $\Delta H_{303} = -20{,}820$ cal.
(2) $2(HCl \cdot 12.73H_2O) = 2H^+(soln) + 2Cl^-(soln) + 25.46H_2O(soln)$, $\Delta H_{303} = 0$
(3) $FeCl_2(s) = Fe^{++}(soln) + 2Cl^-(soln)$, $\Delta H_{303} = -15{,}000$ cal.
(4) $25.46H_2O(l) = 25.46H_2O(soln)$, $\Delta H_{303} = -2{,}030$ cal.
(a) Find ΔH_{303} for reaction (5).
(5) $Fe(s) + 2(HCl \cdot 12.73H_2O) = FeCl_2(s) + H_2(g) + 25.46H_2O(l)$
(b) ΔH_f° for HCl + ΔH solution to form HCl·12.73H$_2$O is −38,900 cal. Find the heat of formation of ferrous chloride [M. F. Koehler, and J. P. Coughlin, *J. Phys. Chem.*, **63**, 605 (1959)].

14. Combining the two equations
$Hg(CH_3)_2(l) + Br_2(l) = CH_3Br (g) + HgBrCH_3(s)$, $\Delta H = -43.37$ kcal.
$Hg(CH_3)_2(l) + HgBr_2(s) = 2HgBrCH_3(s)$, $\Delta H = -14.59$ kcal.
together with $\Delta H_f(HgBr_2, s) = -40.64$ kcal. mole^{-1} and $\Delta H_f(CH_3Br, g) = -8.6$ kcal. mole^{-1}, find $\Delta H_f(Hg(CH_3)_2, l)$ [K. Hartley, H. O. Pritchard, and H. A. Skinner, *Trans. Faraday Soc.*, **46**, 1019 (1950)].

15. From the emf of the Daniell galvanic cell at 25° (1.1 volt) and the heats of formation for Zn^{++} (aq.) and Cu^{++}(aq.)
(a) find ΔH and ΔE for Zn (s) + Cu^{++}(aq.) = Zn^{++}(aq.) + Cu (s).
(b) Find q_{rev} for the cell reaction.

16. Within the context of Chapters 1 to 3, how does the internal combustion engine convert the energy of a chemical reaction into work?

17. In an actual thermochemical measurement (e.g., heat of combustion), the products are finally present at a temperature somewhat different from that of the reactants initially.

$$aA(T) + bB(T) = mM(T + \Delta T) + nN(T + \Delta T)$$

Given the measured heat effect q and given the temperature-independent mean molar heat capacities $\bar{C}_A$, $\bar{C}_B$, etc., all at constant volume, show how to evaluate the isothermal heat of reaction at T and constant volume. Use diagram and equation to answer.

18. Given S(rhombic) = S(monoclinic), $\Delta H_{368.5} = 96$ cal. and C_P(rh.) = 3.52 + 6.3 × $10^{-3}T$, C_P(mon.) = 3.64 + 6.8 × $10^{-3}T$
(a) Find ΔH_{298} for the transition.
(b) Let S(mon.) at 20° convert adiabatically to S(rh.). What will be the final temperature? Explain clearly the principle involved.

19. From the appropriate heats of formation, find the heat of combustion of normal hexane (g) at 25°.

20. Find ΔH_{298} for the thermite reaction:

$$2Al + Fe_2O_3 \rightarrow 2Fe + Al_2O_3$$

21. The value of the bond dissociation energy of water is $D_{H-OH} = 119$ kcal. $mole^{-1}$. Find the heat of formation of the OH radical.

22. D_{Cl_2} is 28.5 kcal.; D_{H-OH} is 119 kcal. Assuming that the heats of solution of Cl and OH in water are the same, find ΔH_{298} for

$$OH^-_{(aq.)} + Cl_{(aq.)} \rightarrow OH_{(aq.)} + Cl^-_{(aq.)}$$

23. Bond dissociation can be induced by electron impact.
(a) What is the minimum electron energy in e. v. which just suffices to decompose hydrogen into atoms?
(b) Find the heats of formation of H and of H^+. The ionization potential of H is 13.595 e.v.

24. From information in the text find ΔH_{298} for the ion-molecule reaction $CH_3^+(g) + CH_4(g) \rightarrow C_2H_5^+(g) + H_2(g)$.

25. For the reaction $NH_3(g) + H^+(g) \rightarrow NH_4^+(g)$, $\Delta H_{298} = -220$ kcal. Find ΔH_{298} for $C_2H_5^+(g) + NH_3(g) \rightarrow NH_4^+(g) + C_2H_4(g)$. The ionization potential of H is 13.595 e.v.

26. A water heater is required to heat 200 l. of water per hour from 20° to 60°.
(a) Using methane as fuel and $1\frac{1}{2}$ times the stoichiometric requirement of air, how many liters per hour of methane at 20° and 1 atm. will be required? Assume perfect heat exchange and ignore heat losses. Use values of C_P from Table 2.1.
(b) How many kilowatts of electric energy would be required?

27. From the bond dissociation energy $D_{CH_3-H} = 103$ kcal. $mole^{-1}$ and heats of formation find the C—C bond dissociation energy in ethane.

28. Given the bond dissociation energies
$$H_2 = 2H, \qquad \Delta H = 103 \text{ kcal. mole}^{-1}$$
$$H_2O = H + OH, \qquad \Delta H = 119 \text{ kcal. mole}^{-1}$$
$$O_2 = 2O, \qquad \Delta H = 118 \text{ kcal. mole}^{-1}$$
find (a) the standard heat of formation of the OH radical and (b) the bond dissociation energy of the OH radical.

29. The following standard heats of formation are available for urea, CH_4ON_2:

State	ΔH°_{f298}
crystal	−79.634 kcal. mole⁻¹

Sol. in	10 H_2O	-75.970
	20 H_2O	-76.107
	50 H_2O	-76.219
	100 H_2O	-76.259
	200 H_2O	-76.281

Treat these data graphically and estimate the heat effect in the following processes at 25° and 1 atm.:

(a) 1.0 g. of crystaline urea is dissolved in 10 ml. of water.

(b) 1.0 g. of urea is dissolved in the solution formed in part (a).

(c) 90 ml. of water is added to the solution formed in part (a).

30. For the change in state

$$H_2O(l) = H_2O(g), \qquad \Delta H_{373} = 9700 \text{ cal. mole.}^{-1}$$

the molar heat capacities approximate 18 cal. mole^{-1} deg.$^{-1}$ and 9 cal. mole^{-1} deg.$^{-1}$ for liquid and vapor.

(a) Given $(\partial \Delta H / \partial T) = C_P(\text{vap.}) - C_P(\text{liq.})$ write the appropriate *integral* equation using T and 0 as limits.

(b) State the corresponding numerical equation which can be solved for one parameter, ΔH_0.

(c) Express ΔH_T for the vaporization of water as a function of T.

31. Find the value of ΔH_{1000} for the process

$$\tfrac{1}{2} H_2 \text{ (g)} + \tfrac{1}{2} Br_2 \text{ (g)} = HBr \text{ (g)}$$

by graphical treatment of the following data:

T (°K)	300	400	500	600	700	800	900	1000
C_P (Br_2)	8.622	8.777	8.859	8.911	8.948	8.977	9.001	9.022
C_P (HBr)	6.964	6.983	7.039	7.141	7.274	7.426	7.580	7.730
C_P (H_2)	6.930	6.944	6.967	7.000	7.042	7.095	7.157	7.228

[From A. R. Gordon and C. Barnes, *J. Chem. Phys.*, **1**, 692 (1933).]

Plot $[C_P \text{ (HBr)} - \tfrac{1}{2}C_P \text{ (}H_2\text{)} - \tfrac{1}{2}C_P \text{ (}Br_2\text{)}]$ versus T and evaluate $\int \Delta C_P \, dT$ graphically.

32. Obtain an expression equivalent to equation (3.21) applicable to constant volume adiabatic processes.

33. Estimate the temperature which develops when the following reaction occurs explosively at constant volume with an initial temperature of 25°:

$$CH_4 \text{ (g)} + 2O_2 \text{ (g)} + 8N_2 \text{ (g)} = CO_2 \text{ (g)} + 2 H_2O \text{ (g)} + 8 N_2 \text{ (g)}$$

Since the reaction is fast it may be considered adiabatic. Take $C_P(H_2O, g) = 12$ cal. deg.$^{-1}$, C_P (N_2, g) = 8 cal. deg.$^{-1}$, C_P (CO_2, g) = 13 cal. deg.$^{-1}$

34. Estimate the adiabatic flame temperature when methane is burned at constant pressure with twice the stoichiometric requirement of air. Use values of C_P given in problem 33 and C_P (O_2, g) = 8 cal. deg.$^{-1}$ mole^{-1}.

35. Find ΔH_{500} for the process

$$C_2H_4 \text{ (g)} + H_2 \text{ (g)} = C_2H_6 \text{ (g)}$$

36. Find ΔH_0^o for combustion of ethane and the heat of combustion at 300° and 1 atm.

37. The standard heat of formation of tin telluride, SnTe, is -14.65 kcal. mole^{-1}, and its heat of sublimation is 53.1 kcal. mole^{-1}. The heats of sublimation of Sn(s) and Te(s) are 72.0 and 46.5 kcal. mole^{-1} respectively, all at 298°K. Find the bond dissociation energy, D_{SnTe} [C. Hirayama, Y. Ichikawa, and A. M. DeRoo, *J. Phys. Chem.*, **67**, 1039 (1963)].

4

SECOND LAW
OF THERMODYNAMICS

4.1 Spontaneous Changes

The first law of thermodynamics deals with the conservation of energy (heat and work) in physical and chemical processes. We specify the initial and final states of the system and associate a unique value of ΔE or ΔH with the change. However, nothing in these considerations gives information as to whether or not the specified change can occur spontaneously. The information derived from the first law describes only what happens *if* and *when* the specified change occurs. The question of whether or not the specified change *can* occur spontaneously is one with which the second law of thermodynamics deals. (The question of when in time it will occur is treated by chemical kinetics.)

In order to gain some insight into the factors which determine whether or not a given change can occur spontaneously, let us first examine some simple processes to which ordinary experience and common sense can be applied. Consider a sample of gas confined in a rigid container which is connected by a stopcock to another evacuated container. If the stopcock is opened we know from experience that the gas will expand spontaneously to fill the larger volume; in fact, we know that whenever the external pressure is appreciably less than the gas pressure, spontaneous expansion can occur. Conversely, we know that whenever the external pressure is appreciably greater than the gas pressure, compression can occur spontaneously. In the realm of chemistry, a typical spontaneous process is observed when zinc metal is placed in contact with aqueous copper sulfate. Zinc dissolves and cupric ion is reduced to copper metal. These are phenomena which can be readily observed, but many other processes which are spontaneous in the broadest sense of the word are not observed to take place in finite time. Among these is the reaction of hydrogen and oxygen at room temperature, the classic example of a chemical reaction which is "spontaneous" but in the absence of a catalyst proceeds at an infinitesimally small rate. In order to convey the proper breadth of meaning we shall use the term *permitted* change to characterize spontaneous gas expansion and chemical reactions as well as the "spontaneous" phenomena which may have vanishingly small rates. In a thermodynamic context *permitted* must be understood as *not forbidden*, although the process may not occur to a measurable extent.

There are other processes which cannot occur and are, therefore, called *forbidden*. For every change in state which can occur spontaneously, the corresponding reverse change cannot occur. If a system changes from state A to state B without external aid, then it never changes from state B to state A without external aid. This statement holds both for the isolated system ($q = w = 0$) and for the isothermal system at constant volume ($w = 0$, $q \neq 0$).

In reality, processes either do or do not occur. In ideality, the intermediate *reversible* process can be imagined. An example of reversibility, involving isothermal gas expansion which produces maximum work, was discussed in Chapter 2.

4.2 A Criterion of Forbiddenness

The classification of physical-chemical processes as *permitted*, *reversible*, or *forbidden* is simply a statement of experience. We now proceed to develop a more formal criterion of forbiddenness. Like the first law of thermodynamics, such a principle is to be discovered, not derived from other principles. It has already been shown that the first law does not provide such a principle.

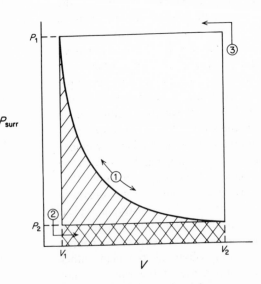

FIG. 4.1. Isothermal gas volume changes.

Consider the work done by the gas in the three types of expansion indicated in Fig. 4.1, given by $P_{surr.} \, dV_{syst.}$ discussed in Chapter 2. It was shown there that the maximum work would be done in the *reversible* expansion along path (1), that is, when the pressure on the gas is at all times only infinitesimally less than the pressure of the gas. This condition leads to the expression $w_{max.} = \int_{V_1}^{V_2} P_{gas} \, dV$, and the value of this integral corresponds to the area marked ⬚ in Fig. 4.1. On the other hand, in a *permitted* or *irreversible* expansion such as that indicated by path (2) in Fig. 4.1, the work done by the gas is given by $w = P_2 \, \Delta V \, (P_{surr.} = P_2,$ a constant), and the value of this work term is given by the area marked ⬚ in Fig. 4.1.

Other possible paths of *irreversible* expansion can be readily imagined, but in all such cases it is apparent that the work done by the gas would be less than the maximum work which could be obtained by expansion between the fixed initial and final volumes, since in an *irreversible* or *permitted* expansion the external pressure must be appreciably less than the gas pressure. In a *forbidden* expansion against pressure greater than gas pressure, work done by the gas would have to be greater than the maximum work. Such an expansion is never observed.

We recognize a quantitative distinction between the three classes of events:

$$Permitted \text{ process } w < w_{max.}$$

$$Reversible \text{ process } w = w_{max.} \tag{4.1}$$

$$Forbidden \text{ process } w > w_{max.}$$

This distinction applies also to isothermal gas compression, if proper regard to sign is observed. In compression, work done *by* the gas is negative. In an *irreversible* compression the pressure on the gas is at all times greater than the gas pressure and, therefore, the work done *on* the gas is greater than the minimum required, which is to say that work done *by* the gas is less (more negative) than $w_{max.}$.

It should be recalled from the discussion in Chapter 2 that the variable amount of work done by the system in an isothermal gas expansion does not contradict the principle of energy conservation. For given initial and final states ΔE has a unique value (zero for isothermal expansion of an *ideal* gas) and q, the heat absorbed by the system, varies according to the manner of expansion in such a fashion that $\Delta E = q - w$ is independent of path.

4.3 Equivalent Reversible Processes

We have argued above that the characteristic of a *permitted* process is that the work done by the system is less than the maximum work possible for the specified change. Thus the permissibility of a proposed process will depend on the comparison of w and $w_{max.}$ for the process. It has been shown in Chapter 2 that $w_{max.}$ has a unique value for an isothermal gas expansion between given initial and final states. Therefore, we could proceed to state more formally the characteristics of *permitted* gas volume changes at constant temperature, but this would be trivial. In order to give this concept more general applicability we must ask whether or not the isothermal maximum work is a function of state; that is, does its value depend on the nature of the process or only on the initial and final states?

It is possible to construct a galvanic cell (see Chapter 2) in which the electrode reactions are the oxidation and reduction of hydrogen. The arrangement is indicated in Fig. 4.2. If hydrogen gas were bubbled over both electrodes at the same pressure, no potential difference would be found between them. If, on the other hand, the pressure of hydrogen is different at the two electrodes (either by dilution with an inert gas, or by placing the electrodes at different depths in the solution), a small potential difference appears, in the sense that there will be a tendency for electrons to flow through the external circuit from

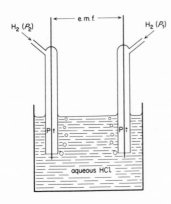

FIG. 4.2. Galvanic cell with hydrogen electrodes.

the electrode with the higher hydrogen pressure, P_2, to that with the lower hydrogen pressure, P_1. This means that at the former electrode the reaction

$$H_2(P_2) = 2H^+ + 2e$$

is occurring, while at the latter the reaction

$$2e + 2H^+ = H_2(P_1)$$

is occurring. The net effect of these reactions is

$$H_2(P_2) = H_2(P_1)$$

that is, hydrogen is being transferred from a region of higher pressure to a region of lower pressure and some electric energy is produced. The decrease in potential energy of the gas is equal to the electric energy produced in the surroundings. Recalling the discussion in Chapter 2 concerning the conditions for obtaining maximum work from a given amount of chemical change, we see that this is approached as the current drain is reduced to smaller and smaller values. The zero current potential, or emf, multiplied by the amount of electric charge transfer associated with unit chemical reaction ($2 \times 96,487$ coulombs for the reaction given above) gives the maximum work available from the process. Computation of maximum work in this fashion is analogous to the computation of maximum work by direct gas expansion, in the sense that it is presumed that the work is accomplished against an opposing force only infinitesimally less than the driving force. This *reversible* electrochemical process thus constitutes an alternate reversible path to gas expansion, and we ask whether or not the maximum work is the same for both paths of an isothermal change in state.

The foregoing details are given only to illustrate the possibility of carrying out a specified change in state by alternate *reversible* paths. In returning to the question of whether or not $w_{max.}$ in an isothermal change in state is a function of state only, or also depends on the path, we shall not confine ourselves to the particular alternate processes described, but will make the arguments more general.

Figure 4.3 represents alternate isothermal processes connecting the same initial and final states. Let $w'_{max.}$ and $w''_{max.}$ be the maximum work for the change in state from A to B by the alternate processes (1) and (2), respectively. Now suppose that

$$w'_{max.} > w''_{max.}$$

Let the system change from state A to state B via process (1) and return to the initial state via process (2). In the first half of the cycle work is done by the system, and in the second half work is done on the system. The difference between these two quantities is the net work output for the cycle. This will reach a limiting maximum value when the processes (1) and (2) are carried out reversibly.

That is, the work done by the system will be maximized at $w'_{max.}$ and the work done on the system will be minimized at $w''_{max.}$. Since we have postulated that $w'_{max.} > w''_{max.}$, the cycle has resulted in net work being done by the system on the surroundings.[1] This, of course, must be compensated by net heat absorption ($q'_{rev.} > q''_{rev.}$), since $\Delta E = 0$ for the cycle. There is nothing to prevent indefinite repetition of the cycle, since the system always returns to its initial state. Each repetition converts heat from the surroundings to work on the surroundings. We conclude that *if $w'_{max.} > w''_{max.}$, a cyclic process can convert heat into work isothermally*. This result is not contrary to the first law, which requires only that $q = w$ in a cyclic process, but a little consideration will show that it is contrary to experience. If permitted, it should be possible to supply the work to drive an ocean liner from the thermal energy of the ocean; it should be possible to supply work to operate a refrigerator from the thermal energy of the room and thus to create a temperature gradient without depending on an external source of energy; it should be possible to use work withdrawn as heat from a thermal reservoir at one temperature to be dissipated as heat (perhaps by friction) in a body at a higher temperature and thus to bring about the flow of heat from a lower to a higher temperature without supplying work. Experience denies all of these possibilities, and these denials are forms of the second law of thermodynamics as applied to isothermal processes, another form of which is that *an isothermal process whose only result is the conversion of heat into work is impossible*. Also equivalent to this is the answer to the question proposed above: *The maximum work obtainable from an isothermal process is a function only of the initial and final states and not of the path*. The unlimited isothermal conversion of heat to work is termed perpetual motion of the second kind. The second law *forbids* such a conversion.

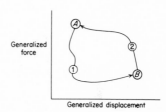

Generalized force

Generalized displacement

FIG. 4.3. Indicator diagram for an isothermal change in state.

The equivalent conclusions reached above represent the most important step in our discussion of *permitted* processes, for it was previously shown that for a specific path (such as simple expansion) from initial to final state, the change is *permitted* if $w < w_{max.}$. Now it has been shown that if we can compute $w_{max.}$ for *any one isothermal path* from initial to final state, we know its value for all possible paths. That is, $w_{max.}$ is *a function of state for the isothermal process*. For example, isothermal expansion of an ideal gas from V_1 to V_2 can yield maximum work $nRT \ln V_2/V_1$, and therefore any process which achieves the same result (and no other result) has the same value of $w_{max.}$. In other words, for any equivalent process, that is, any other process which brings about the same change in state, the work performed by that process may be less than the maximum work for that change in state but cannot exceed it ($w \le w_{max.}$). We

---

[1]For the purpose of this discussion we could as well have postulated that $w'_{max.} < w''_{max.}$ and reversed the direction of the cycle.

will illustrate later how $w_{max.}$ may be calculated indirectly and then used to predict the permissibility of chemical reaction.

4.4 Recapitulation

Before proceeding to more formal statements and applications of the second law of thermodynamics let us recapitulate our progress. We have argued that an inevitable characteristic of any permitted ("spontaneous") process is its inefficiency, that is, it does work less than the maximum work possible for the change specified. Therefore, it behooved us to examine more closely the nature of the maximum work and it was shown that, *in isothermal processes, the maximum work is dependent only on the initial and final states of the system, not on the path.* This principle is a result of experience and is a limited statement of the second law of thermodynamics.

Since $w_{max.}$ for an isothermal process is a function of initial and final states only, its value can be computed in principle without any knowledge of how the change in state is actually accomplished. For example, in the isothermal change in state

$$\text{gas}\ (P_1,\ V_1,\ T) = \text{gas}\ (P_2,\ V_2,\ T)$$

it has been shown that

$$w_{max.} = \int_{V_1}^{V_2} P\ dV$$

regardless of how the change in state is carried out. Although methods of computing $w_{max.}$ in chemical processes have yet to be shown, the preceding arguments concerning the value of $w_{max.}$ apply. For instance, for an isothermal change in state such as

$$\text{H}_2\ (\text{g}) + \tfrac{1}{2}\ \text{O}_2\ (\text{g}) = \text{H}_2\text{O}\ (\text{l})$$

at 1 atm. total pressure and 25° there exists a unique value of $w_{max.}$ independent of path.

Having shown that the relative values of w and $w_{max.}$ in an isothermal process provide a distinction between permitted, reversible, and forbidden processes, we now proceed to develop more general methods which will apply to a variety of physical and chemical changes. These changes will usually be studied under either of two conditions: The system may be confined in a rigid container at constant volume, and consequently no work of expansion is done (T, V constant). Alternatively, the system may be maintained at a constant external pressure, in which case the process may be accompanied by a change in volume, and work of expansion $P\ \Delta V$ may be done (T, P constant). In either case, unless otherwise noted, it is presumed that no provision is made for any other kind of work (such as electric work) to be done by the system in the course of the physical or chemical change under study.

4.5 The Work Content

For any change in state at constant volume w is necessarily zero.

The *ability* to produce work, measured by $w_{max.}$ for the same change in state under reversible conditions, is not necessarily zero. The classification of isothermal processes at constant volume becomes:

$$\text{\textit{Permitted} process } 0 < w_{max.}$$

$$\text{\textit{Reversible} process } 0 = w_{max.} \tag{4.2}$$

$$\text{\textit{Forbidden} process } 0 > w_{max.}$$

Since $w_{max.}$ is determined by the initial and final states, within our experience, there must be a correlative thermodynamic property of the system, the *Helmholtz free energy*, or the *work content*. Designating this property by A, we postulate that

$$A_2 - A_1 = \Delta A = -w_{max.} \text{ (isothermal)} \tag{4.3}$$

or
$$dA_T = -dw_{max.}$$

According to this postulate, which is a limited statement of the second law of thermodynamics, the amount of work which can be performed in any isothermal process is completely determined by the initial and final states of the system. For a given change in state, $A_2 - A_1$ does not depend at all upon the amount of work actually performed.

The change in work content can be measured or calculated, in principle, for any change in state whatever. However, we see by equation (4.3) that ΔA is a criterion of reversibility for constant volume, constant temperature processes (with no provision for electric or other work), as follows:

$$\text{\textit{Permitted} process } \Delta A_{V,T} < 0$$

$$\text{\textit{Reversible} process } \Delta A_{V,T} = 0 \tag{4.4}$$

$$\text{\textit{Forbidden} process } \Delta A_{V,T} > 0$$

When we consider that any process that can occur or can be imagined must fall into one of these three classes, and in particular when we consider the dominant role that equilibrium processes hold in chemistry, the potential significance of these relations (4.4) can be appreciated. It is important, then, to consider the means of measuring ΔA.

The process of isothermal pressure-volume change of a pure substance, so often examined, will prove to be of the greatest importance. Since

$$dA_T = -dw_{max.} = -PdV$$

it is necessary to know the dependence of P on V for the substance under study and then to evaluate the integral

$$\Delta A_T = -\int_{V_1}^{V_2} PdV \tag{4.5}$$

for the specified change. $\int PdV$ is usually negligible for solids and liquids. For the ideal gas

$$P = \frac{nRT}{V}$$

and

$$\Delta A_T = -\int_{V_1}^{V_2} \frac{nRT}{V} \, dV$$

$$= -nRT \ln \frac{V_2}{V_1} = nRT \ln \frac{P_2}{P_1} \tag{4.6}$$

EXERCISE 4.1

Compute ΔA for the following process, assuming the gas to be ideal.

$$20 \text{ g. He } (1 \text{ atm., } 25°) = 20 \text{ g. He } (15 \text{ atm., } 25°)$$

Ans. $\Delta A = 8000$ cal.

For many processes $\Delta A_T = -w_{max.}$ can be evaluated directly. To illustrate, in the Daniell cell

$$\text{Zn (s)} + \text{CuSO}_4 \text{ (aq.)} = \text{ZnSO}_4 \text{ (aq.)} + \text{Cu (s)}$$

it was shown that $w_{max.}$ (elect.) may be computed from the zero current potential of the cell. Very little volume change occurs in the discharge of such a cell and, therefore, $w_{max.}$ (elect.) is almost precisely $w_{max.}$ (total) $= -\Delta A$. In the case cited it was shown that $w_{max.} = 212{,}000$ joules [$\Delta A = -212{,}000$ joules]; therefore, we find that when zinc, copper, copper sulfate solution, and zinc sulfate solution are mixed in a closed container (with no provision for electric work) the process of oxidation of zinc and the reduction of copper ion is permitted.

4.6 The Gibbs Free Energy

When physical or chemical changes occur in systems subjected to a constant pressure such as that of the atmosphere, a change in the volume of the system may occur. If there is no provision for other work, e.g., electric, the work done by the system will be $P_{surr.} \, \Delta V = P_{syst.} \, \Delta V$. For instance, in the reaction of 1 mole of hydrogen gas with $\frac{1}{2}$ mole of oxygen gas to form 1 mole of water vapor at 373°K and 1 atm., the volume of the system decreases, corresponding to a decrease in the number of moles of gas from 1.5 to 1.0. At 373°K and 1 atm. total pressure, this volume change amounts to

$$\Delta V = \frac{\Delta nRT}{P} = -\frac{0.5 \times 0.082 \times 373}{1} = -15.3 \text{ l.}$$

and the work done by the system is

$$P \, \Delta V = -15.3 \text{ l. atm.}$$

The amount of expansion work in a specified constant pressure process is independent of whether the process is permitted or forbidden, since this work is determined entirely by the pressure and the initial and final volumes. Therefore, the total work done in a constant pressure, constant temperature process taking place in a system in which nonexpansion work is excluded is always $P \, \Delta V$. For such processes, the classification given in equation (4.1) becomes

Permitted process $P\Delta V < w_{max.}$

Reversible process $P\Delta V = w_{max.}$

Forbidden process $P\Delta V > w_{max.}$

That is, a permitted process is inefficient, and the work done (always $P\Delta V$) is less than the maximum work for the specified change in state. When a permitted process occurs under these conditions, the ability to do work decreases.

Rearranging the above relations and using the previously defined property ΔA, we may state the classification thus:

$$\text{\textit{Permitted} process} \quad \Delta A_{T,P} + P\Delta V < 0$$

$$\text{\textit{Reversible} process} \quad \Delta A_{T,P} + P\Delta V = 0 \qquad (4.7)$$

$$\text{\textit{Forbidden} process} \quad \Delta A_{T,P} + P\Delta V > 0$$

The frequent occurrence and practical importance of processes which take place at constant pressure and temperature lend importance to the function $\Delta A + P\Delta V$. The corresponding property, $A + PV$, is clearly a property of state and is called the *Gibbs free energy*, with symbol F.

$$F = A + PV \qquad (4.8)$$

The free energy has a unique value for each state of a system. An isothermal change from state 1 to state 2 is accompanied by a change in the free energy of the system given by

$$F_2 - F_1 = A_2 - A_1 + P_2V_2 - P_1V_1$$

$$\Delta F = \Delta A + \Delta(PV) \qquad (4.9)$$

As in the case of E, H, and A, the absolute value of F cannot be known, but changes in F, that is, values of ΔF for specified changes in state, can in principle be calculated or measured.

4.7 ΔF for Gas Expansion

The free energy change in isothermal pressure-volume changes (involving no change in physical or chemical state) is obtained by writing equation (4.8) in differential form.

$$dF = dA + PdV + VdP$$

It was shown that in such changes $dA = -PdV$; it follows that

$$dF = VdP$$

Expressing the restriction of constant temperature formally gives

$$(\partial F/\partial P)_T = V \qquad (4.10)$$

For a finite change

$$\Delta F_T = \int_{P_1}^{P_2} VdP$$

EXERCISE 4.2

Evaluate ΔF_{298} for

$$H_2O \ (1, 1 \text{ atm.}) = H_2O \ (1, 100 \text{ atm.})$$

Ans. 43 cal.

When the ideal gas law can be applied

$$\Delta F_T = \int_{P_1}^{P_2} \frac{nRT}{P} \, dP$$

$$= nRT \ln \frac{P_2}{P_1} = nRT \ln \frac{V_1}{V_2} \tag{4.11}$$

Comparison of equations (4.11) and (4.6) shows that for an isothermal pressure-volume change at constant n, ΔA_T and ΔF_T are identical for an ideal gas. The same conclusion is reached by inspecting equation (4.9), since at constant temperature, $PV = $ constant and $\Delta(PV) = 0$.

EXERCISE 4.3

Evaluate ΔF and ΔA for the isothermal process

$$H_2 \text{ (g, 1 atm.)} = H_2 \text{ (g, 0.01 atm.)}$$

carried out with 10 g. of hydrogen at 100°.

Ans. $\Delta A_{373} = \Delta F_{373} = -17{,}200$ cal.

4.8 ΔF at Constant Pressure

For any change in which the initial and final pressures are identical, equation (4.9) simplifies to

$$\Delta F_{T,P} = \Delta A + P\Delta V \tag{4.12}$$

and the classification given in equation (4.7) simplifies to

$$\begin{aligned} &\textit{Permitted } \text{process} \quad \Delta F_{T,P} < 0 \\ &\textit{Reversible } \text{process} \quad \Delta F_{T,P} = 0 \\ &\textit{Forbidden } \text{process} \quad \Delta F_{T,P} > 0 \end{aligned} \tag{4.13}$$

Since, for a process at constant temperature and pressure

$$-\Delta F_{T,P} = w_{\text{max.}} - P\Delta V = w_{\text{max.}} - w_{\text{expansion}}$$

the decrease in F under such conditions may be called *net work*, that is, maximum work less the inevitable and unavailable work of expansion due to a change in the volume of the system. Thus arises the term *free energy*, meaning available energy.

The vaporization of water at 100° and 1 atm. is accompanied by zero change in free energy, $w_{\text{max.}}$ being exactly equal to $w_{\text{exp.}}$. On the other hand, for

$$\text{Zn (s)} + 2\text{HCl (aq.)} = \text{ZnCl}_2 \text{ (aq.)} + \text{H}_2 \text{ (g)}$$

$w_{\text{max.}}$ is large enough so that if the process were carried out in a galvanic cell electric work would be done in addition to the inevitable work of expansion accompanying the formation of a gas. Therefore, ΔF is negative and the process is permitted. When the volume decreases, as

$$2 \text{ AgCl (s)} + \text{H}_2 \text{ (g)} = 2 \text{ Ag(s)} + 2\text{HCl (aq.)}$$

the atmosphere does work on the system and increases the net work available; i.e., if $w_{\text{exp.}}$ is negative, the net work is greater than $w_{\text{max.}}$. This does not constitute a contradiction, since $w_{max.}$ is a property of the system whereas the net work includes work contributed by the surroundings.

Let us evaluate $\Delta F_{T,P} = \Delta A + \Delta PV$ for

$$H_2O \text{ (l, 1 atm., 373°K)} = H_2O \text{ (g, 1 atm., 373°K)}$$

The value of $\Delta A_{373} = -w_{max.}$ is obtained from the fact that the saturation vapor pressure of water at 373°K is 1 atm., and, therefore,

$$w_{max.} = P\Delta V = 1 \times (V_g - V_1)$$

Neglecting V_1 in comparison with V_g, and assuming the gas to be ideal, we have

$$w_{max.} = P\Delta V = 1 \times RT/\text{mole vaporized}$$

For the second term, ΔPV, we see that this also is $P\,\Delta V$, since P is constant and has the same value as $w_{max.}$. Therefore,

$$\Delta F_{373} = \Delta A_{373} + P\Delta V = -w_{max.} + P\Delta V = 0$$

Since $\Delta F = 0$ for the process described, it follows that for any path leading from the specified initial state to the specified final state $\Delta F_{373} = 0$. That is to say, when water vapor at 100° expands against the atmosphere at 760 mm., it cannot perform any additional work.

To compute ΔF_T for any process it is necessary to know ΔA_T or $w_{max.}$. In the example just given, the process was in fact a reversible one and $w_{max.}$ was easily and directly evaluated. To compute ΔF_T for an irreversible process it is necessary and sufficient to accomplish the same change in state by any reversible process for which $w_{max.}$ is calculable.

An example of an irreversible process for which we can calculate ΔF is

(i) $H_2O \text{ (l, 373°K, 700 mm.)} = H_2O \text{ (g, 373°K, 700 mm.)}$

To accomplish this change in reversible fashion, the following sequence of processes may be used, each of which is to be conducted reversibly:

(ii) Isothermal compression of liquid water

$$H_2O(\text{l, 373°K, 700 mm.}) = H_2O \text{ (l, 373°K, 760 mm.)}$$

(iii) Isothermal vaporization of water

$$H_2O \text{ (l, 373°K, 760 mm.)} = H_2O \text{ (g, 373°K, 760 mm.)}$$

(iv) Isothermal expansion of water vapor

$$H_2O \text{ (g, 373°K, 760 mm.)} = H_2O \text{ (g, 373°K, 700 mm.)}$$

Since ΔF is a function of state, it follows that

$$\Delta F \text{ (i)} = \Delta F \text{ (ii)} + \Delta F \text{ (iii)} + \Delta F \text{ (iv)}$$

ΔF may be evaluated for each of the reversible steps as follows:

$$\Delta F \text{ (ii)} = n \int V_M dP = nV_M(P_2 - P_1)$$

$$= n(0.018)\left(1 - \frac{700}{760}\right) \text{ l. atm.}$$

(if V_M, the molar volume of liquid water, is assumed to be independent of pressure).

$$\Delta F \text{ (iii)} = 0 \text{ (see preceding discussion)}$$

$$\Delta F \text{ (iv)} = nRT \ln\left(\frac{P_2}{P_1}\right)$$

$$= n(0.082) \times 373 \ln\left(\frac{700}{760}\right) \text{l. atm.}$$

Since ΔF (ii) is quite small compared to ΔF (iv), the following approximation is possible:

$$\Delta F \text{ (i)} = \Delta F \text{ (iv)} = nRT \ln\left(\frac{P}{P_{eq.}}\right).$$

where P is the pressure exerted by the surroundings on the system and $P_{eq.}$ is the equilibrium vapor pressure of water at the specified temperature. In the example described above, ΔF (vaporization H_2O at 700 mm., 373°K) $= -2.52$ l. atm. mole^{-1} and the sign indicates that the process is permitted.

EXERCISE 4.4

Evaluate ΔF for the hypothetical process

$$H_2O \text{ (l, 100°, 800 mm.)} = H_2O \text{ (g, 100°, 800 mm.)}$$

and show that the result is consistent with experience.

Ans. $\Delta F_{373} = +1.57$ l. atm. mole^{-1}.

This process is forbidden.

4.9 ΔF for Chemical Change

In the preceding examples it has been shown how ΔF_T may be calculated for a simple physical change. Let us now consider a chemical process,

$$Mg(OH)_2 \text{ (s, } T, P) = MgO \text{ (s, } T, P) + H_2O \text{ (g, } T, P)$$

The equilibrium pressure of water vapor in this system will be designated $P_{eq.}$. Now, by analogy with the preceding case ΔF_T may be computed for this process from consideration of a sequence of reversible processes resulting in the same net change in state.

(i) $Mg(OH)_2 \text{ (s, } T, P) = Mg(OH)_2 \text{(s, } T, P_{eq.})$

(ii) $Mg(OH)_2 \text{ (s, } T, P_{eq.}) = MgO \text{ (s, } T, P_{eq.}) + H_2O \text{(g, } T, P_{eq.})$

(iii) $MgO \text{ (s, } T, P_{eq.}) = MgO \text{ (s, } T, P)$

(iv) $H_2O \text{ (g, } T, P_{eq.}) = H_2O \text{ (g, } T, P)$

ΔF (i) and ΔF (iii) are very small compared to ΔF (iv), and ΔF (ii) is precisely zero. Therefore, to a good approximation, ΔF for the process of interest is given by ΔF (iv).

$$\Delta F = nRT \ln\left(\frac{P}{P_{eq.}}\right)$$

At 25°, the equilibrium pressure of water vapor over $Mg(OH)_2$ (s) is 4.5×10^{-4} mm. Therefore, if we wish to compute ΔF for the dehydration process at P_{H_2O}

$= 20$ mm. and 298°K, we have

$$\Delta F_{298} = n \times 0.082 \times 298 \ln \left(\frac{20}{4.5 \times 10^{-4}} \right) = 261 \text{ l. atm. mole}^{-1}$$

This process is forbidden. The reverse process

$$H_2O \text{ (g, 20 mm., 25°)} + MgO \text{ (s, 20 mm., 25°)} = Mg(OH)_2(s, 20 \text{ mm., } 25°)$$

is permitted, since the value of ΔF is equal and opposite in sign to that for the dehydration process at the same temperature and pressure.

It would appear that at 25° and $P_{H_2O} = 20$ mm. dehydration of $Mg(OH)_2$ cannot occur spontaneously in an isolated system. The dehydration process becomes permitted under different conditions. For instance, if P_{H_2O} is less than the equilibrium water vapor pressure (4.5×10^{-4} mm.), the value of ΔF is negative and the process is permitted.

EXERCISE 4.5

Evaluate ΔF for the process of dehydration of $Mg(OH)_2$ at 25° and 0.1 mm. pressure. $\qquad$ *Ans.* $\Delta F_{298} = 132$ l. atm. mole^{-1}.

A chemical change with specified initial and final pressures may be forbidden at one temperature but permitted at another. Thus, the decomposition of $Mg(OH)_2$ is forbidden at 25° and 1 atm. The equilibrium vapor pressure of water in this system increases with increasing temperature and at temperatures above 260° exceeds 1 atm. Therefore, at 1 atm. and a temperature above 260°, ΔF is negative and the decomposition is permitted. The value of the isothermal free energy change is in general a function of temperature, and changing temperature is an important way to change forbidden processes to permitted processes.

Another means of accomplishing a given change in state when it is normally forbidden is to couple the process for which $\Delta F(a) > 0$ with another for which $\Delta F(b) < 0$ such that $\Delta F(a) + \Delta F(b) < 0$. For example, consider the reaction

$$CaO \text{ (s, 20 mm., 25°)} + H_2O \text{ (g, 20 mm., 25°)} = Ca(OH)_2(s, 20 \text{ mm., } 25°)$$

In this system, the equilibrium vapor pressure of water is 4.7×10^{-9} mm. and

$$\Delta F_{298, 20mm.} = -n \times 0.082 \times 298 \ln \left(\frac{20}{4.7 \times 10^{-9}} \right) = -542 \text{ l. atm. mole}^{-1}$$

Now, if this process is coupled with the dehydration of $Mg(OH)_2$ in a single system at 25° and 20 mm., the net result is

$$Mg(OH)_2(s) + CaO(s) = MgO(s) + Ca(OH)_2(s)$$

and the value of ΔF is obtained by algebraic addition of the values for the two partial processes.

$$\Delta F_{298, 20mm.} = 261 - 542 = -281 \text{ l. atm. mole}^{-1} = -6.81 \text{ kcal. mole}^{-1}$$

This result indicates that dehydration of $Mg(OH)_2$ by CaO to form MgO and $Ca(OH)_2$ is permitted at 20 mm. and 25°. The expression for ΔF, obtained by addition of the expressions for the two partial processes, is

$$\Delta F = n_{\text{Mg(OH)}_2} RT \ln \left(\frac{P}{P_{\text{eq., Mg(OH)}_2}} \right) - n_{\text{Ca(OH)}_2} RT \ln \left(\frac{P}{P_{\text{eq., Ca(OH)}_2}} \right)$$

$$n_{\text{Ca(OH)}_2} = n_{\text{Mg(OH)}_2} = n_{\text{H}_2\text{O}}$$

$$\Delta F = n_{\text{H}_2\text{O}} RT \ln \left(\frac{P_{\text{eq., Ca(OH)}_2}}{P_{\text{eq., Mg(OH)}_2}} \right)$$

The pressure on the system, P, disappears from the expression, and the value of ΔF depends only on the relative equilibrium water vapor pressures of the two hydrates.

This method of computing ΔF depends on the principle that F is an extensive property of state. For any reaction

$$a\text{A} + b\text{B} + \ldots = m\text{M} + n\text{N} + \ldots$$

it follows that

$$\Delta F = mF(\text{M}) + nF(\text{N}) + \ldots - aF(\text{A}) - bF(\text{B}) - \ldots$$

When two or more processes are combined, as

$$a\text{A} + b\text{B} + \ldots = j\text{J} + k\text{K} + \ldots = m\text{M} + n\text{N} + \ldots$$

the net free energy change is the algebraic sum of the free energy changes for the individual steps.

$$\Delta F(\text{A} - \text{M}) = \Delta F(\text{A} - \text{J}) + \Delta F(\text{J} - \text{M})$$

This operation is completely analogous to Hess's law of thermochemistry, equation (3.8).

EXERCISE 4.6

The equilibrium vapor pressure of water in a system containing $\text{CdBr}_2 \cdot 4\text{H}_2\text{O}$ (s) and CdBr_2 (s) at 25° is 30 mm. Evaluate ΔF_{298} for

$$\text{CdBr}_2 \cdot 4\,\text{H}_2\text{O (s)} + 4\,\text{CaO} = \text{CdBr}_2 \text{ (s)} + 4\,\text{Ca(OH)}_2 \text{ (s)}$$

Ans. $\Delta F_{298} = -53.6$ kcal.

4.10 ΔF for Galvanic Cells

We have seen how ΔF may be calculated for gas expansion, and how closely $\Delta F = RT \ln P_2/P_1$ is related to whether or not particular chemical processes can occur. There is another important class of chemical processes for which ΔF can be evaluated even more directly. For the Daniell cell reaction,

$$\text{Zn(s)} + \text{Cu}^{++}(1M) = \text{Zn}^{++}(1M) + \text{Cu(s)}$$

as well as for any isothermal process at constant pressure, $\Delta F_{T,P} = -w_{\text{max.}} + P\Delta V$. For any galvanic cell, both expansion work and electric work are involved. Their combined value is characteristic for a given reversible process. The maximum electrical work does not include expansion work. It is a direct measure of maximum net work, ΔF.

Since
$$\Delta F_{T,\,P} = -w_{\mathrm{max.}} + P\Delta V$$

$$w_{\mathrm{max.}} = w\,(\mathrm{elect.}) + w\,(\mathrm{exp.})$$

$$\Delta F_{T,\,P} = -w\,(\mathrm{elect.})$$

It was concluded in Chapter 2 that the maximum electric work is obtained from a galvanic cell reaction when a vanishingly small current is drawn from the device. (Let it be clear that we mean the maximum electric work for a fixed amount of chemical change.) The corresponding emf of the cell has its maximum value for the given cell, since (electric work) = (potential difference) × (charge transferred). For 1 gram-equivalent of chemical reaction, the charge transferred is that of 6.02×10^{23} electrons or 96,487 coulombs; therefore, to maximize electric work per unit reaction, one must maximize the emf. The maximum value of w (elect.), which is $-\Delta F$, is, therefore, given by

$$w(\mathrm{elect.}) = -\Delta F = n\mathscr{F}\mathscr{E} \qquad (4.14)$$

where n is the number of equivalents of reaction, $\mathscr{E}$ is the zero current potential (emf) and $\mathscr{F}$ is the faraday. By convention the anode (the electrode at which oxidation occurs) is usually taken to be negative in potential with respect to the cathode (the electrode at which reduction occurs) in the spontaneous discharge of the cell. For the Daniell cell, whose reaction is given above, the value of $\mathscr{E}$ is 1.10 v. at 25° and the Zn electrode is the anode. Therefore, the oxidation of 1 g. at. wt. of zinc (two equivalents) under the conditions specified is accompanied by a free energy change given by

$$\Delta F = -2 \text{ equiv.} \times 1.10 \text{ v.} \times 96,487 \text{ amp. sec. equiv.}^{-1}$$

$$= -2.12 \times 10^5 \text{ joules}$$

$$= -50.7 \text{ kcal.}$$

To measure the free energy change of any reaction in a galvanic cell, it is necessary only to measure the intensity factor of energy, the potential. Since $\Delta F = -n\mathscr{F}\mathscr{E}$, the capacity factor of energy can be determined from a knowledge of the nature of the process occurring and the value of $\mathscr{F}$, common to all oxidation-reduction processes.

Having evaluated ΔF for a cell reaction, we may apply the criterion of equation (4.13) to the process at constant temperature and pressure *and in the absence of any provision for electric work*. That is, we may conclude that a cell reaction which has a positive emf will be permitted as written when the terminals of the cell are short-circuited or when the same system is assembled in a beaker with no provisions for electric work.

The reversible emf of a galvanic cell depends on the nature of the substances involved and also upon the concentrations of these substances in a fashion which will be discussed in a later chapter. For the present, we will indicate the nature of this dependence as follows: For a galvanic cell whose reaction is

$$\mathrm{Fe\ (s)} + \mathrm{Cd^{++}\ (1\ }M) = \mathrm{Fe^{++}\ (1\ }M) + \mathrm{Cd\ (s)}$$

the reversible emf is 0.04 v. (iron anode). The corresponding free energy change per unit reaction is given by

$$\Delta F = -2 \times 96{,}487 \times 0.04 = -7.7 \times 10^3 \text{ joules}$$

This is to say that if we mix the substances at the specified concentrations with no provision for electric work, the reaction written above is permitted. If the rate is not too small for observation, the concentration of Cd^{++} will decrease and the concentration of Fe^{++} will increase until eventually a state is reached where no further net change occurs. This condition is reached when the concentration of Fe^{++} is about 20 times the concentration of Cd^{++}. This is the state of chemical equilibrium in which there is no further tendency to react.

When a galvanic cell is constructed with the reactants and products at this equilibrium concentration ratio of 20/1 (e.g., $Fe^{++} = 1\ M$, $Cd^{++} = 0.05\ M$), the reversible emf will be zero. This is an experimental fact, but it is also clearly predictable from the second law of thermodynamics and its consequence which we have developed, namely, that if ΔF is zero for a constant pressure isothermal process, then the process is neither permitted nor forbidden. This means that there is no tendency for either the forward or reverse reaction to occur spontaneously, as is in fact the case.

If a galvanic cell with a concentration ratio $Fe^{++}/Cd^{++} > 20$ is constructed, the reversible emf of the cell will again have a finite value, but of a polarity opposite to that of the original cell, i.e., the Cd electrode will be the anode in spontaneous discharge, and cadmium will be oxidized. Since cadmium is being oxidized, the reaction

$$\text{Fe (s)} + \text{Cd}^{++} \text{ (aq.)} = \text{Fe}^{++} \text{ (aq.)} + \text{Cd (s)}$$

with $(Fe^{++})/(Cd^{++}) > 20$ is proceeding from right to left. The free energy change for the forward reaction must be positive, since it is the reverse of the permitted process. To be consistent with the sign convention adopted, we must assign a negative emf to the cell for the reaction as written. A resulting corollary is that a negative emf denotes a forbidden process. The reverse reaction

$$\text{Cd (s)} + \text{Fe}^{++} \text{ (aq.)} = \text{Cd}^{++} \text{ (aq.)} + \text{Fe (s)}$$

$$\frac{(\text{Fe}^{++})}{(\text{Cd}^{++})} > 20$$

will now have a negative free energy change, a positive emf, and is a permitted process, with $\Delta F = -n\mathscr{F}\mathscr{E} < 0$. The relation between ΔF and electric work is a very useful and important one which will be used repeatedly.

We can also use galvanic cells to illustrate further the principle that a process, which by itself has a positive value of ΔF and is, therefore, forbidden, may be made to proceed through the expedient of coupling it with another process having a negative ΔF whose magnitude is greater than the first. This principle of the additivity of free energy changes applies even more evidently to the additivity of emf's. That is, since for processes (a), (b), . . .

$$\Delta F \text{ (net)} = \Delta F (a) + \Delta F (b) + \cdots$$

we have also, keeping n the same throughout,

$$n\mathscr{F}\mathscr{E} \text{ (net)} = n\mathscr{F}\mathscr{E}\ (a) + n\mathscr{F}\mathscr{E}\ (b) + \ldots$$

Since n and $\mathscr{F}$ are common factors,

$$\mathscr{E} \text{ (net)} = \mathscr{E}\ (a) + \mathscr{E}\ (b) + \ldots$$

This result is consistent with the common observation that when cells are connected in series their emf's combine algebraically. This may be illustrated by combining the two cells previously discussed, as indicated in Fig. 4.4. There are two possible ways of connecting the cells. When we connect terminals 2 and 3 and then measure the reversible emf across 1 and 4, experience leads us to expect a value of $1.10 + 0.04 = 1.14$ v., and this is in fact the observation. On the other hand, when we reverse the polarity of one cell, connecting terminals 2 and 4 and then measure the reversible emf across 1 and 3, we find $1.10 - 0.04 = 1.06$ v. In the latter case the net process which occurs on spontaneous discharge (no electric work) is

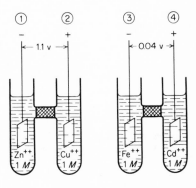

FIG. 4.4. Coupled galvanic cells.

$$\text{Zn (s)} + \text{Cu}^{++}\ (1\ M) + \text{Cd (s)} + \text{Fe}^{++}\ (1\ M)$$
$$= \text{Zn}^{++}(1\ M) + \text{Cu (s)} + \text{Cd}^{++}(1\ M) + \text{Fe (s)}$$

and the ΔF for this process is given by

$$\Delta F = -2(1.10 - 0.04)96{,}487$$
$$= -2.05 \times 10^5 \text{ joules}$$

Note that in this instance the permitted reaction involves oxidation of cadmium and reduction of iron, which was forbidden when the iron-cadmium cell was considered alone.

EXERCISE 4.7

A galvanic cell is constructed with a silver electrode in contact with a solution of silver salt ($1\ M$) and a mercury electrode in contact with a solution of mercuric salt ($1\ M$). It is found that the silver electrode is the anode and that the reversible emf is 0.05 v. Write the cell reaction and compute ΔF for that process.

$$\textit{Ans.}\ 2\ \text{Ag (s)} + \text{Hg}^{++}\ (1\ M) = 2\ \text{Ag}^+\ (1\ M) + \text{Hg (l)}$$
$$\Delta F = -9650 \text{ joules.}$$

4.11 Temperature Dependence of Maximum Work Functions

Up to this point we have considered only isothermal processes, since the demonstration that maximum work is a function of state alone was limited by this condition. Now, it is well-known, and was mentioned in the preceding section, that a process which is forbidden at one temperature may become permitted at another, even though all conditions other than temperature remain fixed. For instance, the vaporization of water at 90° and 1 atm. is forbidden, with a positive value of ΔF. However, at 110° and 1 atm. vaporization is a permitted process with a negative value of ΔF. It is essential to develop a method of computing the variation of ΔF with temperature, and thus to be able to make statements about the relative values of isothermal ΔF's at different temperatures. Let it be clear that we are not now prepared to discuss in detail the variation with temperature of the work content A or the free energy content F, but rather the relation between the value of ΔA or ΔF for an isothermal process at one temperature and the value of ΔA or ΔF for the corresponding isothermal process at another temperature.

In order to obtain the temperature dependence of ΔA_T, we re-examine equation (4.6), which applies to an ideal gas.

$$\Delta A_T = -nRT \ln \left(\frac{V_2}{V_1} \right)$$

Let the initial and final volumes V_1 and V_2 be fixed and take the temperature derivative of ΔA_T.

$$\frac{d\Delta A_T}{dT} = -nR \ln \left(\frac{V_2}{V_1} \right)$$

Since

$$\Delta A_T = -w_{\mathrm{max.}}$$

and since it has been shown that in the isothermal expansion of an ideal gas

$$\Delta E = 0$$

then

$$\Delta A_T = -w_{\mathrm{max.}} = -q_{\mathrm{rev.}} = -nRT \ln \left(\frac{V_2}{V_1} \right)$$

Therefore, the temperature derivative given above may be expressed

$$\frac{d\Delta A_T}{dT} = \frac{-q_{\mathrm{rev.}}}{T} \qquad (4.15)$$

The temperature derivative of the isothermal quantity ΔA_T is to be understood in the sense

$$\frac{d\Delta A_T}{dT} = \lim_{(T_2 - T_1) \to 0} \left(\frac{\Delta A_2 - \Delta A_1}{T_2 - T_1} \right)$$

4.12 Temperature Dependence of ΔF

We are concerned generally much more with the Gibbs free energy than with the Helmholtz free energy. The temperature dependence of ΔF to be considered now is limited to isothermal expansion of the ideal gas, but it will be shown in section 6.6 that the same result can be obtained without this restriction.

For isothermal expansion of an ideal gas

$$\Delta F_T = nRT \ln \left(\frac{P_2}{P_1} \right)$$

Remembering that T is constant, we express this relation by

$$F_2 - F_1 = nRT \ln P_2 - nRT \ln P_1$$

The temperature dependence of free energy for F_2 is to be taken at the constant pressure P_2, and for F_1 at P_1. Then representing this difference by

$$\left(\frac{\partial F_2}{\partial T} \right)_{P_2} - \left(\frac{\partial F_1}{\partial T} \right)_{P_1} = \left(\frac{\partial \Delta F_T}{\partial T} \right)_P$$

we have

$$\left(\frac{\partial \Delta F_T}{\partial T} \right)_P = nR \ln \left(\frac{P_2}{P_1} \right)$$

Since

$$\Delta F_T = -w_{\text{max.}} = -q_{\text{rev.}} = nRT \ln \left(\frac{P_2}{P_1} \right)$$

for an isothermal gas expansion, then

$$\left(\frac{\partial \Delta F_T}{\partial T} \right)_P = \frac{-q_{\text{rev.}}}{T} \qquad (4.16)$$

For any isothermal process it follows from the first and second laws that

$$q_{\text{rev.}} = \Delta E_T + w_{\text{max.}} = \Delta E_T - \Delta A_T$$

(For isothermal expansion of an ideal gas $\Delta E = 0$, but this is not the case for all isothermal processes.) Adding and subtracting ΔPV gives

$$q_{\text{rev.}} = (\Delta E_T + \Delta PV) - (\Delta A_T + \Delta PV) = \Delta H_T - \Delta F_T.$$

Equation (4.16) can then be written

$$\left(\frac{\partial \Delta F_T}{\partial T} \right)_P = \frac{\Delta F_T - \Delta H_T}{T} \qquad (4.17)$$

which is the *Gibbs-Helmholtz equation*. A more convenient form of this equation can be obtained by taking

$$\left[\frac{\partial (\Delta F_T / T)}{\partial T} \right]_P = \frac{1}{T} \left(\frac{\partial \Delta F_T}{\partial T} \right)_P - \frac{\Delta F_T}{T^2}$$

Combining with equation (4.17) gives

$$\left[\frac{\partial (\Delta F_T / T)}{\partial T} \right]_P = \frac{-\Delta H_T}{T^2} \qquad (4.18)$$

It was shown before for the process

$$H_2O \text{ (l, 1 atm., } T) = H_2O \text{ (g, 1 atm., } T)$$

that the value of ΔF is zero when $T = 373°K$. We may use equation (4.17) to compute the numerical value of $\partial(\Delta F)/\partial T$ at 1 atm. and 373°K, since we know both ΔF and ΔH under these conditions:

$$\left(\frac{\partial \Delta F_T}{\partial T}\right)_P = \frac{\Delta F_T - \Delta H_T}{T} = \frac{0 - 9710 \text{ cal. mole}^{-1}}{373}$$

$$= -26.0 \text{ cal. deg.}^{-1} \text{ mole}^{-1}$$

This derivative is negative, indicating that the value of ΔF will decrease and become negative as temperature increases, in keeping with the fact that vaporization at 1 atm. is permitted at temperatures above 373°K and forbidden at temperatures below 373°K.

Over a limited range of temperature, or when ΔH is nearly constant, equation (4.18) integrates readily.

$$\int_{\Delta F_1/T_1}^{\Delta F_2/T_2} d(\Delta F/T) = -\int_{T_1}^{T_2} \Delta H \frac{dT}{T^2}$$

$$\frac{\Delta F_2}{T_2} - \frac{\Delta F_1}{T_1} = \Delta H \left(\frac{1}{T_2} - \frac{1}{T_1}\right)$$

which rearranges to

$$\Delta F_2 = \Delta H + T_2 \left(\frac{\Delta F_1 - \Delta H}{T_1}\right) \tag{4.19}$$

As a matter of convenience, we may omit the subscript $_T$ for ΔF and ΔH, although the condition remains. Also, when a partial differential equation is to be integrated, we revert to standard notation. Again, the restrictions are not removed. Thus, the integral equation (4.19) is strictly valid only for processes at constant pressure. When the parameters of the equation are not very sensitive to moderate changes in pressure, which is frequently the case, this restriction may be ignored.

Equation (4.19) may be illustrated by evaluating ΔF for the vaporization of water at 400°K and 1 atm., ΔH being taken to be constant. Remembering that $\Delta F_{373} = 0$, one obtains

$$\Delta F_{400} = 9710 \text{ cal.} + \frac{400 \,(0\text{–}9710 \text{ cal.})}{373°K}$$

$$= -690 \text{ cal. mole}^{-1}$$

The accuracy of the calculation could be improved by using the value of ΔH corresponding to the average temperature, $\frac{1}{2}(T_2 + T_1)$.

EXERCISE 4.8

In a preceding section it was shown that ΔF of vaporization of water at 373°K and 700 mm. is $nR \times 373 \times \ln (700/760)$. Calculate the value of ΔF of vaporization of water at 363°K and 700 mm.

Ans. $\Delta F_{363} = 200 \text{ cal. mole}^{-1}$.

This method of calculating the variation of ΔF with temperature can be applied to any process for which the necessary data are available. These are the value of ΔF at some one temperature and the value of ΔH for the process. For instance, the reaction between Hg(g) and $\frac{1}{2}$ O$_2$(g) to produce HgO(s) at 25° and 1 atm. can be shown to have $\Delta F = -21.58 \text{ kcal. mole}^{-1}$. From tables of heats of formation it can also be shown that ΔH for this process is

—36.22 kcal. mole^{-1}. It follows then that

$$\left(\frac{\partial \Delta F}{\partial T}\right)_P = \frac{-21{,}580 - (-36{,}220)}{298°} = 49.2 \text{ cal. mole}^{-1} \text{ deg.}^{-1}$$

indicating that ΔF becomes zero at a lower temperature. We can estimate the temperature T_2 at which the process becomes reversible (i.e. reaches equilibrium) by setting $\Delta F_2 = 0$ in equation (4.19):

$$0 = -36{,}220 + T_2 (49.2), \qquad T_2 = 737°K$$

The answer must be considered inaccurate, since the approximation of constant ΔH is involved.

We may also apply the Gibbs-Helmholtz equation to a consideration of the temperature coefficient of the reversible emf of a galvanic cell. Replacing ΔF by $-n\mathscr{F}\mathscr{E}$ in the two forms of the Gibbs-Helmholtz equation, we have

$$n\mathscr{F}\left(\frac{\partial \mathscr{E}}{\partial T}\right)_P = \frac{n\mathscr{F}\mathscr{E} + \Delta H}{T} \tag{4.20}$$

$$\mathscr{E} = -\frac{\Delta H}{n\mathscr{F}} + T\left(\frac{\partial \mathscr{E}}{\partial T}\right)_P \tag{4.21}$$

provided ΔH is constant over the temperature interval involved. We see that here also the value of the reversible emf at various temperatures may be calculated if the value at some one temperature is known, together with the ΔH for the process. Examples of this application will be given in a later chapter on electromotive force.

SUMMARY, CHAPTER 4

1. Classification of isothermal processes (the second law of thermodynamics)

    Permitted $w < w_{\text{max.}}$

    Reversible $w = w_{\text{max.}}$

    Forbidden $w > w_{\text{max.}}$

2. For processes at const. T, V in closed systems

    Permitted $0 < w_{\text{max.}} = -\Delta A$

    Reversible $0 = w_{\text{max.}} = -\Delta A$

    Forbidden $0 > w_{\text{max.}} = -\Delta A$

3. For processes at const. T, P in closed systems

    Permitted $0 < w_{\text{max.}} - P\Delta V = -(\Delta A + P\Delta V) = -\Delta F$

    Reversible $0 = w_{\text{max.}} - P\Delta V = -(\Delta A + P\Delta V) = -\Delta F$

    Forbidden $0 > w_{\text{max.}} - P\Delta V = -(\Delta A + P\Delta V) = -\Delta F$

4. Evaluation of ΔF: $\Delta F(AD) = \Delta F(AB) + \Delta F(BC) + \Delta F(CD)$

    Ideal gas: $\Delta F_T = nRT \ln (P_2/P_1) = nRT \ln (V_1/V_2)$

Vaporization: $\Delta F_T = nRT \ln (P/P_{eq.})$

Reactions in a galvanic cell

$$\Delta F_T = -n\mathscr{F}\mathscr{E}_T$$

5. Temperature dependence of ΔF_T

$$\left(\frac{\partial \Delta F_T}{\partial T}\right)_P = -\frac{q_{rev.}}{T} = \frac{\Delta F - \Delta H}{T}$$

Gibbs-Helmholtz equation

$$\left(\frac{\partial(\Delta F_T/T)}{\partial T}\right)_P = -\frac{\Delta H}{T^2}$$

PROBLEMS, CHAPTER 4

1. Evaluate w and ΔA for the expansion of one mole of ideal gas at 300°K from 10 atm. to 1 atm.

(a) By free expansion into an evacuated vessel.

(b) Against a constant $P_{surr.} = 1$ atm.

(c) Reversibly.   *Ans.* (a) $\Delta A = -1371$ cal. (b) $w = 537$ cal.

2. For the processes in Problem 1, find ΔE and ΔH.

3. A lead storage battery generates an emf of 6 v.; its internal resistance is 0.05 ohm.

(a) What fraction of the energy it expends is wasted by ohmic internal resistance at a current of 1 ma.?

(b) What fraction at a current of 1 amp.? *Ans.* (a)8.35×10^{-6}, (b)8.35×10^{-3}.

4. A galvanic cell is constructed so that the cell reaction is

$$H_2 (P_1 = 1 \text{ atm.}) = H_2 (P_2 = 0.1 \text{ atm.})$$

(a) What is the maximum electric work obtainable from the cell at 25°?

Ans. (a) 5680 joules.

(b) What is the emf of the cell?   (b) 0.0296 v.

(c) What is the temperature coefficient of the emf?   (c) 9.9×10^{-5} v. deg^{-1}.

5. In the case of a cell such as that described in the preceding problem, what ratio of pressures P_1/P_2 would be required to produce an emf of 0.1 v.?

Ans. 2.41×10^3.

6. Using the data in the text (p. 37), evaluate ΔA for

(a) H_2O (s, 0°, 1 atm.) $= H_2O$ (1, 0°, 1 atm.).   *Ans.* (a) 1.42×10^{-3} l. atm.

(b) H_2O (l, 100°, 1 atm.) $= H_2O$ (g, 100°, 1 atm.).   (b) -30.6 l. atm.

(c) H_2O (g, 100°, 1 atm.) $= H_2O$ (g, 100°, 0.1 atm.).   (c) -70.4 l. atm.

7. For gases which obey the equation of state $PV = RT + bP$, find expressions for ΔA and ΔF for isothermal expansion

(a) In terms of V_1 and V_2.

(b) In terms of P_1 and P_2.   *Ans.* $\Delta A = RT \ln (V_1 - b)/(V_2 - b)$.

8. At 30° the equilibrium vapor pressure of water is 31.82 mm. Hg. Compute ΔF for the process

$$H_2O \text{ (l, 1 atm., 30°)} = H_2O \text{ (g, 1 atm., 30°)} \qquad \textit{Ans. } 1.90 \text{ kcal.}$$

9. The equilibrium vapor pressure of water over solid $BaCl_2 \cdot H_2O$ at 25° is 2.5 mm. Find ΔF for $BaCl_2 \cdot H_2O$ (s) = $BaCl_2$ (s) + H_2O (g) at 25° and 1 mm.

Ans. −545 cal.

10. Using data from the text and the preceding problem, find ΔF_{298} for $Ca(OH)_2(s) + BaCl_2(s) = CaO$ (s) + $BaCl_2 \cdot H_2O(s)$ *Ans.* 12.0 kcal.

11. At 80° the equilibrium vapor pressure of benzene is 1 atm. Therefore, $\Delta F_{353} = 0$ for the process

$$C_6H_6 \text{ (l, 1 atm., 80°)} = C_6H_6 \text{ (g, 1 atm., 80°)}$$

The heat of vaporization of benzene is 7350 cal. mole^{-1}.
(a) Evaluate ΔF for the corresponding process at 298°K.
(b) Compute the pressure at which $\Delta F_{298} = 0$, i.e., the equilibrium vapor pressure of benzene at 25°.   *Ans.* (a) + 1.14 kcal. (b) 110 mm.

12. The vapor pressure of supercooled liquid water at −5° is 3.16 mm. The vapor pressure of ice at −5° is 3.01 mm. Compute ΔF for

$$H_2O \text{ (s, 1 atm., −5°)} = H_2O \text{ (l, 1 atm., −5°)} \qquad \textit{Ans.} \text{ 25.9 cal.}$$

13. For the process

$$CaCO_3 \text{ (s)} = CaO \text{ (s)} + CO_2 \text{ (g)}$$

the equilibrium pressure of CO_2 is 1 atm. at 900°
(a) Find ΔF_{1173} for the process when $P_{CO_2} = 0.5$ atm.
(b) The value of ΔH_{1173} is 43,000 cal. mole^{-1}. At what temperature will the equilibrium pressure of CO_2 be 0.5 atm.?   *Ans.* (a)−1.61 kcal. (b) 1133°K.

---

14. Develop an expression for ΔA for reversible, isothermal expansion of gas obeying van der Waals equation.

15. Two galvanic cells are constructed as follows:
(a) H_2 (1 atm.) + 2 AgCl (s) = 2 HCl (1 M) + 2 Ag (s) for which $\mathscr{E}_{298} = 0.222$ v.
(b) H_2 (1 atm.) + 2 AgBr (s) = 2 HBr (1 M) + 2 Ag(s) for which $\mathscr{E}_{298} = 0.073$ v.
Couple the two cells in opposition so that cell *a* runs forward and cell *b* runs in reverse. Write the chemical equation for the net process and compute ΔF_{298}.

16. An aqueous solution of electrolyte is decomposed at 25° electrolytically and reversibly according to the equation

$$H_2O \text{ (l)} = \tfrac{1}{2} O_2 \text{ (g)} + H_2(g)$$

The combined gases are collected in a previously evacuated container at constant volume and caused to react, reforming water which returns to the solution at 25°, liberating 60 kcal. net heat to the surroundings over the entire cycle. Calculate $\mathscr{E}$.

17. From the densities of ice and water at 0° (0.917 and 1.000 g. cc.$^{-1}$),
(a) Find ΔF for H_2O (s, 2 atm.) = H_2O (l, 2 atm.).
(b) Find the approximate compensating change in temperature which would give $\Delta F = 0$ at 2 atm. for melting ice.

18. When the process Pb^{++} (aq.) + Cd = Cd^{++}(aq.) + Pb occurs in a galvanic cell at 25° under reversible conditions, w(elect.) = 13 kcal. When the same change in state occurs isothermally with no provision for electric work, 18 kcal. of heat is lost to the surroundings. Determine $q_{rev.}$.

19.   For the cell described in the preceding problem,

$$\mathscr{E} = 0.277 \text{ v. at } 25°.$$

(a) Find ΔF_{298}.
(b) Find $\mathscr{E}$ at 50°.

20.   (a) Devise and describe an isothermal reversible procedure for transferring one mole of volatile component A from a binary solution obeying Raoult's law from mole fraction X'_A to X''_A, when the second component is nonvolatile. The volumes of solution are taken so large that composition is sensibly constant.
(b) Express ΔF_T as a function of X_A.

21.   According to the principle of Le Chatelier, increasing the pressure on a system in a state of equilibrium will shift the position of equilibrium in that direction which will tend to offset the increased pressure. Explain this principle in terms of ΔF.

22.   For the reaction 2C (graphite) $+ 3H_2$ (g) $+$ S (rhombic) $= C_2H_5SH(l)$, for all substances in their standard states, $\Delta H°_{298} = -17.61$ kcal., $\Delta F°_{298} = -1.36$ kcal.
(a) For the preceding reaction, find P_{H_2} at which $\Delta F_{298} = 0$.
(b) Taking $\Delta H°$ constant, find the temperature at which $\Delta F° = 0$. Integrate equation (4.18) for the general case that

$$\Delta H_T = \Delta H_0 + \Delta aT + (\Delta b/2)T^2 + (\Delta c/3)T^3$$

23.   At $-5°$ the vapor pressure of ice is 3.01 mm. Find ΔF for

$$H_2O \text{ (g, 1 mm., } -5°) = H_2O \text{ (s, 100 mm., } -5°)$$

24.   Two galvanic cells are constructed as follows:
(a) H_2 (1 atm.) $+ 2$ AgCl (s) $= 2$ HCl (0.0050 m) $+ 2$ Ag (s)
(b) H_2 (1 atm.) $+ 2$ AgCl (s) $= 2$ HCl (0.050 m) $+ 2$ Ag (s)
and the emf's at 25° are 0.49844 and 0.38589 v., respectively. Couple the two cells in opposition so that cell a runs forward and cell b in reverse.
(a) What is the net emf of the combination?
(b) Combine the opposed cell reactions and write the net process.
(c) Evaluate ΔF for the net process.

25.   At 25° the partial pressure of H_2S over its aqueous solutions is 1.00 atm. at 0.10 molal and 2.00 atm. at 0.20 molal. Describe a procedure to effect the process

$$H_2S \text{ (0.1 } m) = H_2S \text{ (0.2 } m)$$

in a reversible fashion and evaluate ΔF_{298} for the change in state. The amounts of solution are so large that transfer of one mole of H_2S does not affect the concentration.

26.   The heat effects which attend a given change in state when carried out reversibly and irreversibly are not, in general, the same. This can be demonstrated by using equation (4.16) to obtain $q_{rev.}$ and (4.17) to obtain ΔH. The emf of the cell whose reaction is

$$H_2 + 2 \text{ AgCl} = 2 \text{ HCl (0.100 } m) + 2 \text{ Ag}$$

is 0.35240 v. at 25° and $d\mathscr{E}/dT = -0.0019$ v. deg.$^{-1}$ Find ΔH and $q_{rev.}$.

27. At 300° the decomposition

$$NH_4I (s) = NH_3 (g) + HI (g)$$

reaches an equilibrium state for which $P_{NH_3} = P_{HI} = 44.6$ mm.

(a) Find ΔF_{573} when $P_{NH_3} = 30$ mm. and $P_{HI} = 50$ mm.

(b) If P_{NH_3} is held at 30 mm. what value of P_{HI} will make the process reversible at 300°?

28. Two galvanic cells are constructed as follows:

(a) $Cu^{++}(1\ M) + H_2(1\ atm.) = Cu (s) + 2H^+(1\ M)$

(b) $Zn (s) + 2H^+(1\ M) = Zn^{++}(1\ M) + H_2 (1\ atm.)$

When they are coupled so that both cells run forward, as written, what is their combined emf at 25°?

5

CHEMICAL EQUILIBRIUM
IN GASEOUS SYSTEMS

5.1 Equilibrium States

In the preceding chapter it was shown that the value of the free energy change (ΔF) in a constant temperature, constant pressure process in an isolated system can be used to classify the process as *permitted, reversible,* or *forbidden.* If the specified temperature and pressures of substances present are such that the free energy change in the process of interest is zero, there is no tendency for the process to occur in either direction, and the system is in an *equilibrium state.*

Consider a system consisting of gaseous hydrogen, nitrogen, and ammonia. In order to characterize the state of a mixture, it is necessary to specify not only the temperature and the total pressure of the system, but also the composition. If the total pressure and temperature are fixed, and if the system exchanges no work with the surroundings other than expansion work, then the sign of the free energy change for the process is a criterion of permissibility.

If one chooses an initial composition of the system quite at random, the composition almost certainly changes with time. Regardless of the composition of the starting mixture, if reaction is possible, the composition of the system eventually reaches a value which no longer changes with time. That is, the system comes to equilibrium.

There is no unique composition of the system at equilibrium. In fact, an infinite number of different equilibrium compositions are possible at constant total pressure and constant temperature. To illustrate, let the initial composition of the system be a moles of nitrogen, b moles of hydrogen, and c moles of ammonia. Let the number of moles of ammonia formed in the course of equilibration be x.

Initial moles a b c

$$N_2 \; + \; 3H_2 \; = \; 2NH_3$$

Equil. moles $a - \tfrac{1}{2}x$ $b - \tfrac{3}{2}x$ $c + x$

The value of x is found from experiment, but the values of a, b, and c can be selected arbitrarily by the experimenter. *They have no relation to the stoichiometric coefficients.* Thus, with an infinite choice of initial compositions, it is possible to have an infinite variety of equilibrium states. Application of the second law of thermodynamics reveals a useful relationship describing these equilibrium states which will now be examined.

EXERCISE 5.1

1.165 moles of nitrogen and 0.465 mole of hydrogen are equilibrated in a 1 l. vessel at 450°. At equilibrium 0.0845 mole of ammonia is present. Find the amounts of nitrogen and hydrogen and the partial pressures of all components at equilibrium.   *Ans.* $n_{N_2} = 1.123$; $n_{H_2} = 0.338$; $P_{N_2} = 66.5$ atm; $P_{H_2} = 20$ atm.; $P_{NH_3} = 5$ atm.

5.2 Free Energy Changes of Isothermal Reactions in Ideal Gases

Consider the generalized system consisting of a mixture of ideal gases A, B, ..., M, N, ... among which chemical interactions can occur as described by the stoichiometric equation

$$aA + bB + \ldots = mM + nN + \ldots$$

The free energy change for this process at constant temperature depends on the partial pressures P_A, P_B, ..., P_M, P_N, ... In order to evaluate the free energy change at fixed partial pressures of the components, we may imagine that the system consists of very large amounts of material, so that the unit process described produces no appreciable change in partial pressures. Then if a moles of A at P_A react with b moles of B at P_B to form m moles of M at P_M and n moles of N at P_N, etc.,

$$\Delta F_T = mF(M) + nF(N) + \ldots - aF(A) - bF(B) - \ldots$$

where $F(M)$ is the molar free energy of M at P_M, etc., all at one temperature T.

The molar free energy of each substance is a function of the partial pressure of that substance,

$$dF_T = VdP \tag{5.1}$$

For an ideal gas, this equation becomes

$$dF_T = \frac{nRT}{P} dP$$

Previously, this expression was integrated between the limits P_1 and P_2 to obtain the change in free energy as a function of pressure. For the present purpose the indefinite integral will be more suitable. For one mole of ideal gas the constant of integration is the molar free energy of the gas at unit pressure (when $P = 1$, $\ln P = 0$), a value denoted by F_T^o.

$$F_T = RT \ln P + F_T^o \qquad (5.2)$$

Equation (5.2), therefore, does not yield values of F_T, since F_T^o is not known, but rather gives the relationship between the free energy at an arbitrary pressure P and the free energy at unit pressure. The same relation could have been obtained by equation (4.11), thus, for one mole

$$\Delta F_T = F_T(\text{state } 2) - F_T(\text{state } 1) = RT \ln (P_2/P_1)$$

Let $P_1 = 1$; that is, let state 1 be the *standard state*

$$F_T(\text{state } 2) = RT \ln P_2 + F_T^o$$

Equation (5.2) applies to each of the components of a system and may be used to expand the expression for ΔF_T.

$$\Delta F_T = mF_T^o(M) + nF_T^o(N) + \ldots - aF_T^o(A) - bF_T^o(B) - \ldots + mRT \ln P_M$$
$$+ nRT \ln P_N + \ldots - aRT \ln P_A - bRT \ln P_B - \ldots \qquad (5.3)$$

Representing the coefficient of the ith component by ν_i and summing over all terms gives

$$\Delta F_T = \sum_i \nu_i F_{iT}^o + \sum_i \nu_i RT \ln P_i \qquad (5.4)$$

The first term on the right-hand side of equation (5.4) is a collection of constants of integration from equation (5.2) for each substance.

$$\sum_i \nu_i F_{iT}^o = mF_T^o(M) + nF_T^o(N) + \ldots - aF_T^o(A) - bF_T^o(B) - \ldots \qquad (5.5)$$

It is the change in free energy for the process

$$aA(P_A = 1) + bB(P_B = 1) + \ldots = mM(P_M = 1) + nN(P_N = 1) + \ldots$$

and is called the *standard free energy change*, ΔF_T^o. Thus, for

$$N_2 + 3H_2 = 2NH_3$$

it is the free energy change for the uniquely defined process at temperature T

$$N_2(P_{N_2} = 1 \text{ atm.}) + 3H_2(P_{H_2} = 1 \text{ atm.}) = 2NH_3(P_{NH_3} = 1 \text{ atm.})$$
$$\Delta F_T^o = 2F_T^o(NH_3) - F_T^o(N_2) - 3F_T^o(H_2)$$

Stoichiometry dictates the ratios of the coefficients in the chemical equations but not their absolute values. The choice of the unit of reaction is always arbitrary, and different circumstances may favor one choice in preference to another. If $a, b, \ldots, m, n, \ldots$ represent any set of coefficients consistent with the stoichiometry of the process

(i) $$aA + bB + \ldots = mM + nN + \ldots$$

every coefficient can be multiplied by the same constant α

(ii) $$\alpha a\mathrm{A} + \alpha b\mathrm{B} + \ldots = \alpha m\mathrm{M} + \alpha n\mathrm{N} + \ldots$$

since the stoichiometry requires only that

$$\frac{\text{(coefficient of A)}}{\text{(coefficient of B)}} = \frac{a}{b}, \text{ etc.}$$

For the processes (i) and (ii) (at the same temperature) it also follows that

$$\alpha \Delta F(\mathrm{i}) = \Delta F(\mathrm{ii})$$

Negative values of α are evidently permitted.

The value of ΔF_T^o is not completely established until the choice of standard state has been specified. Although one atmosphere is almost always chosen, this is a completely arbitrary choice. For instance, if the unit of pressure is 1 mm. Hg, then the standard free energy change for ammonia synthesis would be that for the process

$$\mathrm{N_2}(P = 1 \text{ mm.}) + 3\mathrm{H_2}(P = 1 \text{ mm.}) = 2\mathrm{NH_3}(P = 1 \text{ mm.}).$$

This possibility of multiple standard states arises from equation (5.2), because $F_T = F_T^o$ whenever $P = 1$ for each pressure unit chosen. Values of F_T^o also depend on the unit of mass, the customary choice being the gram mole.

EXERCISE 5.2

Given $\Delta F_{723}^o = 7.16$ kcal. for the synthesis of 1 gram mole of ammonia from the elements, find the corresponding standard free energy of formation of 1 pound mole of ammonia.   *Ans.* 3245 kcal.

5.3   The Reaction Function

To consider the second term on the right-hand side of equation (5.4), it is helpful to repeat the development of that equation by a slightly different method.

Remembering that ΔF_T is independent of path and depends only upon initial and final states, we demonstrate its relation to the corresponding ΔF_T^o in the diagram:

$$aA(P_A) \quad + \quad bB(P_B) \quad + \ldots \xrightarrow{\Delta F_T} \quad mM(P_M) \quad + \quad nN(P_N) \quad + \ldots$$
$$\downarrow \Delta F(A) \qquad \downarrow \Delta F(B) \qquad\qquad \uparrow \Delta F(M) \qquad \uparrow \Delta F(N)$$
$$aA(P_A = 1) + bB(P_B = 1) + \ldots \xrightarrow{\Delta F^o_T} mM(P_M = 1) + nN(P_N = 1) + \ldots$$

The quantities $\Delta F(A)$, $\Delta F(B)$, $\Delta F(M)$, $\Delta F(N)$ represent the free energy changes for the processes of changing the pressures of the reactants and products from the arbitrary pressures P_i to unit pressure, or inversely.

$$\Delta F(A) = aRT \ln \frac{1 \text{ unit}}{P_A \text{ units}}$$

$$\Delta F(M) = mRT \ln \frac{P_M \text{ units}}{1 \text{ unit}}, \text{ etc.}$$

If we now abbreviate these expressions to

$$\Delta F(A) = -aRT \ln P_A, \qquad \Delta F(M) = mRT \ln P_M, \text{ etc.}$$

it is to be remembered that each partial pressure is expressed as a ratio in units of the standard state pressure and is, therefore, dimensionless. Consequently, the pressures P_A, P_B, P_M, P_N, etc., must be expressed as multiples of the unit standard state pressure.

It is clear from the diagram that the difference between ΔF_T and ΔF_T^o is equal to the sum of the terms $\Delta F(A)$, $\Delta F(B)$, $\Delta F(M)$, $\Delta F(N)$, etc. This difference

$$\Delta F_T - \Delta F_T^o = mRT \ln P_M + nRT \ln P_N + \ldots - aRT \ln P_A - bRT \ln P_B - \ldots$$

is equivalent to equation (5.4). It is convenient to express the righthand side of this equation in the form

$$\Delta F_T - \Delta F_T^o = RT \ln \frac{P_M^m P_N^n \ldots}{P_A^a P_B^b \ldots}$$

$$= RT \ln \prod_i (P_i^{v_i}) \qquad (5.6)$$

The function of pressures $\prod_i (P_i^{v_i})$ has a characteristic algebraic form which justifies our giving it a special designation as the *reaction function* of pressures and representing its value by Q_P.[1]

$$\prod_i (P_i^{v_i}) = \frac{P_M^m P_N^n \ldots}{P_A^a P_B^b \ldots} = Q_P \qquad (5.7)$$

The relationship represented by the diagram above is conveniently abbreviated

$$\Delta F_T - \Delta F_T^o = RT \ln Q_P \qquad (5.8)$$

It is to be emphasized that neither equation (5.4) nor equation (5.8) is restricted to reversible processes, or to equilibrium states. The reaction function may have any value at all, since, for any given process, the pressures of reactants and products can be adjusted to whatever values we please. For the process

$$N_2 + 3H_2 = 2NH_3$$

and

$$Q_P = \frac{P_{NH_3}^2}{P_{N_2} P_{H_2}^3} \text{ (atm.}^{-2})$$

$\Delta F_{723}^o = 7160 \text{ cal mole}^{-1}$, and ΔF_{723} for formation of 2 moles of ammonia when $P_{NH_3} = 10$ atm., $P_{N_2} = 1$ atm. and $P_{H_2} = 2$ atm. can be computed as follows.

$$Q_P = \frac{10^2}{1 \cdot 2^3} \text{ (atm.}^{-2})$$

$$\Delta F_{723} = 14{,}320 + 1.987 \times 723 \times 2.303 \times \log 12.5 = 17{,}940 \text{ cal.}$$

---

[1]The partial pressures in the reaction function are dimensionless and, therefore, Q_P is dimensionless. Nevertheless, its numerical value depends on the choice of standard states, and it is helpful to specify this choice by assigning appropriate pressure units to Q_P, which will be shown in parentheses.

Therefore the process

$$N_2 \ (1 \text{ atm.}) + 3H_2 \ (2 \text{ atm.}) = 2NH_3 \ (10 \text{ atm.})$$

is forbidden. This is not to be understood as meaning that ammonia cannot be synthesized from the elements. A similar computation for the process

$$N_2 \ (10 \text{ atm.}) + 3H_2 \ (50 \text{ atm.}) = 2NH_3 \ (1 \text{ atm.})$$

yields

$$\Delta F_{723} = 14{,}320 + 1.987 \times 723 \times 2.303 \times \log \frac{1^2}{10 \cdot 50^3} = -5850 \text{ cal.}$$

This process is permitted.

EXERCISE 5.3

Compute ΔF^o_{723} for

$$N_2 + 3 H_2 = 2 NH_3$$

when the standard state is chosen to be 1 mm. Hg. That is, compute ΔF_{723} for

$$N_2 \ (1 \text{ mm.}) + 3 H_2 \ (1 \text{ mm.}) = 2 NH_3 \ (1 \text{ mm.})$$

Ans. 33,420 cal.

It should be evident from the preceding considerations that there is an unambiguous relationship between the stoichiometric equation describing a process and the appropriate reaction function. In the preceding section it was pointed out that if the coefficients in the stoichiometric equation are multiplied by a constant factor α, the value of ΔF is multiplied by the same factor. The right-hand side of equation (5.8) is also multiplied by the same factor, leading to

$$\alpha \Delta F_T - \alpha \Delta F^o_T = RT \ln (Q_P)^\alpha$$

For example, for

$$\tfrac{1}{2} N_2 + \tfrac{3}{2} H_2 = NH_3$$

$$\Delta F^o_{723} = 7160 \text{ cal.}$$

Q_P for this process is formulated

$$Q_P = \frac{P_{NH_3}}{P_{N_2}^{1/2} P_{H_2}^{3/2}} \ (\text{atm.}^{-1})$$

and the free energy change when $P_{NH_3} = 10$ atm., $P_{N_2} = 1$ atm., and $P_{H_2} = 2$ atm. is given by

$$\Delta F_{723} = 7160 + 1.987 \times 723 \times 2.303 \times \log \frac{10}{1^{1/2} \cdot 2^{3/2}} = 8970 \text{ cal.}$$

Note that giving the factor α negative values is equivalent to a statement of the reverse reaction:

$$2NH_3 = 3H_2 + N_2$$

$$\Delta F_{723} = -14{,}320 + RT \ln \frac{P_{H_2}^3 P_{N_2}}{P_{NH_3}^2}$$

EXERCISE 5.4

If $P_{NH_3} = 1$ atm. and $P_{H_2} = 2$ atm., what value must P_{N_2} have in order that ΔF_{723} shall be zero? *Ans.* 2.66×10^3 atm.

5.4 The Equilibrium Reaction Function

Of the various sets of pressures which can be chosen for processes such as the preceding, we are particularly interested in those sets for which $\Delta F = 0$, since these are sets corresponding to equilibrium states of the system. According to equation (5.8), a simple relationship exists between the *standard free energy change* and the reaction function of the *equilibrium* pressures, designated by $\mathscr{P}_i$, since $\Delta F_T = 0$ for an equilibrium set of pressures.

$$\Delta F_T^o = -RT \ln \prod_i (\mathscr{P}_i^{\nu_i})$$

$$= -RT \ln \frac{\mathscr{P}_M^m \mathscr{P}_N^n \cdots}{\mathscr{P}_A^a \mathscr{P}_B^b \cdots} \tag{5.9}$$

The *equilibrium function* of pressures $\prod_i (\mathscr{P}_i^{\nu_i})$ has the same algebraic form as the reaction function, but refers only to certain sets of pressures, namely, those for which $\Delta F_T = 0$. The numerical value of the equilibrium function is designated[2] by $K_{\mathscr{P}}$.

$$\frac{\mathscr{P}_M^m \mathscr{P}_N^n \cdots}{\mathscr{P}_A^a \mathscr{P}_B^b \cdots} = K_{\mathscr{P}} \tag{5.10}$$

This expression is often called the *mass action law*.

It was shown that the standard free energy change ΔF^o has a fixed value for a given process at a given temperature. It follows from equation (5.9) that $K_{\mathscr{P}}$ also *has a fixed value for a given process at a given temperature*. For this reason, $K_{\mathscr{P}}$ is called the *equilibrium constant*. The relation between $K_{\mathscr{P}}$ and ΔF_T^o is given by

$$\Delta F_T^o = -RT \ln K_{\mathscr{P}} \tag{5.11}$$

To illustrate, let us consider the process

$$A + B = C$$

taking $K_{\mathscr{P}} = 10$ (atm.$^{-1}$), and let the initial partial pressures be P_A, P_B with $P_C = 0$. The partial pressures at equilibrium become

$$\mathscr{P}_A = P_A - \mathscr{P}_C; \qquad \mathscr{P}_B = P_B - \mathscr{P}_C$$

$$\frac{\mathscr{P}_C}{(P_A - \mathscr{P}_C)(P_B - \mathscr{P}_C)} = 10 \text{ atm.}^{-1}$$

Since an infinite variety of initial pressures P_A, P_B, and P_C are permitted, no two of which lead to the same equilibrium state, there is an infinite number of sets of values for $\mathscr{P}_A$, $\mathscr{P}_B$, and $\mathscr{P}_C$. For instance, if $P_A = 0.1$ atm., $P_B = 0.5$ atm.,

---

[2]The previous remarks concerning units in Q_P apply equally to $K_{\mathscr{P}}$ and appropriate units will be given in parentheses.

and $P_C = 0$, substitution yields

$$10\mathscr{P}_C^2 - 7\mathscr{P}_C + 0.5 = 0$$

whose solutions are

$$\mathscr{P}_C = 0.62 \text{ and } 0.0808 \text{ atm.}$$

The first is impossible, since $\mathscr{P}_C$ cannot exceed either P_A or P_B. Therefore,

$$\mathscr{P}_C = 0.0808 \text{ atm.}; \qquad \mathscr{P}_A = 0.0192 \text{ atm.}; \qquad \mathscr{P}_B = 0.4192 \text{ atm.}$$

EXERCISE 5.5

Let $P_A = 1$ atm., $P_B = 0.5$ atm. and $P_C = 0$ for the process

$$A + B = C; \qquad K_{\mathscr{P}} = 10 \, (\text{atm.}^{-1})$$

Find the equilibrium pressures.

Ans. $\mathscr{P}_C = 0.426$ atm.; $\mathscr{P}_A = 0.574$ atm.; $\mathscr{P}_B = 0.074$ atm.

In the synthesis of ammonia it is found that if a 3:1 mixture of hydrogen and nitrogen is heated to a temperature of 450° at a total pressure of 50 atm., reaction occurs until the mole per cent of ammonia is 9.17. (The rate of approach to this equilibrium state may be increased by the use of catalysts, but the equilibrium composition is not affected by their presence.) The composition of the system in the equilibrium state is

$$\mathscr{P}_{NH_3} = 4.58 \text{ atm.}; \qquad \mathscr{P}_{H_2} = 33.99 \text{ atm.}; \qquad \mathscr{P}_{N_2} = 11.33 \text{ atm.}$$

The value of $K_{\mathscr{P}}$, may be computed for

$$N_2 + 3H_2 = 2NH_3$$

$$K_{\mathscr{P}} = \frac{\mathscr{P}_{NH_3}^2}{\mathscr{P}_{N_2}\mathscr{P}_{H_2}^3}$$

$$K_{\mathscr{P}} = \frac{4.58^2}{11.33 \cdot 33.99^3} = 4.70 \times 10^{-5} \, (\text{atm.}^{-2})$$

EXERCISE 5.6

Compute the equilibrium pressure of ammonia at 723°K when $\mathscr{P}_{N_2} = 10$ atm. and $\mathscr{P}_{H_2} = 10$ atm. $\qquad$ *Ans.* 0.685 atm.

5.5 The Reaction Isotherm

The free energy change which accompanies a process may be stated in compact form by combining equations (5.8) and (5.11) to obtain

$$\Delta F_T = RT \ln \frac{Q_P}{K_{\mathscr{P}}} \tag{5.12}$$

This relation is called the reaction isotherm, since it may be applied to the description of the permissibility of reaction throughout the course of an isothermal chemical change. A graphical representation of ΔF_T as a function of the ratio $Q_P/K_{\mathscr{P}}$ is given in Fig. 5.1.

Suppose that a system is displaced from a state of equilibrium until $Q_P < K_{\mathscr{P}}$, either by augmenting the pressures of the reactants or by diminishing the

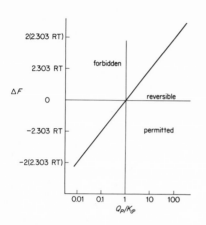

FIG. 5.1. The reaction isotherm.

pressures of the products. By equation (5.12), $\Delta F_T < 0$, and the conversion of "reactants" to "products" is permitted. On the other hand, if a system is displaced from an equilibrium state until $Q_P > K_{\mathscr{P}}$, either by augmenting the pressures of the products or by diminishing the pressures of the reactants, then $\Delta F_T > 0$, and the conversion of "reactants" to "products" is forbidden. That is, the conversion of "products" to "reactants" is permitted. These relations may be summarized thus:

$$Q_P < K_{\mathscr{P}}, \quad \Delta F < 0 \quad \text{forward process permitted}$$
$$Q_P = K_{\mathscr{P}}, \quad \Delta F = 0 \quad \text{process reversible (equil. state)}$$
$$Q_P > K_{\mathscr{P}}, \quad \Delta F > 0 \quad \text{forward process forbidden (reverse process permitted)}$$

Note that in either case the direction of the permitted process is such as to make the value of Q_P approach that of $K_{\mathscr{P}}$. This is a most important result, namely, that *the direction of the permitted process is always toward an equilibrium state.* It follows that when the pressure of one of the components of a system previously at equilibrium is increased, the process which consumes that component becomes permitted. The student may have previously encountered a qualitative statement of this behavior known as the *principle of Le Chatelier,* which states that *any change in the variables that characterize the state of a system in equilibrium causes a shift in the position of equilibrium in a direction that tends to counteract the change in the variable under consideration.*

The ammonia synthesis may be used to illustrate the principles stated above. Values of ΔF_{723} for

$$N_2 + 3H_2 = 2NH_3$$

under various conditions are summarized in Table 5.1.

TABLE 5.1

VALUES OF ΔF_{723} FOR THE PROCESS

$$N_2 + 3H_2 = 2NH_3$$

Case	P_{N_2} (atm.)	P_{H_2} (atm.)	P_{NH_3} (atm.)	Q_P	$K_{\mathscr{P}}$	ΔF (cal.)
1	1.00	1.00	1.00	1.00	4.7×10^{-5}	14,320
2	10.00	20.00	4.58	2.6×10^{-4}	4.7×10^{-5}	2,460
3	11.33	33.99	4.58	4.7×10^{-5}	4.7×10^{-5}	0
4	1.00	1.00	6.86×10^{-3}	4.7×10^{-5}	4.7×10^{-5}	0
5	20.00	33.99	4.58	2.7×10^{-5}	4.7×10^{-5}	−796
6	10.00	50.00	1.00	8.0×10^{-7}	4.7×10^{-5}	−5,850

Comparison of case 1 with case 4 shows that an increase in the pressure of ammonia above the equilibrium value makes the reverse reaction permitted.

Comparison of case 2 with case 3 shows that decreasing the nitrogen and hydrogen pressures below the equilibrium values also makes the reverse reaction permitted.

Comparison of case 5 with case 3 shows that increase of the nitrogen pressure above the equilibrium value makes the forward reaction permitted.

Comparison of the fifth and sixth columns of the table shows that the critical factor in the determination of permissibility is the relation of Q_P to the fixed value of $K_{\mathscr{P}}$.

EXERCISE 5.7

The volume of a system in the equilibrium state described in case 3 of Table 5.1 is increased by a factor of two, thus decreasing temporarily the pressures of all components to one-half their equilibrium values. What process will be permitted and what will be the value of ΔF_{723}?

$$Ans.\ 2\,NH_3 = N_2 + 3\,H_2; \ \Delta F_{723} = -1990\ cal.$$

5.6   The Equilibrium Function of Mole Fractions

The preceding descriptions of equilibrium states in terms of the partial pressures are often useful but equivalent descriptions in terms of mole fractions or numbers of moles of components (mole numbers) are sometimes to be preferred. Remembering that partial pressure P_i, mole fraction X_i, and total pressure P_t are related by

$$P_i = X_i P_t$$

we may expand the equilibrium function of pressures thus:

$$\Pi_i(\mathscr{P}_i^{\nu_i}) = \Pi_i(X_i^{\nu_i}\mathscr{P}_t^{\nu_i})$$

$$\frac{\mathscr{P}_M^m \mathscr{P}_N^n \ldots}{\mathscr{P}_A^a \mathscr{P}_B^b \ldots} = \frac{X_M^m X_N^n \ldots}{X_A^a X_B^b \ldots} \times \frac{\mathscr{P}_t^m \mathscr{P}_t^n \ldots}{\mathscr{P}_t^a \mathscr{P}_t^b \ldots}$$

$$K_{\mathscr{P}} = K_X \mathscr{P}_t^{\Delta\nu} \tag{5.13}$$

By analogy, K_X is the value of $\Pi_i(X_i^{\nu_i})$ and

$$\Delta\nu = m + n + \ldots - a - b - \ldots$$

It is to be observed that K_X is not an "equilibrium constant" with regard to variations in $\mathscr{P}_t$ except for $\Delta\nu = 0$. K_X is simply the value of the equilibrium function of the mole fractions.

Equation (5.13) may be modified by remembering that

$$X_i = \frac{n_i}{n_t}$$

With this substitution we have

$$\Pi_i(\mathscr{P}_i^{\nu_i}) = \Pi_i(n_i^{\nu_i}n_t^{-\nu_i}\mathscr{P}_t^{\nu_i})$$

$$\frac{\mathscr{P}_M^m \mathscr{P}_N^n \ldots}{\mathscr{P}_A^a \mathscr{P}_B^b \ldots} = \frac{n_M^m n_N^n \ldots}{n_A^a n_B^b \ldots} \times \frac{n_t^a n_t^b \ldots}{n_t^m n_t^n \ldots} \times \frac{\mathscr{P}_t^m \mathscr{P}_t^n \ldots}{\mathscr{P}_t^a \mathscr{P}_t^b \ldots} \tag{5.14}$$

$$K_{\mathscr{P}} = K_n \times (n_t)^{-\Delta\nu} \times (\mathscr{P}_t)^{\Delta\nu}$$

Again, by analogy, K_n is the value of $\prod_i(n_i^{\nu_i})$, and this quantity is not an "equilibrium constant" with regard to variations in P_t *except for* $\Delta\nu = 0$. K_n is simply the value of the equilibrium function of the mole numbers.

EXERCISE 5.8

The dissociation process

$$A_2 = 2\,A$$

occurs to the extent that $X_A = 0.01$ at 1 atm. total pressure. Compute the approximate value of X_A at 10 atm. total pressure. (Let $X_{A_2} \cong 1$.)

Ans. 3.16×10^{-3}.

While $K_{\mathscr{P}}$ is not altered by variations in total pressure at constant temperature (for an ideal gas), the position of equilibrium, as expressed by composition, does change with change in total pressure, unless $\Delta\nu = 0$. The function $\prod_i(X_i^{\nu_i})$ is convenient for this examination. By equation (5.13) it appears that an increase in $\mathscr{P}_t$ must cause a decrease in K_X for $\Delta\nu > 0$. Similarly, decreasing $\mathscr{P}_t$ increases K_X for $\Delta\nu > 0$. When $\Delta\nu < 0$ the effect is reversed. Clearly, an increase in K_X corresponds to conversion of reactants to products; a decrease in K_X corresponds to the reverse process. Equation (5.13) is a quantitative statement of the principle of Le Chatelier for total pressure variations. These regularities may be summarized thus:

$\Delta\mathscr{P}_t$	$\Delta\nu$	$\Delta K_{\mathscr{P}}$	ΔK_X	Equilibrium shifts
$+$	$+$	0	$-$	$\leftarrow$
$+$	$-$	0	$+$	$\rightarrow$
$+$	0	0	0	$\rightleftharpoons$
$-$	$+$	0	$+$	$\rightarrow$
$-$	$-$	0	$-$	$\leftarrow$
$-$	0	0	0	$\rightleftharpoons$

5.7 Equilibrium Computations

The equilibrium constant is a most important thermodynamic property of a chemical system. It can be directly determined by analysis of an equilibrium state of the system. That is, the substances are mixed and react until an equilibrium state is attained, at which time the composition of the system is determined.

Absence of observable change is a necessary but not a sufficient condition to characterize an equilibrium state. No observable change will occur when a system is in an equilibrium state, but, on the other hand, absence of observable reaction may indicate only that the rate of approach to an equilibrium state is negligible. The difficulty of ensuring that the state observed by analysis is indeed an equilibrium state is usually surmounted by approaching the equilibrium from several initial states and requiring that all values of the supposed equilibrium constant agree within experimental error. Net chemical change stops when an equilibrium state is reached, but nonthermodynamic methods demonstrate that a dynamic balance of forward and reverse processes—not complete cessation of reaction—is responsible.

Before proceeding to numerical calculations relating to equilibrium, let us first examine in algebraic terms the generalized process

$$aA + bB + \ldots = mM + nN + \ldots$$

When the initial composition of the system is known, it is convenient to state this information by giving the number of moles of each substance. Let the initial composition of the system be α moles of A, β moles of B, ... μ moles of M, ν moles of N, ... The ratios $\alpha : \beta : \mu : \nu$ need not be the same as $a : b : m : n$; that is, the initial amounts of reactants and products are not necessarily in stoichiometric ratios.

The equilibrium composition is related to the initial composition as follows: In the change from initial state to equilibrium state the *changes* in the amounts of reactants and products are proportional to the stoichiometric coefficients. Let the number of moles of M formed be mx. Since

$$axA + bxB + \ldots = mxM + nxN + \ldots$$

it follows that ax moles of A and bx moles of B have been consumed in the formation of mx moles of M and nx moles of N, etc. The various mole numbers at equilibrium are, therefore,

$$\alpha - ax \qquad \beta - bx \qquad \mu + mx \qquad \nu + nx$$

It may happen that the amount of M decreases in the course of equilibration, in which case the numerical value of x will be negative.

The equilibrium composition of the system may also be given in terms of mole fractions. Representing the total number of moles in the system at equilibrium by n_t, that is,

$$n_t = \alpha - ax + \beta - bx + \mu + mx + \nu + nx + \ldots$$

we have $\qquad X_A = \dfrac{\alpha - ax}{n_t}, \qquad X_M = \dfrac{\mu + mx}{n_t}$, etc.

The equilibrium mole fractions may be inserted in equation (5.13) and the equilibrium mole numbers in equation (5.14).

$$K_{\mathscr{P}} = K_n n_t^{-\Delta \nu} \mathscr{P}_t^{\Delta \nu} = \frac{(\mu + mx)^m (\nu + nx)^n}{(\alpha - ax)^a (\beta - bx)^b} n_t^{-\Delta \nu} \mathscr{P}_t^{\Delta \nu} \qquad (5.15)$$

This expression relates the equilibrium constant and the various experimental characteristics of a system. In general, the measurement of an equilibrium constant is accomplished by mixing known amounts of reagents (α, β, μ, ν, etc., are known), equilibrating, and measuring the extent of reaction (x measured) or the equilibrium amounts of reagents ($\mu + mx$, etc.) at a known total pressure $\mathscr{P}_t$. On the other hand, the value of $K_{\mathscr{P}}$ may be known and used to find the equilibrium composition of a system with a chosen initial composition.

The equilibrium between N_2O_4 and NO_2 is conveniently measurable in the interval 25–45° [F. H. Verhoeck and F. Daniels, *J. Am. Chem. Soc.*, **53**, 1250 (1931)]. Some of the data appear in Table 5.2.

TABLE 5.2

THE DISSOCIATION EQUILIBRIUM $N_2O_4 = 2NO_2$

Temp. (°C)	$c^0 N_2O_4$ (mole l.$^{-1}$)	P_t, equil. (atm.)	$K_{\mathscr{P}}$ (atm.)
25	4.49×10^{-3}	0.157	0.142
25	29.68×10^{-3}	0.862	0.126
35	6.28×10^{-3}	0.238	0.317
35	27.72×10^{-3}	0.890	—
45	10.15×10^{-3}	0.406	0.649
45	19.84×10^{-3}	0.744	0.628

In these experiments the initial amount of product was always zero ($\mu = 0$), and equation (5.15) simplifies to

$$K_{\mathscr{P}} = \frac{(2x)^2}{\alpha - x}(\alpha + x)^{-1}\mathscr{P}_t \tag{5.16}$$

The initial state of the system is described by $c^0_{N_2O_4}$, the number of formula weights of N_2O_4 per l. present in the system, without regard to extent of dissociation. The equilibrium state of the system is characterized by the measured total pressure, $\mathscr{P}_t$. Choosing V l. of the gaseous sample for consideration at temperature T, we have the following mole numbers:

	Initial	*Equilibrium*
N_2O_4	$\alpha = c^0 V$	$(\alpha - x) = c^0 V - x$
NO_2	$\mu = 0$	$(\mu + 2x) = 2x$
		$n_t = c^0 V + x$

The value of x may be obtained from

$$c^0 V + x = \frac{\mathscr{P}_t V}{RT}$$

Substituting for x and α in equation (5.16), one obtains

$$K_{\mathscr{P}} = \frac{4(\mathscr{P}_t V/RT - c^0 V)^2}{2c^0 V - \mathscr{P}_t V/RT} \cdot \left(\frac{\mathscr{P}_t V}{RT}\right)^{-1}\mathscr{P}_t$$

After simplification

$$K_{\mathscr{P}} = \frac{4(\mathscr{P}_t/RT - c^0)^2}{2c^0 - \mathscr{P}_t/RT}RT$$

From the first entry in Table 5.2 we compute $K_{\mathscr{P}}$ at 25° as follows:

$$\frac{\mathscr{P}_t}{RT} = 6.42 \times 10^{-3} \text{ mole l.}^{-1}$$

$$\left(\frac{\mathscr{P}_t}{RT} - c^0\right) = 1.93 \times 10^{-3} \text{ mole l.}^{-1}$$

$$2c^0 - \frac{\mathscr{P}_t}{RT} = 2.56 \times 10^{-3} \text{ mole l.}^{-1}$$

$$RT = 24.47 \text{ atm. l. mole}^{-1}$$

$$K_{\mathscr{P}} = \frac{4(1.93 \times 10^{-3})^2}{2.56 \times 10^{-3}} \times 24.47 = 0.142 \text{ (atm.)}$$

The small trend in $K_{\mathscr{P}}$ at each temperature with increasing pressure which appears in the results quoted in Table 5.2 is the result of the further dissociation of NO_2 into NO and O_2.

EXERCISE 5.9

Complete Table 5.2 by computing $K_{\mathscr{P}}$ for the conditions described in the fourth line of the table.   *Ans.* $K_{\mathscr{P}} = 0.285$ (atm.)

As a variation of the preceding computation we may ask to what extent N_2O_4 dissociates at 1 atm. and 45° [taking $K_{\mathscr{P}} = 0.649$ (atm.)]. In this case it is convenient to select an initial state consisting of 1 mole of N_2O_4 and then to solve for the value of x as a measure of the fraction dissociated. We have

	Initial	*Equilibrium*
N_2O_4	$\alpha = 1$	$\alpha - x = 1 - x$
NO_2	$\mu = 0$	$\mu + 2x = 2x$
		$n_t = 1 + x$

Substitution in equation (5.16) yields

$$0.649 \text{ (atm.)} = \frac{(2x)^2}{(1 - x)(1 + x)} \, 1 \text{ atm.,} \qquad x = 0.374$$

EXERCISE 5.10

At what total pressure is N_2O_4 50% dissociated at 45°?   *Ans.* 0.49 atm.

Another type of dissociation is illustrated by

$$2HI(g) = H_2(g) + I_2(g)$$

This equilibrium has been studied by A. H. Taylor and R. H. Crist [*J. Am. Chem. Soc.*, **63**, 1377 (1941)] at temperatures in the range 390–490°. In one procedure, a sample of pure hydrogen iodide was equilibrated at the desired temperature, then cooled quickly (the rate of the reaction is negligible at room temperature) and analyzed for hydrogen iodide and iodine. The equilibrium data for this procedure in Table 5.3 are designated by d (for decomposition).

In the second procedure, a known quantity of hydrogen was added to an unmeasured amount of iodine. When equilibrium had been reached, the

TABLE 5.3

THE EQUILIBRIUM $2HI = H_2 + I_2$

Temp. (°K)		H_2 (init. m/cc. $\times 10^5$)	I_2 (equil. m/cc. $\times 10^5$)	H_2 (equil. m/cc. $\times 10^5$)	HI (equil. m/cc. $\times 10^5$)	$K_{\mathscr{P}}$ (obs.) $\times 10^2$	$K_{\mathscr{P}}$ (corr.) $\times 10^2$
763.8	c	1.173	0.1185	0.4262	1.494	2.244	2.196
763.8	d	0	0.2424	0.2424	1.641	2.182	2.172
730.8	c	1.228	0.1524	—	1.687	—	2.018
730.8	d	0	0.1696	0.1696	1.181	2.063	2.007
698.6	c	1.134	0.0738	0.4565	1.354	1.835	1.812
698.6	d	0	0.0479	0.0479	0.353	1.840	1.812
666.8	c	1.119	0.1295	0.3258	1.587	1.676	1.642
666.8	d	0	0.1395	0.1395	1.079	1.672	1.644

sample was analyzed for hydrogen iodide and iodine. These data, in Table 5.3, are designated by c (for combination). In these experiments a small correction was necessary for loss of hydrogen by diffusion through the walls of the vessel. This loss will be largest at the highest temperatures, where the rate of diffusion is greatest, and in mixtures containing the most hydrogen. The values of the equilibrium constants have been corrected for this loss.

In this reaction $\Delta \nu = 0$, and equation (5.15) reduces to

$$K_{\mathscr{P}} = \frac{(\mu + x)(\nu + x)}{(\alpha - 2x)^2} \tag{5.17}$$

For the decomposition experiments we have

	Initial	*Equilibrium*
HI	α	$\alpha - 2x = n_{HI}$
I_2	$\mu = 0$	$x = n_{I_2}$
H_2	$\nu = 0$	$x = n_{H_2}$

$$K_{\mathscr{P}} = \frac{x^2}{(\alpha - 2x)^2} = \frac{n_{H_2} n_{I_2}}{n_{HI}^2}$$

The equilibrium values n_{HI} and $n_{I_2} = n_{H_2}$ are determined experimentally, and for the second line in Table 5.3 we obtain

$$K_{\mathscr{P}} = \frac{(0.2424)^2}{(1.641)^2} = 2.182 \times 10^{-2}$$

For the combination experiments we have

	Initial	*Equilibrium*
HI	$\alpha = 0$	$0 - 2x = n_{HI}$
I_2	μ	$\mu + x = n_{I_2}$
H_2	ν	$\nu + x = n_{H_2}$

The equilibrium values of n_{HI} and n_{I_2} are again measured, and the value of ν, the initial amount of hydrogen, is known. Since $n_{HI} = -2x$ (this is a case in which "products" are consumed), the value of n_{H_2} is

$$n_{H_2} = \nu - \tfrac{1}{2} n_{HI}$$

That is, each mole of hydrogen iodide formed consumes $\tfrac{1}{2}$ mole of hydrogen.

$$K_{\mathscr{P}} = \frac{n_{I_2}(n_{H_2}^0 - \tfrac{1}{2} n_{HI})}{n_{HI}^2}$$

The first line of data in Table 5.3 gives

$$K_{\mathscr{P}} = \frac{0.1185(1.173 - 1.494/2)}{1.494^2} = 2.244 \times 10^{-2}$$

EXERCISE 5.11

Complete the third line of Table 5.3.

$$\text{\textit{Ans.} } n_{H_2} = 0.384 \times 10^{-5}, \qquad K_{\mathscr{P}} = 2.057 \times 10^{-2}.$$

To find the extent of dissociation of hydrogen iodide at 698.6°K, when $K_{\mathscr{P}} = 1.812 \times 10^{-2}$, it is convenient to choose 2 moles of hydrogen iodide initially. The amount dissociating is taken as x. Choosing the mole number of reactant decomposing equal to its coefficient in the stoichiometric equation facilitates the solution.

	Initial	Equilibrium
HI	$\alpha = 2$	$\alpha - 2x = 2 - 2x$
I_2	$\mu = 0$	$\mu + x = x$
H_2	$v = 0$	$v + x = x$

Substituting these quantities in equation (5.17), we obtain

$$K_{\mathscr{P}} = \frac{x^2}{(2 - 2x)^2}$$

When $\Delta v = 0$, as in this case, the extent of dissociation is not dependent on total pressure.

If the system contains initially any of the products as well as hydrogen iodide, the extent of dissociation is decreased in accordance with the principle of Le Chatelier. For example, let the system consist initially of equimolar quantities of hydrogen and hydrogen iodide. In this case

	Initial	Equilibrium
HI	$\alpha = 2$	$\alpha - 2x = 2 - 2x$
I_2	$\mu = 0$	$\mu + x = x$
H_2	$v = 2$	$v + x = 2 + x$

$$K_{\mathscr{P}} = 1.812 \times 10^{-2} = \frac{x(2 + x)}{(2 - 2x)^2}$$

$$x = 0.033$$

EXERCISE 5.12

If 1 mole of iodine and 3 moles of hydrogen are equilibrated at 666.8°K, how much hydrogen iodide will be formed?   *Ans.* $n_{HI} = 1.94$.

As a final illustration we examine once more the synthesis of ammonia, for which data are given in Table 5.4 [A. T. Larson and R. L. Dodge, *J. Am.*

TABLE 5.4

THE EQUILIBRIUM $\frac{1}{2}N_2 + \frac{3}{2}H_2 = NH_3$

Initial comp.: 76.2% H_2, 23.5% N_2, 0.3% Ar

Temp. (°C)	P_t (atm.)	% NH_3 at equil.	$K_{\mathscr{P}}$ (atm.$^{-1}$)
350	10	7.35	0.0266
350	50	25.11	—
400	10	3.85	0.0129
400	50	15.11	0.0130
450	10	2.04	0.00659
450	50	9.17	0.00690
500	10	1.20	0.00381
500	50	5.58	0.00388

Chem. Soc., **45**, 2918 (1923)]. The small trend in the values of $K_{\mathscr{P}}$ with pressure is an effect of gas imperfection which will be discussed in a later section.

For the process

$$\tfrac{1}{2}N_2 + \tfrac{3}{2}H_2 = NH_3$$

equation (5.15) becomes

$$K_{\mathscr{P}} = \frac{\mu + x}{(\alpha - \tfrac{1}{2}x)^{1/2}(\beta - \tfrac{3}{2}x)^{3/2}}\, n_t P_t^{-1} \tag{5.18}$$

To evaluate $K_{\mathscr{P}}$ for one of the mixtures described in Table 5.4 it is first necessary to establish the relation between X_{NH_3} and the various mole numbers at equilibrium. That is,

$$X_{NH_3} = \frac{n_{NH_3}}{n_t} = \frac{(\mu + x)}{\alpha - \tfrac{1}{2}x + \beta - \tfrac{3}{2}x + \mu + x}$$

For the cases being considered $\mu = 0$ and

$$X_{NH_3} = \frac{x}{\alpha + \beta - x}$$

For 1 mole of the initial reaction mixture at 500° and 10 atm.,

$$X_{NH_3} = 0.0120 = \frac{x}{1 - x}$$

$$x = 0.0119$$

	Initial	*Equilibrium*
N_2	$\alpha = 0.235$	$\alpha - \tfrac{1}{2}x = 0.229$
H_2	$\beta = 0.762$	$\beta - \tfrac{3}{2}x = 0.744$
NH_3	$\mu = 0$	$\mu + x = \underline{0.0119}$
		$n_t = \overline{0.985}$

$$K_{\mathscr{P}} = \frac{0.0119}{(0.229)^{1/2}(0.744)^{3/2}} \times 0.985 \times 10^{-1}$$

EXERCISE 5.13

Compute the value of $K_{\mathscr{P}}$ in line 2 of Table 5.4.   *Ans.* 0.0278.

5.8 Temperature Dependence of Equilibrium Functions

The temperature derivative of the equilibrium constant may be obtained from a rearranged form of equation (5.11); thus

$$\Delta F_T^\circ/T = -R \ln K_{\mathscr{P}}$$

$$\frac{d(\Delta F_T^\circ/T)}{dT} = -R \frac{d \ln K_{\mathscr{P}}}{dT} \tag{5.19}$$

The Gibbs-Helmholtz equation (4.18)

$$\left[\frac{\partial(\Delta F_T/T)}{\partial T}\right]_P = \frac{-\Delta H_T}{T^2}$$

gives the value of the left-hand side of equation (5.19), yielding

$$\left(\frac{\partial \ln K}{\partial T}\right)_P = \frac{\Delta H_T^o}{RT^2} \quad \text{or} \quad \left(\frac{\partial \ln K}{\partial(1/T)}\right)_P = \frac{-\Delta H_T^o}{R} \tag{5.20}$$

This is *van't Hoff's equation.*

It was shown previously that multiplying all coefficients of the chemical equation by a factor α leads to

$$\alpha \, \Delta F^o = -RT \ln K_{\mathscr{P}}^{\alpha}$$

Dropping subscripts for convenience, it follows that

$$-\frac{d(\alpha \, \Delta F^o/T)}{dT} = \frac{\alpha \, \Delta H^o}{T^2} = R\frac{d \ln (K_{\mathscr{P}})^{\alpha}}{dT}$$

This is to say that the enthalpy term in equation (5.20) applies to the standard process of interest. For $\alpha = 2$, ΔF^o is doubled, ΔH^o is doubled, while $K_{\mathscr{P}}$ is squared. When $\alpha = -1$ (viz., for the reverse process), both the ΔF^o and ΔH^o change sign, while $K_{\mathscr{P}}$ is inverted.

Equation (5.20) shows that if $\ln K_{\mathscr{P}}$ (or $\log K_{\mathscr{P}}$) is plotted against $1/T$, the slope of the resulting curve at any point will be proportional to ΔH^o for the process. Such a graph appears in Fig. 5.2 for the dissociation of hydrogen iodide, the data of Table 5.3 being used. It should be noted that the points fit a straight line, indicating that ΔH^o is practically independent of temperature in the range covered.

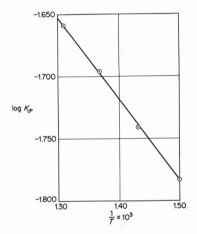

FIG. 5.2. Temperature dependence of $K_{\mathscr{P}}$ for $2HI = H_2 + I_2$.

EXERCISE 5.14

Estimate the slope of the line drawn through the data in Fig. 5.2 and use this in equation (5.20) to obtain a value of ΔH^o. Compare with the result of the succeeding example.

Whenever the temperature dependence of ΔH^o may be ignored, either because it is small or because one is dealing with a small range of temperature, equation (5.20) integrates to

$$\ln \frac{K_2}{K_1} = \frac{-\Delta H}{R}\left(\frac{1}{T_2} - \frac{1}{T_1}\right)$$

$$\log \frac{K_2}{K_1} = \frac{\Delta H}{2.3\,R}\left(\frac{T_2 - T_1}{T_2 T_1}\right) \tag{5.21}$$

where K_2 represents the value of $K_{\mathscr{P}}$ at T_2 and K_1 the value of $K_{\mathscr{P}}$ at T_1. In this approximation ΔH applies almost precisely to the average temperature, $\frac{1}{2}(T_1 + T_2)$. The distinction between ΔH^o and ΔH is insignificant in this approximation.

Application of equation (5.21) may be illustrated with data from Table 5.3. For 666.8°K and 763.8°K

$$\log \frac{2.184 \times 10^{-2}}{1.643 \times 10^{-2}} = \frac{\Delta H_{715.3}}{2.303 \times 1.987} \cdot \frac{763.8 - 666.8}{763.8 \times 666.8}$$

$$\Delta H_{715.3} = 2969 \text{ cal.}$$

Note that the equilibrium function used in Table 5.3 corresponds to

$$2HI = H_2 + I_2$$

and, therefore, ΔH is for decomposition of 2 moles of hydrogen iodide. The ΔH of formation per mole of hydrogen iodide is opposite in sign and one-half as great.

EXERCISE 5.15

Use the result above to find $K_{\mathcal{P}}$ at 500°K for

$$HI = \tfrac{1}{2} I_2 + \tfrac{1}{2} H_2$$

Ans. 8.7×10^{-2}.

Equation (5.20) is a quantitative statement of the principle of Le Chatelier with regard to temperature variations. Its qualitative consequences are summarized as follows:

ΔH	ΔT	$\Delta K_{\mathcal{P}}$	Equilibrium shift
$-$	$+$	$-$	$\leftarrow$
$+$	$+$	$+$	$\rightarrow$
$-$	$-$	$+$	$\rightarrow$
$+$	$-$	$-$	$\leftarrow$
0	$\pm$	0	$\rightleftharpoons$

If the precision required or the temperature interval is such that it is unsatisfactory to assume that ΔH is independent of temperature, an expression such as equation (3.20)

$$\Delta H_T^o = \Delta H_0^o + \Delta a T + \frac{\Delta b}{2} T^2 + \frac{\Delta c}{3} T^3$$

may be inserted in equation (5.20) before integration, yielding

$$\frac{d \ln K_{\mathcal{P}}}{dT} = \frac{\Delta H_0^o}{RT^2} + \frac{\Delta a}{RT} + \frac{\Delta b}{2R} + \frac{\Delta c T}{3R} \tag{5.22}$$

This expression integrates to give

$$\ln K_{\mathcal{P}} = -\frac{\Delta H_0^o}{RT} + \frac{\Delta a}{R} \ln T + \frac{\Delta b}{2R} T + \frac{\Delta c}{6R} T^2 + I \tag{5.23}$$

where I is a constant of integration.

From the observed values of $K_{\mathcal{P}}$ at two temperatures and C_P data from Table 2.1, the constants ΔH_0^o and I in equation (5.23) may be evaluated. For

$$\tfrac{1}{2} N_2 + \tfrac{3}{2} H_2 = NH_3$$

we have

$$\Delta a = -7.493, \qquad \Delta b = 7.562 \times 10^{-3}, \qquad \Delta c = -14.49 \times 10^{-7}$$

Substitution of $K_{\mathcal{P}} = 0.0270$ at 350° and $K_{\mathcal{P}} = 0.00670$ at 450° in equation (5.23) yields the simultaneous equations

$$2.3 \log 0.0270 = \frac{-\Delta H_0^o}{1.987 \times 623} - \frac{7.493}{1.987} 2.3 \log 623$$

$$+ \frac{7.562 \times 10^{-3}}{2 \times 1.987} \times 623 - \frac{14.49 \times 10^{-7}}{6 \times 1.987} \times 623^2 + I$$

$$2.3 \log 0.00670 = \frac{-\Delta H_0^o}{1.987 \times 723} - \frac{7.493}{1.987} 2.3 \log 723$$

$$+ \frac{7.562 \times 10^{-3}}{2 \times 1.987} \times 723 - \frac{14.49 \times 10^{-7}}{6 \times 1.987} \times 723^2 + I$$

whose solution is

$$\Delta H_0^o = -8977 \text{ cal.}, \qquad I = 12.26$$

Substitution of these values yields

$$\ln K_{\mathscr{P}} = \frac{8977}{RT} - \frac{7.493}{R} \ln T + \frac{7.562 \times 10^{-3}}{2R} T - \frac{14.49 \times 10^{-7}}{6R} T^2 + 12.26$$

which applies to the temperature range over which the empirical heat capacity equations are valid.

EXERCISE 5.16

From the information given above, find $K_{\mathscr{P}}$ and ΔF^o at 1000°K for

$$\tfrac{1}{2} N_2 + \tfrac{3}{2} H_2 = NH_3$$

$$Ans. \ K_{\mathscr{P}} = 5.6 \times 10^{-4}; \qquad \Delta F_{1000}^o = 14.89 \text{ kcal.}$$

5.9 Additivity of Free Energies; Standard Free Energies of Formation

The free energy is a property of state, and the value of ΔF depends only on the initial and final state, regardless of path. In this respect, F completely resembles H, and the algebra of thermochemistry, as expressed by Hess's law, is applicable by direct analogy to free energy calculations. For example, it is found that for the reaction

(i) $$N_2(g) + 2O_2(g) = 2NO_2(g)$$
$$\Delta F_{298}^o = 24.780 \text{ kcal.}$$

From preceding sections we find for

(ii) $$2NO_2(g) = N_2O_4(g)$$
$$\Delta F_{298}^o = -1.100 \text{ kcal.}$$

These two equations combine to give

(iii) $$N_2(g) + 2O_2(g) = N_2O_4(g)$$

and the corresponding relation of the free energy changes is

$$\Delta F_{298}^o(\text{iii}) = \Delta F_{298}^o(\text{i}) + \Delta F_{298}^o(\text{ii}) = 23.680 \text{ kcal.}$$

Note that addition of ΔF^o's is equivalent to multiplication of equilibrium functions.

$$\Delta F^o_{298}(\text{i}) = -RT \ln \frac{\mathscr{P}^2_{NO_2}}{\mathscr{P}_{N_2}\mathscr{P}^2_{O_2}}$$

$$\Delta F^o_{298}(\text{ii}) = -RT \ln \frac{\mathscr{P}_{N_2O_4}}{\mathscr{P}^2_{NO_2}}$$

$$\Delta F^o_{298}(\text{iii}) = -RT \ln \frac{\mathscr{P}^2_{NO_2}}{\mathscr{P}_{N_2}\mathscr{P}^2_{O_2}} \times \frac{\mathscr{P}_{N_2O_4}}{\mathscr{P}^2_{NO_2}}$$

$$\Delta F^o_{298}(\text{iii}) = -RT \ln \frac{\mathscr{P}_{N_2O_4}}{\mathscr{P}_{N_2}\mathscr{P}^2_{O_2}}$$

EXERCISE 5.17

From study of the further dissociation of NO_2 formed from N_2O_4 it has been found that for the reaction

$$NO\,(g) + \tfrac{1}{2}\,O_2\,(g) = NO_2\,(g)$$
$$\Delta F^o_{298} = -8.329 \text{ kcal.}$$

Compute the value of ΔF^o_{298} for the reaction

$$\tfrac{1}{2}\,N_2\,(g) + \tfrac{1}{2}\,O_2\,(g) = NO\,(g)$$

Ans. 20.719 kcal.

By means of the operations illustrated above values of ΔF^o for various processes may be reduced for tabulation to *standard free energies of formation from the elements*. The Gibbs-Helmholtz equation may be used further to reduce all values to a single temperature, usually 25° (298.15°K). A brief list of such values is given in Table 5.5. Some pure solids and liquids, as well as gases, are included. This information, together with the Gibbs-Helmholtz equation and values of ΔH, permits the calculation of equilibrium constants over a wide range of temperatures.

The procedure to be followed for computing free energy changes of chemical reactions from free energies of formation ΔF^o_f resembles that for enthalpy change. Thus, to find ΔF^o_{298} for

(i)
$$C_2H_2(g) + H_2(g) = C_2H_4(g)$$

we use the data of Table 5.5:

(ii)
$$H_2(g) + 2C(s) = C_2H_2(g)$$
$$\Delta F^o_f = 50.000 \text{ kcal.}$$

(iii)
$$2H_2(g) + 2C(s) = C_2H_4(g)$$
$$\Delta F^o_f = 16.282 \text{ kcal.}$$

$$\Delta F^o_{298}(\text{i}) = \Delta F^o_f(\text{iii}) - \Delta F^o_f(\text{ii})$$
$$= -33.718 \text{ kcal.}$$

$$K_{\mathscr{P}} = 5.19 \times 10^{24} \text{ (atm.}^{-1}) = \frac{\mathscr{P}_{C_2H_4}}{\mathscr{P}_{C_2H_2}\mathscr{P}_{H_2}}$$

TABLE 5.5

STANDARD MOLAR FREE ENERGIES OF FORMATION AT 25°*

Substance	ΔF^o_{298} (kcal. mole^{-1})	Substance		ΔF^o_{298} (kcal. mole^{-1})
H_2O (g)	-54.6352	methane,	CH_4 (g)	-12.140
H_2O (l)	-56.6902	ethane,	C_2H_6 (g)	-7.860
HCl (g)	-22.769	propane,	C_3H_8 (g)	-5.614
HBr (g)	-12.72	normal butane,	C_4H_{10} (g)	-3.754
HI (g)	0.31	isobutane,	C_4H_{10} (g)	-4.296
SO_2 (g)	-71.79	normal pentane,	C_5H_{12} (g)	-1.96
SO_3 (g)	-88.52	normal hexane,	C_6H_{14} (g)	0.05
H_2S (g)	-7.892	benzene,	C_6H_6 (g)	30.989
NO (g)	20.719	benzene,	C_6H_6 (l)	29.756
NO_2 (g)	12.390	ethylene,	C_2H_4 (g)	16.282
NH_3 (g)	-3.976	acetylene,	C_2H_2 (g)	50.000
CO (g)	-32.8079	formaldehyde,	HCHO (g)	-26.3
CO_2 (g)	-94.2598	acetaldehyde,	CH_3CHO (g)	-31.96
AgCl (s)	-26.224	methanol,	CH_3OH (l)	-39.73
AgBr (s)	-22.930	ethanol,	C_2H_5OH (l)	-41.77
Fe_2O_3 (s)	-177.1	formic acid,	HCOOH (l)	-82.7
Al_2O_3 (s)	-376.77	acetic acid,	CH_3COOH (l)	-93.8
NaCl (s)	-91.785			

* From *Selected Values of Chemical Thermodynamic Properties*, Circular 500, National Bureau of Standards, 1952; and from *Selected Values of the Properties of Hydrocarbons*, Circular C461, National Bureau of Standards, 1947.

From the heats of formation, as shown in Chapter 3, we obtain

$$\Delta H^o_{298}(i) = -41.698 \text{ kcal.}$$

With this datum it is possible to estimate $K_{\mathscr{P}}$ at some temperature other than 25°, say 500°. Taking ΔH independent of temperature, we find that equation (5.21) yields

$$\log \frac{K_{773}}{5.13 \times 10^{24}} = \frac{-41,698}{2.303 \times 1.987} \frac{475}{298 \times 773}$$

$$K_{773} = 8.4 \times 10^5 \text{ (atm.}^{-1})$$

To obtain the equilibrium constant at 298° K for

(iv) $$C_2H_4(g) + H_2(g) = C_2H_6(g)$$

we also require the free energy of formation of ethane.

(v) $$3H_2(g) + 2C(s) = C_2H_6(g)$$

$$\Delta F^o_f = -7.860 \text{ kcal.}$$

These data combine to give

$$\Delta F^o_{298}(iv) = \Delta F^o_f(v) - \Delta F^o_f(iii)$$
$$= -24.142 \text{ kcal.}$$

$$K_{\mathscr{P}} = \frac{\mathscr{P}_{C_2H_6}}{\mathscr{P}_{H_2}\mathscr{P}_{C_2H_4}} = 5.0 \times 10^{17} \text{ (atm.}^{-1})$$

Obviously the equilibrium state in this system at 25° lies very far in the direction of complete hydrogenation, although the rate of hydrogenation at room temperature is negligible in the absence of a catalyst. Conversely, ethane has very little tendency to lose hydrogen at room temperature, and no catalyst can change this situation so long as the products of the decomposition are not removed.

Let us examine the possibility that ethylene may disproportionate to ethane and acetylene by computing the equilibrium constant for the process

(vi) $$2C_2H_4(g) = C_2H_2(g) + C_2H_6(g)$$

The value of ΔF^o_{298} for this process is obtained from the free energies of formation given above.

$$\Delta F^o_{298}\,(vi) = \Delta F^o_f(ii) + \Delta F^o_f(v) - 2\Delta F^o_f(iii)$$
$$= 9.576 \text{ kcal.}$$

$$K_{\mathscr{P}} = \frac{\mathscr{P}_{C_2H_2}\mathscr{P}_{C_2H_6}}{\mathscr{P}^2_{C_2H_4}} = 9.6 \times 10^{-8} \text{ (atm.)}$$

Very large or very small values of equilibrium constants such as those found above often permit considerable simplification of the calculation. For example, to compute the extent of disproportionation of ethylene at one atmosphere pressure we have

	Initial	*Equilibrium*
C_2H_4	$\alpha = 2$	$\alpha - 2x = 2 - 2x$
C_2H_2	$\mu = 0$	$\mu + x = x$
C_2H_6	$\nu = 0$	$\nu + x = x$

$$K_{\mathscr{P}} = 9.6 \times 10^{-8} = \frac{x^2}{(2-2x)^2}$$

Clearly, $x \ll 1$ and we make a justifiable approximation:

$$9.6 \times 10^{-8} = \frac{x^2}{2^2}$$

$$x = 6.2 \times 10^{-4}$$

EXERCISE 5.18

Compute the value of ΔF^o_{298} for the process

$$2\,CH_4 = C_2H_6 + H_2$$

and the extent of dissociation of CH_4 in this fashion.

Ans. $\Delta F^o_{298} = 16.42$ kcal., $1.0 \times 10^{-4}\%$.

5.10 The Free Energy Function

Information useful for calculating equilibrium constants is most commonly available in terms of $(F^o_T - H^o_0)/T$, the free energy function. It will be shown in Chapter 17 that values of this function can be calculated for gases from spectroscopic data. Using the third law of thermodynamics, to be discussed in Chapter 6, we can evaluate the free energy function from heat capacity data. For any reaction, including formation of compounds from the elements,

$$\Delta \frac{F_T^o - H_0^o}{T} = \frac{\Delta F_T^o}{T} - \frac{\Delta H_0^o}{T} \tag{5.24}$$

It follows that

$$\frac{\Delta F_T^o}{T} = \frac{\Delta H_0^o}{T} + \Delta \frac{F_T^o - H_0^o}{T} \tag{5.25}$$

Combining equations (5.11) and (5.25) gives

$$-R \ln K_{\mathscr{P}} = \frac{\Delta H_0^o}{T} + \Delta \frac{F_T^o - H_0^o}{T} \tag{5.26}$$

In the preceding equations ΔH_0^o is the actual heat of reaction at $0°K$. It should not be confused with the constant of integration in equation (3.20). The quantity ΔH_0^o is equal to the difference of the standard heats of formation at $0°K$, by equation (3.9). Some values of these functions are listed in Table 5.6.

TABLE 5.6

THE THERMODYNAMIC FUNCTIONS*

Substance	$-(F_T^o - H_0^o)/T$ cal. deg.$^{-1}$ mole^{-1}				ΔH_0^o
	298°K	500°K	1000°K	1500°K	kcal. mole^{-1}
H_2 (g)	24.42	27.95	32.74	35.59	0
I_2 (g)	54.18	58.46	64.40	67.96	15.656
O_2 (g)	42.06	45.68	50.70	53.81	0
HI (g)	42.40	45.99	50.90	53.90	6.7
CO (g)	40.25	43.86	48.77	51.78	−27.202
CO_2 (g)	43.56	47.67	54.11	58.48	−93.969
H_2O (g)	37.17	41.29	47.01	50.60	−57.107
CH_4 (g)	36.46	40.75	47.65	52.84	−15.99
C_2H_2 (g)	39.98	44.51	52.01	57.23	54.33
C_2H_4 (g)	43.98	48.74	57.29	63.94	14.52
C_2H_6 (g)	45.27	50.77	61.11	69.46	−16.52
C_3H_6 (g)	52.95	59.32	71.57	81.43	8.47
C_3H_8 (g)	52.73	59.81	74.10	85.86	−19.48
C_4H_{10} (g)	58.54	67.91	86.60	101.95	−23.67

* From F. D. Rossini et al., *Selected Values of Physical and Thermodynamic Properties of Hydrocarbons and Related Compounds*, Pittsburgh: Carnegie Press, 1953, and from G. N. Lewis, M. Randall, K. S. Pitzer, and L. Brewer, *Thermodynamics*, 2d ed., New York: McGraw-Hill Book Company, 1961.

EXERCISE 5.19

Find ΔF_{1000}^O for $2 \, C_2H_4 = C_4H_{10}$. *Ans.* −24.73 kcal.

5.11 Systems of Real Gases: The Fugacity

The entire consideration of equilibrium in gaseous systems has been restricted to ideal gases and their mixtures. Such a development is not completely realistic, since there are no ideal gases, but it has the advantage of providing a simple working model. We have seen that many gaseous systems do, in fact, approach rather closely to the behavior of ideal gaseous systems, and we may, therefore, consider the preceding equations as good first approximations for real equilibrium reaction mixtures at moderate pressures. Whenever such approximations are not permissible, and this will tend to be the case at high pressure and low temperature, a more nearly correct treatment must be used.

There are two evident approaches to the problem of improving the description of a gaseous system at equilibrium. The first adopts the previous approach to equilibrium through the free energy function, and we have the usual relation between the free energy change at arbitrary pressures ΔF_T and the free energy change at unit pressures ΔF_T^o, the standard free energy change.

$$aA(P_A) \quad + \quad bB(P_B) \quad + \ldots \xrightarrow{\Delta F_T} \quad mM(P_M) \quad + \quad nN(P_N) \quad + \ldots$$

$$\Bigg\downarrow \Delta F(A) \quad \Bigg\downarrow \Delta F(B) \qquad \qquad \Bigg\uparrow \Delta F(M) \quad \Bigg\uparrow \Delta F(N)$$

$$aA(P_A = 1) + bB(P_B = 1) + \ldots \xrightarrow{\Delta F^o_T} mM(P_M = 1) + nN(P_N = 1) + \ldots$$

$$\Delta F_T = \Delta F_T^o + \Delta F(A) + \Delta F(B) + \Delta F(M) + \Delta F(N)$$

The inaccuracies attending the use of the perfect gas law at this stage of the earlier development can be avoided by using modified equations of state. To illustrate, let us use $P(V - nb) = nRT$. Then in place of

$$\Delta F_T(A) = \int_{P_A}^1 V\, dP = aRT \ln \frac{1}{P_A}, \text{ etc.}$$

we have

$$\Delta F_T(A) = \int_{P_A}^1 V\, dP = \int_{P_A}^1 \left(\frac{aRT}{P_A} + ab_A \right) dP_A$$

$$= aRT \ln \frac{1}{P_A} + ab_A(1 - P_A)$$

Continuing by analogy with the prior development, we find that

$$\Delta F_T - \Delta F_T^o = RT \ln \frac{P_M^m P_N^n \cdots}{P_A^a P_B^b \cdots} + ab_A(1 - P_A) + bb_B(1 - P_B) \tag{5.27}$$

$$+ mb_M(P_M - 1) + nb_N(P_N - 1), \text{ etc.}$$

It should be evident that when $\Delta F_T = 0$ it will no longer follow that the equilibrium function $\prod_i (\mathscr{P}_i^{\nu_i})$ will be constant—unless the summation

$$ab_A(1 - \mathscr{P}_A) + bb_B(1 - \mathscr{P}_B) + mb_M(\mathscr{P}_M - 1) + nb_N(\mathscr{P}_N - 1)$$

happens to be zero. That is, the gas imperfections of the reactants would need to exactly compensate those of the products. Equation (5.27) is valid provided that the equation of state employed is valid in the pressure and temperature interval of interest, but the method becomes increasingly awkward as more reliable and more complicated equations of state are employed. Each choice of equation of state would lead to a new type of equilibrium function. We must try something else.

There is clearly an advantage of mathematical simplicity in the familiar type of equilibrium function, $\Pi(P_i^{\nu_i})$. This function follows from the relations $dF = VdP \cong RTd \ln P$. To retain the same type of equilibrium function and yet to avoid the errors inherent in describing real gases by the perfect gas equation, let us define f, the *fugacity*, by

$$dF_T = VdP = RTd \ln f \tag{5.28}$$

It should be remembered at this point that $dF_T = VdP$ is exact and involves no assumption as to the nature of the gas while $dF_T = RTd \ln f$ is correct by definition. Since V and P are experimental quantities, the relation $V\,dP = RT\,d \ln f$ furnishes an experimental basis for evaluating f. It is important to observe that the definition of fugacity has operational significance. It is also worth mentioning that any understanding of fugacity which we acquire must derive from equation (5.28).

For an isothermal change in state of a real gas

$$dF_T = RT\,d \ln f$$
$$\Delta F_{T\,\text{real}} = RT \ln \frac{f_2}{f_1} \tag{5.29}$$

which is to be compared with

$$\Delta F_{T\,\text{ideal}} = RT \ln \frac{P_2}{P_1}$$

for an ideal gas. Let us once more examine the problem of the equilibrium process, beginning with the familiar diagram but replacing all P_i's by the analogous f_i's.

$$aA(f_A) \quad + bB(f_B) \quad + \ldots \xrightarrow{\Delta F_T} mM(f_M) \quad + nN(f_N) \quad + \ldots$$

$$\Big\downarrow \Delta F(A) \quad \Big\downarrow \Delta F(B) \qquad\qquad \Big\uparrow \Delta F(M) \quad \Big\uparrow \Delta F(N)$$

$$aA(f_A = 1) + bB(f_B = 1) + \ldots \xrightarrow{\Delta F^o_T} mM(f_M = 1) + nN(f_N = 1) + \ldots$$

Once more

$$\Delta F_T - \Delta F^o_T = \Delta F(A) + \Delta F(B) + \ldots + \Delta F(M) + \Delta F(N) + \ldots$$
$$= aRT \ln \frac{1}{f_A} + \ldots + mRT \ln \frac{f_M}{1} + \ldots$$
$$= RT \ln \frac{f_M^m f_N^n \cdots}{f_A^a f_B^b \cdots}$$
$$= RT \ln \Pi_i (f_i^{\nu_i})$$

At equilibrium $\qquad\qquad\qquad \Delta F = 0$

and $\qquad\qquad\qquad \Delta F^o_T = -RT \ln \Pi_i (f_i^{\nu_i})_{\text{equil.}}$

Since ΔF^o_T is a fixed quantity it follows that the value of the equilibrium function of fugacities,

$$K_f = \Pi_i (f_i^{\nu_i})_{\text{equil.}}$$

is a constant in real gas systems. The data in Table 5.7 show that $K_{\mathscr{P}}$ is not a constant in the ammonia equilibrium when the pressure is high, but that at low pressures the value of $K_{\mathscr{P}}$ approaches a fixed limit. That is, in any real gas system at sufficiently low pressures

$$\Pi_i (f_i^{\nu_i})_{\text{equil.}} = \Pi_i (\mathscr{P}_i^{\nu_i}) \times \text{const.} \tag{5.30}$$

It is common practice to complement the definition of fugacity given in equation (5.28) by the additional stipulation that in the limit of very low pressure the fugacity approaches the pressure ($f \to P$ as $P \to 0$); f and P are now completely interchangeable at sufficiently low pressure, and the constant in equation (5.30) becomes unity.

The ratio of the fugacity to the pressure is called the *activity coefficient* γ.

$$\frac{f}{P} = \gamma \tag{5.31}$$

At low pressures the activity coefficient approaches unity.

It remains to be shown that f_i can be evaluated for pure gases or mixtures of gases. Let us first consider the simple case of a pure gas. From equation (5.28)

$$\int_1^2 d \ln f = \ln \frac{f_2}{f_1} = \frac{1}{RT} \int_1^2 V \, dP \tag{5.32}$$

The factor V on the right-hand side of equation (5.32) refers to the observed molar volume of the gas, an experimental quantity. This may also be expressed as the ideal molar volume RT/P, with a correction term $-\alpha$ representing the molar deviation from ideality, which is also a quantity derivable from experiment. That is,

$$V_{\text{obs.}} = V_{\text{ideal}} - \alpha$$

Using this terminology, we write equation (5.32) in the form

$$RT \ln \frac{f_2}{f_1} = \int_1^2 \left(\frac{RT}{P} - \alpha \right) dP$$

$$RT \ln \frac{f_2}{f_1} = RT \ln \frac{P_2}{P_1} - \int_1^2 \alpha \, dP \tag{5.33}$$

or

$$RT \ln \frac{P_1 f_2}{f_1} = RT \ln P_2 - \int_1^2 \alpha \, dP$$

Since $f \to P$ as $P \to 0$, then $f_1 = P_1$ at sufficiently small pressure. Letting state 2 refer to any state by removing the subscript, we have

$$RT \ln f = RT \ln P - \int_0^P \alpha \, dP$$

or

$$\ln \gamma = \ln \frac{f}{P} = -\frac{1}{RT} \int_0^P \alpha \, dP \tag{5.34}$$

TABLE 5.7

EQUILIBRIUM IN THE AMMONIA SYNTHESIS

$$\tfrac{1}{2}N_2 + \tfrac{3}{2}H_2 = NH_3$$

$450°$; initial mixture, $N_2/H_2 = \tfrac{1}{3}$

P_t (atm.)	% NH_3 equil.	$K_{\mathscr{P}} \times 10^3$	$K_f \times 10^3$
10	2.04	6.59	6.55
30	5.80	6.76	6.59
50	9.17	6.90	6.50
100	16.35	7.25	6.36
300	35.5	8.84	6.08
600	53.6	12.94	6.42
1000	69.4	23.28	10.10

The right-hand side of this equation may be evaluated graphically by measuring the area under the curve obtained by plotting α, the deviation of the molar volume from ideality, versus P. Thus, experimental data on the molar volume of a real gas as a function of pressure can be used to obtain numerical values of γ and f.

Evaluation of fugacities through use of equation (5.34) may also be performed analytically if a suitable equation of state is available for the gas in question. As a simple example we take the equation of state $P(V - b) = RT$ (1 mole) discussed in Chapter 1. In this case α is given by

$$\alpha = V_{\text{ideal}} - V_{\text{obs.}} = \frac{RT}{P} - \left(\frac{RT}{P} + b\right) = -b$$

and equation (5.34) becomes

$$\ln \gamma = \frac{bP}{RT}$$

SUMMARY, CHAPTER 5

1. Free energy of an ideal gas
   $F_T = RT \ln P + F_T^o$, where $F_T^o =$ molar free energy at unit pressure.

2. Free energy change in an isothermal ideal gas reaction
   $$aA + bB + \ldots = mM + nN + \ldots$$
   $$\Delta F_T = \sum_i \nu_i F_i^o + \sum_i \nu_i RT \ln P_i$$

3. The reaction function
   $$\Delta F_T - \Delta F_T^o = RT \ln Q_P$$
   $$Q_P = \Pi_i (P_i^{\nu_i}) = \frac{P_M^m P_N^n \ldots}{P_A^a P_B^b \ldots}$$

4. The equilibrium function
    At equilibrium: $\Delta F_{T,P} = 0$

    $$\Delta F_T^o = -RT \ln K_{\mathscr{P}}$$

    $$K_{\mathscr{P}} = \prod_i (\mathscr{P}_i^{\nu_i}) = \frac{\mathscr{P}_M^m \mathscr{P}_N^n \cdots}{\mathscr{P}_A^a \mathscr{P}_B^b \cdots}$$

5. The reaction isotherm

    $$\Delta F_T = RT \ln (Q_P/K_{\mathscr{P}})$$

    $Q_P < K_{\mathscr{P}}$ forward process permitted

6. The equilibrium function of mole fractions

    $K_x = K_{\mathscr{P}} \times \mathscr{P}_t^{-\Delta \nu}$, where $\Delta \nu = m + n + \ldots - a - b - \ldots$
    $K_{\mathscr{P}} = K_n n_t^{-\Delta \nu} P_t^{\Delta \nu}$; when $\Delta \nu = 0$, $K_{\mathscr{P}} = K_n = K_x$

7. Relation of initial and equilibrium states

	Initial	Equilibrium
A	α	$\alpha - ax$
B	β	$\beta - bx$
M	μ	$\mu + mx$
N	ν	$\nu + nx$

    $$K_{\mathscr{P}} = \frac{(\mu + mx)^m (\nu + nx)^n}{(\alpha - ax)^a (\beta - bx)^b} n_t^{-\Delta \nu} P_t^{\Delta \nu}$$

8. Temperature dependence

    $$\frac{d \ln K}{d(1/T)} = \frac{-\Delta H^o}{R}; \text{ if } \Delta H^o = \Delta H \text{ is assumed constant}$$

    $$\log \frac{K_2}{K_1} = \frac{\Delta H}{2.3R} \left(\frac{T_2 - T_1}{T_2 T_1} \right)$$

9. Additivity of free energies

    $$\Delta F(A - M) = \Delta F(A - J) + \Delta F(J - M)$$

10. Real gas equilibria
    Fugacity defined by $dF = RT \, d \ln f$ and $f \to P$ as $P \to 0$
    Activity coefficient: $\gamma = f/P$

    $$\Delta F_T - \Delta F_T^o = RT \ln \prod_i (f_i^{\nu_i})$$

    $$\Delta F_T^o = -RT \ln K_f$$

PROBLEMS, CHAPTER 5

1. For each of the following reactions
(a) Evaluate ΔF_{298}^o.
(b) Evaluate ΔH_{298}^o.
(c) State whether $K_{\mathscr{P}}$ increases or decreases with increasing temperature.
(d) State the effect of increasing the volume of the system on K_x.

(i) O_2 (g) $+ 2$ NO (g) $= 2$ NO_2 (g)
(ii) NO_2 (g) $+$ CO (g) $=$ NO (g) $+ CO_2$ (g)
(iii) 2 HI (g) $+ Cl_2$ (g) $= 2$ HCl (g) $+ I_2$ (s)
Ans. $\Delta F = -16.66, -53.12, -46.16$ kcal.; $\Delta H = -27.02, -54.12, -56.53$ kcal.

2. The accompanying figure (Prob. Fig. 5.2) describes semi-quantitatively the temperature dependence of K for several reactions. Correlate each curve with one of the following, where all data refer to a common temperature.

Reaction (i) $\Delta F^o = -12$ kcal., $\Delta H = 20$ kcal.
Reaction (ii) $\Delta F^o = -8$ kcal., $\Delta H = 20$ kcal.
Reaction (iii) $\Delta F^o = -5$ kcal., $\Delta H = -10$ kcal.
Reaction (iv) $\Delta F^o = -5$ kcal., $\Delta H = 12$ kcal.

3. Using data from Table 5.6, find the value of $K_{\mathscr{P}}$ at 25° for
$$HI \text{ (g)} = \tfrac{1}{2} H_2 \text{ (g)} + \tfrac{1}{2} I_2 \text{ (g)}$$
Ans. 3.12×10^{-2}.

4. Given that $\Delta F^o_{298} = 16.77$ kcal. for
$$\tfrac{1}{2} I_2 \text{ (g)} = I \text{ (g)}$$
find the extent of dissociation of iodine vapor to atoms
(a) At 1 mm.
(b) At 10^{-6} mm.   *Ans.* (a) $\alpha = 7.1 \times 10^{-12}$, (b) $\alpha = 7.1 \times 10^{-9}$

5. Using data from Table 5.5, find the fractional extent of reaction for SO_3 (g) $= SO_2$ (g) $+ \tfrac{1}{2} O_2$ (g) at 25° when the partial pressure of oxygen is maintained at 10^{-6} mm.
Ans. 1.5×10^{-8}.

6. Find the equilibrium composition for $n\text{-}C_4H_{10} = i\text{-}C_4H_{10}$ at 25°.   *Ans.* $X_{iC_4H_{10}} = 0.715$.

7. Equimolar quantities of hydrogen and hydrogen iodide are mixed at 666.8°K.
(a) Find the composition of the system at equilibrium.
(b) Evaluate $\Delta F^o_{666.8}$ for the forward reaction.
Ans. (a) $x_{I_2} = 7.61 \times 10^{-3}$,
(b) $\Delta F^o_{666.8} = 5.44$ kcal.

8. Find $\Delta F_{666.8}$ for the process H_2 (g, 0.1 atm) $+ I_2$ (g, 0.01 atm.) $= 2$ HI (g, 1 atm.).
Ans. 3.71 kcal.

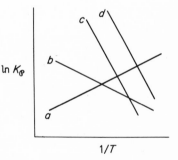

PROB. FIG. 5.2.

9. If equimolar quantities of hydrogen, iodine, and hydrogen iodide are heated to 666.8°K, what reaction will tend to occur? What is $\Delta F_{666.8}$ for the reaction? See Table 5.3 for data.   *Ans.* -5.44 kcal.

10. A mixture containing a mole ratio of nitrogen to hydrogen of $1:2$ is heated to 400° at a total pressure of 10 atm. Will the system contain as much as 1 mole per cent ammonia at equilibrium?

11. For the dissociation of phosgene
$$COCl_2 \text{ (g)} = CO \text{ (g)} + Cl_2 \text{ (g)}$$

the value of $K_{\mathscr{P}}$ at $100°$ is 6.7×10^{-9} (atm.) Find the fraction of phosgene dissociated at $100°$ under the following circumstances:

(a) 1 mole of phosgene in a 100 l. vessel.

(b) 1 mole of phosgene in a 1 l. vessel.

(c) 1 mole of phosgene in a 100 l. vessel containing chlorine at a partial pressure of 1 atm.

(d) 1 mole of phosgene in a 100 l. vessel containing nitrogen at a partial pressure of 1 atm.

Ans. (a) 1.48×10^{-4}, (b) 1.48×10^{-5}, (c) 6.7×10^{-9}, (d) 1.48×10^{-4}.

12. A vessel having a volume of 503 ml. was filled at $50°$ with methanol vapor at a partial pressure of 37.6 mm. and with 0.0686 g. of nitrosyl chloride. After equilibration the partial pressure of nitrosyl chloride was found to be 20.7 mm. Find $K_{\mathscr{P}}$ for the reaction

$$CH_3OH + NOCl = CH_3ONO + HCl$$

Ans. 1.33.

13. Given the standard free energies of formation of the three isomeric pentanes, find their mole fractions in the equilibrium mixture at $600°K$.

$$\Delta F^o_{600} \text{ (n-pentane)} = 33,790 \text{ cal. mole}^{-1}$$
$$\Delta F^o_{600} \text{ (isopentane)} = 32,660 \text{ cal. mole}^{-1}$$
$$\Delta F^c_{600} \text{ (neopentane)} = 35,080 \text{ cal. mole}^{-1}$$

Ans. $X_n = 0.255$, $X_{neo} = 0.084$.

14. One g. of iodine and 100 mm. partial pressure of hydrogen is introduced into a 1 l. vessel at $25°$. The vessel is then heated to $666.8°K$. From data in Table 5.3 find the amount of hydrogen iodide at equilibrium.

Ans. 3.4×10^{-3} mole.

15. From the data in Tables 5.5 and 3.2 find $K_{\mathscr{P}}$ at $200°$ for

$$CO \text{ (g)} + H_2O \text{ (g)} = CO_2 \text{ (g)} + H_2 \text{ (g)}$$

Ans. 213.

16. Given $\Delta F^o_{2000} = 2240$ cal. and $\Delta F^o_{2200} = -3560$ cal. for

$$Cl_2 \text{ (g)} = 2 Cl \text{ (g)}$$

find ΔH^o_{2100}.

Ans. 60 kcal.

---

17. An equimolar mixture of nitrogen and hydrogen at $500°$ and 50 atm. is equilibrated. By the method of successive approximations find X_{NH_3} at equilibrium.

Ans. $X_{NH_3} = 0.042$.

18. A reaction mixture contains 0.2 mole A, 1.0 mole AB initially. At equilibrium, 0.1 mole B is present at 2 atm. total pressure, unmeasured amounts of A and AB are also present. How much B will be present at equilibrium when the same mixture is expanded to 1 atm. total pressure?

19. For the reaction system $3A \text{ (g)} + 2B \text{ (g)} = 4C \text{ (g)} + D \text{ (g)}$ a mixture at $500°K$ contains initially 0.65 moles A, 0.40 moles B, 0.80 moles C and 0 moles D in a volume of 10 l. Letting $n_D = x$ at equilibrium,

(a) Express n_A, n_B, n_C in terms of x.

(b) For $x = 0.10$ mole, evaluate n_A, etc.

(c) Evaluate $K_{\mathscr{P}}$.

20. A reaction system described by A (g) + 3B (g) = 2C (g) consists initially of 25 mole per cent A, 50 mole per cent B, 10 mole per cent C, and 15 mole per cent inert gas, D. At equilibrium the system contains 20 mole per cent C when $P_{total} = 4$ atm.

(a) Find the mole per cent of A, B, and x (where $x = n_A$) at equilibrium.

(b) Find $K_{\mathscr{P}}$.

(c) How is the position of equilibrium affected by adding D at constant total pressure?

21. The compounds A, B, and C are interconvertible in the gaseous state. That is, (i) A (g) = B (g), and (ii) A (g) = C (g). Given ΔF_f^o (A) = 10 kcal., ΔF_f^o (B) = 11 kcal., and ΔF_f^o (C) = 14 kcal., all at 298°K,

(a) Evaluate $K_{\mathscr{P}}$ for reactions (i) and (ii) at 298°K.

(b) Find the equilibrium composition.

22. In the vapor of HCN both of the following reactions occur: 2 HCN = (HCN)$_2$, $K_{\mathscr{P}} = 0.095$; 3 HCN = (HCN)$_3$, $K_{\mathscr{P}} = 0.055$.

(a) Find the composition, in mole percentage, of hydrogen cyanide vapor at $P_{total} = 100$ mm.

(b) Find $K_{\mathscr{P}}$ for (HCN)$_3$ (g) = HCN (g) + (HCN)$_2$ (g) [W. F. Giauque and R. A. Ruehrwein, *J. Am. Chem. Soc.*, **61**, 2626 (1939)].

23. From the data in Table 5.5, find the vapor pressure of benzene at 25°.

24. For the processes

(i) C_2H_6 (g) = C_2H_4 (g) + H_2 (g)

(ii) C_2H_6 (g) + I_2 (s) = C_2H_4 (g) + 2 HI (g)

(a) Evaluate ΔF_{298}^o in each case.

(b) From a thermodynamic point of view, what is the role of iodine in dehydrogenation?

25. Vapor density measurements on acetic acid vapor yield apparent molecular weights which are in excess of the formula weight, 60, indicating that the acid dimerizes. The following values of r = (obs. mol. wt./formula wt.) have been obtained at the indicated temperatures and total pressures.

t (°C)	110	132	156	184
r	1.51	1.33	1.19	1.10
P mm.	453	403	473	553

Find $K_{\mathscr{P}}$ at each temperature and obtain ΔH for

$$2 \ CH_3COOH \ (g) = (CH_3COOH)_2 \ (g)$$

26. For the reaction

$$N_2 \ (g) + O_2 \ (g) = 2 \ NO \ (g)$$

$K_{\mathscr{P}} = 1.21 \times 10^{-4}$ at 1800 °K and $K_{\mathscr{P}} = 4.08 \times 10^{-4}$ at 2000°K. Find

(a) ΔF_{2000}^o per mole of NO.

(b) ΔH_{1900} per mole of NO.

(c) $K_{\mathscr{P}}$ at 2500°K, taking ΔH independent of temperature.

27. For the dissociation reaction

$$2 CO_2 (g) = 2 CO (g) + O_2 (g)$$

$K_{\mathscr{P}} = 4 \times 10^{-21}$ at $1000°K$ and $K_{\mathscr{P}} = 1.025 \times 10^{-12}$ at $1400°K$. Use this information with data from Table 2.1 to solve simultaneous equations obtained from equation (5.23) and obtain ΔH_0^o, I, and ΔF_{298}^o.

28. For the reaction

$$C_3H_8 (g) = C_3H_6 (g) + H_2 (g)$$

the equilibrium constants were found to be $5.17 \pm 0.15 \times 10^{-4}$ (atm.) at $648.2°K$ and $3.67 \pm 0.17 \times 10^{-5}$ (atm.) at $583.2°K$. Find the value of ΔH at the mean temperature and the uncertainty in ΔH from the corresponding uncertainty in the equilibrium constants.

29. A gas mixture at $451.4°$ and constant volume consists initially of C_2H_6, 1 atm.; C_2H_4, x atm.; and H_2, y atm. At equilibrium it consists of C_2H_6, 0.976 atm.; C_2H_4, 0.1941 atm.; and H_2, 0.02728 atm.

(a) Find the values of x and y in the initial mixture.

(b) If the ΔH of hydrogenation of the ethylene is -32.6 kcal., what is the value of $K_{\mathscr{P}}$ at $450°$ for

$$C_2H_6 = C_2H_4 + H_2$$

30. For a reaction of the type $A (g) + B (g) = M (g) + N (g)$, and for the case that $P(V - b) = RT$ is applicable, under what condition is $\mathscr{P}_M \mathscr{P}_N / \mathscr{P}_A \mathscr{P}_B =$ constant?

31. Consider that $P = (n/V) RT = cRT$, where c is concentration of gas (e.g., mole lit.$^{-1}$).

(a) Derive an expression for K_c in terms of $K_{\mathscr{P}}$.

(b) Derive an expression for $d \ln K_c / dT$.

32. In a reacting system described by $A (g) + 2B (g) = 3C (g)$ the mole numbers at equilibrium are $n_A = 4.5$, $n_B = 6.5$, $n_C = 2.0$ at $400°K$. Given $\Delta H_{400}^o = 46$ kcal.,

(a) Evaluate the equilibrium constant at $400°K$.

(b) Find ΔF_{400}^o.

(c) Find, within 1 per cent, K_{401}/K_{400}.

33. The fractional extent of dissociation, α, of F_2 has been measured with the following results:

°K	513	565	604	658
α	0.007	0.035	0.097	0.247
$P_{atm.} \times 10^7$	6.89	7.23	7.47	7.80

Evaluate $K_{\mathscr{P}}$ at each temperature and find ΔH for $\frac{1}{2} F_2 (g) = F (g)$.
[H. Wise, *J. Phys. Chem.*, **58**, 389 (1954)].

34. The vapor pressure of water at $0°$ and 1 atm. is 4.58 mm. Find ΔF for

(a) $H_2O (1, 0°, 1 \text{ atm.}) = H_2O (1, 0°, 4.58 \text{ mm.})$.

(b) $H_2O (1, 0°, 4.58 \text{ mm.}) = H_2O (g, 0°, 4.58 \text{ mm.})$.

(c) $H_2O (1, 0°, 1 \text{ atm.}) = H_2O (s, 0°, 1 \text{ atm.})$.

(d) $H_2O (s, 0°, 4.58 \text{ mm.}) = H_2O (g, 0°, 4.58 \text{ mm.})$.

(e) $H_2O (1, 0°, 1 \text{ atm.}) = H_2O (g, 0°, 4.58 \text{ mm.})$.

(f) For the process H_2O (s, $t°$, 4.58 mm.) $= H_2O$ (1, $t°$, 4.58 mm.), $\Delta F = 0$. Find $t°$.

35. Show by thermodynamic considerations that the equilibrium composition of a chemical reaction mixture cannot depend upon the presence or absence of a catalyst (e.g., platinum).

36. Show mathematically that no two equilibrium compositions for the reaction system $aA + bB = cC + dD$ can be the same for different initial mole number ratios $\alpha : \beta : \gamma : \delta$.

37. Consider the reaction

$$aA + bB = mM$$

and its equilibrium function in the form

$$K_{\mathscr{P}} = \frac{n_M^m}{n_A^a n_B^b}\left(\frac{P_t}{n_t}\right)^{m-a-b}$$

Using previously defined symbols and for the case that $K_{\mathscr{P}} \ll 1$, so that at constant total pressure

$$K' = n_M^m \alpha^{-a}\beta^{-b}$$

show that the yield of M is a maximum for $\alpha + \beta = $ constant when the ratio $\rho = \alpha/\beta$ is the same as the stoichiometric ratio a/b.

38. At somewhat elevated temperatures elemental iodine reacts with paraffinic hydrocarbons to produce olefins, diolefins, and acetylenes of the same carbon skeleton as the reactant.

$$C_nH_{2n+1} \text{ (g)} + I_2 \text{ (g)} = C_nH_{2n} \text{ (g)} + 2HI \text{ (g)}; \qquad K_A$$
$$C_nH_{2n} \text{ (g)} + I_2 \text{ (g)} = C_nH_{2n-2} \text{ (g)} + 2HI \text{ (g)}; \qquad K_B$$

(a) Using the data of Table 5.6, find K_A and K_B at 500°K and at 1000°K for C_2H_6, C_2H_4, and C_2H_2.
(b) By interpolating with $\ln K = -\Delta H/RT + $ const., find K_A and K_B at 958°K.
(c) Calculate the expected distribution for moles of C_2H_6, C_2H_4, and C_2H_2 per 100 moles C_2H_6 initially present.
(d) In an actual run at 685° and 1 atm. the initial ratio I_2/C_2H_6 was 4.6 and 24 per cent of I_2 subsequently reacted. On the basis of 100 moles C_2H_6 initially present, 1.9 C_2H_6, 72.0 C_2H_4, and 10.0 C_2H_2 were present at equilibrium. Evaluate K_A and K_B from these measurements [J. H. Raley, R. D. Mullineux, and C. W. Bittner, *J. Am. Chem. Soc.*, **85**, 3174 (1963)].

6

ENTROPY
AND THE THIRD LAW
OF THERMODYNAMICS

6.1 Heat Engines

In Chapter 4 it was shown that $w_{\text{max.}}$ in an isothermal process depends only on the initial and final states of the system and not on the path. In order to extend this method to the study of the influence of temperature on forbiddenness, it is necessary to examine the temperature dependence of $w_{\text{max.}}$. This was done for the case of ideal gas expansions in section 4.11 and will now be developed in more general fashion.

The first examination of the temperature dependence of $w_{\text{max.}}$ arose from studies of the behavior of cyclic heat engines. The common steam engine is an example of this type of device, and cyclic operation is clearly a requirement for any practical heat engine. A working fluid (e. g., steam) is heated, expands to perform work, and is cooled, losing heat to the surroundings. The operations are performed on the working fluid in cycles. That is, the working fluid passes repeatedly through the same physical states. The net effect of the cyclic process is the conversion of heat into work.

Although work (mechanical or electric) can always be completely converted into heat, it is a fact of common observation that the converse is not true. Even with the utmost refinements, it is found that the working fluid of a cyclic heat engine delivers work equivalent to only a fraction of the heat absorbed by the fluid. This is not a contradiction of the first law of thermodynamics, which denies the possibility of creating or destroying energy, since the working fluid must always lose heat to the surroundings or to some body at a temperature below that of the heat source. A heat engine cannot operate until

146

a temperature difference is established between a *source* of heat and a *sink* (which may be the surroundings).

The essential features of a cyclic heat engine are indicated in Fig. 6.1. The working fluid absorbs heat $|q_2|$[1] from the *source* at temperature T_2, performs some work $|w|$ on the surroundings, and loses some heat $|q_1|$ to the low temperature *sink* at T_1.

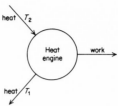

In the course of a complete cycle, that is, for an operation which returns the fluid to its original state, the first law of thermodynamics states that the net heat absorbed by the fluid $|q_2| - |q_1|$ must be equal to the net work done by the fluid $|w|$, since $\Delta E_{\text{cycle}} = 0$.

FIG. 6.1. Heat engine.

$$|w| = |q_2| - |q_1| \tag{6.1}$$

The efficiency η of the cyclic heat engine is defined as the ratio of *work done to heat absorbed from the high temperature source.*

$$\eta = \frac{|w|}{|q_2|} = \frac{|q_2| - |q_1|}{|q_2|} \tag{6.2}$$

It is always less than unity. Actually, the efficiency of a simple steam engine is commonly less than 0.20, that is, 80 per cent of the heat absorbed from the source is lost as heat to the surroundings. Even when a heat engine is operated in more and more nearly reversible fashion, the limiting efficiency is less than unity.

$$\eta_{\text{lim.}} = \frac{|w_{\text{max.}}|}{|q_{2\,\text{rev.}}|} = \frac{|q_{2\,\text{rev.}}| - |q_{1\,\text{rev}}|}{|q_{2\,\text{rev.}}|} \tag{6.3}$$

Apparently, nature has placed some limitations on our ability to convert heat into work.

Another type of device which belongs in the general class of cyclic heat engines is more commonly known as a refrigerator or heat pump. In this device, heat is absorbed by a working fluid from a low temperature region (cold box), work is done on the fluid, and heat is released to a high temperature region (surroundings). That is, each of the operations indicated in Fig. 6.1 is reversed. Again, the first law of thermodynamics requires that the heat delivered to the surroundings must be equal to the sum of work done on the fluid plus heat absorbed from the cold box.

$$|q_2| = |w| + |q_1| \tag{6.4}$$

For a given amount of heat withdrawn from the cold box, $|q_1|$, the coefficient of performance of the heat pump,

$$\eta = \frac{|w|}{|q_2|} = \frac{|w|}{|w| + |q_1|} \tag{6.5}$$

---

[1]The symbols $|q_2|$ and $|q_1|$ are used to denote the absolute amount of heat absorbed or evolved by the system without regard to sign. The same applies to $|w|$.

decreases as the device is operated in more and more nearly reversible fashion. That is, $|w|$ decreases, and the limiting value of $|w|/|q_2|$ is

$$\eta_{\text{lim.}} = \frac{|w_{\text{max.}}|}{|q_{2\,\text{rev.}}|} = \frac{|w_{\text{max.}}|}{|w_{\text{max.}}| + |q_{1\,\text{rev.}}|} \tag{6.6}$$

Practical experience indicates that the limiting value of the coefficient of performance of a heat pump is *not* zero. Indeed, this would correspond to flow of heat from T_1 to T_2 with no expenditure of work. All experience denies this possibility. Even with the most efficient machine operating in reversible fashion, a finite amount of work must be done to remove heat $|q_1|$ from the cold box.

We now inquire into the nature of this limit on $|w|/|q_2|$ and ask what experimental circumstances govern its value.

6.2 Efficiency of Heat Engines

The quantitative relationship between operating temperatures and limiting efficiency will be developed later, but for the moment we turn to the question of whether or not the nature of the working fluid influences the limiting efficiency. That is, for the same operating temperatures can one working fluid have a *limiting* efficiency different from another?

Let us assume that we have two different cyclic heat engines, A and B, operating between the same two temperatures, and that the limiting efficiency of A is greater than that of B.

$$\frac{|w_{\text{max.}}|(A)}{|q_{2\,\text{rev.}}|(A)} > \frac{|w_{\text{max.}}|(B)}{|q_{2\,\text{rev.}}|(B)} \tag{6.7}$$

Let the heat engine B operate as a heat pump so as to exactly consume the work output of engine A, as indicated in Fig. 6.2. That is,

$$|w_{\text{max.}}|(A) = |w_{\text{max.}}|(B) \tag{6.8}$$

From relation (6.7) it follows that

$$|q_{2\,\text{rev.}}|(B) > |q_{2\,\text{rev.}}|(A) \tag{6.9}$$

The consequence of assuming unequal limiting efficiencies would be to deliver more heat to the source at T_2 by the heat pump B than would be removed from the source by the engine A. Since both devices operate in cycles, they experience no net change in state. Their coupled operation would produce no effect other than pumping heat from a lower to a higher temperature, which is contrary to all experience. We conclude that *the limiting efficiency of all heat engines is the same for all*

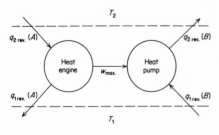

FIG. 6.2. Coupled heat engines.

working fluids for any assigned temperatures of heat source and heat sink.

To examine the effect of operating temperatures upon the limiting efficiency of a heat engine, it will be convenient to select an ideal gas as the working fluid, following a path known as the Carnot cycle. There are four reversible steps, indicated in Fig. 6.3.

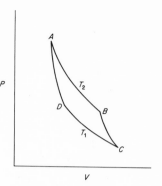

FIG. 6.3. Carnot cycle.

Step AB—isothermal expansion; $\Delta E_{T_2} = 0$

$$q_{2\text{ rev.}} = w_{\text{max.}} = nRT_2 \ln \frac{V_B}{V_A} \qquad (6.10)$$

Step BC—adiabatic expansion; $q = 0$

$$w_{\text{max.}} = -\Delta E = \int_{T_1}^{T_2} nC_V\, dT \qquad (6.11)$$

Step CD—isothermal compression; $\Delta E_{T_1} = 0$

$$q_{1\text{ rev.}} = w_{\text{max.}} = nRT_1 \ln \frac{V_D}{V_C} \qquad (6.12)$$

Step DA—adiabatic compression; $q = 0$

$$w_{\text{max.}} = -\Delta E = -\int_{T_1}^{T_2} nC_V\, dT \qquad (6.13)$$

The sum of all four work terms is

$$w_{\text{max.}} \text{ (cycle)} = nRT_2 \ln \frac{V_B}{V_A} - nRT_1 \ln \frac{V_C}{V_D} \qquad (6.14)$$

From equation (2.36) which describes adiabatic reversible expansion of an ideal gas

$$+ R \ln \frac{V_C}{V_B} = C_V \ln \frac{T_2}{T_1} = + R \ln \frac{V_D}{V_A} \qquad (6.15)$$

and, therefore,

$$\frac{V_C}{V_B} = \frac{V_D}{V_A}$$

or

$$\frac{V_C}{V_D} = \frac{V_B}{V_A} \qquad (6.16)$$

Equation (6.14) simplifies to

$$|w_{\text{max.}}| \text{(cycle)} = (T_2 - T_1)nR \ln (V_B/V_A) \qquad (6.17)$$

and the limiting efficiency is given by equations (6.10) and (6.17),

$$\eta_{\text{lim.}} = \frac{|w_{\text{max.}}|}{|q_{2\text{ rev.}}|} = \frac{T_2 - T_1}{T_2} \qquad (6.18)$$

The temperatures T_1 and T_2 in equation (6.18) were introduced by employing the ideal gas law and are, therefore, the ideal gas or absolute temperatures. By the argument given at the beginning of this section, equation (6.18) applies to all cyclic heat engines, regardless of the nature of the working fluid. It is effectively a statement of the second law of thermodynamics. The ideal gas temperature, therefore, appears in a thermodynamic law of general validity and may be identified with so-called thermodynamic or Kelvin temperature (cf. section 1.4). The centigrade degree is arbitrary, however, since any measure of temperature which is proportional to T would satisfy equation (6.18).

Since equation (6.18) describes the limiting efficiency of any heat engine, a steam engine operating between 100° and 25° has a limiting efficiency given by

$$\eta_{\text{lim.}} = \frac{373° - 298°}{373°} = 0.201$$

For a refrigerator which keeps the cold box temperature at 0° and delivers heat to the room at 25°, the coefficient of performance is

$$\eta_{\text{lim.}} = \frac{298° - 273°}{298°} = 0.084$$

Since this is

$$\frac{|w_{\text{max.}}|}{|q_{2\,\text{rev.}}|} = \frac{|w_{\text{max.}}|}{|w_{\text{max.}}| + |q_{1\,\text{rev.}}|}$$

the reciprocal of $\eta_{\text{lim.}}$ will give the relation of $|w_{\text{max.}}|$ and $|q_{1\,\text{rev.}}|$.

$$\frac{1}{\eta_{\text{lim.}}} = 1 + \frac{|q_{1\,\text{rev.}}|}{|w_{\text{max.}}|}$$

$$\frac{|q_{1\,\text{rev.}}|}{|w_{\text{max.}}|} = \frac{1}{\eta_{\text{lim.}}} - 1 = 10.8 \tag{6.19}$$

Equation (6.19) shows that in the present example the minimum work input to the refrigerator must be 1/10.8 cal. per calorie of heat removed from the cold box.

EXERCISE 6.1

In thermodynamic terms, why is it advantageous to operate a steam engine at large positive pressure?

6.3 The Entropy

From equation (6.18), by the substitution $|w_{\text{max.}}| = |q_{2\,\text{rev.}}| - |q_{1\,\text{rev.}}|$, an important relation is obtained:

$$\frac{|q_{2\,\text{rev.}}| - |q_{1\,\text{rev.}}|}{|q_{2\,\text{rev.}}|} = \frac{T_2 - T_1}{T_2}$$

$$\frac{|q_{2\,\text{rev.}}|}{T_2} = \frac{|q_{1\,\text{rev.}}|}{T_1} \tag{6.20}$$

Since $q = 0$ for the adiabatic steps (BC and DA) in the Carnot cycle, it follows that for the complete cycle

$$\Sigma \frac{q_{\text{rev.}}}{T} = \frac{|q_{2\ \text{rev.}}|}{T_2} - \frac{|q_{1\ \text{rev.}}|}{T_1} = 0 \qquad (6.21)$$

Although this relation has been demonstrated only for the Carnot cycle, which consists of two isothermal and two adiabatic steps, it can be shown that it also applies to any other cyclic process. Furthermore, the relation is independent of the nature of the working fluid, and consequently we shall take equation (6.21) to be applicable to *all cyclic* processes. That is, for any cyclic process

$$\int_{\text{cycle}} \frac{dq_{\text{rev.}}}{T} = 0$$

We conclude that $dq_{\text{rev.}}/T$ is the differential of a new thermodynamic function whose value depends only on the initial and final states of the system. The corresponding property of the system, called the *entropy S*, is, therefore, a thermodynamic *property of state* and is defined by the equation

$$dS = \frac{dq_{\text{rev.}}}{T} \qquad (6.22)$$

As stated, the change in the value of this property in a cyclic process is zero.

$$\Delta S_{\text{cycle}} = \int_{\text{cycle}} \frac{dq_{\text{rev.}}}{T} = 0 \qquad (6.23)$$

It will be remembered that ΔH_{cycle} and ΔF_{cycle} are also zero. By analogy to those functions of state, the entropy change for a given change in state can be measured or computed, but the absolute value of S cannot be determined.

The value of ΔS for a given change in state is given by integrating equation (6.22).

$$\Delta S = S_2 - S_1 = \int \frac{dq_{\text{rev.}}}{T} \qquad (6.24)$$

That is, in order to evaluate ΔS, we must accomplish the change in state reversibly and measure the corresponding heat effect at each temperature. The value of ΔS so obtained, however, is not restricted to the reversible process but applies rigorously to the same change in state by any path whatever.

Since $T\,dS = dq_{\text{rev.}}$, and since it may be stated quite generally that a change in energy is given by the product of a generalized force times a generalized displacement, it appears that entropy is the generalized displacement factor in reversible heat flow. Temperature is the corresponding generalized force.

For a change in the temperature of n moles of a substance from T_1 to T_2, $dq_{\text{rev.}}$ is given by $C\,dT$. Therefore, for a temperature change at constant volume

$$S_2 - S_1 = \int_{T_1}^{T_2} n\frac{C_V\,dT}{T} \qquad (6.25)$$

and for a temperature change at constant pressure

$$S_2 - S_1 = \int_{T_1}^{T_2} n\frac{C_P\,dT}{T} \qquad (6.26)$$

When C_P may be considered independent of temperature, integration of equation (6.26) yields

$$S_2 - S_1 = nC_P \ln \frac{T_2}{T_1} \tag{6.27}$$

For example, for the change in state

$$H_2(g, 1 \text{ atm.}, 0°) = H_2(g, 1 \text{ atm.}, 100°)$$

$$S_{373} - S_{273} = 5 \times 2.303 \log \frac{373°}{273°} = 1.56 \text{ cal. deg}^{-1}$$

EXERCISE 6.2

Develop an expression for $S_2 - S_1$ for the constant pressure change of 1 mole of hydrogen from T_1 to T_2 when C_P is given by an empirical equation of the form used in Table 2.1. $\quad\quad Ans.\ a \ln \frac{T_2}{T_1} + b(T_2 - T_1) + \frac{c}{2}(T_2^2 - T_1^2).$

For an isothermal volume change of an ideal gas $dE = 0$ and $dq_{\text{rev.}} = dw_{\text{max.}}$ It follows that

$$S_2 - S_1 = \int_1^2 \frac{dw_{\text{max.}}}{T}$$

$$= \int_{V_1}^{V_2} \frac{P\,dV}{T} = \int_{V_1}^{V_2} \frac{nR\,dV}{V}$$

$$= nR \ln \frac{V_2}{V_1} = nR \ln \frac{P_1}{P_2} \tag{6.28}$$

For example, for the change in state

$$1 \text{ g. O}_2 \text{ (g, 1 atm., 25°)} = 1\text{g. O}_2 \text{ (g, 0.1 atm., 25°)}$$

$$S_2 - S_1 = \frac{1.987 \times 2.303}{32} \log \frac{1}{0.1}$$

$$= 0.143 \text{ cal. deg.}^{-1}$$

Consider two boxes at $0°$, separated by a removable partition, each having a volume of 11.2 1., one containing 0.5 mole of hydrogen and the other 0.5 mole of deuterium. When the partition is removed, the gases mix, and the final state of the system is one mole of a uniform mixture in a volume of 22.4 1. Experience tells us that the reverse process does not occur spontaneously. There is no significant entropy change arising from specific interactions between H_2 and D_2 since they are nearly ideal gases; the net result is equivalent to the sum of the entropy change for expanding 0.5 mole of hydrogen from 11.2 1. to 22.4 1. at $0°$ with the corresponding entropy change for deuterium. Each of these can be evaluated by equation (6.28):

$$\Delta S_{D_2} = 0.5\,R \ln \frac{22.4}{11.2}$$

$$\Delta S_{H_2} = 0.5\,R \ln \frac{22.4}{11.2}$$

The entropy change is a function only of the mole numbers and volumes. For mixing any amounts of gases A and B at a common temperature and pressure, it follows that

$$\Delta S_{\text{mix.}} = n_A R \ln \frac{V_A + V_B}{V_A} + n_B R \ln \frac{V_A + V_B}{V_B} \qquad (6.29)$$

The problem of finding ΔS for

$$aA (V_A, T_A) + bB (V_B, T_B) = (a + b) M (V_M, T_M)$$

where M refers to mixture, is resolvable into the component entropy effects for changing temperature (by equations 6.25 or 6.26), changing pressure (by equation 6.28), and finally mixing (by equation 6.29). For one mole of mixture this is more conveniently expressed in terms of mole fractions as

$$\Delta S_{\text{mix.}} = - X_A R \ln X_A - X_B R \ln X_B \qquad (6.30)$$

Similarly, for mixing any number of gases at a common temperature and pressure, the entropy of mixing, per mole of mixture, can easily be shown to be

$$\Delta S_{\text{mix.}} = -R \sum X_i \ln X_i \qquad (6.31)$$

It can also be shown that equations (6.29)–(6.31) apply as well to mixing two liquids which form a solution obeying Raoult's law.

As a final instance of the computation of entropy changes in simple physical processes, consider the phase changes, such as fusion and vaporization. For each change, such as

$$H_2O (l, P, T) = H_2O (g, P, T)$$

there is for any given pressure only one temperature at which the process is reversible. At a pressure of 1 atm. the vaporization of water is reversible only at 100°. At the equilibrium pressure and temperature

$$\Delta H = q_{\text{rev.}}$$

and, therefore,

$$\Delta S_T = \frac{\Delta H_T}{T} \qquad (6.32)$$

Equation (6.32) applies to reversible, isothermal processes such as

$$H_2O(l, 1 \text{ atm.}, 100°) = H_2O(g, 1 \text{ atm.}, 100°)$$

for which

$$\Delta S_{373} = \frac{9713}{373°} = 26.0 \text{ cal. deg.}^{-1} \text{ mole}^{-1}$$

At 25°, the equilibrium vapor pressure of water is 23.6 mm. and, therefore, equation (6.32) applies to

$$H_2O(l, 23.6 \text{ mm.}) = H_2O(g, 23.6 \text{ mm})$$

for which

$$\Delta H_{298} = 10,520 \text{ cal. mole}^{-1}$$

Therefore,

$$\Delta S_{298} = \frac{10,520}{298°} = 35.3 \text{ cal. deg.}^{-1} \text{ mole}^{-1}$$

On the other hand, the hypothetical process

$$H_2O(l, 1 \text{ atm., } 25°) = H_2O(g, 1 \text{ atm., } 25°)$$

is not reversible and equation (6.32) *cannot* be directly applied. That is, whereas dS always equals $dq_{rev.}/T$, replacement of $q_{rev.}$ by ΔH is possible only for reversible processes.

In order to evaluate ΔS for the change in state specified above, it is necessary to devise an equivalent reversible process such as

(i) $\quad H_2O$ (l, 1 atm., 298°K) $= H_2O$ (l, 1 atm., 373°K)

(ii) $\quad H_2O$ (l, 1 atm., 373°K) $= H_2O$ (g, 1 atm., 373°K)

(iii) $\quad H_2O$ (g, 1 atm., 373°K) $= H_2O$ (g, 1 atm., 298°K)

Using $C_P(H_2O, l) = 18$ cal. deg.$^{-1}$ mole^{-1} and $C_P(H_2O, g) = 9$ cal. deg.$^{-1}$ mole^{-1} in equation (6.26) for processes (i) and (iii), and equation (6.32) for process (ii), we obtain

$$\Delta S_{298} = 18 \ln \frac{373°}{298°} + \frac{9713}{373°} + 9 \ln \frac{298°}{373°} = 28.0 \text{ cal. deg.}^{-1} \text{ mole}^{-1}$$

EXERCISE 6.3

Compute ΔS at $-10°$ for

$$H_2O \text{ (s, 1 atm.) } = H_2O \text{ (l, 1 atm.)}$$

Take C_P $(H_2O, s) = 9$ cal. deg.$^{-1}$ mole^{-1} and ΔH_{273} (fusion) $= 1440$ cal. mole^{-1}.

Ans. $\Delta S_{263} = 4.93$ cal. deg.$^{-1}$ mole^{-1}.

6.4 Reversibility and Irreversibility

Let us examine the mutual interactions of a system and its surroundings during a reversible process. Heat gained by one is lost by the other, and for reversible heat transfer the two temperatures must be the same at every stage of the process. That is,

$$\int \frac{dq_{rev.}}{T} = - \int \frac{dq_{rev.}}{T}$$
$$\text{system} \qquad\qquad \text{surroundings.}$$

It follows that $\Delta S_{syst.} + \Delta S_{surr.} = \Delta S_{net} = 0$. By extension, for a (system + surroundings) complex of many parts, $\Sigma \Delta S_i = 0$ for any reversible process. Now, any combination of a system and its immediate surroundings constitutes an isolated system which can exchange neither heat nor work with any other part of the universe. *For any reversible change in an isolated system*, $\Delta S = 0$.

The permitted irreversible process is characterized by performing less work $w'_{irrev.}$ than could have been performed by the corresponding reversible change in state, $w'_{rev.}$. Since $\Delta E'_{rev.} = \Delta E'_{irrev.}$, it follows that, for the system:

$$(q'_{rev.} - w'_{rev.})_{syst.} = (q'_{irrev.} - w'_{irrev.})_{syst.} \tag{6.33}$$

$$(q'_{rev.} - q'_{irrev.})_{syst.} = (w'_{rev.} - w'_{irrev.})_{syst.} > 0 \tag{6.34}$$

Let us now restore the system reversibly to its initial state, transferring heat $q''_{rev.}$ and work $w''_{rev.}$ from the surroundings to the system. The net entropy change in the combined, isolated, complex is zero. Although the system in its final state is unchanged, the surroundings have been degraded. For this reversible process $\Delta S''_{syst.} + \Delta S''_{surr.} = 0$. Also, the system has been returned to its initial state, and $\Delta S'_{syst.} + \Delta S''_{syst.} = 0$. Consequently, ΔS_{net} for the entire operation is

$$\Delta S_{net} = (\Delta S'_{syst.} + \Delta S'_{surr.})_{irrev.} + (\Delta S''_{syst.} + \Delta S''_{surr.})_{rev.}$$

or

$$\Delta S_{net} = \Delta S'_{syst.} + \Delta S'_{surr.} = \Delta S'_{surr.} + \Delta S''_{surr.} \tag{6.35}$$

The amount of work $w''_{rev.}$ required to restore the system equals in magnitude (but differs in sign from) the maximum work $w'_{rev.}$ which could have been produced by the system in the forward process:

$$(w'_{rev.} + w''_{rev.})_{syst.} = 0 \tag{6.36}$$

Correspondingly,

$$(q'_{rev.} + q''_{rev.})_{syst.} = 0 \tag{6.37}$$

Combining equations (6.34) and (6.37) gives

$$(q''_{rev.} + q'_{irrev.})_{syst.} < 0 \tag{6.38}$$

and, with changed signs, for the surroundings:

$$(q''_{rev.} + q'_{irrev.})_{surr.} > 0 \tag{6.39}$$

For changes at constant temperature, we divide both sides of the inequality (6.39) by T and obtain, by equations (6.35) and (6.39),

$$\Delta S_{net} = (\Delta S'_{irrev.} + \Delta S''_{rev.})_{surr.} > 0 \tag{6.40}$$

For nonisothermal processes it would be necessary to resolve the reversible steps into differential isothermal steps, with $dq_{rev.}/T = dS$, and connect them by differential adiabatic reversible steps with $dq_{rev.} = 0$, $dS = 0$. Again, it can be shown, both system and surroundings being taken into consideration, that *for any irreversible change there is a net increase in entropy.*

EXERCISE 6.4

One mole of steam at 100°, and 1 atm. and 100 g. of ice at 0°, 1 atm., comprise the initial state of an isolated system. What is the final state, and what is the net entropy change?   *Ans.* Final temp. 30°, $\Delta S = 9.9$ cal. deg.$^{-1}$

6.5 Entropy and Free Energy

It has been shown in Chapter 4 that the Gibbs free energy F and the Helmholtz free energy A are important thermodynamic functions of state. These properties can now be fully *defined* in terms of the entropy, the earlier restriction to isothermal processes being removed:

$$A = E - TS \tag{6.41}$$

$$F = H - TS \tag{6.42}$$

Since E, H, and S are properties of state, it follows that A and F are also. For any given process, the values of ΔA and ΔF depend only upon initial and final states, and not on the path.

$$A_2 - A_1 = E_2 - E_1 - (T_2 S_2 - T_1 S_1)$$
$$\Delta A = \Delta E - \Delta TS \tag{6.43}$$

$$F_2 - F_1 = H_2 - H_1 - (T_2 S_2 - T_1 S_1)$$
$$\Delta F = \Delta H - \Delta TS \tag{6.44}$$

Although ΔF can now be computed, in principle, for any change in state including one in which the initial and final temperatures are not the same, this thermodynamic function is principally used for constant pressure, constant temperature changes. For an isothermal change in state

$$\Delta F_T = \Delta H_T - T \Delta S_T \tag{6.45}$$

Since

$$\Delta H = \Delta E + \Delta PV$$

then

$$\Delta F_T = \Delta E_T + \Delta(PV)_T - T \Delta S_T \tag{6.46}$$

For an isothermal change

$$T \Delta S = q_{rev.}$$

and from the first law $\Delta E = q_{rev.} - w_{max.}$. Therefore,

$$- \Delta F_T = w_{max.} - \Delta PV \tag{6.47}$$

For a constant pressure change in state

$$- \Delta F_{T, P} = w_{max.} - P \Delta V \tag{6.48}$$

which conforms with the limited definition of ΔF given in Chapter 4. $w_{max.}$ includes all possible kinds of work, that is, electric work as well as expansion work. If we separate the work term into expansion work w and all other kinds of work, $w_{max., net}$, so that

$$w_{max.} = w_{max., net} + w_{exp.}$$

and substitute in equation (6.48), we obtain

$$- \Delta F_{T,P} = w_{max., net} \tag{6.49}$$

since $w_{exp.} = P \Delta V$ at constant pressure. This is to say that the decrease in free energy is a measure of the maximum *net* work obtainable from the specified change.

EXERCISE 6.5

Starting with equation (6.43), show that, for an isothermal change in state

$$-\Delta A = w_{max.}.$$

To repeat briefly the argument concerning ΔF as a criterion of reversibility in a constant pressure, constant temperature change, we recall that the distinguishing feature of a permitted process is that w is less than $w_{max.}$. Now, if a change in state, such as a chemical reaction, is carried out in an open vessel at constant temperature, with no provision for electric or other work, there still occurs the unavailable work of expansion against the constant pressure of the surroundings, $P \Delta V$. Therefore, in such a system a process for which $w_{max.}$ (a function of state) exceeds $P \Delta V$ is a permitted change. That is, $\Delta F < 0$. If $w_{max.} = P \Delta V$, $\Delta F = 0$ and the process is reversible. When $\Delta F > 0$, the process is forbidden.

Returning to the relation given for ΔF in a constant temperature change (equation 6.45), we note that the term $T \Delta S$ is sometimes called the *unavailable energy*. Since

$$\Delta F = -w_{max.} + \Delta PV = \Delta H - T \Delta S$$

and since

$$\Delta E = \Delta H - \Delta PV$$

then

$$-w_{max.} = \Delta E - T \Delta S \tag{6.50}$$

This equation shows that the maximum work available from a change in state is less than the internal energy change ΔE by the amount $T \Delta S$. That is, an amount of energy $T \Delta S$ is not available for conversion into work, even when the change is carried out reversibly. This situation is similar to that which is found with heat engines, in which only part of the heat absorbed from the source can be converted into work.

For any isothermal change in state, the value of ΔF may be computed by equation (6.45). For example, it has been shown that for

$$H_2O(l, 1 \text{ atm.}, 100°) = H_2O(g, 1 \text{ atm.}, 100°)$$

$$\Delta H_{373.16} = 9713 \text{ cal. mole}^{-1}$$

and

$$\Delta S_{373.16} = 26.0 \text{ cal. deg}^{-1} \text{ mole}^{-1}$$

Therefore,

$$\Delta F_{373.16} = 9713 - 373.16 \times 26.0 = 0 \text{ cal. mole}^{-1}$$

This process is, of course, reversible.

On the other hand, for

$$H_2O(l, 1 \text{ atm.}, 25°) = H_2O(g, 1 \text{ atm.}, 25°)$$

$$\Delta H_{298} = 10,520 \text{ cal. mole}^{-1}$$

and

$$\Delta S_{298} = 28.0 \text{ cal. deg.}^{-1} \text{ mole}^{-1}$$

Therefore,

$$\Delta F_{298} = 10,520 - 298° \times 28.0 = 2170 \text{ cal. mole}^{-1}$$

and this process is forbidden under the conditions specified.

EXERCISE 6.6

Compute ΔF at $-10°$ for

$$H_2O(l, 1 \text{ atm.}) = H_2O(s, 1 \text{ atm.})$$

See Exercise 6.3 for data.   *Ans.* $\Delta F_{263} \cong -54 \text{ cal. mole}^{-1}$.

If ΔF and ΔH are known for some isothermal change, equation (6.45) may be used to compute ΔS. It was shown in Chapter 5 that evaluation of the equilibrium function yields a value of $\Delta F_T^o = -RT \ln K$. For example, for

$$N_2(g, 1 \text{ atm.}) + 3H_2(g, 1 \text{ atm.}) = 2NH_3(g, 1 \text{ atm.})$$
$$\Delta F_{298}^o = -7.95 \text{ kcal.}$$

From Chapter 3

$$\Delta H_{298}^o = -22.08 \text{ kcal.}$$

Therefore,

$$\Delta S_{298}^o = \frac{\Delta H_{298}^o - \Delta F_{298}^o}{298.2^\circ} = -47.45 \text{ cal. deg.}^{-1}$$

EXERCISE 6.7

From data given in Chapters 3 and 5 compute ΔS_{298}^o for

$$H_2 \text{ (g, 1 atm.)} + I_2 \text{ (s, 1 atm.)} = 2 \text{ HI (g, 1 atm.)}$$

Ans. $\Delta S_{298}^o = 39.5 \text{ cal. deg.}^{-1}$.

6.6 Pressure and Temperature Dependence of Free Energy

Substituting $H = E + PV$ in equation (6.42), we obtain

$$F = E + PV - TS \tag{6.51}$$

Consider a pure substance, whose free energy content is related to other properties by equation (6.51). An infinitesimal change in the pressure, volume, and temperature of that substance is accompanied by a free energy change

$$dF = dE + P\,dV + V\,dP - T\,dS - S\,dT \tag{6.52}$$

If the system is in temperature and pressure equilibrium with its surroundings and only expansion work is done

$$P\,dV = dw_{max.} \quad \text{and} \quad T\,dS = dq_{rev.}$$

From the first law

$$dE = dq_{rev.} - dw_{max.}$$

Therefore, equation (6.52) simplifies to

$$dF = V\,dP - S\,dT \tag{6.53}$$

for a pure substance. The free energy is a function of P and T, and this dependence can be expressed by the total differential

$$dF = \left(\frac{\partial F}{\partial P}\right)_T dP + \left(\frac{\partial F}{\partial T}\right)_P dT \tag{6.54}$$

Comparing the coefficients of dP in equations (6.53) and (6.54) gives

$$\left(\frac{\partial F}{\partial P}\right)_T = V \tag{6.55}$$

which was obtained previously as equation (4.10). Similarly,

$$\left(\frac{\partial F}{\partial T}\right)_P = -S \tag{6.56}$$

For any process

$$aA + bB + \ldots = mM + nN + \ldots$$

which can represent either a simple change in phase or a chemical reaction, the change in free energy at constant temperature and pressure is given by

$$\Delta F_{T,P} = mF_{T,P}(M) + nF_{T,P}(N) + \ldots - aF_{T,P}(A) - bF_{T,P}(B) - \ldots$$

For a small change in the temperature or pressure

$$d\Delta F = mdF(M) + \ldots - adF(A) - \ldots$$

Each of these differential changes can be described by equation (6.53), with P and T the same for all substances:

$$adF(A) = aV(A)\,dP - aS(A)\,dT$$

$$\vdots \qquad \vdots \qquad \vdots$$

$$mdF(M) = mV(M)\,dP - mS(M)\,dT$$

$$\vdots \qquad \vdots \qquad \vdots$$

Following familiar patterns (cf. Chapter 3)

$$d\Delta F_{T,P} = \Delta V_{T,P}\,dP - \Delta S_{T,P}\,dT \tag{6.57}$$

At constant temperature

$$\left(\frac{\partial \Delta F_{T,P}}{\partial P}\right)_T = \Delta V_{T,P} \tag{6.58}$$

and at constant pressure

$$\left(\frac{\partial \Delta F_{T,P}}{\partial T}\right)_P = -\Delta S_{T,P} = \frac{\Delta F_{T,P} - \Delta H_{T,P}}{T} \tag{6.59}$$

This is the Gibbs-Helmholtz equation previously given as equation (4.17), since $\Delta S = q_{rev.}/T$. However, the chain of reasoning which has been used in the present development contains none of the limitations which were present in the arguments which lead to equation (4.17). Equation (6.54) applies to all types of substances, and to chemical change as well as physical change.

     The remainder of the development of useful forms of the Gibbs-Helmholtz equation follows much the same pattern as used in Chapter 4, except that we now have ΔS instead of $q_{rev.}/T$. The principal utility of the Gibbs-Helmholtz equation lies in its application to the temperature dependence of the equilibrium constant (see section 5.8), which is related to the standard free energy change by

$$\Delta F_T^o = -RT \ln K_{\mathscr{P}}$$

or

$$\frac{\Delta F_T^o}{T} = -R \ln K_{\mathscr{P}}$$

The temperature derivative for this property is obtained as follows: Since

$$\frac{\partial}{\partial T}\left(\frac{\Delta F_T^o}{T}\right) = \frac{1}{T}\frac{\partial(\Delta F_T^o)}{\partial T} - \frac{\Delta F_T^o}{T^2}$$

the Gibbs-Helmholtz equation yields

$$\frac{\partial}{\partial T}\left(\frac{\Delta F_T^o}{T}\right) = \frac{\Delta F_T^o - \Delta H_T^o}{T^2} - \frac{\Delta F_T^o}{T^2}$$

$$\frac{\partial}{\partial T}\left(\frac{\Delta F_T^o}{T}\right) = -\frac{\Delta H_T^o}{T^2}$$

$$\frac{\partial}{\partial T}(\ln K_{\mathscr{P}}) = \frac{\Delta H_T^o}{RT^2}$$

$$\frac{\partial \ln K_{\mathscr{P}}}{\partial (1/T)} = -\frac{\Delta H_T^o}{R}$$

For the case that ΔH^o may be considered to be independent of temperature, integration gives

$$\ln \frac{K_2}{K_1} = \frac{\Delta H^o}{R}\left(\frac{1}{T_1} - \frac{1}{T_2}\right) \tag{6.60}$$

The use of this equation has been demonstrated in section 5.8.

6.7 Entropy and Probability

Thermodynamics has been developed thus far in a strictly classical manner without invoking concepts of the structure of matter. The approach has been macroscopic, rather than microscopic. The consideration of entropy could be concluded in the same way, but it will be particularly advantageous now to examine entropy effects from a molecular point of view.

In order better to understand the physical significance of the property entropy, it should be noted that the changes which are accompanied by an increase in entropy have a common characteristic. They result in increased molecular disorder. In fusion the system changes from the highly ordered arrangement of a crystal lattice to the irregular molecular arrangement of the liquid state. In vaporization the molecules are released from the confined motion of the liquid state. As the temperature of a substance—solid, liquid, or gas—is increased, an increasingly chaotic and disordered motion of the molecules occurs. The entropy change associated with expanding gases and mixing liquids can be related to the increased freedom of position in space of the individual molecules. Such concepts can be described qualitatively and quantitatively in terms of probabilities.

Consider a system of n objects introduced at random into an equal number of boxes or cells, with n_1 objects in the first cell, n_2 in the second, and so on. The number of possible arrangements, or ways of mixing, is given by

$$W = \frac{n!}{n_1!\, n_2! \dots n_i! \dots} \tag{6.61}$$

For large n we may use Stirling's approximation (see Appendix 1)

$$\ln n! = n \ln n - n \tag{6.62}$$

from which it follows that

$$\ln W = n \ln n - n - \sum (n_i \ln n_i - n_i) = n \ln n - \sum n_i \ln n_i \tag{6.63}$$

Clearly,

$$n \ln n = n_1 \ln n + n_2 \ln n + \ldots = \sum n_i \ln n$$

and equation (6.63) can be written

$$\ln W = - \sum n_i \ln \left(\frac{n_i}{n}\right) = - \sum n_i \ln X_i \tag{6.64}$$

where $X_i = n_i/n$. Dividing both sides of equation (6.64) by n, we obtain

$$\frac{1}{n} \ln W = - \sum X_i \ln X_i \tag{6.65}$$

The similarity of this equation to equation (6.31) suggests that entropy is a function of probability. Multiplying both sides of equation (6.65) by the gas constant R and taking $n = N = 6 \times 10^{23}$ gives

$$\frac{R}{N} \ln W = k \ln W = - R \sum X_i \ln X_i$$

These relations suggest, but do not prove,

$$S = k \ln W \tag{6.66}$$

This is Boltzmann's equation relating entropy and probability; k is known as Boltzmann's constant.

When one mole of a gas, confined in volume V_1, is given access to an additional volume V_2, it expands to fill the available volume. The entropy of the initial state of the system is related to the chance W_1 of finding all N molecules in V_1, $[V_1/(V_1 + V_2)]^N$. The chance of finding a given molecule in V_1 is $V_1/(V_1 + V_2)$. The chance of finding all N molecules in $V_1 + V_2$, corresponding to the final state of the system, is $W_2 = 1$. Then, by equation (6.66),

$$S_2 - S_1 = k \ln \frac{W_2}{W_1} = k \ln \frac{1}{[V_1/(V_1 + V_2)]^N} = R \ln \frac{V_1 + V_2}{V_1} \tag{6.67}$$

The preceding considerations apply equally well to a superficially dissimilar problem, that of arranging molecules in a crystal. Suppose that small, nearly symmetric molecules can be arranged head-to-tail, as (I): $AB - AB - AB - \ldots$ or, randomly, (II): $AB - BA - AB - AB - \ldots$ For N molecules, $W_I = 1^N = 1$ and $W_{II} = (\frac{1}{2})^N$. The ΔS between these two states is

$$S_{II} - S_I = k \ln \frac{W_{II}}{W_I} = k \ln (\tfrac{1}{2})^N = - R \ln 2$$

This effect has been observed for crystals of CO, NO, N_2O and other molecules.

6.8 The Third Law of Thermodynamics

It has been observed that entropies of systems increase with rising temperature, and this is related to increasing disorder. We are led to ask how the entropy of a system behaves as the temperature decreases and approaches zero. Some insight was gained by the observation of processes in galvanic cells [T. W. Richards, *Z. Physik. Chem.*, **42**, 129 (1902)] for which

$d\ \Delta F/dT = -\ \Delta S$ approaches zero as the temperature decreases. W. Nernst proposed in 1906 that ΔS of a transformation approached zero in the limit of $0°K$. It has since been shown that $\Delta S_0 = 0$ cannot be expected to apply unless only perfect crystalline substances are involved. They must be free of mixing or randomness. With this limitation, then, it has been proposed that at $0°K$ $\sum S_{0,\ \text{products}} = \sum S_{0,\ \text{reactants}}$. Let us consider a simple example. $\sum S_0 = S_0(\text{AC}) + S_0(\text{BD}) - S_0(\text{AB}) - S_0(\text{CD}) = 0$ for the process

$$\text{AB} + \text{CD} = \text{AC} + \text{BD}.$$

Similarly, $\Delta S_0 = S_0(\text{AD}) + S_0(\text{BC}) - S_0(\text{AB}) - S_0(\text{CD}) = 0$ for the process

$$\text{AB} + \text{CD} = \text{AD} + \text{BC}$$

In order for ΔS_0 to be zero for all processes involving perfect, crystalline substances, it would be necessary for S_0 (A) to be the same whether the atom or group A is combined with B, C, or D—or is uncombined. Since the numbers and kinds of atoms always balance in chemical equations, nothing is to be gained by always including such terms as S_0 (A), etc., and our bookkeeping will be unaffected by adopting the proposal of Max Planck (1912): *the entropy of every pure, perfect crystalline substance is zero at the absolute zero of temperature.* This is the third law of thermodynamics.

The third law supports the postulate that the entropy of a system is related to its probability, $S = k \ln W$. The number of ways in which the molecules of a system can be arranged depends in part, as shown, upon the number of accessible "cells," or "boxes," or available space. It depends in part upon geometric relationships, as AB-AB and AB-BA. By extension, it depends upon anything which causes one molecule M to differ from another, M*. It will be shown in Chapter 17 that differences of internal energy act in this way. These energy differences disappear at $0°K$, including the translational energy which causes the randomness of disordered motion. Even the oscillatory motion of molecules in crystals finally vanishes at absolute zero, except for an irreducible "zero-point" vibration. For systems of one molecular species, in perfectly ordered crystals, the arrangement is unique and $W_0 = 1$. That is, $S_0 = k \ln W_0 = 0$.

6.9 Third Law Entropies

For any system, S_T is given by

$$S_T = \int_0^T \frac{C_P\ dT}{T} + S_0 \tag{6.68}$$

For a pure substance, invoking the third law, we have

$$S_T = \int_0^T \frac{C_P\ dT}{T} \tag{6.69}$$

The great importance of equation (6.69) in its application to chemistry lies in the possibility of evaluating the entropy change for a chemical reaction:

$$\Delta S_T = m S_T(\text{M}) + n S_T(\text{N}) + \ldots - a S_T(\text{A}) - b S_T(\text{B}) - \ldots \tag{6.70}$$

By the methods of Chapter 3 it is possible to evaluate the enthalpy change:

$$\Delta H_T = m\,\Delta H_f(M) + n\,\Delta H_f(N) + \ldots - a\,\Delta H_f(A) - b\,\Delta H_f(B) - \ldots$$

The position of chemical equilibrium can finally be obtained from $\Delta F = \Delta H - T\,\Delta S$, exclusively in terms of thermal measurements. Other methods of evaluating the thermodynamic state functions will be developed in Chapter 17.

The third law is a discovery, based on fact and amply tested. One method of demonstrating its validity consists in comparing measurements of S_T for a substance by two paths. From heat capacity measurements on rhombic (r) sulfur [E. D. Eastman and W. C. McGavock, *J. Am. Chem. Soc.*, **59**, 145 (1937)], $S_{386.6}(r) - S_0(r) = 8.827 \pm 0.06$ cal. deg.$^{-1}$ mole^{-1}. From the heat of transition

$$S_{386.6}(m) - S_{386.6}(r) = 0.258 \pm 0.03 \text{ cal. deg.}^{-1} \text{ mole}^{-1}$$

and therefore

$$S_{386.6}(m) - S_0(r) = 9.085 \pm 0.07 \text{ cal. deg.}^{-1} \text{ mole}^{-1}$$

When equation (6.69) was applied to measurements on pure, supercooled monoclinic (m) sulfur,

$$S_{386.6}(m) - S_0(m) = 9.04 \pm 0.10 \text{ cal. deg.}^{-1} \text{ mole}^{-1}$$

Within experimental error, $S_0(m) = S_0(r)$.

The procedure for evaluating S_T of a substance which undergoes one or more phase changes, beginning with the crystalline substance at 0°K, involves summing all terms of the type $\int C\,d\ln T$ for heating and all terms of the type $\Delta H/T$ for phase change. The simplest type of calculation for a gas would be

$$S_T = \int_0^{T_1} C(c)\,d\ln T + \Delta H(\text{fus.})/T_1$$

$$+ \int_{T_1}^{T_2} C(l)\,d\ln T + \Delta H(\text{vap.})/T_2 + \int_{T_2}^{T} C(g)\,d\ln T \qquad (6.71)$$

where T_1 is the melting point and T_2 the boiling point of the substance.

Let us consider the computation of S_{298}^0 in detail for chlorine gas. The data in Fig. 6.4 represent experimental measurements of C_P for solid and liquid

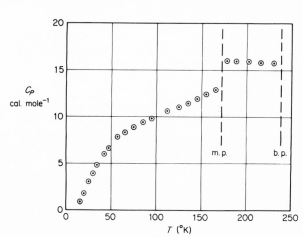

FIG. 6.4. Heat capacity of chlorine [W. F. Giauque and G. M. Powell, *J. Am. Chem. Soc.*, **61**, 1970 (1939)].

chlorine at various temperatures. Discontinuities in the heat capacity appear at 171.12°K, the melting point, and at 239.05°K, the normal boiling point.

The lowest temperature at which the heat capacity of solid chlorine has been measured is 15°K. A theory of low temperature heat capacity, due to P. Debye, gives

$$C_P = kT^3 \qquad (6.72)$$

where k is a constant. Using equation (6.69) (taking $S_0 = 0$), we may evaluate S_{15}

$$S_T = \int_0^T \frac{C_P \, dT}{T} = \int_0^T kT^2 \, dT$$

$$= \tfrac{1}{3}kT^3 = \tfrac{1}{3}C_P \text{ at } T$$

$$S_{15} = \frac{0.89}{3} = 0.30 \text{ cal. deg.}^{-1} \text{ mole}^{-1}$$

This is a small contribution to the total entropy at 298°K and an inaccuracy in the theory introduces no great error.[2]

The entropy change for heating solid chlorine from 15°K to its melting point, 171.12°K, is obtained by graphical evaluation of

$$S_{171.12} - S_{15} = \int_{15}^{171.12} C_P \, d \ln T$$

This is indicated in Fig. 6.5, where C_P is plotted versus $\ln T$. The area under the curve between limits is 16.57 cal. deg.$^{-1}$ mole^{-1}.

The measured $\Delta H_{171.12}$ of fusion is 1531 cal. mole^{-1} and, therefore,

$$\Delta S_{171.12} \text{ (fusion)} = \frac{1531}{171.12°} = 8.90 \text{ cal. deg.}^{-1} \text{ mole}^{-1}$$

From 171.12°K to 239.05°K, the entropy change for heating the liquid is evaluated by measuring the area

$$S_{239.05} - S_{171.12} = \int_{171.12}^{239.05} C_P \, d \ln T$$

under the curve between the given limits. The value of ΔS for this change is 5.23 cal. deg.$^{-1}$ mole^{-1}.

EXERCISE 6.8

From Fig. 6.4 estimate the mean value of C_P (Cl_2, l) between 171°K and 239°K. Find ΔS for this temperature change by application of equation (6.27) and compare with the graphical result.

At 239.05°K, the normal boiling point, the ΔH of vaporization is observed to be 4878 cal. mole^{-1}. Therefore,

$$\Delta S_{239.05} \text{(vap.)} = \frac{4878}{239.05°} = 20.41 \text{ cal. deg.}^{-1} \text{ mole}^{-1}$$

Tabulating these entropy terms, we have

---

[2] A more precise theoretical treatment gives 0.33 instead of 0.30.

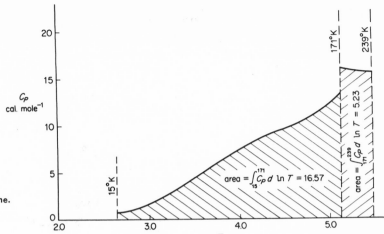

FIG. 6.5. Entropy of chlorine.

Temp. °K	Method	ΔS
0–15	Debye theory	0.33
15–171.12	graphical	16.57
171.12	$\Delta H/T$	8.90
171.12–239.05	graphical	5.23
239.05	$\Delta H/T$	20.41
		51.44 cal. deg.$^{-1}$ mole^{-1}

This is the measured third law entropy of gaseous chlorine at 1 atm. and 239.05°K. The standard entropy at this temperature differs by a small correction of $+ 0.12$ cal. deg.$^{-1}$ mole^{-1} for the gas imperfection of chlorine at this temperature. With this correction,

$$S^o_{239.05} \, (Cl_2) = 51.56 \text{ cal. deg.}^{-1} \text{ mole}^{-1}$$

To find $S^o_{298.10}$, C_P for chlorine gas from 239.05°K to 298.10°K is needed. This is practically constant at 8.20 cal. deg.$^{-1}$ mole^{-1} over this temperature range, and therefore

$$S_{298.10} - S_{239.05} = 8.20 \times 2.3 \log \frac{298.10°}{239.05°} = 1.83 \text{ cal. deg.}^{-1} \text{ mole}^{-1}$$

and

$$S^o_{298} = 51.56 + 1.83 = 53.39 \text{ cal. deg.}^{-1} \text{ mole}^{-1}$$

It is also possible to calculate S^o_{298} from a complete knowledge of the molecular properties such as atomic masses, interatomic distances, vibration frequencies, etc. These properties are obtained by detailed analysis of molecular spectra, as indicated in Chapter 17. The entropies in Table 6.1 include values obtained from this source as well as from heat capacity measurements.

The standard entropy change for any process

$$aA + bB + \ldots = mM + nN + \ldots$$

involving substances for which S_T^o is known can be computed simply by

$$\Delta S_T^o = mS_T^o(M) + nS_T^o(N) + \ldots - aS_T^o(A) - bS_T^o(B) - \ldots$$

For example, ΔS_{298}^o for

$$\tfrac{1}{2}N_2(g) + \tfrac{2}{3}H_2(g) = NH_3(g)$$

is

$$\Delta S_{298}^o = S_{298}^o(NH_3) - \tfrac{1}{2}S_{298}^o(N_2) - \tfrac{3}{2}S_{298}^o(H_2)$$
$$\Delta S_{298}^o = 46.01 - \tfrac{1}{2}(45.77) - \tfrac{3}{2}(31.21)$$
$$= -23.67 \text{ cal. deg.}^{-1} \text{ mole}^{-1}$$

The value of ΔS^o, together with the value of ΔH^o at the same temperature, gives ΔF^o. For the synthesis of ammonia

$$\Delta F_{298}^o = \Delta H_{298}^o - T\Delta S_{298}^o$$
$$= -11,040 - 298°(-23.67)$$
$$= -3990 \text{ cal. mole}^{-1}$$

The agreement of this value of ΔF_{298}^o with that given in Chapter 5 represents a successful test of the validity of the third law of thermodynamics. It is important to realize that the present value is obtained without any use of equilibrium data. That is, the third law permits a prediction of the equilibrium state in a chemical system from measurements of the properties of the components and the ΔH for the change.

TABLE 6.1

THIRD LAW ENTROPIES*

Substance	S_{298}^o (cal. deg.$^{-1}$ mole^{-1})	Substance		S_{298}^o (cal. deg.$^{-1}$ mole^{-1})
O_2 (g)	49.003		H_2S (g)	49.15
H_2 (g)	31.211		NO (g)	50.339
N_2 (g)	45.767		NO_2 (g)	57.47
C (graphite)	1.3609		NH_3 (g)	46.01
Cl_2 (g)	53.286		CO (g)	47.301
Br_2 (g)	58.639		CO_2 (g)	51.061
I_2 (s)	27.9	methane,	CH_4 (g)	44.50
S (rhombic)	7.62	ethane,	C_2H_6 (g)	54.85
H_2O (g)	45.106	propane,	C_3H_8 (g)	64.51
H_2O (l)	16.716	normal butane,	C_4H_{10} (g)	74.10
HCl (g)	44.617	isobutane,	C_4H_{10} (g)	70.42
HBr (g)	47.437	normal pentane,	C_5H_{12} (g)	83.27
HI (g)	49.314	normal hexane,	C_6H_{14} (g)	92.45
SO_2 (g)	59.40	benzene,	C_6H_6 (g)	64.34
SO_3 (g)	61.24	ethylene,	C_2H_4 (g)	52.45
		acetylene,	C_2H_2 (g)	47.997

*From *Selected Values of Chemical Thermodynamic Properties*, Circular 500, National Bureau of Standards, 1952, and *Selected Values of the Properties of Hydrocarbons*, Circular C461, National Bureau of Standards, 1947.

The value of ΔS^o for a chemical change at some temperature other than 25° is obtained by application of equation (6.27) to each of the reactants and products. When the heat capacities may be considered constant, the general expression is

$$\Delta S_2 - \Delta S_1 = \Delta C_P \ln \frac{T_2}{T_1}$$

EXERCISE 6.9

Use data from Table 6.1 and the heat capacities from Table 2.1 to find ΔS_{373} for the combustion of methane to form carbon dioxide and water vapor.

Ans. $-.71$ cal. deg. $^{-1}$ mole $^{-1}$.

SUMMARY, CHAPTER 6

1. Limiting efficiency of cyclic heat engines

$$\eta_{\text{lim.}} = \frac{w_{\text{max.}}}{q_2} = \frac{T_2 - T_1}{T_2}$$

2. The entropy, defined by $dS = \dfrac{dq_{\text{rev.}}}{T}$

    For heat absorption

$$S_2 - S_1 = \int_{T_1}^{T_2} \frac{C\, dT}{T}$$

    For isothermal ideal gas changes

$$\Delta S = nR \ln \frac{V_2}{V_1} = nR \ln \frac{P_1}{P_2}$$

    For reversible phase transformations

$$\Delta S = \frac{\Delta H}{T}$$

    For mixing

$$\Delta S_{\text{mix.}} = - R \sum X_i \ln X_i$$

3. The Helmholtz free energy, defined by

$$A = E - TS$$

    The Gibbs free energy, defined by

$$F = H - TS$$

    For an isothermal change

$$\Delta A = \Delta E - T\,\Delta S = - w_{\text{max., tot.}}$$

$$\Delta F = \Delta H - T\,\Delta S = - w_{\text{max., net.}}$$

    For pressure and temperature changes of a pure substance

$$dF = \left(\frac{\partial F}{\partial P}\right)_T dP + \left(\frac{\partial F}{\partial T}\right)_P dT = V\, dP - S\, dT$$

    At constant temperature

$$dF = V\, dP$$

For ideal gas expansion

$$\Delta F = RT \ln \frac{P_2}{P_1}$$

At constant pressure

$$dF = -S \, dT$$

For a chemical reaction or phase transformation

$$\left[\frac{\partial(\Delta F)}{\partial T}\right]_p = -\Delta S$$

$$\frac{\partial(\Delta F/T)}{\partial T} = -\frac{\Delta H}{T^2}$$

$$\frac{\partial \ln K_{\mathscr{P}}}{\partial 1/T} = \frac{\Delta H}{R}$$

4. The third law of thermodynamics

Probability

$$S = k \ln W$$

Third law

$$S_0 = 0$$

Third law entropy

$$S_T = S_0 + \int_0^T C \, d \ln T$$

Evaluate $\int_0^T C \, d \ln T$ from heat capacity data.

Application of data on S_T^o to chemical reactions

$$\Delta S_T^o = m S_T^o(M) + n S_T^o(N) + \ldots - a S_T^o(A) - b S_T^o(B) - \ldots$$

PROBLEMS, CHAPTER 6

1. If the heat sink of a cyclic heat engine is at $0°$, what must be the temperature of the heat source for the engine to have a limiting efficiency of 0.5?

Ans. $273°$.

2. What is the minimum work per hr. which must be expended to keep a refrigerator at a temperature of $-5°$ when the room temperature is $30°$ and heat flows into the refrigerator at a rate of 1000 kcal. hr.$^{-1}$? How much heat hr.$^{-1}$ is liberated to the room?   *Ans.* 130 kcal. hr.$^{-1}$, 1130 kcal.hr.$^{-1}$.

3. A sample of ideal gas is carried through a reversible Carnot cycle. It absorbs 1000 cal. at $400°K$ (step I), expands adiabatically to $300°K$ (step II), releases x cal. at $300°K$ (step III), and is restored adiabatically to the initial state (step IV).

(a) Evaluate ΔS for each step.

(b) Evaluate x (step III).

(c) Evaluate $w_{max.}$ for the cycle.

Ans. (a) $\Delta S(I) = 2.50$ cal. deg.$^{-1}$, $\Delta S(II) = 0$, $\Delta S(III) = -2.50$ cal. deg.$^{-1}$, $\Delta S(IV) = 0$ cal. deg.$^{-1}$, (b) -750 cal., (c) 250 cal.

4. Find ΔS_{268} for H_2O (l, $-5°$) = H_2O (s, $-5°$), using C_P (H_2O, l) = 18 cal. deg.$^{-1}$ mole^{-1}, C_P (H_2O, s) = 9 cal. deg.$^{-1}$ mole^{-1}, and ΔH_{273} (H_2O, fusion) = 1440 cal. mole^{-1}.   *Ans.* -5.11 cal. deg.$^{-1}$.

5. Using data in Table 6.1, find ΔS_{298}^0 for combustion of ethane to form carbon dioxide and liquid water. Compare $T\,\Delta S$ for this reaction with the heat of combustion from Table 3.1.   *Ans.* $\Delta S = -74.1$ cal. deg.$^{-1}$ mole^{-1}.

6. Evaluate ΔS for

$$H_2O \text{ (l, 1 atm., } 125°) = H_2O \text{ (g, 1 atm., } 125°)$$

Some of the following data may be useful: C_P (H_2O, l) = 18 cal. deg.$^{-1}$ mole^{-1}; C_P (H_2O, g) = 9 cal. deg.$^{-1}$ mole^{-1}; ΔH_{373} (H_2O, vap.) = 9713 cal. mole^{-1}; ΔH_{398} (H_2O, vap.) = 9400 cal. mole^{-1}; vapor pressure at 125°, 1740.5 mm.

Ans. 25.4 cal. deg.$^{-1}$.

7. In the temperature range 300–1000°K, the molar heat capacity at constant pressure of water vapor is given by $7.0 + 3.0 \times 10^{-3}\,T$ cal. deg.$^{-1}$ (see Exercise 2.3). Find S_{1000}^0 for water vapor.   *Ans.* 55.6 cal. deg.$^{-1}$ mole^{-1}.

8. Devise and describe a reversible path for the process

$$H_2O \text{ (l, 3 atm. } 125°) = H_2O \text{ (g, 1 atm., } 100°)$$

Use data from Problem 6 to evaluate ΔS for the system.

Ans. 24.9 cal. deg.$^{-1}$ mole^{-1}.

9. From the data of Problem 5, find ΔF_{298}^0 for the combustion of ethane.

Ans. -351 kcal. mole^{-1}.

10. One mole of helium at 1 atm. and 25° expands isothermally into a connecting 10 l. evacuated container. Evaluate q, ΔH, ΔF, and ΔS.

Ans. $q = \Delta H = 0$, $\Delta F = -203$ cal., $\Delta S = 0.681$ cal. deg.$^{-1}$.

---

11. Find $\Delta S_{\text{system}} + \Delta S_{\text{surroundings}}$ for the irreversible process described in problem 10.

12. When the reaction

$$Cd \text{ (s)} + Pb \text{ } (NO_3)_2 \text{ (aq., 1 M)} = Cd \text{ } (NO_3)_2 \text{ (aq., 1 M)} + Pb \text{ (s)}$$

occurs without producing any electric work, the heat liberated at 25° is 17,690 cal. When the same reaction occurs reversibly in a galvanic cell, it produces electric work equivalent to 12,750 cal.
(a) Find $q_{\text{rev.}}$, the heat effect which accompanies the reversible operation of the cell.
(b) Find ΔS_{298} for the reaction written above.

13. For each of the following changes, state whether ΔH, ΔS, and ΔF are positive, negative, zero, or indeterminate:
(a) Vaporization of water at 120° and 1 atm.
(b) Melting of ice at 0° and 1 atm.
(c) Mixing of ideal gases at constant T and P.
(d) Expansion of an ideal gas into a vacuum.
(e) Adiabatic, reversible expansion of an ideal gas.

14. What is the maximum work in joules hr.$^{-1}$ which can be produced by a cyclic heat engine operating between 0° and 100° and consuming 10^6 cal. hr.$^{-1}$?

15. From data in Table 6.1, find the change in ΔF^o per degree at 298°K for

$$\tfrac{1}{2} N_2 \text{ (g)} + \tfrac{3}{2} H_2 \text{ (g)} = NH_3 \text{ (g)}$$

16. Find ΔS for

$$N_2 \text{ (g, 1 atm., 25°)} = N_2 \text{ (g, 10 atm., 100°)}$$

17. Find the molar entropy of N_2O at its normal boiling point from the following data [R. W. Blue and W. F. Giauque, *J. Am. Chem. Soc.*, **57**, 991 (1935)]: $S_{14} = 0.214$ cal. deg.$^{-1}$ mole^{-1}; melting point $= 182.26°$K; heat of fusion $= 1563$ cal. mole^{-1}; normal boiling point $= 184.59°$K; heat of vaporization $= 3958$ cal. mole^{-1}. The heat capacity at various temperatures is

T (°K)			20	30	40	50	60	70
C_P (cal. deg.$^{-1}$ mole^{-1})			1.51	3.46	5.13	6.52	7.56	8.32
80	90	100	110	120	130	140	150	
8.95	9.44	9.90	10.32	10.77	11.25	11.72	12.19	
160	170	180	182.26 $-$ 184.59°K					
12.71	13.30	13.98	C_P (l) 18.57					

18. Evaluate ΔS for releasing 1 mole O_2 at 25°, 1 atm., into the air at the same temperature and pressure.

19. It is notoriously difficult to reduce systems to low temperatures and keep them there. Liquids with low boiling points are commonly used as refrigerants. Heat leaking into the system is offset by the latent heat of vaporization. According to Trouton's rule, $\Delta S_{vap.} \cong 21$ cal. deg.$^{-1}$ mole^{-1} at the boiling point. How many moles of refrigerant must evaporate per kcal. leaking into the system when the refrigerant is
  (a) Liquid nitrogen, b. p. $= 77°$K?
  (b) Liquid hydrogen, b. p. $= 20.4°$K?
  (c) Liquid helium, b. p. $= 4.2°$K?

20. At 473°K, Ag_2O is in equilibrium with oxygen when $P_{O_2} = 1.35$ atm. Evaluate ΔS_{473} for the process

$$2 Ag_2O \text{ (s)} = 4 Ag \text{ (s)} + O_2 \text{ (g)}$$

at a constant pressure of 1 atm., given $\Delta H_{473} = -14.4$ kcal.

21. For two liquids A and B which obey Raoult's law, $\Delta H_{mix.} = 0$ and consequently $\Delta H_{vap.}$ (A) and $\Delta H_{vap.}$ (B) are the same for the pure liquids and for the mixture. Devise and describe a reversible process for mixing two liquids, and show that $q_{rev.}/T = -R (X_A \ln X_A + X_B \ln X_B)$.

22. An ideal, monatomic gas expands reversibly and adiabatically from P_1, V_1, T_1 to P_2, V_2, T_2 and $\Delta S = 0$. Replace this process by a sequence of reversible processes, none of which is adiabatic, and show that the sum of the component entropy changes is zero.

23. In a refrigerator, or heat pump, the work $w_{rev.}$ is required to deliver heat $q_{rev.}$ from the system at T_1 to the surroundings at T_2, where $T_2 > T_1$. Show that $|w_{rev.}|/|q_{rev.}| = (T_2 - T_1)/T_1$.

24. Find $w_{rev.}$ required to remove $q_{rev.} = 1$ kcal. to a room at 298°K from a system to be maintained at the temperature of
  (a) Boiling nitrogen, 77°K.
  (b) Boiling hydrogen, 20.4°K.
  (c) Boiling helium, 4.2°K.
  (d) Absolute zero.

25. According to Hildebrand's rule, entropies of vaporization of many "normal" liquids are nearly equal when compared at equal vapor concentrations. Specifically, $\Delta S' = \Delta H'_{vap.}/T' \cong 27$ cal. mole^{-1} deg.$^{-1}$ when T' is the temperature at which vapor concentration is 5×10^{-3} mole l.$^{-1}$ and $\Delta H'_{vap.}$ is the heat of vaporization at T'. Show, in a qualitative way, that $\Delta S' =$ const. may be expected from $S = k \ln W$.

26. As $T \to 0$, S_0 for nitrous oxide attains a limiting value 1.14 cal. mole^{-1} deg.$^{-1}$. This value can be understood in terms of nearly random NNO and ONN arrangements of the almost symmetrical molecules in the crystal lattice. Complete randomness would lead to $S_0 = R \ln 2$. What would be the ratio of vapor pressures of N_2O from such an imperfect crystal and from a perfectly random crystal if $\Delta H_{vap.}$ is the same?

27. The equilibrium vapor pressure of water vapor over $Ca(OH)_2$ at 25° is 0.8 mm. Values of ΔH^0_f at 298°K for $Ca(OH)_2(s)$, $CaO(s)$ and $H_2O(g)$ are -235.65, -151.79, and -57.11 kcal. mole^{-1}, respectively. Ignoring minor effects, find ΔS_{298} for $Ca(OH_2)(s) = CaO(s) + H_2O(g)$.

28. The entropy of crystalline nitric oxide approaches $\frac{1}{2} R \ln 2$ as the temperature approaches zero. Show that this value would be consistent with a dimer having a rectangular structure, and randomly oriented as

$$\begin{array}{ccc} \text{N O} & & \text{O N} \\ & \text{and} & \\ \text{O N} & & \text{N O} \end{array}$$

in the crystal [W. J. Dulmage, E. A. Meyers, and W. N. Lipscomb, *J. Chem. Phys.*, **19**, 1432 (1951)].

7

PHASE EQUILIBRIA
AND COLLIGATIVE
PROPERTIES

7.1 Vaporization Equilibria

The second law of thermodynamics applies as well to various phase equilibria as it does to chemical equilibria. Both the methods to be used and the relationships to be developed will closely resemble those of Chapter 5. This similarity is not accidental, but real and fundamental, and deserves careful attention.

The isothermal free energy changes for some process at each of two temperatures can be related by considering the cycle

$$\text{Reactants (any state, } T) \quad \xrightarrow{\Delta F_T} \quad \text{Products (any state, } T)$$
$$\downarrow \qquad\qquad\qquad\qquad\qquad\qquad\qquad \uparrow$$
$$\text{Reactants (standard state, } T) \quad \xrightarrow{\Delta F^o_T} \quad \text{Products (standard state, } T)$$

The expression obtained will be of the form

$$\Delta F_T = \Delta F^o_T + RT \ln Q \tag{7.1}$$

where Q is the reaction function of properties describing the states of the system to which ΔF_T applies. ΔF^o_T is the corresponding standard free energy change, that is, the free energy change for the process in which reactants and products are in their standard states.

For any reversible change at constant temperature and pressure $\Delta F = 0$. That is, for the change in state

$$\text{Reactants (equil. state, } T) \rightarrow \text{Products (equil. state, } T)$$

172

$$\Delta F_T = 0 = \Delta F_T^o + RT \ln K \tag{7.2}$$

where K is the equilibrium function (see section 5.9). It has the same mathematical form as the reaction function, but refers to the equilibrium state (or states) of the system. Since ΔF_T^o is the free energy change for a uniquely defined change in state, it has a single numerical value for a given system at a given temperature. It follows that K also has a unique value, called the equilibrium constant.

The equilibrium to be considered first is vaporization of a pure liquid or pure solid. If the uniform pressure on a system consisting of liquid (or solid) plus vapor equals the vapor pressure at that temperature, the system is in an equilibrium state. Other pressures are possible, but do not correspond to equilibrium states.

In general terms, isothermal vaporization of a liquid may be represented by

$$A(l, P) = A(g, P) \text{ at constant } T$$

where P is any pressure, not necessarily the vapor pressure. An expression for ΔF_T may be obtained by use of an isothermal cycle

$$
\begin{array}{ccc}
A(l, P) & \xrightarrow{\Delta F_T} & A(g, P) \\
\Delta F_T(i) \downarrow \cong 0 & \Delta F_T(iii) \uparrow = RT \ln\left(\dfrac{P}{1}\right) \\
A(l, P = 1) & \xrightarrow{\Delta F_T(ii) = \Delta F_T^o} & A(g, P = 1)
\end{array}
$$

Since F is a property of state, ΔF does not depend on path and

$$\Delta F_T = \Delta F_T(i) + \Delta F_T(ii) + \Delta F_T(iii) \tag{7.3}$$

The dependence of free energy on pressure at constant temperature is given by equation (6.55).

$$dF_T = V\, dP \tag{7.4}$$

Considering the vapor to be an ideal gas, we have

$$\Delta F_T(iii) = RT \ln\left(\frac{P}{1}\right) \text{ per mole} \tag{7.5}$$

Except near the critical temperature, the molar volume of a liquid is much less than the molar volume of its vapor and

$$\Delta F_T(i) \cong 0$$

$\Delta F_T(ii)$ for vaporization of liquid at 1 atm. will be designated the standard free energy of vaporization $\Delta F_T^o(\text{vap.})$. Substituting these expressions into equation (7.3) gives

$$\Delta F_T = \Delta F_T^o(\text{vap.}) + RT \ln P \tag{7.6}$$

When the pressure P is the equilibrium vapor pressure $\mathscr{P}$, $\Delta F_T = 0$.

$$\Delta F_T = 0 = \Delta F_T^o(\text{vap.}) + RT \ln \mathscr{P}$$

$$\Delta F_T^o(\text{vap.}) = -RT \ln \mathscr{P} \tag{7.7}$$

This is a specific example of equation (7.2) and in this case $K = \mathscr{P}$. For example, the vapor pressure of water at 25° is 23.6 mm., or 0.0311 atm.

$$\Delta F_{298}^0(\text{vap. } H_2O) = -1.987 \times 298° \ln 0.0311$$

$$= 2057 \text{ cal. mole}^{-1}$$

This is the free energy change for

$$H_2O(l, 1 \text{ atm.}) = H_2O(g, 1 \text{ atm.})$$

which is evidently a forbidden change at 25°.

EXERCISE 7.1

The vapor pressure of ice at $-10°$ is 2.0 mm. Compute ΔF_{263}^0 for

$$H_2O \text{ (s)} = H_2O \text{ (g)}$$

when the standard state of the vapor is taken to be 1 atm.   *Ans.* 3105 cal. mole⁻¹.

7.2 Temperature Dependence of Vapor Pressure

Since $\mathscr{P}$, the equilibrium vapor pressure, is the equilibrium function in a liquid-vapor or solid-vapor system, its temperature dependence may be obtained by application of the Gibbs-Helmholtz equation in the form

$$\frac{d(\Delta F/T)}{dT} = -\frac{\Delta H}{T^2} \tag{7.8}$$

Since

$$\ln \mathscr{P} = \frac{-\Delta F^0 \text{ (vap.)}}{RT}$$

then

$$\frac{d \ln \mathscr{P}}{dT} = \frac{\Delta H^0 \text{ (vap.)}}{RT^2} \tag{7.9}$$

where ΔH^0(vap.) is the change in heat content for the standard change in state

$$A(l, P = 1, T) = A(g, P = 1, T)$$

When ΔH^0(vap.) may be considered independent of temperature, equation (7.9) integrates to

$$\ln \mathscr{P} = \frac{-\Delta H^0 \text{ (vap.)}}{RT} + \text{const.}$$

or

$$\ln \frac{\mathscr{P}_2}{\mathscr{P}_1} = \frac{\Delta H^0 \text{ (vap.)}}{R} \left(\frac{T_2 - T_1}{T_2 T_1}\right) \tag{7.10}$$

Equation (7.10) may be demonstrated graphically by plotting $\log \mathscr{P}$ versus $1/T$ (°K), as shown in Fig. 7.1. The experimental points lie on a practically straight line of slope $-\Delta H^0$(vap.)/2.3 R. ΔH^0(vap.) of both liquids and solids is invariably positive, and the curves have negative slope.

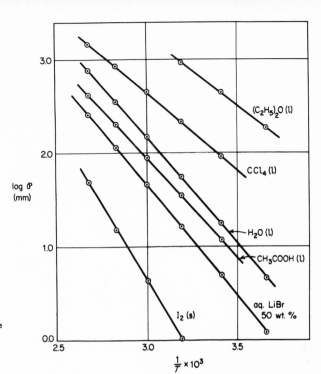

FIG. 7.1. Vapor pressure—temperature relationship.

EXERCISE 7.2

From the slope of the appropriate curve in Fig. 7.1 estimate ΔH° (vap.) for carbon tetrachloride.   *Ans.* 7.5 kcal. mole^{-1}.

Analytical use of equation (7.10) may be demonstrated by calculation of ΔH° (vap.) of water from data given previously.

$$\log \frac{760}{23.6} = \frac{\Delta H^\circ \text{ (vap.)}}{2.3\,R} \left(\frac{373^\circ - 298^\circ}{373^\circ \times 298^\circ} \right)$$

$$\Delta H^\circ \text{ (vap.)} = 10{,}230 \text{ cal. mole}^{-1}$$

Note that the unit of pressure used is immaterial, since only the ratio of pressures is used. Furthermore, the difference between ΔH°(vap.) and ΔH(vap.) is small, and the distinction is not ordinarily noted. The value of ΔH thus obtained from the vapor pressure at two temperatures is, to a good approximation, that for the mean temperature; i.e., $(100 + 25)/2 = 62.5^\circ$. A more precise value of ΔH at any temperature is obtained from the slope of the $\log \mathscr{P}$ versus $1/T$ plot. This is not quite a straight line, because of the small variation of ΔH°(vap.) with temperature and because of the use of the ideal gas law in deriving equations (7.4) and (7.10).

EXERCISE 7.3

Use equation (7.10) and the result of the preceding example to compute the vapor pressure of water at 50°.   *Ans.* 90 mm.

According to Trouton's rule (cf. problem 6.19), the molar heat of vaporization in calories is approximately 21 times the absolute boiling point. Equivalently, $\Delta S(\text{vap.}) \cong 21$ cal. deg.$^{-1}$ mole^{-1}. Values of $\Delta H(\text{vap.})$ and $\Delta S(\text{vap.})$ in Table 7.1 show that this is often, but not always, obeyed. Water and several other substances do not fit this generalization very well and are said to be abnormal liquids. Hydrocarbons usually have normal constants. The rule permits estimation of the vapor pressures of a liquid over a range of temperature from a knowledge of its normal boiling point.

TABLE 7.1

VAPORIZATION OF LIQUIDS

Substance	Normal boiling point (°C)	$\Delta H^o(\text{vap.})$ (cal. mole^{-1})	$\Delta S^o(\text{vap.})$ (cal. deg.$^{-1}$ mole^{-1})
Water, H_2O	100.0	9717	26.04
Carbon tetrachloride, CCl_4	76.7	7170	20.5
Acetic acid, CH_3COOH	118.2	5830	14.9
Ethanol, C_2H_5OH	78.5	9220	26.22
Normal butane, C_4H_{10}	−0.5	5320	19.63
Normal pentane, C_5H_{12}	36.1	6160	19.92
Normal hexane, C_6H_{14}	68.7	6896	20.17
Benzene, C_6H_6	80.1	7353	20.81
Toluene, C_7H_8	110.6	8000	20.85
Ethyl benzene, C_8H_{10}	136.2	8600	21.01
Cyclohexane, C_6H_{12}	80.7	7190	20.3

EXERCISE 7.4

The normal boiling point of 2-methyl hexane is 90°. Estimate its vapor pressure at 0°.   *Ans.* 23.4 mm.

7.3 Vapor Pressure of Solutions

When a volatile substance is present in a homogeneous solution, its partial vapor pressure over the solution is always less than the vapor pressure of the pure substance at the same temperature. For a solution of fixed composition, the partial vapor pressure of any volatile component behaves very much like the vapor pressure of a pure liquid with respect to variation of temperature.

For the sake of simplicity, consider a solution which consists of a volatile solvent and a nonvolatile solute. In this case the vapor pressure of the solution is that of the solvent over the solution. By a simple modification of the treatment used in sections 7.1 and 7.2 we shall show that the temperature dependence of the vapor pressure of such a solution obeys the same law as that for a pure liquid.

The change in state of interest here is

$$A(\text{soln.}, X_A, P) = A(g, P)$$

at constant temperature and where X_A is the mole fraction of the volatile solvent in the solution. Employing the same type of cycle used previously, namely,

$$A\ (\text{soln.},\ X_A,\ P) \xrightarrow{\ \Delta F\ } A\ (\text{g},\ P)$$
$$\Delta F\ \Big| \cong 0 \qquad\qquad \Delta F\ \Big| = RT\ln\left(\frac{P}{1}\right)$$
$$A\ (\text{soln.},\ X_A,\ P=1) \xrightarrow{\ \Delta F^{o}\ } A\ (\text{g},\ P=1)$$

and the same approximation with respect to $\Delta F(i)$ (solution subjected only to the pressure of vapor), we obtain for the change of interest

$$\Delta F_T = \Delta F_T^o(\text{vap. soln.}) + RT\ln P \tag{7.11}$$

When $P = \mathscr{P}$, the equilibrium vapor pressure of the solution at the temperature of interest, $\Delta F_T = 0$ and

$$\Delta F_T^o(\text{vap. soln.}) = -RT\ln\mathscr{P} \tag{7.12}$$

ΔF_T^o(vap. soln.) is to be distinguished from ΔF_T^o(vap.) employed in the preceding section, since the change so specified is not vaporization of the pure liquid. It is, rather, vaporization of the liquid from a solution, in which its free energy content is less than in the pure liquid state. To illustrate this difference, consider the fact that the vapor pressure of pure liquid water at 25° is 23.6 mm., whereas its vapor pressure over a solution containing 5 moles of sucrose $(C_{12}H_{22}O_{11})$ in 1000 g. of water is 20.7 mm. Therefore, from the pure liquid

$$\Delta F_{298}^o(\text{vap.}) = 2057\ \text{cal. mole}^{-1}$$

as computed previously, whereas for the sucrose solution

$$\Delta F_{298}^o(\text{vap. soln.}) = -\ 1.987 \times 298° \times 2.303\ \log\ (20.7/760)$$
$$= 2135\ \text{cal. mole}^{-1}$$

EXERCISE 7.5

From the data given above compute ΔF_{298} for
$$H_2O\ (l) = H_2O\ (\text{in 5 molal sucrose soln.})$$

Ans. $\Delta F_{298} = -78$ cal.

The equilibrium function in this type of system is simply $K = \mathscr{P}$, and the Gibbs-Helmholtz equation applies.

$$\ln\frac{\mathscr{P}_2}{\mathscr{P}_1} = \frac{\Delta H^o\ (\text{vap. soln.})}{R}\left(\frac{T_2 - T_1}{T_2 T_1}\right) \tag{7.13}$$

This equation is applied in exactly the same fashion as equation (7.10). A graphical illustration is given in Fig. 7.1. ΔH^o(vap. soln.) from either graphical or analytical application of equation (7.13) is the heat of vaporization of the solvent *from the solution* and may differ from that obtained for the pure liquid. If there is an appreciable ΔH for the formation of the solution from the pure components, ΔH^o(vap. soln.) will differ from ΔH^o(vap.) by this amount. This will result in a difference in the slopes of the curves for the pure solvent and the solution.

It can be shown that solutions which obey Raoult's law ($P = P^0 X$, equation 1.24) are produced isothermally without change in enthalpy. That is, $\Delta H_T = 0$ for

$$n_A A(l) + n_B B(l) = \text{soln. A, B}(X_A, X_B)$$

If Raoult's law applies, then

$$\ln \mathscr{P}_A = \ln \mathscr{P}_A^0 + \ln X_A \tag{7.14}$$

and the temperature derivative at fixed composition is

$$\left(\frac{\partial \ln \mathscr{P}_A}{\partial T} \right)_{X_A} = \left(\frac{\partial \ln \mathscr{P}_A^0}{\partial T} \right)_{X_A=1} \tag{7.15}$$

That is, the temperature derivative of the logarithm of the vapor pressure of A (or B) over the solution is the same as that for the pure liquid, and it follows that

$$\Delta H^o(\text{vap. soln.}) = \Delta H^o(\text{vap. solvent})$$

Combining the thermochemical equations, we have

$$\text{A (pure liq.)} = \text{A (g, 1 atm.)}; \quad \Delta H^o \text{ (vap. solvent)}$$
$$\text{A (g, 1 atm.)} = \text{A (soln.)}; \quad -\Delta H^o \text{ (vap. soln.)}$$

$$\overline{\text{A (pure liq.)} = \text{A (soln.)}; \quad \Delta H^o \text{ (soln.)} = 0}$$

It is evident that the enthalpy change in forming a Raoult's law solution is zero.

7.4 Heterogeneous Chemical Equilibria

The thermodynamic treatment of chemical equilibria involving gases and pure solids (or gases and pure liquids) is closely related to that employed for vaporization. Consider the generalized chemical change

$$a\text{A(s)} + b\text{B(g)} = m\text{M(s)} + n\text{N(g)}$$

in which, for purposes of illustration, A and M are taken to be pure solids and N and B ideal gases. The equilibrium function for such a system is developed by the familiar procedure of relating the change of interest to the change for standard states by means of the isothermal cycle

$$
\begin{array}{ccc}
a\text{A (s)} + b\text{B (g, } P_B) & \xrightarrow{\Delta F} & m\text{M (s)} + n\text{N (g, } P_N) \\
\end{array}
$$

$$\left|\Delta F = 0 \quad \right| \Delta F = bRT \ln\frac{1}{P_B} \quad \right| \Delta F = 0 \quad \right| \Delta F = nRT \ln\frac{P_N}{1}$$

$$a\text{A (s)} + b\text{B (g, } P_B = 1) \xrightarrow{\Delta F^o} m\text{M (s)} + n\text{N (g, } P_N = 1)$$

The most convenient choice of standard state for a pure solid or liquid is the pure state itself, and we neglect the small pressure dependence of the free energy. If solid or liquid solutions are involved, the dependence of free energy on concentration must be considered, as shown in the next section. The pressure dependence of the free energy of B and N may be given as usual for ideal gases, and

$$\Delta F_T = \Delta F_T^o + RT \ln Q_P \qquad (7.16)$$

where

$$Q_P = P_N^n / P_B^b$$

is the reaction function of pressures. It resembles the function used for all-gas systems, but the reason that P_A and P_M do not appear in the functions Q and K is not that these pressures are negligibly small, since solids may have vapor pressures of many atm. (e.g., solid CO_2). Rather, P_A and P_M do not enter into Q_P because the terms in $\int VdP$ for solids (and liquids) contribute little to the summation of free energy terms.

For a set of pressures corresponding to an equilibrium state, $\Delta F_T = 0$ for the process, and

$$0 = \Delta F_T^o + RT \ln K_{\mathscr{P}}$$
$$\Delta F_T^o = - RT \ln K_{\mathscr{P}} \qquad (7.17)$$

The decomposition of calcium carbonate illustrates the application of equations (7.16) and (7.17).

$$CaCO_3(s) = CaO(s) + CO_2(g)$$

At $800°$, $\mathscr{P}_{CO_2} = 167$ mm., provided both solid phases are also present, and

$$K_{\mathscr{P}} = \mathscr{P}_{CO_2}$$

When the conventional standard states are adopted, the value of $K_{\mathscr{P}}$ is

$$K_{\mathscr{P}} = 167/760 = 0.220 (atm.)$$

From equation (7.17) we obtain

$$\Delta F_{1073}^o = - 1.987 \times 1073 \times 2.303 \log 0.220 = 3.23 \text{ kcal. mole}^{-1}$$

This is the free energy change for

$$CaCO_3(s) = CaO(s) + CO_2(g, 1 \text{ atm.})$$

at $800°$, which is evidently a forbidden change. That is, at $800°$ in a system containing the two solids and carbon dioxide at 1 atm., the reaction to form calcium carbonate is permitted.

The equilibrium state of the system $CaCO_3$—CaO—CO_2 at any temperature is described by a single pressure, that of carbon dioxide, which can have only one value at a given temperature. However, when two or more gaseous substances are involved in the reaction of interest, an infinite number of equilibrium states is possible. An example is

$$NH_4HS(s) = NH_3(g) + H_2S(g)$$

At $25°$, the total gas pressure at equilibrium is 481 mm., consisting of equimolar amounts of ammonia and hydrogen sulfide, and, therefore,

$$K_{\mathscr{P}} = \mathscr{P}_{NH_3} \cdot \mathscr{P}_{H_2S}$$

$$= \left(\frac{\mathscr{P}_{total}}{2}\right)^2 = \left(\frac{481/760}{2}\right)^2 = 0.10 \, (atm.^2)$$

At any combination of pressures for which

$$\mathscr{P}_{NH_3} \, \mathscr{P}_{H_2S} < 0.10 \, (atm.)^2$$

it is not possible for NH_4HS to form. It is possible, by addition of one of the products to the system, to decrease the degree of dissociation of the solid. For instance, if the ammonia pressure is increased to 1 atm., the equilibrium pressure of hydrogen sulfide is decreased.

$$K_{\mathscr{P}} = 0.10 = 1 \times \mathscr{P}_{H_2S}$$
$$\mathscr{P}_{H_2S} = 0.10 \, atm.$$

whereas previously the hydrogen sulfide pressure was 0.316 atm.

EXERCISE 7.6

The standard free energy of formation of gaseous hydrogen sulfide from rhombic sulfur and hydrogen at 25° is -7.892 kcal. mole^{-1}. Formulate the equilibrium function for the reaction

$$S \, (rhombic) + H_2 \, (g) = H_2S \, (g)$$

and compute the equilibrium constant at 25°.

Ans. $K_{\mathscr{P}} = \mathscr{P}_{H_2S}/\mathscr{P}_{H_2} = 6.13 \times 10^5$.

The temperature dependence of the equilibrium constant in a heterogeneous reaction is obtained in the usual fashion by application of the Gibbs-Helmholtz equation (6.60) to equation (7.17).

$$\ln \frac{K_2}{K_1} = \frac{\Delta H^o}{R} \left(\frac{T_2 - T_1}{T_2 T_1}\right) \tag{7.18}$$

In the system $CaCO_3$—CaO—CO_2, the equilibrium constant is simply the equilibrium pressure of carbon dioxide, and from its dependence on temperature, ΔH^o for the reaction is obtained. For example, the carbon dioxide pressure is 167 mm. at 800° and 372 mm. at 850°. From these data we find

$$\log \frac{372}{167} = \frac{\Delta H^o}{2.303 \times 1.987} \left(\frac{1123 - 1073}{1123 \times 1073}\right)$$

$$\Delta H^o = 38.35 \, kcal. \, mole^{-1}$$

The standard change in enthalpy corresponds to the process

$$CaCO_3(s, 1 \, atm.) = CaO(s, 1 \, atm.) + CO_2(g, 1 \, atm.)$$

at the mean temperature, 825°.

EXERCISE 7.7

The total vapor pressure of ammonium bisulfide, NH_4HS, is 355 mm. at 20° and 481 mm. at 25°. What is ΔH^o for this dissociation? *Ans.* 21.1 kcal. mole^{-1}.

7.5   Free Energy of Dilution

In general, mixing will produce free energy changes, both because of entropy effects and also because of changes in enthalpy for nonideal solutions. For gases, only the entropy effect was found to be important, and the corresponding free energy change was shown to be equivalent to gas expansion. Composition, as such, did not affect the results. The case is rather different for liquids. In order to consider equilibrium phenomena involving solutions, whether phase change or chemical change, it is necessary to consider first the effect of composition upon free energy.

In order to examine the thermodynamic behavior of solutions, it is a great advantage to take the mole number n as continuously variable. Such systems are said to be *open*, and those with n constant are *closed*. In order to apply equation (6.54) to open systems, we must write

$$dF = \left(\frac{\partial F}{\partial P}\right)_{T,\, n_1,\, n_2\ldots} dP + \left(\frac{\partial F}{\partial T}\right)_{P,\, n_1,\, n_2\ldots} dT$$

$$+ \left(\frac{\partial F}{\partial n_1}\right)_{P,\, T,\, n_2\ldots} dn_1 + \left(\frac{\partial F}{\partial n_2}\right)_{P,\, T,\, n_1\ldots} dn_2 + \ldots$$

$$= VdP - SdT + \mu_1 dn_1 + \mu_2 dn_2 + \ldots \tag{7.19}$$

The coefficient μ is called the *chemical potential* or the *partial molar free energy*.

At constant temperature and pressure,

$$dF_{T,P} = \sum \mu_i \, dn_i \tag{7.20}$$

For a single pure substance, at one atmosphere,

$$dF^o_{T,P} = \mu^o \, dn$$

The chemical potential of a substance is the increase in free energy of the system caused by adding one mole of that substance. At constant T and P the chemical potential of each component of a solution depends upon the environment. For each solute it depends upon the solvent, and in each solvent it depends upon the composition. When a substance is transferred from one environment to another, the free energy change per mole is the difference of the chemical potentials.

When a solution is produced by adding n_1, n_2 . . . moles of its components in constant proportion, composition is constant and each μ_i is constant. Equation (7.20) integrates to give

$$F_{T,P} = \sum \mu_i \, n_i + \text{const.} \tag{7.21}$$

When the restriction of constant composition is removed from equation (7.21), the total change in $F_{T,P}$ arising from changing mole numbers, and changing environment is given by

$$dF_{T,P} = \sum \mu_i \, dn_i + \sum n_i \, d\mu_i \tag{7.22}$$

Combining equations (7.20) and (7.22) gives

$$\sum n_i \, d\mu_i = 0 \tag{7.23}$$

For the case of a binary solution, denoting solvent and solute by subscripts 1 and 2, we have

$$n_1 \, d\mu_1 + n_2 \, d\mu_2 = X_1 \, d\mu_1 + X_2 \, d\mu_2 = 0 \tag{7.24}$$

since both terms may be divided by $n_1 + n_2$. This is a form of the *Gibbs-Duhem equation*. The chemical potentials of the two components of the solution are closely interrelated. The close relation between $d\mu_1$ and $d\mu_2$ will be found to lead to a corresponding interdependence of dP_1 and dP_2. Figure 1.11 demonstrates this effect.

Let us examine now one volatile component A in a solution at some initial composition X' and some final composition X''. To evaluate $\Delta F = n(\mu'' - \mu')$ we choose an isothermal cycle:

$$
\begin{array}{ccc}
\text{A (soln., } X') & \xrightarrow{\;\;\Delta F\;\;} & \text{A (soln., } X'') \\[2pt]
\Big\downarrow {\scriptstyle \Delta F \text{ (i)}} \;{\scriptstyle =0} & & \Big\uparrow {\scriptstyle \Delta F \text{ (iii)}} \;{\scriptstyle =0} \\[2pt]
\text{A (g, } P') & \xrightarrow[\Delta F(\text{ii})=nRT\ln(P''/P')]{} & \text{A (g, } P'')
\end{array}
$$

Step (i) is the vaporization of A from solution at a partial pressure P_1' which is the equilibrium vapor pressure. Since this is a reversible change, $\Delta F_{T,P}(\text{i}) = 0$. Step (ii) is the change from P' to P'', the equilibrium vapor pressure over the solution of composition X''. Integration of equation (7.4), the vapor being taken to be an ideal gas, gives $\Delta F(\text{ii})$. Step(iii) is the reversible condensation of gaseous A at P'' to the solution at X'' and $\Delta F_{T,P}(\text{iii}) = 0$. Therefore,

$$\Delta F = n(\mu'' - \mu') = nRT \ln (P''/P') \tag{7.25}$$

Equation (7.25) involves no assumption about the solution but is limited to moderate vapor pressures for which the ideal gas law is applicable.

EXERCISE 7.8

At 25° the vapor pressure of water over a 5 molal solution of sucrose is 20.7 mm., whereas the vapor pressure of pure water at this temperature is 23.6 mm. Use equation (7.25) to compute ΔF_{298} for

$$H_2O \text{ (l)} = H_2O \text{ (in 5 molal sucrose solution)}$$

Ans. −78 cal. mole⁻¹.

EXERCISE 7.9

In the preceding cycle, replace X'' by any composition X, and let $X' = 1$. The corresponding vapor pressures are P and P^0. With composition variable, show that equation (7.25) leads to

$$d\mu = RT \, d \ln P$$

For components of solutions which obey Raoult's law (Chapter 1)

$$P_A = X_A \, P_A^0$$

the ratio of vapor pressures becomes

$$\frac{P''}{P'} = \frac{X'' P^0}{X' P^0}$$

Equation (7.25), for $n = 1$, becomes

$$\Delta F_T = \mu'' - \mu' = RT \ln \frac{X''}{X'} \tag{7.26}$$

When one state refers to the pure solvent, then equation (7.26), for any solvent composition X_1, becomes

$$\mu_1 - \mu_1^0 = RT \ln X_1 \tag{7.27}$$

and

$$d\mu_1 = RT \, d \ln X_1 \tag{7.28}$$

EXERCISE 7.10

Show, by analogy with the preceding development, that when the volatile component obeys Henry's law (Chapter 1), equation (7.26) is valid for the solute. Show also that equation (7.27) is invalid.

When one component of a binary solution obeys Raoult's law and equation (7.28) applies, equation (7.24) can be used to discover how P_2 depends upon X_2 for the second component, or solute. By substitution,

$$n_1 \, RT \, d \ln X_1 + n_2 \, d\mu_2 = 0$$

Divide each term by n_2, then replace n_1/n_2 by X_1/X_2, and $d \ln X_1$ by dX_1/X_1, to give

$$d\mu_2 = -RT \frac{dX_1}{X_2}$$

Since $\qquad\qquad X_1 + X_2 = 1$ and $dX_2 = -dX_1$, then

$$d\mu_2 = RT \frac{dX_2}{X_2}$$

Integrating between $X_2 = 1$ and any X_2 and using equation (7.25), we have

$$\mu_2 - \mu_2^0 = RT \ln \left(\frac{P_2}{P_2^0} \right) = RT \ln X_2$$

or

$$P_2 = X_2 P_2^0$$

That is, when one component of a binary solution obeys Raoult's law, the second component must also.

EXERCISE 7.11

Evaluate ΔF_{298} for mixing 2 moles of A and 8 moles of B to form an ideal solution. Consider both

$$2A(X_A = 1) = 2A(X_A = 0.2)$$

and

$$8B(X_B = 1) = 8B(X_B = 0.8)$$

7.6 Boiling Point Elevation

Adding a nonvolatile solute to a volatile solvent lowers the vapor pressure of the solution. It can be shown that $\Delta P_{vap.}$ uniquely determines the associated boiling point raising, freezing point lowering, and osmotic pressure —the *colligative properties*.

Consider a simple experimental situation. Heat is steadily supplied to a volatile solvent until it boils at constant temperature at the prevailing atmospheric pressure. A nonvolatile solute is added, momentarily lowering the vapor pressure. Ebullition stops until the temperature of the solution rises, increasing the vapor pressure until it again equals atmospheric pressure and boiling resumes. These effects are indicated in Fig. 1.9.

A relation between boiling point elevation and composition of the solution may be obtained for an ideal (Raoult's law) solution as follows: The change in state under consideration is the constant temperature, constant pressure vaporization of solvent A from a solution in which it is present at mole fraction X_1 near unity. The pressure is constant at 1 atm. This change in state may be related to vaporization of pure liquid by the isothermal cycle

$$\text{A (soln., } X_1) \xrightarrow{\quad \Delta F \quad} \text{A (g, } P = 1)$$

$$\Delta F \text{ (i)} \Big| = RT \ln (1/X_1)$$

$$\text{A (l, } X_1 = 1) \xrightarrow{\quad \Delta F\text{(ii)} \quad}$$

Step (i) is the reverse of dilution of the solvent from the pure state to mole fraction X_1. The free energy change is given by equation (7.26). Step (ii) is the vaporization of the pure solvent ($X_1 = 1$) at 1 atm. ΔF(ii) is the standard free energy of vaporization as defined in section 7.1. Therefore, for the change of interest

$$\Delta F_T = \Delta F_T^o + RT \ln \left(\frac{1}{X_1}\right) \tag{7.29}$$

and since this is an equilibrium phenomenon, that is, the temperature is adjusted until the vapor pressure of the solution is 1 atm., $\Delta F_T = 0$.

$$\Delta F_T^o(\text{vap.}) = -RT \ln \left(\frac{1}{X_1}\right) \tag{7.30}$$

In this case the equilibrium function is

$$K = \frac{1}{X_1}$$

and its temperature dependence is obtained by applying the Gibbs-Helmholtz equation.

$$\ln \left(\frac{X_1''}{X_1'}\right) = \frac{\Delta H^o \text{ (vap.)}}{R} \left(\frac{T'' - T'}{T''T'}\right) \tag{7.31}$$

We are concerned here with the relation between the boiling points of solvent

($X_1' = 1$ at T') and solution ($X_1'' < 1$ at T''). The boiling point raising is $\Delta T_b = T'' - T'$ and equation (7.31) becomes

$$\Delta T_b = -\frac{RT''\,T'}{\Delta H^\circ\,(\text{vap.})}\ln X_1'' \tag{7.32}$$

A simpler, approximate equation is usually adequate. The boiling points of solvent and solution differ but little and we replace $T''\,T'$ by T_b^2 where T_b now represents, for convenience, the boiling point of pure solvent. Also, for small solute concentrations $X_2 \ll 1$; $-\ln X_1 = -\ln(1 - X_2)$ may be expanded in series

$$-\ln (1 - X_2) = X_2 + \tfrac{1}{2}X_2^2 + \tfrac{1}{3}X_2^3 + \cdots$$

and the higher terms neglected.

With these approximations, we have

$$\Delta T_b = \frac{RT_b^2\,X_2}{\Delta H^\circ\,(\text{vap.})} \tag{7.33}$$

That is, the boiling point elevation is proportional to the *mole fraction of solute*. In dilute solutions $n_2 \ll n_1$ and n_2 may be neglected in the denominator of the mole fraction yielding

$$\Delta T_b = \frac{RT_b^2}{\Delta H^\circ\,(\text{vap.})} \times \frac{n_2}{n_1} = \frac{RT_b^2}{\Delta H^\circ\,(\text{vap.})} \times \frac{W_2 M_1}{W_1 M_2} \tag{7.34}$$

Equation (7.34) is often used to estimate the molecular weight of a solute, assuming that this property is fixed and unchanged by the process of dissolution. For example, suppose that 5 g. of an unknown solute is dissolved in 100 g. of water and that this solution is found to have a normal boiling point of 100.40°. $\Delta T_b \doteq 0.40°$ and all quantities in equation (7.34) are known except M_2.

$$M_2 = \frac{RT_b^2}{\Delta H^\circ\,(\text{vap.})} \times \frac{W_2 \times M_1}{W_1} \times \frac{1}{\Delta T_b}$$

$$= \frac{1.987 \times 373^{\circ2}}{9717} \times \frac{5 \times 18}{100} \times \frac{1}{0.40°} = 64.0$$

It should be noted that if any kind of reaction occurs between solvent molecules or between solvent and solute, the "molecular weight" obtained by use of equation (7.34) will not necessarily have a simple meaning. However, equation (7.33) correctly gives the mole fraction of solute, which may consist of more than one species, or a species different from that used in making up the solution.

Since a single solvent A may be employed in boiling point measurements with several different solutes, the properties of the solvent appearing on the right-hand side of equation (7.34) are collected for convenience into a single factor. It is also customary to express the concentration of solute in molal units. (A 1 m solution contains 1 mole of solute in 1000 g. of solvent.) The molality $m = (W_2/M_2)/(W_1/1000)$ and therefore by substitution in equation (7.34)

$$\Delta T_b = \frac{RT_b^2 \times M_1}{\Delta H^\circ \text{(vap.) } 1000} m \tag{7.35}$$

$$\Delta T_b = K_b m$$

The factor $RT^2 M_1/[\Delta H^\circ(\text{vap.}) \times 1000]$ is called the *molal boiling point elevation constant* K_b, that is, the boiling elevation for a 1 m ideal solution. In the case of water, its value is

$$K_b = \frac{1.987 \times 373^{\circ 2} \times 18}{9717 \times 1000} = 0.51^\circ \text{ molal}^{-1}$$

TABLE 7.2

MOLAL BOILING POINT AND FREEZING POINT CONSTANTS

Liquid	t_f (°C)	K_f (deg. mol.$^{-1}$)	t_b (°C)	K_b (deg. mol.$^{-1}$)
Acetic acid, CH_3COOH	16.55	3.9	118.1	3.0
Benzene, C_6H_6	5.45	5.1	80.1	2.53
Camphor, $C_{10}H_{16}O$	178.4	40.0	—	—
Carbon tetrachloride, CCl_4	−22.8	—	76.8	5.03
n-Hexane, C_6H_{14}	−94.3	—	69.0	2.75
Naphthalene, $C_{10}H_8$	80.1	6.90	217.9	—
Nitrobenzene, $C_6H_5NO_2$	5.82	8.1	210.9	5.24
Water, H_2O	0.0	1.853	100.0	0.51

EXERCISE 7.12

Compute the molecular weight of a solute which in a 6 weight per cent solution in carbon tetrachloride elevates the boiling point by 1.815°.   *Ans. M = 177.*

7.7 Freezing Point Depression

When the temperature of a solution is lowered, the solid phase which separates may be pure solute, pure solvent, or a solid homogeneous mixture (a solid solution). The first of these three cases will be treated quantitatively in Chapter 8. The second case is considered here under its usual title of freezing point depression, and the third case is reserved as a problem. However, these three processes are fundamentally the same and a general treatment can be developed which includes all cases.

When pure solid solvent separates at constant pressure from a solution upon cooling, the "freezing point" of the solution is the equilibrium temperature at which the crystallization just begins. This temperature is always less than the freezing point of the pure solvent. This is a well known fact qualitatively described in Fig. 1.9, but it is also a necessary consequence of the second law of thermodynamics for solutions whose behavior approximates Raoult's law.

The change in state under consideration is

$$A(s) = A(\text{soln., } X_1)$$

at constant temperature and pressure. This is related to the standard process, fusion to form the pure liquid, by the isothermal cycle

$$
\begin{array}{ccc}
A\,(s) & \xrightarrow{\ \ \Delta F\ \ } & A\,(\text{soln.},\,X_1) \\
\Big| & & \Big\uparrow\ \Delta F\,(\text{ii}) = RT\ln X_1 \\
\underset{\Delta F(\text{i})=\Delta F^{o}\text{fusion}}{\underline{\hspace{3cm}}} & \longrightarrow & A\,(l)
\end{array}
$$

Step (i) is the fusion of the pure substance and

$$\Delta F_T(\text{i}) = \Delta F_T^o(\text{fusion})$$

but note that the temperature at which this change is specified is not the equilibrium fusion temperature for pure A and, therefore, ΔF_T^o (fusion) is not zero. Step (ii) corresponds to dissolving 1 mole of A in a very large amount of solution of composition X_1:

$$\Delta F_T(\text{ii}) = RT\ln X_1 \tag{7.36}$$

For the change in state of interest and when T is the equilibrium temperature for the solution at its freezing point

$$\Delta F_T = 0 = \Delta F_T^o\,(\text{fusion}) + RT\ln X_1$$

or

$$\Delta F_T^o\,(\text{fusion}) = -RT\ln X_1 \tag{7.37}$$

In this instance, the equilibrium function is

$$K = X_1$$

and the temperature dependence of X_1 in equilibrium with pure solid solvent is given by

$$\ln\left(\frac{X_1''}{X_1'}\right) = \frac{\Delta H^o\,(\text{fusion})}{R}\left(\frac{T''-T'}{T''T'}\right) \tag{7.38}$$

T' is the freezing temperature of the pure solvent ($X_1 = 1$), T'' is the freezing temperature of the solution ($X_1 < 1$), and $T' - T''$ is the freezing point depression ΔT_f, given by

$$\Delta T_f = -\frac{RT''T'}{\Delta H^o\,(\text{fusion})}\ln X_1 \tag{7.39}$$

Equation (7.39) is completely analogous to equation (7.32) and for dilute solutions (X_1 near unity) the same approximations may be made. Replacing T' and T'' by T_f, the freezing point of the pure solvent, we obtain

$$\Delta T_f = \frac{RT_f^2}{\Delta H^o\,(\text{fusion})}\,X_2 \tag{7.40}$$

and

$$\Delta T_f = \frac{RT_f^2}{\Delta H^o\,(\text{fusion})} \times \frac{W_2 M_1}{W_1 M_2} \tag{7.41}$$

EXERCISE 7.13

The freezing point of pure benzene, C_6H_6, is 5.45° and its heat of fusion is 2351 cal. mole^{-1}. Compute the freezing point of a solution containing 1 weight per cent of naphthalene, $C_{10}H_8$, in benzene.   *Ans.* 5.04°.

As in the case of boiling point elevation, the properties of the solvent which appear in equation (7.41) may be collected into a *molal freezing point depression constant*, K_f.

$$\Delta T_f = K_f m$$

where

$$K_f = \frac{RT_f^2 M_1}{\Delta H^\circ \text{(fusion)} \cdot 1000} \tag{7.42}$$

Values of K_f for various liquids are given in Table 7.2.

EXERCISE 7.14

Compute the molal freezing point constant for water. ΔH° (fusion) = 1440 cal. mole^{-1}.   *Ans.* $K_f(H_2O) = 1.85°$ mol.$^{-1}$.

7.8 Osmotic pressure

When two samples of a pure liquid at common temperature and pressure are connected through a membrane permeable to the substance, no net transport occurs across the barrier. (In fact, a dynamic equilibrium exists, as could be shown by using H_2O and D_2O.) When a solute is added to the liquid on one side of the membrane, chosen to be impermeable to the solute, solvent passes spontaneously through the membrane into the solution. The phenomenon is *osmosis*. The free energy of the system decreases when osmosis occurs, since

$$\Delta F' = \mu_1'(\text{solution}) - \mu_1^0(\text{solvent}) = RT \ln X_1 \tag{7.43}$$

by equation (7.26). When a pressure Π is applied to the solution in excess of that on the solvent, just sufficient to stop osmosis, the system is in a state of equilibrium. The chemical potential of pure solvent at P equals the chemical potential of solvent in solution at $P + \Pi$. Increasing pressure on the solution changes its chemical potential to μ_1'' (solution). The corresponding free energy change is

$$\Delta F'' = \mu_1'' \text{ (solution)} - \mu_1' \text{ (solution)} = \int_P^{P+\Pi} V_{\text{solvent}} \, dP \tag{7.44}$$

When the two effects balance

$$\Delta F' + \Delta F'' = 0 = RT \ln X_1 + \Pi V_{\text{solvent}} \tag{7.45}$$

For solutions which obey Raoult's law V_{solvent} can be identified with the molar volume of the pure solvent, designated V_1. By methods used previously (section 7.6), $\ln X_1 = \ln (1 - X_2) \cong -X_2$. A convenient, final form of the equation for osmotic pressure is

$$\Pi V_1 = RTX_2 \tag{7.46}$$

Measurement of osmotic pressure is far more sensitive for measuring molecular weight at very small solute concentrations than either boiling point raising or freezing point lowering.

EXERCISE 7.15

An aqueous solution containing 1 per cent of protein by weight has an osmotic pressure of 1.0 mm. Hg at 25°. Estimate the molecular weight of the protein. Estimate the freezing point lowering of the solution.   *Ans. $M \cong 2 \times 10^5$.*

7.9 The Clapeyron Equation

In systems of arbitrarily fixed composition, with two phases, the temperature and pressure at equilibrium are interdependent. Only one of the two is independently variable, and the system is said to be univariant. The simplest example is a system of one component with two phases (viz., $1 + v$, $s + v$, $1 + s$, $s' + s''$). Representing the two phases by α and β, we can represent the transition of interest by

$$A(\alpha, P, T) = A(\beta, P, T)$$

There is an infinite number of temperature-pressure combinations which correspond to equilibrium states of the system. For any equilibrium state

$$F_{P,T}(\alpha) = F_{P,T}(\beta)$$

since the phase transition involves no change in free energy for the reversible process at constant pressure and temperature.

Let the pressure be changed from P to $P + dP$, and the system restored to equilibrium by an appropriate change in temperature from T to $T + dT$. Then

$$F_{P,T}(\alpha) + dF(\alpha) = F_{P,T}(\beta) + dF(\beta)$$

since the new state is also an equilibrium state. Therefore

$$dF(\alpha) = dF(\beta) \tag{7.47}$$

Equation (7.47) states that if the system is to remain in an equilibrium state, any change in pressure and temperature must be such that the changes in free energy of the two phases will be equal.

Equation (6.53) gives the temperature and pressure dependence of the free energy of a pure substance and may be applied to each phase, yielding

$$V(\alpha)dP - S(\alpha)dT = V(\beta)dP - S(\beta)dT \tag{7.48}$$

Rearranging, we obtain

$$\frac{dP}{dT} = \frac{S(\beta) - S(\alpha)}{V(\beta) - V(\alpha)} = \frac{\Delta S}{\Delta V} \tag{7.49}$$

Since the phase change is isothermal and reversible, $\Delta S = \Delta H/T$ and

$$\frac{dP}{dT} = \frac{\Delta H}{T \Delta V} \tag{7.50}$$

This is the Clapeyron equation, which describes the relation between change in pressure and change in temperature for a univariant phase equilibrium of any kind. For example, the ΔH of fusion of ice is 1440 cal. mole^{-1} or 59.6 l. atm. mole^{-1}. ΔV is obtained by comparing the density of ice at $0°$ (0.917 g. cc.$^{-1}$) and that of water at $0°$ (1.000 g. cc.$^{-1}$).

$$V(\mathrm{l}) - V(\mathrm{s}) = \left(\frac{1}{1.000} - \frac{1}{0.917}\right) \times 18 \times 10^{-3}\,\mathrm{l.\ mole^{-1}}$$

$$= -1.63 \times 10^{-3}\,\mathrm{l.\ mole^{-1}}$$

Therefore,

$$\frac{dP}{dT} = \frac{59.6}{273° \times (-1.63 \times 10^{-3})} = -134\,\mathrm{atm.\ deg.^{-1}}$$

or

$$\frac{dT}{dP} = -0.0075\,\mathrm{deg.\ atm.^{-1}}$$

The freezing point of water will decrease by $0.0075°$ for each atmosphere of pressure increase. (Over a small range of temperature ΔH and ΔV are practically independent of pressure and temperature and $dT \cong \Delta T$, $dP \cong \Delta P$.)

The freezing point of water is ordinarily observed with the system at 1 atm. and this defines $0°$C. However, if the freezing point is observed for water in a closed vessel from which all gases (e.g., air) except water vapor are excluded, the pressure on the system is that of the vapor, or 4.58 mm. at $0°$. According to the result obtained above, the decrease in pressure will increase the melting point by $0.0075°$. An additional increase of $0.0025°$ is to be expected due to the removal of dissolved air. The equilibrium temperature at which solid, liquid, and vapor coexist as pure phases is called the *triple point*.

EXERCISE 7.16

At $-38.87°$, the melting point of mercury at 1 atm., the density of the liquid is 13.69 g. cc.$^{-1}$ and the density of the solid is 14.19 g. cc.$^{-1}$ The heat of fusion is 2.33 cal. g.$^{-1}$ Estimate the melting point of mercury at 1000 atm.   *Ans.* $-32.6°$.

For vaporization equilibria, simplifying assumptions are possible which transform equation (7.50) to the form of equation (7.9). Consider that

$$\Delta V = V(\mathrm{g}) - V(\mathrm{l\ or\ s})$$

and except near the critical temperature the volume of the solid or liquid is negligible in comparison to the vapor. Further, if the vapor is taken to be an ideal gas, so that $V(\mathrm{g}) = RT/P$ per mole, we obtain

$$\frac{d\mathscr{P}}{dT} = \frac{\Delta H(\mathrm{vap.})\mathscr{P}}{RT^2}$$

or

$$\frac{d\ln\mathscr{P}}{dT} = \frac{\Delta H(\mathrm{vap.})}{RT^2} \tag{7.51}$$

which corresponds to equation (7.9) and is known as the Clapeyron-Clausius equation.

SUMMARY, CHAPTER 7

1. Vaporization of pure solids, liquids, and solutions

$$\Delta F_T^o(\text{vap.}) = -RT \ln \mathscr{P}$$

$$\ln \frac{\mathscr{P}_2}{\mathscr{P}_1} = \frac{\Delta H^o(\text{vap.})}{R}\left(\frac{T_2 - T_1}{T_2 T_1}\right)$$

2. Heterogeneous chemical equilibrium

$$a\text{A}(s) + b\text{B}(g) = m\text{M}(s) + n\text{N}(g)$$

$$\Delta F_T = \Delta F_T^o + RT \ln Q_P$$

$$\Delta F_T^o = -RT \ln K_{\mathscr{P}}$$

$$K_{\mathscr{P}} = \frac{\mathscr{P}_N^n}{\mathscr{P}_B^b}$$

3. Free energy of dilution (ideal solution)

$$dF = VdP - SdT + \mu_1 dn_1 + \mu_2 dn_2 + \cdots$$

$$X_1 d\mu_1 + X_2 d\mu_2 = 0 \text{ (binary solution)}$$

$$\Delta F = RT \ln \frac{P''}{P'} \text{ (any solution)}$$

$$= RT \ln \frac{X''}{X'} \text{ (ideal solution)}$$

4. Boiling point elevation; freezing point lowering (ideal dilute solution)

$$\Delta T = \frac{RT^2}{\Delta H} X_{\text{solute}}$$

$$\Delta T = Km$$

5. Osmotic pressure (ideal dilute solution)

$$\Pi V = RT \, X_{\text{solute}}$$

6. Clapeyron equation (any two phases)

$$\frac{dP}{dT} = \frac{\Delta H}{T\Delta V}$$

Clapeyron-Clausius equation (ideal vapor)

$$\frac{d\ln \mathscr{P}}{dT} = \frac{\Delta H}{RT^2}$$

PROBLEMS, CHAPTER 7

1. The vapor pressure of water is 23.76 mm. at 25°. Given ΔF_f^o of H_2O (l) equal to -56.6902 kcal. mole^{-1} at 25°, find ΔF_f^o of H_2O (g) and compare with the result of Table 5.5.

2. The heat of vaporization of water is 9.7 kcal. mole^{-1} at 100°. Find the vapor pressure of water at 99°.   *Ans.* 733.3 mm.

3. The vapor pressure of benzene is 115 mm. at 30° and 181 mm. at 40°. Find the vapor pressure of benzene at 20°.   *Ans.* 70.8 mm.

4. From the data of Table 7.1, calculate the vapor pressure of carbon tetra-chloride at 70°.   *Ans.* 622 mm.

5. The vapor pressure of solid carbon dioxide is 1.0 atm. at −78° and 2.0 atm. at −69°. The vapor pressure of liquid carbon dioxide is 6.7 atm. at −50° and 14.1 atm. at −30°. Find the temperature and pressure at the triple point of carbon dioxide.   *Ans.* −53.5°, 5.9 atm.

6. The normal boiling point of cyclohexane is 81.4°. Use Trouton's rule to estimate the vapor pressure at 25°.   *Ans.* 103 mm.

7. Show that a simple expression for correction of observed boiling points to normal boiling points of the form

$$\Delta T = 1.25 \times 10^{-4} \, T_{\text{obs}}. \; [P(\text{mm.}) - 760]$$

can be obtained from equation (7.9) and Trouton's rule by use of approximations appropriate for small changes in T and P.

8. The vapor pressure of water is 355 mm. at 80°, and for 50 weight per cent LiBr solution it is 114 mm. at the same temperature. Calculate ΔF_{353} for adding one mole of H_2O (l) to a very large volume of 50 per cent LiBr solution.

Ans. −798 cal.

9. The vapor pressure of water for 50 weight per cent LiBr aqueous solution is 256 mm. at 100°. Referring to problem 8, find ΔH (vap.) of water from this solution at 90°.   *Ans.* 10.60 kcal.

10. From the result of Problem 9, find the enthalpy change for adding one mole of H_2O (l) to a very large amount of 50 per cent LiBr solution.   *Ans.* .88 kcal.

11. One g. of gaseous H_2S is admitted to a 1 l. bulb initially containing NH_3 at 1 atm. At 25°, how much solid NH_4HS will be present at equilibrium?

Ans. 0.0210 moles.

12. In the reduction of iron oxide according to

$$Fe_3O_4(s) + H_2(g) = 3FeO(s) + H_2O(g)$$

at a total pressure of 1 atm., the equilibrium composition of the gas phase is 44 mole per cent H_2 at 678° and 27 mole per cent H_2 at 772°. Find ΔH for the process.   *Ans.* 15.8 kcal.

13. The equilibrium $2 FeCl_3(s) = Fe_2Cl_6(g)$ obeys the equation log P(mm.) $= -6887 \, T^{-1} + 14.52$.

(a) Calculate the equilibrium pressure at 120°.

(b) Find ΔH(vap.).

[R. R. Hammer and N. W. Gregory, *J. Phys. Chem.*, **66**, 1705 (1962).]

Ans. (a) $P = 1.0 \times 10^{-3}$ mm (b) 31.5 kcal.

14. A solution containing 122 g. of benzoic acid, C_6H_5COOH, in 1000 g. of benzene, C_6H_6, boils at 81.5°. Find the apparent molecular weight of benzoic acid (which dimerizes) in the solution and the degree of dimerization.

Ans. 81 per cent dimer.

15. One g. of naphthalene in 50 g. of a certain solvent raises the boiling point by 0.40°; 1.20 g. of an unknown X in 60 g. of the same solvent raises the boiling point 0.55°. What is the molecular weight of X?   *Ans.* 93.

16. Heat is abstracted from a solution of urea in water until a quantity of ice forms and the temperature of the solution in equilibrium with it becomes −1.25°. What is the composition of this solution?   *Ans.* 0.67 m.

17. Calculate and compare the approximate numerical values of $\Delta P/P$, ΔT_f, ΔT_b, and Π at 25° for a 1.0 wt. per cent aqueous solution of protein having a molecular weight of 60,000.   *Ans.* $\Delta P/P = 3 \times 10^{-6}$;
$$\Delta T_f = 3.1 \times 10^{-4}; \Delta T_b = 0.85 \times 10^{-4}; \Pi = 3.1 \text{ mm.}$$

---

18. Find ΔF_{373}^{0} for vaporization of water when the standard state of the vapor is chosen to be 1 mm. pressure.

19. From data in Table 7.1 find the vapor pressure of *n*-butane at 25°.

20. The vapor pressure of supercooled liquid water is 2.149 mm. at −10° and 4.579 mm. at 0°. The vapor pressure of ice at −10° is 1.950 mm. From these data find the heat of fusion of ice.

21. Find ΔF_{298} for a system in which 100 g. of cyclohexane, C_6H_{12}, is mixed with 100 g. of benzene, C_6H_6, assuming that an ideal solution is formed.

22. Iodine reacts slowly with cyclohexene, C_6H_{10}, to form an unstable diiodide. If 0.01 mole of iodine is added to 0.25 mole of cyclohexene, what is the boiling point elevation

(a) If no reaction occurs?

(b) If substantially complete reaction occurs?

For cyclohexene, $t_b = 83°$. Use Trouton's rule to find ΔH(vap.) and neglect the volatility of the solutes.

23. When one mole of A(solvent) is added to a very large amount of its solution with B(nonvolatile solute) at X_B and temperature T, the attendant heat effect is ΔH_S. When pure A is vaporized at T, the heat effect is ΔH_V^0. The $P_A - T$ dependence of the solution obeys the Clapeyron-Clausius equation, from which one obtains a heat effect ΔH_{CC}.

(a) Complete the accompanying diagram which demonstrates the relationships among the various heat effects ΔH_1, ΔH_2, etc.

(b) State the fundamental principle employed to establish the relationships.

(c) Identify $\Delta H_1 \ldots \Delta H_5$.

$$\text{A (liq., } X_A = 1, T) \xrightarrow{1} \text{A (soln. } X_A, T)$$

A (liq., $X_A = 1, T$) ——1——→ A (soln. X_A, T)

| 2 ↓   5 ↗   ↑ 4 |
| 3 |

A ( )——3——→ A ( )

24. Use equation (7.24) and the result of exercise 7.9 to establish a relation between dP_1 and dP_2 for solvent and solute at constant temperature with composition variable. Use Fig. 1.11 to test approximately the result obtained, for $X_1 = X_2 = 0.5$.

25. A substance B (s) melts at T_f, absorbing heat ΔH_f (B), and B (l) forms an ideal solution with A (l). When B (s) dissolves in A (l) at a temperature just below T_f, what is the integral heat of solution?

26. When the solid phase which separates from a solution on cooling is a solid solution, equation (7.40) does not apply. The binary system A-B forms a solid solution as well as a liquid solution. Both solutions obey Raoult's law. Show that the equilibrium function corresponding to

$$A(\text{solid soln., } X_A') = A(\text{liquid soln., } X_A'')$$

is

$$K = X_A''/X_A'$$

Consider A the solvent and use the method of section 7.7 to find an expression for ΔT_f in terms of these compositions and of physical constants of the solvent.

27. A brief, correct derivation of the equation for b.p. raising begins: when $P_1 = P_1^0 X_1$ and $P_1 = P_{atm.} = $ const., then $\ln P_1 = \ln X_1 + \ln P^0$ and $d \ln P_1/dT = 0 = d \ln X_1/dT + d \ln P^0/dT$. Complete the derivation, remembering that X_1 is the independent variable.

28. In an experimental measurement of molecular weight by boiling point raising in Exercise 7.12, the boiling point of the solvent was measured at a barometric pressure 756.8 mm. and that of the solution, somewhat later, at 755.6 mm. What correction should be applied to ΔT_b?

29. The m.p. of Hg at 1 atm. is $-38.87°$; the heat of fusion is 2.33 cal./g.; the density of the liquid is 13.69 g./cc.$^{-1}$; the density of the solid is 14.19 g.cc.$^{-1}$. Calculate the change of melting point for a pressure increase of 2 atm.

30. It has been established that the decomposition pressure of CO_2 in equilibrium with $CaCO_3$ and CaO is independent of the relative amounts of the two solid phases, as long as some of each is present. From this fact, show that $CaCO_3(s)$ decomposes at phase boundary surfaces, and does not decompose homogeneously.

31. The vapor pressure P of a solution of nonvolatile solute is a function of temperature T and of solvent mole fraction X_1. That is,

$$dP = \left(\frac{\partial P}{\partial T}\right)_{X_1} dT + \left(\frac{\partial P}{\partial X_1}\right)_T dX_1$$

Complete each of the following equations in the most nearly appropriate manner as applied to the measurement of boiling point raising for determination of molecular weight.

$$dP =$$

$$\left(\frac{\partial P}{\partial T}\right)_{X_1} =$$

$$\left(\frac{\partial P}{\partial X_1}\right)_T =$$

Use the preceding relations to obtain a differential equation suitable to describe b.p. raising.

32. Monoclinic sulfur is stable above 368.5°K at 1 atm. and $\Delta F_{298}^0 = 18$ cal. mole^{-1} for S (rhombic) $=$ S (monoclinic). The density of rhombic sulfur is 2.07 g. cc.$^{-1}$. At what applied pressure will rhombic sulfur have the same vapor pressure as monoclinic sulfur has at an applied pressure of 1 atm. Consider both at 25°?

33. The Clapeyron equation can be shown to apply to phase transitions in systems of fixed composition. As an example, for aqueous sucrose solutions P_{H_2O} is a function of T alone for any given composition. Derive equation (7.51) for vapor-solution equilibria of such systems and explain precisely the significance of ΔH.

8

EQUILIBRIA
IN SOLUTIONS
OF NONELECTROLYTES

8.1 Ideal Solutions

A thermodynamic description of equilibria in solutions requires a knowledge of the functional dependence of chemical potential upon concentration. For volatile substances whose vapors approximate ideal gas behavior, the fundamental relation was shown to be (Exercise 7.9):

$$d\mu_i = RT \, d\ln P_i \tag{8.1}$$

When P is known as a function of composition at constant T, for the solvent (component 1),

$$P_1 = P_1^0 X_1$$

$$\ln P_1 = \ln P_1^0 + \ln X_1$$

$$d\ln P_1 = 0 + d\ln X_1$$

and

$$d\mu_1 = RT \, d\ln X_1 \tag{8.2}$$

Raoult's law always applies to the major component of a solution as X_1 approaches unity, but often does not apply to minor components. For sufficiently dilute solutions Henry's law is applicable, and such solutions are also termed ideal with respect to solute behavior. In such case, at constant T, for the solute (component 2),

$$P_2 = k \, X_2$$

$$\ln P_2 = \ln k + \ln X_2$$

$$d\ln P_2 = 0 + d\ln X_2$$

and

$$d\mu_2 = RT\,d\ln X_2 \tag{8.3}$$

In sufficiently dilute solution all measures of composition of solute are proportional to each other. Accordingly, Henry's law may be expressed in terms of molality $(P = k_m m)$ or molarity $(P = k_M M)$ as well as in terms of mole fraction. It will be convenient to represent any measure of composition of solute in dilute solution by the generalized symbol c. Then, provided P is proportional to c, equation (8.1) gives

$$d\mu = RT\,d\ln c \tag{8.4}$$

and

$$\mu = \mu_c^0 + RT\ln c \tag{8.5}$$

where μ_c^0 pertains to solute at $c = 1$. Each choice of concentration unit establishes a corresponding standard state. For solutions which obey Henry's law up to $1\,m$, μ_m^0 in the molal scale refers to the experimentally realizable $1\,m$ solution, at each temperature. When Henry's law is not obeyed, μ_m^0 (or μ_c^0 in general) is best considered simply as a constant of integration which need not be visualized (cf. section 8.6).

Henry's law has limited validity for real solutions and often applies only at rather low concentrations. Also, the state at unit concentration may not be experimentally accessible because of a limited solubility. In either case equation (8.4) is limited to the concentration range to which Henry's law applies, and this restriction applies equally to equation (8.5). The standard state is no longer the real solution at unit concentration, say $m = 1$, but a hypothetical state which can be partly described as having the solute vapor pressure which a $1\,m$ solution would have *if* Henry's law were valid at $1\,m$. This hypothetical state is indicated by the point A in Fig. 8.1, which corresponds to the extrapolation of the Henry's law line to $1\,m$ solute concentration. Since by definition this hypothetical state satisfies Henry's law, for the process

A(hyp. std. state) $= A$

$(m$, Henry's law region$)$

$$\mu = \mu_m^0 + RT\ln\frac{m}{1}$$

When composition is expressed in terms of mole fraction, the standard state of the solute will be experimentally accessible only for solutions which obey Raoult's law over the entire range $X_2 = 0$ to $X_2 = 1$. For all other solutions it refers to the hypothetical state described by extrapolation from the very dilute solution to pure liquid solute at $X_2 = 1$. One such state is indicated by point B in Fig. 8.1. For the change in state

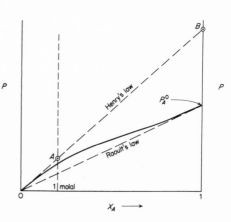

FIG. 8.1. Standard states for solutes.

$$A(\text{hyp. std. state}) = A(X_2, \text{Henry's law region})$$

$$\mu = \mu_x^0 + RT \ln \frac{X_2}{1}$$

For any real change in state within the Henry's law region, as

$$A(m') = A(m'')$$

or

$$A(X_2') = A(X_2'')$$

the isothermal change in free energy, the free energy of dilution, is readily obtained from equations (8.6) and (8.7).

$$\Delta F_T = n(\mu'' - \mu') = nRT \ln \frac{m''}{m'} \tag{8.6}$$

or

$$\Delta F_T = n(\mu'' - \mu') = nRT \ln \frac{X_2''}{X_2'} \tag{8.7}$$

The parameters μ_m^0 and μ_x^0 vanish and the experimental inaccessibility of the corresponding standard states is unimportant.

EXERCISE 8.1

Find ΔF_{298} for the solute when a Henry's law solution containing 0.1 mole of solute in 100 g. of solvent is diluted by addition of 900 g. of solvent.

Ans. $\Delta F_{298} = -136$ cal.

8.2 Solubility

Many solutions exhibit a natural upper limit of solute concentration called the solubility. It is characterized by the fact that at constant temperature and pressure the pure solute is in equilibrium with the dissolved solute. The free energy change for dissolving solute in solution approaches zero as the concentration approaches saturation. Representing the molar free energy of pure substance at 1 atm. by μ_2^*, and that of solute in the saturated solution by $\mu_{2,\,\text{sat.}}$, then we have $\mu_2^* = \mu_{2,\,\text{sat.}}$.

The significant free energy changes for solutions can be related by the cycle

$$\text{A (pure subs.)} \xrightarrow{\Delta F} \text{A (soln., } c)$$

$$\Delta F(i) \bigg| = \Delta F^0 \qquad \Delta F(ii) \bigg| = RT \ln (c/1)$$

$$\longrightarrow \text{A (soln., std. state)}$$

In step (i) pure solute dissolves to form solution in a standard state.

$$\Delta F(i) = \Delta F^0 = \mu_2^0 - \mu_2^*$$

In step (ii) the solute is transferred from its standard state to any arbitrarily chosen concentration. For solutions which obey Henry's law,

$$\Delta F(ii) = \mu_2 - \mu_2^0 = RT \ln c$$

In general, dissolving solute to yield any concentration c gives the free energy change

$$\Delta F_T = \Delta F_T^0 + RT \ln c$$

When pure solute dissolves to give the saturated solution at concentration $c_{sat.}$,

$$\Delta F_T = 0 = \Delta F_T^0 + RT \ln c_{sat.} \tag{8.8}$$

EXERCISE 8.2

The solubility of iodine in water at 25° is 0.29 g.l.$^{-1}$. Find ΔF_{298}^0 for
$I_2(s) = I_2(m = 1)$.   *Ans.* 3920 cal. mole^{-1}.

Equation (8.8) is a familiar relation between the standard free energy change and the corresponding equilibrium function. In this instance, $K = c_{sat.}$. Application of the Gibbs-Helmholtz equation leads to an expression of the solubility (equilibrium constant) as a function of temperature:

$$\frac{d \ln c_{sat.}}{dT} = \frac{\Delta H^0}{RT^2} \tag{8.9}$$

The enthalpy term in various applications of van't Hoff's equation is always the heat effect for the given process involving standard states. In this case it is the standard heat of solution.

For solid solutes which obey Raoult's law, ΔH^0 has special significance. The vapor pressure P_{solid}^0 of a pure solid substance at any temperature below its freezing point is less than that of the supercooled liquid, P_{liquid}^0 (cf. section 1.9) at the same temperature. Raoult's law applies only to liquids and in such instances must be understood in the sense $P = X P_{liquid}^0$. The partial pressure of the dissolved substance over any saturated solution is necessarily equal to that of the pure solid solute and $P_{solid}^0 = X_{sat.} P_{liquid}^0$. An immediate conclusion is that the solubility of a given solute is the same in all solutions obeying Raoult's law at a given temperature, since P_{solid}^0 and P_{liquid}^0 are functions of the solute alone. Further, the heat of solution at any composition is the heat of fusion of the pure solute, since the net process can be resolved into two steps:

A (pure solid)   = A (pure liquid), $\Delta H(i) = \Delta H_{fusion}$
A (pure liquid) = A (solution), $\Delta H(ii) = 0$

A (pure solid)   = A (solution), $\Delta H_{soln.} = \Delta H_{fusion}$

It has already been shown (section 7.3) that $\Delta H(ii) = 0$ for solutions which obey Raoult's law.

Some examples of the temperature dependence of solubility appear in Fig. 8.2. For gaseous solutes the heat of solution is normally exothermic and approximates $-\Delta H_{vap.}$ for the solute. For nonideal liquid mixtures (immiscible liquids

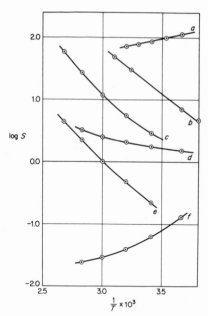

FIG. 8.2. Solubility vs. temperature. $S =$ grams solute/ 1000 grams solvent. a—ethyl acetate in water, b —I_2 in CCl_4, c—benzoic acid in H_2O, d—C_6H_6 in H_2O, e—I_2 in H_2O, f—C_2H_6 in H_2O.

are necessarily nonideal in respect to Raoult's law), $\Delta H_{soln.}$ may be positive or negative.

8.3 Distribution Coefficients

An equilibrium related to solubility is that involved in the distribution of a solute between two immiscible liquids. For example, at 20° the solubility of iodine in water is 0.29 g. l.$^{-1}$, whereas its solubility in carbon tetrachloride, which is practically immiscible with water, is 15.8 g. l.$^{-1}$. If a mixture of the two liquids is equilibrated at 20° with excess solid iodine, each liquid becomes saturated with iodine at the concentrations given. That is, the presence of a second, immiscible liquid phase does not alter the solubility.

We now ask what is the nature of the equilibrium state when the amount of solute is not sufficient to saturate the two liquids. That is, what is the equilibrium function corresponding to

$$A \text{ (soln. in } Q, c_Q) = A \text{ (soln. in R, } c_R)$$

where Q and R represent the two immiscible liquids and c_Q and c_R are not necessarily the saturation values? The change of interest is related to the standard change by the isothermal cycle

$$A \text{ (soln. in } Q, c_Q) \xrightarrow{\ \Delta F \text{(dist.)}\ } A \text{ (soln. in R, } c_R)$$

$$\Delta F(i) \Big| = RT \ln (1/c_Q) \qquad\qquad \Delta F(iii) \Big| = RT \ln (c_R/1)$$

$$A \text{ (soln. in } Q, \text{ std. state)} \xrightarrow{\ \Delta F(ii) = \Delta F^0 \text{(dist.)}\ } A \text{ (soln. in } R, \text{ std. state)}$$

Steps (i) and (iii) are dilution processes. Step (ii) is the standard process, namely, the transfer of solute from its standard state in solvent Q to its standard state in solvent R.

$$\Delta F_T \text{ (dist.)} = \Delta F_T^0 \text{ (dist.)} + RT \ln \frac{c_R}{c_Q} \qquad (8.10)$$

For equilibrium values of c_Q and c_R, $\Delta F_T = 0$ and

$$0 = \Delta F_T^0 \text{ (dist.)} + RT \ln \frac{c_R}{c_Q}$$

$$\Delta F_T^0 \text{ (dist.)} = -RT \ln K \qquad (8.11)$$

The value of the equilibrium function in this case is called a *distribution coefficient.*

$$K = \frac{c_R}{c_Q} \qquad (8.12)$$

That is, the ratio of concentrations in the two phases is constant for a given system and temperature.

Equation (8.11) may be valid in dilute solution even when it fails (because of deviations from Henry's law) at higher concentrations. When the solute is sparingly soluble, then Henry's law and equation (8.11) may be valid for the saturated solutions as well. If this is the case, then in the saturated solutions

$$K = \frac{c_R \text{ (sat.)}}{c_Q \text{ (sat.)}} \tag{8.13}$$

and the distribution constant may be evaluated from the ratio of solubilities in the two solvents.

Some solutes have different molecular forms in different solvents. For example, picric acid, $C_6H_2(NO_2)_3OH$, exists largely as the undissociated molecular species in benzene solution, but dissociates as an acid in water forming a positive and a negative ion. In this case the distribution equilibrium is

$$H^+ \text{ (aq.)} + P^- \text{ (aq.)} = HP \text{ (benzene)}$$

and the equilibrium function is

$$K = \frac{c_{HP \text{ (benzene)}}}{c_{H^+ \text{ (aq.)}} \times c_{P^- \text{ (aq.)}}}$$

Benzoic acid, C_6H_5COOH, exists as a dimer, $(HB)_2$, in benzene solution, and as the practically undissociated acid, HB, in water.

$$2HB \text{ (aq.)} = (HB)_2 \text{ (benzene)}$$

The equilibrium function is, therefore,

$$K = \frac{c_{(HB)_2 \text{ (benzene)}}}{c^2_{HB \text{ (aq.)}}}$$

Analysis of the benzene layer by acidimetry gives the number of equivalents of benzoic acid per liter of solution. The molar concentration of the species $(HB)_2$ is half as great. That is, in the benzene layer, $c_{(HB)_2} = \frac{1}{2}c_{HB}$ and the equilibrium function may be written

$$K = \frac{c_{HB \text{ (benzene)}}}{2\,c^2_{HB \text{ (aq.)}}}$$

Table 8.1 gives some results for this system. The constancy of the values obtained in the fourth column supports the proposed dimerization. Note that the ratio of concentrations in the two phases (third column) is not constant.

TABLE 8.1

DISTRIBUTION OF BENZOIC ACID BETWEEN WATER AND BENZENE AT 6°

$c_{HB \text{ (aq.)}}$ $m/l.$	$c_{HB \text{ (benzene)}}$ $m/l.$	$\dfrac{c_{HB \text{ (benzene)}}}{c_{HB \text{ (aq.)}}}$	$\dfrac{c_{HB \text{ (benzene)}}}{c^2_{HB \text{ (aq.)}}}$ $(m/l.)^{-1}$
0.00329	0.0156	4.75	1.44×10^3
0.00579	0.0495	8.55	1.48×10^3
0.00749	0.0835	11.14	1.49×10^3
0.0114	0.195	17.1	1.50×10^3

One l. of 0.01 M solution of benzoic acid in water is extracted with 1 l. of benzene. What per cent of the benzoic acid will be left in the water?   *Ans.* 23%.

8.4 Chemical Equilibrium in Ideal Solutions

The thermodynamic description of chemical equilibrium among solutes in dilute solution is altogether similar to the preceding treatments. Let c_A, c_B, c_M, c_N, etc., represent any arbitrary concentrations of reacting substances which obey Henry's law and, therefore, equation (8.5). The pertinent free energy changes are summarized by the following cycle:

$$aA\,(c_A)\quad+\quad bB\,(c_B)+\ldots\quad\xrightarrow{\Delta F_T}\quad mM\,(c_M)\quad+\quad nN\,(c_N)+\ldots$$

$$\Delta F_T = \left| aRT \ln (1/c_A)\right. \qquad \Delta F_T = \left| mRT\ln(c_M/1)\right.$$

$$\Delta F_T = \left| bRT\ln(1/c_B)\right. \qquad \Delta F_T = \left| nRT\ln(c_N/1)\right.$$

$$aA\,(\text{std. st.}) + bB\,(\text{std. st.}) + \ldots \xrightarrow{\Delta F_T^0} mM\,(\text{std. st.}) + nN\,(\text{std. st.}) + \ldots$$

The change in free energy for the over-all reaction at arbitrary concentrations is

$$\Delta F_T = m\mu_M + n\mu_N + \ldots - a\mu_A - b\mu_B - \ldots \tag{8.14}$$

and for the corresponding standard reaction it is

$$\Delta F_T^0 = m\mu_M^0 + n\mu_N^0 + \ldots - a\mu_A^0 - b\mu_B^0 - \ldots \tag{8.15}$$

The sum of all free energy terms for processes involving changes in solute concentration is given by

$$\Sigma\, \Delta F_T = RT \ln\left(\frac{c_M^m\, c_N^n\ldots}{c_A^a\, c_B^b\ldots}\right) \tag{8.16}$$

The reaction quotient is represented again by Q, and combining equations (8.14) through (8.16) gives

$$\Delta F_T = \Delta F_T^0 + RT \ln Q \tag{8.17}$$

For a set of equilibrium concentrations, $\Delta F_T = 0$ and

$$0 = \Delta F_T^0 + RT \ln K_c$$

$$\Delta F_T^0 = -RT \ln K_c \tag{8.18}$$

where K_c is the equilibrium function of concentrations.

$$K_c = \left(\frac{c_M^m\, c_N^n\ldots}{c_A^a\, c_B^b\ldots}\right)_{\text{equil.}} \tag{8.19}$$

Since ΔF_T^0 is the free energy change for a uniquely defined change in state, namely, that involving the standard states of all reactants and products, it follows that K_c has a unique numerical value for a given system at a given temperature. This value is of course the equilibrium constant for the reaction.

Equation (8.19) is valid for any of the usual concentration units, including molality, molarity, and mole fraction, so long as the solutes obey Henry's law. Of course, the numerical value of the equilibrium constant will depend on the choice of units, as will the corresponding value of ΔF_T^0 obtained from equation (8.18), since the standard process is different for each choice.

Equations (8.18) and (8.19) have much the same meaning and applicability as the corresponding equations developed in Chapter 5 for gaseous systems. For example, the dissociation of N_2O_4 has been studied in dilute carbon tetrachloride solution. [K. Atwood and G. K. Rollefson, *J. Chem. Phys.*, **9**, 506 (1941).]

$$N_2O_4 = 2NO_2$$

The equilibrium constants were expressed in terms of the equilibrium mole fractions of N_2O_4 and NO_2, with results shown in Table 8.2. The value of the equilibrium function shows relatively little variation over a wide range of concentrations.

TABLE 8.2

DISSOCIATION OF N_2O_4 IN CCl_4 AT 25°

$X_{NO_2} \times 10^5$	$K = \dfrac{X^2_{NO_2}}{X_{N_2O_4}} \times 10^5$
1.1	5.65
9.7	5.55
38.6	6.34
96.5	6.49
145.0	5.68

Since only rather dilute solutions are involved, where $n_{NO_2} \ll n_{CCl_4}$ and $n_{N_2O_4} \ll n_{CCl_4}$, the equilibrium function of mole fractions may be written

$$K_x = \frac{X^2_{NO_2}}{X_{N_2O_4}} = \frac{n^2_{NO_2}}{n_{N_2O_4}} \cdot \frac{1}{n_{CCl_4}}$$

The number of moles of carbon tetrachloride is given by

$$n_{CCl_4} = \frac{V_{CCl_4} \times \rho_{CCl_4}}{M_{CCl_4}} = V_{CCl_4} \times 10.4$$

where V_{CCl_4} is the volume of solvent (or solution) in liters and ρ_{CCl_4} is the density. Letting the degree of dissociation of N_2O_4 be α and n_0 the initial number of moles of N_2O_4, we have

$$K_x = \frac{4\alpha^2}{1-\alpha} \cdot \frac{n_0}{V_{CCl_4} \times 10.4}$$

$$\frac{4\alpha^2}{1-\alpha} = \frac{K_x \times 10.4}{c_0}$$

where c_0 is the initial concentration of N_2O_4 in molar units. For example, when $c_0 = 0.01\ M$,

$$\frac{4\alpha^2}{1-\alpha} = \frac{6.0 \times 10^{-5} \times 10.4}{0.01}$$

$$\alpha = 0.117$$

From the form of this equation, it is evident that the degree of dissociation will increase with decreasing N_2O_4 concentration, in keeping with the principle of Le Chatelier.

EXERCISE 8.4

Estimate the initial concentration of N_2O_4 at which 50% dissociation will occur in carbon tetrachloride solution at 25°. *Ans.* 3.12×10^{-4}.

Another example of an equilibrium to which equations (8.18) and (8.19) apply is the iodination of cyclohexene.

$$C_6H_{10} + I_2 = C_6H_{10}I_2$$

The equilibrium function is

$$K = \frac{c_{C_6H_{10}I_2}}{c_{C_6H_{10}}c_{I_2}}$$

Substituting $c_i = n_i/V$, where V is the volume of solution, we obtain

$$K = \frac{n_{C_6H_{10}I_2}}{n_{C_6H_{10}}n_{I_2}} V$$

which shows that the position of equilibrium is a function of concentration as before.

The equilibrium constant for this system at 25° is 20 (m/l.)$^{-1}$ in carbon tetrachloride. If a solution of initial concentration $c_{0,C_6H_{10}}$ in cyclohexene and c_{0,I_2} in iodine is prepared, equilibration will result in the formation of an equilibrium concentration of cyclohexene diiodide, $c_{C_6H_{10}I_2}$. For each mole of diiodide formed, a mole of iodine and a mole of cyclohexene are consumed. Therefore,

$$K = \frac{c_{C_6H_{10}I_2}}{(c_{0,C_6H_{10}} - c_{C_6H_{10}I_2})(c_{0,I_2} - c_{C_6H_{10}I_2})}$$

For example, if

$$c_{0,C_6H_{10}} = c_{0,I_2} = 0.01 \text{ M}$$

$$20 = \frac{x}{(0.01 - x)(0.01 - x)}$$

$$c_{C_6H_{10}I_2} = x = 0.0015 \text{ or } 0.0685 \text{ M}$$

This quadratic equation has two positive roots, but only 0.0015 M is physically real, since the equilibrium concentration of cyclohexene diiodide cannot exceed 0.01 M, the initial concentration of cyclohexene and iodine.

EXERCISE 8.5

Starting with $c_{0,C_6H_{10}} = 0.01$ M, what initial concentration of iodine will be required to produce 50% conversion of cyclohexene into the iodide at 25° in carbon tetrachloride? *Ans.* 0.055 M.

Application of the Gibbs-Helmholtz equation to equation (8.18) gives the temperature dependence of the equilibrium constant in the usual form.

$$\ln \frac{K_2}{K_1} = \frac{\Delta H^0}{R} \left(\frac{T_2 - T_1}{T_2 T_1} \right) \tag{8.20}$$

where ΔH^0 is the change in heat content for the standard change in state, taken to be independent of temperature.

EXERCISE 8.6

The equilibrium constant for the iodination of cyclohexene in carbon tetrachloride solution is 13 $(M)^{-1}$ at 35°. Compute ΔH^0 for the process.

Ans. -7.9 kcal. mole^{-1}.

The classic case of solution equilibrium is the esterification reaction

$$CH_3COOH + C_2H_5OH = CH_3COOC_2H_5 + H_2O$$

first studied by M. Berthelot and L. St. Gilles [*Ann. chim. phys.*, **68,** 225 (1863)]. In this reaction, the total number of moles of substance does not change, and therefore, as shown for gas phase reactions,

$$K_c = K_n = \frac{n_{ester} \cdot n_{water}}{n_{acid} \cdot n_{alcohol}} \tag{8.21}$$

This system is usually studied by taking some arbitrary number of moles of acetic acid, α; alcohol, β; ester, μ; and water, ν. These substances can hardly be expected to form an ideal solution, and therefore it is somewhat fortuitous that the value of K_n is relatively constant for various initial states.

The number of moles of acetic acid, $\alpha - x$, is measured at equilibrium. Since the decrease in amount of acetic acid is equal to the decrease in alcohol and to the increase in ester and water,

$$K_n = \frac{(\mu + x)(\nu + x)}{(\alpha - x)(\beta - x)}$$

When 1 mole of acetic acid is mixed with 2 moles of ethanol at 100°, the amount of acetic acid at equilibrium is 0.150 mole. That is, $x = 0.850$, and

$$K_n = \frac{(0.850)(0.850)}{(1 - 0.850)(2 - 0.850)} = 4.2$$

If large amounts of ester and water, with small amounts of acetic acid and alcohol are present initially, the approach to equilibrium may *increase* the amount of acetic acid and alcohol in the system. In this case the value of x, as defined above, would be negative.

EXERCISE 8.7

Find the equilibrium composition of the system at 100° when 1 mole of ethyl acetate and 1 mole of water are mixed.

Ans. $X_{ester} = X_{H_2O} = 0.33$; $X_{acid} = X_{alcohol} = 0.17$.

8.5 Real Solutions

Up to this point all discussions of equilibria involving solutions have presumed that Raoult's law applies to the solvent and Henry's law to the solute. These relations have been used to obtain the concentration dependence of the free energy (equations 7.26, 8.6, and 8.7). Although the description of the standard states of solutes has taken into account deviations from these ideal relations, the application of equilibrium functions has been restricted to situations in which approximately ideal behavior has been found.

The limitation of the simple descriptions of equilibria in solution which have been examined so far arises from the necessity to express the free energy of dilution in terms of some measurable property and from the mathematical convenience of inaccurate laws. Let us reconsider the problem of evaluating the free energy change for isothermally transferring a component of a solution from one composition to another. In the isothermal cycle

$$
\begin{array}{ccc}
\text{A (soln., } X') & \xrightarrow{\quad \Delta F \quad} & \text{A (soln., } X'') \\[1mm]
\Delta F \Big|=0 \Big\downarrow & & \Big\uparrow \Delta F \Big|=0 \\[1mm]
\text{A (g, } P') & \xrightarrow[\quad]{\Delta F = nRT \ln (P''/P')} & \text{A (g, } P'')
\end{array}
$$

P' and P'' are the equilibrium vapor pressures over the solutions containing A at mole fractions X' and X''. To be entirely correct it would be necessary to use fugacity, not pressure, but for the majority of processes of interest the inaccuracy is not great. The net change in free energy per mole of substance transported from one solution to the other—whether by osmosis, electrolysis, or vaporization—is given by

$$
\Delta F_T = RT \ln \frac{P''}{P'}
$$

If either Henry's law or Raoult's law is invoked at this point, replacing P''/P' by c''/c', in whatever units, the consequence is the same as replacing equation (8.1) by (8.2). It would be possible to correlate pressure and composition by using empirical descriptions, such as $P = aX + bX^2 + \ldots$, but the equilibrium functions would become unmanageable. The device which has been generally adopted closely resembles the one employed for gaseous systems (section 5.11). We define the *activity a* for a component of a solution so that the equilibrium function of the activities will be correct. That is,

$$
K_a = \frac{a_M^m \, a_N^n \cdots}{a_A^a \, a_B^b \cdots} \tag{8.22}
$$

and the value of K_a will be constant without respect to the applicability of Raoult's law or Henry's law.

8.6 The Activity

In terms of our experience with other equilibrium functions, we may expect to be able to develop equation (8.22) from an expression of the type

$$
d\mu = RT \, d \ln a \tag{8.23}
$$

for which the corresponding integral is

$$
\mu = \mu^0 + \int RT \, d \ln a \tag{8.24}
$$

These equations define activity so that it is proportional to fugacity. A proportionality constant remains to be chosen, and it will be an advantage to complete the definition of a by specifying

$$a = \frac{f}{f^0} \qquad (8.25)$$

For a gas, $f^0 = 1$ atm. and $a = f$. The activity and fugacity are, therefore, interchangeable for gases, except that f is dimensioned, whereas a is dimensionless.

For the solvent in solution it is necessary to make a further choice in order to relate activity to concentration. Recalling that $f \cong P$ for substances in the gaseous state at moderate pressure, we find that equation (8.25) becomes

$$a \cong \frac{P}{P^0} \qquad (8.26)$$

The resemblance of equation (8.26) to Raoult's law is striking and suggests that, for the solvent, the standard state be chosen for convenience as $a_1 = 1$ when $X_1 = 1$ at each temperature. On this basis $a_1 = X_1$ for solutions which obey Raoult's law, apart from deviations of the vapor from ideal behavior. Even for highly nonideal solutions (cf. Fig. 1.11), $a \cong P/P^0$ for moderate vapor pressures. Equation (8.25) is evidently a complete analog of Raoult's law, and the similarity is altogether intentional.

EXERCISE 8.8

The vapor pressure of water over 5 m sucrose ($X_{H_2O} = 0.918$) is 20.7 mm. at 25° and $P^0_{H_2O} = 23.6$ mm. Find a_{H_2O} for the solution and compare with X_{H_2O}.

Ans. a = 0.878.

To correlate activity and concentration units for solutes, one may choose mole fraction, molality, molarity, or other units. To establish a suitable correlation it is well to remember that solutes exhibit their simplest behavior in very dilute solutions. Accordingly, we choose the infinitely dilute solution as the *correlation reference state* for given solute and solvent at each temperature. In practical terms we say that $a_2 \to X_2$ as $X_2 \to 0$, or $a_2 \to m$ as $m \to 0$ and the like. In terms of f and a, Henry's law is exactly

$$f_2 = k\, a_2 \qquad (8.27)$$

at all concentrations, where k is some constant. As a frequently admissible approximation

$$P_2 \cong k_X a_2 \qquad (8.28)$$

or

$$P_2 \cong k_m a_2 \qquad (8.29)$$

where the values of the proportionality constants depend upon whether a_2 and X_2 or a_2 and m are correlated. To the same degree of approximation

$$P_2 \cong k_X X_2 \tag{8.30}$$

or

$$P_2 \cong k_m m \tag{8.31}$$

within the range of validity of Henry's law. That is, $a = X$ or $a = m$ in the limit of very dilute solutions for which k_X or k_m can be evaluated. These experimental constants, in turn, lead to values of activities by equations (8.28) and (8.29) and measured pressures.

The system ethanol-chloroform, for which data appear in Table 8.3, is rather nonideal and may be used to illustrate some of the methods of calculating activities. It should be observed that as $X_{C_2H_5OH}$ approaches unity, $a_{C_2H_5OH}$ $= P_{C_2H_5OH}/P^0_{C_2H_5OH}$ approaches the mole fraction. That is, Raoult's law applies to the solvent and $a_{C_2H_5OH} \cong X_{C_2H_5OH}$. In the same range of composition, but for the minor component, P_{CHCl_3}/X_{CHCl_3} is approximately constant. The solute nearly obeys Henry's law. The limiting value of P/X can be estimated graphically, by extrapolating to the infinitely dilute solution (Fig. 8.3), to be 428. At any composition, therefore, $a_{CHCl_3} = P_{CHCl_3}/428$. As might be expected, values of a_{CHCl_3} and X_{CHCl_3} correspond fairly well in dilute solutions but differ considerably at higher concentrations. On this same basis a_{CHCl_3} at $X_{CHCl_3} = 1$ is 0.690, whereas the alternative choice ($a \rightarrow X$, $X \rightarrow 1$) would give $a_{CHCl_3} = 1$. The choice of correlation reference state is arbitrary. In either case activity is proportional to the partial vapor pressure.

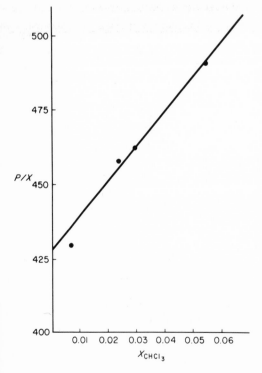

FIG. 8.3. Extrapolation of Henry's law constant to infinitely dilute solution.

It is often convenient to resolve a thermodynamic function of activities into the corresponding function of the concentrations and another function which corrects for nonideality. The simplest correlation of activity and composition is one of the form

$$a = \gamma X \tag{8.32}$$

where γ is the defined *activity coefficient*. Analogous relations apply to other composition units. This same device has been employed previously for converting pressure to fugacity.

EXERCISE 8.9

Evaluate a_{CHCl_3} at 35° from the data of Table 8.3 at $X_{CHCl_3} = 0.0400$ for the correlation reference state $X_{CHCl_3} = 1$.

Ans. $a_{CHCl_3} = 0.968$.

EXERCISE 8.10

Show that the difference in chemical potential of a solute between solutions at X'_2, a'_2 and X''_2, a''_2 is given by $\Delta F = \mu''_2 - \mu'_2 = RT \ln a''_2/a'_2$.

TABLE 8.3
VAPOR PRESSURES OF CHLOROFORM AND ETHANOL AT 35°

$X_{C_2H_5OH}$	$P_{C_2H_5OH}$ mm.	P_{CHCl_3} mm.	$\dfrac{P_{C_2H_5OH}}{P^0_{C_2H_5OH}}$	$\dfrac{P_{CHCl_3}}{X_{CHCl_3}}$	a_{CHCl_3}
0	0	295.11			0.690
0.0384	17.81	286.10	0.1733	297.5	0.668
0.0400	18.13	285.56	0.1764	297.5	0.667
0.0414	18.69	285.48	0.1818	297.8	0.667
0.0440	19.42	285.45	0.1889	298.6	0.667
. . .	. . .	. . .	. . .	. . .	. . .
0.1517	37.27	268.98	0.3626	317.1	0.628
. . .	. . .	. . .	. . .	. . .	. . .
0.9458	96.93	26.61	0.9431	491	0.0622
0.9703	99.86	13.75	0.9716	463	0.0321
0.9759	100.28	11.03	0.9757	458	0.0258
0.9938	102.21	2.66	0.9945	430	0.0062
1.	102.78			(428)	

G. Scatchard and C. L. Raymond, *J. Am. Chem. Soc.*, **60**, 1278 (1938).

8.7 Chemical Equilibrium in Real Solutions

The use of the property activity, rather than one of the more direct measures of composition such as mole fraction, molality, or molarity, permits the redevelopment of the equilibrium function in a form precisely applicable to real solutions. Since the equation for the free energy of dilution in terms of activities has exactly the same mathematical form as that applying to ideal solutions [Exercise 8.10 and equations (8.6), (8.7)], the development is precisely the same as that for equation (8.19).

The generalized chemical change is related to the standard change by the isothermal cycle

$$aA\,(a_A) \quad + \quad bB\,(a_B) + \dots \quad \xrightarrow{\Delta F_T} \quad mM\,(a_M) \quad + \quad nN\,(a_N) + \dots$$

$$\Delta F_T = \left| aRT\ln(1/a_A) \right| \quad \Delta F_T = \left| bRT\ln(1/a_B) \right| \qquad \Delta F_T = \left| mRT\ln(a_M/1) \right| \quad \Delta F_T = \left| nRT\ln(a_N/1) \right|$$

$$aA\,(a_A = 1) + bB\,(a_B = 1) + \dots \xrightarrow{\Delta F_T^0} mM\,(a_M = 1) + nN\,(a_N = 1) + \dots$$

Then

$$\Delta F_T = \Delta F_T^0 + RT\ln Q_a \qquad (8.33)$$

where

$$Q_a = \left(\frac{a_M^m\, a_N^n \dots}{a_A^a\, a_B^b \dots}\right)_{\text{arbitrary}}$$

and ΔF_T^0 is the standard free energy change, that is, for unit *activities* of reactants and products. Q_a is the reaction function of activities, each of which can be chosen arbitrarily. When the activities of reactants and products are those corresponding to an equilibrium state, $\Delta F_T = 0$.

$$0 = \Delta F_T^0 + RT\ln K_a$$

or

$$\Delta F_T^o = -RT \ln K_a \qquad (8.34)$$

where K_a is the value of the equilibrium function of activities.

$$K_a = \left(\frac{a_M^m \, a_N^n \ldots}{a_A^a \, a_B^b \ldots} \right)_{\text{equil.}} \qquad (8.35)$$

The activity of each substance factors into a concentration and an activity coefficient, for example $a = X\gamma$, and the activity coefficients are collected separately.

$$K_a = \frac{X_M^m \, X_N^n \ldots}{X_A^a \, X_B^b \ldots} \frac{\gamma_M^m \, \gamma_N^n \ldots}{\gamma_A^a \, \gamma_B^b \ldots} \qquad (8.36)$$

For convenience let

$$K_a = K_X \, K_\gamma$$

Since it is K_a, not K_X, which is related to the standard free energy change by equation (8.34), it is K_a which is the equilibrium constant, having a unique value for a given system and temperature. The value of K_X is expected to depend on the composition of the system, since the activity coefficients vary with composition. For example, in the esterification equilibrium, treated as an ideal system in section 8.4, if various mixtures of acetic acid, alcohol, and water are equilibrated at 25°, and the value of $K_X = K_n$ computed for the equilibrium composition, the results shown in Table 8.4 are obtained. The variation in K_n is to be attributed to variations in the activity coefficients with the composition (equilibrium) of the system. The value of K_γ and hence K_n is also affected by the presence of salts such as sodium bromide and sodium chloride which do not appear in the chemical equation.

TABLE 8.4

THE ESTERIFICATION EQUILIBRIUM

| | Initial mixture (moles) | | |
Acetic acid	Alcohol	Water	K_n
1	1	0	3.79
3	1	0	4.73
1	3	0	2.45
1	1	23	3.56

The treatment of solution equilibria given in section 8.4 implicitly assumes that K_γ is unity. This is a good approximation in many dilute real solutions, since

$$a \longrightarrow X \qquad \text{and} \qquad \gamma \longrightarrow 1$$

as the concentration approaches zero. In some concentrated solutions, for example, in the esterification equilibrium, the activity coefficients are probably substantially different from unity. However, since the value of K_n is not a strong function of composition, we conclude that the γ's change in such a fashion that K_γ remains nearly constant.

SUMMARY, CHAPTER 8

1.   Free energy of dilution

$$\Delta F_T = nRT \ln \frac{P_2}{P_1}$$

For Henry's law solutions, $P = kX$

$$\Delta F_T = nRT \ln \frac{X_2''}{X_2'}$$

For dilute solutions, $X \ll 1$

$$\Delta F_T = nRT \ln \frac{c''}{c'}$$

Standard states $X = 1$, $c = 1$ may be hypothetical.

2.   Solubility

$$\Delta F_T^o \, (\text{soln.}) = -RT \ln c \, (\text{sat.})$$

$$\ln \frac{c_2}{c_1} = \frac{\Delta H}{R} \left(\frac{T_2 - T_1}{T_2 T_1} \right)$$

3.   Distribution between immiscible solvents Q and R

$$\Delta F_T^o \, (\text{dist.}) = -RT \ln K$$

$$K = \frac{c_R}{c_Q} = \frac{c_R \, (\text{sat.})}{c_Q \, (\text{sat.})}$$

4.   Chemical equilibrium

$$\Delta F_T = \Delta F_T^o + RT \ln Q$$

$$\Delta F_T^o = -RT \ln K$$

$$K = \frac{c_M^m \, c_N^n \, \cdots}{c_A^a \, c_B^b \, \cdots} \quad (\text{dilute solution})$$

$$\ln \frac{K_2}{K_1} = \frac{\Delta H}{R} \left(\frac{T_2 - T_1}{T_2 T_1} \right)$$

5.   Activity

$$d\mu = RT \, d \ln a$$

$$\mu = \mu^o + RT \ln a$$

$$\Delta F_T = n(\mu'' - \mu') = nRT \ln \frac{a''}{a'}$$

Correlation reference state, solvent

$$a \rightarrow 1 \quad \text{as} \quad X \rightarrow 1$$

Correlation reference state, solute

$$a \rightarrow X \quad \text{as} \quad X \rightarrow 0$$

6. Chemical equilibrium in real solutions

$$\Delta F_T^0 = -RT \ln K_a$$

$$\frac{a_M^m a_N^n}{a_A^a a_B^b} = \frac{X_M^m X_N^n}{X_A^a X_B^b} \cdot \frac{\gamma_M^m \gamma_N^n}{\gamma_A^a \gamma_B^b}$$

PROBLEMS, CHAPTER 8

1. Succinic acid, $C_4H_6O_4$, is practically undissociated in its saturated aqueous solution. Its solubility given in grams per 100 g. of water is

Temp. (°C)	0°	12.5°	25°	37.5°	50°
Solubility	2.75	4.92	8.35	14.00	21.40

Plot log solubility versus $1/T$ and find ΔH (soln.). *Ans.* 7.3 kcal.

2. The solubility of succinimide hydrate, $C_4H_7O_3N$, in alcohol is 3.4 g./100 g. at 10° and 6.6 g./100 g. at 25°. Find ΔH, ΔF, and ΔS at 25° for the solution of 1 mole of this substance in a large amount of solution containing 1.0 g./100 g. *Ans.* $\Delta H = 7.4$ kcal., $\Delta F = -1.15$ kcal., $\Delta S = 28.7$ cal. deg.$^{-1}$.

3. From the solubilities of iodine in water and carbon tetrachloride as given in the text, find ΔF_{293} for

$$I_2 \ (H_2O, \ 0.1 \ g.l.^{-1}) = I_2 \ (CCl_4, \ 0.1 \ g.l.^{-1})$$

Ans. -2.33 kcal.

4. A saturated aqueous solution of benzoic acid, $C_7H_6O_2$, at 6° contains 0.19 g./100 g. Use data from Table 8.1 to find the solubility of benzoic acid in benzene at 6°. *Ans.* 0.36 mole l.$^{-1}$.

5. From data on the equilibrium

$$C_6H_{10} \ (CCl_4) + I_2 \ (CCl_4) = C_6H_{10}I_2 \ (CCl_4)$$

and the solubility of I_2 in CCl_4, which is 20 g./1000 g. at 25°, find ΔF_{298}^0 for

$$C_6H_{10} \ (CCl_4) + I_2 \ (s) = C_6H_{10}I_2 \ (CCl_4)$$

using 1 mole l.$^{-1}$ as the standard state of the dissolved substances. The density of CCl_4 is 1.6 g.cc.$^{-1}$. *Ans.* $\Delta F^0 = -548$ cal.

6. The vapor pressure of pure benzene at 22° is 85 mm., and its solubility in water is 0.82 g.l.$^{-1}$. Assuming Henry's law,
(a) what is the partial vapor pressure of benzene over an aqueous solution containing 0.5 g.l.$^{-1}$ at 22°?
(b) What is the activity of benzene in the latter solution relative to $a = 1$ in the pure liquid? *Ans.* (a) 9.8×10^{-3} mm., (b) 1.15×10^{-4} mm.

---

7. Iodine is to be extracted from a fixed quantity of water by a fixed total quantity of carbon tetrachloride. Show that the total amount of iodine removed from the water layer increases with n, the number of portions into which the total quantity of carbon tetrachloride is divided.

8. In Exercise 8.3 it was found that when 1 l. of 0.01 M aqueous benzoic acid is equilibrated with 1 l. of benzene, 77% of the benzoic acid is found in the benzene layer. If the same amount of benzoic acid is distributed between 5 l. of water and 5 l. of benzene, what per cent will remain in the water layer?

9. For the reaction

$$C_6H_{10} + I_2 = C_6H_{10}I_2$$

the equilibrium constant in CCl_4 at 35° is 13 $(m/l.)^{-1}$. A solution contains initially $C_6H_{10}I_2$ at 0.01 M. What is the degree of dissociation of the diiodide at equilibrium?

10. It has been found by optical methods that the degree of dissociation of BrCl in carbon tetrachloride is 43 % at 25°. Find K and ΔF^0_{298} for

$$BrCl\,(CCl_4) = \tfrac{1}{2}\,Br_2\,(CCl_4) + \tfrac{1}{2}\,Cl_2\,(CCl_4)$$

11. Show that the enthalpy term of equation (8.9) corresponds to $-\Delta H_{vap.}$ for gaseous solutes which obey Raoult's law.

12. The solubility of iodine in water is 0.29 g.l.$^{-1}$ at 20° and 0.52 g.l.$^{-1}$ at 40°. Find $\Delta H_{soln.}$ for the process.

13. A binary solution obeys Raoult's law over the entire range of composition. Expressing composition in terms of mole fraction, show that equations (8.8) and (8.9) apply equally to both components. How is the result related to the phenomenon of freezing point lowering?

14. Show that $\Delta F_A = RT \ln X_A$ for a component of solution which obeys either Raoult's law or Henry's law when one mole of the substance A is added to a very large volume of solution in which its composition is X_A.

15. From the result of the preceding problem, show that the free energy change which attends the formation of one mole of ideal solution with constituents A and B is given by

$$\Delta F_{mixing} = X_A\,RT \ln X_A + X_B\,RT \ln X_B$$

16. From the result of the preceding problem, show that the entropy of mixing for a binary solution which obeys Raoult's law is given by

$$\Delta S_{mixing} = -X_A\,R \ln X_A - X_B\,R \ln X_B$$

17. Develop an expression for ΔF_{mixing} of a nonideal binary solution in terms of P_A and P_B. Use the data of Table 8.3 to calculate ΔF for mixing 0.1517 moles of ethanol and 0.8483 moles of chloroform at 35°.

18. From the data for the solubility of sulfur in *n*-hexane, construct a graph of log (solubility) versus $1/T$. Considering the allotropy of sulfur, how do you explain the difference in the slopes at high and low temperatures? If sulfur exists in these solutions largely as S_8, what are the equations describing the two processes? Evaluate ΔH for each. To what process does the difference between these two quantities refer?

Temp. (°C)	40	60	80	100	120	130	140
Solubility (g. S/100 g. soln.)	0.55	1.0	1.7	2.8	4.4	5.2	6.0

9

PHASE DIAGRAMS

9.1 The Gibbs Phase Rule

The phase rule of J. Willard Gibbs provides a general and useful connection between the *number of phases*, the *number of components*, and the *number of independent variables* (*or degrees of freedom*) which must be specified in order to characterize a system.

A *phase* is that portion of a system which is homogeneous throughout. That is, the physical properties of a phase are uniform. The phase may or may not be continuous. Both a single block of ice and a mass of cracked ice represent a single phase. A system consisting of more than one phase is said to be heterogeneous. The heterogeneous system (ice-water) consists of two phases, and if there is vapor in the system, this constitutes a third phase. An entirely gaseous system at equilibrium is always homogeneous, regardless of the number of components present, and therefore constitutes a single phase. Liquid substances exhibit varying degrees of miscibility, and a mixture of liquids may form one, two, or more distinct phases. Some combinations of substances form homogeneous, crystalline mixtures of variable composition called solid solutions, but often solid mixtures are heterogeneous, consisting of two or more phases.

The *composition* of each phase in a system is described by specifying the concentrations of all components. A given component need not appear in all phases of a system. The components of a system are commonly taken to be the fewest substances which can be combined to produce every composition of every phase in the system. For example, the system ice–water–water-vapor has one component, H_2O. Choosing H_2 and O_2 as the components would be incorrect, because this would permit variations in composition outside the limit specified for the system, namely, $n_H : n_O = 2:1$.

For considerations of phase equilibria it is the *number* of independently variable substances, not their nature, which is important. This will be referred to as the *number of components c*. In describing the phase relations of ice–water–water-vapor we are not concerned with hydrogen and oxygen as such. All phases, therefore, have the same composition, viz., H_2O and $c = 1$. Additions of other components would, of course, give rise to new systems. Thus, $H_2O + NaCl$ constitutes a two-component system. The liquid phase contains both components, but the solid phase is under some circumstances pure H_2O, and under others, pure NaCl. The vapor phase is pure H_2O under all ordinary conditions.

Consider the value of c in the system $CaCO_3 - CaO - CO_2$. To obtain any combination of these three phases (two solid, one gas) requires at least two components, most conveniently CaO and CO_2. Freedom to choose n_{CaO} and n_{CO_2} suffices to prepare any amount of any phase. Choosing $CaCO_3$ would not do this, since then n_{CaO}/n_{CO_2} must always be unity. Choosing any other pair such as $CaCO_3$ and CaO would be correct but artificial, because it would involve negative values of n_{CaO} or n_{CO_2}.

After the phases and components present in a system have been specified, there remains a number of additional variables which may be specified in order to complete the exact description of the system. Some of these are pressure, temperature, volume, energy content, and entropy. In a system containing more than one component, the concentrations of the components in the various phases should also be included in the list. The extensive properties, such as volume or energy content, need not concern us, since the important characteristics of phase equilibria, such as freezing point or solubility, are intensive properties. These are unaffected by the amounts of phases present. For example, at a given temperature the equilibrium pressure in the system water–water-vapor is independent of the volume of either phase, so long as they are both present. Furthermore, the number of intensive properties which must be specified is limited, since they are not all independent. In sufficiently simple systems this can be determined by inspection. For example, in a system consisting of a pure gas, specification of the temperature and density uniquely determines the pressure, heat capacity, etc. The state of this system is uniquely characterized by specification of two intensive properties and the system is, therefore, said to have two *degrees of freedom*. On the other hand, the one-component, two-phase system water–water-vapor is uniquely characterized by specification of only one intensive property, such as temperature, since at a given temperature the equilibrium vapor pressure of water has a fixed value. Conversely, if the pressure is specified, the temperature is determined, namely, that temperature at which the equilibrium vapor pressure of water has the chosen value. Such a system has one degree of freedom. Evidently, the *number of degrees of freedom* or *variance f is the minimum number of independent variables which must be specified in order to characterize the system.*

The Gibbs phase rule can now be formulated as follows: Consider a system of p phases (A, B, C, etc.) and c components (1, 2, 3, etc.) in an equilibrium state, as indicated in Fig. 9.1. To assess the number of independent variables, we begin by specifying the concentration of each component in each phase, $p \times c$ quantities. In addition, we specify the temperature and pressure of the system as a whole, these properties being uniform throughout in an equilibrium state. The total number of variables v specified is, therefore,

$$v = pc + 2 \tag{9.1}$$

However, these are not all independent variables. In each phase containing c components it is necessary to specify only the concentration of $c - 1$ components, since only one possible concentration of the remaining component is consistent with this specification. For example, if the composition of the phases is given in mole fraction units, the sum $X_1 + X_2 + X_3 + \ldots = 1$. Therefore, we reduce the number of variables by one for each phase, obtaining

$$v = pc + 2 - p \tag{9.2}$$

Next, when the concentrations of the components in the various phases, X_{1A}, X_{1B}, X_{1C}, ... represent an equilibrium distribution, then a specification of X_{1A} automatically determines X_{1B}, X_{1C}, etc. (see section 8.3). Therefore, for each one of the c components, $p - 1$ composition variables are not independent, and we obtain

$$v = pc + 2 - p - c(p - 1) \tag{9.3}$$

The dependent variables having been eliminated, the quantity remaining is the number of independent variables or the number of *degrees of freedom f*.

$$f = c - p + 2 \tag{9.4}$$

This is a statement of the *Gibbs phase rule*, and its application will be demonstrated in the succeeding sections.

	Components		
Phases	1 , 2 , 3 , • • •		
A	X_{1A} X_{2A} X_{3A} • • •		
B	X_{1B} X_{2B} X_{3B} • • •		
C	X_{1C} X_{2C} X_{3C} • • •		
• • •	• • •		

FIG. 9.1. Phase equilibria.

9.2 One-Component Systems

We consider first the phase equilibria between the various forms of a single substance, and as an example the ice–water–water-vapor system is described in Fig. 9.2. In order to display the data over a wide range of conditions, the pressure and temperature scales are nonlinear. The curve AB describes the vapor-liquid equilibrium; that is, each point on the curve represents the equilibrium vapor pressure at the corresponding temperature. In a similar manner the curve AD describes the solid-vapor equilibrium. These curves meet at A and the Clausius-Clapeyron equation permits extrapolation along the dashed lines. An equilibrium between a supercooled liquid and its vapor can be treated validly by thermodynamics, even though there is a more stable state of the system, namely, ice-vapor. Experimental observations can be made corresponding to points on the curve AC which describes the vapor pressure of supercooled water, but superheated ice is not accessible to experimental test.

Curve AF describes the water-ice equilibrium and displays the decrease in melting point with increased pressure described quantitatively by the Clapeyron equation (7.50). There is no vapor phase present in the system in this region.

The Gibbs phase rule for a one-component system reduces to $f = 1 - p + 2 = 3 - p$, showing that when only one phase is present, there are two degrees of freedom. That is, there is a wide range of temperature and pressure over which the vapor alone can exist. Choosing a temperature does not determine the pressure, or vice versa. However, a specification of these two variables determines the density, heat capacity, etc., so the number of independent variables is two.

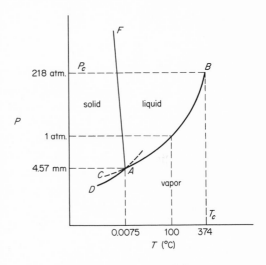

FIG. 9.2. The system H_2O (not to scale).

The three curves in Fig. 9.2 represent conditions for equilibria between two phases: curve AB, liquid-vapor; curve AD, solid-vapor; curve AF, solid-liquid. In a system of one component, the presence of two phases at equilibrium reduces the number of degrees of freedom to one, as shown by equation (9.4). For example, there is a wide range of temperature over which liquid and vapor can exist at equilibrium, but if the temperature is specified, the equilibrium pressure of the system is fixed and is not an independent variable. Conversely, if a pressure is specified, the temperature at which the two phases can be at equilibrium is fixed. For the other two equilibria the same restrictions appear.

The point of intersection of the three curves in Fig. 9.2 is called a *triple point*, since it describes three phases, solid, liquid, and vapor, at equilibrium. The phase rule shows that in such a case the number of degrees of freedom is zero. That is, there are no independent variables. There is only one temperature and one pressure at which this equilibrium can be established.

It should be noted, as in Chapter 7, that the triple point of water does not lie at 0°C, since the latter is defined as the freezing point of water at a pressure of 1 atm. On the other hand, the triple point is the freezing point of water under its own equilibrium vapor pressure, which is 4.57 mm. at this temperature.

A second example of a one-component system, sulfur, is shown in Fig.

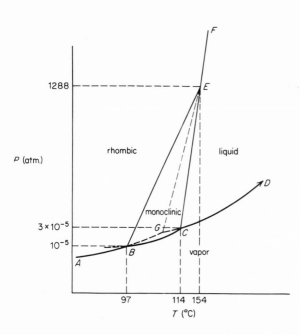

FIG. 9.3. The system sulfur (not to scale).

9.3. Again, the scale of values on the pressure and temperature axes is nonlinear. Two crystal forms (rhombic and monoclinic) of solid sulfur are observed, the former being the stable form at room temperature.

The curves again describe two-phase equilibria in this one-component system and, therefore, describe systems with one degree of freedom, by application of equation (9.4). Curve CD describes the vapor pressure of liquid sulfur as a function of temperature, curve BC the vapor pressure of monoclinic sulfur, and curve AB the vapor pressure of rhombic sulfur. These three curves can be quantitatively described by the Clausius-Clapeyron equation (7.9). Curve CE describes the equilibrium between liquid and monoclinic crystals, that is, the variation of the melting point of monoclinic sulfur with pressure, according to equation (7.50). At pressures above 1288 atm. the monoclinic form is no longer stable, and the rhombic form melts directly to the liquid, an equilibrium described by curve EF. At pressures below 1288 atm. the rhombic form equilibrates with the monoclinic form at temperatures and pressures described by curve BE. In this case the curve describes the equilibrium between two solid phases. In such a change the equilibrium state is attained rather slowly, and it is possible to superheat the rhombic form and observe its vapor pressure along curve BG and its melting point along curve GE. The slow attainment of the equilibrium state in the rhombic-monoclinic transformation is responsible for the observation of an indefinite melting point of sulfur.

When two solid phases occur in a one-component system, four triple points can arise: s'-s''-l; s'-s''-v; s'-l-v; s''-l-v. The phase rule does not predict whether or not all triple points are experimentally accessible. In the present case experiment shows that S_r-1-v is metastable. The stable triple points are B, which describes the equilibrium S_r-S_m-v; the point C, which describes the equilibrium S_m-1-v; and the point E, which describes the equilibrium S_m-S_r-1. Each of these points represents a one-component system containing three phases, and therefore each has no degrees of freedom. That is, there is only one temperature and pressure at which each of these equilibria can be established.

EXERCISE 9.1

From the slopes of the curves in Fig. 9.3 establish the relative densities of monoclinic, rhombic, and liquid sulfur by application of equation (7.50).

$$Ans. \rho_1 < \rho_m < \rho_r.$$

9.3 Two-Component Vapor-Liquid Systems

When a two-component system is considered, the compositions of each phase of the system, as well as temperature and pressure, become important experimental variables. Therefore, for complete description of such a system a three dimensional diagram would be useful. Since such diagrams are difficult to construct the usual practice is to fix one variable, say the pressure, and to display the relation between the other two in a conventional two-dimensional diagram. When a vapor phase is absent, this restriction is not important, since it has been shown for condensed phases (Chapter 7) that equilibrium temperatures are insensitive to moderate changes in pressure.

A phase diagram describing vapor-liquid equilibrium in a two-component system of liquids forming an ideal solution has already been given (see Fig. 1.10). Figure 9.4(a) describes the vapor-liquid equilibrium in the system benzene-toluene, which is nearly ideal, at constant temperature. Figure 9.4(b) describes the same system at constant pressure. The composition of the system is plotted along the horizontal axis in mole fraction units, while the pressure or temperature appears on the vertical axis. In Fig. 9.4(a) the upper curve gives the relation between the pressure and the composition of the liquid

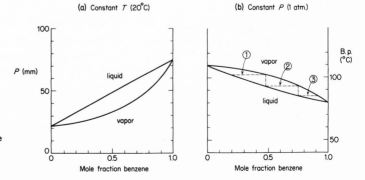

FIG. 9.4. Phase diagrams of the system benzene—toluene.

phase at equilibrium, while the lower curve relates the pressure and the composition of the vapor at equilibrium. That is, any pair of points on the two curves connected by a horizontal line represent the compositions of the liquid and vapor at equilibrium at the chosen pressure. For an ideal system, such pairs of points obey Raoult's law. For a real system, this relationship must be determined by experiment, but in either case it is unique. That is, for a liquid of given composition there is only one possible vapor composition at equilibrium. The gross composition of the system will vary with the relative amounts of the two phases and is, therefore, not an intensive property within our present usage. In Fig. 9.4(b) the same system is described at a fixed pressure, showing the relation between vapor-liquid equilibrium temperature and composition, and again, any pair of points on the two curves connected by a horizontal line represent the equilibrium compositions of the liquid and vapor at the chosen temperature.

For two-component systems, the phase rule shows that when two phases are present there are two degrees of freedom ($f = 2 - 2 + 2 = 2$). In Fig. 9.4 one variable has already been fixed, the temperature in (a) and the pressure in (b). There remains, in either instance, one variable subject to arbitrary choice if the system is to contain two phases at equilibrium. In (a), for a given choice of liquid and corresponding vapor composition, there is only one equilibrium pressure. In (b) when the composition is chosen, the equilibrium temperature is established. Conversely, if in case (a) a pressure is selected (within the range P_A^0 to P_B^0), the compositions of the two phases are determined, and if in case (b) a temperature is selected (within the range T_B^0 to T_A^0), the compositions of the two phases are again fixed.

Many two-component vapor-liquid systems deviate considerably from the ideal behavior described in Fig. 9.4. Two extreme cases are shown in Figs. 9.5 and 9.6. For each system (a) is a pressure-composition diagram at constant

FIG. 9.5. Phase diagrams of the system ethanol—benzene.

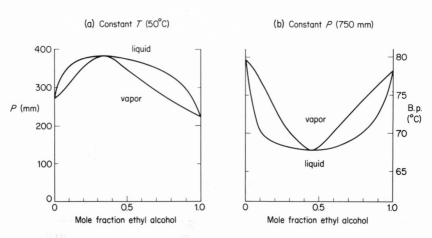

(a) Constant T (50°C)   (b) Constant P (750 mm)

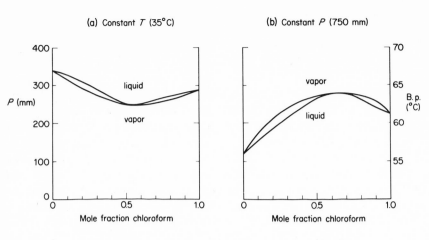

FIG. 9.6. Phase diagrams of the system acetone—chloroform.

temperature, and (b) is a temperature-composition diagram at constant pressure. The pressure chosen may be 1 atm., in which case the (b) figure is called a boiling point diagram.

The system ethanol-benzene, described in Fig. 9.5, shows a maximum in the vapor pressure curve and a corresponding minimum in the boiling temperature. At a pressure of 1 atm. the minimum boiling point is observed at 0.45 mole fraction of alcohol. The coincidence of the two curves at this point signifies that the compositions of vapor and liquid under these conditions are identical. Such a mixture is known as an *azeotrope*.

The system acetone-chloroform, described in Fig. 9.6, shows a minimum in the vapor pressure curve and a corresponding maximum in the boiling temperature. At a pressure of 1 atm. the maximum boiling point is observed at 0.65 mole fraction of chloroform. This is also an azeotropic mixture, since the compositions of vapor and liquid are identical.

EXERCISE 9.2

A liquid mixture consisting of 0.25 mole fraction of chloroform in acetone is gradually warmed through the temperature range 25° − 100° at a constant pressure of 1 atm. Describe the number and nature of the phases present at all stages of this process.

9.4 Distillation Processes

Information such as that in these diagrams provides the basic data describing the equilibrium state in processes of evaporation and condensation. For illustration we will briefly consider two such processes: free boiling and fractional distillation. In free boiling we assume that small increments of vapor in equilibrium with the liquid are continuously formed, removed, and discarded.

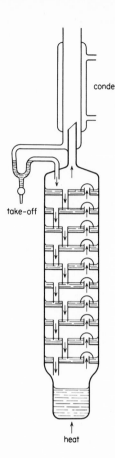

condenser

take-off

heat

FIG. 9.7. Fractionating column.

In fractional distillation a series of liquid-vapor equilibrations is accomplished in a device such as that shown in Fig. 9.7. Heat is supplied to boil the liquid in the lower reservoir, or "still pot." The vapor flowing up the column is brought into intimate contact with the liquid retained in each compartment to hasten equilibration. At the top of the column a reflux condenser returns part or all of the mixture as liquid which flows down through the column. The middle portion of the device is insulated so that no net condensation occurs here to interfere with the equilibration of liquid and vapor phases at the various levels. Ideally, in each stage or "plate" of such a column, vapor-liquid equilibrium is attained, and the net effect is one of a series of successive evaporations and condensations of the charge. Product is usually removed by diverting part of the liquid condensing at the head of the column.

An equimolar mixture of benzene and toluene at a pressure of 1 atm. boils at 92.5°, according to Fig. 9.4(b). The composition of the vapor in equilibrium with the boiling liquid is $X_{benzene} = 0.775$, and we see that the vapor is richer in the more volatile component, benzene. Continued free boiling, with removal of this vapor, depletes the liquid phase in benzene and results in a gradual increase in the boiling point of the liquid. Eventually its composition approaches pure toluene. This is the nature of the result of free boiling of any mixture of liquids when no maximum or minimum in the boiling point curve occurs. For example, commercial liquid air is a mixture of liquid nitrogen (b.p. $= -195.8°$) and liquid oxygen (b.p. $= -183°$), and evaporation of this mixture results in enrichment of the remaining liquid in the less volatile component, oxygen.

In fractional distillation of a mixture such as benzene and toluene, the vapor-liquid equilibration at each plate produces material successively richer in the more volatile component, benzene, toward the top of the column. It cannot be expected that an exact vapor-liquid equilibrium is attained at each level in the column, but the observed separation is often stated in terms of the *number of theoretical plates*. This is the number of vapor-liquid equilibrations required to obtain the observed enrichment. For example, suppose that after operation of a certain column for a period of time at total reflux on a mixture of benzene and toluene the composition of the liquid in the still pot is $X_{benzene} = 0.20$, while the composition of the vapor at the head of the column is $X_{benzene} = 0.91$. Figure 9.4 (b) may be used to estimate the number of theoretical plates by the simple process of counting the number of equilibration steps between these two compositions as indicated in the figure. It can be seen that through improvements in the design of a fractionating column so as to increase the number of theoretical plates, practically pure benzene can be obtained from the mixture.

EXERCISE 9.3

If a still pot is charged with a mixture containing 25 mole per cent of benzene in toluene, estimate the composition of the vapor at the head of a column with three theoretical plates. (Assume that the composition of the material in the still pot does not change.)   *Ans.* $X_{benzene} = 0.94$.

Liquid-vapor systems which form azeotropes yield distinctive results when subjected to free boiling or fractional distillation. In a system such as ethanol-benzene, which forms a minimum-boiling azeotrope, free boiling of any mixture containing initially $X_{alcohol} < 0.45$ produces a vapor which has a higher concentration of alcohol than the parent liquid, and, therefore, upon continued boiling the composition of the remaining liquid approaches pure benzene as the boiling point rises. In fractional distillation, no matter how effective the column, the vapor at the head of the column cannot exceed $X_{alcohol} = 0.45$. In the ethanol-water system, it is the formation of such a minimum-boiling azeotrope at 96% ethanol which prevents the separation of absolute ethanol by fractional distillation of this two-component system.

Free boiling of an ethanol-benzene mixture in which $X_{alcohol} > 0.45$ yields a vapor which has a lower concentration of alcohol than the parent liquid, and with continued boiling the liquid composition approaches pure alcohol. Fractional distillation tends to yield the minimum-boiling azeotrope at the head of the column, while the still pot becomes enriched in alcohol.

For a liquid mixture which forms a maximum-boiling azeotrope, such as the acetone-chloroform system (Fig. 9.6), free boiling of any mixture tends to yield the azeotrope. Regardless of whether the initial composition is greater or less than that of the azeotrope, the composition of the liquid remaining upon free boiling approaches that of the azeotrope as the boiling point rises. This behavior is utilized in the HCl-H_2O system, which forms a maximum-boiling azeotrope at 1 atm., 108.6°, and 20.22 weight per cent HCl, to prepare standard solutions of the acid.

Fractional distillation of a system forming a maximum-boiling azeotrope can yield either pure component at the head of the column, depending on initial composition, while the liquid in the still pot always approaches the composition of the azeotrope.

9.5 Two-Component Systems Exhibiting Two Liquid Phases

Certain pairs of liquids are practically insoluble in each other. When benzene and water are mixed at 25°, two liquid phases are formed: one is 99.91 mole per cent H_2O; the other is 99.81 mole per cent benzene. The mutual solubility of two such liquids usually changes with temperature, and this infor-

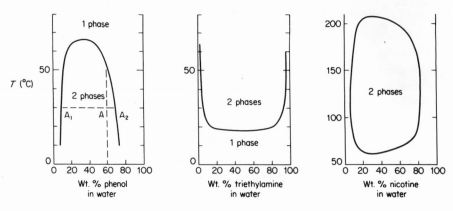

FIG. 9.8. Miscibility of liquid pairs.

mation can be expressed in the form of phase diagrams such as those in Fig. 9.8. The information shown refers to a constant pressure of 1 atm.

The curves of Fig. 9.8 describe the limits of solubility, and the region enclosed is called a two-phase region, since systems of gross composition and temperature such as those represented by the points A will form two phases of compositions given by points A_1 and A_2, the intersections of a horizontal line with the solubility curve. For example, at 30° a mixture of 60% phenol with water will yield two liquid layers, one containing 9% phenol and the other 70% phenol.

EXERCISE 9.4

Sixty grams of phenol is mixed with 40 g. of water at 30°. How many grams of each liquid phase will be formed?   *Ans.* 16.4 g. 9% phenol; 83.6 g. 70% phenol.

Figure 9.8 shows that the mutual solubilities of phenol and water increase with increasing temperature and that the two liquids become miscible in all proportions at 66°. This is called the *upper consolute temperature*. The system triethylamine-water shows the opposite (and less common) behavior, an increase in mutual solubilities with descreasing temperature. This system has a *lower consolute temperature* of 18.5°. The system nicotine-water is quite unusual in that it has both an upper and a lower consolute temperature.

We shall begin discussion of the vaporization equilibria involving two-phase liquid systems by considering the extreme case of an immiscible liquid pair, that is, a liquid pair whose mutual solubilities are so small that the vapor pressures of the two mutually saturated liquid phases are practically those of the pure substances. In such a case, the total vapor pressure over the two-phase liquid system is simply equal to the sum of the vapor pressures of the two pure substances. The presence of a second liquid phase does not affect the vaporization equilibrium of the first.

It is evident that the sum of the two vapor pressures will reach that of the atmosphere at a temperature below the boiling point of either pure liquid, and, therefore, the boiling point of the two-phase system is less than that of either component. This behavior is the basis for the technique of steam distillation in which an organic substance immiscible with water may be distilled at a temperature less than 100°, even though its own boiling point may be considerably higher. This is often advantageous in purification without the thermal decomposition which might occur in simple distillation of the pure substance.

Partially miscible liquids illustrate an extreme case of deviation from ideality, and for those ranges of concentrations in which a homogeneous liquid phase is formed the phase diagram has the usual appearance, as seen in the areas outside the vertical lines in Fig. 9.9. In Fig. 9.9 (a), showing equilibrium pressure as a function of composition, the curve AB describes the composition of the liquid in equilibrium with vapor of composition given by the point at the same pressure on curve AC. In Fig. 9.9(b), showing the equilibrium temperature as a function of composition at 1 atm., the curve AB describes the equilibrium vaporization temperature of liquid solutions of isobutanol in water, and the composition of the vapor formed at a given temperature is given by the curve AC. The solubility of isobutanol in water varies slightly with temperature, as indicated by the curve DB. The point B represents the composition of a saturated solution of isobutanol in water at the equilibrium vaporization temperature, and the point C represents the composition of the vapor in equilibrium with this solution.

Figure 9.9 describes the course of events when a liquid mixture of isobutanol and water is warmed. For any mixture containing less than 8.5% or more than 78% isobutanol, the liquid phase is homogeneous with boiling points given by curves AB and EF, respectively. The composition of the vapor in equilibrium with these liquids at the boiling points is given by curves AC and CF, respectively. However, a system of gross composition between 8.5% and 77% isobutanol will have two liquid layers, and regardless of their relative amounts, so long as two liquids are present, boiling will occur at 89° and 1 atm. The composition of the vapor in equilibrium with the two liquid phases is given by point C, 67% isobutanol. According to the phase rule, at this point $f = 2 - 3 + 2 = 1$. Since the pressure has been arbitrarily selected, no degrees of freedom remain, and a constant boiling point will be observed until one of the liquid phases disappears. For example, if the gross composition of the system is 50% isobutanol,

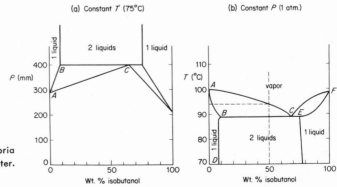

(a) Constant T (75°C)   (b) Constant P (1 atm.)

FIG. 9.9. Vapor—liquid equilibria for the system isobutanol—water.

as indicated by the vertical dashed line, the 77% butanol liquid phase will disappear first, leaving the 8.5% butanol liquid phase. At this time only two phases remain, one liquid and one vapor, and the equilibrium temperature is no longer fixed. Further boiling results in an increase in temperature with change in the liquid composition along line BA until, at approximately 94°, the last of the liquid disappears.

EXERCISE 9.5

From the data given in Fig. 9.9 (a) describe the number and nature of the phases present at various temperatures as a mixture of 50% isobutanol and water vapor is compressed at 75°.

Ans. First liquid, 7% isobutanol forms at 375 mm.; 2 liquid phases, 8.5% isobutanol, 77% isobutanol form at 400 mm. Above 400 mm., no vapor phase.

9.6 Solid-Liquid Equilibria in Two-Component Systems

We now consider solid-liquid equilibria in two-component systems, that is, the phenomena of freezing and melting. We shall confine our discussion to systems in which the liquid phase, or *melt*, is at all times homogeneous, but will include cases in which more than one solid phase is formed.

Information concerning solid-liquid equilibria can be obtained by observing the cooling curve in the region of the freezing point. The sample is heated to a temperature at which it is completely liquefied and then allowed to cool slowly with an approximately constant rate of heat loss. The temperature of the sample is observed and plotted as a function of time. This type of measurement is combined with microscopic, X-ray, or chemical identification of the solid formed in order to characterize the number and nature of the phases present at the fusion equilibrium temperature. Such experiments are ordinarily performed at 1 atm., and, therefore, one variable has been initially fixed.

For pure substances the typical cooling resembles Fig. 9.10. At a constant rate of heat loss the temperature of the melt falls in an approximately linear fashion with time (segment AB). Some supercooling of the melt may occur (segment BC), but when the solid phase forms, the temperature of the system rises abruptly to the equilibrium fusion temperature T_f. With two phases present in a one-component system, the phase rule predicts one degree of freedom ($f = 1 - 2 + 2 = 1$), and since the pressure has already been arbitrarily selected, the temperature is invariant. Heat loss by the system corresponds to the latent heat of crystallization of the sample, and the temperature remains constant until all of the liquid freezes (segment DE). This constancy of temperature during crystallization (or melting) is an important practical criterion of purity. After

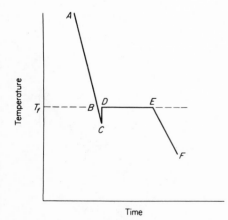

FIG. 9.10. Cooling curve for a pure substance.

complete solidification the system again contains only one phase, and loss of heat is accompanied by a decrease in the temperature of the solid (segment *EF*).

In one simple type of two-component system the two solids exhibit no mutual solubility or compound formation. That is, the solid consists either of one phase, one of the pure substances, or of two phases, the two pure substances, present as a heterogeneous mixture. The phase diagram for a system of this type at 1 atm. is shown in Fig. 9.11. The descending curves may be said to describe the depression of the freezing point of Cd by addition of Bi and the depression of the freezing point of Bi by addition of Cd. It should be noted that the quantitative thermodynamic treatment of freezing point depression previously given (section 7.7) applies only to ideal solutions, whereas the more concentrated solutions containing comparable amounts of the two components are usually not ideal.

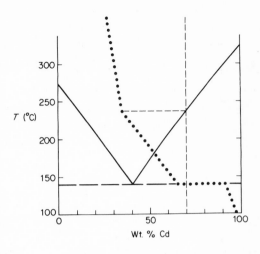

FIG. 9.11. The system cadmium—bismuth.

The cooling curve for a melt containing approximately 70% Cd is superimposed on the phase diagram. The first appearance of a solid phase occurs at approximately 235°, and the solid which appears is pure Cd. This enriches the melt in Bi with a consequent further depression of the freezing point, and the slope of the cooling curve is diminished due to release of heat of crystallization. During this stage of the cooling process there are two phases present, the melt and pure solid Cd. According to the phase rule, for a two-phase two-component system $f = 2$. Of these two degrees of freedom one has been utilized by choosing to work at atmospheric pressure.[1] The remaining degree of freedom may be either temperature or composition. That is, we may regard temperature as the independent variable, in which case the equilibrium composition is fixed by the curve, or on the other hand the composition of the melt may be regarded as the independent variable, in which case the equilibrium temperature is fixed.

As the temperature continues to fall, the amount of solid Cd increases. That is, the solubility of Cd in the melt decreases with decreasing temperature. The composition of the melt at any temperature is given by constructing the appropriate horizontal and noting its point of intersection with the freezing point curve. For example, if a system of gross composition 70% Cd is cooled to 200°, the composition of the remaining melt will be approximately 57% Cd. (See Fig. 9.11.)

Temperature decrease with formation of pure solid Cd continues until the

---

[1]As shown previously, solid-liquid equilibria are insensitive to pressure changes, and only large variations have an appreciable effect on the temperature-composition relation.

temperature indicated by the dashed line is reached, when the composition of the remaining melt is 40% Cd. This temperature, 140°, is the lowest freezing point which can be observed in the system. This temperature and composition of melt characterize the *eutectic point*, at which the solution is mutually saturated with respect to the pure solids. Upon further cooling the remaining melt freezes, without change in composition, forming the eutectic mixture of two pure solids, Cd and Bi. The crystals which separate have a characteristic fine-grained appearance. The number of phases present at the eutectic temperature is three, one liquid and two solid, and according to the phase rule $f = 1$. Since pressure has been fixed, no further degrees of freedom remain. The temperature during this stage of solidification is constant, and this portion of the cooling curve is called the *eutectic halt*. For a given two-component system the eutectic temperature is as well defined as the freezing point of a pure compound. In fact, the cooling curve for a solution of eutectic composition has the same form as that for a pure substance, the distinctions being that the melting point is lower than that for either pure component and the solid formed can be seen, upon microscopic examination, to be heterogeneous, consisting of a minute dispersion of the two solids.

Two pure substances often combine in simple proportions to form one or more compounds, recognizable by their distinctive crystal structure in the solid state. For example, zinc and magnesium form the intermetallic compound $MgZn_2$. Evidence for this compound is found in the phase diagram, shown in Fig. 9.12, in the occurrence of a maximum in the freezing points of the mixtures. The melting point of the compound $MgZn_2$ is 590°, and it contains 15.65 weight per cent magnesium. The regions on each side of this compound may be regarded as independent phase diagrams for the systems Zn-$MgZn_2$ and $MgZn_2$-Mg. In the former system a eutectic point is found at 368° and 3.2% magnesium (79% Zn and 21% $MgZn_2$), and in the latter system a eutectic point is found at 347° and 49% magnesium (61% $MgZn_2$ and 39% Mg). Upon cooling a melt containing 40% Mg, the first solid which separates (at *ca.* 425°) will be the pure phase $MgZn_2$. This continues to separate while the temperature falls to 347°, at which the eutectic halt occurs, and further solidification yields the eutectic mixture of $MgZn_2$ and Mg.

Some compounds are stable in the crystalline state at moderate temperatures but upon warming decompose before reaching a true melting point. This behavior is indicated in the system K-Na, shown in Fig. 9.13. The compound KNa_2 is stable below 7°, but decomposes at this temperature, yielding a melt containing 56% K and pure solid Na. Such a phase transformation temperature is known as an *incongruent melting point*. Note

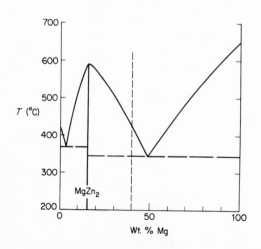

FIG. 9.12. The system magnesium—zinc.

that during the course of this decomposition three phases are present in this two-component system. According to the phase rule, there is one degree of freedom, and since the pressure is fixed, the temperature is invariant, as with the melting of a pure substance. However, one of the products of this "melting" process is a solid.

It is instructive to follow the cooling curve of a melt having a composition in the range 46–56% K, as indicated by the vertical dashed line in Fig. 9.13. A solid phase, pure Na, first appears at *ca.* 15°, depleting the melt of Na and depressing the freezing point. When the composition of the remaining melt reaches 56% K and the temperature 7°, reaction between the melt and pure Na occurs to form the com-

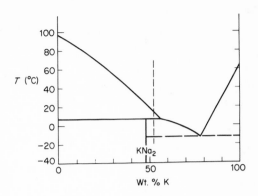

FIG. 9.13. The system potassium—sodium.

pound KNa_2. Since three phases are present during this process, an invariant temperature is observed, which is called a *peritectic halt*. The original melt contained more K than required for formation of the compound, so that when the Na has been completely converted into KNa_2 some melt will still remain. In practice, such a reaction involving two solid phases may be quite slow, and the peritectic halt may be difficult to observe. The cooling curve from this point on will have the usual form, a decline in temperature as solid KNa_2 is formed and the melt grows richer in K, followed by a eutectic halt at $-12°$. When the original melt contains more than 56% K, only the eutectic halt will be observed, and when it contains less than 46% K, only the peritectic halt will be observed.

EXERCISE 9.6

Sketch the cooling curves and specify the number and nature of the phases present during cooling of melts containing 40% and 60% K in Na.

FIG. 9.14. The system lead—bismuth.

In many systems, particularly those involving two metals, it is observed that a significant mutual solubility of the solids occurs. That is, a small amount of one solid can be incorporated in the crystal lattice of the other without formation of a second phase. A system showing this behavior is described in the phase diagram of Fig. 9.14. When a melt containing less than 37% Bi is cooled, it is found that the first solid which forms is the solid solution α (Bi in Pb). For a melt containing 15% Bi, the first solid appears at a temperature of *ca.* 280°, and the

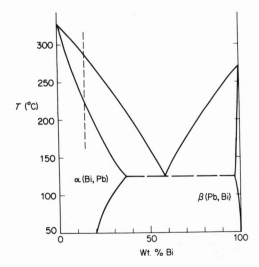

solid solution contains 5% Bi. Further cooling produces more of this solid phase containing increasing proportions of Bi, until at *ca.* 220° complete solidification has occurred. At no time are more than two phases present, and therefore no halt is observed. The eutectic halt will be observed only for systems containing between 37% and 97.3% Bi, and the two phases of the eutectic mixture are the two solid solutions rather than the pure substances.

The phase diagram for the system Pb-Bi shows that the solubility of Bi in Pb changes with temperature and that solid solutions containing 18–37% Bi become supersaturated at low temperatures. A slow transformation to a more dilute solid solution of Bi in Pb with the formation of a second phase should occur and should be microscopically recognizable.

9.7 Three-Component Systems

Complete description of a three-component or ternary system would require a four-dimensional figure, since four variables must be specified: two compositions, pressure, and temperature. If any two of the variables are arbitrarily fixed, a two-dimensional graph may be used.

The solubility behavior of a three-component liquid system as a function of composition at fixed pressure and temperature can be represented as shown for the system phenol-water-acetone in Fig. 9.15. A triangular set of coordinates is used in which each apex represents a pure component, and compositions corresponding to less than 100% of that component are measured on a scale normal to the opposite leg of the triangle. On such a diagram the three percentages represented by any given point always total 100. For example, the point marked *O* in the figure represents a system containing 15% water, 35% phenol, and 50% acetone. Points along a given side of a triangle represent zero per cent of the component found at the opposite apex, that is, two-component systems. For example, the horizontal side of the triangle in Fig. 9.15 represents phenol-water systems and corresponds to a horizontal line across Fig. 9.8 (a), since temperature as well as pressure is fixed.

The curve shown in the graph separates the region of compositions in which two liquid phases are formed from that in which a single homogeneous liquid phase is formed. Although phenol and water at this temperature and pressure are only partly miscible, the addition of acetone increases their mutual solubility until, at concentrations of acetone in excess of 43%, all proportions of phenol and water are miscible. (Very small additions of acetone actually diminish the mutual solubilities of phenol and water to a slight

FIG. 9.15. The ternary system phenol—water—acetone at 30° and 1 atm.

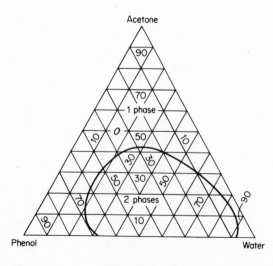

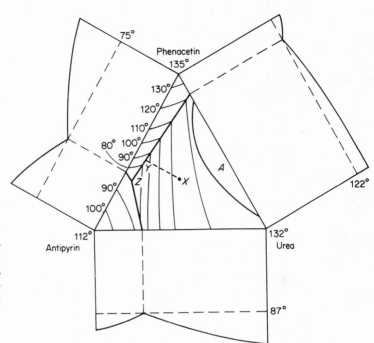

FIG. 9.16. The system an-
tipyrin — urea — phenacetin
[from   Landolt-Bornstein,
Physikalisch-Chemische Ta-
bellen, Erg. IIIa, Julius
Springer, Berlin, 1955].

extent.) The two-component systems, acetone-water and acetone-phenol, are
miscible in all proportions. However, addition of the third component to
either of these systems can cause separation into two phases. For example,
if we begin with a 50–50 water-acetone mixture and add phenol, two liquid
phases will appear when the system contains more than 20% and less than
65% phenol.

Freezing-point data for a three-component system require a three-dimensional figure which can be displayed in the form shown in Fig. 9.16. The composition axes of the central triangle are arranged in the same way as in Fig.
9.15. The face of the triangle is drawn as a contour map, showing isothermal
lines. The heavy lines show the eutectic compositions, with a ternary eutectic
point at 59% antipyrin, 6% urea, 35% phenacetin, and 69°. The region *A*
represents a region of liquid immiscibility. Attached to each side of the triangle
are the corresponding two-component phase diagrams.

Upon cooling a three-component liquid belonging to a system such as that
shown in Fig. 9.16, for example, an equimolar mixture of antipyrin, urea, and
phenacetin, the first solid which separates will be one of the pure components;
in the example given, urea at *ca.* 112° (point *X*). As the melt is depleted in urea,
the equilibrium temperature decreases along the line *XY* until at *ca.* 85° (point
Y) two solid phases, urea and phenacetin, form. This enriches the melt in
antipyrin, and the temperature falls still further along the line *YZ* until the
ternary eutectic point at 69° (point *Z*) is reached and a third solid phase, antipyrin, forms together with the other two. In a three-component system a

constant temperature is obtained only when four phases are present, in this case three solids and one liquid, for according to the phase rule $f = 3 - 4 + 2 = 1$, and the pressure has been arbitrarily fixed.

SUMMARY, CHAPTER 9

1. *The Gibbs phase rule:* $f = c - p + 2$

2. *One-component systems:* $f = 3 - p$
   One phase, $f = 2$
   Two phases, $f = 1$
   Three phases, triple point, $f = 0$

3. *Two-component vapor-liquid systems:* $f = 4 - p$
   For vapor-one liquid equilibria, constant T or P, $f = 1$
   For vapor-two liquid equilibria, constant T or P, $f = 0$

4. *Solid-liquid equilibria*
   Two components, pressure fixed: $f = 3 - p$
     Liquid, one solid, $f = 1$
     Liquid, two solids; eutectic, peritectic, $f = 0$
   Three components, pressure fixed, $f = 4 - p$
     Liquid, two solids, $f = 1$
     Liquid, three solids; ternary eutectic, $f = 0$

PROBLEMS, CHAPTER 9

1. In the equilibrium

$$CaCO_3 \text{ (s)} \rightleftharpoons CaO \text{ (s)} + CO_2 \text{ (g)}$$

we have seen that at each temperature there is a characteristic dissociation pressure $P = K$. Does the system consist of pure crystals of $CaCO_3$ mixed with pure crystals of CaO, or does it contain crystals in which $CaCO_3$ and CaO are molecularly dispersed (a solid solution)? Only one of these alternatives is thermodynamically allowed. Explain.

2. From the data given below construct a graph of liquid and vapor composition versus boiling point and describe the result of (a) free boiling and (b) fractional distillation of a mixture containing 50 mole per cent of carbon tetrachloride in ethyl alcohol.

B.p. (°C)		77.9	72.8	68.0	65.0	63.6	64.3	75.9
Mole per cent	liquid	0	6.4	17.6	33.6	63	72.8	100
CCl_4 in C_2H_5OH	vapor	0	25	45	55	63	67	100

3. Use the data given below for the liquid-vapor system chloroform in benzene to estimate the composition of the first distillate when a large quantity of 50% chloroform in benzene is distilled in a fractionating column of 4 theoretical plates.

T (°C)		80.6	79.0	77.3	75.3	74.0	71.9	68.9	61.4
Mole per cent	liquid	0	15	29	44	54	66	79	100
$CHCl_3$ in C_6H_6	vapor	0	20	40	60	70	80	90	100

4. At 20° the mutual solubility of methyl ethyl ketone and water is such that one layer contains 22.6 wt. % and the second contains 90.1 wt. % methyl ethyl ketone. How much of each layer will be formed when 50 g. of water and 50 g. of methyl ethyl ketone are mixed?

5. From the data given below for the vapor-liquid system furfural-water construct a phase diagram showing vapor and liquid composition at the boiling point and also the mutual solubility of the two liquids below the boiling point.

B.p. (°C)		100	98.1	97.9	97.9	100.6	122.5	155	162
Mole per cent ⎱ liquid		0	2	9.2	50	80	92	96	100
furfural ⎰ vapor		0	8	9.2	9.2	11	32	81	100

Temp. (°C)		90	80	60
Mutual solubility ⎱				
Mole per cent ⎬ L_I		3.4	3.0	2.2
furfural ⎰ L_{II}		55	60	67

Describe the number and nature of phases present when a mixture containing 60 mole per cent furfural is warmed.

6. Obtain an expression for the composition of the vapor X'_A as a function of the composition of the liquid X_A at constant temperature in a two-component system forming an ideal solution.

7. From the following set of cooling curves for the system $PbSO_4$–K_2SO_4 construct the phase diagram for the system. The melting points of the pure substances are 1070° and 1080°C, respectively. What is the formula of the compound formed?

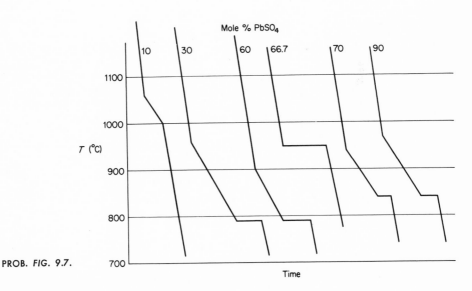

PROB. FIG. 9.7.

8. Using Figs. 9.12, 9.13, and 9.14, sketch the cooling curves for melts containing (a) 10 wt. % Mg in Zn. (b) 20 wt. % Mg in Zn. (c) 20 wt. % K in Na. (d) 70 wt. % K in Na. (e) 20 wt. % Bi in Pb. (f) 40 wt. % Bi in Pb

9. Magnesium melts at 651° and nickel at 1450°. These elements form two compounds in the solid state, Mg_2Ni, which shows an incongruent melting point at 770° yielding liquid containing 38 wt. % Ni and the compound $MgNi_2$. The latter compound melts at 1180°. Two eutectics are found; one at 510° and 28% Ni, the other at 1080° and 88% Ni. Use this information to sketch the phase diagram.

10. The following phase diagram describes the system silver-tin. What is the formula of the compound formed? Construct cooling curves for melts containing 30, 60, and 90% silver.

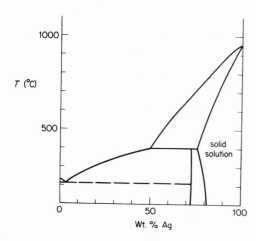

PROB. FIG. 9.10.

11. The data given below are the weight per cent compositions of the two layers formed in various mixtures of water, ether, and methanol. Use the data to construct the ternary solubility diagram, indicating the two-phase region.

Wt. % methanol		0	10	20	30
Wt. % water	L_I	93	82	70	45
	L_{II}	1	6	15	40

10

ELECTROCHEMISTRY

10.1 Faraday's Law

In 1887 Svante Arrhenius proposed that acids, bases, and salts dissociate in aqueous solutions to form positive and negative ions. Upon application of an electric field, conduction of electric current in such electrolyte solutions takes place through the migration of these ions, rather than by migration of electrons as in the metals.

It is the nature of electrolytic conduction that electric charge is transferred between ions in solution and the electrodes which are immersed in the solution and connect with the external circuit. When negative electric charge enters the solution, it effects chemical reactions of reduction. The electrode at which reduction occurs is the *cathode*, and the positively charged ions which migrate toward it are *cations*. At the other electrode, the *anode*, reactions of oxidation provide a mechanism for transferring electrons from the solution to the metallic circuit. The negative ions which migrate toward this electrode are *anions*. For example, if two metallic silver electrodes are dipped into a solution of silver nitrate, as shown in Fig. 10.1, and an electric current is passed through the system, the following processes occur: Current is carried through the electrolyte by the migration of anions (NO_3^-) toward the anode and cations (Ag^+) toward the cathode. At the cathode silver ions are discharged by acquisition of an electron from the cathode, and deposit on the cathode as metallic silver. At the anode silver enters the solution as silver ions, liberating electrons to the external circuit.

The processes which occur at electrodes depend on the sign of the electrode, its composition, the nature and concentrations of the ions in solution, and the

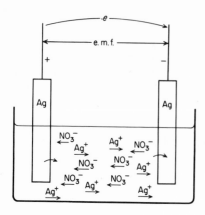

FIG. 10.1. Electrolysis of silver nitrate solution.

applied voltage. Those reactions tend to occur which are thermodynamically allowed, viz, for which $-n\mathscr{F}\mathscr{E} + \Delta F$ (reaction) < 0. If two or more reactions are chemically possible, that reaction involving the smallest value of ΔF will occur first as the applied voltage is gradually increased. With further increase in applied voltage, other reactions will set in as they become allowed. Electrode reactions may involve the electrodes themselves (as in the Daniell cell), or coatings upon the electrodes (as in the lead storage battery), or only ions in solution. For the present we shall write simple electrode reactions that express the net change which occurs, but do not portray the mechanism of the process. For example, in the electrolysis of aqueous silver nitrate between platinum electrodes, the anode reaction can no longer be oxidation of silver, and it is observed that the electrode reactions are

$$Ag^+ \text{ (aq.)} + e = Ag \text{ (s)} \quad \text{at the cathode}$$

and

$$\tfrac{1}{2} H_2O \text{ (l)} = \tfrac{1}{4} O_2 \text{ (g)} + H^+ \text{ (aq.)} + e \quad \text{at the anode}$$

In the electrolysis of dilute aqueous sulfuric acid between platinum electrodes, hydrogen is evolved at the cathode and oxygen at the anode. The electrode reactions used to represent this are

$$H^+ \text{ (aq.)} + e = \tfrac{1}{2} H_2 \text{ (g)} \quad \text{at the cathode}$$

and

$$\tfrac{1}{2} H_2O \text{ (l)} = \tfrac{1}{4} O_2 \text{ (g)} + H^+ \text{ (aq.)} + e \quad \text{at the anode.}$$

A precise quantitative relation exists between the amount of charge passed through the system and the amount of chemical reaction occurring at the electrodes. This relation is known as *Faraday's law*, which states that *96,487 coulombs (1 coulomb = 1 ampere-second) of electricity produce a chemical change of 1 gram-equivalent*. For example, the passage of 96,487 coulombs of electric charge through the electrolysis cell shown in Fig. 10.1 will result in the deposition of 107.87 g. of silver on the cathode, and loss of 107.87 g. of silver from the anode. Such a cell is often used as a *coulometer*, which measures the total charge passing through an electric circuit in terms of the weight of silver deposited.

EXERCISE 10.1

A silver coulometer is connected in series with a cell for electrolysis of water. One gram of silver is deposited on the cathode of the coulometer. How many grams of oxygen and hydrogen will be evolved from the electrolysis of water?
Ans. 0.0742 g. O_2; 0.00934 g. H_2.

Faraday's law is exact because 1 gram-equivalent of chemical change in an electrolytic cell necessarily involves Avogadro's number of electrons in reduction at the cathode and a like number in oxidation at the anode. An ion with a positive valence number of 2, such as Cu^{++}, requires two units of electrons for reduction to the metal, and therefore one unit of electrons will reduce 1 gram-equivalent weight, or $\frac{1}{2}$ gram-atomic weight. The experimental determination of the *faraday*, which is equal to 96,487 coulombs, may be combined with the experimental value of the charge on the electron (see Chapter 13), 1.60210×10^{-19} coulomb, to obtain a value of Avogadro's number.

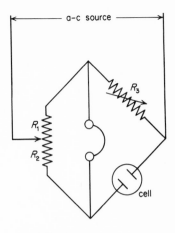

FIG. 10.2. Wheatstone bridge.

$$\frac{96,487}{1.60210 \times 10^{-19}} = 6.0225 \times 10^{23}$$

This is the number of electronic charges in 1 faraday and, therefore, the number of atoms in 1 gram-atomic weight.

10.2 Conductance

The resistance which electrolyte solutions offer to the flow of current gives some useful insights into their nature. *Ohm's law* defines the resistance R of a conductor as the proportionality factor relating current I to potential difference V across the conductor.

$$V = RI \tag{10.1}$$

A potential difference of 1 v. will produce a current of 1 amp. through a resistance of 1 ohm.

Conductance l is the reciprocal of resistance and the unit of conductance is the mho or ohm^{-1}.

$$l = \frac{I}{V} \tag{10.2}$$

The resistance or conductance of electrolyte solutions is usually measured with a Wheatstone bridge, as shown in Fig. 10.2. Alternating rather than direct current is used so that the electrode reactions that occur in one half cycle will be reversed in the other half cycle. Thus products of electrolysis do not accumulate at the electrodes, and the electrolyte is not consumed. When audio frequencies are used (commonly 1000 cycles per second), earphones serve as convenient null detectors.

The observed conductance will depend on the spacing and size of the electrodes as well as on the nature of the electrolyte solution. If the electrodes constitute the ends of a cylindrical vessel, the observed conductance of a given solution will be directly proportional to the cross-sectional area of the electrodes A, and inversely proportional to the distance between the electrodes d.

A property of the electrolyte solution itself is the *specific conductance L*, defined as the conductance of a sample between electrodes of 1 sq. cm. area, which are 1 cm. apart. The relation of the specific conductance to the observed conductance is

$$L = l\frac{d}{A} \tag{10.3}$$

In practice it is difficult to construct a conductivity cell in which d and A are precisely known. Therefore it is customary to measure the resistance of a solution of known specific conductance and thus obtain the *cell constant k*, relating observed resistance to specific conductance. The same cell may then be used for measurements on solutions of unknown conductance. For example, it is found that $0.02000\,M$ aqueous potassium chloride, for which $L_{25°} = 0.002768$ ohm^{-1}cm.$^{-1}$, in a certain conductance cell has a resistance of 145.0 ohms. The resistance is inversely proportional to the specific conductance, the proportionality factor being the cell constant.

$$L = \frac{k}{R} \tag{10.4}$$

Therefore, for the cell in question

$$k = 145.0 \times 0.002768 = 0.4014 \text{ cm.}^{-1}$$

When filled with $0.00250\,M$ potassium sulfate, the same cell has a resistance of 575 ohms. The specific conductance of the latter solution is, therefore,

$$L = \frac{0.4014}{575} = 0.000698 \text{ ohm}^{-1} \text{ cm.}^{-1}$$

EXERCISE 10.2

What is the resistance at 25° of a 0.0200 M aqueous potassium chloride solution in a cell whose effective interelectrode dimensions are $d = 3$ cm. and $A = 6$ cm.^{2}?

Ans. 181 ohms.

These calculations neglect solvent conductivity. In most aqueous solutions this assumption is justified, since the specific conductance of pure water at 25° is only 6.2×10^{-8} ohm^{-1} cm.$^{-1}$. In practice it is difficult to prepare water with this small conductance, since a very small amount of electrolyte impurity can produce a comparable conductance. For example, one part per million by weight of potassium chloride ($1.33 \times 10^{-5}\,M$) will produce a specific conductance of approximately 2×10^{-6} ohm^{-1} cm.$^{-1}$.

10.3 Equivalent Conductance

The specific conductance of strong electrolytes, such as sodium chloride, is only approximately proportional to the number of ions per unit volume. To examine this behavior it is convenient to refer the electric conductivity to 1 gram-equivalent of electrolyte. The *equivalent conductance* Λ is defined by

$$\Lambda = VL = \frac{1000}{c}L \tag{10.5}$$

where V is the volume of solution (in milliliters) containing 1 gram-equivalent of electrolyte, and c is the concentration in gram-equivalents per liter.

The concept of equivalent conductance may be illustrated by considering a conductivity cell having parallel electrodes 1 cm. apart and of indefinite extent. Using a solution of any concentration let this vessel be filled with a volume of solution containing 1 gram-equivalent of electrolyte. (For a 1 normal solution, 1 equivalent is contained in 1 l. of solution, and 1000 cm.² of each electrode surface is covered.) Dilution of the solution in this cell with consequent decrease in the specific conductance L, produces a corresponding increase in the area of the electrodes covered. Evidently the equivalent conductance is the conductance of 1 gram-equivalent of solute between electrodes 1 cm. apart, regardless of the concentration.

EXERCISE 10.3

From the specific conductance of 0.0200 M potassium chloride given above, compute the equivalent conductance.   *Ans.* 138.4 ohm⁻¹ eq.⁻¹ cm.².

The observed dependence of equivalent conductance on concentration is shown for several electrolytes in Fig. 10.3. The horizontal axis is the square root of concentration, which simplifies extrapolation to infinitely dilute solution for reasons which will be discussed in a later section.

For a large group of substances called *strong electrolytes* the equivalent conductance lies above *ca.* 100 ohm⁻¹eq.⁻¹cm.² in solutions of moderate concentration. In these solutions Λ increases slowly with increasing dilution, as shown in Fig. 10.3. This behavior is not to be attributed to increasing dissociation, for these electrolytes are thought to be completely dissociated at all concentrations. Rather, the increase in Λ with dilution is to be attributed to decreasing interionic forces which inhibit migration in the electric field. Extrapolation of the curve to zero concentration

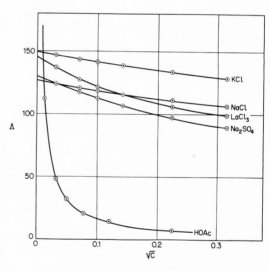

FIG. 10.3. Equivalent conductance vs. concentration.

yields Λ_0, the *equivalent conductance* of the electrolyte at *infinite dilution*, a measure of the "natural" conductance of the ions subject only to the viscous drag of the solvent.

In 1875 F. Kohlrausch came to the conclusion that at *infinite dilution* the cations and anions behave independently and that the total equivalent conductance of the electrolyte is equal to the sum of the equivalent conductances of the cations and anions. The evaluation of the individual ionic conductances at infinite dilution will be described in a succeeding section, but the validity of

TABLE 10.1

EQUIVALENT CONDUCTANCES OF STRONG ELECTROLYTES
IN AQUEOUS SOLUTION AT INFINITE DILUTION AND 25°*

Substance	Λ_0 (ohm^{-1}eq.$^{-1}$cm.^{2})	Substance	Λ_0 (ohm^{-1}eq.$^{-1}$cm.^{2})
HCl	426.16	NaOH	247.8
LiCl	115.03	AgNO$_3$	133.36
NaCl	126.45	MgCl$_2$	129.40
KCl	149.86	CaCl$_2$	135.84
NH$_4$Cl	149.7	BaCl$_2$	139.98
KBr	151.9	LaCl$_3$	145.8
KI	150.38	KIO$_4$	127.92
NaI	126.94	KClO$_4$	140.04
KNO$_3$	144.96	NaOAc	91.0

* From G.F.A. Kortum and J.O'M. Bockris, *Textbook of Electrochemistry*, Elsevier Press, Inc., New York, 1951.

this conclusion may be demonstrated by taking values of the equivalent conductance at infinite dilution, Λ_0 being taken from Table 10.1. According to Kohlrausch's law, Λ_0 for any strong electrolyte such as KCl may be separated into a simple sum of equivalent ionic conductivities, thus:

$$\Lambda_0(\text{KCl}) = \lambda_0(\text{K}^+) + \lambda_0(\text{Cl}^-) \tag{10.6}$$

It follows that the difference between $\Lambda_0(\text{KCl})$ and $\Lambda_0(\text{KI})$ is simply the difference between $\lambda_0(\text{Cl}^-)$ and $\lambda_0(\text{I}^-)$. This may be tested by obtaining the same difference from $\Lambda_0(\text{NaCl})$ and $\Lambda_0(\text{NaI})$, as follows:

$$\Lambda_0(\text{KCl}) - \Lambda_0(\text{KI}) = \lambda_0(\text{Cl}^-) - \lambda_0(\text{I}^-)$$
$$149.86 - 150.38 = -0.52 \text{ ohm}^{-1}\text{eq.}^{-1}\text{cm.}^2$$
$$\Lambda_0(\text{NaCl}) - \Lambda_0(\text{NaI}) = \lambda_0(\text{Cl}^-) - \lambda_0(\text{I}^-)$$
$$126.45 - 126.94 = -0.49 \text{ ohm}^{-1}\text{eq.}^{-1}\text{cm.}^2$$

The concentration dependence of the equivalent conductance of weak electrolytes is in marked contrast to that of strong electrolytes. Figure 10.3 illustrates this behavior for acetic acid, a typical weak electrolyte. The equivalent conductance is small at high concentrations and increases markedly with increasing dilution. Since conductivity is a measure of the number of ions present, it is necessary to suppose that one equivalent of acetic acid furnishes comparatively few ions. That is, acetic acid dissociates incompletely according to

$$\text{CH}_3\text{COOH} = \text{H}^+ + \text{CH}_3\text{COO}^-$$

and the conductivity is to be attributed to the ions. According to the principle of Le Chatelier, the degree of dissociation increases with dilution, giving rise to an increasing equivalent conductance with decreasing concentration. At infinite dilution the acid would presumably be completely dissociated and show an equivalent conductance comparable with that of the strong electrolytes, but this is beyond the range of measurement or extrapolation.

If a weak electrolyte dissociates to the fractional extent α, then by an extension of Kohlrausch's law of the intrinsic conductivities of individual ions we expect that

$$\Lambda = \alpha \Lambda_0 \tag{10.7}$$

This relation is valid at vanishingly small ion concentrations and a useful first approximation in fairly dilute solutions. The value of Λ_0 for a weak electrolyte such as acetic acid may be obtained by application of Kohlrausch's law to measurements of Λ_0 for strong electrolytes involving the same ions. For example, since for acetic acid

$$\Lambda_0(\text{HOAc}) = \lambda_0(\text{H}^+) + \lambda_0(\text{OAc}^-)$$

its value may be obtained from

$$\Lambda_0(\text{HCl}) + \Lambda_0(\text{NaOAc}) - \Lambda_0(\text{NaCl})$$

Using values from Table 10.1, we obtain

$$\Lambda_0(\text{HOAc}) = 426.16 + 91.0 - 126.45$$
$$= 390.7 \text{ ohm}^{-1}\text{eq.}^{-1}\text{cm.}^2$$

Comparison of this calculated value of $\Lambda_0(\text{HOAc})$ with the observed value of $\Lambda(\text{HOAc})$ at some finite concentration yields the degree of dissociation α of the acid. For example, the observed value of $\Lambda(\text{HOAc})$ at 0.01 M is 16.3 ohm^{-1} eq.$^{-1}$cm.^{2} Therefore,

$$\alpha = \frac{16.3}{391} = 0.0417$$

EXERCISE 10.4

Combine the values of Λ_0 for a strong acid, a strong base, and the corresponding salt from Table 10.1 to compute the sum

$$\lambda_0(\text{H}^+) + \lambda_0(\text{OH}^-)$$

Compare this value with the observed conductance of pure water ($L = 6.2 \times 10^{-8}$ ohm^{-1}cm.$^{-1}$) to obtain a value for the degree of dissociation of water.

Ans. $\alpha = 2.0 \times 10^{-9}$.

10.4 Ionic Mobilities—Transference Number

Because of differences in size, charge, and degree of hydration, the cations and anions of a given electrolyte do not, in general, migrate with the same velocity. The *transference number n* is the fraction of total current carried by one ionic species.

$$n_+ = \frac{i_+}{i_+ + i_-}, \qquad n_- = \frac{i_-}{i_+ + i_-} \tag{10.8}$$

Transference numbers are most precisely evaluated by observation of *ion mobilities* in a moving boundary apparatus, sketched in Fig. 10.4. Two electrolyte solutions, having one ion in common, are carefully introduced so that a sharp boundary is formed as

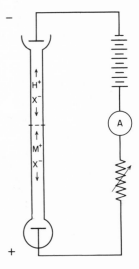

FIG. 10.4. Moving boundary apparatus.

indicated. We may imagine that these two electrolytes are a strong acid and its salt. Then the position of the boundary can be observed with an acid-base indicator or by the change of refractive index of the solution at the boundary.

An electric field is applied to the cell in such a sense that the faster ion (H^+) precedes the slower ion (M^+) toward the cathode. Under these circumstances the boundary will remain sharply defined, because any tendency of the faster ion (H^+) to outrun the slower ion (M^+) will reduce the concentration of electrolyte at the boundary, thus increasing the resistance and the potential gradient along the tube in that region. This will tend to speed up the slower ion (M^+). On the other hand, if the slower ions (M^+) diffuse ahead of the boundary they enter a region of lower resistance and lower potential gradient and, therefore, tend to slow down. Thus, the boundary formed with the ion of higher mobility preceding the one of lower mobility remains sharply defined.

A steady current I is passed through the solution for t seconds, causing the boundary to migrate toward the cathode, sweeping out a volume V liters. This is accompanied by the migration of $\mathscr{F} c_+ V$ coulombs of positive charge past an arbitrary reference plane in the acid solution. The transference number of the cation (H^+) in this solution is obtained from

$$n_+ = \frac{\mathscr{F} c_+ V}{It} \tag{10.9}$$

and

$$n_- = 1 - n_+$$

Table 10.2 shows that the transference number is not a strong function of concentration.

TABLE 10.2

CATION TRANSFERENCE NUMBERS IN AQUEOUS SOLUTION AT 25°*

Electrolyte	0.10 N	0.01 N	∞ dilute (extrapolated)
HCl	0.8314	0.8251	0.8209
NaOAc	0.5594	0.5537	0.5507
KNO$_3$	0.5103	0.5084	0.5072
KCl	0.4898	0.4902	0.4906
LiCl	0.3168	0.3289	0.3364
AgNO$_3$	0.4682	0.4648	0.4643
Na$_2$SO$_4$	0.3828	0.3848	0.386
LaCl$_3$	0.4375	0.4625	0.477

* From G.F.A. Kortum and J.O'M. Bockris, *Textbook of Electrochemistry*, Elsevier Press, Inc., New York, 1951.

EXERCISE 10.5

Use data from Table 10.2 to find the linear velocity of H^+ in 0.1 N HCl when subjected to a potential gradient of 1 v. cm.$^{-1}$. The specific conductance of 0.1 N HCl is 0.0391 ohm^{-1}cm.$^{-1}$. *Ans.* 3.37 × 10^{-3} cm.sec.$^{-1}$.

Since $\lambda_+/\Lambda = n_+$, the fraction of current carried by the cation, the transference numbers may be used to obtain values of *equivalent ionic conductances*.

$$\lambda_+ = \Lambda n_+$$
$$\lambda_- = \Lambda n_- \qquad (10.10)$$

Table 10.3 gives some values obtained in this manner.

EXERCISE 10.6

Use data from Table 10.3 to compute the equivalent conductance at infinite dilution of $NaNO_3$. Also find the transference numbers of the cation and anion in this electrolyte.   *Ans.* $\Lambda_0 = 121.55$ ohm^{-1}, $n_+ = 0.412$, $n_- = 0.588$.

TABLE 10.3

EQUIVALENT IONIC CONDUCTANCES IN AQUEOUS SOLUTION AT INFINITE
DILUTION AND 25°*

Cations	λ_0(ohm^{-1})	Anions	λ_0(ohm^{-1})
H^+	349.8	OH^-	197.6
Li^+	38.69	Cl^-	76.34
Na^+	50.11	Br^-	78.3
K^+	73.52	I^-	76.8
NH_4^+	73.4	NO_3^-	71.44
Ag^+	61.92	CH_3COO^-	40.9
$\frac{1}{2} Ca^{++}$ (†)	59.50	$\frac{1}{2} SO_4^=$	80.0
$\frac{1}{2} Ba^{++}$ (†)	63.64	IO_4^-	54.83
$\frac{1}{3} La^{+++}$	69.5	ClO_4^-	67.32

* From G.F.A. Kortum and J.O'M. Bockris, *Textbook of Electrochemistry*, Elsevier Press, Inc., New York, 1951.

(†) The factor $\frac{1}{2}$ is used as a reminder that this is the conductance of 1 gram-*equivalent*.

10.5 Galvanic Cells

A galvanic cell liberates the free energy change of a chemical reaction as externally available electric energy, which is proportional to the difference of electric potential (or emf) between the electrodes. The emf of the cell is determined by the relative tendencies of oxidation and reduction processes at the electrodes. When the electrodes are not externally connected, no current flows and no reactions occur at the electrodes in a properly designed cell. The electrode processes exert a joint push-pull action which circulates electrons through the cell and the external circuit. Electron releasing reactions of chemical oxidation occur at the anode, by definition. The external circuit conducts the electrons to the cathode, where they are consumed by chemical reduction. A half cell may take a variety of forms, but always contains coupled chemical species in two valence states. For example, the two half cells constituting the Daniell cell are (a) zinc metal in contact with a zinc salt solution, which is the anode, and (b) copper metal in contact with copper salt solution, the cathode. At the anode the process is

$$Zn = Zn^{++} (aq.) + 2e$$

and at the cathode it is

$$2e + Cu^{++} (aq.) = Cu$$

The algebraic sum of the half cell reactions is the net *cell reaction:*

$$Zn + Cu^{++} (aq.) = Cu + Zn^{++} (aq.)$$

It is convenient to describe galvanic cells or single electrodes by an abbreviated notation together with appropriate conventions concerning the relationship between these descriptions and the corresponding chemical reactions. The most important single consideration throughout is this: the galvanic cell is a device for effecting electrochemical processes in a reversible manner and for measuring the free energy change from the emf. Any conventions used for cells must be compatible with other thermodynamic conventions. It will be necessary to interconvert the representation of a galvanic cell and a corresponding chemical equation which describes the cell process. There is an important difference between them, since a chemical equation connotes extensive properties, such as heat of reaction, whereas the essential characteristic of a galvanic cell is its emf, an intensive property. Accordingly, the representation of a galvanic cell must clearly indicate substances, their states and concentrations, as well as any other factor which may affect the emf. A common form of notation is now described.

1. A seat of emf between electrode and electrolyte, or between two electrolyte solutions, is represented by a vertical line, as $Zn \mid Zn^{+2}$.

2. The sequence electrode $\mid$ electrolyte represents oxidation, while electrolyte $\mid$ electrode represents reduction. Examples are

$Zn \mid Zn^{+2} (aq., m)$	$Zn = Zn^{+2} (aq., m) + 2e$
$Zn^{+2} (aq., m) \mid Zn$	$2e + Zn^{+2} (aq., m) = Zn$
$Ag^+ (aq., m) \mid Ag$	$e + Ag^+ (aq., m) = Ag$
$Ag, AgCl (s) \mid Cl^- (aq., m)$	$Ag + Cl^- (aq., m) = AgCl + e$

3. The metallic electrode is to be represented according to rule 2, even when it does not react chemically, as, for example, in:

$Pt, H_2 (P) \mid H^+ (aq., m)$	$\frac{1}{2} H_2 (P) = H^+ (aq., m) + e$
$Pt \mid Fe^{+2} (aq., m), Fe^{+3} (aq., m')$	$Fe^{+2} (aq., m) = Fe^{+3} (aq., m') + e$
$Pt, Cl_2 (P) \mid Cl^- (aq., m)$	$Cl^- (aq., m) = \frac{1}{2} Cl_2 (P) + e$

4. A combination of any two single electrodes constitutes a complete cell, the electrode arbitrarily placed on the left being the anode and that on the right the cathode, thus:

$$Zn \mid ZnSO_4 (aq., m_1) \mid CuSO_4 (aq., m_2) \mid Cu$$

The *cell reaction* is the algebraic sum of the electrode reactions

$$Zn + Cu^{+2} (aq., m_2) = Zn^{+2} (aq., m_1) + Cu$$

'n this cell the junction of the two solutions is a source of emf as exemplified by the fact that the observed potential depends to a small extent on the nature of the anions present in the two solutions. The emf which develops at a iquid junction corresponds to the free energy change of transferring the migrating ions from one environment to the other. This *junction potential* is often diminished by use of a *salt bridge*, which consists of a tube filled with a solution of potassium chloride connecting the two electrode compartments. This device permits flow of current by migration of ions and reduces the net junction potential to a very small value. The salt bridge is indicated by two vertical lines, and when it is used, the nature of the anions has practically no effect on the emf and need not be specified, as in

$$Zn\,|\,Zn^{+2} (aq., m_1)\,\|\,Cu^{+2} (aq., m_2)\,|\,Cu$$

Although cells with liquid junctions or salt bridges are commonly used for practical measurements, it is preferable to use cells without liquid junctions for thermodynamic measurements. A single electrolyte solution may furnish the ions for both electrodes, as in the cell

$$Pt, H_2 (P_1)\,|\,H^+ (aq., m_1),\ Cl^- (aq., m_2)\,|\,Cl_2 (P_2), Pt$$

for which the cell reaction is found by adding the electrode reactions thus:

$$\tfrac{1}{2} H_2 (P_1) = H^+ (aq., m_1) + e$$
$$e + \tfrac{1}{2} Cl_2 (P_2) = Cl^- (aq., m_2)$$
$$\overline{\tfrac{1}{2} H_2 (P_1) + \tfrac{1}{2} Cl_2 (P_2) = H^+ (aq., m_1) + Cl^- (aq., m_2)}$$

In such a cell it is possible to vary the concentrations of reacting cation and anion independently by using two electrolytes, an acid other than HCl and a chloride salt.

5. The sign of the emf is considered positive when the cell reaction is a permitted process. For

$$Zn\,|\,Zn^{+2} (1\ m)\,\|\,Cu^{+2} (1\ m)\,|\,Cu$$

the cell reaction, $Zn + Cu^{+2} (1\ m) = Cu + Zn^{+2} (1\ m)$, is permitted and $\mathcal{E} = 1.1$ v., whereas for the cell

$$Cu\,|\,Cu^{+2} (1\ m)\,\|\,Zn^{+2} (1\ m)\,|\,Zn$$

the cell reaction, $Cu + Zn^{+2} (1\ m) = Cu^{+2} (1\ m) + Zn$ is forbidden and $\mathcal{E} = -1.1$ v.

As a further example of the connection between the galvanic cell and the cell reaction, consider the cell

$$Pt\,|\,Fe^{+2} (m_1),\ Fe^{+3} (m_2)\,\|\,Zn^{+2} (m_3)\,|\,Zn$$

The cell reaction is obtained by addition of electrode reactions with such coefficients that the number of equivalents oxidized is equal to the number reduced:

$$2 \, Fe^{+2} \, (m_1) = 2 \, Fe^{+3} \, (m_2) + 2e$$
$$\underline{2e + Zn^{+2} \, (m_3) = Zn}$$
$$2 \, Fe^{+2} \, (m_1) + Zn^{+2} \, (m_3) = 2 \, Fe^{+3} \, (m_2) + Zn$$

When all concentrations are unity, the observed emf is -1.5 v., showing that the cell reaction as written is forbidden.

EXERCISE 10.7

Combining two of the electrodes described above formulate a galvanic cell in which the cell reaction is

$$Zn^{+2} \, (m_1) + H_2 \, (P) = Zn + 2 \, H^+ \, (m_2)$$

Ans. Pt., $H_2 \, (P) \, | \, H^+ \, (m_2) \, \| \, Zn^{+2} \, (m_1) \, | \, Zn$.

A galvanic cell consisting of two electrodes of the same type which differ only in concentrations of reagents is called a *concentration cell*. For example, in the cell

$$Pt, H_2 \, (P_1) \, | \, H^+ \, (m_1) \, \| \, H^+ \, (m_2) \, | \, H_2 \, (P_2), \, Pt$$

with cell reaction

$$\tfrac{1}{2} \, H_2 \, (P_1) + H^+ \, (m_2) = \tfrac{1}{2} \, H_2 \, (P_2) + H^+ \, (m_1)$$

an emf is developed only when $P_1 \neq P_2$ or $m_1 \neq m_2$. The liquid junctions in this cell make it unsatisfactory for precise thermodynamic measurements, and for such purposes the double concentration cell

$$Pt, H_2 \, (P) \, | \, HCl \, (m_1) \, | \, Cl_2 \, (P), \, Pt\text{-}Pt, \, Cl_2 \, (P) \, | \, HCl \, (m_2) \, | \, H_2 \, (P), \, Pt$$

where all gas pressures are equal and the emf depends only on the relative values of m_1 and m_2, may be used.

EXERCISE 10.8

Write the reaction occurring in the double concentration cell formulated above.

Ans. $HCl \, (m_2) = HCl \, (m_1)$.

10.6 Thermodynamics of Galvanic Cells

Electric energy is measured as the product of an intensity factor $\mathscr{E}$ (potential difference or emf in volts) and a capacity factor q (the electric charge in coulombs). That is,

$$w \, \text{(elect.)} = q \mathscr{E} \tag{10.11}$$

The electric charge q is proportional to the number of equivalents reacting,

$$q = n \mathscr{F} \tag{10.12}$$

where $\mathscr{F}$ is the faraday. Remembering that electric energy is free energy, we see that the reversible emf, $\mathscr{E}$, is a thermodynamic property since

$$-\Delta F = w \, \text{(elect.)} = n \mathscr{F} \mathscr{E} \tag{10.13}$$

At each electrode of a galvanic cell a unit positive test charge would experience an *electric potential*, $\mathscr{V}_{\text{right}}$ or $\mathscr{V}_{\text{left}}$. The measured difference in electric potential between the two electrodes is related to the emf of the cell by definition as

$$\mathcal{E} = \mathscr{V}_{\text{right}} - \mathscr{V}_{\text{left}} = \Delta\mathscr{V} \qquad (10.14)$$

and the sign of $\Delta\mathscr{V}$ is established by experiment.

The cell potential difference is measured by balancing it against an adjustable, known potential difference. A heavy duty working cell provides current for IR drop across the precision resistance shown in Fig. 10.5. When a sensitive galvanometer is used to detect the position of balance, very little current flows from the unknown cell. The potential difference so measured corresponds to reversible operation. It is the reversible emf of the cell, $\mathcal{E}$.

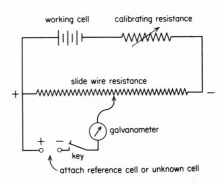

A galvanic cell offers an unusually clear example of *thermodynamic reversibility*. When the emf of the cell is opposed by an equal and opposite emf, no reaction occurs and no current flows. When the emf of the cell exceeds the opposing emf very slightly, a small current flows and a chemical reaction accompanied by a decrease in free energy occurs in the cell. When the opposing emf slightly exceeds the emf of the cell, the reverse chemical reaction occurs in the cell, one which is accompanied by a positive free energy change.

FIG. 10.5. Potentiometer.

Whether or not a given reaction can be made to take place reversibly in a galvanic cell depends somewhat on the skill and persistence of the investigator. The technique for equilibrating H_2 and H^+ (aq.) at an electrode is known; that for O_2 and OH^- (aq.) is not. If the latter were feasible, then from the emf of the cell

$$\text{Pt, } H_2 \,|\, H^+ \text{ (aq.), } OH^- \text{ (aq.)} \,|\, O_2\text{, Pt}$$

the free energy change for the reaction

$$H_2 \text{ (g)} + \tfrac{1}{2} O_2 \text{ (g)} = H_2O \text{ (l)}$$

could be evaluated directly. Our inability to make this measurement has no thermodynamic significance; it is merely an inconvenience. The free energy change depends only on the initial and final states, not on the path, and the free energy of formation of water can be evaluated by alternate methods.

Let us review the relation between electric work and free energy change. The maximum electric work is a direct measure of the free energy change for the cell reaction. Since

$$\Delta F_T = -(w_{\text{max.}} - P\Delta V) \qquad (10.15)$$

for a constant temperature, constant pressure change, and

$$w_{\text{max.}} = w_{\text{max.}} \text{ (elect.)} + P\Delta V$$

it follows that

$$\Delta F_T = -w_{\text{max.}} \text{ (elect.)} = -n\mathscr{F}\mathcal{E}_T \qquad (10.16)$$

EXERCISE 10.9

The emf at 25° for the cell

$$\text{Pt, H}_2 \text{ (1 atm.)} \,|\, \text{HCl (aq., 1 } m) \,|\, \text{Cl}_2 \text{ (1 atm.) Pt}$$

is 1.36 v. Use this information to compute the free energy of formation of hydrochloric acid in 1 M solution at 25°. *Ans.* −31.4 kcal.

Pencil-and-paper processes occur with either positive or negative free energy changes. It follows from equation (10.13) that corresponding cells may have negative or positive electromotive forces. By the second convention of section 10.5, the electrode on the left-hand side of the pencil-and-paper cell is the anode. (This confusion does not arise in the laboratory, where the anode is recognized as the negative electrode by virtue of the electrons released by anodic oxidation.) In fact, oxidation at this electrode and reduction at the right-hand electrode may be forbidden because of a positive ΔF (reaction). We persist with the cell formulation but assign a negative emf. To illustrate, the Daniell cell may be expressed as

$$\text{Cu} \,|\, \text{Cu}^{+2} \text{ (aq., 1 } M) \,\|\, \text{Zn}^{+2} \text{ (aq., 1 } M) \,|\, \text{Zn}$$

and the conventional way to write the cell reaction is

$$\text{Cu} + \text{Zn}^{+2} \text{ (aq., 1 } M) = \text{Cu}^{+2} \text{ (aq., 1 } M) + \text{Zn}$$

This change in state, at 25° and 1 atm. is forbidden, having a free energy change

$$\Delta F_{298} = 50,800 \text{ cal./g.-atom}$$

but the reaction will occur as written when this amount of free energy is supplied from an external source. The emf of the cell above is, therefore, given as −1.1 v. By convention, the cell reaction is always written with the electrode on the left as anode. If the emf is positive, the chemical change specified can supply energy; if negative, the cell must be supplied with energy for this change to occur.

The temperature dependence of the emf of a galvanic cell has been given briefly in Chapter 4, equation (4.20), and will be reviewed here. The derivative of ΔF_T with respect to temperature, according to equation (6.56), is

$$\left(\frac{\partial \Delta F_T}{\partial T}\right)_P = -\Delta S_{T,P} \tag{10.17}$$

Therefore, the derivative of $\mathscr{E}_T$ with respect to temperature (at constant pressure)

$$\left(\frac{\partial \mathscr{E}_T}{\partial T}\right)_P = \frac{\Delta S_T}{n\mathscr{F}} \tag{10.18}$$

yields a value of ΔS_T for the cell reaction. Since

$$\Delta H_T = \Delta F_T + T\,\Delta S_T$$

it follows that ΔH_T for the cell reaction is given by

$$\Delta H_T = -n\mathscr{F}\mathscr{E}_T + Tn\mathscr{F}\left(\frac{\partial \mathscr{E}_T}{\partial T}\right)_P \tag{10.19}$$

EXERCISE 10.10

For the cell

$$\text{Zn} \,|\, \text{ZnCl}_2 \,(0.555 \; m) \,|\, \text{AgCl, Ag}$$

$$\mathscr{E}_{273} = 1.015 \text{ v. and } \partial\mathscr{E}/\partial T = -0.000492 \text{ v. deg.}^{-1}$$

Calculate ΔF_{273}, ΔS_{273}, and ΔH_{273} for the cell reaction

$$\text{Zn} + 2\,\text{AgCl} = \text{ZnCl}_2 \,(0.555 \; m) + 2\,\text{Ag}$$

$$\text{Ans. } \Delta F_{273} = -46.8 \text{ kcal.}; \quad \Delta S_{273} = -22.7 \text{ cal. deg.}^{-1};$$
$$\Delta H_{273} = -53.0 \text{ kcal.}$$

10.7 Concentration Dependence of EMF

The concentration dependence of the free energy change for a constant temperature, constant pressure change in state has been given in several instances in Chapters 5 through 8. By application of the familiar cycle relating the process of interest to the corresponding standard process, a similar expression applying to electrolytic solutions can be obtained. Choosing as our example a reaction in which a solid and a gas as well as electrolyte solutions are involved, we have

$$X_2(g, P_{X_2}) \quad + M(s) \xrightarrow{\;\Delta F_T\;} \quad M^{+2}(a_{M^{+2}}) \quad + \quad 2X^-(a_{X^-})$$

$$\Delta F_T = \left| RT \ln (1/P_{X_2}) \quad \Delta F_T \right| = 0 \qquad \Delta F_T = \left| RT \ln (a_{M^{+2}}) \; \Delta F_T = \right| 2RT \ln (a_{X^-})$$

$$X_2(g, P_{X_2} = 1) + M(s) \xrightarrow{\;\Delta F_T^0\;} M^{+2}(a_{M^{+2}} = 1) + 2X^-(a_{X^-} = 1)$$

$$\Delta F_T = \Delta F_T^0 + RT \ln Q \tag{10.20}$$

where

$$\Delta F_T = \mu_{M^{+2}} + 2\,\mu_{X^-} - \mu_M - \mu_{X_2}$$

$$\Delta F_T^0 = \mu_{M^{+2}}^0 + 2\,\mu_{X^-}^0 - \mu_M^0 - \mu_{X_2}^0$$

and

$$Q = \frac{a_{M^{+2}} a_{X^-}^2}{P_{X_2}}$$

Although the cycle and equation (10.20) are not completely general, the extension to other types of reactions should be obvious. It is assumed that the gas X_2 is ideal and that the free energy of the pure solid M is fixed. (To be precise, the fugacity should be used instead of the pressure.)

As shown in Chapter 8, the activity a is defined in such a way as to make equation (10.20) completely rigorous. The reference state used in the consideration of electrolytic solutions is the infinitely dilute solution, and the concentration unit is usually the molality m (approximately equal to the molarity M in dilute aqueous solutions) so that

$$a \longrightarrow m \quad \text{as} \quad m \longrightarrow 0$$

In solutions of finite concentration the ratio of the activity to the molality is the activity coefficient γ.

$$\gamma = \frac{a}{m}$$

For the galvanic cell corresponding to the reaction above, namely,

$$M \mid M^{+2}(a_{M^{+2}}), X^-(a_{X^-}) \mid X_2(P_{X_2}), Pt$$

the dependence of the emf on the activities of its components follows from equations (10.20) and (10.16).

$$- n\mathscr{F}\mathscr{E}_T = \Delta F_T^0 + RT \ln Q \tag{10.21}$$

ΔF_T^0 is uniquely related to the emf of the cell in which all activities and pressures are unity, namely,

$$M \mid M^{+2}(a_{M^{+2}} = 1), X^-(a_{X^-} = 1) \mid X_2(P_{X_2} = 1), Pt$$

For this cell $Q = 1$, and $\Delta F_T = \Delta F_T^0$.

Therefore,

$$- n\mathscr{F}\mathscr{E}_T^0 = \Delta F_T^0 \tag{10.22}$$

where $\mathscr{E}_T^0$ is the *standard emf* of the cell. Equation (10.21) now becomes

$$\mathscr{E}_T = \mathscr{E}_T^0 - \frac{RT}{n\mathscr{F}} \ln Q \tag{10.23}$$

When $\mathscr{E}$ is expressed in v. and $\mathscr{F}$ in coul. equiv.$^{-1}$, R should be 8.3143 j. deg.$^{-1}$ mole^{-1}.

In equation (10.23) the term in $\ln Q$ describes the dependence of $\mathscr{E}$ on composition. However, the value of this term is clearly independent of the choice of coefficients for the cell reaction. For the preceding illustration when $n = 2$ we have

$$\tfrac{1}{2} \ln \frac{a_{M^{+2}} a_{X^-}^2}{P_{X_2}}$$

whereas if $n = 1$, we have

$$\ln \frac{a_{M^{+2}}^{1/2} a_{X^-}}{P_{X_2}^{1/2}}$$

and the value of the second term of equation (10.23) is the same in either case. This is a consequence of the fact that the emf is an intensive property, independent of the amounts of materials involved. On the other hand, the free energy change, $\Delta F_T = -n\mathscr{F}\mathscr{E}_T$, represents a change in an extensive property, and as such its value depends on n.

Methods for evaluating a and $\mathscr{E}^0$ will be described later, but an approximate application of equation (10.23) is possible when $a \cong m$, that is, for dilute solutions. Consider again the cell

$$Pt, H_2 \mid HCl \, (aq.) \mid Cl_2, Pt$$

When $a_{HCl} = 1$ and $P_{H_2} = P_{Cl_2} = 1$, i.e., for all reacting substances in their standard states, the emf is $\mathscr{E}_{298}^0 = 1.36$ v. For any other composition, such as

$$Pt, H_2 \, (1 \text{ atm.}) \mid H^+ \, (10^{-5} \, m), Cl^- \, (10^{-1} \, m) \mid Cl_2 \, (10^{-2} \text{ atm.}), Pt$$

we find by equation (10.23)

$$\mathscr{E}_{298} = 1.36 - \frac{0.0592}{2} \log \frac{m_{\text{H}}^2 \cdot m_{\text{Cl}^-}^2}{P_{\text{H}_2} P_{\text{Cl}_2}}$$

$$= 1.36 - \frac{0.0592}{2} \log \frac{(10^{-5})^2 (10^{-1})^2}{10^{-2}}$$

$$= 1.36 + 0.30 = 1.66 \text{ v.}$$

EXERCISE 10.11

Find $\mathscr{E}_{298}$ for the cell

$$\text{Cd} \,|\, \text{Cd}^{+2}\,(10^{-1}\,m) \,\|\, \text{Sn}^{+2}\,(10^{-2}\,m),\ \text{Sn}^{+4}\,(10^{-5}\,m)\,|\, \text{Pt}$$

$\mathscr{E}_{298}^0$ for this cell is 0.55 v.   *Ans.* $\mathscr{E}_{298} = 0.49$ v.

10.8 Determination of the Standard EMF

It is neither practical nor necessary to measure directly the standard emf of a cell. This would require preparing a cell in which all reagents are present at unit activity; it can sometimes be done, but it serves no useful purpose. The solute at unit activity is a convenient concept, but not a useful reagent. Somewhat analogously, a standard emf is a parameter of an equation, but not a useful working standard.

It is convenient to treat each type of ion of an electrolyte as an independent species with its own activity coefficient. That is, for a cation whose molal concentration is m_+ we write $a_+ = \gamma_+ m_+$ and for an anion, $a_- = \gamma_- m_-$, where γ_+ and γ_- are the ionic activity coefficients and a_+ and a_- are the ionic activities. However, it is never possible to make observations on cations or anions alone, but only on the electrolytic solution. The quantity which emerges from such observations is the activity of the electrolyte rather than the individual ion activities. For reasons which will become evident, it is convenient to define the relationship between the activity of the electrolyte a and the activities of the individual ions, a_+ and a_-, by

$$a = a_+ \times a_- \tag{10.24}$$

in the case of a 1-1 electrolyte. Since $m_+ = m_- = m$, then

$$a = m_+ \gamma_+ \times m_- \gamma_- = m^2 \,(\gamma_+ \gamma_-)$$

and we define the mean activity coefficient of the electrolyte $\gamma_\pm$ by

$$\gamma_\pm = (\gamma_+ \gamma_-)^{1/2} \tag{10.25}$$

so

$$a = m^2 \gamma_\pm^2$$

For other types of electrolytes analogous definitions of the activity of the electrolyte and the mean activity coefficient are used. For example, in the case of a 2-1 electrolyte, $\text{M}^{+2}\text{X}_2^-$,

$$a = a_+ a_-^2 = m_+ \gamma_+ m_-^2 \gamma_-^2$$

and

$$\gamma_\pm = (\gamma_+ \gamma_-^2)^{1/3}$$

so

$$a = 4m^3\gamma_\pm^3$$

The value of $\mathscr{E}^0$ in equation (10.23) is determined by a procedure which takes advantage of the fact that, by definition, $a \to m$ as $m \to 0$. Emf measurements are made at a series of lower concentrations, and the value of $\mathscr{E}^0$ obtained by extrapolation to infinitely dilute solution. For example, the emf of the cell

$$\text{Pt, H}_2\ (1\ \text{atm.})\,|\,\text{HCl}\ (m)\,|\,\text{AgCl (s), Ag}$$

has been accurately determined [H. S. Harned and R. W. Ehlers, *J. Am. Chem. Soc.*, **54**, 1350 (1932)] for various concentrations of HCl. The cell reaction is

$$\text{H}_2\ (1\ \text{atm.}) + 2\ \text{AgCl (s)} = 2\ \text{H}^+\ (\text{aq.,}\ m) + 2\ \text{Cl}^-\ (\text{aq.,}\ m) + 2\ \text{Ag (s)}$$

and, therefore, the expression for the activity dependence of the emf is

$$\mathscr{E}_T = \mathscr{E}_T^0 - \frac{RT}{2\mathscr{F}} \ln a_{\text{H}^+}^2 a_{\text{Cl}^-}^2$$

Substituting by equations (10.24) and (10.25), we have at 25°

$$\mathscr{E}_{298} = \mathscr{E}_{298}^0 - 0.1183 \log m - 0.1183 \log \gamma_\pm \tag{10.26}$$

The quantity $\mathscr{E}_{298} + 0.1183 \log m$, if plotted versus concentration m and extrapolated to $m = 0$, would give as intercept $\mathscr{E}_{298}^0$, since as $m \to 0$, $\gamma_\pm \to 1$ and $\log \gamma_\pm \to 0$. However, such a plot is nonlinear because of the dependence of $\gamma_\pm$ on m, which makes extrapolation difficult. In section 10.11 we shall discuss the Debye-Hückel theory of electrolyte activity, which gives the dependence of $\gamma_\pm$ on m in aqueous solution at 25° in the form of a limiting law precisely valid for 1-1 electrolytes in infinitely dilute solution.

$$\log \gamma_\pm = -0.509\sqrt{m} \tag{10.27}$$

Substitution of this expression in equation (10.26) does not constitute a further

FIG. 10.6. Determination of $\mathscr{E}^0$.

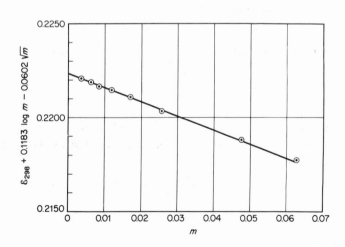

$\mathscr{E}_{298} + 0.1183 \log m - 0.0602 \sqrt{m}$

m

assumption, but assists in obtaining a linear plot for extrapolation. We obtain

$$\mathscr{E}_{298} + 0.1183 \log m - 0.0602\sqrt{m} = \mathscr{E}_{298}^0 \qquad (10.28)$$

If equation (10.27) were a precise description of the dependence of $\gamma_\pm$ on m at finite concentrations, the left-hand side of equation (10.28) would be independent of m. This is not the case, as shown in Fig. 10.6 but fortunately this quantity varies linearly with m, permitting a precise extrapolation to $m = 0$ for a value of $\mathscr{E}_{298}^0$. The intercept in the present example is $\mathscr{E}_{298}^0 = 0.2224$ v.

The value of $\mathscr{E}_{298}^0$ for the cell in question having been determined the value of $\gamma_\pm$ at any concentration can be obtained by substituting the measured emf in equation (10.26). Values of $\gamma_\pm$ for several electrolytes are given in Fig. 10.7. Note that the 1-1 electrolytes give rise to a family of converging curves at low concentrations. The same is true of other charge types, but only one example is given in each class.

EXERCISE 10.12

For the cell

$$\text{Pt, H}_2 \text{ (1 atm.)} \,|\, \text{HCl (0.01710 } m) \,|\, \text{AgCl (s), Ag}$$

$\mathscr{E}_{298}$ is 0.43783. Calculate $\gamma_\pm$ for hydrochloric acid at this concentration.

Ans. $\gamma_\pm = 0.884$.

10.9 Standard Electrode Oxidation Potentials

Galvanic cells can be formally divided into half cells and, apart from occasional incompatibilities of the electrolytes, all possible cells can be constructed from combinations of a limited number of half cells. Each half cell may be considered formally to have its proper single electrode potential by referring it to the unit positive test charge. Individual electrode potentials are not measurable in practice, although a given electrode must always make the same contribution to the emf of any cell which contains it. Qualitatively, however, electrodes which tend strongly to oxidation will have potentials

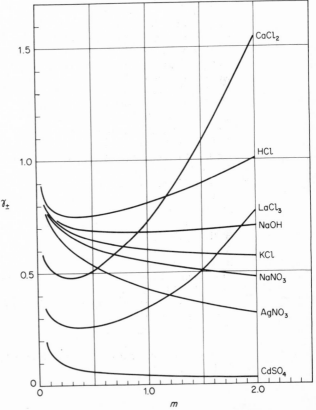

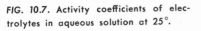

FIG. 10.7. Activity coefficients of electrolytes in aqueous solution at 25°.

negative with respect to electrodes tending to reduction. All single electrode potentials $\mathscr{V}_a, \mathscr{V}_b, \mathscr{V}_c, \ldots$ can be measured as differences against the potential of some one standard reference electrode, $\mathscr{V}_s$, by constructing the appropriate cells. Let the reference half cell be on the right, arbitrarily. Then the emf's of these cells can be represented: $\mathscr{E}_{sa} = \mathscr{V}_s - \mathscr{V}_a; \mathscr{E}_{sb} = \mathscr{V}_s - \mathscr{V}_b$, etc. Combining the half cells differently, say a with b, gives: $\mathscr{E}_{ab} = \mathscr{V}_a - \mathscr{V}_b$. The value of $\mathscr{E}_{ab}$ is predictable from the measurements already performed, since $\mathscr{E}_{ab} = \mathscr{E}_{sb} - \mathscr{E}_{sa}$. The absolute potential of the reference electrode does not appear in the final result, and formally it may be assigned any value, the most convenient being zero. Conventionally, then, the potential difference of a test half cell (on the left) coupled with a reference half cell is the *relative* single

TABLE 10.4

POTENTIALS OF STANDARD HALF CELLS*

$\mathscr{E}^0$ = oxidation potential (emf), $\mathscr{V}^0$ = electrode potential

Electrode Reaction	$\mathscr{E}^0_{298}$	$\mathscr{V}^0_{298}$
Li (s) = Li+ (aq.) + e	3.045	−3.045
K (s) = K+ (aq.) + e	2.925	−2.925
Na (s) = Na+ (aq.) + e	2.714	−2.714
Mg (s) = Mg+2 (aq.) + 2e	2.37	−2.37
Mn (s) = Mn+2 (aq.) + 2e	1.18	−1.18
Zn (s) = Zn+2 (aq.) + 2e	0.763	−0.763
Cr (s) = Cr+2 (aq.) + 2e	0.74	−0.74
Fe (s) = Fe+2 (aq.) + 2e	0.440	−0.440
Cr+2 (aq.) = Cr+3 (aq.) + e	0.41	−0.41
Cd (s) = Cd+2 (aq.) + 2e	0.403	−0.403
Pb (s) + 2 I− (aq.) = PbI2 (s) + 2e	0.365	−0.365
Ni (s) = Ni+2 (aq.) + 2e	0.250	−0.250
Ag (s) + I− (aq.) = AgI (s) + e	0.151	−0.151
Sn (s) = Sn+2 (aq.) + 2e	0.136	−0.136
Pb (s) = Pb+2 (aq.) + 2e	0.126	−0.126
½ H2 (g) = H+ (aq.) + e	0.000	0.000
Ti+3 (aq.) = Ti+4 (aq.) + e	−0.04	0.04
Ag (s) + Br− (aq.) = AgBr (s) + e	−0.071	0.071
Sn+2 (aq.) = Sn+4 (aq.) + 2e	−0.15	0.15
Hg (l) + Cl− (aq., 1 N) = ½ Hg2Cl2 (s) + e (N calomel)	−0.2802	0.2802
Cu+ (aq.) = Cu+2 (aq.) + e	−0.153	0.153
Ag (s) + Cl− (aq.) = AgCl (s) + e	−0.2224	0.2224
I− (aq.) = ½ I2 (s) + e	−0.5355	0.5355
Fe+2 (aq.) = Fe+3 (aq.) + e	−0.771	0.771
½ C6H6O2 (aq.) = ½ C6H4O2 (aq.) + H+ (aq.) + e (quinhydrone)	−0.6996	0.6996
Hg (l) = ½ Hg2+2 (aq.) + e	−0.789	0.789
Ag (s) = Ag+ (aq.) + e	−0.7991	0.7991
Br− (aq.) = ½ Br2 (l) + e	−1.0652	1.0652
2 Cr+3 (aq.) + 7 H2O = Cr2O7= (aq.) + 14 H+ (aq.) + 6e	−1.33	1.33
Cl− (aq.) = ½ Cl2 (g) + e	−1.3595	1.3595
Mn+2 (aq.) + 4 H2O = MnO4− (aq.) + 8 H+ (aq.) + 5e	−1.51	1.51
Ce+3 (aq.) = Ce+4 (aq.) + e	−1.61	1.61
Co+2 (aq.) = Co+3 (aq.) + e	−1.82	1.82

*From W. M. Latimer, *Oxidation Potentials*, 2nd ed., Prentice-Hall, Inc., Englewood Cliffs, N.J., 1952.

electrode oxidation potential, or emf, and: $\mathscr{E}_{sa} = -\mathscr{V}_a$. We might equally well have adopted the convention that the reference electrode shall be at the left of the cell and report all single electrode *reduction* potentials. Many prefer this convention. It should be noted that signs of electric potentials $\mathscr{V}$ have been established by another convention based upon experimental test, and therefore, the signs of two electrode potentials are not affected by the order of representation of the electrodes. By our convention $\mathscr{E}_{cell} = \mathscr{V}_{right} - \mathscr{V}_{left}$; therefore, interchanging the two half cells will change the sign of the emf and $\mathscr{E}_{as} = -\mathscr{E}_{sa} = \mathscr{V}_a - \mathscr{V}_s$. Relative emf's of single electrodes such as $\mathscr{E}(M, M^+)$ and $\mathscr{E}(M^+, M)$ differ in sign, but the corresponding potentials $\mathscr{V}(M, M^+)$ and $\mathscr{V}(M^+, M)$ do not.

The choice of reference electrode has already been anticipated in part by the convention (section 3.7) that $\Delta H^0 = 0$ for the standard reaction

$$\tfrac{1}{2} H_2 (f = 1) = H^+ (a = 1) + e$$

It is convenient to extend this convention and to let $\Delta F_f^0(H^+) = 0$ for the same reaction. For the electrode, represented Pt, $H_2 | H^+$, both $\mathscr{E}^0$ and $\mathscr{V}^0$ are zero. By these conventions the (oxidation) emf's of half cells represented by the diagrams

$$Zn \,|\, Zn^{+2}$$
$$Pt,\, Cl_2 \,|\, Cl^-$$
$$Ag,\, AgCl \,|\, Cl^-$$
$$Pt \,|\, Fe^{+2},\, Fe^{+3}$$

are defined to be the emf's of the cells

$$Zn \,|\, Zn^{+2} \| H^+ \,|\, H_2,\, Pt$$
$$Pt,\, Cl_2 \,|\, Cl^- \| H^+ \,|\, H_2,\, Pt$$
$$Ag,\, AgCl \,|\, Cl^- \| H^+ \,|\, H_2,\, Pt$$
$$Pt \,|\, Fe^{+2},\, Fe^{+3} \| H^+ \,|\, H_2,\, Pt$$

The corresponding cell reactions are

$$\tfrac{1}{2} Zn + H^+ = \tfrac{1}{2} Zn^{+2} + \tfrac{1}{2} H_2$$
$$Cl^- + H^+ = \tfrac{1}{2} Cl_2 + \tfrac{1}{2} H_2$$
$$Ag + Cl^- + H^+ = AgCl + \tfrac{1}{2} H_2$$
$$Fe^{+2} + H^+ = Fe^{+3} + \tfrac{1}{2} H_2$$

When the half cell diagram is written

$$Zn^{+2} \,|\, Zn$$

the (reduction) emf of the electrode is that of the cell

$$Pt,\, H_2 \,|\, H^+ \| Zn^{+2},\, Zn$$

for which the reaction is

$$\tfrac{1}{2} H_2 + \tfrac{1}{2} Zn^{+2} = H^+ + \tfrac{1}{2} Zn$$

Standard relative electrode oxidation potentials $\mathscr{E}^0$, and electrode potentials $\mathscr{V}^0$ appear in Table 10.4. The standard emf of any cell for which the single electrode potentials are known can be obtained by appropriate combination. As an example, in terms of electrode potentials $\mathscr{V}$

$$\text{Zn} \,|\, \text{Zn}^{+2} \,\|\, \text{Cu}^+, \text{Cu}^{+2} \,|\, \text{Pt}$$

$$\text{Zn} + 2\,\text{Cu}^{+2} = \text{Zn}^{+2} + 2\,\text{Cu}^+$$

$$\mathscr{E}^0_{298} = \mathscr{V}^0\,(\text{Cu}^+, \text{Cu}^{+2}) - \mathscr{V}^0\,(\text{Zn}, \text{Zn}^{+2})$$

$$= 0.153 \text{ v.} - (-0.763 \text{ v}) = 0.916 \text{ v.}$$

As a second example, in terms of oxidation emf's

$$\text{Ag} \,|\, \text{Ag}^+ \,\|\, \text{Cd}^{+2} \,|\, \text{Cd}, \qquad 2\,\text{Ag} + \text{Cd}^{+2} = 2\,\text{Ag}^+ + \text{Cd}$$

we find

$$\mathscr{E}^0_{298} = \mathscr{E}^0_{298}\,(\text{Ag}, \text{Ag}^+) - \mathscr{E}^0_{298}\,(\text{Cd}, \text{Cd}^{+2})$$

$$= -0.799 - (0.403) = -1.202 \text{ v.}$$

The positive sign in the first example signifies that the zinc electrode is the actual anode and that the standard cell reaction is permitted as written. The negative sign in the second example signifies that the cadmium electrode is, in practice, the anode and that the standard cell reaction is forbidden as written.

EXERCISE 10.13

Formulate a cell in which the cell reaction is

$$2\,\text{Fe}^{+2}\,(a = 1) + \text{Ni}^{+2}\,(a = 1) = 2\,\text{Fe}^{+3}\,(a = 1) + \text{Ni (s)}$$

and determine whether the change is permitted.

Ans. $\mathscr{E}^0_{298} = -1.021$ v.; change forbidden.

In an actual cell the sign of $\mathscr{E}_{\text{cell}}$ and of $\Delta F(\text{reaction})$ depend both upon the values of $\mathscr{E}^0_{\text{cell}}$ and of the activities of all reacting substances. For example, let us compute the emf of the cell

$$\text{Pt} \,|\, \text{Fe}^{+2}\,(a = 10^{-4}),\ \text{Fe}^{+3}\,(a = 1) \,\|\, \text{Hg}_2^{+2}\,(a = 1) \,|\, \text{Hg}$$

for which the cell reaction is

$$2\,\text{Fe}^{+2} + \text{Hg}_2^{+2} = 2\,\text{Hg} + 2\,\text{Fe}^{+3}$$

$$\mathscr{E}^0_{298} = \mathscr{E}^0_{298}\,(\text{Fe}^{+2}, \text{Fe}^{+3}) - \mathscr{E}^0_{298}\,(\text{Hg}, \text{Hg}_2^{+2})$$

$$= -0.771 - (-0.789) = 0.018 \text{ v.}$$

Therefore, the standard process is permitted, but for $\mathscr{E}_{298}$ we find

$$\mathscr{E}_{298} = \mathscr{E}^0_{298} - \frac{0.0592}{2} \log \frac{a^2_{\text{Fe}^{+3}}}{a^2_{\text{Fe}^{+2}} a_{\text{Hg}_2^{+2}}}$$

$$= 0.018 - \frac{0.0592}{2} \log 10^8$$

$$= 0.018 - 0.2368 = -0.218 \text{ v.}$$

Therefore, the process specified in the cell is forbidden, and the reverse process is permitted.

10.10 Applications of EMF Measurements

It has already been shown that the measured emf of a galvanic cell at several temperatures gives important information about the thermodynamics of the corresponding cell reaction. The ΔF for the cell reaction is directly proportional to the emf and ΔS is directly proportional to its temperature derivative. Likewise, ΔF^0 for the cell reaction is directly proportional to $\mathscr{E}^0$. Now, since

$$\Delta F_T^0 = -RT \ln K \tag{10.29}$$

it follows that

$$\mathscr{E}_T^0 = \left(\frac{RT}{n\mathscr{F}}\right) \ln K \tag{10.30}$$

where K is the equilibrium constant. Therefore, galvanic cell measurements can provide information about the equilibrium states in many systems. For example, in the cell

$$Ag \,|\, Ag^+ \,(aq.) \,\|\, Cl^- \,(aq.) \,|\, AgCl \,(s), \, Ag$$

the cell reaction is simply the dissolution of silver chloride.

$$AgCl \,(s) = Ag^+ \,(aq.) + Cl^- \,(aq.)$$

From Table 10.4 we find

$$\mathscr{E}_{298}^0 = \mathscr{E}_{298}^0 \,(Ag, Ag^+) - \mathscr{E}_{298}^0 \,(Ag, AgCl, Cl^-)$$
$$= -0.7991 - (-0.2224) = -0.5767 \text{ v.}$$

According to equation (10.30),

$$-0.5767 = 0.0592 \log (a_{Ag^+} a_{Cl^-})_{eq.}$$

$$(a_{Ag^+} \times a_{Cl^-})_{eq.} = K = 1.8 \times 10^{-10} \text{ (moles}^2 \text{ kg.}^{-2})$$

This is the solubility product of silver chloride.

As another example, consider the process

$$2\, Ti^{+3} + Sn^{+4} = 2\, Ti^{+4} + Sn^{+2}$$

From Table 10.4

$$\mathscr{E}_{298}^0 = \mathscr{E}_{298}^0 \,(Ti^{+3}, Ti^{+4}) - \mathscr{E}_{298}^0 \,(Sn^{+2}, Sn^{+4})$$
$$= -0.04 - (-0.15) = 0.11 \text{ v.}$$

Therefore,

$$0.11 = \frac{0.0592}{2} \log \left(\frac{a_{Ti^{+4}}^2 a_{Sn^{+2}}}{a_{Ti^{+3}}^2 a_{Sn^{+4}}}\right)_{eq.}$$

and

$$K = 5.2 \times 10^3$$

EXERCISE 10.14

From data in Table 10.4 estimate the equilibrium constant in the oxidation of Ce^{+3} to Ce^{+4} by Cl_2.   *Ans.* 5.85×10^{-5} (moles kg.$^{-1}$ atm.$^{-1/2}$).

Galvanic cells are often used to determine the activities of ions in aqueous solutions, particularly of hydrogen ion activity. This is usually given in terms of the pH scale,

$$pH = -\log a_{H^+} \tag{10.31}$$

Any one of several cells in which the emf depends on the hydrogen ion activity may be used. The most obvious is a cell using a hydrogen electrode. The other electrode may be any convenient one, and for this purpose the *normal calomel electrode* is often used. The electrode potential of the latter is included in Table 10.4. The value given there is not the standard electrode potential, but rather the potential of the electrode in which the potassium chloride concentration is 1 normal. The potassium chloride solution can also serve as a salt bridge. The complete cell is

$$\text{Pt, H}_2 \text{ (1 atm.)} \,|\, \text{H}^+ \,(a_{H^+}) \,\|\, \text{KCl (1 } N) \,|\, \underset{\text{normal calomel electrode}}{\text{Hg}_2\text{Cl}_2, \text{ Hg}}$$

The cell reaction is

$$\text{H}_2 \text{ (1 atm.)} + \text{Hg}_2\text{Cl}_2 = 2 \text{ Hg} + 2 \text{ Cl}^- \text{ (1 } N) + 2 \text{ H}^+ \,(a_{H^+})$$

Since the only variable to be considered is a_{H^+}, it is most convenient to state the emf as the difference

$$\mathscr{E} \text{ (cell)} = \mathscr{E} \text{ (H}_2, \text{ H}^+) - \mathscr{E} \text{ (}N \text{ calomel)} \tag{10.32}$$

and to give the dependence of $\mathscr{E}$ (H$_2$, H$^+$) on a_{H^+} thus (since $P_{H_2} = 1$):

$$\mathscr{E}(\text{cell}) = \mathscr{E}^0(\text{H}_2, \text{H}^+) - \frac{RT}{n\mathscr{F}} \ln a_{H^+}^2 - \mathscr{E}(N \text{ calomel})$$

Since $\mathscr{E}^0$ (H$_2$, H$^+$) = 0,

$$\mathscr{E}(\text{cell}) = -\frac{0.0592}{2} \log a_{H^+}^2 - \mathscr{E}(N \text{ calomel})$$
$$= +0.0592 \text{ pH} - \mathscr{E}(N \text{ calomel}) \tag{10.33}$$

It is necessary only to insert the known value of $\mathscr{E}(N$ calomel) from Table 10.4 and rearrange to obtain

$$pH = \frac{\mathscr{E}(\text{cell}) - 0.2802}{0.0592} \tag{10.34}$$

EXERCISE 10.15

If the hydrogen pressure in the cell described above is 0.9 atm. instead of 1 atm. what error in pH will result? *Ans.* 0.023 pH units.

Another electrode often used for hydrogen ion measurements is the quinhydrone electrode. This consists of an inert metal such as platinum in contact with a saturated solution of quinhydrone. The latter is a compound consisting of equimolar portions of quinone, $C_6H_4O_2$, and hydroquinone, $C_6H_4(OH)_2$. It may also be regarded as the dimer of semiquinone, $C_6H_4O_2H$, which in solution establishes the equilibrium

$$(\text{C}_6\text{H}_4\text{O}_2\text{H})_2 = \text{C}_6\text{H}_4\text{O}_2 + \text{C}_6\text{H}_4(\text{OH})_2$$

This is a convenient way to maintain a 1-1 proportion of quinone and hydro-quinone. Hydroquinone is a weak dibasic acid which dissociates to $C_6H_4O_2^=$ $+ 2\,H^+$. The electrode reaction is

$$C_6H_4(OH)_2 = C_6H_4O_2 + 2\,H^+ + 2e$$

which may be abbreviated

$$QH_2 = Q + 2\,H^+ + 2e$$

The expression for the oxidation potential of this electrode is

$$\mathscr{E} = \mathscr{E}^0 - \frac{RT}{2\mathscr{F}} \ln \frac{a_Q a_{H^+}^2}{a_{QH_2}}$$

and since there are equimolar amounts of quinone and hydroquinone

$$\mathscr{E} = \mathscr{E}^0\,(Q, QH_2) + 0.0592\,pH$$

In combination with a normal calomel electrode, the cell is

$$Pt\,|\,Q, QH_2,\,H^+\,\|\,KCl\,(1\ N)\,|\,Hg_2Cl_2,\,Hg$$

and the emf of the cell depends on the pH of the left-hand solution as follows:

$$\mathscr{E}\,(cell) = \mathscr{E}^0\,(Q, QH_2) + 0.0592\,pH - \mathscr{E}\,(N\ calomel)$$

Using values from Table 10.4 this may be rearranged to

$$pH = \frac{\mathscr{E}\,(cell) + 0.4194}{0.0592} \tag{10.35}$$

It must be realized that single ion activities cannot be measured and the very definition of pH is thermodynamically unsound. The concept of acidity, or pH, can be given only limited operational meaning. In the context of one measurement just described, equation (10.35) defines pH. The limitation arises from the inaccuracy of the implied assumption that no free energy change accompanies the transport of ions across the liquid junction between the half cells.

A thermodynamically acceptable description of acidity has already been developed for aqueous hydrochloric acid, viz.,

$$Pt,\,H_2\,|\,HCl\,(m)\,|\,AgCl,\,Ag$$

for which, at 25°,

$$\mathscr{E} = \mathscr{E}^0 - 0.1183 \log a_H \cdot a_{Cl^-}$$

The function $a_H \cdot a_{Cl^-}$ cannot be resolved, and a_{H^+} is undefined, because it cannot be measured. To the extent that the difference between $\gamma_{H^+} \cdot \gamma_{Cl^-}$ and unity can be ignored, m_{H^+} serves to measure acidity for dilute aqueous solutions of fully ionized acids.

Galvanic cells may also be used to follow the course of many kinds of oxidation-reduction titrations. For example, in the oxidation of ferrous ion by ceric ion the ferrous-ferric electrode, in conjunction with a reference electrode,

$$Pt\,|\,Fe^{+2},\,Fe^{+3}\,\|\,KCl\,(1\ N)\,|\,Hg_2Cl_2,\,Hg$$

will have an emf given by

$$\mathscr{E} = \mathscr{E}^0(Fe^{+2}, Fe^{+3}) - \frac{RT}{n\mathscr{F}} \ln \frac{a_{Fe^{+3}}}{a_{Fe^{+2}}} - \mathscr{E} \ (N \text{ calomel})$$

If ceric ion is added to the ferrous ion solution, the reaction

$$Fe^{+2} + Ce^{+4} = Fe^{+3} + Ce^{+3}$$

which has a very large equilibrium constant, will occur until either Fe^{+2} or Ce^{+4} is virtually exhausted. If enough Ce^{+4} is added to oxidize 50% of the Fe^{+2} originally present, then $a_{Fe^{+2}} \cong a_{Fe^{+3}}$ and

$$\mathscr{E} = \mathscr{E}^0(Fe^{+2}, Fe^{+3}) - 0 - \mathscr{E} \ (N \text{ calomel})$$
$$= -0.771 - (-0.280) = -0.491 \text{ v}.$$

At 90% oxidation of Fe^{+2} to Fe^{+3}, $a_{Fe^{+3}} \cong 9 \times a_{Fe^{+2}}$ and

$$\mathscr{E} = \mathscr{E}^0(Fe^{+2}, Fe^{+3}) - 0.0592 \log (9/1) - \mathscr{E} \ (N \text{ calomel}) = -0.547 \text{ v}.$$

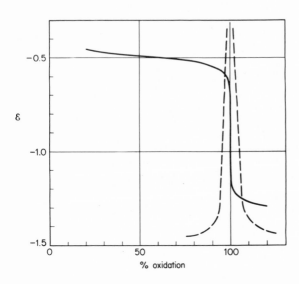

FIG. 10.8. Potentiometric titration. $Fe^{+2} + Ce^{+4}$ = $Fe^{+3} + Ce^{+3}$ vs. N calomel.

and so forth. The variation of the emf of the cell with the extent of oxidation of the ion is shown in Fig. 10.8. For points corresponding to oxidation of Fe^{+2}, the cell is to be regarded as though the anode is Ce^{+3}, Ce^{+4}, and its emf will be given by

$$\mathscr{E} = \mathscr{E}^0(Ce^{+3}, Ce^{+4}) - 0.0592 \log \frac{a_{Ce^{+4}}}{a_{Ce^{+3}}} - \mathscr{E} \ (N \text{ calomel})$$

For example, when a 10% excess of Ce^{+4} has been added, $a_{Ce^{+4}} \cong \frac{1}{10} a_{Ce^{+3}}$ and

$$\mathscr{E} = -1.61 - 0.0592 \log (1/10) - (-0.280) = -1.27 \text{ v}.$$

Note in Fig. 10.8 that the most rapid change in emf versus reagent added occurs at the equivalence point. This may be emphasized by plotting $\Delta \mathscr{E}/\Delta \%$

as shown by the dashed line. This function exhibits a sharp maximum at the equivalence point.

EXERCISE 10.16

Show that the cell

$$Pt \,|\, Ce^{+3}, Ce^{+4} \,\|\, KCl \,(1\ N) \,|\, Hg_2Cl_2, Hg$$

has the same emf as the cell

$$Pt \,|\, Fe^{+2}, Fe^{+3} \,\|\, KCl \,(1\ N) \,|\, Hg_2Cl_2, Hg,$$

when the activities of Ce^{+3}, Ce^{+4}, Fe^{+2} and Fe^{+3} have their equilibrium values related by

$$K = \frac{a_{Fe^{+3}} a_{Ce^{+3}}}{a_{Fe^{+2}} a_{Ce^{+4}}}$$

10.11 Debye-Hückel Theory

The differences between activities and concentrations of electrolytes, illustrated in Fig. 10.7, are mostly much greater than were previously found for nonelectrolytes, and activity coefficients may easily be as small as 0.1. Deviations from ideality are frequently important at concentrations of solute much less than 0.01 m and the device of letting $a \rightarrow m$ as $m \rightarrow 0$ encounters serious problems. In part, reliable experimental measurements become increasingly difficult in very dilute solutions; in part, extrapolating results from even the most dilute solutions to infinite dilution can be very uncertain on a merely empirical basis. According to one of these (G. N. Lewis and M. Randall, 1921), for sufficiently dilute solutions the activity coefficients of electrolytes of a given charge type depend chiefly on the *ionic strength* μ of the solution, defined by equation (10.36).

$$\mu = \tfrac{1}{2} \sum_i m_i Z_i^2 \tag{10.36}$$

where m_i is the concentration of each ion present in the solution and Z_i is the charge on that ion. The correlation between activity coefficient and ionic strength becomes increasingly accurate with increasing dilution.

It was pointed out in connection with Fig. 10.7 that the curves of activity coefficient versus concentration for electrolytes of a given charge type form a family which converges with decreasing concentration. For example, among the 1-1 electrolytes at 0.1 m some mean activity coefficients are 0.78 for NaCl, 0.77 for KCl. The curves are practically indistinguishable at lower concentrations, but above 0.1 m the differences become increasingly significant.

The ionic strength is a property of the solution as a whole and at constant low ionic strength the activity coefficient of a given electrolyte is found to have a nearly constant value regardless of the actual composition of the solution. For example, the mean activity coefficient of sodium chloride 0.001 m in NaCl is 0.966, but in a solution 0.001 m in NaCl and 0.099 m in KBr, $\mu = 0.1$ and we may expect the mean activity coefficient of sodium chloride to be approximately 0.78. (See Fig. 10.7.)

The activity coefficient of an electrolyte also depends on its charge type. For example, in the case of a 2-1 electrolyte, for which

$$m = m_+ = \tfrac{1}{2} m_-$$

$$\mu = \tfrac{1}{2}(m \times 2^2 + 2m \times 1^2) = 3m$$

an ionic strength of 0.1 is achieved at a concentration of 0.033 m. Figure 10.7 shows that the activity coefficient of calcium chloride at this concentration is approximately 0.60. By the same token, we may predict that the activity coefficient of magnesium bromide in 0.033 m solution will be approximately the same. Furthermore, in a solution containing 0.01 m barium bromide and 0.07 m sodium chloride the ionic strength is

$$\mu = \tfrac{1}{2}(m_{\mathrm{Ba^{++}}} \times 2^2 + m_{\mathrm{Br^-}} \times 1^2 + m_{\mathrm{Na^+}} \times 1^2 + m_{\mathrm{Cl^-}} \times 1^2)$$
$$= \tfrac{1}{2}(0.01 \times 4 + 0.02 + 0.07 + 0.07) = 0.1$$

and therefore $\gamma_\pm$ (BaBr$_2$) $\cong 0.60$ and $\gamma_\pm$ (NaCl) $\cong 0.78$.

Lewis discovered empirically that in solutions of low ionic strength ($\mu \leq 0.1$) the logarithm of the activity coefficient of electrolytes of a given charge type is a linear function of the square root of the ionic strength of the solution, i.e.,

$$\log \gamma_\pm = k\sqrt{\mu} \qquad (10.37)$$

where k depends on the charge type of the electrolyte in question. In 1923 P. Debye and E. Hückel developed a theoretical expression for the prediction of activity coefficients as a function of electrolyte charge type and ionic strength. That theory is based on a consideration of the consequences of the electrostatic forces between ions in solution. Although these are subject to a continuous random motion, on the average each positive ion will "see" more negative ions than positive, and vice versa. That is, each ion will be surrounded by a fluctuating *ion atmosphere* of net opposite charge. Dilution of the solution involves work against the net coulombic attraction between the ion and its neighbors. This work is in addition to the free energy change for dilution of an ideal solution in which such forces are not considered. Since, by definition, $a \rightarrow m$ as $m \rightarrow 0$, the difference between the actual and ideal free energy of dilution is a measure of the activity coefficient of the ions.

Through evaluation of the electrostatic work of dilution, Debye and Hückel obtained an expression for the activity coefficient of an ion. When approximations appropriate to dilute solutions are made, the *Debye-Hückel limiting law* is obtained in the form

$$-\ln \gamma_i = \frac{e^3 Z_i^2}{(\epsilon k T)^{3/2}} \sqrt{\frac{2\pi N \mu}{1000}} \qquad (10.38)$$

where γ_i = activity coefficient of ion species i.

   e = electronic charge, 4.803×10^{-10} e.s.u.

   Z_i = number of unit charges on ion species i.

   ϵ = dielectric constant of the medium, 78.56 for H$_2$O at 25°

   k = gas constant per molecule = 1.3805×10^{-16} erg. deg.$^{-1}$.

   T = Kelvin temperature.

   N = Avogadro number, 6.023×10^{23}.

   μ = ionic strength of the solution.

At 25° the constants in equation (10.38) may be combined to give

$$- \log \gamma_i = 0.509 \, Z_i^2 \sqrt{\mu} \tag{10.39}$$

Only the mean activity coefficient, $\gamma_\pm$, is experimentally accessible, and for an electrolyte which dissociates into cations of charge Z_+ and anions of charge Z_-,

$$A_a B_b = a A^{Z_+} + b B^{Z_-}$$

the mean activity coefficient is related to the ion activity coefficients by

$$\gamma_\pm = (\gamma_+^a \gamma_-^b)^{1/(a+b)} \tag{10.40}$$

Substitution of equation (10.39) in (10.40) yields

$$-\log \gamma_\pm = 0.509 \, Z_+ Z_- \sqrt{\mu} \tag{10.41}$$

The validity of this equation may be tested by plotting $-\log \gamma_\pm$ versus $\sqrt{\mu}$ which should give a straight line of slope 0.51 for a 1-1 electrolyte, a slope 0.51×2 for a 2-1 electrolyte and so on. Data which can be subjected to this test will be given in the next section.

EXERCISE 10.17

Estimate the mean activity coefficient of barium bromide and of sodium chloride in a solution of ionic strength 0.1. Compare with data given above.

Ans. $\gamma_\pm$ (BaBr$_2$) $= 0.48$; $\gamma_\pm$ (NaCl) $= 0.69$.

10.12 Solubility of Strong Electrolytes

It has been indicated that for a change in state involving an electrolyte solution the usual form for the expression of ΔF_T applies;

$$\Delta F_T = \Delta F_T^0 + RT \ln Q_a \tag{10.42}$$

where Q_a is the reaction function of activities. In this kind of chemical change, as in any other, $\Delta F_T = 0$ for reaction at equilibrium and, therefore,

$$\Delta F_T^0 = - RT \ln K_a \tag{10.43}$$

where K_a is the value of the equilibrium function of activities. ΔF_T^0 has a unique value for a given reaction at a given temperature, and, therefore, K_a also has a unique value, called the equilibrium constant. This is to be distinguished from the value of the corresponding equilibrium function of concentrations, which is inexact and not constant.

The change of state involved in the dissolving of a strong electrolyte may be represented for ionic crystals in general by

$$A_a B_b \, (s) = a A^{Z_+} \, (aq.) + b B^{Z_-} \, (aq.)$$

and the corresponding equilibrium function is

$$K_a = a_+^a a_-^b \tag{10.44}$$

where Z_+ is the charge on the cation whose activity is a_+ and Z_- is the charge on the anion whose activity is a_-. If the solid phase is at all times pure $A_a B_b$

(s), which is the standard state, its activity is unity and does not appear in the equilibrium function.

Factoring the activities

$$K_a = m_+^a m_-^b \gamma_+^a \gamma_-^b \qquad (10.45)$$

and substituting the mean activity coefficient, we have

$$K_a = m_+^a m_-^b \, (\gamma_\pm)^{a+b} \qquad (10.46)$$

For example, in the case of silver chloride

$$\text{AgCl (s)} = \text{Ag}^+ \text{(aq.)} + \text{Cl}^- \text{(aq.)}$$

$$K_a = m_{\text{Ag}^+} m_{\text{Cl}^-} \gamma_\pm^2$$

It is customary in elementary considerations to take the mean activity coefficient to be approximately unity, in other words, to consider the value of the equilibrium function of concentrations to be constant. In dealing with solutions of very insoluble electrolytes, with no added salts, the ionic strength is small, and the approximation is justified. To illustrate, the measured solubility of silver chloride in water at 20° is 1.5×10^{-4} g./100 g., or 1.05×10^{-5} m. If no other source of silver or chloride ions is present, $m_{\text{Ag}^+} = m_{\text{Cl}^-} = 1.05 \times 10^{-5}$ at equilibrium, and

$$K_a = (1.05 \times 10^{-5})^2 = 1.10 \times 10^{-10} \text{ (moles}^2 \text{ kg.}^{-2})$$

The ionic strength of this solution is 1.05×10^{-5}, and the mean activity coefficient predicted by the Debye-Hückel limiting law at 20° is

$$-\log \gamma_\pm = 0.523 \sqrt{1.05 \times 10^{-5}}$$

$$\gamma_\pm = 0.996$$

On the other hand, for a somewhat more soluble 2-1 electrolyte, lead iodide,

$$\text{PbI}_2 \text{ (s)} = \text{Pb}^{+2} \text{(aq.)} + 2\,\text{I}^- \text{(aq.)}$$

$$K_a = m_{\text{Pb}^{+2}} m_{\text{I}^-}^2 \gamma_\pm^3$$

the solubility is 6.8×10^{-2} g./100 g. and at equilibrium $m_{\text{Pb}^{+2}} = 1.47 \times 10^{-3}$ and $m_{\text{I}^-} = 2.94 \times 10^{-3}$. As a first approximation we take $\gamma_\pm = 1$ and find

$$K_a \cong (1.47 \times 10^{-3})(2.94 \times 10^{-3})^2 = 1.27 \times 10^{-8} \text{ (moles}^3 \text{ kg.}^{-3})$$

However, the ionic strength of the solution is

$$\mu = \tfrac{1}{2}(1.47 \times 10^{-3} \times 2^2 + 2.94 \times 10^{-3} \times 1^2) = 4.41 \times 10^{-3}$$

At this ionic strength the mean activity coefficient of a 2-1 electrolyte, by the Debye-Hückel limiting law, is given by

$$-\log \gamma_\pm = 0.523 \times 2 \sqrt{4.41 \times 10^{-3}}$$

$$\gamma_\pm = 0.86$$

Therefore, the value of K_a is estimated to be

$$K_a = 1.27 \times 10^{-8} (0.86)^3 = 0.81 \times 10^{-8} \text{ (moles}^3 \text{ kg.}^{-3})$$

The activity coefficient represents a significant correction to the concentration in this case.

The presence of added salts in the solution, even though they have no ion in common with the substance of interest, can have, through their effect on the activity coefficient, a substantial effect on the solubility. For example, let us estimate the solubility of silver chloride in 0.1 m potassium nitrate solution, whose ionic strength is 0.1 In this solution $\gamma_\pm$ for a 1-1 electrolyte is 0.78 (see above) and, therefore, at 20°

$$K_a = m_{Ag^+} \cdot m_{Cl^-} (0.78)^2 = 1.10 \times 10^{-10}$$

Since

$$m_{Ag^+} = m_{Cl^-}$$

$$m_{Ag^+} = \frac{(1.10 \times 10^{-10})^{1/2}}{0.78} = 1.35 \times 10^{-5} \text{ moles kg.}^{-1}$$

Thus, the solubility of silver chloride is increased by ~30% when the ionic strength of the solution is 0.1 instead of ~0, but the activity remains the same. This is known as a *salt effect*.

EXERCISE 10.18

Estimate the solubility of silver chloride in 0.1 m KCl at 20°, (a) assuming $\gamma_\pm = 1$, and (b) using $\gamma_\pm = 0.78$.   *Ans.* (a) 1.10×10^{-9} m, (b) 1.81×10^{-9} m.

Careful study of the salt effect on solubility has provided one means of verifying the Debye-Hückel limiting law. J.N. Bronsted and V. K. La Mer [*J. Am. Chem. Soc.*, **46**, 555 (1942)] determined the solubility of complex cobalt ammine salts of three charge types, a 1-1 salt, a 1-2 salt and a 3-1 salt. Various electrolytes were added to the solution to alter the ionic strength. From the solubility of the complex cobalt ammine salt, the mean activity coefficient was computed and plotted as shown in Fig. 10.9. The linear dependence on $\mu^{1/2}$ and the relation of the slopes to charge type are in good agreement with the theory.

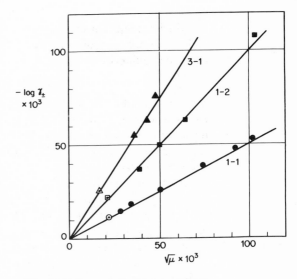

FIG. 10.9. Test of the Debye—Hückel limiting law. ⊙ 1-1 salt in water ● with added electrolytes; ⊡ 1-2 salt in water ■ with added electrolytes; △ 3-1 salt in water ▲ with added electrolytes solid lines, D-H limiting law.

10.13 Acids and Bases

The definition of an acid as a substance with an ionizable proton, and a base as a substance with an ionizable hydroxyl group, is useful in aqueous systems, but inadequate in nonaqueous systems. Although we will be primarily concerned with the former, it is advantageous to adopt the broader view of Bronsted and of Lowry, which defines an *acid* as a *proton donor* and a *base* as a *proton acceptor*. The loss of a proton by an acid produces a substance which is capable of accepting a proton, namely a base. Conversely, the gain of a proton by a base produces a substance capable of donating a proton, an acid. Two substances which are related by the difference of one proton are said to be *conjugate acid and base*. Formally they are related by

$$HA = H^+ + A^-; \quad \text{or} \quad HB^+ = B + H^+$$

where A^- is the base conjugate to the acid HA and HB^+ is the acid conjugate to the base B. In electrolytic solutions free H^+ cannot exist, and an acid can only transfer a proton to a suitable acceptor by a process of the type

$$HA + B = HB^+ + A^-$$

The strength of an acid HA is commonly defined in terms of the equilibrium constant K_{HA} of this reaction which clearly involves the inseparable basicity of the proton acceptor, B. Two acids can be compared with each other by referring both to a common base. Thus, for a second acid HA', with equilibrium constant $K_{HA'}$,

$$HA' + B = HB^+ + A'^-$$

Combining the equations gives

$$HA + A'^- = HA' + A^-$$

for which the equilibrium constant is $K_{HA}/K_{HA'}$ and does not involve the basicity of B. In aqueous media water is the common proton acceptor and for strong acids the equilibrium

$$HA + H_2O = H_3O^+ + A^-$$

lies immeasurably far to the right. In such cases K_{HA} cannot be measured, and strong acids cannot be compared in terms of $K_{HA}/K_{HA'}$, since neither constant, nor their ratio, can be measured. The only strong acid species present is H_3O^+, the hydronium ion. The species H_3O^+ is known in the attenuated gaseous state, and the reaction $H^+ + H_2O = H_3O^+$ is exothermic by approximately 170 kcal. Other gaseous species $H^+ (H_2O)_n$ with $n = 2$ to 5 also exist, but the energy of binding each additional H_2O decreases very rapidly and the value of n is unknown for aqueous $H^+(H_2O)_n$. The symbol H^+ is used for the solvated proton unless the proton-accepting role of the solvent B is to be explicitly shown, when the proton is represented by HB^+, and so forth.

The extent to which an acid HA undergoes proton donation to the solvent B depends upon the energetics of several processes:

$HA(g) = H(g) + A(g)$ bond dissociation energy

$H(g) = H^+(g) + e$ ionization of H

$A(g) + e = A^-(g)$ electron affinity of A

$H^+(g) + B(g) = HB^+(g)$ proton affinity of B

$$HB^+(g) = HB^+(\text{solution}) \quad \text{solvation energy of } HB^+$$

$$A^-(g) = A^-(\text{solution}) \quad \text{solvation energy of } A^-$$

The great difference in acidity of CH_4 and HCl, for example, arises almost entirely from the electron affinities of Cl (3.6 ev) and CH_3 (1.0 ev). All other energy terms are equal, or nearly so. One of the major differences between solvents in their ability to promote ionic dissociation of acids arises from differences in proton affinity (viz., basicity). Whether or not the ion pair arising from proton transfer conducts an electric current efficiently is a quite different matter, depending upon ion separation which is determined by the dielectric constant of the solvent, ϵ. The coulombic force of attraction f between ions of charge $+e$ and $-e$ at a separation r is

$$f = \frac{-e^2}{\epsilon r^2} \tag{10.47}$$

The great differences in the extent of electrolytic conduction in water ($\epsilon \cong 80$) and in hydrocarbons ($\epsilon \cong 2.5$) are consistent with this effect.

The preceding discussion of acids necessarily includes a description of bases. Thus, in aqueous solutions a substance B is a base if it removes a proton from water by the reaction

$$B + H_2O = BH^+ + OH^-$$

An example is ammonia. The equilibrium constant K_B for such a reaction is often termed the ionization constant of the base. The reaction is, in fact, formally indistinguishable from the ionization of an acid.

$$HA + B = A^- + HB^+$$

The only difference is that in one instance we emphasize the proton donor, in the other we emphasize the proton acceptor. There is a tendency to ignore the role of the solvent water as acid or base, for example, and to confer the determining effect upon the solute as base or acid. The self-hydrolysis of water involves both the acid and base functions, since

$$H_2O + H_2O = H_3O^+ + OH^-$$

and

$$K_W = \frac{a_{H_3O^+} a_{OH^-}}{a_{H_2O}^2}$$

In pure water $a_{H_2O} = 1$ and in dilute solutions $a_{H_2O} \cong 1$, so that

$$K_W = a_{H_3O^+} a_{OH^-}$$

10.14 Weak Acids and Bases

An acid which transfers protons to the solvent to a limited degree is said to be weak. For the process

$$HA + H_2O = H_3O^+ + A^-$$

the equilibrium expression is

$$K_{HA} = \frac{a_{H_3O^+} a_{A^-}}{a_{HA} a_{H_2O}} \tag{10.48}$$

In dilute aqueous solutions $a_{H_2O} \cong 1$ and

$$K_{HA} = \frac{a_{H_3O^+} a_{A^-}}{a_{HA}} \tag{10.49}$$

This expression corresponds formally to the process

$$HA = H^+ + A^-$$

and so gives rise to the conventional formula

$$K_{HA} = \frac{a_{H^+} a_{A^-}}{a_{HA}} \tag{10.50}$$

Acetic acid is a typical example, for which $K_{HA} = 1.8 \times 10^{-5}$ at 25° in water. Provided no other electrolytes are present, the ionic strength is small, and it is often permissible to replace activities by concentrations. Another useful approximation, valid for all but very weak acids, is to neglect the self-dissociation of water and to set

$$m_{H^+} \cong m_{OAc^-}$$

Thus, in 0.1 m acetic acid $m_{H^+} \cong m_{OAc^-} \cong 1.4 \times 10^{-3}$. The contribution to m_{H^+} from water itself can be established by estimating the equivalent m_{OH^-}. At 25° the value of K_W is 1.00×10^{-14} and

$$m_{OH^-} \cong \frac{10^{-14}}{1.4 \times 10^{-3}} \cong 7 \times 10^{-12}$$

The approximation is, therefore, justified.

The ionization constant of a weak acid is most easily measured in an appropriate galvanic cell. The following cell was used for acetic acid [H. S. Harned and R. W. Ehlers, *J. Am. Chem. Soc.*, **54**, 1350 (1932)]:

$$Pt, \ H_2 \mid HOAc \ (m_1), \ NaOAc \ (m_2), \ NaCl \ (m_3) \mid AgCl, \ Ag$$

All solutes were present in one solution without liquid junction. The cell reaction is

$$\tfrac{1}{2} H_2 + AgCl = H^+ + Cl^- + Ag$$

The value of a_{H^+} is, of course, established by the chosen concentrations m_{HOAc} and m_{OAc^-} and the corresponding activity coefficients through the relation

$$K_{HA} = \frac{a_{H^+} a_{OAc^-}}{a_{HOAc}} = \frac{m_{H^+} m_{OAc^-}}{m_{HOAc}} \frac{\gamma_{H^+} \gamma_{OAc^-}}{\gamma_{HOAc}} \tag{10.51}$$

The emf of the cell is given by

$$\mathscr{E} = \mathscr{E}^0 - \frac{RT}{\mathscr{F}} \ln a_{H^+} a_{Cl^-}$$

$$= \mathscr{E}^0 - \frac{RT}{\mathscr{F}} \ln \frac{m_{Cl^-} m_{HOAc}}{m_{OAc^-}} - \frac{RT}{\mathscr{F}} \ln \frac{\gamma_{Cl^-} \gamma_{HOAc}}{\gamma_{OAc^-}} - \frac{RT}{\mathscr{F}} \ln K_{HA} \tag{10.52}$$

Since HOAc is electrically neutral, $\gamma_{HOAc} = 1$ in sufficiently dilute solutions. Also, the Debye-Hückel limiting law gives $\gamma_{Cl^-} = \gamma_{OAc^-}$, and the term involving activity coefficients is approximately zero. For one experiment at 25°, m_1 = m_{HOAc} = 0.012035, $m_2 = m_{OAc^-}$ = 0.011582, $m_3 = m_{Cl^-}$ = 0.012426 and $\mathscr{E} = 0.61583$ v. From the same research, $\mathscr{E}^0 = 0.22239$ v. The function of molalities, in these symbols, is $m_3(m_1 - m_{H^+})/(m_2 + m_{H^+})$. Since m_{H^+} is evidently very small, it is permissible to use the approximation $m_{H^+} = K_{HA} m_1/m_2 = 1.9 \times 10^{-5}$. The adjusted concentrations become $m_1' = 0.012016$ and $m_2' = 0.011563$. Solving equation (10.52) gives $K_{HA} = 1.725 \times 10^{-5}$. Extrapolating other measurements at several ionic strengths to infinite dilution leads to the value $K_{HA} = 1.754 \times 10^{-5}$ at 25°. The ionization constants of several acids and bases appear in Table 10.5.

EXERCISE 10.19

Solve equation (10.51) using values of m_1', m_2' and m_3 given in the text to evaluate K_{HA} for acetic acid. *Ans.* $K_{HA} = 1.725 \times 10^{-5}$.

The fractional degree of dissociation α of a weak acid is a function of the nominal concentration of acid, m_0: $m_{H^+} = m_{A^-} = m_0\alpha$; $m_{HA} = m_0(1 - \alpha)$. Substituting into equation (10.51) gives

$$K_A = \frac{m_0\alpha^2}{1 - \alpha}\gamma_\pm^2 \qquad (10.53)$$

TABLE 10.5

DISSOCIATION CONSTANTS OF WEAK ACIDS AND
HYDROLYSIS CONSTANTS OF WEAK BASES (25°)

Acids	K_A	Bases	K_B
Acetic acid, CH_3COOH	1.75×10^{-5}	Ammonia, NH_3	1.8×10^{-5}
Arsenic acid, H_3AsO_4 (1)	2.5×10^{-4}	*sec.* Butylamine, $C_4H_{11}N$	4.4×10^{-4}
(2)	5.6×10^{-8}	Diethylamine, $C_4H_{11}N$	1.26×10^{-3}
(3)	3.0×10^{-13}	Dimethylamine, C_2H_7N	5.2×10^{-4}
Boric acid, H_3BO_3	6.0×10^{-10}	Ethylamine, C_2H_7N	5.6×10^{-4}
Carbonic acid, H_2CO_3 (1)	4.2×10^{-7}	Hydrazine, $N_2H_4.H_2O$	3×10^{-6}
(2)	4.8×10^{-11}	Methylamine, CH_5N	5×10^{-4}
Formic acid, $HCOOH$	1.77×10^{-4}	Phenylhydrazine, $C_6H_8N_2$	1.6×10^{-9}
Hydrogen sulfide, H_2S (1)	1.0×10^{-7}	Pyridine, C_5H_5N	2.3×10^{-9}
(2)	1.3×10^{-13}	Silver hydroxide, $AgOH$	1.1×10^{-4}
Hypochlorous acid, $HClO$	3.2×10^{-8}	Urea, CH_4ON_2	1.5×10^{-14}
Oxalic acid, $H_2C_2O_4$ (1)	3.8×10^{-2}		
(2)	5.0×10^{-5}		
Phosphoric acid, H_3PO_4 (1)	7.5×10^{-3}		
(2)	6.2×10^{-8}		
(3)	1×10^{-12}		

For the related process of hydrolysis of the conjugate base

$$A^- + H_2O = HA + OH^-$$

the expression for equilibrium is

$$K_B = \frac{a_{HA}a_{OH^-}}{a_{A^-}\cdot a_{H_2O}} = \frac{a_{HA}a_{OH^-}}{a_{A^-}} \qquad (10.54)$$

and K_B is the hydrolysis constant. The hydrolysis of bases does not depend upon the electric charge type, and it is worth restating the preceding relations for any base B^Z, where Z is electric charge:

$$B^Z + H_2O = HB^{Z+1} + OH^-$$

$$K_B = \frac{a_{HB}^{Z+1} a_{OH^-}}{a_{B^Z}} \tag{10.55}$$

Equation (10.55) applies as well to ammonia as to acetate ion.

EXERCISE 10.20

Show that equations (10.50) and (10.55) are related by $K_B K_A = K_W$.

SUMMARY, CHAPTER 10

1. Faraday's law

    1 gram-equivalent of electrolysis requires 96,487 coulombs.

2. Conductance

$$l = \frac{1}{R} = \frac{I}{V}$$

Specific conductance

$$L = l\frac{d}{A}$$

Equivalent conductance, Λ; at infinite dilution, Λ_0

$$\Lambda = \frac{1000}{c}L$$

Kohlrausch's law

$$\Lambda = \lambda_+ + \lambda_-$$

Degree of dissociation

$$\alpha = \frac{\Lambda}{\Lambda_0}$$

Transference number

$$n_+ = \frac{i_+}{i_+ + i_-}, \qquad n_- = \frac{i_-}{i_+ + i_-}$$

Equivalent ionic conductances

$$\lambda_+ = \Lambda n_+, \qquad \lambda_- = \Lambda n_-$$

3. Galvanic cells—by convention, left-hand electrode is the anode, at which oxidation occurs; +emf, cell reaction permitted; −emf, cell reaction forbidden.

$$\Delta F_T = - w \text{ (elect.)} = - n\mathscr{F}\mathscr{E}_T$$

$$\Delta S_{T,P} = n\mathscr{F}\left(\frac{\partial \mathscr{E}_T}{\partial T}\right)_P$$

$$\Delta H_T = - n\mathscr{F}\mathscr{E}_T + Tn\mathscr{F}\left(\frac{\partial \mathscr{E}_T}{\partial T}\right)_P$$

$$\mathscr{E}_T = \mathscr{E}_T^0 - \frac{RT}{n\mathscr{F}} \ln Q$$

Standard electrode oxidation potentials (emf's)

$$\mathscr{E} \text{ (cell)} = \mathscr{E} \text{ (anode)} - \mathscr{E} \text{ (cathode)}$$

By convention, for Pt, $H_2(g)\,|\,H^+(aq.)$,

$$\mathscr{E}^0_T = 0, \qquad \left(\frac{\partial \mathscr{E}^0}{\partial T}\right)_P = 0$$

4. Applications of galvanic cells
   Equilibria

$$\mathscr{E}^0_T = \frac{RT}{n\mathscr{F}} \ln K$$

   pH measurement

$$\mathscr{E} \text{ (cell)} = a \times \text{pH} + b$$

   where a and b depend on nature of cell used
   Redox titration

$$\mathscr{E} \text{ (cell)} = \text{const.} - \frac{RT}{n\mathscr{F}} \ln \frac{a_{\text{ox.}}}{a_{\text{red.}}}$$

5. Electrolyte activities

$$a = \gamma m$$

   Ionic strength

$$\mu = \tfrac{1}{2} \sum c_i Z_i^2$$

   Debye-Hückle limiting law at $25°$

$$-\log \gamma_\pm = 0.509\, Z_+ Z_- \sqrt{\mu}$$

6. Solubility product

$$A_a B_b \text{ (s)} = a A^{Z^+} \text{ (aq.)} + b B^{Z^-} \text{ (aq.)}$$

$$K_a = m_+^a\, m_-^b\, (\gamma_\pm)^{a+b}$$

7. Acid dissociation

$$\text{HA} + H_2O = H_3O^+ + A^-$$

$$K_A = \frac{a_{H_3O^+} a_{A^-}}{a_{HA}}$$

8. Base hydrolysis

$$B + H_2O = BH^+ + OH^-$$

$$K_B = \frac{a_{BH^+}\, a_{OH^-}}{a_B}$$

9. Ion product of water

$$2\,H_2O = H_3O^+ + OH^-$$

$$K_W = a_{H_3O^+} a_{OH^-}$$

For a conjugate acid and base

$$K_A \times K_B = K_W$$

PROBLEMS, CHAPTER 10

1. A certain divalent metal salt solution is electrolyzed in series with a silver coulometer. After 1 hr. the weight of silver deposited is 0.5094 g. and the weight of the unknown metal deposited is 0.2653 g.
(a) What is the atomic weight of the unknown?
(b) What was the average current during the electrolysis?

Ans. (a) 112.3, (b) 0.1266 amp.

2. It is found that when a certain conductance cell is filled with 0.0200 M aqueous potassium chloride, the resistance is 175 ohms. When the same cell is filled with 0.01 M aqueous sodium acetate, the resistance is 579 ohms. The specific conductance of 0.0200 M potassium chloride is 27.7×10^{-4} ohm^{-1}cm.$^{-1}$. Find the equivalent conductance of the sodium acetate solution.

Ans. 83.7.

3. From data in Table 10.1 find Λ_0 for the weak electrolyte NH_4OH. In 0.1 M solution this substance is 1.34% dissociated. What is the specific conductance of such a solution?

Ans. $\Lambda_0 = 271$, $L = 3.63 \times 10^{-4}$.

4. In a moving boundary apparatus a 0.1 N solution of potassium acetate is electrolyzed at a steady current of 0.1 amp. After 1000 sec. it is found that the cation boundary has swept out a volume of 6.84 cc. What is the transference number of the anion in this solution?

Ans. $n_- = 0.340$.

5. From the data in Tables 10.1 and 10.2 find the equivalent ionic conductances of Li^+ and Cl^- at infinite dilution.

Ans. $\lambda_+ = 38.70$.

6. Use the data of Table 10.3 to estimate the specific conductance of 0.01 M $Ca(NO_3)_2$. Assume that at this concentration $\Lambda = \Lambda_0$. Find the transference number of the cation.

Ans. $L = 2.62 \times 10^{-3}$, $n_+ = 0.454$.

7. A sample of water having a specific conductance of 1.12×10^{-6} ohm^{-1} cm.$^{-1}$ was saturated with silver chloride, whereupon the specific conductance rose to 2.85×10^{-6} ohm^{-1} cm.$^{-1}$. Find the solubility of silver chloride, a strong electrolyte.

Ans. $c = 1.25 \times 10^{-5}$ M.

8. The equivalent conductance of the sodium salt of crotonic acid at infinite dilution is 88.30 ohm^{-1}eq.$^{-1}$cm.^{2}. The equivalent conductance of crotonic acid at 1.7×10^{-3} N is 39.47 ohm^{-1}eq.$^{-1}$cm.^{2}. Find the degree of dissociation of crotonic acid in this solution.

Ans. 10%.

9. Formulate the galvanic cells corresponding to the following reactions and calculate ΔF_{298}^0 for each reaction:
(a) $Ag \, (s) + H^+ \, (aq.) = Ag^+ \, (aq.) + \frac{1}{2} H_2 \, (g)$
(b) $Cd \, (s) + 2 \, H^+ \, (aq.) = Cd^{+2} \, (aq.) + H_2 \, (g)$
(c) $Pb \, (s) + 2 \, AgI = PbI_2 \, (s) + 2 \, Ag \, (s)$
(d) $Br_2 \, (l) + 2 \, Ce^{+3} \, (aq.) = 2 \, Br^- \, (aq.) + 2 \, Ce^{+4} \, (aq.)$

Ans. (a) 18.43 kcal., (c) -9.87 kcal.

10. Find $\mathscr{E}_{298}$ for the following cells:
(a) $Zn \,|\, Zn^{+2} \, (a = 0.001) \,\|\, \begin{matrix} Fe^{+2} \, (a = 0.001) \\ Fe^{+3} \, (a = 0.1) \end{matrix} \,\Big|\, Pt$
(b) $Ag \,|\, Ag^+ \, (a = 0.1) \,\|\, Cd^{+2} \, (a = 0.1) \,|\, Cd$
(c) $Ag, AgBr \, (s) \,|\, HBr \, (a = 0.01) \,|\, H_2 \, (1 \text{ atm.}), Pt$

Ans. (a) 1.74 v.

11. Estimate the mean activity coefficient of the first salt mentioned in each of the following mixed salt solutions:
(a) 0.01 m CaCl$_2$, 0.05 m NaCl.
(b) 0.01 m FeSO$_4$, 0.02 m Na$_2$SO$_4$.
(c) 0.02 m NaCl, 0.01 m LaCl$_3$ *Ans.* (a) $\gamma_\pm = 0.52$.

12. The solubility of silver sulfate, Ag$_2$SO$_4$, in water at 25° is 0.79 g./100 g. Find K_a (a) neglecting activity considerations, and (b) using Debye-Hückel limiting law to estimate $\gamma_\pm$.   *Ans.* (a) 6.5×10^{-5}, (b) 9.4×10^{-6}.

13. Find the pH of the following solutions, letting $a = m$:
(a) 0.1 m hypochlorous acid.
(b) 0.01 m sodium hypochlorite.
(c) 0.1 m phenylhydrazine.
(d) 0.01 m phenylhydrazine hydrochloride.   *Ans.* (a) 4.25, (b)9.75.

14. Find the pH at the first and second end points in the titration of 0.01 M H$_2$CO$_3$ with 0.01 M strong base.   *Ans.* First end point, pH $=9.0$.

---

15. For the cell

$$\text{Ag, AgCl (s)} \,|\, \text{HCl (1 } m) \,|\, \text{H}_2 \text{ (1 atm.), Pt}$$

$\mathscr{E}_{298} = -0.2333$ v. Find $\gamma_\pm$ for HCl in 1 m solution.

16. From the data in Table 10.4 find the equilibrium constants for the following reactions:
(a) AgBr (s) = Ag$^+$ (aq.) + Br$^-$ (aq.)
(b) Sn^{+2} (aq.) + I$_2$ (s) = Sn^{+4} (aq.) + 2 I$^-$ (aq.)
(c) 5 Ce^{+3} (aq.) + MnO$_4^-$ (aq.) + 8 H$^+$ (aq.)
$$= 5 \text{ Ce}^{+4} \text{ (aq.)} + \text{Mn}^{+2} \text{ (aq.)} + 4 \text{ H}_2\text{O}$$

17. Find $\mathscr{E}_{298}$ for the following cell

$$\text{Pt} \,|\, \text{Q, QH}_2, \text{H}_2\text{O} \,\|\, \text{KCl (1 } N) \,|\, \text{Hg}_2\text{Cl}_2, \text{Hg}$$

from the fact that in water with no added acid or base $a_{H^+} = 10^{-7}$.

18. Show that in the cell

$$\text{Pt} \,|\, \text{Fe}^{+2}, \text{Fe}^{+3} \,\|\, \text{KCl (1 } N) \,|\, \text{Hg}_2\text{Cl}_2, \text{Hg}$$

when the ferrous ion is titrated to equivalence with ceric ion (so that total Ce = total Fe) that the emf at equivalence is

$$\mathscr{E} = \tfrac{1}{2} [\mathscr{E}^0(\text{Ce}^{+3}, \text{Ce}^{+4}) + \mathscr{E}^0(\text{Fe}^{+2}, \text{Fe}^{+3})] - \mathscr{E}(\text{N.C.E.})$$

Find $\mathscr{E}_{298}$ for the cell at the equivalence point.

19. The cell

$$\text{Cd} \,|\, \text{CdCl}_2 \text{ (1 } m) \,|\, \text{AgCl, Ag}$$

has $\mathscr{E}_{298} = 0.675$ v. and $d\mathscr{E}/dT = -0.00065$ v. deg.$^{-1}$ Find ΔH_{298} and ΔS_{298} for the reaction

$$\text{Cd} + 2 \text{ AgCl} = \text{Cd}^{+2} + 2 \text{ Cl}^- + 2 \text{ Ag}$$

20. The emf of the cell

$$\text{Pt, H}_2 \text{ (1 atm.)} \,|\, \text{HBr (} m) \,|\, \text{AgBr (s), Ag}$$

was measured at various molalities m of HBr, with the following results:

m	0.0004042	0.0008444	0.001355	0.001850	0.00239(
$\mathscr{E}_{298}$	0.47381	0.43636	0.41243	0.39667	0.38383

Find $\mathscr{E}_{298}^{0}$ and the mean activity coefficient of HBr at the highest concentration

21. A conductance cell with an effective cross section of 10 cm.^{2} and an inter-electrode distance of 5 cm. is used in the conductimetric titration of 0.1 N acetic acid with 0.1 N sodium hydroxide. Neglecting ionization of acetic acid, find the actual resistance of the cell at 90%, 100%, and 110% neutralization. Assume that $\Lambda/\Lambda_0 = 0.90$ for all strong electrolytes in the system.

22. The cell

$$\text{Pt, H}_2 \text{ (1 atm.)} \,|\, \text{H}^+ \text{ (pH} = \text{?), I}^- \,(a = 1) \,|\, \text{AgI (s), Ag}$$

is constructed to measure pH. At what pH will the cell have $\mathscr{E}_{298} = 0$?

23. A solution of stannous salt is to be titrated with a ceric solution, using a platinum electrode and normal calomel reference electrode. What is $\mathscr{E}_{298}$ when the titration is 99% complete?

24. Silver ion forms an ammine complex $\text{Ag(NH}_3)_2^+$ and in 0.1 m ammonia the solubility of silver chloride is 6.8×10^{-3} m. Find the equilibrium constant for dissociation of the complex. Let $a = m$. K_a for AgCl is 1.1×10^{-3} m^2 kg^{-2}.

$$\text{Ag(NH}_3)_2^+ = \text{Ag}^+ + 2\,\text{NH}_3$$

25. Consider the equilibrium

$$\text{I}_2 + \text{I}^- = \text{I}_3^-$$

in aqueous solution, for which $K = 720$ (l. mole^{-1}). Show that when $m_{\text{I}^-} \gg m_{\text{I}_2}$ initially the ratio I_3^-/I_2 is independent of m_{I_2} and proportional to m_{I^-}. Find the value of the ratio in 0.01 m iodide.

26. Find $m_{\text{H}_3\text{O}^+}$ in a solution resulting from the addition of 25 ml. of 0.1 m ammonium hydroxide to 50 ml. of 0.1 m formic acid.

27. A solution is 0.20 N in formic acid and 0.05 N in hypochlorous acid. When 10 ml. of 0.1 N sodium hydroxide is added to 40 ml. of the solution of acids, find the concentrations of hypochlorite ion, formate ion and hydronium ion.

28. The heat of neutralization of strong acid by strong base is 13,800 cal. mole^{-1}. Find the value of K_W at 50° and find $a_{\text{H}_3\text{O}^+} = a_{\text{OH}^-}$ in pure water at this temperature.

29. Show in general that the minimum slope of the curve of pH versus per cent neutralization is found at 50% neutralization.

11

RATES OF
CHEMICAL REACTION

1.1 Equilibrium and Reaction Rate

A reaction with a large increase in the standard free energy cannot produce a good yield of product, since at equilibrium the concentrations of reactants will be much greater than the concentrations of products. On the other hand, a large decrease in the standard free energy assures a large yield of product at equilibrium but gives no indication of the rate of approach to equilibrium. For example, the standard free energy of formation of $H_2O(l)$ from the elements at 25° is -57 kcal. per mole, and yet hydrogen and oxygen do not react in the pure state at this temperature.

Suppose that the reactants A and B can produce two sets of products M,N and R,S by competitive processes and that the standard free energy change for formation of M,N is much more favorable than for formation of R,S. That is, the standard free energy content of M,N is much less than R,S. It does not follow that the relative yields at every state prior to establishment of the equilibrium shall be in the sense M,N > R,S. In fact, the products R,S may be in equilibrium with the reactants before the products M,N are detectable. As an example, consider the following reactions:

$$C_6H_6 \text{ (l)} + 3Cl_2 \text{ (g)} = 6C \text{ (s)} + 6HCl \text{ (g)}, \qquad \Delta F^o_{298} = -166 \text{ kcal. mole}^{-1}$$

$$C_6H_6 \text{ (l)} + Cl_2 \text{ (g)} = C_6H_5Cl \text{ (l)} + HCl \text{ (g)}, \qquad \Delta F^o_{298} = -24.4 \text{ kcal. mole}^{-1}$$

Although the free energy change for the first reaction considerably exceeds that of the second, nevertheless the latter is experimentally feasible, and the former does not occur to any measurable extent.

We know from thermodynamics that the ultimate position of equilibrium

275

in a chemical system does not depend upon reaction paths. It is easily show that the rate of approach to equilibrium does depend strongly upon the reaction path. For example, the immeasurably slow reaction in the dark between pur hydrogen and chlorine becomes explosive when a trace of sodium vapor introduced. In either case the standard free energy of formation of hydroge chloride gas is -23 kcal. per mole. We may well ask why a reaction which i quite slow under one set of conditions becomes quite rapid under differer conditions.

It is one of the chief functions of chemical kinetics to propose and test *mechanism*, or detailed description of the reaction path, as an explanation of what is observed. To illustrate, in the case described above it appears tha reaction by simple collision between hydrogen molecules and chlorine molecule does not produce hydrogen chloride at an appreciable rate. On the other hand sodium vapor reacts readily with chlorine to produce chlorine atoms

$$Na + Cl_2 \longrightarrow NaCl + Cl$$

which react efficiently with hydrogen,

$$Cl + H_2 \longrightarrow HCl + H$$

producing the product, hydrogen chloride. From the facts (a) that the reaction is extremely rapid and (b) that the amount of hydrogen chloride produce is much greater than the amount of sodium initially present, it is possible t conclude that the hydrogen atoms produced in the second step react efficientl with molecular chlorine

$$H + Cl_2 \longrightarrow HCl + Cl$$

to produce another molecule of product and another chlorine atom. The latte can react with hydrogen as before, thus leading to a *chain reaction* in whic many molecules of product are produced for each chlorine atom initially gen erated by the sodium.

An indispensable prerequisite to the study of the chemical kinetics of reaction system is a careful test of the nature of the reaction which is occurring Changes in concentrations should be measured quantitatively for as man of the reactants and products as are required to establish the process or proces ses involved. When the stoichiometry of a reaction under study has been estab lished as

$$aA + bB + \ldots = mM + nN + \ldots$$

the next step is to observe the rate of the reaction by repeated measurement of the concentration of a reactant or product at known times and at constan temperature. The choice of substance to be measured is arbitrary and may b dictated by experimental convenience, since the stoichiometric coefficient give relations between the rates of consumption and production of reactant and products,

$$\frac{-1}{a} \cdot \frac{dc_A}{dt} = \frac{-1}{b} \cdot \frac{dc_B}{dt} = \frac{1}{m} \cdot \frac{dc_M}{dt} = \frac{1}{n} \cdot \frac{dc_N}{dt} \tag{11.1}$$

where c_A, c_B, c_M and c_N are the instantaneous concentrations and t is time.

In some instances the rate law takes the form of a simple proportionality between the rate and the concentrations of reactants, but it will not be of such a simple form if there are two or more simultaneous or competing processes. In such cases the experimenter may attempt to isolate one process by a proper choice of temperature, concentration, solvent, or other condition. If the reaction is known to be reversible, the back reaction can usually be avoided by measuring rates during the early stages of the reaction when c_A, c_B are near their maximum values and c_M, c_N are still small. The reverse reaction can be similarly isolated by beginning with M and N. The experimenter eventually succeeds, we shall suppose, in securing an adequate rate law for the widest practicable range of experimental conditions.

11.2   Order of Reaction Rates

Chemical reactions may be simple or complex. Complex reactions involve two or more component steps which are rate controlling and will be discussed later. Simple reactions can be described in terms of a single rate-controlling process, say

$$aA + bB + \ldots = mM + nN + \ldots$$

and the rate law takes the simple form

$$\frac{-dc_A}{dt} = kc_A^\alpha c_B^\beta \ldots \tag{11.2}$$

The exponents α and β cannot be predicted but must be established by observation of the dependence of rate on concentration. The value of the sum $\alpha + \beta \ldots$ is the *order* of the reaction. The order with respect to A is α; the order with respect to B is β.

The constant k is the *specific velocity constant* or *rate constant*. Its value depends upon the nature of the reaction, and for reactions in solution it may also depend upon the solvent. It is a function of temperature, but it is not a function of concentration. The significance of k becomes apparent by letting $c_A = c_B = \ldots = 1$, when $-dc_A/dt = k$. That is, k is the reaction velocity at unit concentration of each reagent. The dimension of k follows from

$$k = \frac{-dc/dt}{c^{\alpha+\beta+\ldots}}$$

and is (concentration)$^{1-\alpha-\beta\ldots}$ (time)$^{-1}$. Choosing liters, moles, and seconds, we find that this becomes, for a first-order reaction, sec.$^{-1}$, and for a second-order reaction, liter-mole^{-1} sec.$^{-1}$.

The decomposition of nitrogen pentoxide is described by the stoichiometric equation

$$2N_2O_5 = 2N_2O_4 + O_2$$

The time dependence of the yield of oxygen in carbon tetrachloride solution at 45° has been measured [H. Eyring and F. Daniels, *J. Am. Chem. Soc.*, **52,** 1472 (1930)], and from this the concentration of nitrogen pentoxide remaining at any time can be computed, with the results shown in Table 11.1. These data are displayed in Fig. 11.1, where the descending curve describes the instanta-

TABLE 11.1

DECOMPOSITION OF N_2O_5 IN CCl_4 AT 45°

Time (sec.)	Moles O_2 (from 1 l.)	$c_{N_2O_5}$ (moles l.$^{-1}$)	k (sec.$^{-1}$ × 10^4)
0	0.000	5.33	—
82	0.14	5.04	6.97
162	0.27	4.78	6.67
409	0.62	4.06	6.57
604	0.96	3.36	6.37
1129	1.44	2.37	6.67
1721	1.83	1.57	6.95
1929	1.94	1.36	6.99
3399	2.34	0.53	6.69

neous concentration of unreacted nitrogen pentoxide as a function of time. The corresponding instantaneous rate of decomposition, or reaction velocity,

$$\frac{-dc_{N_2O_5}}{dt} = \text{slope}$$

is seen to vary with the value of $c_{N_2O_5}$. The relationship between rate and concentration may be examined by plotting $\Delta c/\Delta t$ against the average concentration for each interval, as in Fig. 11.2. With the exception of one point, evidently due to an experimental error, the relation is linear and

$$\frac{-dc_{N_2O_5}}{dt} = kc_{N_2O_5}$$

Referring to equation (11.2), we may say that this is a first-order reaction.

The rate of reaction could as well have been described in terms of oxygen produced as of nitrogen pentoxide consumed. It follows from stoichiometry that

moles N_2O_5 decomposed $= 2 \times$ moles O_2 produced

and from equation 11.1 that

rate of N_2O_5 decomposition $= 2 \times$ rate of O_2 production

Figure 11.1 also shows this relationship.

EXERCISE 11.1

Letting x and x_∞ denote moles of oxygen produced at times t and ∞, show that for the decomposition of nitrogen pentoxide

$$dx/dt = k(x_\infty - x)$$

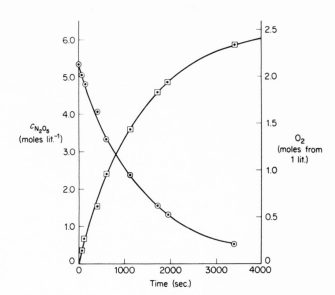

FIG. 11.1. Decomposition of N_2O_5.
- ⊙ concentration of N_2O_5 (left hand scale)
- ⊡ oxygen yield (right hand scale)

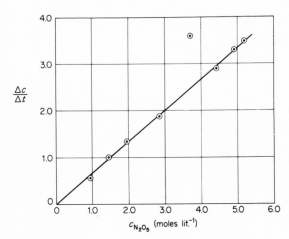

FIG. 11.2. Rate of decomposition of N_2O_5 as a function of its concentration.

The saponification of ethyl acetate, an ester,

$$CH_3COOC_2H_5 + OH^- = CH_3COO^- + C_2H_5OH$$

is described by the rate equation

$$\frac{-dc_{ester}}{dt} = kc_{ester}c_{base}$$

The rate is first order in concentration of ester and first order in concentration of base. It is a second-order reaction.

The reaction between nitric oxide and oxygen

$$2NO + O_2 = 2NO_2$$

obeys the rate equation

$$\frac{-dc_{NO}}{dt} = kc_{NO}^2 c_{O_2}$$

The overall rate is third order. It is said to be second order in nitric oxide and first order in oxygen. We might also say that it is zero order in nitrogen dioxide.

During the early stages of reaction between ethylene and iodine,

$$C_2H_4 + I_2 = C_2H_4I_2$$

when the reverse reaction may be ignored, the rate of formation of ethylene diiodide is given by

$$\frac{-dc_{I_2}}{dt} = kc_{C_2H_4} c_{I_2}^{3/2}$$

and the reaction is of the $\frac{5}{2}$ order.

It will be found that the coefficients of the chemical equation and the exponents of the rate equation often correspond to one another. That they do not necessarily correspond is illustrated by the formation of ethylene diiodide, as indicated above. In the case of the inversion of sucrose

$$C_{12}H_{22}O_{11} + H_2O = C_6H_{12}O_6 \text{ (glucose)} + C_6H_{12}O_6 \text{ (fructose)}$$

the rate of reaction is described by

$$\frac{-dc_{\text{sucrose}}}{dt} = kc_{H^+} c_{\text{sucrose}} c_{H_2O}$$

The rate is proportional to the concentration of acid, but since the acid is not consumed it does not appear in the stoichiometric equation. Water is consumed in the chemical reaction, but in dilute aqueous solution the fractional change in its concentration during the reaction is very small. For purposes of rate measurements the concentration of water is constant, and the factor c_{H_2O} may be replaced by the number it represents; more frequently it is combined with the specific velocity constant, thus: $kc_{H_2O} = k'$. The factor c_{H^+} is also constant within any single experiment, and we may write

$$k_{\text{observed}} = kc_{H_2O} c_{H^+} = k' c_{H^+}$$

$$\frac{-dc_{\text{sucrose}}}{dt} = k_{\text{obs.}} c_{\text{sucrose}}$$

Then $k_{\text{obs.}}$ will change from one experiment to another as c_{H^+} is varied while k' will remain constant.

EXERCISE 11.2

From the following data for the inversion of sucrose, show that the rate is first-order in c_{H^+}.

Inversion velocity (min.$^{-1} \times 10^4$)	18.3	13.0	9.2	3.8
Hydrogen ion concentration (moles l.$^{-1} \times 10^3$)	9.84	6.99	4.98	2.06

11.3 First-Order Reaction Rates

A first-order rate law is

$$\frac{-dc}{dt} = kc \tag{11.3}$$

where c is the concentration of reacting substance. That is, a first-order reaction rate is proportional to the concentration of the substance reacting. When the reaction has proceeded halfway to completion the rate is only half the initial rate, and so on. Dividing both sides of equation (11.3) by c gives

$$-\frac{1}{c} \cdot \frac{dc}{dt} = k \tag{11.4}$$

It follows that the fractional rate of change in concentration does not vary with time or concentration. The concentration can be replaced by the amount, as moles or molecules, irrespective of the volume. The specific velocity constant has the meaning of fractional change per unit time, and its dimension is reciprocal time, e.g., sec.$^{-1}$.

EXERCISE 11.3

For N_2O_5 at $35°$, $k = 1.4 \times 10^{-4}$ sec.$^{-1}$. At any moment, what is the rate of reaction expressed as per cent per minute?

Ans. 0.84% min.$^{-1}$.

Simple radioactive decay follows the first-order rate law. A milligram of radium disintegrates at a rate of 3.7×10^7 atoms sec.$^{-1}$. Since there are 2.65×10^{18} atoms, the fractional rate of change is $3.7 \times 10^7 / 2.65 \times 10^{18} = 1.40 \times 10^{-11}$ sec.$^{-1}$. The same sample after an interval of 1622 years will disintegrate at the rate of 1.85×10^7 atoms of radium per second but there will be only 1.325×10^{18} atoms remaining in the sample, and, therefore, the fractional rate of change per second is still $1.85 \times 10^7 / 1.325 \times 10^{18} = 1.40 \times 10^{-11}$.

Integrating equation (11.4) gives

$$-\int \frac{dc}{c} = k \int dt \tag{11.5}$$

$$-\ln c = kt + I \tag{11.6}$$

where I is the constant of integration. Equation (11.6) shows that a graph of $\ln c$ is linear in t with a slope equal to $-k$. If $\log c$ is employed, the slope is $-k/2.303$. Figure 11.3 demonstrates this relationship for the decomposition of nitrogen pentoxide.

EXERCISE 11.4

From the slope of the line in Fig. 11.3 obtain a value of the first-order rate constant for the reaction and compare with the values given in Table 11.1.

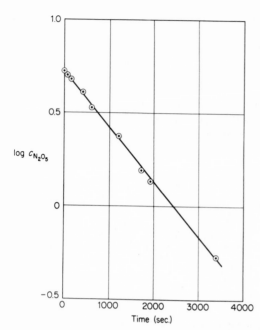

FIG. 11.3. Test of the first-order rate law. Decomposition of N_2O_5 in CCl_4 at 45°.

Letting $c_0 = c$ at $t = 0$, equation (11.6) may be written

$$\ln c_0 - \ln c = \ln \frac{c_0}{c} = kt \qquad (11.7)$$

This equation has been used to obtain the values of the rate constant given in Table 11.1. For example, from the data at 0 and 162 sec.,

$$2.303 \log \frac{5.33}{4.78} = 162k$$

$$k = 6.72 \times 10^{-4} \text{ sec.}^{-1}$$

EXERCISE 11.5

Calculate the time required for the concentration of nitrogen pentoxide to decrease by a factor of $\frac{1}{4}$ in carbon tetrachloride solution at 45°. Use the value of k obtained in Exercise 11.4. *Ans.* 35 min.

The time required for one-half the reactant to decompose is the *half life* $t_{1/2}$. Substituting $c = c_0/2$ in equation (11.7) gives

$$t_{1/2} = k^{-1} \ln 2 \qquad (11.8)$$

which shows that the half life is independent of initial concentration or amount. For radioactive decay it is customary to characterize the decay rate by giving the half life rather than the rate constant.

EXERCISE 11.6

Show that for radioactive decay $n = n_0 e^{-kt}$ where n is the number of atoms.

From an inspection of the first-order rate equation, (11.7), it is seen that the ratio of concentrations may be replaced by the ratio of the values of any property which is proportional to the concentration. Thus, if $c = a\pi$, where π is the value of an appropriate physical property and a is a constant of proportion, then

$$\frac{c_0}{c} = \frac{a\pi_0}{a\pi} = \frac{\pi_0}{\pi}$$

For gaseous substances $c = P/RT$ and $c_0/c = P_0/P$, where P is the pressure of reactant, but not necessarily the total pressure. For example, in the first-order gas phase reaction

$$SO_2Cl_2 = SO_2 + Cl_2$$

the total pressure (at constant V and T) approaches twice the initial pressure of SO_2Cl_2 as the pressure of SO_2Cl_2 approaches zero. Since two moles of products are produced for each mole of reactant consumed, the total pressure at any instant is given by

$$P_{total} = P + 2(P_0 - P)$$

where P is the instantaneous pressure of SO_2Cl_2. Rearranging to obtain P, we find

$$\frac{P_0}{P} = \frac{P_0}{2P_0 - P_{total}}$$

As a final example of first-order kinetics, consider the decomposition of di-t-butyl peroxide in the vapor phase at 140–160°. [J.H. Raley, F.F. Rust and W.E. Vaughan, *J. Am. Chem. Soc.*, **70,** 88 (1948)]. By analysis the reaction was found to yield acetone and ethane,

$$(CH_3)_3COOC(CH_3)_3 = 2(CH_3)_2CO + C_2H_6$$

TABLE 11.2

DECOMPOSITION OF DI-t-BUTYL PEROXIDE AT 147.2°

t (min.)	0	6	14	20
P_t (mm.)	179.5	198.6	221.2	237.3
t	26	34	40	46
P_t	252.5	271.3	284.9	297.1

The rate of reaction was measured by following with a manometer the increase in pressure of the gaseous reaction system maintained at constant temperature and constant volume. If we let P_0 be the pressure of peroxide at $t = 0$, the final pressure of products will be $3P_0$ at $t = \infty$. At an intermediate time the combined pressure of reactant and products is P_t and $\frac{1}{2}(P_t - P_0)$ is the decrease in pressure of peroxide. The partial pressure of peroxide remaining is $P_0 - \frac{1}{2}(P_t - P_0)$. Typical results in Table 11.2 have been graphed in Fig. 11.4, and the data are seen to conform to the first-order rate law.

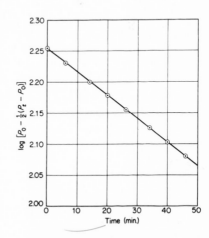

FIG. 11.4. Decomposition of di-t-butyl peroxide.

EXERCISE 11.7

From the values of P_t at $t = 0$ and $t = 20$ in Table 11.2, evaluate the first-order specific velocity constant.

Ans. $k = 1.46 \times 10^{-4}$ sec.$^{-1}$

11.4 Second-Order Reaction Rates

The general form of the second-order rate law is

$$\frac{-dc_A}{dt} = k c_A c_B \tag{11.9}$$

That is, the rate of the reaction is proportional to the second power of concentration and the dimension of the rate constant is $(\text{concentration})^{-1} (\text{time})^{-1}$. The special case, in which $c_A = c_B$ at all times, or in which A and B are identical, will be treated later.

When the stoichiometric equation is of the form

$$A + B = \text{products}$$

and $c_A \neq c_B$, let a and b represent c_A and c_B at $t = 0$, and let $a - x$ and $b - x$ represent c_A and c_B at any time t. With the new variable x, which represents the amount of reactants consumed at time t, equation (11.9) becomes

$$\frac{dx}{dt} = k(a - x)(b - x) \tag{11.10}$$

This equation integrates, by the method of partial fractions, to

$$\frac{1}{a - b} \ln \frac{b(a - x)}{a(b - x)} = kt \tag{11.11}$$

The reaction of n-propyl bromide with thiosulfate ion,

$$C_3H_7Br + S_2O_3^= = C_3H_7SSO_3^- + Br^-$$

has been studied by T.I. Crowell and L.P. Hammett [*J. Am. Chem. Soc.*, **70**, 3444 (1948)]. Samples of volume 10.02 cc. were withdrawn from a reaction mixture at various times after mixing and titrated with 0.02572 N iodine solution, yielding the results indicated in Table 11.3. In each instance the concentra-

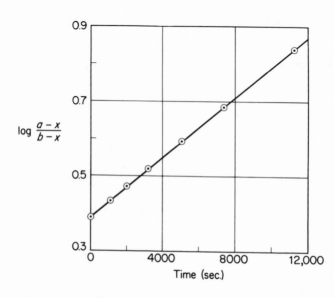

FIG. 11.5. Reaction of n-propyl bromide with thiosulfate.

TABLE 11.3

REACTION OF n-PROPYL BROMIDE WITH THIOSULFATE

Time (sec.)	I_2 titer (cc.)	$k \times 10^6$ (moles/l.)$^{-1}$(sec.)$^{-1}$
0	37.63	—
1110	35.20	1658
2010	33.63	1644
3192	31.90	1649
5052	29.86	1636
7380	28.04	1618
11232	26.01	1618
		Average 1637
∞	22.24	

tion of thiosulfate ion is given by the iodine titer multiplied by the volumetric factor N_{I_2}, $V_{\text{soln.}} = 0.00257$. The various factors appearing in equation (11.11) are obtained from the experimental data as follows:

$$a - x = 0.00257 \, V_t = 33.63 \times 0.00257 = 86.5 \times 10^{-3} \text{ at 2010 sec.}$$
$$a = 0.00257 \, V_0 = 37.63 \times 0.00257 = 96.8 \times 10^{-3}$$
$$b = (V_0 - V_\infty) \, 0.00257 = 15.39 \times 0.00257 = 39.5 \times 10^{-3}$$
$$a - b = V_\infty 0.00257 = 22.24 \times 0.00257 = 57.2 \times 10^{-3}$$
$$b - x = (a - x) - (a - b) = (V_t - V_\infty) \, 0.00257$$
$$= 11.39 \times 0.00257 = 29.2 \times 10^{-3} \text{ at 2010 sec.}$$

The values of the rate constant so obtained appear in the third column of Table 11.3.

Such data can also be represented graphically, as shown in Fig. 11.5. Inspection of equation (11.11) shows that a plot of the left-hand side of the equation versus time should be a straight line with zero intercept. For simplicity, the ordinate can be $\ln (a - x)/(b - x)$, for which an intercept of $\ln (a/b)$ is obtained as shown in Fig. 11.5. The slope of the line is $k(a - b)$ or, if logarithms to the base 10 are used, $k(a - b)/2.303$.

EXERCISE 11.8

Measure the slope of the line in Fig. 11.5; compute the value of k and compare with the average value given in Table 11.3.

When $c_A = c_B$ the left-hand side of equation (11.11) becomes indeterminate, and Fig. 11.5 becomes useless. In fact, the errors situation becomes rapidly worse as c_A approaches c_B and the experimenter should choose appreciably different initial concentrations of A and B if possible or, alternatively, should use identical concentrations and equation (11.13).

EXERCISE 11.9

Substitute $b = a + \delta$ in equation (11.11) and evaluate the indeterminate form obtained as $\delta \to 0$. Show that an equation identical with 11.13 is obtained where $c_0 = a$ and $c = a - x$.

When the second-order rate law applies to the decomposition of a single substance, equation (11.9) becomes

$$\frac{-dc}{dt} = kc^2 \tag{11.12}$$

and the integral is

$$\frac{1}{c} - \frac{1}{c_0} = kt \tag{11.13}$$

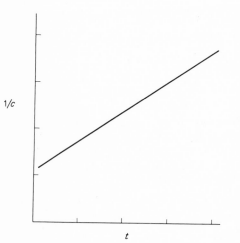

1/c

t

These equations also apply to the general second-order rate equation (11.10), when $c_A = c_B$. Equation (11.13) shows that a graph of $1/c$ versus will be linear with slope k and intercept $1/c_0$, as indicated in Fig. 11.6.

A very well-known example of a second-order reaction is the decomposition of hydrogen iodide. For a complete description of the rate process over a wide range of experimental conditions, it is necessary to consider both forward and reverse reactions. At early stages of the decomposition, however, the reverse reaction may be ignored

FIG. 11.6. Second-order reaction $c_A = c_B$.

without serious error. The rate of this reaction was measured [G.B. Kistia-kowsky, *J. Am. Chem. Soc.*, **50**, 2315 (1928)] by heating silica bulbs containing hydrogen iodide for various times in a molten lead bath. The samples were rapidly cooled and analyzed for hydrogen iodide and for iodine. Some typical results appear in Table 11.4.

TABLE 11.4

DECOMPOSITION OF HYDROGEN IODIDE AT 321.4°

Initial HI (moles/l.)	Time (sec.)	Decomp. (%)	k (moles/l.)$^{-1}$ sec.$^{-1}$ $\times 10^6$
0.0234	82,800	0.826	3.96
0.3279	16,800	2.071	3.87
0.9381	5,400	1.903	3.76

EXERCISE 11.10

Substitute the appropriate data for one of the experiments described in Table 11.4 in equation (11.13) and confirm the value of k in the table.

The half life of a second-order reaction may be obtained by substituting $c = c_0/2$ at $t = t_{1/2}$ in equation (11.13) to give

$$t_{1/2} = \frac{1}{kc_0} \qquad (11.14)$$

In contrast to a first-order reaction, the half life depends on the initial concentration.

To illustrate the contrast between first-order and second-order kinetics, consider the following hypothetical example: A substance A, initially present at a concentration of 1 mole per l., decomposes at such a rate that after 1 hr. its concentration has fallen to $\frac{1}{2}$ mole per l. Evidently the half life of this reaction is 1 hr. under these conditions. If the reaction is first order, we can predict that, since the half life is independent of concentration, the concentration after 2 hr. will be $\frac{1}{4}$ mole per l., after 3 hr., $\frac{1}{8}$ mole per l. and so forth, as indicated in Table 11.5. However, if the reaction is second order, equation (11.14) indicates that the half life for an initial concentration of $\frac{1}{2}$ mole per l. will be twice as great as the original half life. Therefore, it will require 2 additional hours for the

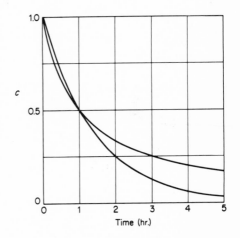

FIG. 11.7. Contrast of first- and second-order kinetics.

concentration to fall to $\frac{1}{4}$ mole per l., and so forth, as shown in Table 11.5. The two cases are illustrated graphically in Fig. 11.7, which also shows that interpretation would be unreliable for a limited period of observation.

TABLE 11.5

CONTRAST OF FIRST- AND SECOND-ORDER KINETICS

Time (hr.)	Concentration (moles/l.)		
	First order		Second order
0	1.000		1.000
1	0.500	(observed)	0.500
2	0.250	(predicted)	—
3	0.125		0.250

EXERCISE 11.11

For the system described in Table 11.5, calculate the concentration of reactant at 2 hrs. if the reaction is second order.   *Ans.* 0.333 moles/l.

11.5 Reversible Reactions

All reactions are reversible in principle, and in the equilibrium state the rate of the forward reaction is equal to the rate of the reverse reaction. (This fact is often used in the "kinetic derivation" of the equilibrium function, with the implicit assumption that the reaction rate law can be deduced from the stoichiometric equation.) If in a given system the equilibrium state is one in which both reactants and products are present in appreciable amounts, it follows that, except for the earliest stages of the reaction, reactants are being regenerated as well as consumed. This process must also be included in the rate law describing the change in concentration of the reactants with time.

In a simple type of reversible reaction both the forward and reverse reactions are first order. The reaction may be represented by

$$A \underset{k_{-1}}{\overset{k_1}{\rightleftharpoons}} B$$

and the corresponding rate equation is

$$\frac{-dc_A}{dt} = k_1 c_A - k_{-1} c_B \tag{11.15}$$

If we represent the concentrations of A and B at zero time by a and b, and those at time t by $a - x$ and $b + x$, equation (11.15) becomes

$$\frac{dx}{dt} = k_1(a - x) - k_{-1}(b + x) \tag{11.16}$$

At equilibrium the net rate is zero and

$$k_1(a - x_e) = k_{-1}(b + x_e)$$

The value of x in the equilibrium state is x_e, a constant independent of time in a given experiment. Solving for b, we obtain

$$b = \frac{k_1}{k_{-1}}(a - x_e) - x_e$$

Substituting this expression in equation (11.16) yields

$$\frac{dx}{dt} = (k_1 + k_{-1})(x_e - x) \tag{11.17}$$

Integrating from $x = x_0$ at $t = 0$ to x at t gives

$$(k_1 + k_{-1})t = \ln \frac{x_e - x_0}{x_e - x} \tag{11.18}$$

This rate equation is formally quite similar to the first-order rate equation (11.7), except that the measured rate constant is now the sum of the forward and reverse rate constants. If π is some property which is linear in x, then the change in x can be replaced by the change in this property.

$$(k_1 + k_{-1})t = \ln \frac{\pi_e - \pi_0}{\pi_e - \pi} \tag{11.19}$$

An example of the reversible first-order reaction is the mutarotation of

α-d-glucose to the stereoisomeric β-d-glucose which has been extensively studied. The process of interest may be represented formally by

$$\alpha G \underset{k_{-1}}{\overset{k_1}{\rightleftharpoons}} \beta G$$

The two substances may be distinguished by the difference in the degree to which they rotate plane-polarized light. The optical rotation due to each substance is proportional to its concentration, and the optical rotations caused by two such substances in the same solution are additive. It is convenient to follow the course of the reaction by periodic polarimetric measurements of a solution of glucose. In this case the physical property π in equation (11.19) becomes the observed optical rotation α. Typical observations are shown in Fig. 11.8, where log $(\alpha - \alpha_e)$ is plotted versus time. In this form, the term log $(\alpha_0 - \alpha_e)$, which is constant, becomes the intercept.

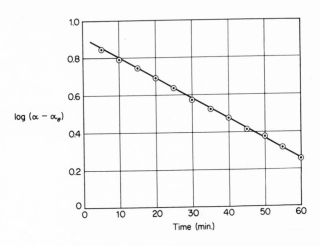

FIG. 11.8. Mutarotation of glucose. (From a student experiment.)

EXERCISE 11.12

From Fig. 11.8 estimate $k_{obs.}$ for the mutarotation of α-d-glucose.

Ans. $k_{obs.} = 2.4 \times 10^{-2}$ min.$^{-1}$.

If the value of the equilibrium constant for the reaction is known, the observed rate constant, $k_1 + k_{-1}$, can be separated to yield the values of the individual rate constants, since at equilibrium

$$\frac{k_1}{k_{-1}} = \frac{(b + x_e)}{(a - x_e)} = K_{eq.}$$

Therefore,

$$k_{obs.} = k_1 + \frac{k_1}{K_{eq.}} \quad \text{and} \quad k_1 = \frac{k_{obs.}K_{eq.}}{1 + K_{eq.}}$$

For the mutarotation of glucose, the equilibrium state corresponds to 63.6% β-d-glucose. Therefore, $K_{eq.} = c_\beta/c_\alpha = 1.75$. From the value of $k_{obs.}$ we find $k_1 = 1.5 \times 10^{-2}$ and $k_{-1} = 0.86 \times 10^{-2}$.

11.6 Complex Reactions

Chemical systems in which a single rate process occurs are uncommon. Many reactions exhibit complications such as side reactions and formation of unstable intermediates. Indeed, one of the chief aims of chemical kinetics is the discovery and elucidation of such complexities.

If a single set of reactants produces two or more sets of products at comparable rates, then the consumption of reactants by all such processes must be taken into account in formulating the rate law. The mathematical treatment is quite straightforward when the competing reactions are of the same order. Thus, if the substance A decomposes by two simultaneous first-order processes to yield M and N

$$A \xrightarrow{k_M} M$$
$$\xrightarrow{k_N} N$$

the differential rate law is

$$\frac{-dc_A}{dt} = k_M c_A + k_N c_A \tag{11.20}$$

Combining constants, we find that this integrates to the familiar form of the first-order rate law:

$$\ln \frac{c_{0,A}}{c_A} = k_{obs.} t \tag{11.21}$$

where

$$k_{obs.} = k_M + k_N$$

In order to find the individual values of k_M and k_N, it is necessary only to measure the ratio c_M/c_N at any time during the course of the reaction.

EXERCISE 11.13

Derive the integrated rate law for production of M in the case described above.

$$Ans. (M) = \frac{k_M c_{0,A}}{k_M + k_N} (1 - e^{-(k_M + k_N)t}).$$

Many chemical reactions take place in steps, each described by an appropriate rate equation. For example, consider the generalized reaction $A \longrightarrow Z$, which proceeds by two first-order steps $A \xrightarrow{k_1} M$ and $M \xrightarrow{k_2} Z$. Since the rate of decomposition of A is unaffected by the fate of M, the usual first-order rate law applies (equation 11.3). The integrated form, equation (11.7), may be written

$$c_A = c_{0,A} e^{-k_1 t} \tag{11.22}$$

The substance M is being formed from A and is decomposing to form Z. Therefore, the differential rate law has two terms.

$$\frac{dc_M}{dt} = k_1 c_A - k_2 c_M \tag{11.23}$$

Substituting c_A from equation (11.22) and integrating gives

$$c_M = \frac{k_1 c_{0,A}}{k_2 - k_1} (e^{-k_1 t} - e^{-k_2 t}) + c_{0,M} e^{-k_2 t} \tag{11.24}$$

Note that the second term in equation (11.24) describes the first-order decomposition of M for the special case that $c_{0,A} = 0$.

In many instances, the only substance initially present will be A, that is, $c_{0,M} = c_{0,Z} = 0$. In this event, the first term of equation (11.24) describes the time dependence of c_M. Since at any time $c_A + c_M + c_Z = c_{0,A}$, solving for c_Z by substitution with equations (11.22) and (11.24) yields

$$c_Z = c_{0,A} \left[1 - \frac{k_2}{k_2 - k_1} e^{-k_1 t} + \frac{k_1}{k_2 - k_1} e^{-k_2 t} \right] \tag{11.25}$$

An example of a rate process which would be expected to obey consecutive first-order kinetics is the acid catalyzed hydrolysis of the normal ester of a dibasic acid. If a comparatively weak acid is produced, so that in the presence of added strong acid c_{H^+} is constant, the rate of each step varies only with the concentration of ester R_2A.

$$R_2A + H_2O \xrightarrow[H^+]{k_1} ROH + HAR$$

$$HAR + H_2O \xrightarrow[H^+]{k_2} H_2A + ROH$$

It might also be expected that for a symmetric acid $k_1 = 2k_2$ since there are two hydrolyzable groups in the former case and one in the latter. To illustrate, consider such an ester present initially at 1 mole per l. That is, let $c_{0,A} = 1.00$ and $c_{0,M} = c_{0,Z} = 0$. The time dependence of c_A, c_M, and c_Z is shown in Fig. 11.9 for $k_1 = 2k_2 = 1.0$ min.$^{-1}$. Note that the concentration of the intermediate M goes through a maximum.

In one common type of complex reaction the reactant, in a rapidly established equilibrium, yields an intermediate which decomposes to the ultimate product. As a simple example, consider

$$A \underset{k_{-1}}{\overset{k_1}{\rightleftharpoons}} M, \qquad M \xrightarrow{k_2} Z$$

where $k_2 \ll k_1 \ll k_{-1}$. Since for the first step $K_{eq.} = k_1/k_{-1}$, the second inequality corresponds to $K_{eq.} \ll 1$. That is, very little of the reactant A is at any time present in the form M. Therefore, the loss of A is measured by the gain in Z,

$$\frac{-dc_A}{dt} = \frac{dc_Z}{dt} = k_2 c_M \tag{11.26}$$

and c_M is related to c_A by the equilibrium function

$$K_{eq.} = \frac{c_M}{c_A}$$

Therefore,

$$\frac{-dc_A}{dt} = \frac{dc_Z}{dt} = k_2 K_{eq.} c_A \tag{11.27}$$

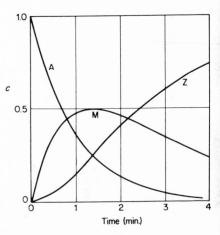

FIG. 11.9. Time dependence of concentrations in a complex reaction.

and the reaction follows a first-order rate law in spite of the complexity. The observed rate constant $k_{obs.} = k_2 K_{eq.}$

An example of this type of complexity is the reaction between nitric oxide and oxygen

$$2NO + O_2 = 2NO_2$$

which follows a third-order law [M. Bodenstein, *Z. physik. Chem.*, **100**, 68 (1922)], i.e.,

$$\frac{-dc_{NO}}{dt} = kc_{NO}^2 c_{O_2}$$

The reaction was interpreted as being termolecular, but the possibility exists that the reaction is complex, involving the equilibrium

$$2NO \rightleftharpoons N_2O_2 \quad K_{eq}$$

followed by the rate-determining step

$$N_2O_2 + O_2 \xrightarrow{k_2} 2NO_2$$

This mechanism yields

$$\frac{-dc_{NO}}{dt} = \frac{dc_{NO_2}}{dt} = k_2 c_{N_2O_2} c_{O_2}$$

Since

$$K_{eq.} = \frac{c_{N_2O_2}}{c_{NO}^2}$$

the observed rate law would be

$$\frac{-dc_{NO}}{dt} = \frac{dc_{NO_2}}{dt} = k_{obs.} c_{NO}^2 c_{O_2}$$

where

$$k_{obs.} = k_2 K_{eq.}.$$

A further remark on the relationship between the equilibrium function and the rate equations for forward and reverse reactions is appropriate. Consider any reaction for which the stoichiometric equation is

$$aA + bB = mM + nN$$

The rate equations may be represented in the form

$$\text{forward rate} = k' c_A^\alpha c_B^\beta$$

$$\text{reverse rate} = k'' c_M^\mu c_N^\nu$$

Although α, β, μ, ν are sometimes the same as a, b, m, n, there is not necessarily such a correspondence. In fact, the concentration of a reagent may not even appear in the rate equation, or, on the other hand, a factor may be required for a substance which does not appear in the stoichiometric equation. Stoichiometry establishes only the ratios $a : b, a : m, a : n$, etc. There is no simple principle which predicts α, β, μ, ν or even the form of the rate equation. It can only be said of the forward and reverse rate equations that they may be equated at equilibrium and that the resulting function of the concentrations, e.g.,

$$\frac{c_M^\mu c_N^\nu}{c_A^\alpha c_B^\beta} = \frac{k'}{k''}$$

must resolve to the appropriate equilibrium function

$$\frac{c_M^m c_N^n}{c_A^a c_B^b} = K_{eq.}$$

This is illustrated by the kinetics for the iodination of ethylene, mentioned previously, for which

$$\text{forward rate} = k' c_{C_2H_4} \, c_{I_2}^{3/2}$$

$$\text{reverse rate} = k'' c_{C_2H_4I_2} \, c_{I_2}^{1/2}$$

These rate equations evidently combine to give the correct equilibrium expression, but they are not predictable from the stoichiometric equation

$$C_2H_4 + I_2 = C_2H_4I_2$$

11.7 Temperature Dependence—Activation Energy

A quantitative expression of the temperature dependence of reaction rate constants, proposed in 1889 by Svante Arrhenius, is

$$\frac{d \ln k}{dT} = \frac{E_a}{RT^2} \tag{11.28}$$

or

$$k = Ae^{-E_a/RT} \tag{11.29}$$

where A and E_a are constants for a given reaction.

Following the general form of Arrhenius's argument for a first-order reaction, let us postulate that only "active" molecules can react and that they are in equilibrium with "passive" molecules of the same chemical species. Thus,

$$M_{passive} \rightleftharpoons M_{active}$$

$$K_a = \frac{c_{M_a}}{c_{M_p}}$$

and

$$\text{rate} = kc_{M_a} = kK_a c_{M_p}$$

If $c_{M_a} \ll c_{M_p}$, then the concentration of passive molecules may be replaced by the concentration of all M molecules c_M and the rate is directly proportional to the total concentration,

$$\text{rate} = k_{obs.} c_M$$

The observed rate constant includes the equilibrium constant for activation,

K_a, as a factor. It is postulated that the rate constant for decomposition of the activated complex, k, has a negligible temperature dependence. Since

$$k_{obs.} = kK_a$$

and

$$\ln k_{obs.} = \ln K_a + \ln k$$

it follows, after applying van't Hoff's equation, that

$$\frac{d \ln k_{obs.}}{dT} = \frac{d \ln K_a}{dT} = \frac{E_a}{RT^2} \tag{11.30}$$

where E_a is the *energy of activation* per mole for converting passive molecules to active molecules. If both rate and equilibrium are measured at constant pressure, it would be correct to employ H_a, the heat or enthalpy of activation.

Arrhenius considered that the active and passive forms were related somewhat as isomeric species. It is now thought that activation of a molecule consists in raising it to a high energy level whether by thermal collision, absorption of light, or otherwise.

The Arrhenius equation, (11.28), integrates to

$$\ln k = \frac{-E_a}{R} \frac{1}{T} + \ln A \tag{11.31}$$

or

$$\log \frac{k_2}{k_1} = \frac{E_a}{2.303\,R} \frac{T_2 - T_1}{T_2 T_1} \tag{11.32}$$

and a plot of $\log k$ versus $1/T$ should be a straight line with slope $-E_a/2.303\,R$.

EXERCISE 11.14

If the rate constant for a reaction is twice as great at 35° as at 25°, estimate the energy of activation by equation (11.32).   *Ans.* 12.6 kcal. mole^{-1}.

The first stage of a kinetic study is commonly to find a suitable rate equation to describe the time dependence of the course of reaction. The measurement of the rate is only the tool to be used. It is seldom the primary objective. The next step is to determine the temperature dependence of the rate constant and to measure the energy of activation. (The final and most important step, to explain the results, will concern us for the rest of this chapter.) To illustrate, consider again the decomposition of di-t-butyl peroxide for which measurements

TABLE 11.6

THE DECOMPOSITION OF DI-t-BUTYL PEROXIDE AT VARIOUS TEMPERATURES

Solvent	Temp. 125°	$k \times 10^5\ sec.^{-1}$ 135°	145°	E_a kcal. mole^{-1}	A $\times 10^6\ sec.^{-1}$
Cumene	1.6	5.2	15.6	37.5	0.63
t-Butyl benzene	1.5	5.0	15.1	38.0	1.1
tri-n-Butyl amine	1.7	4.2	16.0	37.0	0.35
Vapor	1.1	3.6	11.5	39.1	3.2

at different temperatures in several solvents are given in Table 11.6 and in Fig. 11.10 [J.H. Raley, F.F. Rust, and W.E. Vaughan, *J. Am. Chem. Soc.*, **70**, 1336 (1948)]. In each solvent the rate constants conform to the linear dependence of log k versus $1/T$ as required by the Arrhenius equation (11.28). It is worth noting that the rate constant and the activation energy are scarcely affected by the solvent.

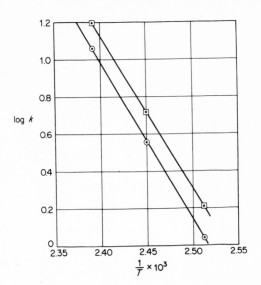

FIG. 11.10. Temperature dependence of the rate of decomposition of di-*t*-butyl peroxide.
⊙ vapor   ▢ cumene solution

EXERCISE 11.15

From the rate constants given in Table 11.6 for the decomposition of di-*t*-butyl peroxide in *t*-butyl benzene find the value of E_a by plotting log k versus $1/T$. Also find the value of A. Compare with the values given in the table.

There are no known instances of unimolecular or bimolecular rate constants which fail to conform to the Arrhenius temperature dependence. Results which are inconsistent with the equation are usually to be regarded as resulting from faulty experimental techniques or an improper choice of rate equation.

11.8 The Activated Complex

All chemical rate processes are now described as proceeding through the formation of intermediate *activated complexes*. If all activated complexes were to decompose or rearrange to produce reaction product, then the observed rate of reaction would be equal to the rate of formation of the complex. Each component rate process in a chemical reaction is considered to involve a single species of activated complex in effective equilibrium with reactants, thus:

$$aA + bB \rightleftharpoons \text{complex} \longrightarrow \text{products}$$

Reactions are said to be *unimolecular, bimolecular,* or *termolecular* when one, two, or three molecules are required to produce the activated complex. The internal energy of the complex is greater than that of either reactants or products and the energy of formation of the activated complex from the reactants is identified with the energy of activation for the reaction. The structure of the complex is postulated to be intermediate between that of the reactants and that of the products. This is certainly a very reasonable postulate. Thus, in a bimolecular reaction between two diatomic molecules the valence bonds between A—B and C—D have stretched and weakened in the complex, while those between A—C and B—D have begun to form.

$$
AB + CD \overset{E'_a}{\rightleftharpoons}
\begin{array}{c}
A - - B \\
| \qquad | \\
| \qquad | \\
C - - D
\end{array}
\underset{E''_a}{\rightleftharpoons} AC + BD
$$

$$\Delta E$$

The reverse reaction proceeds through the same activated complex as that for the forward reaction.

It is postulated that the activated complex, once formed from reactants or products, has approximately equal probabilities of decomposing into reactants or products. That is, the rate-determining step for the reaction is the formation of the activated complex, a bimolecular process in this instance. The decomposition of the activated complex however, is necessarily a unimolecular process, regardless of the mechanism of formation. It was shown previously that this type of complexity will lead to a second-order rate law.

At equilibrium the rates of the forward and reverse reaction are equal.

$$k'c_{AB}c_{CD} = k''c_{AC}c_{BD}$$

$$\frac{k'}{k''} = \frac{c_{AC}c_{BD}}{c_{AB}c_{CD}} = K_{eq.} \tag{11.33}$$

The temperature dependence of the equilibrium constant in a constant-volume process is given by an equation analogous to (6.60):

$$\frac{d \ln K_{eq.}}{dT} = \frac{d \ln k'/k''}{dT} = \frac{\Delta E}{RT^2}$$

According to the Arrhenius equation,

$$\frac{d \ln k'}{dT} - \frac{d \ln k''}{dT} = \frac{E'_a}{RT^2} - \frac{E''_a}{RT^2}$$

and we infer, by comparison, that the energy change for the forward reaction is equal to the difference between the activation energies of the forward and reverse reactions.

$$\Delta E = E'_a - E''_a \tag{11.34}$$

This relationship is further illustrated in Fig. 11.11.

The utility of equation (11.34) may be demonstrated by applying it to a decomposition of the type

$$A : B = A \cdot + B \cdot$$

where A· and B· are atoms or free radicals. It is generally assumed that atoms and free radicals combine without activation energy. It follows from equation (11.34) that the activation energy for the forward reaction

$$E'_a = \Delta E - 0$$

is equal to the thermodynamic ΔE for the reaction.

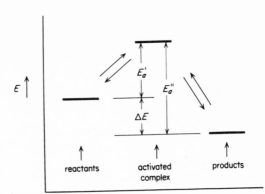

FIG. 11.11. Relation between the activation
energies and the internal energy change
for a reversible reaction.

The energy of activation for the unimolecular decomposition of di-t-butyl peroxide, which can be represented RO-OR, has been previously given as 39.1 kcal. mole^{-1}. If the rate-determining process is dissociation into two butoxy free radicals, then the activation energy is to be identified with the thermodynamic ΔE for breaking the RO-OR, bond, viz., the bond dissociation energy D(RO-OR).

To be consistent with the view adopted, it appears that a unimolecular rate process is to be described in terms of the unimolecular decomposition of an isolated, activated molecule M*.

$$M^* \xrightarrow{k_1} \text{products}$$

and

$$\text{rate} = k_1 c_{M^*} \tag{11.35}$$

A difficulty arises when we try to account for the manner of forming activated molecules. If the process

$$M + X \underset{k_{-2}}{\overset{k_2}{\rightleftharpoons}} M^* + X$$

where X is any molecule in the system, including M, is proposed by analogy with the bimolecular case, then it would appear that

$$\text{rate of reaction} = \text{rate of activation} = k_2 c_M c_X$$

or if the system consists of pure M

$$\text{rate of reaction} = k_2 c_M^2$$

That is, the rate of activation would be proportional to the collision frequency which varies as the square of the concentration.

It was at one time seriously proposed that the activation process was absorption of radiation from the surroundings, but all attempts to detect this radiation were unsuccessful. The difficulty was resolved in 1922 by F.A. Lindemann as follows: Since the activated species M* is a transient intermediate which never accounts for a significant fraction of the reacting system, it may be expected that at any instant the rate of formation and the rate of disappearance of M* are equal. That is,

$$k_2 c_M c_X = k_{-2} c_{M*} c_X + k_1 c_{M*}$$ (11.36)

Suppose that the rate of unimolecular decomposition of M* is small compared to the rate of collisional deactivation. That is, if $k_{-2} c_{M*} c_X \gg k_1 c_{M*}$, then to a very good approximation

$$k_2 c_M c_X = k_{-2} c_{M*} c_X$$

and

$$c_{M*} = K^*_{eq.} c_M$$ (11.37)

The observed rate law, obtained by substitution in equation (11.35), becomes first order.

$$\text{rate} = k_1 K^*_{eq.} c_M$$ (11.38)

It is a consequence of this proposal that at sufficiently low total gas pressure (c_X) the rate of deactivating collisions can be made arbitrarily small so that when the rate of deactivation becomes much smaller than the rate of decomposition, practically all M* will form products. That is, when $k_{-2} c_{M*} c_X \ll k_1 c_{M*}$,

$$k_2 c_M c_X = k_1 c_{M*}$$

and

$$c_{M*} = \frac{k_2 c_M c_X}{k_1}$$

If the system consists of pure M,

$$c_{M*} = \frac{k_2 c_M^2}{k_1}$$

Therefore, at sufficiently low pressure the measured rate is that of the bimolecular activation process which varies as the square of the pressure.

$$\text{rate} = k_2 c_M^2$$ (11.39)

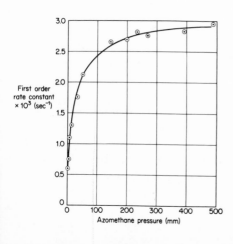

FIG. 11.12. Test of the Lindemann hypothesis in first order decomposition of azomethane.

First order rate constant × 10³ (sec⁻¹)

Azomethane pressure (mm)

At intermediate pressures a complex rate law is to be expected. If the rate constant for a first-order reaction is measured at a series of decreasing pressures, it is to be expected that the first-order rate constant will exhibit a "falling off" at lower pressures, that is, a lack of constancy with pressure, indicating the increasing inadequacy of the simple first-order rate law.

Several attempts have been made to test this aspect of the Lindemann hypothesis, but it is difficult to find cases in which it is certain that no complexities other than that indicated above are involved. A reaction which appears to meet this test is the decomposition of azomethane.

$$CH_3NNCH_3 = N_2 + C_2H_6$$

The first-order rate constant was measured by H.C. Ramsperger [*J. Am. Chem. Soc.*, **49,** 1495 (1927)] over a range of pressures with the results indicated in Fig. 11.12. It is seen that the rate constant does indeed fall off with decreasing pressure. It has also been shown that addition of an inert gas to the system increases the rate constant toward the high pressure value.

11.9 Kinetic Theory of Gases

The next stage in our development of chemical kinetics will be a consideration of the detailed nature of the atomic and molecular encounters which govern the rates of chemical reactions. These processes are best understood for those reactions which occur between simple molecules in the gas phase, and, therefore, we must first briefly describe some of the molecular properties of gases.

There is a relatively simple molecular model which successfully describes the principal features of the macroscopic behavior of gases. We present here a simplified treatment of this theory. The nature of the modifications required to adapt the theory to the description of real gases also reveals important facts about the nature of this state of matter.

The basic postulates of the simplified kinetic theory of gases are as follows:

1. A gas consists of uniform particles which are in constant motion. The absolute temperature of the system is taken to be proportional to the average kinetic energy of the molecules.

2. The diameter of the molecules is very small compared to the average distance between them.

3. Collisions of molecules with each other and with the walls of the vessel are strictly elastic. That is, translational energy is conserved, and no changes in the internal energy of the molecules occur as a result of collisions. (For polyatomic molecules this is true on the average, but not for individual collisions.)

Consider a sample of gas confined in a cubical container with an edge of length *l*. The molecules are in chaotic motion, colliding with each other and with the walls of the container. Let us adopt a set of rectangular coordinates perpendicular to the faces of the cube, as in Fig. 11.13. The velocity *c* of any molecule is a vector and may be resolved into components c_x, c_y, c_z, parallel to the axes. It is easily

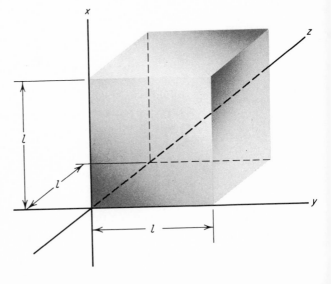

FIG. 11.13. Kinetic theory model.

shown that

$$c^2 = c_x^2 + c_y^2 + c_z^2 \tag{11.40}$$

In fact, we are only concerned here with the magnitude of the velocity and, therefore, also use c to represent molecular speed.

The pressure which the gas exerts on the walls of the container is due to molecular impacts. In a perfectly elastic collision of a molecule with a wall, the component of velocity perpendicular to that wall simply reverses its sign. That is, a molecule having a positive component of velocity c_x which collides with the wall parallel to the yz plane will, after collision, have an equal but negative component of velocity $-c_x$. Its components of velocity c_y and c_z will be unchanged in the collision.

The collision described produces a change in momentum of $2mc_x$, where m is the mass of the molecule. The rate of collision of a molecule with both walls parallel to the yz plane is c_x/l, since the distance l must be traversed between collisions. The rate of collisions at one wall is $c_x/2l$ and the rate of momentum change is

$$\frac{c_x}{2l} 2mc_x = \frac{mc_x^2}{l} \tag{11.41}$$

Individual molecular velocities will be shown to have a wide distribution. Therefore, in computing the total rate of momentum change at the wall for n molecules in the container we must use the average value of c_x^2 denoted by $\overline{c_x^2}$. (This is distinct from the square of the average velocity.) The average rate of momentum change at one wall is, therefore, $nm\overline{c_x^2}/l$, and this is the force exerted by the molecules on the wall. Since pressure is force per unit area

$$P = \frac{nm\overline{c_x^2}}{l^3} = \frac{nm\overline{c_x^2}}{V} \tag{11.42}$$

where V is the volume of the container.

There is no net transport of gas with respect to the coordinate system and the three axes are indistinguishable, so that

$$\overline{c_x^2} = \overline{c_y^2} = \overline{c_z^2}$$

and from equation (11.40) $3\overline{c_x^2} = \overline{c^2}$. Therefore, equation (11.42) may be written:

$$P = \frac{1}{3} \frac{nm\overline{c^2}}{V} \tag{11.43}$$

which is the basic equation of the kinetic theory of gases.

It can be shown that equation (11.43) conforms to the equation of state for an ideal gas. It was postulated that the absolute temperature of a gas is proportional to the average kinetic energy of the molecules. That is,

$$\tfrac{1}{2}nm\overline{c^2} = \text{const. } T \tag{11.44}$$

Substitution of this relation in equation (11.43) yields

$$\frac{PV}{T} = \frac{2 \text{ const.}}{3} = n'R \tag{11.45}$$

(Note the distinction between n, the number of molecules in the container, and n', the number of moles.) Since the right-hand side of equation (11.45) is a constant, this relationship between P, V, and T corresponds to the ideal gas law.

The value of the proportionality constant in equation (11.44) can be obtained from the gas constant R, as indicated in equation (11.45). Substituting, we find

$$\tfrac{1}{2}nm\overline{c^2} = \tfrac{3}{2}n'RT \tag{11.46}$$

If we consider a molar volume of gas, then $n' = 1$ and $n = 6.02(10)^{23}$, or N, Avogadro's number. Since $Nm = M$, the molecular weight,

$$\overline{c^2} = \frac{3RT}{M} \tag{11.47}$$

From equation (11.47) we obtain an expression for the root-mean-square molecular speed u, defined by $u = \sqrt{\overline{c^2}}$.

$$u = \sqrt{\frac{3RT}{M}} \tag{11.48}$$

This is not greatly different from the average molecular speed $\bar{c}$ given by

$$\bar{c} = \sqrt{\frac{8RT}{\pi M}} \tag{11.49}$$

which is obtained from the Maxwell-Boltzmann distribution law, equation 17.70.

EXERCISE 11.16

Use equations (11.48) and (11.49) to calculate the root-mean-square velocity and the average speed of nitrogen molecules at $0°$ in meters sec.$^{-1}$.

Ans. $u = 493$ meters sec.$^{-1}$; $\bar{c} = 454$ meters sec.$^{-1}$.

In equation (11.49) we see the basis for *Graham's law* of molecular effusion which states that *if two gases effuse through a small hole, it is found that their relative rates of effusion are inversely proportional to the square root of their molecular weights*. Evidently the rate of effusion is proportional to the average molecular speed, and, therefore,

$$\frac{\bar{c}_1}{\bar{c}_2} = \frac{\sqrt{8RT/\pi M_1}}{\sqrt{8RT/\pi M_2}} = \sqrt{\frac{M_2}{M_1}} \tag{11.50}$$

The use of an average value of the molecular speed in the preceding relations implies that this property of the system is independent of time as must be the case for a sample having a constant temperature. On the other hand, the velocities of the individual molecules are continually changing, both in magnitude and direction, as a result of molecular collisions. Although the total kinetic energy and momentum of the two particles involved in a collision does not change, in general energy will be transferred between them, because most collisions are not simple "head on" collisions, but glancing blows of molecules moving at odd angles. It is easy to imagine that a particular molecule in a succession of collisions may be reduced to a very small kinetic energy or, conversely, may acquire a very high kinetic energy. Thus, there must exist at any instant a distribution of molecular velocities and energies which can be described in a statistical manner. This distribution function D can be given in the form

$$\frac{dn}{n} = D\, dc$$

where dn/n is the fraction of molecules having speeds between the values c and $c + dc$.

J. C. Maxwell and L. Boltzmann treated this situation by considering the effect of random collisions upon the distribution of molecular velocities. They demonstrated that there is a unique distribution which does not change with time and which must therefore describe the system at thermal equilibrium. The distribution function of molecular speeds is derived in Chapter 17 and is found to be

$$\frac{dn}{n} = 4\pi \left(\frac{m}{2\pi kT}\right)^{3/2} e^{-mc^2/2kT}\, c^2\, dc \tag{11.51}$$

where m = molecular mass, k = gas constant per molecule, and T = Kelvin temperature. This is one form of the *Maxwell-Boltzmann distribution law* and is illustrated in Fig. 11.14, where the ordinate is the value of D. The speed cor-

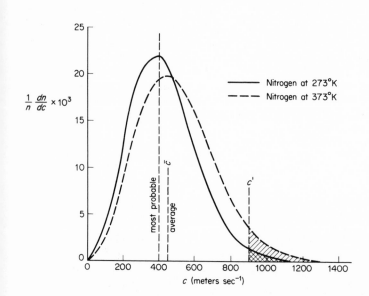

FIG. 11.14. Distribution of molecular speeds.

responding to the maximum of the curve is the most probable speed. Since the curve is not symmetrical, the average speed $\bar{c}$ is slightly greater than the most probable speed. The fraction of molecules having speeds greater than a particular value, such as c', is given by the ratio of the area under the curve from c' to infinity to the total area under the curve.

The temperature dependence of the distribution function is indicated by the dashed curve for a higher temperature in Fig. 11.14. It is evident that raising the temperature increases the fraction of molecules having energies above a given value. This is responsible for the increase of reaction rates with temperature, as will be shown in the next section.

11.10 Theory of Reaction Rates

It has been proposed that bimolecular reaction processes occur when two reacting molecules collide with relative energy $\geq E_a$. That is to say,

$$\text{rate} = Z \cdot P(E)$$

where Z is the collision rate and where $P(E)$ is the fraction of collisions in which the relative energy E_a is equalled or exceeded.

To evaluate Z, the number of collisions per cubic centimeter per second in a system of identical molecules, we consider that a collision occurs when the centers of two molecules approach within distance d, the molecular diameter (in centimeters). In one second a molecule sweeps out a volume $\pi d^2 \bar{c}$, where $\bar{c}$ is the average molecular speed (in cm. sec.$^{-1}$). That is, it will collide with any other molecules whose centers lie within this volume, as indicated in Fig. 11.15. The number of collisions per second made by the molecule of interest is $\pi d^2 \bar{c} n$ when there are n molecules per cc. Since this is the collision rate for 1 molecule, we multiply by n to obtain the number of collisions per cc. for all molecules and by $\frac{1}{2}$ to avoid counting each collision twice, obtaining

$$Z = \tfrac{1}{2}\pi d^2 \bar{c} n^2 \qquad (11.52)$$

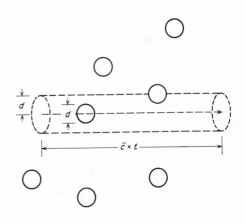

FIG. 11.15. Molecular collisions.

This equation is slightly inaccurate, due to some approximations used in the derivation, but it is quite adequate for our purpose.

Values of d, the collision diameter, may be obtained from measurements of gas viscosities and related properties using equations developed from the kinetic theory of gases (see E.H. Kennard, *Kinetic Theory of Gases*, Chapter 4, McGraw-Hill, New York, 1938). This aspect of the theory will not be treated here. Other sources of such information, such as crystal densities, van der Waals constants, b, etc., are also available.

EXERCISE 11.17

The collision diameter of the hydrogen iodide molecule is $3(10)^{-8}$ cm. Find the number of molecular collisions per cubic centimeter of gas at $0°$ and 1 atm. in 1 sec.   *Ans.* 2.17×10^{28} cc.$^{-1}$ sec.$^{-1}$

The average time between gas collisions for a single molecule is a usefu number. Dividing the answer to Exercise 11.16 by the number of molecules pe cubic centimeter, we obtain

$$\frac{2.17 \times 10^{28}}{6.02 \times 10^{23}/22,400} = 8.08 \times 10^8 \text{ collisions per second}$$

or approximately 10^{-9} second average time between collisions. This is a ver short time, but it is long compared to the rate of molecular vibrations, which occur on a time scale of 10^{-13} second. That is, approximately 10^4 internal mole cular vibrations occur for each collision in the gas phase. On the other hand an electronically excited molecule usually requires a time greater than 10^{-9} sec to emit light (see Problem 26) and can be completely "quenched" by collision at ordinary pressure.

It has been postulated that reaction occurs between two molecules when they collide with a *relative* translational energy equal to or greater than the Arrhenius activation energy E_a. For distribution of *relative* kinetic energy in such a collision, Maxwell's distribution law (see Chapter 17) takes the form

$$\frac{dn}{n} = \frac{1}{RT} e^{-E/RT} dE \tag{11.53}$$

Integrating from E_a to infinity gives

$$\frac{n_{E_a}}{n} = P(E_a) = e^{-E_a/RT} \tag{11.54}$$

which is the fraction of collisions in which $E \geq E_a$. Although $P(E)$ covers the range from E_a to infinity, the shape of the curves in Fig. 11.14 indicates that very few molecules have energies substantially greater than E_a when this is several times the average energy.

The basic equation of the *collision theory* of reaction rate becomes

$$\text{rate} = Ze^{-E_a/RT} = kn^2 \tag{11.55}$$

which is seen to have the exponential factor required by the Arrhenius equa- tion. Evidently the collision number Z is to be associated with the frequency factor A of the Arrhenius equation. However, the collision number, given by equation (11.52), is temperature dependent in that the molecular velocity is proportional to $T^{1/2}$. That is, the collision theory indicates that the tem- perature dependence of the rate constant should be

$$k = \text{const. } T^{1/2} e^{-E_a/RT}$$

or

$$\ln k = \ln \text{const.} + \frac{1}{2} \ln T - \frac{E_a}{RT} \tag{11.56}$$

and

$$\frac{d \ln k}{dT} = \frac{1}{2T} + \frac{E_a}{RT^2} \tag{11.57}$$

In the systems usually studied it is not possible to detect the influence of the first term in $1/T$, especially when E_a has a substantial value.

The collision theory does not permit the complete prediction of reaction rates from molecular properties, since the theory does not provide a method of predicting the activation energy. However, the collision number Z in equation (11.55) can be compared with the observed frequency factor A in equation (11.29). For example, the rate constant for decomposition of hydrogen iodide is observed to be $7.26 \times 10^{10} \, e^{-E_a/RT}$ at 700°K where the value of E_a is 43,700 cal. mole^{-1}. The units of this rate constant are mole^{-1} l. sec.$^{-1}$. That is, the rate is measured in moles reacting per liter per second. The collision number at 700°K when n corresponds to 1 mole l.$^{-1}$ is given by

$$Z = \frac{\pi}{2} (3 \times 10^{-8})^2 \sqrt{\frac{8 \times 8.3 \times 10^7 \times 700}{3.14 \times 128}} \left(\frac{6 \times 10^{23}}{10^3}\right)^2$$

$$= 1.75 \times 10^{31} \text{ collisions cc.}^{-1} \text{ sec.}^{-1}$$

Converting to moles l.$^{-1}$ sec.$^{-1}$ of HI consumed, we have

$$\text{rate} = 2 \times \frac{1.75 \times 10^{31} \times 10^3}{6 \times 10^{23}} = 5.8 \times 10^{10}$$

which is rather good agreement with the experimental value, in view of the approximations. Only a few simple second-order gas phase reactions are adequately described by this theory. In some cases the frequency factor is substantially less than the collision number, and it was formerly proposed that some geometrical requirement has to be fulfilled in the collision, in a kind of lock-and-key effect. This may be described by a *steric factor*, a number less than unity which gives the probability that a given collision will satisfy this requirement. This factor is taken to be independent of the energy requirement.

When the observed frequency factor is substantially greater than the predicted value, one suspects that the reaction is not a simple bimolecular process and that a chain mechanism such as that described in section 11.1 applies.

The next major development of the theory of reaction rates is found in the work of Eyring and others (see S. Glasstone, K.J. Laidler, and H. Eyring, *The Theory of Rate Processes*, McGraw-Hill, New York, 1941) who considered the activation process in detail. This theory of the transition state postulates that the products are formed by decomposition of an *activated complex* formed by the reacting species. If the activated complex is in equilibrium with the reactants, then for the bimolecular process

$$A + B \rightleftharpoons AB^* \longrightarrow \text{products}$$

$$c_{AB^*} = K_{eq}^* . \, c_A c_B$$

The rate constant for the unimolecular decomposition of the activated complex is defined by the equation

$$\text{rate of product formation} = k^* c_{AB^*}$$

If the activated molecule AB^* requires a mean time $t^* = 1/k^*$ to attain a critical configuration which always decomposes to product, the rate constant may be expressed roughly as $k^* = 1/t^* = \nu^*$. That is, ν^* is a fictitious vibration frequency of AB^* which always leads to rupture of the bond. The energy associated with motion of frequency $v^\pm$ along one coordinate is $hv^\pm$ where h is the Planck constant (see Chapter 17). The average energy associated with an nonquantized vibration along one coordinate also equals kT where k is th Boltzmann constant (gas constant per molecule). Equating these two quantitie

$$hv^\pm = kT$$

yields the rate constant

$$k^\pm = v^\pm = kT/h$$

The rate of reaction then becomes

$$\text{rate} = \frac{kT}{h} K^\pm_{eq.} c_A c_B \tag{11.58}$$

Therefore, the observed bimolecular rate constant is

$$\text{rate } k = \frac{kT}{h} K^\pm_{eq.} \tag{11.59}$$

The equilibrium constant $K^\pm_{eq.}$ is expressible in terms of the standard change in free energy, heat content, and entropy of the system in the activation process

$$\Delta F^{0\pm} = \Delta H^{0\pm} - T \Delta S^{0\pm}$$

$$= -RT \ln K^\pm_{eq.} \tag{11.60}$$

$$K^\pm_{eq.} = e^{\Delta S^{0\pm}/R} e^{-\Delta H^{0\pm}/RT} \tag{11.61}$$

Comparison of equation (11.59) with the Arrhenius equation, (11.29), show that the frequency factor is now regarded as composed of a constant kT/h, and a factor depending on the entropy change in the activation process. It wil be shown in Chapter 17 that for the case of two reacting atoms the expression for Z given by the collision theory is obtained as a special case of transition state theory. As the reacting particles increase in complexity, the transition state theory gives a result which diverges from collision theory, which treats molecules as hard structureless spheres; no allowance is made for the effects upon chemical reactivity of internal complexities. The absence of an entropy term is evidence of this inadequacy. Cases in which the frequency factor is much lower than that indicated by collision theory are explained, by transition state theory, in terms of a large negative entropy of activation, that is, by an improbable configuration of the activated complex.

The ultimate success of the transition state theory to predict reaction rates depends on the ability to predict $\Delta H^{0\pm}$ and $\Delta S^{0\pm}$. It is possible to calculate the thermodynamic functions for reactions between molecules for which detailed spectroscopic data are available, as will be shown in a later chapter. Unfortunately, activated complexes are not susceptible to direct examination, but some limited success has been achieved in predicting the properties of such molecules and in turn the changes in enthalpy and entropy which accompany activation.

11.11 Reactions of Atoms and Free Radicals

Many chemical reactions can be understood, from a kinetic point of view, only by postulating the existence of atoms and free radicals as transitory ntermediates. These species usually have such great reactivity that they survive relatively few collisions and rapidly react either with molecules to generate still other radicals, or with other atoms or free radicals. Until recently, the evidence for their existence and importance in reaction mechanisms depended largely on interpretation of kinetic data. However techniques such as flash photolysis and intense radiolysis (Chapter 16) now produce such high concentrations that direct measurements are possible by absorption spectroscopy and electron spin resonance.

The best understood example of a reaction mechanism demonstrating the importance of atoms is the classic hydrogen-bromine reaction. In contrast to the hydrogen-iodine reaction, which follows a simple second-order rate law [rate $= k(H_2)(I_2)$], it was found by M. Bodenstein and S.C. Lind [Z. *Physik.* *Chem.*, **57**, 168 (1907)] that the rate of reaction is described by the empirical equation

$$\frac{d(HBr)}{dt} = \frac{k(H_2)(Br_2)^{1/2}}{1 + k'(HBr)/(Br_2)} \tag{11.62}$$

While k' is found to be temperature-independent and to have a value of approximately 0.1, k has a temperature dependence corresponding to an activation energy of 40,200 cal. mole^{-1}.

The complexity of the rate law was understood only when, thirteen years later, the following mechanism was independently proposed by J.A Christiansen, K.F. Herzfeld, and M. Polanyi. The essence of the mechanism is the proposal that reaction is initiated by the dissociation of molecular bromine.

$$Br_2 \longrightarrow 2Br \qquad k_1$$
$$Br + H_2 \longrightarrow HBr + H \qquad k_2$$
$$H + Br_2 \longrightarrow HBr + Br \qquad k_3$$
$$H + HBr \longrightarrow H_2 + Br \qquad k_4$$
$$Br + Br \longrightarrow Br_2 \qquad k_5$$

The bromine atoms so formed attack hydrogen, forming the product hydrogen bromide and a hydrogen atom. The latter, in turn, attacks bromine, forming another molecule of product and another bromine atom. Thus, the process can be a *chain reaction* in which many molecules of product are formed for each bromine atom originally produced. However, when the concentration of product becomes significant the *inhibition reaction*, step 4, may compete for hydrogen atoms and thus decrease the rate. Bromine atoms which do not react with hydrogen recombine by step 5.

That the proposed mechanism is consistent with the observed rate law can be shown as follows: Hydrogen bromide, the product, is formed in steps 2 and 3, and is consumed in step 4 to give the net rate.

$$\frac{d(HBr)}{dt} = k_2(Br)(H_2) + k_3(H)(Br_2) - k_4(H)(HBr) \tag{11.63}$$

In this equation there appear factors which represent the concentrations of bromine atoms and hydrogen atoms, transitory intermediates which are present in amounts too small for direct measurement. We must, therefore, express their concentrations in terms of measurable quantities. The differential equations describing the time dependence of the atom concentrations are

$$\frac{d(Br)}{dt} = 2k_1(Br_2) - k_2(Br)(H_2) + k_3(H)(Br_2)$$
$$+ k_4(H)(HBr) - 2k_5(Br)^2 \tag{11.64}$$

$$\frac{d(H)}{dt} = k_2(Br)(H_2) - k_3(H)(Br_2) - k_4(H)(HBr) \tag{11.65}$$

An important simplifying approximation can be made, dependent on the fact that the atomic species are extremely reactive. This situation is analogous to the case of successive reactions described in section 11.6 and Fig. 11.9 with $k_2 \gg k_1$. Under these circumstances the concentration of the intermediate quickly reaches a very small *steady-state* concentration which changes only very slowly as the reactants are consumed. Over a short interval of time we take the time derivative of the atom concentration to be zero

$$\frac{d(H)}{dt} = 0, \qquad \frac{d(Br)}{dt} = 0 \tag{11.66}$$

and this permits solution of equations (11.64) and (11.65) as follows: From equation (11.65)

$$k_2(Br)(H_2) = k_3(H)(Br_2) + k_4(H)(HBr)$$

Substituting in equation (11.64) yields

$$k_1(Br_2) = k_5(Br)^2$$

$$(Br) = \sqrt{\frac{k_1}{k_5}}(Br_2) \tag{11.67}$$

Solving equation (11.65) for (H) and substituting for (Br) by equation (11.67), we obtain

$$(H) = \frac{k_2(H_2)\sqrt{\frac{k_1}{k_5}}(Br_2)}{k_3(Br_2) + k_4(HBr)} \tag{11.68}$$

Substituting by equations (11.67) and (11.68) in the rate equation (11.63) for formation of hydrogen bromide yields, with rearrangement,

$$\frac{d(HBr)}{dt} = \frac{2k_2(k_1/k_5)^{1/2}(H_2)(Br_2)^{1/2}}{1 + (k_4/k_3)(HBr)/(Br_2)} \tag{11.69}$$

which is identical in form with the empirical rate equation (11.62).

The ratio of rate constants k_1/k_5 is to be identified with the equilibrium constant for dissociation of bromine, $K_{eq.}$. Also, since

$$\frac{d \ln K_{eq.}}{dT} = \frac{\Delta E}{RT^2} = \frac{d \ln(k_1/k_5)}{dT} = \frac{E_a(1) - E_a(5)}{RT^2} \tag{11.70}$$

the activation energy difference is given by comparison with equation (11.69) as

$$E_a(1) - E_a(5) = \Delta E = 45,200 \text{ cal. mole}^{-1}$$

This value is known both from equilibrium and from spectroscopic data.

The observed temperature dependence of the empirical constant k in equation (11.62) is interpreted as a combination of activation energies for steps 1, 2, and 5.

$$k_{obs.} = A_{obs.}e^{-E_a(obs.)/RT} = A_2 e^{-E_a(2)/RT}\left(\frac{A_1 e^{-E_a(1)/RT}}{A_5 e^{-E_a(5)/RT}}\right)^{1/2}$$

$$= A_2 \left(\frac{A_1}{A_5}\right)^{1/2} e^{-\{E_a(2)+(1/2)[E_a(1)-E_a(5)]\}/RT}$$

That is,

$$E_a(obs.) = E_a(2) + \tfrac{1}{2}[E_a(1) - E_a(5)] \tag{11.71}$$

Combining equations (11.70) and (11.71) yields a value for the activation energy for reaction of a bromine atom with molecular hydrogen.

$$E_a(2) = 40.2 - \tfrac{1}{2}(45.2) = 17.6 \text{ kcal. mole}^{-1}$$

It has been found that organic free radicals are important intermediates in the thermal decomposition of many organic compounds. A technique for detection of such free radicals developed by F. Paneth and W. Hofeditz [*Berichte*, **62**, 1335 (1929)] was applied by F.O. Rice and his collaborators [*J. Am. Chem. Soc.*, **53**, 1959 (1932)] to this problem. The method depends on the fact that many simple free radicals, such as CH_3, react readily with a film or *mirror* of metallic lead on the wall of a glass or silica tube to form the corresponding gaseous lead alkyl. This compound is collected for analysis in a cold trap as indicated in Fig. 11.16. The rate of removal of the mirror is a measure of the

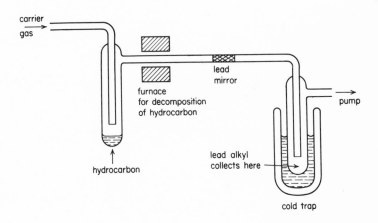

FIG. 11.16. Paneth mirror technique for detection of free radicals.

concentration of free radicals in the gas stream and their nature can be inferred from the composition of the lead alkyl collected.

An important advance in understanding the mechanism of pyrolysis of many organic compounds was achieved by F.O. Rice and K.F. Herzfeld [*J. Am. Chem. Soc.*, **56**, 284 (1934)]. The decomposition of butane will serve as an illustration.

Reaction is initiated by the slow dissociation of a molecule of reactant into free radicals, for example,

$$C_4H_{10} \rightarrow CH_3 + C_3H_7 \quad k_1$$

Chain decomposition proceeds rapidly through free radical attack on the reactant,

$$CH_3 + C_4H_{10} \rightarrow CH_4 + C_4H_9 \quad k_2$$

which produces a stable product and another free radical. The more com plicated free radicals may undergo unimolecular decomposition

$$C_4H_9 \rightarrow CH_3 + C_3H_6 \quad k_3$$

to yield another free radical and a stable molecule. The chain is eventuall terminated by combination of free radicals by such reactions as

$$CH_3 + CH_3 \rightarrow C_2H_6 \quad k_4$$

Regarding CH_3 as the principal chain carrier, we can perform a simplified kinetic analysis of the mechanism. The consumption of C_4H_{10} is principally by radical attack.

$$-\frac{d(C_4H_{10})}{dt} = k_2(CH_3)(C_4H_{10}) \tag{11.72}$$

The steady-state concentration of CH_3 radicals is obtained from the differentia equation

$$\frac{d(CH_3)}{dt} = k_1(C_4H_{10}) - k_4(CH_3)^2 = 0 \tag{11.73}$$

if we note that the steps 2 and 3 taken together do not consume radicals. Solu tion of equation (11.73) for (CH_3) and substitution in equation (11.72) yields

$$-\frac{d(C_4H_{10})}{dt} = k_2 \left(\frac{k_1}{k_4}\right)^{1/2} (C_4H_{10})^{3/2} \tag{11.74}$$

Experimental results indicate that the mechanisms of such reactions are more complicated than we have presumed, involving various other radical-molecule and radical-radical reactions, as well as reactions on the walls of the vessel. These processes further complicate the rate equation. It is fair to say, however, that the observed rate law has approximately the form of equation (11.74) in some simple cases.

Further examples of atom and free-radical reactions will be found in Chapter 16, in connection with studies of photochemistry and radiation chemistry.

11.12 Reactions in Solution—Homogeneous Catalysis

Reaction in solution involving electrolytes may give erratic rate constants unless attention is paid to activity coefficients. The equilibrium function for formation of the activated complex is precise only when formulated in terms of activities. For the generalized reaction between the ions A^{Z_A} and B^{Z_B}, where Z_A and Z_B represent the charges on the ions, we have

$$A^{Z_A} + B^{Z_B} \rightleftharpoons (AB^{\ddagger})^{Z_A + Z_B} \rightarrow \text{products}$$

The equilibrium function is

$$K^{\ddagger} = \frac{a_{AB^{\ddagger}}}{a_A a_B} = \frac{c_{AB^{\ddagger}}}{c_A c_B} \cdot \frac{\gamma_{AB^{\ddagger}}}{\gamma_A \gamma_B} \tag{11.75}$$

and according to the activated complex theory the reaction rate is

$$\text{rate} = \frac{kT}{h} K^{\ddagger}_{\text{eq.}} c_A c_B \frac{\gamma_A \gamma_B}{\gamma_{AB^{\ddagger}}}$$

The specific velocity constant, given by

$$\text{rate } k = \frac{kT}{h} K^{\ddagger}_{\text{eq.}} \frac{\gamma_A \gamma_B}{\gamma_{AB}} \tag{11.76}$$

now contains a factor in the activity coefficients not previously included. Taking the logarithm of the rate constant and substituting by the Debye-Hückel limiting law (equation 10.39) for $\log \gamma$, we have

$$\log \text{rate } k = \log \frac{kT}{h} K^{\ddagger}_{\text{eq.}} + Z_A Z_B \sqrt{\mu} \tag{11.77}$$

which shows the dependence of the specific velocity constant on the ionic strength μ, and on the product of $Z_A Z_B$.

If $\log k$ is plotted versus $\sqrt{\mu}$, as in Fig. 11.17, several possibilities arise. When either Z_A or Z_B is zero, the curves have zero slope. When Z_A and Z_B have the same sign, a positive slope is expected, and when Z_A and Z_B have opposite signs a curve of negative slope is expected. The effects which have just been described are known as primary kinetic salt effects.

Rates of reactions are often greatly accelerated by additives, called catalysts, which undergo no net change as a result of the reaction. Common examples are acids and bases. If the reaction is reversible, the catalyst accelerates the rate of approach to equilibrium, but does not shift the position of equilibrium. It follows that the catalyst increases proportionately the rates of both forward and reverse reactions. A catalyst usually acts by providing a reaction path of lower activation energy than that for the uncatalyzed reaction.

Heterogeneous catalysis, that is, catalysis which depends on the presence

FIG. 11.17. Variation of rate constants with ionic strength [from V. K., LaMer, *Chem. Rev.*, **10**, 179 (1932)].

1. $2[\text{Co(NH}_3)_5 \text{ Br}]^{++} + \text{Hg}^{++} + 2\text{H}_2\text{O}$
   $\longrightarrow 2 \text{ Co}[(\text{NH}_3)_5 \text{ H}_2\text{O}]^{+++} + \text{Hg Br}_2$
2. $\text{S}_2\text{O}_8^{=} + \text{I}^- \longrightarrow \text{I}_2 + 2\text{SO}_4^{=}$
3. $[\text{NO}_2 = \text{N} - \text{COOC}_2 \text{ H}_5]^- + \text{OH}^-$
   $\longrightarrow \text{N}_2\text{O} + \text{CO}_3^{=} + \text{C}_2\text{H}_5\text{OH}$
4. $\text{C}_{12}\text{H}_{22}\text{O}_{11} + \text{OH}^- \longrightarrow$ Invert sugar
5. $\text{H}_2\text{O}_2 + 2\text{H}^+ + 2\text{Br}^- \longrightarrow 2\text{H}_2\text{O} + \text{Br}_2$
6. $[\text{Co(NH}_3)_5\text{Br}]^{++} + \text{OH}^- \longrightarrow$
   $[\text{Co(NH}_3)_5\text{OH}]^{++} + \text{Br}^-$

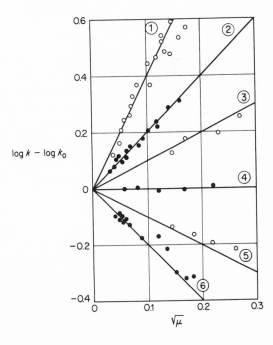

$\log k - \log k_0$

$\sqrt{\mu}$

of a phase boundary, is best considered in connection with surface chemistry Homogeneous catalysis, on the other hand, belongs to the study of th mechanism of homogeneous reactions.

In general terms, the action of a homogeneous catalyst is to form a mor or less stable intermediate with the reactant. This intermediate then react to form the product and to regenerate the catalyst. For the generalized reactio $A + B \rightarrow$ products, catalyzed by X, we propose

$$A + X \underset{k_{-1}}{\overset{k_1}{\rightleftharpoons}} AX \qquad AX + B \overset{k_2}{\rightarrow} product + X$$

The rate equation is

$$rate = k_2(AX)(B) \tag{11.78}$$

Using the steady-state treatment, we obtain

$$\frac{d(AX)}{dt} = k_1(A)(X) - k_{-1}(AX) - k_2(AX)(B) = 0$$

$$(AX) = \frac{k_1(A)(X)}{k_{-1} + k_2(B)} \tag{11.79}$$

Substituting in equation (11.78) we find

$$rate = \frac{k_2(B)k_1(A)(X)}{k_{-1} + k_2(B)} \tag{11.80}$$

A simple rate law is obtained if k_{-1} and $k_2(B)$ have very different values. I $k_{-1} \ll k_2(B)$,

$$rate = k_1(A)(X) \tag{11.81}$$

and if $k_{-1} \gg k_2(B)$

$$rate = \frac{k_1 k_2}{k_{-1}}(A)(B)(X) \tag{11.82}$$

In either event, the rate depends on the concentration of catalyst, although it is neither consumed nor produced in the net reaction.

Many organic reactions are catalyzed by acids and bases. The mutarotation of glucose, described in section 11.5, has been extensively studied from this viewpoint. In any given experiment the rate is first order in glucose, as previously shown, and the value of the observed first-order rate constant varies with pH, as indicated in Fig. 11.18. In the pH range 3–6 the rate is practically independent of pH and can be described by a rate constant k_0 for the uncatalyzed reaction. The increase in rate at pH < 3 can be described by a term which is linear in concentration of H_3O^+ and the increase in rate at pH > 6 by a term which is linear in concentration of OH^-. The net rate constant is

$$k_{obs.} = k_A(H_3O^+) + k_0 + k_B(OH^-)$$

The mutarotation of glucose in aqueous solutions is catalyzed by Brönsted acids and bases in general. Their role can be clarified by examining the mutarotation of tetramethyl glucose in nonaqueous solvents. In pyridine alone, or in cresol alone, the rate of mutarotation is very slow, but it proceeds rapidly in an equimolar mixture of this acid-base solvent pair [T.M. Lowry and

.J. Faulkner, *J. Chem. Soc.*, **127**, 2883 (1925)]. Both base and acid are required, but this requirement cannot be seen in aqueous solutions, since water serves either role and because of its large concentration swamps out small solute effects. The requirement of joint acid-base action has been elaborated in terms of a "push-pull" mechanism involving the concerted acts of proton donation and proton acceptance at different sites of the substrate molecule [C.G. Swain, *J. Am. Chem. Soc.*, **72**, 4578 (1950)]. In aqueous solutions of glucose containing both HA and A⁻, there would then be many rate terms of the general type: rate $= k$ (glucose) (acid) (base). Examples of these acid-base couples would be (HA)

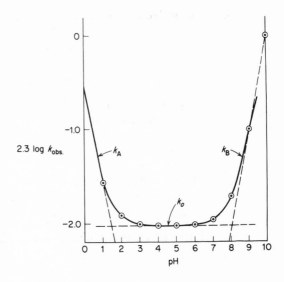

FIG. 11.18. Rate constant $(k_1 + k_{-1})$ for mutarotation of glucose.

(H_2O) and (H^+)(A^-), but the latter would be indistinguishable from the former, since (H^+)(A^-) $= K_{HA}$ (HA).

SUMMARY, CHAPTER 11

1. Reaction order

$$\text{Rate} = -\frac{dc}{dt} = kc_A^\alpha c_B^\beta \ldots$$

Order $= \alpha + \beta + \ldots$

2. First-order reactions

$$-\frac{dc}{dt} = kc, \qquad \ln\frac{c_0}{c} = kt, \qquad c = c_0 e^{-kt}$$

Half life: $t_{1/2} = k^{-1} \ln 2$

3. Second-order reactions

$$-\frac{dc_A}{dt} = kc_A c_B$$

When $(a - x) = c_A \neq c_B = (b - x)$

$$\frac{1}{a - b} \ln \frac{b(a - x)}{a(b - x)} = k$$

When $c_A = c_B = c$

$$\frac{1}{c} - \frac{1}{c_0} = kt$$

Half life: $t_{1/2} = 1/kc_0$

4. Reversible reactions, both first order

$$\frac{dx}{dt} = (k_1 + k_{-1})(x_e - x)$$

$$(k_1 + k_{-1})t = \ln \frac{x_e - x_0}{x_e - x}$$

5. Complex reactions
   Simultaneous first order

$$\ln \frac{c_0}{c} = (k_M + k_N)t$$

Successive first order $A \xrightarrow{k_1} M \xrightarrow{k_2} Z$

$$c_M = \frac{k_1 c_{0,A}}{k_2 - k_1} (e^{-k_1 t} - e^{-k_2 t}) + c_{0,M} e^{-k_2 t}$$

Intermediate in equilibrium with reactants

$$2A \rightleftharpoons A_2$$

$$A_2 + B \longrightarrow \text{products}$$

$$\text{rate} = k K_{eq.}(A)^2(B)$$

6. Activation energy—activated complex

$$\frac{d \ln k}{d(1/T)} = -\frac{E_a}{R}$$

$E_a(\text{forward}) - E_a(\text{reverse}) = \Delta E(\text{thermodynamic})$

7. Kinetic theory of gases

$$P = \frac{nm\overline{c^2}}{3V}$$

Root-mean-square molecular velocity

$$u = \sqrt{\overline{c^2}} = \sqrt{\frac{3RT}{M}}$$

Maxwell-Boltzmann distribution law for relative kinetic energy

$$\frac{dn}{n} = \frac{1}{RT} e^{-E/RT} \, dE$$

8. Theory of reaction rate
   Collision theory

$$\text{rate} = ZP(E)$$

$$Z = \tfrac{1}{2}\pi \, d^2 \bar{c} n^2$$

$$P(E) = e^{-E_a/RT}$$

Activated complex theory

$$\text{rate } k = \frac{kT}{h} K_{eq.}^{\ddagger}$$

$$K_{eq.}^{\ddagger} = e^{\Delta S^{0\ddagger}/R} \; e^{-\Delta H^{0\ddagger}/RT}$$

9. Atom and free radical reactions
    Steady-state approximation

$$\frac{d(\text{radical})}{dt} = 0$$

10. Reactions in solution

$$A + B \rightleftharpoons AB^{\pm} \longrightarrow \text{products}$$

$$\text{rate } k = \frac{kT}{h} K^{\pm}_{\text{eq.}} \frac{\gamma_A \gamma_B}{\gamma_{AB^{\pm}}}$$

Ionic strength effect

$$\log \text{rate } k = \log \frac{kT}{h} K^{\pm}_{\text{eq.}} + Z_A Z_B \sqrt{\mu}$$

Acid-base catalysis

$$k_{\text{obs.}} = k_0 + k_A(H_3O^+) + k_B(OH^-)$$

PROBLEMS, CHAPTER 11

1. The rate of disintegration of a radioactive sample gave the following results:

Days	1	3	5	7	9
Rates	6200	4700	...	2800	2100

Show that the data obey a first-order rate law. Find the half life and evaluate the rate at $t = 5$.   *Ans.* $t_{1/2} = 5.4$ days.

2. A solution of N_2O_5 in CCl_4 at $45°$ produces 5.02 cc. of O_2 in 1198 sec., 7.33 cc. of O_2 in 2315 sec., and a maximum of 9.58 cc. of O_2 after a long time. Show that these results conform to a first-order rate law for decomposition of N_2O_5 and find the first-order rate constant.   *Ans.* $k = 6.2 \times 10^{-4}$ sec.$^{-1}$.

3. The rate constant for the decomposition of hydrogen iodide is 3.96×10^{-6} l. mole^{-1} sec^{-1}. at $321.4°$, and $C_0 = 1$ m.l.$^{-1}$
(a) Find the extent of decomposition after 20 hrs.
(b) Find the half life.   *Ans.* (a) 22%, (b) 2.5×10^5 sec.

4. What are the dimensions of the rate constants in liters, moles and seconds for first-, second-, and third-order reactions?

5. The following data were obtained for the decomposition of di-*t*-butyl peroxide at $154.6°$:

Time (min.)	0	3	6	9	12	15	18
P_{tot} (mm.)	173.5	193.4	211.3	228.6	244.4	259.2	273.9

Plot the appropriate function of pressure versus time to demonstrate first-order kinetics, and obtain the rate constant.   *Ans.* 3.16×10^{-4} sec.$^{-1}$.

6. From the result obtained in Problem 5 find
(a) The time required to produce 30% decomposition at $154.6°$.
(b) The percentage decomposition in 30 min.   *Ans.* (a) 1.13×10^3 sec.

7. Gaseous butadiene dimerizes at $326°$ [W. E. Vaughan, *J. Am. Chem. Soc.*,

54, 3863 (1932)]. Test the following data to determine whether the reaction is of the first or second order, and evaluate k graphically.

Time (min.)	0	3.25	8.02	14.30	24.55	42.50	90.05	∞
P (mm.)	632.0	618.5	599.4	576.1	546.8	509.3	453.3	316.0

Ans. $k = 2.4 \times 10^{-5}$ mm.$^{-1}$ min.$^{-1}$.

8. A solution containing equal concentrations of ethyl acetate and sodium hydroxide is 25% saponified in 5 min. Show that for this system 50% saponification will be reached in 15 min. What will be the percentage of saponification in 10 min.? *Ans.* 40%.

9. The rate of reaction of potassium iodide with ethylene bromide has been studied by R. T. Dillon [*J. Am. Chem. Soc.*, **54**, 952 (1932)]. The stoichiometry of the reaction is

$$C_2H_4Br_2 + 3\,KI = C_2H_4 + 2\,KBr + KI_3$$

and, therefore, the second-order rate law in this case becomes

$$kt = \frac{2.303}{(a - 3b)} \log \frac{b(a/b - 3x)}{a(1 - x)}$$

where a and b are the initial concentrations of potassium iodide and dibromide, respectively, and x is the fraction of dibromide which reacts in time t. For an experiment at 30° in which $a = 0.2152$ M and $b = 0.02450$ M the following data were obtained:

Time (hrs.)	91.4	115.3	136.9	174.4
x	0.1757	0.2154	0.2498	0.3061

Show that these data obey the second-order rate law and find the rate constant. *Ans.* 0.016 mole^{-1} l. hr.$^{-1}$.

10. Express the data of Table 11.3 by a suitable graphical method for testing a second-order rate dependence and evaluate k.

11. Verify the value of k in Table 11.3 for the data at $t = 5052$ sec.

12. If the rate of a reaction doubles from 0° to 10°.

(a) By what factor would the ratio increase when the temperature increases from 100° to 110°?

(b) What is the activation energy? *Ans.* (a) 1.45 (b) 10.6 kcal.

13. The rate constants for the second-order hydrolysis of ethyl m-nitrobenzoate in sodium hydroxide [W. B. S. Newling and C. N. Hinshelwood, *J. Chem. Soc.*, **1936**, 1357] are:

t (°C)	0.1	15.2	24.9	39.9
k (mole^{-1} l. sec.$^{-1}$) × 100	2.31	8.15	17.15	48.8

Plot log k versus $1/T$ and find the activation energy. *Ans.* 13.0 kcal.

14. From gas viscosity measurements the molecular diameter of H_2 molecules is found to be 2.18×10^{-8} cm. Find the number of collisions per cc. per sec. at

(a) 27°, 1 atm.

(b) 327°, 1 atm.

(c) 27°, 0.1 atm. *Ans.* (a) 8.0×10^{28}.

15. Experimental evidence [R. Gomer and G. B. Kistiakowsky, *J. Chem. Phys.*,

19, 85 (1951)] indicates that the reaction $2 CH_3 \rightarrow C_2H_6$ occurs at every collision in the gas phase. Methyl radicals are produced by decomposition of azomethane (CH_3NNCH_3) at $600°K$ at the rate of 10^{15} molecules $cc.^{-1} sec.^{-1}$. Since in the steady state the rate of removal of CH_3 radicals must equal the rate of formation, find the concentration of CH_3 in the reaction system if the collision diameter of CH_3 with CH_3 is 2.3×10^{-8} cm.

16. The half life of radioactive iodine,^{128}I, is 25 min.

(a) Find the rate constant for the decay reaction.

(b) A sample of radioactive iodine is found to be disintegrating at a rate of 1500 atoms $sec.^{-1}$. How many ^{128}I atoms are present in the sample?

(c) What would be the number of ^{128}I atoms present in the sample 50 min. after the observation given in (b)?

17. In acid solutions the following data were obtained for the rate of the reaction $NH_4^+ + NO_2^- = N_2 + 2 H_2O$ [J. H. Dusenbury and R. E. Powell, *J. Am. Chem. Soc.*, **73**, 3266 (1951)]:

HNO_2, mole $l.^{-1}$	0.0092	0.0092	0.0488	0.0249
NH_4^+, mole $l.^{-1}$	0.098	0.049	0.196	0.196
rate, mole $l.^{-1} sec.^{-1} \times 10^{-8}$	34.9	16.6	335	156

Express the rate law.

18. The value of A in the Arrhenius equation is often taken as $10^{13} sec.^{-1}$ for rough calculations of unimolecular reactions. Estimate the temperature at which $t_{1/2} = 1$ sec. for the reaction

$$CH_3I \rightarrow CH_3 + I$$

if the C-I bond dissociation energy is 54.0 kcal. $mole^{-1}$.

19. A mixture of H_2 and C_4H_{10} initially equimolar is admitted to a mass spectrometer from a storage bulb at low pressure through a small orifice.

(a) What is the composition of the gas which emerges from the orifice?

(b) The rate of effusion of either gas is proportional to its partial pressure. After a time it is found that the partial pressure of butane has decreased by 1%. By how much will the hydrogen pressure have decreased?

20. The reaction of nitric oxide with hydrogen

$$2 NO + 2 H_2 = N_2 + 2 H_2O$$

has been studied by following the change in total pressure with time. The initial rate of reaction was found to be proportional to the first power of the hydrogen pressure. At a fixed hydrogen pressure the following rate data were obtained

Initial NO (mm.)	359	300	152
Initial rate (mm. $sec.^{-1}$)	1.50	1.03	0.25

Find the order with respect to NO.

21. The rate equation for a reaction of the nth order when the reactants are present in stoichiometrically equivalent amounts may be written

$$\frac{dx}{dt} = k(a - x)^n$$

Integrate this rate equation, find a general expression for $t_{1/2}$, and show that when $\log t_{1/2}$ is plotted versus $\log a$, a straight line with slope $(1 - n)$ will be obtained.

22. Apply the steady-state treatment to the following mechanism for the decomposition of ozone:

$$O_3 \longrightarrow O_2 + O \qquad k_1$$
$$O_2 + O \longrightarrow O_3 \qquad k_{-1}$$
$$O + O_3 \longrightarrow 2\,O_2 \qquad k_2$$

and obtain a general differential equation for the rate of disappearance of ozone. Except at the very beginning of reaction it is found that the experimental rate law is $-dc_{O_3}/dt = kc_{O_3}^2/c_{O_2}$. What does this imply concerning the relative values of k_{-1} and k_2?

23. The decomposition of gaseous N_2O_5

$$N_2O_5 = 2\,NO_2 + \tfrac{1}{2}\,O_2$$

is found to be first order and was long presumed to be a simple unimolecular reaction. R.A. Ogg [*J. Chem. Phys.*, **18**, 573 (1950)] has shown that the mechanism

$$N_2O_5 \underset{k_{-1}}{\overset{k_1}{\rightleftharpoons}} NO_2 + NO_3 \qquad \text{fast}$$

$$NO_2 + NO_3 \overset{k_2}{\longrightarrow} NO_2 + O_2 + NO \qquad \text{slow}$$

$$NO + NO_3 \overset{k_3}{\longrightarrow} 2\,NO_2 \qquad \text{fast}$$

in which the bimolecular reaction 2 is the rate-determining process, can account for the observed rate law. Apply the steady-state treatment to NO_3 and show that a first-order rate law is obtained.

24. The addition of methyl iodide to pyridine has been studied in several solvents by H.W. Thompson and E.E. Blandon [*J. Chem. Soc.*, **1933**, 1237]. In chloroform the following data were obtained, where a = initial concentration of methyl iodide, b = initial concentration of pyridine, and x = the concentration of quaternary iodide as determined by silver nitrate titration.

temp. = 42.6°	$a = 0.0796$		$b = 0.0790$		
time (min.)	625	840	1149	1438	2647
x(moles l.$^{-1}$) × 10	0.213	0.270	0.335	0.375	0.453

Find the rate constants of this bimolecular reaction.

25. The rate constants for the second-order reaction of hydrogen with iodine are

$T(°K)$	556	629	700	781
k(mole^{-1} l. sec.$^{-1}$)	1.19×10^{-4}	6.76×10^{-3}	1.72×10^{-1}	3.58

(a) Plot log k versus $1/T$ and find E_a.

(b) The equilibrium constant for the reaction is found to be 3.73 at 629°K and 2.43 at 700°K. Find the rate constant and the activation energy for the reverse reaction at 700°.

26. Electronically excited NO fluoresces with a half life approximating 2×10^{-7} sec. at very low pressure of NO. Every collision with added CO_2 "quenches" fluorescence. What pressure of CO_2 is required at 25° to change the apparent half life to 1×10^{-7} sec.? Let $d_{NO} = d_{CO_2} = 4 \times 10^{-8}$ cm. [A.B. Callear and I.W.M. Smith, *Trans. Faraday Soc.*, **59**, 1720 (1964).]

12

SURFACE
CHEMISTRY

12.1 Colloids

Certain solids, such as sulfur and gold, although insoluble in water, can be prepared in the form of superficially homogeneous suspensions stable for relatively long periods of time. These systems represent one type of *colloidal* suspension, or *sol*. They have several peculiar physical and chemical properties which distinguish them from true solutions. For one, the *dispersed phase* can usually be separated from the *dispersion medium* by drastic centrifugation or by passage through a membrane with very fine pores (a technique called *dialysis*), demonstrating the actual heterogeneity of the system. Evidently the particles of the dispersed phase are somewhat larger than atomic dimensions and yet so small that they do not settle in the earth's gravitational field. Other types of colloidally dispersed systems include *aerosol* (solid in gas), *mist* (liquid in gas) and *emulsion* (liquid in liquid).

All colloidal systems are characterized by a stabilized dispersion of particles in a continuous medium. The range of particle size which characterizes a colloidal system is somewhat flexible, depending on the system and the method of examination. As indicated in Table 12.1, colloidal behavior is usually associated with particle sizes ranging from 10^{-5} to 10^{-7} cm. Also included in this table is an estimate of the total surface area per unit volume for various particle sizes (assuming spherical particles). It is evident that this property is inversely proportional to the particle diameter, and that for the smaller particles an appreciable fraction of the atoms or molecules of the particle must lie at the

319

TABLE 12.1

PARTICLE SIZE IN COLLOIDAL SYSTEMS

Particle diameter* (cm.)	Surface area per unit total volume* (cm.^{2} cc.$^{-1}$)	
1	6	
10^{-1}	60	
10^{-2}	600	
10^{-3}	6×10^3	} ordinary suspensions
10^{-4}	6×10^4	
		limit of resolution—optical microscope
10^{-5}	6×10^5	} typical colloidal suspensions
10^{-6}	6×10^6	
10^{-7}	6×10^7	
10^{-8}	6×10^8	

*Assuming spherical particles

surface separating the two phases. For this reason surface phenomena such as adsorption are very important in colloidal systems.

EXERCISE 12.1

The radius of a gold atom is 1.4×10^{-8} cm. Estimate the number of gold atoms in a spherical particle of 20×10^{-8} cm. diameter (neglect voids). Estimate the fraction of atoms lying in the surface of the particle.   *Ans.* 360 atoms; *ca.* 57%.

The most frequently encountered colloidal systems are those in which the dispersed phase is a liquid or solid and the dispersion medium is a liquid, that is, emulsions and sols. Two general categories of such colloids are recognizable. The *lyophobic* (solvent repelling) colloids such as those formed by sulfur and gold are inherently unstable systems which tend eventually to coagulate into the gross solid phase. The maximum concentration of disperse phase for reasonable stability is quite small, and the stability depends strongly on the presence of minor components in the dispersion medium, e.g., electrolytes in water suspensions. Coagulation is not usually reversible. That is, the colloidal system cannot be reformed by simple mixing of the two phases. As the term lyophobic implies, there is little or no attraction between the molecules of the two phases.

There is a second large group of colloidal systems called *lyophilic* (solvent attracting) in which attractive forces between the two phases render the suspension intrinsically stable. Coagulation does not usually occur spontaneously. In fact, the reverse process of dispersion may occur spontaneously when the two phases are mixed. The colloidal systems formed by proteins in aqueous solution and high polymers in organic solvents are typical members of this class.

12.2 Osmotic Pressure of Colloidal Suspensions

It has been shown in Chapter 7 that the osmotic pressure for an ideal solution is proportional to the concentration of solute and inversely proportional to the molecular weight of the solute. In colloidal suspensions it has been found that the osmotic pressure increases more rapidly with concentration than would be expected from the simple relation, and a power series is required to express the concentration dependence.

$$\Pi = Ac + Bc^2 + Cc^3 + \ldots$$

The limiting slope of a plot of Π/c versus c gives A, equal to

$$\lim_{c \to 0} \left(\frac{\Pi}{c} \right) = \frac{RT}{M} \tag{12.1}$$

where M is molecular weight. When R is expressed in units of ergs deg.$^{-1}$ mole^{-1} and c in g. cc.$^{-1}$, then Π is in units of dynes cm^{-2}.

Since the colloidal suspensions to be dealt with usually contain a variety of particle sizes, that is, are *polydisperse*, the molecular weight obtained from measurement of a gross property evidently represents some kind of average. Osmotic pressure measurements give the *number average molecular weight M_n*, which is simply the total weight divided by the total number of particles.

$$M_n = \frac{\sum\limits_i n_i M_i}{\sum\limits_i n_i} \tag{12.2}$$

An interesting case of osmotic equilibrium important in biological systems arises when one of the ions of an electrolyte is so large as to be retained by a membrane which will pass small ions. This is the *Donnan membrane equilibrium* illustrated in Fig. 12.1. Consider two solutions of strong electrolytes Na^+Cl^- and Na^+X^- separated by a membrane which is impermeable to X^-. When the system comes to equilibrium, the activities (approximated by the concentrations) of the diffusible components must be the same on both sides of the membrane.

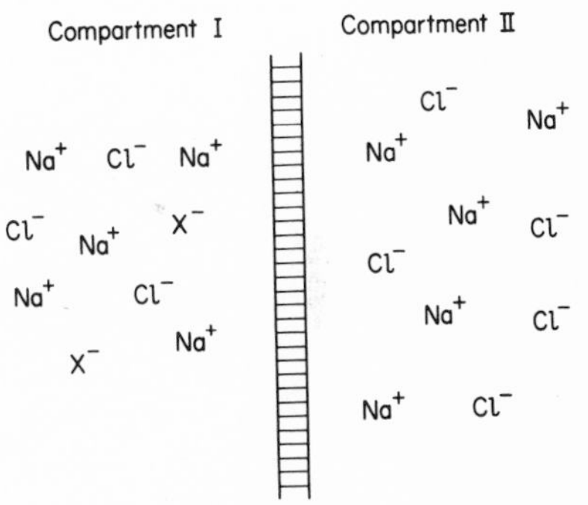

FIG. 12.1. Donnan membrane equilibrium.

$$a_{\text{NaCl}}(\text{I}) = a_{\text{NaCl}}(\text{II})$$

$$c_{\text{Na}^+}(\text{I}) \times c_{\text{Cl}^-}(\text{I}) = c_{\text{Na}^+}(\text{II}) \times c_{\text{Cl}^-}(\text{II}) \tag{12.3}$$

Furthermore, since both compartments remain electrically neutral,

$$c_{\text{Na}^+}(\text{I}) = c_{\text{Cl}^-}(\text{I}) + c_{\text{X}^-}(\text{I}) \quad \text{and} \quad c_{\text{Na}^+}(\text{II}) = c_{\text{Cl}^-}(\text{II}) \tag{12.4}$$

Simultaneous solution of equations (12.3) and (12.4) gives the equilibrium distribution of electrolytes.

$$\left(\frac{c_{\text{NaCl}}(\text{II})}{c_{\text{NaCl}}(\text{I})} \right)^2 = 1 + \frac{c_{\text{NaX}}(\text{I})}{c_{\text{NaCl}}(\text{I})} \tag{12.5}$$

This equation shows that the diffusible electrolyte Na^+Cl^- will not be equally distributed between the two compartments in the presence of NaX. For example, if c_{NaX} (I) $= c_{NaCl}$ (I) then c_{NaCl} (II) $= 1.4\ c_{NaCl}$ (I).

It might be expected that the osmotic pressure difference between the two solutions would be simply that corresponding to the concentration of Na^+X^- in compartment I, but since, when concentrations are expressed in moles per unit volume.

$$\frac{\Pi\ (I) - \Pi\ (II)}{RT} = 2c_{NaX}\ (I) + 2c_{NaCl}\ (I) - 2c_{NaCl}\ (II) \tag{12.6}$$

and c_{NaCl} (II) $> c_{NaCl}$ (I) this is not the case. A simpler relation can be obtained if a large excess of the diffusible electrolyte is used. When c_{NaCl} (II) $\gg c_{NaX}$ (I), by (12.3) and 12.4 c_{NaCl} (I) $= c_{NaCl}$ (II) and

$$\frac{\Pi\ (I) - \Pi\ (II)}{RT} = 2c_{NaX}\ (I) \tag{12.7}$$

The latter technique can be used in osmotic pressure measurements on protein systems.

EXERCISE 12.2

Find the osmotic pressure difference to be expected when c_{NaX} (I) $= c_{NaCl}$ (I) $= 10^{-3}\ M$ at 25°.   *Ans.* 0.0294 atm.

12.3 Viscosity of Colloidal Suspensions

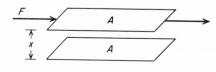

FIG. 12.2. Viscosity.

All liquids exhibit a certain resistance to flow which is measured by the *viscosity coefficient.* Suppose that one plane surface in a body of liquid is caused to move with respect to another by application of a shearing force as indicated in Fig. 12.2. The force F which must be applied to maintain a relative velocity v is proportional to the area of the surfaces, A, and inversely proportional to the distance between them, x. The proportionality constant in this relation is η,

$$F = \eta\frac{vA}{x} \tag{12.8}$$

the viscosity coefficient, which has the dimensions gram cm.$^{-1}$ sec.$^{-1}$ or *poise.* The viscosity of water at 25° is 0.00895 poise, and that of glycerine is 9.54 poise.

The viscosity equation (12.8), in differential form, $dv/dx = F/A\eta$, is applicable to a variety of experimental situations. Examples are rotating concentric cylinders, rotating coplanar circular plates, the terminal velocity of a sphere falling through a fluid, or the rate of flow of a fluid through a capillary tube (viscometer). In the last instance the result is

$$V = \frac{\pi r^4 Pt}{8L\eta} \tag{12.9}$$

where V is the volume of liquid passed through the tube in time t, r is the radius of the tube of length L, and P is the pressure drop through the tube.

Viscosity measurements can be made by comparing the time of flow of an unknown fluid with a liquid of known viscosity in a viscometer. In this case the ratio of pressures is the ratio of densities of the two fluids. Equation (12.9) yields

$$\frac{\eta_1}{\eta_2} = \frac{\rho_1 t_1}{\rho_2 t_2} \qquad (12.10)$$

where ρ is the density and t the time for flow of the same volume of each fluid.

EXERCISE 12.3

A certain volume of water passes through a viscometer in 30 sec. at 25°. How long will it take the same volume of glycerine ($\rho = 1.26$ g. cc.$^{-1}$) to pass? The capillary is to be replaced with another suitable for measuring viscosities of liquids similar to glycerine. By what factor should the radius be increased to give approximately the same time interval?   *Ans.* 2.5×10^4 sec.; *ca.* 5.7.

The presence of colloidal particles suspended in a liquid always increases the viscosity over that of the pure liquid. Einstein showed that for spherical particles at low concentration the fractional increase in viscosity, or *specific viscosity* $\eta_{sp.}$, is strictly proportional to the volume fraction of the suspended material. The true volume fraction of the suspended material cannot be easily calculated from the bulk density but should be proportional to the weight concentration of the suspension. Therefore, the Einstein relation should have the form

$$\eta_{sp.} = \frac{(\eta - \eta_0)}{\eta_0} = kc \qquad (12.11)$$

where η is the viscosity of the suspension, η_0 the viscosity of the pure liquid and c the concentration of the suspension, usually given in grams per 100 ml.

Most natural and artificial polymer molecules are not spherical but either

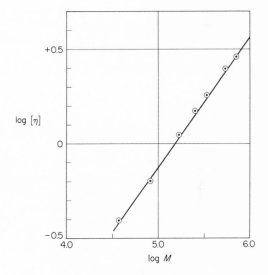

FIG. 12.3. Intrinsic viscosity and molecular weight. Polyisobutylene in n-hexane at 30° [W.R. Krigbaum and P.J. Flory, J. Am. Chem. Soc., **75**, 1775 (1953)].

rodlike or flexible chainlike molecules, and in these cases the specific viscosity increases more rapidly with concentration than is indicated by equation (12.11). This is to say that the viscosity increment per unit concentration, $\eta_{sp.}/c$, called the *intrinsic viscosity* $[\eta]$, increases with concentration. Fortunately, this quantity is usually a linear function of concentration for $\eta_{sp.} < 2$, and it may be obtained accurately as the intercept of a plot of $\eta_{sp.}/c$ versus c.

$$[\eta] = \lim_{c \to 0} \frac{\eta_{sp.}}{c} \tag{12.12}$$

It has been found that for high polymers of a given type the intrinsic viscosity bears a simple relation to the molecular weight of the dispersed particles, as shown in Fig. 12.3. This relationship is summarized in the equation:

$$[\eta] = kM^a \tag{12.13}$$

where k is a proportionality constant characteristic of the dispersed phase and dispersion medium and a (the slope of the line in Fig. 12.3) depends on the shape of the particles. For rigid rodlike particles $a \cong 1.0$ whereas for flexible chainlike molecules $a \cong 0.7$.

Equation (12.13) has been extensively used to determine the molecular weight of high polymers. For polydisperse suspensions the value obtained is evidently an average, and when $a = 1.0$ (rodlike particles) it can be shown that this is the *weight average molecular weight*, defined by

$$M_w = \frac{\sum\limits_i n_i M_i^2}{\sum\limits_i n_i M_i} = \frac{\sum\limits_i c_i M_i}{\sum\limits_i c_i} \tag{12.14}$$

where c is molar concentration.

The contrast between M_n (equation 12.2) and M_w is illustrated in Fig. 12.4, where a typical distribution of molecular weights is shown. M_n corresponds to the maximum of the curve, whereas M_w, which weights larger particles more heavily, has a somewhat higher value.

EXERCISE 12.4

A colloidal suspension contains equal numbers of particles of molecular weight 100,000 and 200,000. Find M_n and M_w.   *Ans.* $M_n = 150,000$; $M_w = 167,000$.

12.4 Brownian Movement and Diffusion

Table 12.1 shows that the particle size range associated with colloidal suspensions is usually less than the resolving power of optical microscopy. Therefore, it is often not possible to see the individual particles of a colloidal suspension in the usual sense. However, the particles can be observed by virtue of the fact that they scatter light. If a suspension is strongly illuminated at right angles to the direction of observation, the position of the particles can be observed as spots of light.

FIG. 12.4. A typical distribution of particle sizes: Number N vs. molecular weight M.

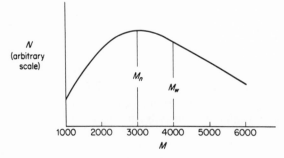

N (arbitrary scale)

M_n

M_w

1000 2000 3000 4000 5000 6000

M

In 1828 the English botanist Robert Brown observed that pollen grains suspended in a liquid execute a continuous irregular motion, now called the *Brownian movement*. With the development of the kinetic theory of gases in the late 1800's, it was realized that this movement is due to random impacts on the particle by the molecules of the liquid. Only for very small particles does the number of impacts from opposite directions become so small that they do not, on the average, cancel out during an observation. It is, of course, this kind of translational molecular motion which is responsible for the macroscopic phenomenon of diffusion.

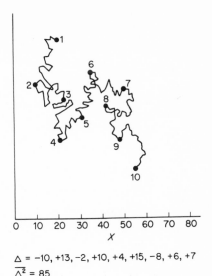

$\Delta = -10, +13, -2, +10, +4, +15, -8, +6, +7$
$\overline{\Delta^2} = 85$

FIG. 12.5. Brownian movement.

If the position of a particle undergoing Brownian movement is observed at equal intervals of time t, a result such as that in Fig. 12.5 is obtained. The net motion parallel to an arbitrary axis is found by projection of the path on that axis, and each increment may be represented by $\Delta_1, \Delta_2, \Delta_3, \ldots$. The observed Δ's vary in magnitude and sign, but if a sufficiently large number of observations is made, the positive and negative values tend to cancel in the average, since there is no net translation of the system. For the same reason the average value of Δ, without regard to sign, is independent of the choice of reference axis.

The connection between the Brownian movement and diffusion can be shown in simplified form by assuming that all displacements have a single value, Δ, corresponding to the average without regard to sign. Consider a small region in a nonuniform suspension where the concentration of particles is a linear function of distance along some arbitrary axis. Migration of particles occurs in both directions across a plane perpendicular to that axis. In the interval of time t all particles lying within a distance Δ of this plane can pass through the plane, but only half will do so, since half the displacements are positive and half negative. This region of interest is indicated in Fig. 12.6. The average concentrations of particles in the two regions on each side of the index plane may be designated n_1 and n_2 particles per unit volume. Since we have specified that the concentration is a linear function of distance, these will correspond to the actual concentrations at planes $\frac{1}{2}\Delta$ on each side of the index plane. These two planes lie at a distance of Δ apart along the concentration axis.

FIG. 12.6. Brownian motion and diffusion.

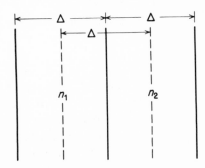

The number of particles crossing the index plane

from left to right is $\frac{1}{2}n_1\Delta$ and from right to left is $\frac{1}{2}n_2\Delta$. The net transfer rate is

$$\frac{dn}{dt} = \frac{\Delta(n_1 - n_2)}{2t} \tag{12.15}$$

The difference in concentrations n_1 and n_2 is, in terms of the concentration gradient dn/dx,

$$n_2 - n_1 = \left(\frac{dn}{dx}\right)\Delta \tag{12.16}$$

Substitution in equation (12.15) gives

$$\frac{dn}{dt} = -\left(\frac{\Delta^2}{2t}\right)\frac{dn}{dx} \tag{12.17}$$

The negative sign shows, as must be the case, that the net transfer is in the direction of decreasing concentration.

Equation (12.17) has the form of Fick's law of diffusion, i.e., the rate of transfer of material across a plane is proportional to the concentration gradient perpendicular to the plane. The proportionality constant is called the *diffusion coefficient D*, and from equation (12.17)

$$D = \frac{\Delta^2}{2t}$$

When the random distribution of displacements actually observed as shown in Fig. 12.5 is used, the same relationship is obtained, except that Δ^2 is replaced by the average of the squares of the displacements

$$D = \frac{\overline{\Delta^2}}{2t} \tag{12.18}$$

The theory of diffusion, developed by Einstein and by von Smoluchowski, gives the relationship between the diffusion coefficient and the frictional coefficient f of a particle as

$$D = \frac{RT}{Nf} \tag{12.19}$$

where N is Avogadro's number. The frictional coefficient is the proportionality constant between the velocity of a particle dx/dt, and the frictional force of resistance to motion. For spherical particles, Stokes's law is

$$f = 6\pi\eta r \tag{12.20}$$

where r is the radius of the particle and η the viscosity of the medium. Substituting in equation (12.18) gives

$$\overline{\Delta^2} = \frac{RTt}{3\pi\eta rN} \tag{12.21}$$

This equation was verified in 1909 by J. Perrin who observed the Brownian movement of relatively large particles, ca. $5(10)^{-5}$ cm. diameter, and obtained an early value of the Avogadro number.

EXERCISE 12.5

Find $\overline{\Delta^2}$ for a time interval of 1000 sec. for the gold particles described in Exercise 12.1 at 25° in water.

Ans. 4.87×10^{-3} cm.

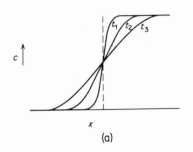

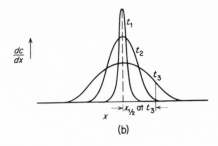

(a)   (b)

FIG. 12.7. Diffusion across a plane boundary.

The diffusion coefficient is usually obtained by observation of macroscopic changes in concentration rather than by use of equation (12.18). In a typical experimental arrangement a sharp boundary is formed between a solution or suspension and the pure solvent. After a time diffusion "blurs" this boundary as shown in Fig. 12.7 (a). The nature of the boundary can be observed with a *schlieren* optical system, which depends on the bending of light rays which pass through regions where the refractive index changes. The refractive index *gradient* and, therefore, the concentration *gradient* is the observed property, which varies as indicated in Fig. 12.7 (b). The variation in this quantity, dc/dx, with time t, and with distance from the original boundary x, is given by

$$\frac{dc}{dx} = \frac{-c_0}{2(\pi Dt)^{1/2}} e^{-x^2/4Dt} \qquad (12.22)$$

where c_0 is the concentration of the solution before diffusion.

For a given time of diffusion the shape of the dc/dx curve is determined by the exponential factor. In fact, the diffusion coefficient can be determined from a measured value of x corresponding to dc/dx equal to half its maximum value at a particular time of diffusion, as in Fig. 12.7 (b). This quantity, $x_{1/2}$, is related to D by

$$\tfrac{1}{2} = e^{-x_{1/2}^2/4Dt}$$

$$D = \frac{x_{1/2}^2}{4t \ln 2} \qquad (12.23)$$

Comparison of equation (12.23) with equation (12.18) shows that $x_{1/2}$ is approximately equal to the root-mean-square distance of Brownian movement, $\sqrt{\overline{\Delta^2}}$.

Some values of diffusion coefficients at 20° in water are given in Table 12.3.

EXERCISE 12.6

From the diffusion coefficient of insulin given in Table 12.2 estimate the time required for $x_{1/2}$ to become 1 mm. at 20° in water.   *Ans.* 4.4(10³) sec.

TABLE 12.2
DIFFUSION AND SEDIMENTATION PROPERTIES OF PROTEINS

Protein	Partial specific volume, $\bar{v}$ (cc. g.$^{-1}$)	Sedimentation coefficient, S_{20} (sec. $\times 10^{13}$)	Diffusion coefficient, D_{20} (cm.^{2} sec.$^{-1} \times 10^7$)	Molecular weight
Insulin	0.749	3.5	8.2	41,000
Hemoglobin	0.749	4.41	6.3	—
Catalase	0.73	11.3	4.1	250,000
Urease	0.73	18.6	3.5	480,000
Tobacco mosaic virus	0.73	185	0.53	31,600,000

12.5 Sedimentation

When the particles of a suspension have a density greater than that of the dispersion medium, they tend to settle under the influence of gravity. However, for small particles the rate of settling is extremely small. The rate of sedimentation can be increased in a high-speed centrifuge. The acceleration G of a centrifugal field is given by

$$G = \omega^2 x \tag{12.24}$$

where ω is the angular velocity and x the distance from the center of rotation. Centrifuges operating at speeds as high as 100,000 r.p.m. with the sample at a radial distance of 5 cm. are used in this type of work. Since the angular velocity in this case is $10^5 \cdot 2\pi/60$ radians per second, the radial acceleration is

$$G = 5(10^5 \cdot 2\pi/60)^2 = 5.5(10)^8 \text{ cm. sec.}^{-2}$$

which is 560,000 times the acceleration of gravity (980 cm. sec.$^{-2}$).

A particle of density ρ suspended in a medium of density ρ_0 has an effective mass (correcting for buoyancy) of $v(\rho - \rho_0)$, where v is its volume. In a centrifugal field, $G = \omega^2 x$, such a particle is subjected to a force

$$F' = v(\rho - \rho_0)\omega^2 x \tag{12.25}$$

The force of resistance to motion is proportional to the velocity of the particle

$$F'' = f\frac{dx}{dt} \tag{12.26}$$

where f is the frictional coefficient, given by Stokes's law, equation (12.20).

The velocity of sedimentation increases until the force of resistance to motion is equal to the centrifugal force, at which point the particle has achieved its terminal velocity. This condition is established in a very short time. Equating the right-hand sides of equations (12.25) and (12.26), we have

$$v(\rho - \rho_0)\omega^2 x = f\frac{dx}{dt} \tag{12.27}$$

For spherical particles $v = \frac{4}{3}\pi r^3, f = 6\pi\eta r$, and

$$S = \frac{dx/dt}{\omega^2 x} = \frac{2r^2(\rho - \rho_0)}{9\eta} \tag{12.28}$$

The left-hand side of equation (12.28), the rate of sedimentation in a unit centrifugal field, is called the *sedimentation coefficient*, symbol S. It has the dimension of time and is usually given in units of 10^{-13} sec., called a *svedberg*.

To illustrate equation (12.28), let us ask what magnitude of centrifugal field will be required to give a velocity of sedimentation of 1 mm. per minute for a typical colloidal suspension with particles of 100Å radius, $\rho = 1.5$, suspended in water. Solving for $\omega^2 x$ yields

$$\omega^2 x = \frac{(dx/dt)9\eta}{2r^2(\rho - \rho_0)} = \frac{(0.1/60) \times 9 \times 0.00895}{2 \times 10^{-12}(1.5 - 1.0)} = 1.35(10)^8 \text{ cm. sec.}^{-2}$$

which is well within the capability of modern centrifuges. The sedimentation coefficient in this example is

$$S = \frac{(0.1/60)}{1.35 \times 10^8} = 124 \text{ svedbergs}$$

The location of the boundary between a sedimenting suspension and the pure liquid above it can be followed by various optical methods, among them the schlieren method mentioned in connection with diffusion measurements. For a monodisperse colloid the boundary remains relatively sharp, and for mixtures of a limited number of well-defined particle sizes a corresponding number of boundaries is to be expected.

For sedimentation over a distance x in time t the sedimentation coefficient is obtained by integration of

$$S\omega^2 \int_0^t dt = \int_{x_1}^{x_2} \frac{dx}{x}$$

$$S = \frac{1}{\omega^2 t} \ln \frac{x_2}{x_1} \tag{12.29}$$

EXERCISE 12.7

The boundary in a monodisperse colloidal suspension in water at 20° moves from a radial distance of 4.4 cm. to 5.0 cm. in 1000 sec. at an angular velocity of 10^4 radians per sec. What is the sedimentation coefficient?   *Ans.* 12.8 svedbergs

Returning to equation (12.27), we replace $v(\rho - \rho_0)$ by $m(1 - \bar{v}\rho_0)$ where $\bar{v}$ is the partial specific volume of the dispersed phase. (Recall that $\bar{v} = 1/\rho$). The relation of the frictional coefficient to the diffusion coefficient is given by equation (12.19). Equation (12.27) may now be written

$$m(1 - \bar{v}\rho_0)\omega^2 x = \frac{RT}{ND} \frac{dx}{dt} \tag{12.30}$$

Collecting factors corresponding to S and noting that $mN = M$, the molecular weight of the particle, gives

$$M = \frac{RTS}{D(1 - \bar{v}\rho_0)} \tag{12.31}$$

In order to combine measurements of D and S they must be corrected to a common basis, usually water at 20°. Some values of S and D so corrected are given in Table 12.2.

EXERCISE 12.8

Complete Table 12.2 by computing the molecular weight of hemoglobin.

Ans. 6.8×10^4.

12.6 Light Scattering

Lord Rayleigh showed in 1871 that the scattering of light by particles smaller than the wave length of light is due to microscopic optical inhomogeneity. For a dilute suspension of spherical particles of radius $< \frac{1}{20}$ the wave length of the incident light, he obtained the following expression for the ratio of the intensity of light i_θ scattered at angle θ to incident light I_0:

$$\frac{i_\theta}{I_0} = \frac{8\pi^4 n r^6}{d^2 (\lambda')^4} \left(\frac{m^2 - 1}{m^2 + 2}\right)^2 (1 + \cos^2 \theta) \tag{12.32}$$

where n is the number of particles per cc., r is the radius of the particles, d is the distance between the observer and the scattering system, λ' is the wave length of light in the dispersion medium, and m is the ratio of the refractive index of the particles to that of the dispersion medium.

The factor $1 + \cos^2 \theta$ (θ is the angle of observation with respect to the beam axis) shows that the scattered intensity is a function of angle θ. A maximum intensity is observed at $\theta = 0°$ and 180° and falls to one-half the maximum at $\theta = 90°$ and 270°. In fact, the scattered light can be resolved into two plane-polarized components: i_1 polarized perpendicular to the plane containing the source of light, the scattering center, and the point of observation; and i_2 polarized in this plane. Figure 12.8 represents the angular dependence of $i_\theta = i_1 + i_2$ in graphical form. It is seen that i_1 is independent of angle, corresponding to the term 1 in $(1 + \cos^2 \theta)$, while i_2 goes to zero at 90° and 270°, as does $\cos^2 \theta$.

The light that we see coming from the sky at an angle from the sun on a clear day is scattered from submicroscopic particles including the molecules of the air. Equation (12.32) shows why this light is predominantly blue, for the factor $(\lambda')^4$ in the denominator requires that the scattered intensity increase with decreasing wave length. Conversely, when we observe the sun directly at sunset through a long atmospheric path, the predominant loss of blue

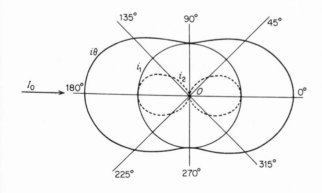

FIG. 12.8. Intensity of scattering by small spherical particles.

light by scattering gives the transmitted light its characteristic red color. When the size of the particle becomes greater than 1/20 of the wavelength, the angular dependence of the scattered light intensities is much more complex than that described by equation (12.32), and is a function of particle size as shown in Fig. 12.9.

12.7 Surface Tension

A drop of liquid in free fall tends to assume the shape of smallest surface area, namely, a spherical one. (Falling in air, the shape is somewhat deformed by the flow of air.) Drops of water on a waxed surface also tend to distorted spheres. These phenomena indicate that the state of minimum energy for a liquid drop is the state of minimum surface. That

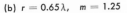

(b) $r = 0.65\lambda$, $m = 1.25$

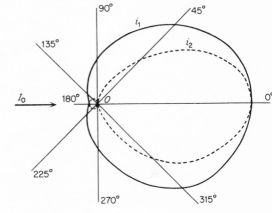

(a) $r = 0.13\lambda$, $m = 1.25$

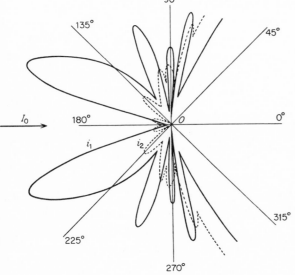

FIG. 12.9. Intensity of scattering by large spherical particles [from M. Bender, *J. Chem. Ed.*, **29**, 15 (1952)].

is, energy must be supplied to increase the surface area of a drop of liquid.

The origin of this characteristic of liquids lies in the attractive forces existing between the molecules. For a molecule in the body of the liquid, these forces tend to cancel as to direction so that there is no net force. On the other hand, a molecule in the surface is acted upon by the attractive forces of the molecules below it, but the opposing forces are absent. This results in a net force directed perpendicular to the surface and into the body of the liquid. In order to increase the surface area of a body of liquid, molecules must move from the body of the liquid to the surface against the forces of molecular attraction. Therefore, work must be done to increase the surface area.

A simple method of defining the work required to increase the surface area of a body of liquid is indicated in Fig. 12.10, which shows a liquid film on a rectangular frame of fine wire. Some force F on the movable side is required to maintain the film at a given area. This force is parallel to the surface of the film and perpendicular to the edge at which the surface meets the movable wire. If the force is increased by an infinitesimal amount, the surface area of the film will increase (if frictional resistance to movement of the wire is neglected). Suppose that the wire moves out a distance d, increasing the surface area of the film by $2dl$. (There are two liquid surfaces, one on each side of the film.) The work done is Fd, and this is proportional to the increase in surface area. The proportionality constant is the surface tension of the liquid, γ.

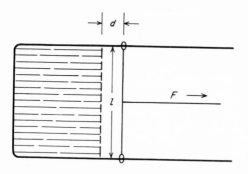

FIG. 12.10. Surface energy.

FIG. 12.11. Capillary rise.

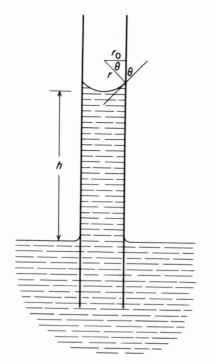

$$Fd = 2dl\gamma$$

$$\gamma = Fd/2dl = \text{energy/area}$$

$$\gamma = F/2l = \text{force/length} \qquad (12.33)$$

Thus, we see that the surface tension is the work required to produce a unit increase in surface area. In the c.g.s. system the units are ergs cm.$^{-2}$ or dynes cm^{-1}.

The rise or depression of liquids in capillary tubes is a common manifestation of surface tension. A liquid rises if it forms a surface which is concave upward, for in this case the pressure above the surface is less than that below. Since the pressure of the gas above the surface is essentially constant and the same as that on the liquid surface in the main reservoir, the liquid rises until the hydrostatic head is equal to ΔP.

The radius of curvature of the liquid, r, may not be the same as that of the capillary tube, r_0, as indicated in Fig. 12.11. That is, the contact angle of the liquid surface with the wall of the capillary, θ, is not necessarily zero. The relationship between r and r_0, by a simple geometric construction, is found to be

$$\cos \theta = \frac{r_0}{r}$$

and the pressure difference across the surface is

$$\Delta P = \frac{2\gamma \cos \theta}{r_0} \qquad (12.34)$$

This is to be equated to the downward pressure of the column of liquid of height h and density ρ.

$$P = \frac{\text{force}}{\text{area}} = \frac{\pi r_0^2 \rho g h}{\pi r_0^2}$$

and

$$\frac{2\gamma \cos \theta}{r_0} = h\rho g$$

Solving for γ yields

$$\gamma = \frac{r_0 \rho g h}{2 \cos \theta} \qquad (12.35)$$

In many cases θ is practically zero, and the use of the approximate form $\gamma = \frac{1}{2} h \rho g r_0$ is justified.

EXERCISE 12.9

A liquid of density 1.5 gm. cm^{-1} rises to a height of 1 cm. in a capillary of 0.5 mm. radius. Given that the contact angle is zero, find γ.   *Ans.* 36.7 dynes cm.$^{-2}$.

12.8 Surface Films

The presence of a solute often has little effect upon the surface tension of a liquid. However, it is found that a few classes of substances such as organic acids, alcohols, and esters exhibit a strong depression of the surface tension even at small solute concentrations. Soaps, the alkali metal salts of fatty acids, are especially active in this respect. For example, a 0.002 N aqueous solution of sodium oleate has a surface tension of 25 dynes cm.$^{-1}$ as compared to 72.8 dynes cm.$^{-1}$ for pure water.

The strong effect of soaps on the surface tension suggests that these substances must be present at much higher concentration in the surface than in the bulk of the liquid phase. They may be said to be *adsorbed* at the interface. J. Willard Gibbs obtained, by rigorous thermodynamic treatment (see W. J. Moore, *Physical Chemistry*, 3rd ed., Prentice-Hall, Inc., Englewood Cliffs, N. J., 1963, p. 737), a relation between the change of surface tension with concentration of solute, $d\gamma/dc$, and the excess concentration of solute in the surface, Γ, in moles cm.$^{-2}$

$$\Gamma = -\frac{c}{RT}\frac{d\gamma}{dc} \qquad (12.36)$$

This equation shows that a substance which is concentrated in the surface (Γ positive) will lower the surface tension ($d\gamma/dc$ negative). Only a substance which is present at lower concentration in the surface than in the main body of liquid (Γ negative) can produce an increase in surface tension ($d\gamma/dc$ positive).

In the light of modern concepts of bond polarity it is not difficult to understand why the long chain fatty acids and their salts should concentrate in the surface of an aqueous solution. The carboxyl group is highly polar and as such is compatible with water. In the low molecular weight acids the influence of this group dominates the character of the molecule. Such acids are soluble in water and do not have a strong effect on the surface tension. As the molecular weight and, therefore, the length of the —CH_2— chain increase, the solubility decreases, and the effect on the surface tension increases. This is to be attributed to the increasing influence of the nonpolar hydrocarbon portion of the molecule.

W. D. Harkins suggested that the fatty acid molecules in the surface of an aqueous solution tend to be oriented in such a fashion that the water soluble carboxyl group or "head" of the molecule is in the body of the solution, while the insoluble hydrocarbon "tail" projects above the surface. This picture received considerable support from the study of the surface films formed by insoluble substances such as the high molecular weight fatty acids. The experimental technique, due to I. Langmuir, consists of allowing an oily film to spread on a clear water surface enclosed by one movable and one fixed barrier. The latter is attached to a delicate torsion balance for measurement of the horizontal force exerted by the film as it is compressed by the movable barrier. The force per unit length of barrier as measured by the torsion balance is called the film pressure, since it is the two-dimensional analog of gas pressure.

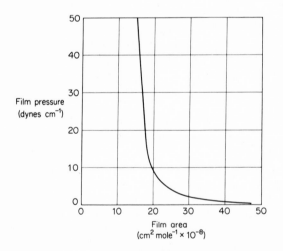

FIG. 12.12. Film pressure vs. area.

Film pressure (dynes cm^{-1})

Film area (cm^2 mole$^{-1} \times 10^{-8}$)

When the film pressure is measured as a function of film area, curves such as that in Fig. 12.12 are obtained. As the area is decreased, the film pressure shows an abrupt increase at an area of ca. 18×10^8 cm^2 mole^{-1}. Langmuir concluded that at this point the surface consists of a tightly packed monomolecular layer of molecules and that further compression must result in "crumpling" the film and formation of multimolecular layers.

If the critical area represents a monomolecular layer, the area per molecule becomes

$$\frac{18 \times 10^8}{6 \times 10^{23}} = 30\text{Å}^2/\text{molecule}$$

The area per molecule is nearly constant for fatty acids over a considerable range of carbon chain lengths. This is to be expected if the carbon chain is oriented vertically with respect to the surface and the area measured is the crosssectional area of the chain. This interpretation is confirmed by X-ray diffraction measurements of similar dimensions in pure solids.

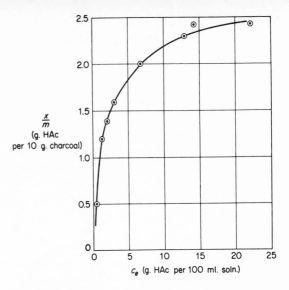

Fig. 12.13. Adsorption isotherm for acetic acid on charcoal.

12.9 Adsorption

When a solid of large surface area per unit mass is exposed to a gas or solution, a significant amount of material may be *adsorbed* on the surface of the solid. The adsorbed substance may be held by a variety of forces, depending on the nature of the system. If these forces are analogous to those responsible for chemical bond formation, i.e., coulombic attraction of oppositely charged ions or electron pair bond formation, the process is called *chemisorption*. The heat of adsorption in such cases is comparable to chemical bond energies, and the process of adsorption is frequently irreversible. Also, it is to be expected that the adsorption will then be limited to a single layer of strongly bound molecules on the surface. In contrast, there are many instances in which the heat of adsorption is rather small and comparable to the heat of condensation. This suggests that the force responsible for the phenomenon is of the nonspecific type known as the van der Waals force, as in liquefaction, and the process is called *physical adsorption*. It would be expected in this case that it will be possible to form multimolecular layers of adsorbed molecules on the surface, with the outer layers behaving approximately as a liquid or solid.

Adsorption can be measured from the depletion of material in the gaseous or liquid phase. For example, if aqueous acetic acid of known concentration c_0 is exposed to powdered charcoal, the concentration of acetic acid decreases to an equilibrium value c_e. From the decrement in concentration the amount of acetic acid adsorbed can be calculated $(c_0 - c_e)V$, where V is the volume of the solution.

For a given system, the amount of material adsorbed is found to be a function of (1) the amount of *adsorbent* (solid phase), (2) the concentration of *adsorbate* (substance adsorbed) in the phase in contact with the surface, and (3) the temperature. If the adsorbent is of uniform particle size, i.e., has a fixed surface area per unit weight, the amount adsorbed at a given concentration and temperature will be proportional to the weight of adsorbent. Therefore, it is customary to give the amount adsorbed in weight, x, per unit weight of adsorbent, m.

When the dependence of adsorption, measured by x/m, on concentration is determined at a fixed temperature the resulting curve is an *adsorption isotherm*.

Such curves often look like Fig. 12.13, where the concentration of interest is the equilibrium concentration of adsorbate.

The shape of the adsorption isotherm suggests that the capacity of the surface for adsorbed material is limited and that at increasing concentrations of adsorbate this capacity is more and more closely approached. Langmuir developed a simple theory of adsorption which satisfactorily describes such systems by assuming that the surface is capable of adsorbing a layer one molecule thick and no more. When adsorption equilibrium is reached, the rate of desorption is equal to the rate of adsorption.

This theory is most easily considered in its application to adsorption of a gas. The rate of adsorption is proportional to the rate of collisions with the surface. This rate, in turn, is proportional to gas pressure and to the fraction of the surface which is unoccupied by adsorbed molecules.

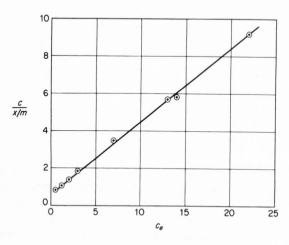

Fig. 12.14. Test of the Langmuir adsorption isotherm.

$$\text{rate of adsorption} = k_1 P(1 - \theta) \tag{12.37}$$

where θ is the fraction of the surface occupied.

The rate of desorption will be proportional to the fraction of surface occupied:

$$\text{rate of desorption} = k_2 \theta \tag{12.38}$$

Equating the right-hand sides of equations (12.37) and (12.38) as the condition for adsorption equilibrium and solving for θ yields

$$\theta = \frac{k_1 P}{(k_1 P + k_2)} \tag{12.39}$$

The weight of substance adsorbed per unit weight of adsorbent, x/m, is proportional to θ, and

$$\frac{x}{m} = \frac{aP}{(1 + bP)} \tag{12.40}$$

or

$$\frac{P}{x/m} = \frac{1}{a} + \frac{bP}{a} \tag{12.41}$$

This shows that a plot of $P/(x/m)$ versus P (or c in the case of adsorption from solution) should be linear. The data of Fig. 12.13 are expressed in this way in Fig. 12.14.

The adsorption of gaseous nitrogen on silica at liquid air temperatures is a typical example of physical adsorption and the adsorption isotherm has the shape shown in Fig. 12.15. The horizontal axis is pressure relative to the saturation vapor pressure of liquid nitrogen at that temperature. The first portion of the curve obeys the Langmuir adsorption isotherm, and it is believed that this corresponds to partial coverage of the surface. The second portion of the curve, at $P/P_0 > ca.$ 0.3, may be due to development of multimolecular layers.

A theory of multilayer adsorption of gases, due to S. Brunauer, P.H. Emmett, and E. Teller [*J. Am. Chem. Soc.*, **60**, 309 (1938)], gives an adsorption isotherm having the correct S shape.

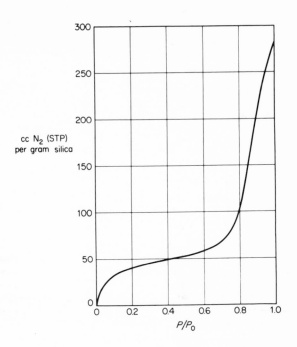

Fig. 12.15. Adsorption of nitrogen on silica at 77°K.

$$V = \frac{V_m C P}{(P_0 - P)[1 + (C - 1)(P/P_0)]}$$

$$(12.42)$$

where V is the volume adsorbed at pressure P, P_0 is the saturation vapor pressure of the adsorbate, V_m is the volume of adsorbed gas corresponding to a monomolecular layer, and C is a constant. For purposes of testing, the equation may be put in the form

$$\frac{P}{V(P_0 - P)} = \frac{1}{V_m C} + \frac{C - 1}{V_m C}\frac{P}{P_0} \qquad (12.43)$$

A plot of the left-hand side of this equation versus P/P_0 should give a straight line with slope $(C - 1)/V_m C$ and intercept $1/V_m C$. Evaluation of these two quantities and simultaneous solution gives V_m, the volume of gas required to form a monomolecular layer. Using a value of the cross-sectional area per molecule obtained from liquid or solid densities, this figure can be used to estimate the surface area of finely divided solids which exhibit this type of adsorption.

12.10 Electrical Properties of Surfaces

If ions of one sign are preferentially adsorbed at a solid solution interface, a net charge or potential difference develops across the interface. This phenomenon was first observed as the *electroosmosis* effect. It is found that when a potential difference is applied to electrodes dipping into an electrolyte

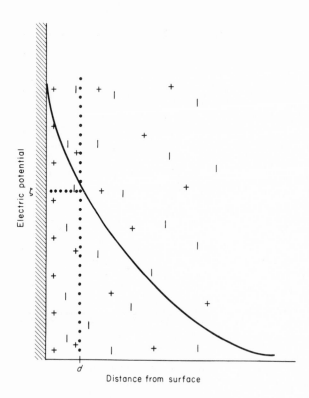

Fig. 12.16. Ion atmosphere at interface. The moving boundary is at d.

solution on opposite sides of a porous plug or fine capillary tube, a flow of solution results. By this same token, when a solution is forced through such a barrier by hydrostatic pressure, a potential difference develops between the solution on one side of the barrier and that on the other. It is called the *streaming potential*.

These phenomena can be understood in terms of an electric double layer illustrated in Fig. 12.16. A layer of ions of one sign (with their associated water of hydration) is firmly adsorbed on the solid surface, the sign of the charge depending upon the nature of the surface and other conditions. The surface as a whole is electrically neutral, and an equal number of opposite electric charges are present in an adjacent ionic atmosphere which, as the term implies, becomes more attenuated as distance from the surface increases. When the solid surface and fluid are in relative motion, there exists a velocity gradient, and a thin film of solvent, together with the ions it contains, is immobilized near the wall. Part of the ion atmosphere moves with the solvent, and part (together with adsorbed ions) effectively belongs to the surface. As a result, the liquid phase and the wall have different net electric charge, and the application of an electric field produces relative motion.

A simple expression can be obtained for the velocity of flow through a capillary in terms of the charge q per unit area and the potential gradient X along the tube. The force causing motion is Xq. An opposing viscous force is given by $\eta v/d$ per unit area, where v is the velocity of solution and d the effective distance from the surface to the moving boundary. These two forces are equal in steady-state flow.

$$Xq = \frac{\eta v}{d} \tag{12.44}$$

Solving for v yields

$$v = \frac{Xqd}{\eta} \tag{12.45}$$

The properties of the diffuse double layer described by q and d are often given in terms of the *zeta potential* ζ, the potential difference of a condenser of charge q per unit area and distance d between plates

$$\zeta = \frac{4\pi q d}{\epsilon} \qquad (12.46)$$

where ϵ is the dielectric constant in the double layer. Substituting for qd in equation (12.44) yields

$$v = \frac{X\zeta\epsilon}{4\pi\eta} \qquad (12.47)$$

The existence of zeta potential at the surface of colloidal particles gives rise to two complementary phenomena. One is the *Dorn effect:* the development of a potential difference upon sedimentation of a suspension. This is analogous to the streaming potential, except that in this case the solid phase moves rather than the liquid. The second phenomenon is more closely related to electro-osmosis and is called *electrophoresis.* In this case a potential gradient applied to a suspension causes migration of the suspended particles in a direction corresponding to their charge. The charge on the particles may be due to absorbed ions, or, as in the case of the proteins, due to the inherent ionizability of certain groups in the molecule.

Since proteins contain both —NH$_2$ and —COOH groups, it is expected that at low pH acidic dissociation will be repressed and base hydrolysis to form —NH$_3^+$ will be favored. Under these conditions the protein molecules should exhibit electrophoretic migration toward the cathode. Conversely, at high pH acidic ionization to form COO$^-$ is favored and base hydrolysis repressed. Migration, therefore, occurs toward the anode. For each protein there will be a particular pH at which equal numbers of positive and negative charges are present, resulting in zero electrophoretic mobility. This is the *isoelectric point.*

The existence of adsorbed ions on the surface of lyophobic colloids has a great deal to do with their stability. The tendency of such particles to coagulate is counteracted by coulombic repulsion of the charged surfaces when such particles approach each other. The stability of such suspensions is strongly dependent on the type and amounts of electrolytes present in the solution.

Lyophobic colloids are coagulated by addition of relatively small amounts of electrolyte to the suspension medium. The critical concentration for coagulation of a particular colloid depends on the nature of the electrolyte. Those most effective are those having multiply charged ions of sign opposite to that of the colloidal particles. For example, the negatively charged colloid arsenic trisulfide is coagulated by 0.040 M KCl and 0.033 M K$_2$SO$_4$, but only 0.00023 M PbCl$_2$ and only 0.000093 M AlCl$_3$ are required. A positively charged suspension is equally sensitive to multiply charged negative ions.

The coagulation behavior of lyophobic colloids can be interpreted as a requirement that the zeta potential be reduced to a certain value before coagulation occurs. This is accomplished by adsorption of oppositely charged ions, the more effective ones being those bearing multiple charges.

SUMMARY, CHAPTER 12

1. Kinetic properties of colloids
   Osmotic pressure

$$\lim_{c \to 0} \left(\frac{\Pi}{c} \right) = \frac{RT}{M}$$

Viscosity, defined by $F = \eta \dfrac{vA}{x}$

$$\eta_{sp.} = \frac{(\eta - \eta_0)}{\eta_0}$$

$$[\eta] = \lim_{c \to 0} \left(\frac{\eta_{sp.}}{c} \right) = kM^a$$

Brownian movement, diffusion

$$\frac{dn}{dt} = -\left(\frac{\overline{\Delta^2}}{2t} \right) \frac{dn}{dx}$$

$$D = \frac{\overline{\Delta^2}}{2t} = \frac{RT}{Nf}$$

At a plane boundary

$$\frac{dc}{dx} = \frac{-c_0}{2(\pi Dt)^{1/2}} e^{-x^2/4Dt}$$

Sedimentation

$$S = \frac{dx/dt}{\omega^2 x} = \frac{2r^2(\rho - \rho_0)}{9\eta}$$

2. Optical properties
   Rayleigh scattering

$$\frac{i_\theta}{I_0} = \frac{8\pi^4 nr^6}{d^2 (\lambda')^4} \left(\frac{m^2 - 1}{m^2 + 2} \right)^2 (1 + \cos^2 \theta)$$

Dissymmetry of scattering, $i_{45°}/i_{135°}$, depends on particle size and shape.

3. Surface properties
   Surface tension

$$\gamma = \frac{F}{2l}$$

Capillary rise

$$\gamma = \frac{r_0 \rho g h}{2 \cos \theta}$$

Gibbs equation for surface concentration, Γ

$$\Gamma = -\frac{c}{RT}\frac{d\gamma}{dc}$$

Langmuir adsorption isotherm (monomolecular layer)

$$\frac{x}{m} = \frac{aP}{(1+bP)}$$

Brunauer-Emmett-Teller adsorption isotherm (multimolecular layer)

$$V = \frac{V_m CP}{(P_0 - P)[1 + (C-1)(P/P_0)]}$$

4. Electrical properties—electrocapillarity, electroosmosis, electrophoresis, streaming potential

Zeta potential,

$$\zeta = \frac{4\pi qd}{\epsilon}$$

Velocity of flow in an electric field

$$v = \frac{X\zeta\epsilon}{4\pi\eta}$$

Isoelectric point—pH of minimum electrophoretic mobility
Coagulation of lyophobic colloids—critical zeta potential

PROBLEMS, CHAPTER 12

1. Estimate the surface area per unit weight for a uniform suspension of spherical particles 10^{-6} cm. in diameter and having a density of 1.5 g. cc.$^{-1}$.
Ans. 4×10^6 cm^2 g^{-1}.

2. A steel ball of density 8.0 g. cc.$^{-1}$ and radius 2 mm. is observed to fall with a terminal velocity of 1.0 cm. sec.$^{-1}$ in a liquid of density 1.8 g. cc.$^{-1}$. Use Stokes's law to find the viscosity of the liquid.   *Ans.* 54 poise

3. Estimate the pressure (in dynes cm.$^{-2}$) required at $25°$ to force water through a tube 1 mm. in radius and 1 meter long at a rate of 1 cc. sec.$^{-1}$. At what rate would glycerine flow through this tube with the same applied pressure?
Ans. 2.28×10^4 dynes cm^{-2}.

4. Find the capillary depression of mercury in a tube of diameter 1 mm. Assume $\theta = 0$. The density is 13.55 g. cc.$^{-1}$; the surface tension is 460 dynes cm^{-1}.
Ans. 1.38 cm.

5. The following values of the specific viscosity versus concentration of polystyrene in benzene were obtained. Plot $\eta_{sp.}/c$ versus c and find the intrinsic viscosity.

c (wt. %)	0.03	0.07	0.12	0.25	0.50
$\eta_{sp.}$	0.123	0.293	0.528	1.19	3.00

Ans. 4.0.

6. The following measurements of osmotic pressure were made on a suspension of polyisobutylene in cyclohexane at 25°.

c (g./100 cc. soln.)	2.00	1.50	1.00	0.50
Π (dynes cm.$^{-2}$) $\times 10^{-3}$	16.09	9.92	5.29	2.03

Plot Π/c versus c and extrapolate to zero concentration. From this limit obtain the number average molecular weight of the polymer. *Ans.* $M_n \cong 87,000$.

7. The following data for intrinsic viscosity versus number average molecular weight were obtained for polyisobutylene in cyclohexane. Plot log $[\eta]$ versus log M_n and find the value of a in equation (12.13).

M_n	202,000	79,300	39,700	13,970	8,170
$[\eta]$	0.866	0.495	0.303	0.165	0.118

Ans. 0.63.

8. The following data were obtained for the adsorption of nitrogen on mica at 90°K. Assume a constant weight of mica.

P (atm.)	12.8	7.3	4.9	3.9	2.8
x (mm.^{3} at 20°, 760 mm.)	25.5	21.6	17.0	15.1	12.0

Show that these data fit the Langmuir adsorption isotherm.

9. Svedberg made the following observations of Brownian movement on a suspension of gold particles in water at 20°:

Time (sec.)	1	2	3	4
Δ (10^{-4} cm.)	4.1	5.8	7.6	8.2

Show that these data obey the law of Brownian movement and, assuming uniform spheres, find the radius of the particles.

10. When 0.2 ml. of a 0.01 M alcoholic solution of palmitic acid was placed on a water surface, the resulting monolayer spread to an area of 2.5×10^3 cm.^{2} Find the cross-sectional area per hydrocarbon chain.

11. A benzene solution containing 7.85 mg. of stearic acid was spread upon an aqueous solution of 10^{-4} M calcium carbonate at pH = 8.5. The area of the film formed was 3.35×10^4 cm.^{2}. When the film was skimmed from the surface its dry weight was 8.1 mg. and it contained 7.1 weight per cent calcium. Find

(a) The area per molecule.

(b) The per cent of the acid converted to the calcium salt.

[I. Langmuir and V. J. Shaeffer, *J. Am. Chem. Soc.*, **58**, 284 (1936)].

Ans. (a) 20.0×10^{-16} cm.^{2}. (b) 100%.

---

12. The viscosities of molten polymers can be represented by log $\eta = A + CM_w^{1/2}$. The polyester formed from 18.87 grams of ϵ-caprolactam and 1.445 grams of stearic acid has a melt viscosity of 10.0 poise at 25°. If $A = -1.32$ and $C = 0.026$, find M_w. [J. R. Schaefgen and P. J. Flory, *J. Am. Chem. Soc.*, **70**, 2709 (1948).]

13. The measured value of the diffusion coefficient of ovalbumin in water at 15.5° is 0.063×10^{-5} cm.^{2} sec.$^{-1}$

(a) Assuming uniform spheres, find the radius of the particles.

(b) Taking the density of the particles as 1.1 g. cc.$^{-1}$ find the molecular weight of this protein.

14. Find the radius of spherical gold particles which fall 1 cm. in water at 20°.
   (a) In 0.5 sec.
   (b) In 7 hrs.
   (c) In 29 days.
The density of gold is 19.3 g. cc.$^{-1}$.

15. A nondiffusible electrolyte NaX is present on one side of a semipermeable membrane at a concentration 0.1 M. Find the ratios of NaCl concentrations on the two sides of the membrane for the case that the concentration of chloride ion in the solution of NaX is (a) 10^{-3} M, (b) 10^{-2} M, (c) 10^{-1} M, and (d) 1.0 M.

16. The following data were obtained for the surface tension at 18° of aqueous solutions of isobutyric acid.

Conc. (M)	0	0.0187	0.0250	0.0500	0.100	0.250
γ (dynes cm.$^{-1}$)	73.0	68.6	67.3	63.3	57.7	48.3
		0.500	1.00			
		40.7	32.6			

   (a) Use these data to test the empirical equation of Szyszkowski [*Z. physik. Chem.*, **64**, 385 (1908)].

$$\frac{(\gamma_0 - \gamma)}{\gamma_0} = B \ln\left(\frac{c}{A} + 1\right)$$

where c is concentration, A ($= 0.051$) is constant for all concentrations of isobutyric acid, and B is found to be the same for all fatty acids. Evaluate B.

   (b) Use the value of B in the preceding equation to evaluate $d\gamma/d \ln c$ at high concentrations where $c \gg A$.

   (c) Use the preceding result to evaluate Γ in the Gibbs equation for high concentrations.

   (d) Find the effective area per molecule in the surface layer of isobutyric acid.

17. For a tube of the construction shown in the figure a sample of liquid assumes an equilibrium position. Explain the effect and show that the equation $\gamma = h\rho g Rr/2(R - r)$ applies where h is the overall height of the liquid column, ρ is the density of the liquid, g is the acceleration of gravity, R and r are the radii of the large and small bore, respectively. Assume that $\theta = 0$. [See. S Natelson and A. H. Pearl, *J. Am. Chem. Soc.*, **57**, 1520 (1935).]

   (a) At 26° for $R = 0.097$ cm., $r = 0.015$ cm., $h = 8.31$ cm. for water. Find γ.

   (b) Show that when the tube is held in a horizontal position and a pressure P applied at the narrow end, $\gamma = PRr/2(R - r)$. Find P for water.

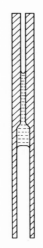

Prob. Fig. 12.17.

18. At sedimentation equilibrium the rate of sedimentation across any plane in the suspension is equal and opposite to the rate of diffusion across that plane. The rate of sedimentation is given by

$$\left(\frac{dn}{dt}\right)_s = \frac{nm_e g}{f}$$

where n is the number of particles per unit volume, m_e is the effective mass per particle and is equal to $\frac{4}{3}\pi r^3(\rho - \rho_0)$, g is the acceleration of gravity, and f is the frictional coefficient. The rate of diffusion is

$$\left(\frac{dn}{dt}\right)_D = -D\frac{dn}{dx} = -\frac{RT}{Nf}\frac{dn}{dx}$$

Equate these expressions and integrate between limits n_1 and n_2, x_1 and x_2 to obtain

$$\ln\left(\frac{n_2}{n_1}\right) = -m_e g(x_2 - x_1)N/RT$$

Perrin used this expression to obtain a value of N from the observation that for gamboge particles of $\rho = 1.195$ and of radius 3.67×10^{-5} cm. in water at 20° ($\rho_0 = 0.998$) the ratio $n_2/n_1 = 0.3$ for $x_2 - x_1 = 0.1$ mm. Find N from these data.

13

ATOMIC
STRUCTURE

13.1 The Electrical Nature of Matter

The phenomena of electrochemistry have already served to demonstrate that some forms of matter are composed of electrically charged particles. In many other circumstances as well, the electrical nature of matter can be observed. In particular, it has been found that although gases are electrical insulators under ordinary circumstances, they can also be made to conduct electric currents. If a potential difference is established between two electrodes in a gas-filled tube, no current flows until a certain critical potential gradient is reached, at which point a visible discharge occurs and current flows readily through the gas. Conduction may be induced at lower potentials by irradiating the tube with X-rays or radiations from radioactive substances; in fact, this phenomenon is used to measure the intensity of the radiations.

An important difference exists between conduction by an electrolytic solution and by a dielectric medium such as a gas. In the former case Ohm's law is obeyed at all values of the applied voltage; in the latter it is not. In electrolytic conduction the ions are present before the field is applied and their velocity increases in proportion to the applied field. In dielectric media, on the contrary, there are no charged particles in the absence of an electric field, and they begin to appear only at rather high field strengths. Presumably the field is responsible for their formation. The study of the nature of the particles produced in gas discharges has furnished important information about the constitution of the atom.

13.2 Cathode Rays

Very early in the study of the nature of the electric discharge in gases, it was noted that a particular radiation seemed to be coming from the cathode. This radiation could pass through an opening in the anode and cause fluorescence in the glass wall of the tube where it struck, as shown in Fig. 13.1.

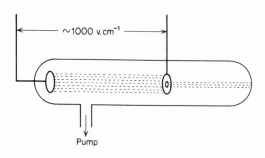

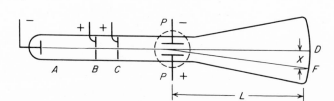

FIG. 13.1. Conduction of electricity in gases.

Simple tests serve to demonstrate that cathode rays are bent by electric and magnetic fields and, therefore, must be a stream of charged particles of finite mass rather than weightless electromagnetic radiations. These particles are called *electrons*, and the direction of curvature indicates that they have a negative charge.

The curvature of cathode rays by electric and magnetic fields was first measured quantitatively by J. J. Thomson in 1897, using an experimental arrangement such as that shown in Fig. 13.2. Cathode rays are generated by electric discharge in a gas at low pressure in chamber *A*, defined into a narrow beam by slits in electrodes *B* and *C*, and produce fluorescence in the glass wall of the tube where they strike, *D*. If a potential difference with the indicated polarity is imposed across the electrodes *PP* through which the beam passes, the position of impact of the cathode rays will be shifted to a point such as *F*.

The behavior of the particles in the region of the electric field is analyzed in

FIG. 13.2. Cathode rays.

detail in Fig. 13.3. In the region between the horizontal lines a uniform electric field exerts a force at right angles to the direction of the ray. The force acting on a particle of mass m and of charge e in an electric field of strength E is Ee. This force produces an acceleration Ee/m directed toward the positive electrode and at right angles to the direction of the ray. If the angle of deflection is small, the time of transit through the field, during which transverse acceleration occurs, is l/v, where v is the velocity of the particles in the ray and l is the distance

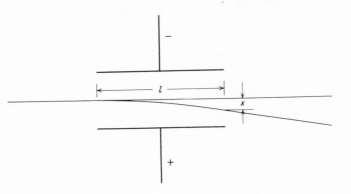

traveled in the field. Applying the simple law of motion for distance traveled under a constant acceleration (distance $= \frac{1}{2}$ acc. $\times$ time^2), we have, for the vertical displacement,

$$x = \frac{Ee}{2m}\left(\frac{l}{v}\right)^2 \tag{13.1}$$

This may be solved for e/m, the charge-to-mass ratio of the particles composing the cathode ray.

$$\frac{e}{m} = \frac{2xv^2}{El^2} \tag{13.2}$$

Actually, the deflection X is measured at some distance L from the region of deflection but by simple proportion, $x/l = X/L$. (See Fig. 13.2).

The velocity of the particles may be obtained by superimposing, in the region of the electric field, a magnetic field of strength H, sufficient to return the beam to the original position D. Such a field will be produced by a magnet with pole pieces above and below the plane of the paper in Figs. 13.2 and 13.3. The force exerted by a magnetic field on a charged particle depends on the velocity of the particle as well as on its charge and is given by Hev. When the forces of the two fields are equal and opposite,

$$Hev = Ee$$

and

$$v = \frac{E}{H} \tag{13.3}$$

Substituting for v in equation (13.2), we have

$$\frac{e}{m} = \frac{2xE}{H^2l^2} \tag{13.4}$$

A consistent set of units must be used for the quantities in equation (13.4). Such a set would be the mks (meter-kilogram-second) system in which E is in volts per meter and H in webers per square meter (1 weber meter^{-2} $= 10^4$ gauss). In this case e/m is obtained in coulombs per kilogram. The most recent value of e/m for cathode rays is 1.7588×10^{11} coulomb kg.$^{-1}$.

In the type of experiment which has just been described it is significant that all particles describe the same trajectory. It follows from equation (13.4) that they must all have a common value of e/m. It would appear highly probable that these particles have common values of e and of m and consist of but one species.

Cathode rays or streams of electrons can also be obtained from heated metals or metal oxides as in the filaments of ratio tubes. In every instance the value of e/m is precisely the same, and it is evident that the electron is a particle common to all kinds of matter.

EXERCISE 13.1

Typical values for the experimental parameters in the Thomson experiment are $E = 10^3$ v. m.$^{-1}$, $l = 10^{-2}$ m., and $x = 10^{-3}$ m. Find the velocity of these electrons. *Ans.* 3.0×10^6 m. sec.$^{-1}$.

13.3 The Charge on the Electron

To evaluate e and m separately requires an independent determination of the charge on the electron, combined with the value of e/m obtained above. The first accurate determination of e was made by R. A. Millikan in 1909 in the classic oil drop experiment. Microscopic droplets of oil produced by an "atomizer" were injected into an air-filled region between two electrodes, as shown in Fig. 13.4. Ionization of the air by X-rays or radioactive radiations caused attachment of one or more electrons to some of the droplets. The motion of these droplets was observed through a microscope. In the absence of an electric field the droplets fall under the influence of gravity, reaching a constant velocity at which the gravitational force is balanced by the viscous resistance of the medium (air). Stokes's law describes the force F on a spherical body of radius r moving through a medium of viscosity η with velocity v.

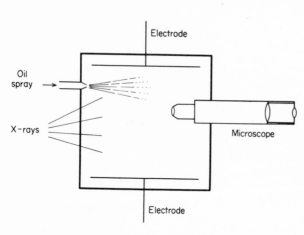

FIG. 13.4. The Millikan oil drop experiment.

$$F = 6\pi\eta rv \tag{13.5}$$

The gravitational force is given by the effective mass of the particle (actual mass less the mass of air displaced) times the acceleration of gravity g.

$$F = \tfrac{4}{3}\pi r^3(\rho - \rho_0)g \tag{13.6}$$

where ρ is the density of the oil and ρ_0 is the density of the medium in which it falls. In free fall, equations (13.5) and (13.6) give, by simultaneous solution, the radius of the droplet from its observed maximum velocity.

$$r = \sqrt{\frac{18\eta v}{4(\rho - \rho_0)g}} \tag{13.7}$$

If the same droplet is subjected to an electric field of such polarity and strength that it neither rises nor falls, then the electric force Ee may be equated to the gravitational force and we have

$$Ee = \tfrac{4}{3}\pi r^3(\rho - \rho_0)g \tag{13.8}$$

Since r is known, measurement of the value of E which fulfills this condition gives e, the charge on the droplet.

More accurate results are obtained by simply measuring a new maximum velocity of fall or rise in the presence of the electric field as compared with that in the absence of the field. In this case a term for the force of resistance of the medium is simply added to the force of the electric field when these forces act in the same direction, or subtracted when they operate in opposite directions. For instance, if the field increases the velocity of descent is

$$Ee + \tfrac{4}{3}\pi r^3(\rho - \rho_0)g = 6\pi\eta rv \tag{13.9}$$

The values of charge obtained by this technique are not all identical, but are small integral multiples of a single quantity, since more than one electron may become attached to a droplet. The most recent value of the charge on the electron is 1.60210×10^{-19} coulomb (4.80298×10^{-10} electrostatic units), and therefore the mass of the electron is 9.1091×10^{-28} g.

The charge on the electron may be combined with the value of the faraday, determined as indicated in Chapter 10, to obtain an accurate value of Avogadro's number N, the number of molecules (atoms) in a gram-molecular (atomic) weight. Since 96,487.0 coulombs are required for liberation of 1 gram-atomic weight of hydrogen or deposition of 1 gram-equivalent weight of any metal, which we assume requires 1 electron,

$$N = \frac{96,487.0}{1.60210 \times 10^{-19}} = 6.02252 \times 10^{23} \text{ atoms per g.-at. wt.}$$

Avogadro's number may in turn be used to compute the mass of any type of atom. For example, the hydrogen atom has a mass of

$$m_H = \frac{1.00797}{6.02252 \times 10^{23}} = 1.67366 \times 10^{-24} \text{ g.}$$

This is the lightest type of atom known.

The mass of the electron is much less than that of any atom. It is only about $\frac{1}{1835}$ as heavy as a hydrogen atom. Therefore, the electron, the negatively charged particle common to all atoms, constitutes only a very minor fraction of the mass of an atom. The positive ion formed by electron loss possesses practically all of the mass of the atom.

EXERCISE 13.2

Find e/m for the helium ion, He^{++}, and compare with that for the electron.
Ans. 4.87×10^7 coulomb kg.$^{-1}$.

13.4   The Nuclear Atom

Having described the charge and mass of the positive and negative electric particles obtainable from atoms, we will now examine information bearing on the spatial distribution of these particles in the atom. Early concepts of this distribution were, of course, rather indefinite, but tended to view the positive portion as extending throughout the volume occupied by the neutral atom, with the light, negative electrons embedded in this matrix.

In 1911 Ernest Rutherford proposed the nuclear theory of atomic structure, based on an analysis of experiments on the scattering of positive ions by metal foils. The positive ions used in the original experiments were alpha particles, a "radiation" emitted by radioactive substances. The alpha particles had been shown to be very energetic helium ions He^{++}, with an atomic mass four times as great as a hydrogen atom. A collimated beam of these particles was directed normal to the surface of a thin sheet of a metal such as gold, and by means of a fluorescent screen placed in various positions, the angular distribution of the scattered particles was observed. The arrangement is indicated in Fig. 13.5.

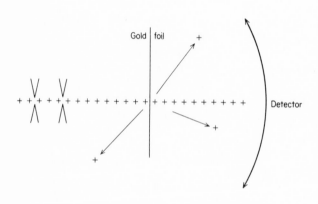

FIG. 13.5. Rutherford scattering experiment.

The most striking qualitative observation made in these experiments was that while most of the alpha particles passed through the foil with little or no deflection, a few were deflected through angles greater than 90°. Although the foil was only $4(10)^{-4}$ cm. thick, it nevertheless constituted a layer of about 10^4 atoms. To understand the significance of the large angle scattering, imagine that rifle bullets are being fired through a thick slab of plastic foam. What would you conclude if something like one in ten thousand of the bullets was deflected back in the general direction of the marksman? Superficially, the target looks like a uniform layer of matter of low density, but the occasional deflection of the projectiles through a large angle indicates small bodies of high density. Since the scattering is a very infrequent occurrence, it is not likely that it can be the result of two or more encounters by the same projectile.

From momentum considerations scattering cannot be due to encounters between the α particle and the electron. The mass of the α particle is about 7300 times that of the electron, and, therefore, the α particle cannot be deflected appreciably by an encounter with an electron. The observed deflection must result from an interaction with the heavy positive portion of the atom. Qualitatively, the fact that deflection is a relatively rare event indicates that this heavy positive portion of the atom occupies very little space. Furthermore, the observation of a small number of very large deflections implies that the positive charge is very highly concentrated in space, thus producing an electrical field of great strength in its immediate vicinity.

On the assumption that the interaction between the α particle and the nucleus can be described by Coulomb's law, Rutherford computed the distribution of scattered α particles as a function of the angle through which they were deflected. He found excellent agreement between calculation and experiment down to interaction distances of $\sim 10^{-12}$ cm. The agreement between model and experiment is taken as evidence that the positive heavy portion of the atom is indeed concentrated in a very small fraction of the total volume occupied by the atom. This portion of the atom is called the *nucleus*. It must be less than 10^{-12} cm. in size. Apparently the heavy positive nucleus has an extension in space only 10^{-5} times that of the whole atom, which extends approximately 10^{-7} cm. In terms of volume, which is proportional to the cube of a linear dimension, the nucleus occupies only about 10^{-15} of the total volume of the atom. The positive charge and most of the mass of the atom is concentrated in this tiny volume, giving the nucleus a density of about 10^{15} gm. cm.$^{-3}$, or 10^6 metric tons per cubic millimeter.

13.5. Isotopes

Rather precise measurements of the atomic weight of many elements where available by 1900, and the accumulated values presented several puzzles. A few of the values, such as C, N, F, H are nearly integral numbers, whereas many others such as B, Mg, Cl are not. Any attempt to find a single unit evenly divisible into all atomic weights will clearly fail. Furthermore, there are three instances (A—K, Co—Ni, Te—I) in which the order of atomic weights does not agree with the logical order of placement in the periodic system.

The atomic weights of the elements were taken to be precisely fixed quantities, since the values determined by different investigators using different sources of the elements gave the same result, within the precision then possible. An exception to this reproducibility was found in the investigations of radioactive substances. The element lead showed appreciable variations in atomic weight depending on its source. Specifically, the atomic weight of lead obtained from uranium deposits may be as low as 206.00 and from thorium deposits as high as 207.9, as compared with the "normal" value of 207.19. This information not only contributed to the understanding of the phenomena of radioactivity but was also the first indication of the solution to the difficulties mentioned above.

As a result of their studies of these and other phenomena associated with radioactivity Rutherford and Frederick Soddy proposed that there could exist several varieties of an element, called *isotopes*, differing only in atomic weight. That is, the nuclear charge of all atoms of an element is the same, but they may occur in several mass varieties. At the same time, the practical invariability of the atomic weight values (with the exception of lead) indicates that the chemical properties of the isotopes of an element must be practically identical. Otherwise, differing sources and chemical treatments would produce variations in the proportions of the several isotopes and hence in atomic weight.

The proposal of isotopes held forth hope of accounting for nonintegral atomic weights by assuming various combinations of isotopes of integral atomic weight. The same concept can account for atomic weight inversions in the periodic system as well as the variable atomic weight of lead. In the latter case, the variation is to be regarded as a consequence of the production of particular lead isotopes by radioactive distintegration.

EXERCISE 13.3

Assuming that the element chlorine is made up of two isotopes having atomic weights of 35 and 37, what must be the per cent abundance of these to give the observed atomic weight of 35.5? *Ans.* 75% ^{35}Cl; 25% ^{37}Cl.

13.6 The Mass Spectrometer

Abundant evidence of the widespread occurrence of isotopes among the elements was soon forthcoming in the study of the positive ions resulting from electron bombardment of atoms. The charge-to-mass ratio of these positive ions was investigated by A. J. Dempster and by F. W. Aston beginning in 1918, using devices which have developed into the modern *mass spectrometer.* A typical experimental arrangement is shown in Fig. 13.6. Electrons from a hot filament are accelerated by a potential of about 70 v. and meet a stream of gas molecules. The positive ions formed by electron impact are accelerated by a potential difference of several thousand volts V, through defining slits into a region of homogeneous magnetic field of strength H. This field is formed by pole pieces lying above and below the plane of the figure so that a semicircular path is followed by the ion beam to the exit slit and collecting electrode. The whole device must be evacuated to a pressure of approximately 10^{-6} mm. Hg to permit transit of the ions from the source region to the collecting electrode without collision.

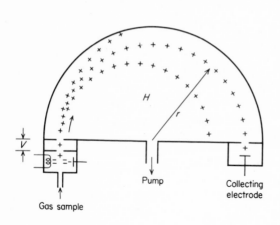

FIG. 13.6. Dempster mass spectrometer.

In acceleration by the potential difference V the positive ions of charge e acquire kinetic energy eV.

$$eV = \tfrac{1}{2}mv^2 \tag{13.10}$$

In the magnetic field of strength H, they are subjected to a radial force Hev and move in a circular path of radius of curvature r.

$$Hev = \frac{mv^2}{r} \tag{13.11}$$

For any given ion the velocity v may be eliminated between (13.10) and (13.11), yielding

$$r = \frac{1}{H} \sqrt{\frac{2Vm}{e}} \tag{13.12}$$

This equation shows that for a given accelerating potential and magnetic field strength, the radius of curvature is determined by the charge-to-mass ratio of the ions. The conditions of ionization in the source region are such that most of the ions are formed by loss of a single electron, and, therefore, most of them have the same charge, 1.602 × 10⁻¹⁹ coulomb. However, the masses of the ions formed, even from a single substance, may have several values, due to the presence of isotopes. These mass varieties give rise to a mass spectrum such as that shown in Fig. 13.7.

In the mass spectrometer a single exit slit and collecting electrode are provided so that only ions having a predetermined radius of curvature pass through and are registered as a current on the collecting electrode. Variation of V or H brings ions of various values of e/m to focus on the exit slit and thus the mass spectrum is scanned. By rearrangement of equation (13.12),

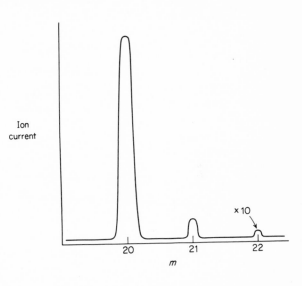

FIG. 13.7. Mass spectrum of neon.

$$\frac{m}{e} = r^2 \frac{H^2}{2V} \tag{13.13}$$

EXERCISE 13.4

Typical operating values for a modern mass spectrometer are $r = 15.0$ cm. and $H = 0.200$ webers m.⁻². What accelerating voltage will be required to detect²⁰ Ne⁺ ions? (Use consistent units, as suggested in section 13.2.)   *Ans.* 2.17 × 10³ v.

Analysis of anode rays as described above shows that, in contrast to cathode rays, many discrete values of m/e are observed. For example, hydrogen gives rise to ions of $m/e = 1.04 \times 10^{-5}$ and 2.08×10^{-5} g. coulomb⁻¹, corresponding to the ions H⁺ and H₂⁺. For many elements, such as that shown in Fig. 13.7, several values of m/e are observed. These can only be attributed to atoms of different mass constituting a single chemical element. In the case of neon three isotopes are observed. With m/e values of 20.7×10^{-5}, 21.75×10^{-5}, and 22.80×10^{-5} g. coulomb⁻¹. Using the value of e, the electronic charge, we may find the masses of these ions to be 33.20×10^{-24}, 34.85×10^{-24}, and 36.51×10^{-24} g.

TABLE 13.1
ISOTOPES OF THE ELEMENTS

Element	Isotopes	Abundance	Atomic weigh
Hydrogen	^1_1H	99.98%	1.00797
	^2_1H	0.02	2.01410
Carbon	$^{12}_6C$	98.9	12.0000
	$^{13}_6C$	1.1	13.0035
Nitrogen	$^{14}_7N$	99.62	14.00307
	$^{15}_7N$	0.38	15.00011
Oxygen	$^{16}_8O$	99.757	15.99491
	$^{17}_8O$	0.039	16.99914
	$^{18}_8O$	0.204	17.99916
Fluorine	$^{19}_9F$	100.	18.99840
Neon	$^{20}_{10}Ne$	90.51	19.99244
	$^{21}_{10}Ne$	0.28	20.99395
	$^{22}_{10}Ne$	9.21	21.99318
Chlorine	$^{35}_{17}Cl$	75.4	34.96885
	$^{37}_{17}Cl$	24.6	36.96590
Tin	$^{112}_{50}Sn$	0.9	111.9040
	$^{114}_{50}Sn$	0.61	113.9030
	$^{115}_{50}Sn$	0.35	114.9035
	$^{116}_{50}Sn$	14.07	115.9021
	$^{117}_{50}Sn$	7.54	116.9031
	$^{118}_{50}Sn$	23.98	117.9018
	$^{119}_{50}Sn$	8.62	118.9034
	$^{120}_{50}Sn$	33.03	119.9021
	$^{122}_{50}Sn$	4.78	121.9034
	$^{124}_{50}Sn$	6.11	123.9052
Iodine	$^{127}_{53}I$	100.	126.9044
Lead	$^{204}_{82}Pb$	1.5	203.9731
	$^{206}_{82}Pb$	23.6	205.9745
	$^{207}_{82}Pb$	22.6	206.9759
	$^{208}_{82}Pb$	52.3	207.9766
Bismuth	$^{209}_{83}Bi$	100.	208.9804
Thorium*	$^{232}_{90}Th$	100.	232.0382
Uranium*	$^{235}_{92}U$	0.71	235.0439
	$^{238}_{92}U$	99.28	238.0508

*Naturally radioactive.

The three isotopes of neon differ in mass by almost exactly the mass of the hydrogen atom, and this indicates a general regularity found among isotopes of a given element: their masses differ by almost exact integral multiples of a unit mass (the hydrogen mass). When the isotopes of one element are compared with those of another element, the same regularity is observed. The isotopic masses are approximately integral multiples of the hydrogen mass. The approximation becomes poorer as the comparison is extended to the full length of the system of elements, and this *mass defect* has an important meaning which is discussed in texts on nuclear chemistry.

Reference to a particular isotope of an element is usually made by giving as a superscript the *mass number* A of that isotope. The mass number will be defined, for the present, as the integer nearest the ratio of the mass of the isotope to the mass of the hydrogen atom. Thus, the isotopes of neon are designated ^{20}Ne, ^{21}Ne, and ^{22}Ne. The mass spectrometer not only measures the relative masses of isotopes, but also the relative abundances of these isotopes in the sample analyzed. The abundances of the isotopes of almost all the elements are found to be practically independent of the source and treatment of the element.

As the basis for a scale of atomic weights physicists and chemists have agreed to define the weight of the most abundant isotope of carbon, ^{12}C, as equal to exactly 12. Table 13.1 lists some important elements, together with abundances and atomic weights.

13.7 X Ray Spectra

In 1895 Wilhelm Roentgen, in the course of investigating the visible and ultraviolet light given off by electrical discharge in gases, found that an unknown radiation (hence, X ray) was emitted which would penetrate consider-

able thicknesses of matter opaque to ordinary light. This radiation could be detected by the fluorescence which it induced in certain solids such as zinc sulfide, by the ionization that it produced in air, and by the darkening of a photographic film protected from all ordinary light. These X rays were not affected by electric or magnetic fields, and were recognized as electromagnetic radiations in the general category of light, but of much shorter wave length.

X radiations arise from electron bombardment of the anode or glass walls of the gas discharge tube in Fig. 13.1. Their wave lengths depend on the energy of the bombarding electrons and also upon the nature of the target. X rays, like the electromagnetic radiations of longer wave length, show the phenomena of reflection, refraction, and diffraction, and these methods can be used to determine their wave lengths.

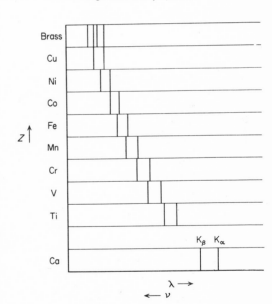

Fig. 13.8. X ray spectra.

The X radiation emitted upon electron bombardment of most of the elements has been studied. In addition to a continuous or polychromatic radiation, each element has its own characteristic emission spectrum consisting of a series of discrete lines, as shown in Fig. 13.8. These lines appear in groups or series and in order of decreasing energy they are designated K, L, M, ...

The wave lengths or frequencies of these lines shift in a regular manner with the position of the element in the periodic system. In 1916 H. G. J. Moseley showed that for a particular line such as the K_α line, the square root of the frequency ν is a linear function of atomic number.

$$\sqrt{\nu} = a(Z - b) \tag{13.14}$$

The values of the parameters a and b are obtained from observations on elements of known atomic number Z.

Prior to the work of Moseley, it was a commonly accepted hypothesis, based on inconclusive evidence, that the number of electrons in the atom, and therefore the charge on the nucleus, is the same as the ordinal number of the atom in the periodic system. Moseley's work established an independent quantitative measure of the atomic number and thus permitted unambiguous recognition of missing or misplaced elements. For example, it is evident in Fig. 13.8 that one element is missing between calcium ($Z = 20$) and titanium ($Z = 22$). This is, of course, scandium ($Z = 21$). Brass is used as a source of zinc radiations, but also contains copper.

13.8 Composition of Nuclei

Inspection of the data on the stable nuclei given in Table 13.1 shows that the atomic mass is not strictly proportional to atomic number. In going from hydrogen to uranium, the atomic number increases by a factor of 92 while the mass number increases by a factor of 238. These facts, together with the existence of isotopes, indicate that there are at least two factors which determine the atomic mass; that is, there are at least two kinds of particles in the atomic nucleus, the principal determinant of atomic mass.

At one time it was proposed that the nucleus consisted of a number of protons equal to the mass number, together with a sufficient number of electrons to reduce the net charge to the observed value of the atomic number. This view is now known to be incorrect for a number of reasons, one of which is that the size (de Broglie wave length—see section 13.15) of an electron is much larger than the size of the atomic nucleus.

A satisfactory explanation of the facts of nuclear composition is found in the proposal of an additional particle, the *neutron*, first observed experimentally by James Chadwick in 1934. This particle has very nearly the same mass as the simplest atomic nucleus, that of ^1H, which is called a *proton*. The neutron has no charge, however, and therefore its addition to a nucleus increases the mass number by one unit without changing the nuclear charge (atomic number).

With these two nucleons, the proton and the neutron, it is possible to account for the composition of all known varieties of atomic nuclei. The *atomic number Z* of an atomic type, or *nuclide*, is equal to the number of protons in the nucleus as well as the number of extranuclear electrons in the neutral atom. The *mass number A* of a nuclide is equal to the number of protons plus neutrons. For example,

the $^{12}_{6}C$ nucleus consists of 6 p, 6 n
the $^{13}_{6}C$ nucleus consists of 6 p, 7 n
the $^{20}_{10}Ne$ nucleus consists of 10 p, 10 n
the $^{21}_{10}Ne$ nucleus consists of 10 p, 11 n
the $^{22}_{10}Ne$ nucleus consists of 10 p, 12 n
the $^{238}_{92}U$ nucleus consists of 92 p, 146 n

It is evident that isotopic nuclides differ only in the number of neutrons in their nuclei.

13.9 Separation of Isotopes

Although it has been found that the relative amounts of the various isotopes of an element are practically independent of source or treatment, some very small differences in chemical and physical properties are to be expected. The difference in properties of the isotopes of an element will in general depend on the ratio of the isotopic masses. Therefore, the greatest differences in isotopic properties are to be found in the light elements where the isotopes exhibit the greatest fractional difference in mass. The isotopes of hydrogen, ^1H and ^2H, differ in mass by a factor of two, and this element will furnish the most outstanding illustration of isotopic differences.

Many physical properties of atoms and molecules depend on atomic mass. For example, gas density depends directly on the masses of the atoms constituting the molecules. This property has been used as a basis for analysis of hydrogen isotope mixtures. Many other gas properties, such as rate of effusion, viscosity and thermal conductivity also depend on molecular mass. For example, the relative rates of effusion of molecular hydrogen containing only ^1H (called *protium*) as compared to molecular hydrogen containing only ^2H (called *deuterium*, symbol D) are given by Graham's law.

$$\frac{R_{H_2}}{R_{D_2}} = \sqrt{\frac{4}{2}} = 1.414$$

The uranium isotope ^{235}U is concentrated for atomic energy use in large amounts by this kind of process, employing the gas UF_6 diffusing repeatedly through very small pores in a metallic barrier. The ideal separation factor α for a single stage in such a process is given by

$$\alpha = \frac{(X_{235}/X_{238})_{final}}{(X_{235}/X_{238})_{initial}} = \sqrt{\frac{352.04}{349.03}} = 1.0043$$

If n stages of effusion are employed, the overall change in concentration is given by

$$\left(\frac{X_{235}}{X_{238}}\right)_{final} = \left(\frac{X_{235}}{X_{238}}\right)_{initial} \alpha^n \tag{13.15}$$

where X_{235} and X_{238} are the mole fractions of $^{235}UF_6$ and $^{238}UF_6$, respectively.

EXERCISE 13.5

What is the minimum number of stages of effusion required to give an equimolar mixture of $^{235}UF_6$ and $^{238}UF_6$, starting with the natural mixture of isotopes?

Ans. n $= 1150$.

Isotope effects are also observable in more complicated physical properties. The specific gravity of D_2O is 1.1059 at 20°, as compared with 0.9982 for H_2O. D_2O (heavy water) freezes at 3.82° and boils at 101.42°. Table 13.2 gives the ratio of vapor pressures of some liquid isotopic compounds at the normal boiling point of the more abundant species (underlined). In each case the lighter compound has the higher vapor pressure.

TABLE 13.2

VAPOR PRESSURES OF ISOTOPIC LIQUIDS

Compounds	P_1/P_2
$^{14}N_2$, $^{15}N_2$	1.0081
$^{14}NH_3$, $^{15}NH_3$	1.00246
NH_3, ND_3	1.110
$H_2^{16}O$, $H_2^{18}O$	1.0046
H_2O, D_2O	1.051

The isotope effect on chemical equilibrium constants is usually quite small but it is significant for the lighter elements. It is best observed by examination of the equilibrium constant for isotopic exchange. For example, if two compounds of hydrogen HX and HY containing significant amounts of both isotopes (the isotopic molecules being designated by DX and DY) are capable of exchanging hydrogen atoms, the process

$$HX + DY = HY + DX$$

occurs until a state of equilibrium is reached. This state is described by the equilibrium function

$$K = \frac{c_{HY} \cdot c_{DX}}{c_{HX} \cdot c_{DY}} \tag{13.16}$$

(taking concentration as the measure of activity). This equation may be rearranged to show the relation between the isotopic constitution of the two molecular species

$$\frac{c_{HY}}{c_{DY}} = K \frac{c_{HX}}{c_{DX}} \tag{13.17}$$

Now if the chemical properties of the isotopic molecules are not identical, that is, if $F^0(HX) \neq F^0(DX)$ and $F^0(HY) \neq F^0(DY)$, the equilibrium constant in equations (13.16) and (13.17) will differ from unity. This means that at equilibrium the isotopic composition in the Y compound will differ from that in the X compound. Several cases in which the equilibrium constant for isotopic exchange has been measured are given in Table 13.3. In the case of the nitrogen isotopic equilibrium, the value indicates that when gaseous ammonia is equilibrated with an ammonium salt solution, the ratio $^{14}N/^{15}N$ in the gas phase will be 1.023 times that ratio in the solution.

These effects are not large enough to cause concern in ordinary chemical manipulation, and the isotopes may be said to have practically identical properties. Nevertheless, it is possible by countercurrent exchange techniques to

TABLE 13.3

ISOTOPIC EXCHANGE EQUILIBRIA

Equilibrium	Equilibrium constant
$^{15}NH_3$ (g) $+$ $^{14}NH_4^+$ (aq.) $=$ $^{14}NH_3$ (g) $+$ $^{15}NH_4^+$ (aq.)	1.023
$H^{12}CN$ (g) $+$ $^{13}CN^-$ (aq.) $=$ $H^{13}CN$ (g) $+$ $^{12}CN^-$ (aq.)	1.013
$^{34}SO_2$ (g) $+$ $H^{32}SO_3^-$(aq.) $=$ $^{32}SO_2$ (g) $+$ $H^{34}SO_3^-$ (aq.)	1.012

repeat the equilibration many times, in a fashion analogous to that used in fractional distillation, and thus to obtain substantial isotopic enrichment by chemical exchange. The exchange of aqueous cyanide with hydrogen cyanide gas has been used to produce 22 atom per cent ^{13}C, as compared to the natural value of 1.1 atom per cent.

The effect of isotopic substitution on the rates of chemical reactions is substantially greater than in the case of equilibria. As compared to the 1% effect quoted in Table 13.3 for an exchange equilibrium with the carbon isotopes, the rate of reaction of molecules containing ^{13}C may be as much as 4% less than for the ^{12}C molecules.

As with other properties, the greatest differences in rates occur between the hydrogen isotopes, and an important method of concentrating deuterium is based on such a phenomenon. When water, which in nature contains about 1 part D to 5,000 parts H, is electrolyzed in alkaline solution, the specific rate of evolution of hydrogen is about five times as great as the rate of evolution of deuterium. That is, hydrogen gas evolved will contain about 1 part D to 25,000 parts H. Thus, as a sample of water is decomposed in this fashion, the residue becomes richer in deuterium. This method is used to produce water containing as much as 99.8% of the heavy isotope. This material now sells for about 30¢ a gram.

13.10 The Quantum Concept

We have now examined part of the experimental evidence upon which a model or theory of atomic structure must be based. This evidence has revealed the existence of a dense, positively charged nucleus containing most of the mass of a given atom, but occupying only $\sim 10^{-15}$ of its volume. The remainder is occupied by electrons. We shall now turn to another important foundation of this model, the quantum concept, introduced by Professor Max Planck in 1901. The basic postulate of the quantum theory of Planck is that electromagnetic radiation can occur only in discrete energy units, or *quanta*, defined by the equation

$$E = h\nu \qquad\qquad (13.18)$$

where E is the energy of a given quantum, h, called the *Planck constant*, has the value 6.6256×10^{-27} erg sec. molecule^{-1}, and ν is the frequency of the radiation. (Recall that $\nu\lambda = c$, where λ is the wave length of the radiation, and c is the velocity of light.)

Although Planck originally introduced this relation in connection with a model for so-called *black body radiation*, its physical significance is more easily appreciated in Einstein's treatment of the photoelectric effect. Experimentally, when metals are exposed to light of appropriate wave length, energetic electrons are emitted. Einstein showed that the maximum kinetic energy of these electrons, E_e, is given by the relation

$$E_e = h\nu - w \tag{13.19}$$

where w is called the work function and is constant for any given metal. The work function is essentially the energy required to produce an electron of zero kinetic energy and is a measure of the binding energy of one of the most loosely bound electrons.

Equation (13.19) makes the striking assertion that the energy of an emitted electron is completely independent of the intensity of the light incident on the metal, and depends only on its frequency. Furthermore, if the frequency of the incident light is too low, an increase in its intensity cannot cause a given surface to emit electrons. Thus, it implies strongly that light is quantized; that is, that it exists in the form of discrete indivisible units.

13.11 Atomic Spectra

The experiments on the photoelectric effect imply quantization of light. Observations of atomic spectra provide evidence that atomic systems too possess a characteristic discreteness. If hydrogen gas is placed in a sufficiently strong electric field or is subjected to an electric discharge, the emission of radiation is observed. The source of this light is the hydrogen atoms produced in the discharge. If this light is analyzed for its constituent frequencies by the use of a spectroscope, it is found to consist of certain discrete frequencies only, as shown in Fig. 13.9. This set of discrete, narrow lines is a part of the emission spectrum of hydrogen. In 1885 J. J. Balmer showed that a group of these lines obeyed a simple empirical relation,

$$\frac{1}{\lambda} = \nu' = R\left(\frac{1}{n'^2} - \frac{1}{n''^2}\right) \tag{13.20}$$

with $n' = 2$. In this relation λ is the wave length of the emitted radiation, ν' (or $1/\lambda$) is the so-called wave number, R is the Rydberg constant, 109,737.31 cm.$^{-1}$ for hydrogen, and n'' is an integer larger than 2. Additional groupings corresponding to other values of n' were also soon recognized, the Lyman, Paschen, Brackett, and Pfund series.

The other elements also show a similar systematic behavior. Furthermore, this characteristic association of the atom with radiation of certain definite frequencies can also be observed in absorption. When light covering a sufficient frequency range is incident upon an assembly of discrete atoms (e.g. Na vapor) characteristic optical absorption spectra are observed. An absorption spectrum always corresponds to an observed emission spectrum, but the reverse is not always true.

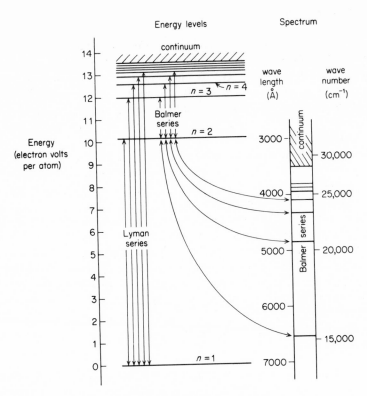

FIG. 13.9. Atomic hydrogen spectrum.

When an atom emits light, its energy is decreased. When it absorbs light, its energy is increased. The change in the energy of the atom, ΔE_a, can be equated to the energy, E, of the light quantum either absorbed or emitted.

$$\Delta E_a = E = h\nu \qquad\qquad (13.21)$$

Since only certain frequencies are observed, the atom undergoes only certain definite changes in energy. This implies the existence of discrete, sharply defined energy levels in the atom. The emission and absorption of radiation may then be understood as resulting from transitions between fixed energy states characteristic of the atom. This was first recognized by Niels Bohr in 1913.[1]

EXERCISE 13.6

One of the important lines in the spectrum of atomic hydrogen lies at $\lambda = 4861$ Å, $\nu = 6.17 \times 10^{14}$ sec.$^{-1}$. What is the corresponding change in the energy content of the hydrogen atom?   *Ans.* 4.09×10^{-12} erg atom^{-1}; 59 kcal. (g.-atom)$^{-1}$.

---

[1]For a fascinating description of the history of this discovery, see W. J. Moore, *Physical Chemistry*, 3rd ed. (Prentice-Hall, Inc., Englewood Cliffs, N. J., 1962), p. 471. The whole topic of the rise of quantum theory is discussed in detail in A. D'Abro, *The Rise of the New Physics* (Dover Publications, Inc., New York, N.Y. 1951).

13.12 The Making of a Model or Theory

The next step in the development of a theory of the hydrogen atom was the coupling of the quantum concept with the nuclear model of Rutherford. The first somewhat satisfactory attempt at this was the model of Bohr, but before examining this we shall briefly discuss the construction of a model.

The construction of a model is essentially an attempt of the human mind to order experimental facts into some satisfying pattern. Such an attempt is not wholly objective, but involves a strong personal element. It is essentially creative. [For an eloquent statement of this position, see Chapter 1 of *The Structure of Physical Chemistry*, by C. N. Hinshelwood, Oxford University Press, London (1952).] In the construction of a model a set of assumptions or postulates are made. The logical consequences of these postulates are then worked out, preferably by the use of mathematics, since errors in logic are thereby minimized. The value of the model is judged by its fit to the experimental observations, and by the character and number of its assumptions. The most satisfactory models are based on a minimal number of *a priori* assumptions. In the last analysis the agreement between the predictions of the model and the experimental observations serves as justification of the postulates chosen.

13.13 The Bohr Model of the Hydrogen Atom

The Bohr model of the hydrogen atom may be based on the following postulates.

I. The Rutherford model is assumed to be correct. The atom consists of a heavy positively charged nucleus around which orbits a light negatively charged electron much as the planets orbit the sun.

II. These orbits are assumed to be stable, and while the electron occupies one of them it cannot radiate energy. This postulate is required because, according to classical physics, electrical charges undergoing accelerated motion radiate energy. Any particle executing circular motion is accelerating, since it is constantly changing its direction and therefore its velocity. (Recall that velocity is a vector quantity and is specified by both a magnitude and a direction.)

III. Emission of radiation occurs whenever the electron moves from an orbit of higher energy to one of lower energy. The frequency of this radiation is given by the relation

$$\nu = \frac{\Delta E}{h}$$

where ΔE is the difference in energy between the orbits.

IV. Only orbits corresponding to certain values of angular momentum, mvr, are allowed. These allowed angular momenta meet the condition

$$mvr_n = \frac{nh}{2\pi} \tag{13.22}$$

where m is the mass of the electron, v is its velocity, r_n is the radius of the orbit corresponding to a given n, n is any integer except 0, and h is Planck's constant. The required concept of quantization is thus introduced as the *a priori* assumption that only certain values of angular momentum are allowed, or that angular momentum is quantized.

On the basis of these postulates the Bohr model can be developed as follows. In stable orbits the centrifugal force arising from the electron's motion must be equal in magnitude to the coulombic force of attraction between the nucleus of charge Ze and the electron of charge e,

$$\frac{(Ze)(e)}{r_n^2} = \frac{mv^2}{r_n}$$

Therefore,

$$r_n = \frac{Ze^2}{mv^2} \tag{13.23}$$

By the postulate of quantization (IV),

$$mvr_n = \frac{nh}{2\pi}$$

Substituting for mv in equation (13.23), we obtain

$$r_n = \frac{n^2h^2}{4\pi^2me^2Z} \tag{13.24}$$

For $n = 1$ this equation yields $r = a_0 = 0.529 \times 10^{-8}$ cm. a_0 has been named the *Bohr radius*.

The total energy E of the electron in a given orbit is equal to the sum of its kinetic energy T and its potential energy V.

$$E = T + V = \tfrac{1}{2}mv^2 - \frac{Ze^2}{r_n}$$

Using (13.23) to substitute for v^2, we have

$$E = T + V = \frac{Ze^2}{2r_n} - \frac{Ze^2}{r_n} = -\frac{Ze^2}{2r_n} \tag{13.25}$$

(The kinetic and potential energies are opposite in sign in agreement with the general relation that force equals the rate of change of energy with distance,

$$F = \frac{dE}{dx}$$

Since the forces act in opposite directions, they must be opposite in sign. Therefore, the values of dE/dx are also opposite in sign.)

We can restate the information contained in equation (13.25) as follows:

$$E = -T = \frac{V}{2} \tag{13.26}$$

We shall take $r = \infty$ where both T and V are zero as our reference point. At $r = \infty$ dissociation is complete. As r decreases, V will decrease and T will increase. E, the total energy, also decreases (equation 13.26), since the absolute value of V is greater than that of T. Equation (13.26) applies generally to systems where only coulombic-type electrostatic potentials are important; in these applications it is known as the *virial theorem*.

Equations (13.24) and (13.25) can be combined to give the equation for the energy of an electron in a given orbit of the hydrogen atom.

$$E_n = \frac{-2\pi^2 m e^4 Z^2}{n^2 h^2} \qquad (13.27)$$

This relationship cannot be checked directly. However, atomic spectral emission lines are postulated to arise from transitions of an electron from a higher energy orbit (designated n'') to one of lower energy (designated n'). The absolute value of the energy difference between these orbits, $|\Delta E|$, can be used to calculate a value for the Rydberg constant which can then be compared to experiment. From (13.27)

$$|\Delta E| = \frac{2\pi^2 m e^4 Z^2}{h^2} \left(\frac{1}{n'^2} - \frac{1}{n''^2} \right) = h\nu \qquad (13.28)$$

For comparison to the Balmer equation we compute the wave number

$$\nu' = \frac{1}{\lambda} = \frac{\nu}{c} = \frac{|\Delta E|}{hc}$$

and substituting, we obtain

$$\nu' = \frac{2\pi^2 m e^4 Z^2}{ch^3} \left(\frac{1}{n'^2} - \frac{1}{n''^2} \right) \qquad (13.29)$$

With equation (13.29) we can compute a value of the Rydberg constant R from fundamental constants. The computed value, 109,737 cm.$^{-1}$, is in satisfactory agreement with the experimental value for hydrogen. Frequencies calculated using this relationship are given in Fig. 13.9.

EXERCISE 13.7

Find the value of ΔE corresponding to transition from $n' = 1$ to $n'' = \infty$ in the hydrogen atom. *Ans.* $\nu' = 109{,}737$ cm.$^{-1}$.

An unexpressed assumption in the above derivation was that the mass of the nucleus is infinitely greater than that of the electron, a good approximation. When the finite mass of the nucleus is considered, the factor $M/(m + M)$ appears in the Rydberg constant, where M is the mass of the nucleus, and this leads to even better agreement between calculated and experimental values.

The Moseley relation, which we have discussed earlier, is entirely compatible with the Bohr model of the atom given in the preceding section, if that model is extended to many-electron systems. The characteristic X ray lines arise from vacancies created in the electron orbits by electron bombardment. When these vacancies are filled by electron transitions from higher orbits, the radiation emitted should have a frequency ($\nu = c\nu'$) given by equation (13.29). The K_a radiation arises from an electron transition from $n = 2$ to $n = 1$. According to equation (13.29), the frequency of such radiation should be proportional to Z^2.

$$\nu = \frac{2\pi^2 me^4 Z^2}{h^3} \left(\frac{1}{1^2} - \frac{1}{2^2} \right) \tag{13.30}$$

However, equation (13.29) was derived from an expression for the permitted orbits of a single electron in the field of a nucleus. In the many-electron atoms the nuclear field is somewhat influenced by the electrons; that is, a screening effect occurs which influences the energy content attributed to the various orbits. This can be allowed for by including a parameter b which reduces the effective nuclear charge. This effect amounts to only about 0.5 units of charge for the K radiation. Thus, we obtain from equation (13.30) an expression of the same form as the Moseley equation (13.14).

$$\nu = \frac{2\pi^2 me^4}{h^3} (Z - b)^2 (0.75)$$

$$\sqrt{\nu} = \sqrt{0.75 \frac{2\pi^2 me^4}{h^3}} (Z - b) \tag{13.31}$$

The computed value of the parameter a agrees satisfactorily with that obtained from the Moseley equation.

EXERCISE 13.8

With the value of R given previously, use equation (13.31) to predict the frequency and wave length of the K_a line for the element calcium. Assume $b = 0.5$.
Ans. $\nu = 9.38 \times 10^{17}$ sec.$^{-1}$; $\lambda = 3.20 \times 10^{-8}$ cm.

13.14 Critical Potentials

The ideas of Bohr regarding the existence of discrete energy levels in atoms were given strong experimental support by the work of James Franck and Gustav Hertz on the determination of critical potentials. A schematic of their apparatus is shown in Fig. 13.10. The filament F provides a source of electrons. These electrons are accelerated by a positive potential on the grid G, this potential being variable so that the maximum energy of the electrons can be controlled. The tube is filled with gaseous atoms at a pressure chosen to give a large number of collisions between electrons and atoms in the region between F and G. However, G and P are spaced so that there are few collisions in the volume between them. A small negative potential is applied

FIG. 13.10. Schematic diagram of Franck-Hertz apparatus for measurement of critical potentials.

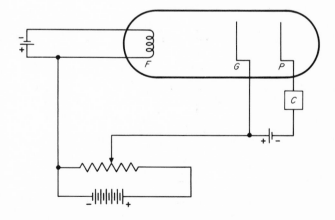

to the plate P, and only electrons with sufficient energy to overcome this potential can reach P. The current reaching P is measured by some device such as an electrometer, C, attached to P.

Electrons emitted from F can be involved in two kinds of collisions, *elastic* and *inelastic*. In an elastic collision total kinetic energy is conserved. Since the mass of the electron is much less than that of the struck atom, it will lose little energy in the collision. In an inelastic collision kinetic energy of the electron can be converted into electronic excitation energy of the atom; that is, an electron in the atom can go from a lower to a higher energy level. In such a collision the impinging electron loses such a large amount of kinetic energy that it cannot overcome the negative retarding potential on the plate P and is returned to the grid.

Since the energy content of the atom and its orbital electrons is sharply quantized, inelastic collisions occur only at energies in excess of well-defined values corresponding to transitions between permitted energy states. That is, with increasing accelerating potential from F to G, it is observed that the plate current drops sharply at certain definite potentials. These *critical potentials* measure the onset of permitted changes in the energy content of the atoms bombarded. For example, helium shows critical potentials at 19.75, 20.55, 21.2, 22.9, 23.6, . . . , and 24.5 v.

The highest critical potential is the *ionization potential;* that is, it measures the minimum energy required to remove an electron completely from the atom. The energy corresponding to this or other critical potentials may also be supplied by absorption of electromagnetic radiation in the form of light, X rays, etc. By suitable modifications of the apparatus, the positive ions thus produced can also be detected.

FIG. 13.11. Ionization potentials.

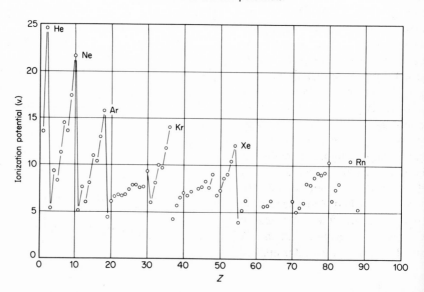

The ionization potential of the one-electron atom, hydrogen, can be pre-
icted from the Bohr formula. Ionization of the normal atom corresponds to
ne transition $n' = 1$, $n'' = \infty$ for which equation (13.29) gives for absorption

$$\nu' = \frac{2\pi^2 me^4 Z^2}{ch^3} \left(\frac{1}{1^2} - \frac{1}{\infty^2} \right) \tag{13.32}$$

$$= R = 109{,}737 \text{ cm.}^{-1}$$

r

$$\Delta E = hc\nu' = 2.1783 \times 10^{-11} \text{ erg atom}^{-1}$$

$$= 13.595 \text{ electron volts atom}^{-1}$$

This transition is indicated as the upper limit of converging energy states in
Fig. 13.9 and is confirmed by direct observation.

The measured ionization potentials of the atoms according to atomic
number are indicated in Fig. 13.11 and show a definite periodicity which may be
correlated with chemical properties. The elements of highest ionization potential
are helium and neon, which seem to be of low chemical reactivity. Each of
these elements is immediately followed by an element of very low ionization
potential, an alkali metal. These elements are very reactive, easily forming
electrovalent compounds in which the alkali metal atom loses an electron to
form a positive ion. [The similar ionization potentials of Xe and O_2 provided
a clue which led to the first synthesis of a noble gas compound by N. Bartlett
Proc. Chem. Soc., 1962, 218).]

EXERCISE 13.9

From the ionization potential of the hydrogen atom given above find the ionization potential of He^+, that is, the energy term in the process

$$He^+ = He^{++} + e$$

Ans. 54.380 electron volt atom^{-1}.

3.15 The Wave Nature of Matter

As we have seen, the old Bohr planetary model of the hydrogen
atom was in satisfactory quantitative agreement with the main features of the
hydrogen atom spectrum. However, it proved impossible to extend this model
to other systems. Thus, it failed to give the observed energy states of the helium
atom, and more seriously, led to a qualitative disagreement with certain experimental results, for example, the influence of a magnetic field on the dielectric
constant of a gas. All attempts to remove these discrepancies by modifications
of the model failed. Clearly, a new approach was desirable.

The foundations for this new approach had been laid by the work of Planck
and Einstein. Einstein had shown that in experiments in which the corpuscular
aspect of radiation was revealed, mechanical properties such as energy and
momentum should be ascribed to the corpuscular photons rather than to the
associated waves. The next step in the development was taken by Louis de
Broglie. He proposed that even when the corpuscular aspect of light was not
apparent, the energy and momentum of radiation should still be attributed to
corpuscular photons.

FIG. 13.12. Schematic diagram of wave associated with an electron constrained to move in a circle. The solid line represents an allowed state, since it fits an integral number of wavelengths to the circumference of the orbit. The state represented by the dashed line is not allowed, since it does not fit an integral number of wavelengths to the circumference of the circle and will therefore destroy itself.

The realization that the corpuscular and wave aspects of radiation were always associated led de Broglie to a brilliant postulate. He assumed that a particle should show the same duality as did radiation. A particle in motion, then, should have associated with it a wave. The energy and momentum of this particle should be related to the frequency and wave length of this associated wave by equations of the same form as those which related the energy and momentum of radiation to its wave length and frequency. Thus, we have the following relationships for particles and their associated waves.

$$E = h\nu \tag{13.33}$$

$$p = \frac{h\nu}{v'} = \frac{h}{\lambda} \tag{13.34}$$

where h is the Planck constant, p is the momentum of the particle, ν is the frequency of the wave associated with the particle, v' is the velocity of the associated wave, and λ is the wave length of that wave ($\nu\lambda = v'$).

This postulate has important experimental consequences. For example, the waves associated with electrons moving at low speeds should have wave lengths of the same dimensions as a crystal lattice, and so should be diffracted by such a lattice (see Chapter 15). Such diffraction was observed by C. Davisson and L. H. Germer, providing striking confirmation of de Broglie's theory.

The wave theory of de Broglie suggested a possible basis for the quantizing conditions introduced by Bohr as a postulate in his development of the planetary model of the hydrogen atom. An electron moving in a circular orbit should have a wave associated with it. A condition for the existence of this wave is that the orbit of the electron be of a circumference equal to some integral number of wave lengths (Fig. 13.12). If this condition is not met, a wave completing a number of out-of-phase cycles will destroy itself. The condition which we have just described is expressed in the equation

$$2\pi r = n\lambda \tag{13.35}$$

Now, since $p = mv$, where v is the particle velocity, by equation (13.34)

$$\lambda = \frac{h}{p} = \frac{h}{mv}$$

Therefore, $2\pi mvr = nh$, and since p_a, the angular momentum, is equal to mvr, we have $p_a = nh/2\pi$, which is Bohr's postulate of quantization of angular momentum. Thus, de Broglie's work indicated the possibility of a description of the hydrogen atom based specifically on a consideration of the wave properties f matter. This description was provided by the wave mechanics of Erwin chrödinger. (As a historical note, an alternate formulation of quantum echanics was developed by Werner Heisenberg at about the same time that chrödinger formulated his wave mechanics.)

3.16 The Heisenberg Uncertainty Principle

While the wave theory of matter resulted in an enormous step for-ard in the description and understanding of the internal structure of the atom, t the same time it indicated that there exists a natural limit on the precision of uch information. Imagine that an attempt is made to determine the "position" f an electron in an atom by some sort of super microscope using exceedingly hort wave length radiation. Evidently the position could not be fixed with reater precision than the wave length of the radiation, and therefore a wave ength somewhat less than the size of an atom would be required. Neglect the orbidding problems of generation and refraction of such radiation and consider he momentum of such quanta. By equation (13.34), $p = h/\lambda$. Interaction of a uantum of this momentum with an orbital electron is in a sense a collision in vhich the electron can gain momentum in an amount between zero and h/λ. "herefore, in the process of measuring the position of the electron to within $\sim\lambda$, its momentum becomes uncertain to within $\sim h/\lambda$. This is the *uncertainty* *rinciple* first stated by Werner Heisenberg in 1928. A common formulation is

$$\Delta p \times \Delta q \approx h \tag{13.36}$$

vhere Δp represents the uncertainty in momentum and Δq the uncertainty in •osition. It can be shown that a similar relation exists between other properties vhose product has the units of h. For instance,

$$\Delta t \times \Delta E \approx h \tag{13.37}$$

That is, the product of the uncertainty in the energy and the uncertainty in the ifetime of an atomic or molecular energy state is h. When an atom or molecule 'emains very briefly in a given energy state, the value of the energy is not well lefined.

The uncertainty principle is a logical consequence of attributing wave pro-•erties to particles, since momentum and wave length are related in reciprocal fashion. The exceedingly small wave length associated with a macroscopic •article such as a rifle bullet introduces an uncertainty in position which is oractically negligible. However, in the realm of atomic structure, precise knowl-:dge of the momentum of an orbital electron is accompanied by an inability to give it a precise location or orbit. It is possible only to give probability distri-oution functions, as shown in the following sections.

13.17 The Wave Equation

Before we examine the Schrödinger wave equation, a brief descrip-tion of wave phenomena is in order. If we pluck a wire fastened at each end and held under tension, it will vibrate. If the wire is plucked in the middle, a possible

(a) $\lambda = \lambda_0$
($n = 1$)

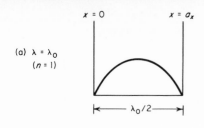

(b) $\lambda = \lambda_0/2$
($n = 2$)

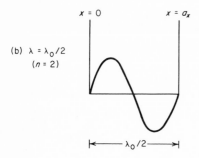

(c) $\lambda = \lambda_0/3$
($n = 3$)

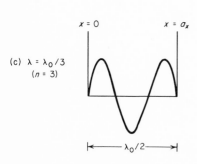

FIG. 13.13. Some allowed vibrations of a string fastened at both ends.

vibration is shown in Fig. 13.13 (a). If the wire is plucked in different fashions, the displacements diagrammed in Figs. 13.13 (b) and (c) become possible. If we designate the wave length in Fig. 13.13 (a) as λ_0 then the wave lengths λ of all the various allowed fundamental vibrations are given by the relation

$$\lambda = \frac{\lambda_0}{n} \tag{13.38}$$

where n is any integer except 0. Only those fundamental vibrations which satisfy equation (13.38) are allowed. What is the source of this limitation on the modes of vibration? It arises from a physical condition imposed by the fact that the two ends of the string are fastened. Only those vibrations are allowed which are compatible with the condition that the ends of the string cannot move.

It is clear that the waves which we have diagrammed can all be represented mathematically as sine functions. We shall represent such wave functions by the symbol ψ. For the waves graphed in Fig. 13.13 a suitable form of the function ψ is

$$\psi = A \sin (360°) \frac{x}{\lambda} = A \sin \frac{2\pi x}{\lambda} \tag{13.39}$$

where A is a constant governing the amplitude or maximum height of the wave, x is the distance from the left origin, and λ is the wave length of the wave. If we now employ equation (13.38), (13.39) becomes

$$\psi = A \sin \left(\frac{2\pi n x}{\lambda_0}\right) \tag{13.40}$$

where, as we have seen, n is any integer.

EXERCISE 13.10

Graph equation (13.38) for $n = 1, 2, 3$ and 4. Assume $A = 1$.

Other functions can also be used to describe waves. For example, the wave shown in Fig. 13.13(a) can be described by a cosine function with the origin selected to coincide with the maximum in the wave. Combinations of sine and cosine functions can also be employed. We are led therefore to seek some property common to these various functions.

A common property is found in their second derivatives. Consider the second derivative of equation (13.39).

$$\frac{d^2\psi}{dx^2} = \frac{-4\pi^2}{\lambda^2} A \sin \frac{2\pi x}{\lambda}$$

r

$$\frac{d^2\psi}{dx^2} = \frac{-4\pi^2}{\lambda^2} \psi \tag{13.41}$$

Equation (13.41) is of fundamental importance. Equations of this form are called wave equations. They will be reduced to an identity by the functions used to describe wave behavior.

EXERCISE 13.11

Show that the set of functions $\psi = A \cos 2\pi x/\lambda$ solves equation (13.41).

Equation (13.41) can be deduced from a rigorous treatment of wave phenomena. Let us therefore postulate that the wave functions describing the de Broglie waves associated with moving particles must be solutions of an equation of the form of equation (13.41). This assumption allows us to relate the kinetic energy T of the moving particle and the wave function ψ.

$$T = \tfrac{1}{2}mv^2$$

By the deBroglie relation $v = h/m\lambda$, and, therefore,

$$T = \frac{h^2}{2m}\frac{1}{\lambda^2}$$

Combining this with equation (13.41) gives

$$T = \frac{-h^2}{8\pi^2 m\psi}\frac{d^2\psi}{dx^2} \tag{13.42}$$

For a particle which possesses both kinetic energy T and potential energy V, we can write $T = E - V$, where E is total energy. Substituting for T in equation (13.42), and rearranging, we have

$$\frac{d^2\psi}{dx^2} = \frac{-8\pi^2 m}{h^2}(E - V)\psi \tag{13.43}$$

This is the Schrödinger equation for one particle in one dimension. Generalizing to three dimensions, this equation becomes

$$\frac{\partial^2\psi}{\partial x^2} + \frac{\partial^2\psi}{\partial y^2} + \frac{\partial^2\psi}{\partial z^2} = \frac{-8\pi^2 m}{h^2}(E - V)\psi \tag{13.44}$$

This equation can be rearranged to give

$$-\frac{h^2}{8\pi^2 m}\left(\frac{\partial^2\psi}{\partial x^2} + \frac{\partial^2\psi}{\partial y^2} + \frac{\partial^2\psi}{\partial z^2}\right) + V\psi = E\psi$$

An often-used shorthand notation for this equation is[2] $H\psi = E\psi$ where

---

[2] H represents a set of instructions to perform various operations on the function ψ. In our example these instructions are as follows: Take the second derivative of ψ with respect to x, holding y and z constant; take the second derivative of ψ with respect to y, holding x and z constant, and add it to the previous result; take the second derivative of z, holding x and y constant. Multiply ψ by V and add this to the other three terms. Multiply this sum by $-h^2/8\pi^2 m$. H is called an operator.

$$H = \frac{-h^2}{8\pi^2 m}\left(\frac{\partial^2}{\partial x^2} + \frac{\partial^2}{\partial y^2} + \frac{\partial^2}{\partial z^2} + V\right)$$

Note carefully that what we have just done does not constitute a derivatio of the Schrödinger equation, but merely relates it to other equations. Th development of this equation and its application to the problem of atom structure must be looked upon as an act of sheer invention justified only by th ability of the scheme erected on it to reproduce experimental observation

The Schrödinger equation will form the basis for the discussion of atomi and molecular structure. We shall postulate that it is the equation obeyed b the ψ functions describing systems containing electrons. In order to determin the mathematical form of this function it is necessary to assume that the po tential energy V is given by the appropriate function of classical physics. Thus for the electron in the hydrogen atom the potential energy is given by th coulombic function, $V = -e^2/r$, just as it is in the Bohr treatment. With th exact form of the potential energy established, it will then be necessary to fin all the ψ functions which reduce equation (13.44) to an identity. In the proces of doing this, values of the total energy E for various states of the system wi be determined. These energy values can then be used to compute spectroscopi frequencies, and these calculated frequencies can be compared to experiment.

13.18 The Interpretation of ψ: The Born Postulate

We now have an equation which can be used to give us a function ψ. A reasonable question which might be asked is, what is the physical sig nificance of this function, ψ? With electromagnetic waves the square of th amplitude of the wave function at any point in space is interpreted as measurin the photon density at that point. Max Born suggested that in wave mechanic ψ^2 be interpreted in a related way. Thus, $\psi^2 dx$ may be interpreted as measurin the probability of finding a particle such as an electron in the region betweer x and $x + dx$. It then follows that the integral of $\psi^2 dx$ over all space must be equal to one, since the probability of finding the electron somewhere in spac must be unity.[3]

$$\int_{-\infty}^{+\infty} \psi^2 \, dx = 1 \tag{13.45}$$

13.19 The Wave Mechanical Model

The model or theory which we are about to examine has a starting

---

[3]Occasionally problems in wave mechanics lead to functions which contain i, $\sqrt{-1}$. As an example consider $\psi = Ae^{+i\phi}$, which describes angular motion. For such a functior $\psi\psi^* \, d\phi$ is considered to be the probability of finding the particle described between ϕ and $\phi + d\phi$. ψ^* is defined as the complex conjugate of ψ; that is, to derive ψ^* from ψ, i is replaced by $-i$. Thus, for the example under consideration,

$$\psi\psi^* d\phi = Ae^{+i\phi} \, Ae^{-i\phi} \, d\phi = A^2 \, d\phi.$$

with integration to be performed from $\phi = 0$ to $\phi = 2\pi$.

oint quite different in character from that of the Bohr planetary model. In the ohr theory a mechanical model consisting of an electron circling a nucleus as a basic postulate. However, wave mechanics begins not with the postulate f a mechanical model, but rather with the postulate of a mathematical relation-nip, the wave equation. Since we feel (usually incorrectly) that we have a better ituitive grasp of mechanical models, we are somewhat annoyed by the choice f the more abstract starting point which a mathematical equation provides. Iowever, the ultimate test of a model is the agreement of its predictions with xperimental observations, and judged by this criterion the wave mechanical iodel is an outstanding success.

We shall begin by making a formal statement of the postulates upon which ve shall base our discussion of a simple one-dimensional problem.[4]

Postulate I. To each system there belongs a function, ψ, which is a solution f the Schrödinger equation for that system.

Postulate II. The function ψ and its slope $d\psi/dx$ are continuous, finite, ind single-valued at every point in space. These are requirements which are net by all functions describing physical waves, for example water waves, sound vaves, and electromagnetic waves.

Postulate III. $\psi\psi^*dx$ represents the probability of finding the particle issociated with the wave function ψ between x and $x + dx$. As a consequence f this assumption

$$\int_{-\infty}^{+\infty} \psi\psi^* \, dx = 1$$

(See Section 13.18).

Our next task is to apply these postulates to some system of interest, and to derive the consequences of this application.

13.20 Particle in a One-Dimensional Box

Although the application of the Schrödinger equation to the simplest real atomic system, the hydrogen atom, is straightforward, it involves mathe-matical functions with which the beginning student of physical chemistry is not usually familiar. Therefore, we shall illustrate the method of approach with an even simpler, but artificial problem, the particle confined in a one-dimen-sional box. We shall find that there is a family of ψ functions which are solutions of the Schrödinger equation for this system, that quantum numbers are found in these functions, and that only certain energies are allowed for the particles; that is, that the energy of the system is quantized. Both the quantum numbers and the quantization of the energy will arise as natural consequences of the postulates which we have made.

We shall define the length of our one-dimensional box as equal to a_x. We shall require that the particle be confined by a potential (wall) of energy V, with V being high enough so that the particle cannot escape. (We shall examine

---

[4]The set of postulates which we make here is not the only possible set, nor is it a com-plete set; however, it is adequate to our purposes.

the question of the value of V later.) The potential V is assumed to affect the particle *only* at the walls of the box. Inside the box $V = 0$, and therefore the wave equation describing this system inside the box will be

$$\frac{d^2\psi}{dx^2} = -\frac{8\pi^2 mE}{h^2}\psi \qquad (13.46)$$

For convenience we shall define our origin as the left wall of the box. The coordinate of the right wall is then $x = a_x$. Our problem now is to find the ψ functions which reduce equation (13.46) to an identity. The term $8\pi^2 mE/h^2$ is constant for any particular value of the energy E. Since the potential energy inside the box is 0, E represents kinetic energy only.

We can rewrite equation (13.46) for a particular value of E as

$$\frac{d^2\psi}{dx^2} = -k^2\psi \qquad (13.47)$$

where

$$k^2 = \frac{8\pi^2 mE}{h^2} \qquad (13.48)$$

The general solution of equation (13.47) is[5]

$$\psi = C_1 e^{ikx} + C_2 e^{-ikx} \qquad (13.49)$$

where C_1 and C_2 are constants. An equivalent and more convenient form of this equation is[5]

$$\psi = A \sin kx + B \cos kx \qquad (13.50)$$

Equation (13.50) represents all the mathematically satisfactory solutions of equation (13.47). However, these solutions do not necessarily satisfy our boundary conditions, and we now must examine equation (13.50) in view of these. We have required that $\psi = 0$ everywhere outside of the box. This means that at the boundary of the box ψ must equal 0 as well and we have a boundary condition to meet. Consider the left wall of the box, where $x = 0$. Since $\cos 0 = 1$, by equation (13.50) $\psi = B$. Therefore, in order to meet our physical condition that $\psi = 0$, B must equal 0. The physically satisfactory solution of equation (13.47) is thus

$$\psi = A \sin kx \qquad (13.51)$$

Note that we have arrived at exactly the function ψ which we discussed earlier as describing the vibrations of a string, as might have been expected intuitively. We have examined this problem in some detail in order to illustrate the interplay between mathematics and the physical situation in deciding the correct solution of the wave equation.

Now let us consider the second boundary, $x = a_x$. Here, too, ψ must equal 0. This means that at $x = a_x$, kx must equal $180°$ (π radians), $360°$ (2π radians), or in general $n\pi$ radians where n is any integer greater than one. Therefore, at $x = a_x$, $ka_x = n\pi$, and

---

[5]These points are discussed in appendix 1.

$$k = \frac{n\pi}{a_x} \tag{13.52}$$

Substituting for k in equation (13.51), we have

$$\psi = A \sin \frac{n\pi x}{a_x} \tag{13.53}$$

There is thus a family of acceptable functions corresponding to $n = 1$, $n = 2$, $n = 3$, etc. These functions are called *eigenfunctions*.

In order to derive the energy formula, equations (13.48) and (13.52) must be combined. The result is

$$E_n = \frac{n^2 h^2}{8m a_x^2} \tag{13.54}$$

Equation (13.54) gives the allowed values of the energy in terms of a set of integers ($n = 1, 2, 3$, etc.), the *quantum numbers* for the system. The allowed values of the energy are called *eigenvalues*.

The value of the constant A may be determined by the use of postulate III. Our problem requires that the particle be inside the box, that is, somewhere between 0 and a_x. Therefore,

$$\int_0^{a_x} A^2 \sin^2 \frac{n\pi x}{a_x} dx = 1 \tag{13.55}$$

The value of A satisfying this relation is[6]

$$A = \sqrt{\frac{2}{a_x}}$$

The wave function now becomes

$$\psi_n = \sqrt{\frac{2}{a_x}} \sin \frac{n\pi}{a_x} \tag{13.56}$$

The process which we have just carried out is called *normalization*, and the wave function ψ_n is now said to be normalized.

The family of functions which we are now considering has another im-

---

[6]In order to integrate this equation, we take advantage of a trigonometric identity.

$$\sin^2 \left(\frac{n\pi x}{a_x}\right) = \frac{1}{2}\left[1 - \cos 2\left(\frac{n\pi x}{a_x}\right)\right]$$

Therefore equation (13.55) becomes

$$A^2\left\{\int_0^{a_x} \left(\frac{dx}{2}\right) - \int_0^{a_x} \frac{1}{2}\left[\cos 2\left(\frac{n\pi x}{a_x}\right)\right] dx\right\} = 1$$

Rewriting gives,

$$A^2\left[\int_0^{a_x} \frac{dx}{2} - \int_0^{a_x} \frac{1}{2} \frac{a_x}{2n\pi} \frac{d}{dx}\left(\sin \frac{2n\pi x}{a_x}\right)\right] = 1$$

Evaluating, we have

$$\frac{A^2 a_x}{2} = 1 \quad \text{and} \quad A = \sqrt{\frac{2}{a_x}}$$

portant property. Consider any two of them, $\psi_l(n = l)$, and $\psi_m(n = m)$ when $l \neq m$. Then[7]

$$\int_0^{a_x} \psi_l \psi_m \, dx = 0$$

Functions which show this type of behavior are said to be *orthogonal* to on another. Orthogonal functions are independent of each other. Exact solution of the Schrödinger equation are always orthogonal.

There are several other points of general interest to be mentioned. First o all, graphs of the wave functions for $n = 1, 2, 3$ are presented in Fig. 13.13 The function for $n = 1$ represents the lowest allowed state of the system. Th wave length cannot be longer than that shown if the wave function is to be zer at both $x = 0$ and $x = a_x$. The energy cannot then be lower than that for thi state, and therefore cannot be 0. The energy of this lowest state is called th *zero point energy*. It is characteristic of systems executing to-and-fro motio (vibrations) that the energy of their lowest allowed state is greater than 0 that is, that a zero point energy exists.

Next, we should note that there is a relation between the kinetic energy o the particle and the curvature of the wave function. For a box of fixed size, a the curvature increases, the number of nodes increases, the wave length there fore decreases, and the kinetic energy increases. These phenomena are a direc consequence of the form of the Schrödinger equation, and so these types o behavior are general.

Our final consideration will be the magnitude of the potential energy *V* required to keep the particle in the box. At the wall of the box the differentia equation which the wave function must fit is

$$\frac{d^2\psi}{dx^2} = -k^2(E - V)\psi \tag{13.57}$$

The solution of equation (13.57) is

$$\psi = C_1 e^{k(E-V)x} + C_2 e^{-k(E-V)x}$$

(See appendix 1 for method of solution.)

---

[7]This can be demonstrated as follows. The two solutions to be considered may be designated

$$\psi_l = \sqrt{\frac{2}{a_x}} \sin\left(\frac{l\pi x}{a_x}\right) \quad \text{and} \quad \psi_m = \sqrt{\frac{2}{a_x}} \sin\left(\frac{m\pi x}{a_x}\right)$$

Assume $l > m$.

$$\int_0^{a_x} \psi_l \psi_m \, dx = \frac{2}{a_x} \int_0^{a_x} \sin\left(\frac{l\pi x}{a_x}\right) \sin\left(\frac{m\pi x}{a_x}\right) dx$$

Applying a trigonometric identity gives

$$\int_0^{a_x} \psi_l \psi_m \, dx = \frac{1}{a_x} \int_0^{a_x} \left[\cos(l - m)\frac{\pi x}{a_x} - \cos(l + m)\frac{\pi x}{a_x}\right] dx$$

$$= \frac{1}{a_x}\left[\frac{a_x}{(l - m)\pi} \sin\left((l - m)\frac{\pi x}{a_x}\right) - \frac{a_x}{(l + m)\pi} \sin\left((l + m)\frac{\pi x}{a_x}\right)\right]_0^{a_x}$$

$$= 0, \text{ since } l \text{ and } m \text{ are integers.}$$

Since we now wish to consider the possibility that the particle can escape 'om the box we shall require only that it be somewhere in space, that is be-ween $x = 0$ and $x = \infty$, rather than *assuming*, as previously, that it will be onfined between $x = 0$ and $x = a_x$. If the particle is to be kept in the box, the estraining potential V must be greater than E, the energy of the particle, and herefore as x goes to infinity the term $C_2 e^{-k(E-V)x}$ goes to infinity. Clearly if the ondition of postulate III is to be met, C_2 must be zero and the acceptable unction becomes

$$\psi = C_1 e^{k(E-V)x} \tag{13.58}$$

As we have seen earlier, if the particle is to be always in the box, ψ as given •y equation (13.58) must equal 0 at the wall. This can only occur if the expo-ent equals $-\infty$. Therefore, V must equal ∞. This is a result completely without •arallel in classical mechanics, where any potential greater than the kinetic nergy of the particle would confine it completely to a classically defined box. Iowever, it is a consequence of our formulation of quantum mechanics that even when the energy of he particle is less than the energy of the confining)otential, there is a finite probability that the par-icle will be found outside any quantum mechanical)ox with a wall of finite thickness. There is much xperimental evidence in agreement with this re-uirement of quantum mechanics. For example, in auclear decay α particles of energy lower than the nergy of the potential barrier of the nucleus have)een observed. These particles could not have sur-nounted the barrier, because to do this their energy nust at least equal the potential energy of the)arrier. Therefore, they are said to have "tunneled" hrough it.

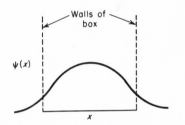

FIG. 13.14. One wave function for particle in one-dimensional box with walls of finite potential.

When the wall potential is finite, the solution cf he wave equation consists of two parts. One part describes the wave function within the field free 'egion of the box and consists of a sine or cosine function. The second is an xponential function and describes the behavior of the particle under the nfluence of the potential. These functions must join smoothly at the wall. One such function is shown in Fig. 13.14.

13.21 The Particle in a Three-Dimensional Rectangular Box

The next problem we shall consider is that of a particle confined to a three-dimensional rectangular box. As before, inside the box we shall set the potential energy of the particle equal to 0, and shall assume that the restraining potential at the walls is infinite. With these assumptions we can write the appropriate wave equation.

$$\frac{\partial^2 \psi}{\partial x^2} + \frac{\partial^2 \psi}{\partial y^2} + \frac{\partial^2 \psi}{\partial z^2} + \frac{8\pi^2 mE}{h^2} \psi = 0 \tag{13.59}$$

Next we shall assume that the function ψ can be written as the product of three functions, one dependent only on x, a second dependent only on y, and a third dependent only on z. $\psi(x, y, z) = X(x)\, Y(y)\, Z(z)$. Upon substitution for ψ equation (13.59) takes the form

$$YZ\frac{\partial^2 X}{\partial x^2} + XZ\frac{\partial^2 Y}{\partial y^2} + XY\frac{\partial^2 Z}{\partial z^2} + \frac{8\pi^2 mE\, XYZ}{h^2} = 0$$

Dividing by $\dfrac{8\pi^2 m}{h^2}\, XYZ$, we find

$$\frac{h^2}{8\pi^2 mX}\frac{\partial^2 X}{\partial x^2} + \frac{h^2}{8\pi^2 mY}\frac{\partial^2 Y}{\partial y^2} + \frac{h^2}{8\pi^2 mZ}\frac{\partial^2 Z}{\partial z^2} + E = 0 \tag{13.60}$$

The first term of equation (13.60) is a function of x only, the second term a function of y only, the third term a function of z only, and the fourth term is a constant. This equation must be true for *all possible combinations of the values* of x, y, and z, since it represents an *identity*. (Note the contrast to the type of algebraic equation which is solved only by specific values of variables.) The only way that this can hold true is for the values of each of the terms to be constant, that is, to be independent of the choice of particular values of x, y, and z. To put it another way, we can choose a particular value of y and a particular value of z. The second (y) and third (z) terms then become constant. Since the fourth term is already constant, the first term becomes equal to a constant for any value of x that we choose. Let us designate this constant as $-E_x$. Then

$$\frac{h^2}{8\pi^2 m}\frac{1}{X}\frac{\partial^2 X}{\partial x^2} = -E_x \tag{13.61}$$

As the result of similar arguments, we can equate the second term of equation (13.60) to a constant $-E_y$ and the third term to a constant $-E_z$. It is clear from equation (13.60) that

$$E = E_x + E_y + E_z \tag{13.62}$$

Equation (13.61) can be rearranged to have the same form as equation (13.46), the equation describing the particle in a one-dimensional box. Therefore, the function X has the form

$$X = \sqrt{\frac{2}{a_x}}\, \sin\left(\frac{n_x \pi x}{a_x}\right) \tag{13.63}$$

and

$$E_{n_x} = \frac{n_x^2 h^2}{8m a_x^2} \tag{13.64}$$

In these equations n_x is a quantum number, and a_x is the box length along the x axis. Similar equations can be written for $Y(y)$ and $Z(z)$. From equation (13.62) the total energy of the particle, $E_{n_x n_y n_z}$, is given by

$$E_{n_x n_y n_z} = \frac{h^2}{8m} \left(\frac{n_x^2}{a_x^2} + \frac{n_y^2}{a_y^2} + \frac{n_z^2}{a_z^2} \right) \tag{13.65}$$

Because this problem involves three variables, there are three quantum numbers. These quantum numbers specify the components into which the kinetic energy can be divided, each component being associated with one of the three axes.

3.22 The Particle in a Cubic Box: An Example of Degeneracy

If the three dimensional box discussed above is cubic, then $a_x = a_y = a_z \equiv a$. Equation (13.65), therefore, becomes

$$E_{n_x n_y n_z} = \frac{h^2}{8ma^2} (n_x^2 + n_y^2 + n_z^2)$$

The lowest energy level will be that for which $n_x = n_y = n_z = 1$. (Recall that $n = 0$ is not allowed.) For this level the energy is given by the relation $E_{1\,1\,1} = 3h^2/8ma^2$. For the next higher level a possible set of quantum numbers is $n_x = 2$, $n_y = 1$, and $n_z = 1$, and $E_{211} = 6h^2/8ma^2$. However, there are two other sets of quantum numbers which will give the same energy: $n_x = 1$, $n_y = 2$, $n_z = 1$; $n_x = 1$, $n_y = 1$, $n_z = 2$. These sets of quantum numbers correspond to different wave functions, $X(x) Y(y) Z(z)$, and, therefore, to different states of the particle in a box. Since there are three such states having the same energy, this is said to be a *triply* or *three-fold degenerate* level. With this we conclude our only detailed discussion of a wave mechanical problem. For the rest of this chapter we shall content ourselves with a presentation of the results of the application of wave mechanics to problems of chemical interest.

EXERCISE 13.12

What is the degeneracy of the level for which $E = 14\, h^2/8ma^2$?   *Ans.* 6 fold.

13.23 The Hydrogen Atom

Hydrogen is the simplest atomic system that we know and the only one for which the Schrödinger equation can provide a wave function without resort to approximations. Consequently, it plays a key role in our discussion of atomic structure. The hydrogen atom consists of a proton and an electron. The potential energy V for the interaction of these two particles is given by Coulomb's law

$$V = -\frac{(Ze)(e)}{r} \tag{13.66}$$

where Z represents the number of unit charges on the nucleus (one for hydrogen), e represents the charge of the electron in electrostatic units, and r represents the distance of separation of the two charges. Since the problem is three-dimensional, three coordinates must be used to describe the position of the electron relative to the proton. The form of Coulomb's law indicates that polar coordinates $(r$, and two angles, θ and $\phi)$ are a more convenient choice than Cartesian coordinates (x, y, and z). The solution to the Schrödinger equation can then be expressed as the product of three functions, one depending on r alone, R; one on the angle θ alone, Θ; and one on the angle ϕ alone, Φ.

$$\psi = R\Theta\Phi \tag{13.67}$$

A few of these functions are given in Table 13.4. In this table a_o is the Bohr radius, and $\rho = (2Z/na_o)r$ where these symbols are defined in the text.

TABLE 13.4

SOME COMPONENT WAVE FUNCTIONS FOR HYDROGEN

Quantum numbers	Functions
$n = 1, \quad l = 0$	$R_{10} = (Z/a_o)^{3/2} 2e^{-\rho/2}$
$n = 2, \quad l = 0$	$R_{20} = \dfrac{(Z/a_o)^{3/2}}{2\sqrt{2}} (2 - \rho)e^{-\rho/2}$
$n = 2, \quad l = 1$	$R_{21} = \dfrac{(Z/a_o)^{3/2}}{2\sqrt{6}} \rho\, e^{-\rho/2}$
$l = 0, m = 0$	$\Theta_{00} = \dfrac{\sqrt{2}}{2}$
$l = 1, m = 0$	$\Theta_{10} = \dfrac{\sqrt{6}}{2} \cos\theta$
$m = 0$	$\Phi_0 = \dfrac{1}{\sqrt{2\pi}}$
$m = 1$	$\Phi_1 = \dfrac{1}{\sqrt{\pi}} \cos\phi$

As is expected from our discussion of the particle in a box, three quantum numbers are associated with these solutions, and are designated by the symbols n, l, and m. For the hydrogen atom the equation for the energy levels is identical to that derived by Bohr on the basis of his mechanical model (equation 13.27), and involves only the quantum number n. The quantum number l specifies the total angular momentum of the system. It is called the *azimuthal quantum number*. The quantum number m specifies the angular momentum about one selected axis. It is called the *magnetic quantum number*.

As in the problem of the particle in a box, the eigenfunctions which are allowed solutions of the Schrödinger equation are characterized by sets of quantum numbers. In the polar coordinate system required for the solution of this problem, more than one quantum number appears in the R and Θ functions. As a result, certain relationships are established in a natural way. As is expected from our discussion of the particle in a box, n may have any integral value (except 0). For any value of n the allowed values of l range from 0 to $(n - 1)$. For any value of l the allowed values of m range from $-l$ through 0 to $+l$. For the lowest quantum number, $n = 1$, there is one eigenfunction. For $n = 2$ there are four eigenfunctions which, according to the restrictions we have outlined above, correspond to the following sets of quantum numbers:

$$l = 0 \quad m = 0 \qquad l = 1 \begin{cases} m = +1 \\ m = 0 \\ m = -1 \end{cases}$$

For hydrogen these levels have the same energy; that is, they are degenerate.

For $n = 3$ there are nine eigenfunctions:

$$l = 0, \quad m = 0 \qquad l = 1 \begin{cases} m = +1 \\ m = 0 \\ m = -1 \end{cases} \qquad l = 2 \begin{cases} m = +2 \\ m = +1 \\ m = 0 \\ m = -1 \\ m = -2 \end{cases}$$

We shall refer to single-particle wave functions which are exact or approximate solutions of the Schrödinger equation as *orbitals*. Each of the eigenfunctions mentioned above can thus be called an *atomic hydrogen orbital*.

The distribution of the electron in space is of particular interest to chemists. As we have discussed earlier, the value of $\psi\psi^* \, d\tau$ for any small element of space $d\tau$, gives the probability of the electrons occupying this element of space. Since the wave functions for hydrogen are complex, we shall begin with a discussion of one component of this wave function, the radial function R. The values of R^2 for some values of n and l are graphed as a function of r, the distance from the nucleus in Fig. 13.15, where it can be seen that R^2 depends on two quantum numbers, n and l. Contrast this to the particle in a box where the corresponding functions $X(x)$, $Y(y)$, and $Z(z)$ each depended on only one quantum number.

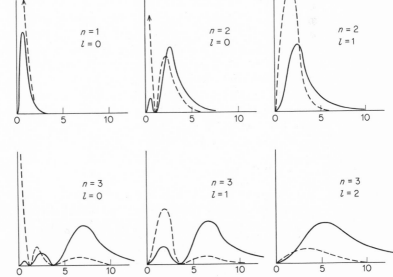

FIG. 13.15. Electron distribution functions.
---- R^2 ——— $r^2 R^2$

Radial distance (A)

There is a considerable advantage in presenting the radial wave function for the hydrogen atom in a different way. We begin by expressing the volume element, $d\tau$, in polar coordinates:[8]

$$d\tau = r^2 \sin \phi \, dr \, d\phi \, d\theta$$

Since $\psi = \psi^*$ the probability of the electron's being in a small volume of space characterized by definite values of r, ϕ, and θ is $\psi^2 r^2 \sin \phi \, dr \, d\phi \, d\theta$. If, at a given value of r, we sum over all possible values of ϕ and θ, the result gives the total probability of the electron's being in the spherical shell between r and $r + dr$. This summation corresponds to the integration[9]

$$\int_0^\pi \int_0^{2\pi} R^2 \Phi^2 \Theta^2 r^2 \sin \phi \, dr \, d\phi \, d\theta = r^2 R^2 dr.$$

$r^2 R^2$ is known as the *radial distribution function*, and is graphed versus r in Fig. 13.15. The area element $r^2 R^2 dr$ at any r represents the probability of the electron's being between r and $r + dr$. Note that the $1s$ function for hydrogen shows a maximum at a value of r equal to the Bohr radius, 0.529 Å. This is the value of r at which there is the highest probability of the electron's being located.

Let us now discuss the two angular functions, Θ and Φ. A three-dimensional representation of the product $\Theta\Phi$ for orbitals with $l = 0$ and $l = 1$ is shown in Fig. 13.16. $\Theta^2\Phi^2$ is also shown, since electron densities will be related to this squared product. Orbitals with $l = 0$ are called s orbitals. For any $n > 1$ three orbitals with $l = 1$ are permitted (p orbitals). They are mutually perpendicular, and one orbital is symmetric around each of the three x, y, and z axes. For any $n > 2$ there are five orbitals with $l = 2$, called d orbitals. For any $n > 3$ there are seven orbitals with $l = 3$, called f orbitals. The angular momentum associated with an orbital increases as l increases, but there is no angular momentum associated with s orbitals, which are completely symmetric about the nucleus.

We have discussed independently the radial and angular distribution of the wave functions for hydrogen. However, the complete wave function is a product of these, and properly should be represented in three dimensions. In Fig. 13.17 sections through such three-dimensional distributions are shown.

By the use of the concept of energy levels designated by three quantum numbers, a system can be developed which explains many of the general observations of atomic spectroscopy. However, certain details cannot be fitted into

---

[8]See C.W. Sherwin, *Introduction to Quantum Mechanics*, Holt, Rinehart, & Winston, Inc., New York (1959), p. 77.

[9]The limits on the integration over ϕ are 0 and π because the ring swept out by integrating over θ from 0 to 2π need only be rotated through π radians to generate a spherical shell. Since the original ψ functions are normalized for these limits, each integration evaluates to 1. If ψ^2 is spherically symmetrical it will not contain ϕ and θ explicitly, and the result of this integration can then be expressed in the alternate form, $\psi^2 4\pi r^2 dr$. In this form $4\pi r^2 dr$ is clearly recognizable as the volume of the spherical shell lying between r and $r + dr$, that is $4/3 \pi r^3 - 4/3\pi(r + dr)^3 = 4\pi r^2 dr$, since terms containing products of differentials are negligibly small and may be dropped.

FIG. 13.16. a) Graphs of $\Theta\Phi$ for the hydrogen atom $l = 0$ and $l = 1$ orbitals. b) Graphs of $[\Theta\Phi]^2$, which together with R^2 determines the electron density in any small volume of space [from W.J. Moore, *Physical Chemistry*, 3rd ed., Prentice-Hall, Inc., Englewood Cliffs, N.J., 1962].

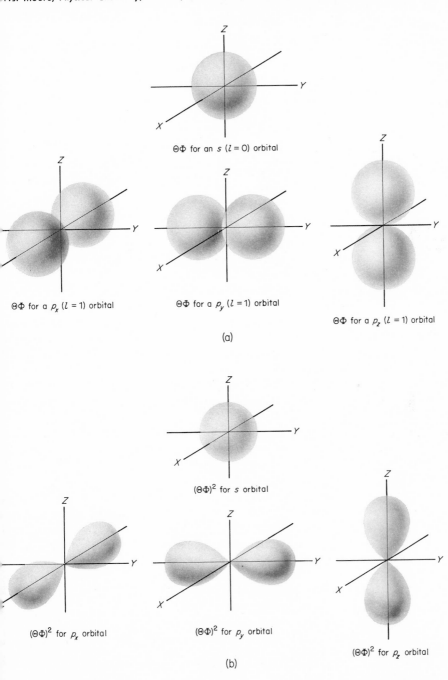

$\Theta\Phi$ for an s ($l = 0$) orbital

$\Theta\Phi$ for a p_x ($l = 1$) orbital

$\Theta\Phi$ for a p_y ($l = 1$) orbital

$\Theta\Phi$ for a p_z ($l = 1$) orbital

(a)

$(\Theta\Phi)^2$ for s orbital

$(\Theta\Phi)^2$ for p_x orbital

$(\Theta\Phi)^2$ for p_y orbital

$(\Theta\Phi)^2$ for p_z orbital

(b)

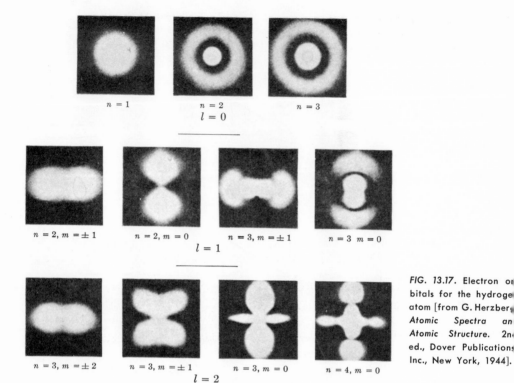

$n = 1$ $n = 2$ $n = 3$
$l = 0$

$n = 2, m = \pm 1$ $n = 2, m = 0$ $n = 3, m = \pm 1$ $n = 3 \; m = 0$
$l = 1$

$n = 3, m = \pm 2$ $n = 3, m = \pm 1$ $n = 3, m = 0$ $n = 4, m = 0$
$l = 2$

FIG. 13.17. Electron orbitals for the hydrogen atom [from G. Herzberg, *Atomic Spectra and Atomic Structure.* 2nd ed., Dover Publications, Inc., New York, 1944].

this general scheme. For example, in the spectra of the alkali metals, where the scheme predicts that only one line, a singlet, should be expected, high resolution shows two closely spaced lines, doublets. Something other than the three quantum numbers that we have so far discussed is required in order adequately to categorize alkali metal electrons. An explanation of this occurrence of doublets was proposed by G. E. Uhlenbeck and S. Goudsmit in 1925. They proposed that the electron has an intrinsic spin, and therefore an intrinsic angular momentum which can either add to or subtract from the angular momentum generated by the movement of the electron through space. About a selected axis this spin angular momentum can have only two values, $+\frac{1}{2}(h/2\pi)$, and $-\frac{1}{2}(h/2\pi)$. There is thus a fourth quantum number s, the spin quantum number, which can have two possible values, $+\frac{1}{2}$ and $-\frac{1}{2}$. In order to specify the state of an electron completely we must give not only the three quantum numbers characterizing its orbital, but also must state whether the spin quantum number is $+\frac{1}{2}$ or $-\frac{1}{2}$.

Since an electron possesses an angular momentum, it has associated with it a magnetic dipole moment. Note the analogy here to a circulating electrical current. Thus, any system with only one electron must be paramagnetic, that is, must be attracted by a magnetic field. For a two-electron system paramagnetism will occur only if the spins of the electron are in the same direction. If they are in opposite directions, they cancel, and there is no net magnetic moment.

This completes the list of quantum numbers needed to describe the state of an electron in the field of a nucleus. The quantum numbers are $n = 1, 2, 3, 4,$ etc., $l = 0, 1, 2, 3, \ldots, (n - 1)$; $m = +l, \ldots, +1, 0, -1, \ldots, -l$; and $s = \pm\frac{1}{2}$. The energy content is determined practically exclusively by n in the case of the hydrogen atom, and, of course, observations on the atomic spectrum of hydrogen are consistent with this model.

13.24 The Periodic System

The experimental basis for our discussion of the electronic structures of many-electron atoms is provided by spectroscopic, magnetic, and chemical experiments. Such experiments are not always easy to interpret uniquely, and thus the correct assignment of an electronic structure is sometimes difficult, but the electronic structures of most atoms have been satisfactorily worked out.

It is the task of quantum mechanics to provide a consistent model for these experimental observations. This cannot be done rigorously for any atom other than hydrogen, since the mathematics required for a rigorous solution of any system more complex than the H atom does not exist. Therefore, approximation methods must be used.

We shall not attempt to discuss such approximation methods here. Instead, we shall limit ourselves to a discussion of the qualitative features of the wave mechanical model of the periodic system. Some rule regarding the type of orbitals occupied by the various electrons in a complex atom is needed, and this is found in the Pauli exclusion principle. For our purposes at this time an adequate statement of the rule is as follows: *No two electrons in any atom may have the same four quantum numbers.* With this restriction we may expect the permitted orbitals to be occupied in the order of increasing energy as we build up the atom by adding protons and electrons to the hydrogen atom. (This is the *Aufbau*, or "building up," principle.)

On the basis of these considerations we see that the lowest or ground state of the hydrogen atom is that for which $n = 1$ ($l = 0$, $m = 0$ and $s = \pm\frac{1}{2}$.) In helium the second electron can also occupy the $n = 1$ orbital, but the two electrons must have values of s opposite in sign in order to satisfy the Pauli principle. A simple notation giving the principal quantum number, designating the value of l by the letter $s(l = 0)$, $p(l = 1)$, $d(l = 2)$, $f(l = 3)$, etc., and the number of electrons in the orbital with a superscript applies as follows to the two atoms thus far described, $H = 1s^1$, $He = 1s^2$.

Before we discuss the lithium atom, the question of the relative energies of the various orbitals must be considered in more detail. As we have mentioned earlier, for the hydrogen atom the energy of the various orbitals is determined to a high degree of approximation by the main quantum number n. However, for more complex atoms the quantum number l is also important. As a first approximation such atoms can be thought of as consisting of two parts, (1) a core made up of the nucleus and all electron shells or subshells which are completely full, and (2) the electron of interest. Assuming now that the orbitals of all atoms are qualitatively similar to those of hydrogen having the same quantum numbers n and l we see an important difference between hydrogen and the other atoms. Consider the lithium atom, which has three protons in its nucleus, and three electrons distributed about that nucleus. The first two of these electrons will occupy the $n = 1$ level, the lowest energy level available. The core of this atom thus consists of a three proton two electron system with a net charge of $+1$. At the $n = 2$ level we have two types of orbitals available, s orbitals and p orbitals. As Fig. 13.15 indicates, an electron in a $2s$ orbital ($l = 0$) has a much higher probability of penetrating into this core than does an electron in a $2p$ orbital ($l = 1$); therefore, the average positive charge to which a $2s$ electron is subjected is higher than that to which a $2p$ electron is subjected. The potential energy term for the $2s$ electron is thus lower (more negative), than that for the $2p$ electron. The third electron will, therefore, occupy the $2s$ orbital, and the configuration of Li is $1s^2, 2s^1$. Similar considerations lead to the conclusion that in general, for more complex atoms, orbitals of the same main quantum number increase in energy as l increases.

The electron configuration of Be is written as $1s^2, 2s^2$, for B as $1s^2, 2s^2, 2p^1$, and for C as $1s^2, 2s^2, 2p^2$. Carbon poses two new problems. There are three equivalent p orbitals. (1) Will the second electron enter the occupied p orbital or a different p orbital? (2) If it enters a different p orbital, will its spin be the same as, or different from, that of the first electron? The first question seems easy to answer. Simple electrostatics tells us that the most stable arrangement of two electrons is one which puts them as far apart as possible, thereby minimizing the repulsive potential between them. Since the p orbitals occupy different regions in space (Fig. 13.16), the most stable arrangement of the two electrons will be that which places them in different orbitals. Now the electron spin must be considered. When electrons are placed in different orbitals, the arrangement in which they have parallel spins is energetically favored over that in which the spins are opposed.[10] Therefore in the lowest energy state the two p electrons of carbon should occupy different orbitals and have the same spin. The atom is thus paramagnetic with a paramagnetism corresponding to that for two electron spins. States in which two electrons have the same spin are known as *triplet states*, because they are triply degenerate. It should be clear to the student that two of the three degenerate states have spin $(+\frac{1}{2}, +\frac{1}{2})$, and $(-\frac{1}{2}, -\frac{1}{2})$. The resultant spins are $+1$ and -1. The intermediate state of resultant spin 0 is also possible (see Chapter 14).

We have seen above that when two electrons are to be distributed in two equivalent atomic orbitals, the triplet state will be lower in energy. This is an

---

[10]Electrons of the same spin tend to keep apart, an effect described as being due to *spin correlation*.

example of *Hund's first rule*, which may be stated as follows: Electrons with the same n and l values will occupy orbitals of different m values, and their spins will be unpaired so far as possible.

In the elements N through Ne the rest of the $2p$ orbitals are occupied. With Na the $3s$ orbital is occupied, and the elements after Na follow a pattern similar to that of the first row elements ending with Ar, $1s^2$, $2s^2$, $2p^6$, $3s^2$, $3p^6$. The parallel between the periodicity of electronic configuration as given by wave mechanics and the chemical properties of the elements is immediately evident. The origin of the first three periods is clear, and certain types of electronic structure can be associated with distinctive chemical properties. For example, after the first short "period" associated with $n = 1$, one s electron, whether $2s$, $3s$, $4s$, $5s$, or $6s$, evidently gives rise to alkali metal properties. On the other hand the configuration s^2, p^6 is that of a rare gas.

In potassium and calcium the $4s$ orbitals are filled. However, beginning with the next element, scandium, the $3d$ rather than the $4p$ shell begins to fill. We thus enter the first group of transition elements. These elements are characterized by multiple valency and by colored compounds. Both of these properties are associated with the fact that the $3d$ and $4s$ levels are close in energy. As a result, the number of electrons involved in bond formation can vary, and electronic transitions can take place at an energy corresponding to that available in a quantum of visible light.

The electronic structures of the transition elements cannot always be predicted on the basis of the simple model that we have presented. The use of hydrogen-like orbitals and the assumption of a definite order of energies which persists from atom to atom for these orbitals leads to a greatly oversimplified model. For example, the configuration of vanadium is $1s^2$, $2s^2$, $2p^6$, $3s^2$, $3p^6$, $3d^3$, $4s^2$, whereas that of chromium, the next element, is $1s^2$, $2s^2$, $2p^6$, $3s^2$, $3p^6$, $3d^5$, $4s^1$. This distribution is favored in chromium because it minimizes unfavorable interactions due both to coulomb repulsion and to spin correlation effects relative to the alternative configuration, $1s^2$, $2s^2$, $2p^6$, $3s^2$, $3p^6$, $3d^4$, $4s^2$, which puts two electrons in the $4s$ orbital. Evidently the reduction in the magnitude of the two unfavorable energy terms is sufficient to outweigh the "normal" difference in energy between the two orbitals. This could not have been predicted in advance from our model. (Note that we have been talking here in terms of a model which makes a useful but completely arbitrary division of the energy of the electron into separate parts.)

After filling the $3d$ orbitals the $4p$ orbitals are filled in the usual way. Then, after strontium, which has a completely filled $5s$ orbital, the $4d$ orbital is filled, beginning a second transition series.

Here we must call attention to a fourth type of orbital with $l = 3$, designated an f orbital. Since, for $l = 3$, m can have any integral value from $+3$ to -3, there are seven f orbitals. These seven orbitals can accommodate fourteen electrons. These $4f$ orbitals are evidently higher in energy than both the $5s$ and $6s$ orbitals and so do not begin to fill until after element 57, lanthanum, which has the electron structure $1s^2$, $2s^2$, $2p^6$, $3s^2$, $3p^6$, $3d^{10}$, $4s^2$, $4p^6$, $4d^{10}$, $5s^2$, $5p^6$, $5d^1$,

$6s^2$. The next element, cerium, has the structure $1s^2$, $2s^2$, $2p^6$, $3s^2$, $3p^6$, $3d^{10}$, $4s^2$, $4p^6$, $4d^{10}$, $4f^2$, $5s^2$, $5p^6$, $6s^2$. The following elements in which the $4f$ shell is being filled are called the lanthanides, or rare earths. When the $4f$ shell is completed, there is a transition series in which the $5d$ shell is filled. Finally the $6p$ shell is filled, and a rare gas configuration is reached.

In the last period the first two elements, francium and radium, have the expected electron structure. The next two elements, actinium and thorium, have electrons in the $6d$ shell. Then with protoactinium the $5f$ shell begins to fill. Thus, we have an actinide series analagous to the lanthanide series, although some of the elements do have $6d$ electrons. The $5f$ shell should be completed in nobelium, $1s^2$, $2s^2$, $2p^6$, $3s^2$, $3p^6$, $3d^{10}$, $4s^2$, $4p^6$, $4d^{10}$, $4f^{14}$, $5s^2$, $5p^6$, $5d^{10}$, $5f^{14}$, $6s^2$, $6p^6$, $7s^2$.

A considerable amount of information regarding the relative energy states of the various orbitals is summarized in Fig. 13.18.

13.25 Electron Configurations of Ions

Electron configurations of negative ions are obtained by addition of electrons to the lowest unoccupied energy level. Electron configurations of positive ions are obtained by subtraction of the most easily removed electrons. Thus, the electron configurations of F^-, Ne, and Na^+ are the same. However, the configurations of other ions are not so easily predicted. For example, on losing two electrons, the Mn atom (outer configuration $3d^5$ $4s^2$) assumes the $3d^5$, $4s^0$ configuration. The objection is often made that this is unreasonable, since the last electron added, a d electron, should have a higher energy than any other electron and, therefore, should be the easiest to remove. However, it should be remembered that in building up the atom we add both a proton and an electron to the previous atom. In ionizing the atom we remove only the electron. The energy relationships need not necessarily be the same, and, indeed, experimental results, the ultimate test of any hypothesis, show that they are not. Thus, a prediction of the relative stabilities of a $4s$ and a $3d$ electron in a given atom cannot safely be made on the basis of the order in which they were filled in building up the given atom from atoms of lower atomic number.

SUMMARY, CHAPTER 13

1. Fundamental atomic properties

Electron $e/m = 1.7588 \times 10^{11}$ coulomb kg.$^{-1}$

$e = 1.602 \times 10^{-19}$ coulomb

$m = 9.11 \times 10^{-28}$ g.

Proton $m = 1.674 \times 10^{-24}$ g.

Nuclear diameter, *ca.* 10^{-12} cm.

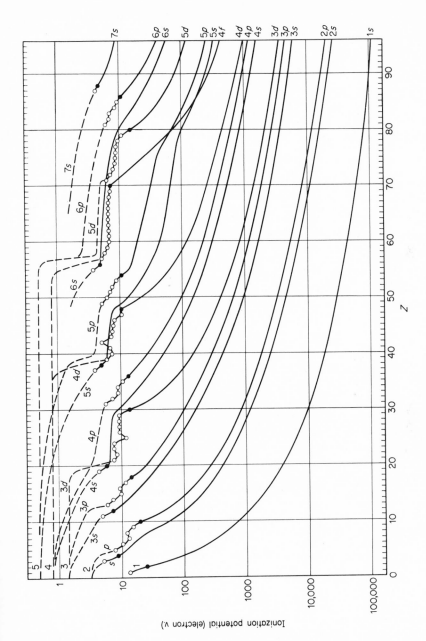

FIG. 13.18. Electron structure of atoms: ● = partly filled subshell; ‖ = filled subshell.

2. Nuclear composition
   Atomic number, Z = no. of protons
   Mass number, A = no. of neutrons + no. of protons
   Isotopes—same Z, different A
   Separation factor

$$\alpha = \sqrt{\frac{M_2}{M_1}}, \text{ for gaseous effusion}$$

   Net separation factor = α^n, where n = no. of stages

3. Quantum theory of electronic energy states
   Energy per quantum

$$E = h\nu; \qquad h = 6.6256 \times 10^{-27} \text{ erg. sec.}$$

   Bohr quantum condition

$$mvr_n = \frac{nh}{2\pi}$$

   Permitted energy states, H atom

$$E_n = -\frac{2\pi^2 me^4 Z^2}{h^2 n^2}$$

   Permitted transitions, the Balmer equation

$$\nu' = \frac{2\pi^2 me^4 Z^2}{ch^3} \left(\frac{1}{n'^2} - \frac{1}{n''^2} \right)$$

$$R = 109,737.31 \text{ cm.}^{-1}$$

   X ray lines, the Moseley equation

$$\sqrt{\nu} = a(Z - b)$$

4. Wave properties of matter
   Wave length of a particle, de Broglie equation

$$\lambda = \frac{h}{mv}$$

   Standing waves, particle in a box, one dimension

$$E_n = \frac{n^2 h^2}{8ma_x^2}$$

   Bohr quantum condition

$$2\pi r_n = n\lambda$$

   Uncertainty principle

$$\Delta p \times \Delta q \approx h$$

5. Atomic orbitals
   ψ, the wave function
   ψ^2, probability distribution function
   $r^2 R^2$, radial distribution function

Quantum numbers, integers describing the eigenfunctions

principal $n = 1, 2, 3, \ldots$

azimuthal $l = 0, 1, \ldots, n - 1$

magnetic $m = -l, \ldots, -1, 0, +1, \ldots, +l$

spin $s = \pm\frac{1}{2}$

PROBLEMS, CHAPTER 13

1. A beam of protons is accelerated from rest to a velocity of 3×10^6 meters sec.$^{-1}$.

(a) What potential difference would be required to achieve this velocity?

(b) If the proton beam is then passed through an electric field such as that described in Exercise 13.1, what deflection (x) would result?

Ans. (a) 4.69×10^4 volts, (b) 5.3×10^{-7} meters.

2. A beam of neon ions is examined in a Dempster mass spectrometer at an accelerating voltage of 1000 v. and a magnetic field strength of 1 weber m.$^{-2}$. Find the linear separation of ^{20}Ne and ^{22}Ne.   *Ans.* 1.0 mm.

3. A drop of oil of density 0.9 g. cm.$^{-3}$ and 10^{-5} cm. radius has one electronic unit of charge.

(a) What will be the velocity of free fall in air? The viscosity of air is 1.87×10^{-4} poise.

(b) What electric field strength will be required to hold the drop stationary? (Note: Use mks units in which $g = 9.80$ meter sec.$^{-2}$)

Ans. (a) 1.05×10^{-4} cm. sec.$^{-1}$, (b) 2.32 volts cm.$^{-1}$.

4. It is found that in a particular mass spectrometer the ion CO_2^+ is focused on the collecting electrode at $V = 1400$ v. and $H = 0.58$ webers m.$^{-2}$.

(a) The voltage shifts to a value of 1000 v. What value of H is now required to focus CO_2^+?

(b) At $H = 0.58$ weber m.$^{-2}$, what voltage would be required to focus CO_2^{++}?

5. A gaseous sample containing 99 mole per cent D_2 and 1 mole per cent H_2 is admitted to a mass spectrometer through a pinhole leak. What will be the relative intensities of the ions D_2^+ and H_2^+ assuming equal ionization efficiencies?

6. The atomic weight of lead obtained from thorium ores is found to be 207.71. Thorium decays to ^{208}Pb. Assuming that the abundance ratio ^{204}Pb: ^{206}Pb: ^{207}Pb is the same as that in ordinary lead, find the isotopic composition of the lead in thorium ore.   *Ans.* ^{208}Pb = 83 atom per cent.

7. The chlorine isotopes are to be fractionated by effusion of HCl gas through a system of 20 stages. Starting with the natural mixture, what is the maximum per cent of ^{35}Cl which can be expected?   *Ans.* 84 per cent.

8. From data in Table 13.3 estimate the minimum number of separation stages required to enrich natural nitrogen to ^{15}N = 10% by exchange of NH_3 (g) with NH_4^+ (aq.).   *Ans.* 148 stages.

9. An attempt is to be made to obtain enriched ^{18}O by fractional distillation of water. From data in Table 13.2 estimate the maximum net separation factor in a column of 100 plates for $H_2{}^{16}O$ and $H_2{}^{18}O$.

10. In the presence of a catalyst, H_2 and D_2 undergo an isotopic exchange reaction to form the mixed molecule HD. Show that if the isotopes had identical chemical properties, the value of the equilibrium constant for the exchange reaction

$$H_2 + D_2 = 2HD$$

$$K = \frac{P_{HD}^2}{P_{H_2} \cdot P_{D_2}}$$

would be 4. Taking this value, find the mole fraction of H_2, D_2, and HD after equilibration of a mixture consisting initially of equimolar amounts of H_2 and D_2.

Ans. $X_{H_2} = X_{D_2} = 0.25$.

11. The work function of cesium metal is 1.81 e.v. Compute the longest wave length of incident light that can eject a photoelectron from Cs.

12. Calculate the frequency in wave numbers and the wave length in angstroms of the first four lines of the Lyman series. (See Fig. 13.9.)

13. From the Bohr equation find the wave length at which the Balmer series converges, i.e, the wave length below which continuous absorption from $n = 2$ is to be expected. *Ans.* 3645 Å.

14. Apply Bohr's equation to He^+ and find the wave length of the first line of the series corresponding to the Balmer series of hydrogen, i.e., $n = 3$ to $n = 2$.

Ans. 1640 Å.

15. A certain spectral line at 4500 Å is found to have a "natural" breadth of 0.1 Å. This is to be taken as a measure of the uncertainty in the energy of the corresponding state. Apply the uncertainty principle to find the lifetime of the state. *Ans.* 6.7×10^{-11} sec.

16. Through what potential difference must protons be accelerated in order that they will have a wave length of 0.1 Å? *Ans.* 8.3 volts.

17. A certain element has a K X ray line with a wave length of 0.5 Å. Assume $b = 0.49$ and use the Rydberg constant to find the atomic number of this element.

Ans. $Z = 50$.

18. From Fig. 13.11 estimate the wave length of light required to ionize gaseous sodium atoms. (*Note:* In the mks system, volt × columb = joule = 10^7 erg.)

Ans. 2.4×10^{-5} cm.

19. For the ground state of the H atom the radial distribution function is almost symmetric about a_0, the Bohr radius, and the uncertainty in electron position can be approximated as a_0. (See Fig. 13.15.) An alternate statement of the uncertainty principle is $\Delta p\, \Delta q \approx h/2\pi$. Use this to show that $\bar{T} \approx 2\pi^2 me^4/h^2$, where $\bar{T}$ is the average kinetic energy of the electron. Compare to the Bohr model.

20. Assume an electron trapped in a one-dimensional box of the dimensions of a typical small nucleus ($r \sim 10^{-13}$ cm.). Calculate the energy of the lowest allowed level in electron volts. Discuss the possibility of electrons being bound in nuclei. (The energies of β particles emitted from nuclei are seldom more than 10^7 e.v.)

21. The walls of a rectangular box containing a particle of electronic mass are infinite. The dimensions of the box are $x = 1 \times 10^{-8}$ cm., $y = 1 \times 10^{-8}$ cm., and $z = 2 \times 10^{-8}$ cm. Compute the energies of the six lowest levels and list all the wave functions that belong to each level.

22. Although positive and negative electrons eventually annihilate each other with resultant production of energy equivalent to their masses, they can form a short-lived complex called *positronium*. Assume a model for this complex similar to the Bohr model for the hydrogen atom.

(a) Compute the energy difference between the ground state and the first excited state. (Use of the electron mass, m_e, in our development of the Bohr model, was an approximation. Properly the reduced mass, μ, must be used. For this problem $\mu = m_e m_p / (m_e + m_p)$, where m_p is the mass of the positive electron (positron).)

(b) Compute the energy required to completely separate the positron and the electron.

(c) Repeat (b) for mesonium, a proton and a negative μ meson of mass 207 times that of the electron.

23. The 1s wave function for the hydrogen atom is

$$\psi_{100} = \frac{1}{\pi^{1/2} a_0^{3/2}} e^{-r/a_0}$$

Compute the probability of an electron being between (a) $r = 0$ and $r = a_0/2$, (b) $r = 0$ and $r = a_0$, and (c) $r = 0$ and $r = \frac{3}{2} a_0$.

24. For $l = 0$ the radial part of the Schrödinger equation for hydrogen reduces to

$$\frac{d^2 R}{dr^2} + \frac{2}{r} \frac{dR}{dr} + \frac{8\pi^2 m}{h^2} (E - V) R = 0$$

The $n = 1$ eigenfunction has the form

$$R = N e^{-\alpha r}$$

where N is a constant, r is the radius, and $\alpha^2 = -(8\pi^2 mE)/h^2$. Use the wave equation to deduce the formula for the energy of this state, and compare to that for the lowest state of the Bohr model.

25. Show that for the ground state of the hydrogen atom the quantum mechanical treatment requires that the most probable value of the radius, r, is a_0, the Bohr radius.

26. A particle of mass m is restricted to rotation at a constant radius r. The correct form of the wave equation for this situation is

$$\frac{1}{r^2} \frac{d^2 \psi}{d\phi^2} + \frac{8\pi^2 m}{h^2} (E - V) \psi = 0$$

where ϕ is the angular coordinate. Assume that the potential energy is zero and show the following:

(a) $\psi_M = \frac{1}{\sqrt{2\pi}} e^{iM\phi}$ and $\frac{1}{\sqrt{2\pi}} e^{-iM\phi}$

(b) $E_M = M^2 h^2 / 8\pi^2 mr^2$, where $M = 0, \pm 1, \pm 2$. Especially consider the reasons why M may equal 0.

14

MOLECULAR STRUCTURE

14.1 The Binding of Atoms

Historically one of the chief pursuits of chemistry has been the search for a model which will describe systems of bound atoms. In principle that search ended with the advent of the quantum theory. In order to obtain the wave function describing the bound system, the exact procedure would involve substitution of all the potential interactions involved in the bound system for V in the wave equation, and solution of the resulting differential equation for the appropriate ψ functions. This method should work equally well for those compounds which we ordinarily think of as ionic, such as sodium chloride, and for those compounds which we ordinarily think of as covalent, such as H_2. Unfortunately, this procedure founders in a sea of mathematical difficulties. Exact solutions of the wave equation for all but the very simplest problems cannot be obtained.

Consequently, simplified approximate descriptions of bound systems must be sought. For ionic bonds the electron distribution is so assymmetric that the valence electrons can be well approximated as belonging almost completely to one of the bound atoms. Thus, sodium chloride can be described to a high degree of approximation as $Na^+ Cl^-$.

In contrast to the ionic bond, the covalent bond can be satisfactorily described only by the use of wave mechanics. The problem may be approached in the following way. Assume a wave function, ψ, as a description of the electron distribution in the system of interest. Then use this function to compute the energy of the system. Modify the wave equation and re-calculate the energy. That function which comes closest to reproducing the experimental binding

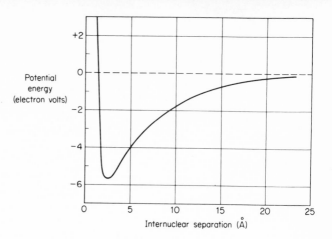

FIG. 14.1. Potential energy of Na^+Cl^-.

energy is assumed to provide the best description of the system. There are various systematic procedures for choosing initial forms for these approximate wave functions. Later in this chapter simplified versions of two will be discussed, the *molecular orbital method*, and the *valence bond method*.

As we discuss these procedures the student should keep clearly in mind that one is not "right" and the other "wrong." They are merely different approximations which emphasize different aspects of the problem. In some problems one of these methods is often found to provide a simpler and more accurate description than the other. On these grounds it is therefore preferred for that particular problem.

14.2 The Ionic Bond

In the last section it has been pointed out that the problem of bonding in compounds such as NaCl could be treated through wave mechanics. However, there is a simpler approach to an adequate description of this type of bonding. In fact, historically the treatment of this problem antedated wave mechanics. The clue to a satisfactory model was provided by observations such as that of electrical conduction by molten NaCl. Such electrical conduction implied the existence of the charged particles Na^+ and Cl^- in molten NaCl and, by extension, in crystalline NaCl as well.

In the most simple model Na^+ and Cl^- ions may be treated as point particles of charge $+e$ and $-e$. The potential energy decrease when these ions are brought to the internuclear separation r, which is 2.5×10^{-8} cm. for gaseous NaCl, may then be calculated by using the coulombic relation:

$$V = -e^2/r = -(4.80 \times 10^{-10} \text{e.s.u.})^2/(2.51 \times 10^{-8}\text{cm.}) = -9.17 \times 10^{-12} \text{ ergs}$$
$$(9.17 \times 10^{-12} \text{ ergs}) (6.24 \times 10^{11}\text{e.v. erg}^{-1}) = -5.73 \text{ e.v.}$$

This simple model thus indicates strong bonding between Na^+ and Cl^-.

According to the coulombic law, the most energetically favorable arrangement of positive and negative point charges would be that in which they are superimposed. However, real ions are not point charges. They consist of a positively charged core surrounded by mobile electrons. As the ions, drawn by the coulombic attraction of their net opposite charges, come close together, repulsion between the groups of electrons belonging to each ion begins to become important. This repulsion shows an r^{-n} dependence where n is in the range from 6 to 12. The interaction between coulombic attraction and this short-range repulsive force results in a minimum in the potential energy curve as shown in Fig. 14.1. This topic is discussed further in Chapter 15.

As with any model this simple electrostatic model for bonding in NaCl must be compared to experimental observation. The prediction of a 5.73 e.v. binding energy between Na^+ and Cl^- in the gas phase cannot be directly verified. However, the basic assumptions of coulombic (r^{-1}) energy terms corresponding to attractions and repulsions, and of strong short-range (r^{-n}) energy terms corresponding to repulsion can be used to calculate the energy evolved in the formation of the NaCl crystal lattice from gaseous Na^+ and Cl^- ions. The calculated value, 7.80 e.v., is to be compared to an experimental value of 8.02 e.v. derived by the use of the Born-Haber cycle (Chapter 15). The model is evidently quite satisfactory.

On the basis of this simple electrostatic model the bond energy of gaseous Na^+Cl^- may be estimated. The reaction of interest is $Na(g) + Cl(g) \rightarrow Na^+Cl^-$ (g). For convenience in calculation, the energy of this reaction may be considered to be the sum of the energies of three individual processes: (1) the energy required to remove an electron from a sodium atom and convert it to a sodium ion, measured by the *ionization potential I* of sodium; (2) the energy evolved when an electron is attached to the chlorine atom to form the chloride ion, measured by the *electron affinity A* of chlorine; (3) the energy evolved when the two ions interact, calculated, as we have seen, by the coulombic law.

(1) $Na(g)$	$\rightarrow Na^+(g) + e$	$q = I$	$=$	5.14 e.v.
(2) $Cl(g) + e$	$\rightarrow Cl^-(g)$	$q = -A$	$=$	-3.62 e.v.
(3) $Na^+(g) + Cl^-(g)$	$\rightarrow Na^+Cl^-(g)$		$q =$	-5.73 e.v.
	$Na(g) + Cl(g) \rightarrow Na^+Cl^-(g)$		$q =$	-4.21 e.v.

As this calculation of the bond energy of NaCl shows, formation of a strong ionic bond will be favored by a low ionization potential (Reaction 1), and by a high electron affinity (reaction 2). Elements of low ionization potential are those which have only one or two electrons in the outermost orbital, and are, therefore, found at the beginning of a period. Elements of high electron affinity need only one or two electrons for completion of a rare gas configuration (s^2p^6), and are, therefore, typically found at the end of a period. The electron affinities of some elements are listed in Table 14.1.

TABLE 14.1

ELECTRON AFFINITIES

Element	A (e.v.)
F	3.448 ± 0.005[1]
Cl	3.613 ± 0.003[1]
Br	3.363 ± 0.003[1]
I	3.063 ± 0.003[1]
O	1.465 ± 0.005[2]
S	$2.07 \ \pm 0.07$[3]

[1]R. S. Berry and C. W. Reimann, *J. Chem. Phys.*, **38**, 1540 (1963).
[2]L. M. Branscomb, D. S. Burch, S. J. Smith, and S. Geltman, *Phys. Rev.*, **111**, 504 (1958).
[3]L. M. Branscomb and S. J. Smith, *J. Chem. Phys.*, **25**, 598 (1956).

14.3 The Covalent Bond

In sodium chloride closed electron shells are assigned both to the sodium ion and to the chloride ion. As a result, the sodium and chloride ions with their associated electrons can be treated as individual charged particles and the laws of classical electrostatics can be used to determine the binding between them. However, there is another large class of compounds which show no physical evidence of the presence of ions. Extreme examples of this class are provided by the diatomic molecules, H_2, N_2, O_2, etc. The atoms in these molecules are strongly bound to each other; that is, the bound state represents a lower total energy (potential plus kinetic) than does the state in which the two atoms are at infinite separation.

$$H + H \longrightarrow H_2 \qquad \Delta E = -103 \text{ kcal. mole}^{-1}$$

$$N + N \longrightarrow N_2 \qquad \Delta E = -225 \text{ kcal. mole}^{-1}$$

$$O + O \longrightarrow O_2 \qquad \Delta E = -117 \text{ kcal. mole}^{-1}$$

Clearly, there is no reason to expect electron transfer in these systems. In fact, in contrast to the situation with NaCl this low total energy cannot be accounted for in terms of a coulombic interaction between two point charges. It can be accounted for only by a description based on wave mechanics. This description must necessarily be approximate, since a complete wave function can be obtained only for a one-electron system.

In order to make the discussion more concrete, we will consider the simplest covalently bonded system, H_2^+. The equilibrium nuclear distance in H_2^+ is 1.06 Å, and the bond dissociation energy is 2.79 e.v.

$$H_2^+ = H^+ + H \qquad \Delta E = 2.79 \text{ e.v.}$$

H_2^+ can be considered to be made up of three particles, two protons, and an electron. Consider now a very simple electrostatic model (not H_2^+) consisting of three point particles, two positively charged at a distance of 1.06 Å, and one negatively charged midway between them. The potential energy of the system in this configuration is 41 e.v. lower than that when the particles are infinitely separated. In terms of electrostatic potential energy, this is an extremely favorable arrangement.

EXERCISE 14.1

Consider coulombic attraction and repulsions and show that the energy of the array described in the preceding paragraph is -41 e.v.

Despite this favorable potential energy, this array is, of course, unrealistic as a model for H_2^+ where the negative particle is an electron. However, we shall explore it further by asking how it might be made more realistic. The answer to this question comes from wave mechanics. The basic difficulty with the proposed electrostatic array as a model for H_2^+ is that the electron must be represented by a highly localized wave function. This results in a very high calculated kinetic energy (Exercise 14.2), the total energy of the system is very high, and the model system is actually unstable.

However, wave mechanics indicates in principle how the model might be altered to be made suitable. In wave mechanics the electron is represented by a probability density distribution function, rather than by a point. This has the effect of "spreading out" the electron. Since with such a function the probability of finding the electron in the most electrostatically favorable position is decreased from the unit probability that we assumed in our electrostatic model, the potential energy resulting from the interaction of this electron with the two protons will increase (become more positive). At the same time, since the wave function describing the electron is less concentrated in space, the kinetic energy calculated from this function will decrease. The eventual result will be a system with some build-up of the electron density distribution function in the internuclear region with a consequent decrease in electrostatic potential energy larger than the accompanying increase in kinetic energy relative to the species H and H^+ at infinite separation.

When electrostatic coulombic type potentials only are considered, the kinetic energy and the potential energy of an equilibrium system are related in quantum mechanical systems exactly as in classical systems. This relation is described by the *Virial theorem*, which states that the energy E of the system is given by the relation $E = -\bar{T} = \bar{V}/2$, where $\bar{T}$ is the average kinetic energy of the electron system and $\bar{V}$ is its average potential energy. Thus, according to this theorem the total energy of a system is directly related to its potential energy. The system H_2^+ shows a bond energy of 2.79 e.v. The Virial theorem requires that this be directly related to the fact that the potential energy of H_2^+ is lower than that of $H + H^+$.

To recapitulate, atoms are bonded covalently because an increase of electron probability in the internuclear region leads to a lowering of the electrostatic potential energy in the bound system relative to the separated atoms. The ionic bond is also explained as resulting from a decrease in electrostatic potential energy. In this fundamental respect there is no difference between the ionic and covalent bonds. We must treat them differently, because, in the ionic bond to a high degree of approximation, electrons may be treated as belonging to individual ions, and the detailed distribution of these electrons is, therefore, relatively unimportant in deciding the interaction between these ions. In our description of the covalent bond in H_2^+ the bonding electron belongs to both the ions being bonded, and as a result the detailed electron distribution is extremely important in any calculation of the energy of this system.

Since mathematical complexities prevent determination of exact wave functions describing electron distributions in chemically bonded systems, approximate wave functions must be used. These approximate wave functions are often synthesized from atomic wave functions, and in the next two sections we shall examine two such methods of synthesis. The results obtained with any wave function are in part a function of the method of synthesis employed, and, therefore, the student should be wary of attaching too much physical significance to these results.

14.4 The Molecular Orbital Approach Using Diatomic Molecules as an Example

To describe exactly an electron in a molecule, a function would be required which describes the interaction of that electron with all the nuclei and all the other electrons of that molecule. Such a function is described as a *molecular orbital*. As we have mentioned earlier, such functions in general are out of reach because of mathematical complexities. A more limited practical goal is the synthesis of suitable approximate functions. Let us consider one such approach to the development of approximate functions to describe the bonding in the hydrogen molecule ion. This system consists of two nuclei, which we shall label A and B, and one electron. If the two nuclei are infinitely separated, then there are two possible energetically equivalent descriptions of the system. The first is $H_A + H_B^+$ with the electron on nucleus A. Its wave function is symbolized by $\psi_A(1)$. The second is $H_A^+ + H_B$, symbolized by the wave function $\psi_B(1)$. When the nuclei are close together, neither of these alone will serve as a description, since each describes the electron as being distributed around one nucleus only, and the electron distribution in H_2^+ must actually be symmetric about both nuclei, since they are equivalent. Two functions can be constructed from $\psi_A(1)$ and $\psi_B(1)$ which reflect this basic requirement, $[\psi_A(1) + \psi_B(1)]$ and $[\psi_A(1) - \psi_B(1)]$. The electron distribution is described by the square of these functions, and for both these functions the requirement that the distribution about A be equivalent to that about B is met. The function $[\psi_A(1) + \psi_B(1)]$ is known as a $\sigma 1s$ molecular orbital. The σ denotes cylindrical symmetry about the internuclear axis, and $1s$ indicates the atomic orbitals from which the molecular orbital was constructed. The function $[\psi_A(1) - \psi_B(1)]$ is known as a σ^*1s molecular orbital, and like the σ $1s$ orbital has cylindrical symmetry about the internuclear axis.

The function $[\psi_A(1) + \psi_B(1)]$ describes a build-up of electron density between the two nuclei. When it is substituted into an appropriate equation, an energy can be calculated for the equilibrium distance of separation of the two nuclei which is 1.76 e.v. lower than the energy when they are completely separated. Consequently, it represents a bonding orbital. (The difference between calculated and observed dissociation energies represents an error of about 37 per cent.) The function $[\psi_A(1) - \psi_B(1)]$ shows a node in the internuclear region with a consequent increase of 1.76 e.v. in energy at the equilibrium distance of separation relative to the separated nuclei. Therefore it represents an unbound state, and it is called an *antibonding* orbital. Since the molecular orbital functions were constructed from a *Linear Combination of Atomic Orbitals*, this is known as the *L.C.A.O.-M.O.* approach.

If we turn now to the problem of the hydrogen molecule, the molecular orbitals should be the same as for the hydrogen molecule ion. H_2 has two electrons, and the Pauli principle allows the placing of both in the bonding orbital so long as their spins are opposed. Therefore, the wave function for this system would be

$$[\psi_A(1) + \psi_B(1)] [\psi_A(2) + \psi_B(2)]$$

The *L.C.A.O.* method can also be applied to the hydrogen orbitals of main quantum number 2. The $2s$ atomic orbitals combine to give both a bonding and an anti-bonding orbital. These are designated as $\sigma 2s$ and $\sigma^* 2s$ orbitals. The p_x atomic orbitals, which we shall designate as those extending along the internuclear axis, also combine to give molecular orbitals of σ symmetry, $\sigma 2p_x$ and $\sigma^* 2p_x$. In contrast, the combination of two $2p_y$ or $2p_z$ orbitals gives rise to molecular orbitals which have a node in a plane passing through the two nuclei. These are called π orbitals. Thus we have the bonding orbitals, $\pi 2p_y$ and $\pi 2p_z$, and the anti-bonding orbitals, $\pi^* 2p_y$ and $\pi^* 2p_z$, which have spatial characteristics quite different from those of the σ orbitals. Schematic diagrams of these orbitals are given in Fig. 14.2. The theoretical treatment also indicates the relative energy of the various orbitals to be in the order $\sigma 1s < \sigma^* 1s < \sigma 2s < \sigma^* 2s < \sigma 2p_x < \pi 2p_y = \pi 2p_z < \pi^* 2p_y = \pi^* 2p_z < \sigma^* 2p_x$.

With this information it is possible to predict the electronic configuration of some simple diatomic molecules, two electrons of opposite spins being placed in each orbital, according to the Pauli principle, as we have seen. H_2 in its lowest electronic energy state (↑↓ in Fig. 14.5) will be expected to have two electrons in the orbital of lowest energy. This configuration is abbreviated $H_2(\sigma 1s)^2$. The first excited state (↑↑ in Fig. 14.5) must be $H_2(\sigma 1s)^1(\sigma^* 1s)^1$, having one bonding and one antibonding electron. The effects of these two electrons cancel, and no bond exists. The hypothetical molecule He_2 would have the configuration $(\sigma 1s)^2(\sigma^* 1s)^2$, that is, two bonding electrons and two antibonding electrons, and again no significant net attraction is observed. For the succeeding diatomic molecules it is presumed that the K shell of the atoms is not involved in the bond, and only the molecular orbitals arising from the second shell are specified. Thus for three of the well-known gaseous diatomic elements we have,

$$N_2: \quad KK(\sigma 2s)^2 (\sigma^* 2s)^2 (\sigma 2p)^2 (\pi 2p)^4$$

$$O_2: \quad KK(\sigma 2s)^2 (\sigma^* 2s)^2 (\sigma 2p)^2 (\pi 2p)^4 (\pi^* 2p)^2$$

$$F_2: \quad KK(\sigma 2s)^2 (\sigma^* 2s)^2 (\sigma 2p)^2 (\pi 2p)^4 (\pi^* 2p)^4$$

There are six net bonding electrons in N_2 which can be said to constitute a triple bond. However, one pair occupies a σ orbital, and the others occupy π orbitals. In O_2 there are only four net bonding electrons, two σ and two π and O_2 is doubly bonded. In both of these cases of multiple bond formation, the molecular orbital treatment indicates that the several bonds are not equivalent.

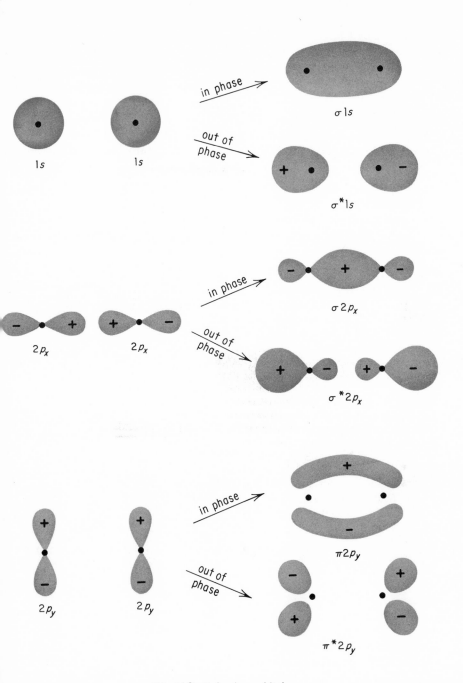

FIG. 14.2. Molecular orbitals.

Finally, in oxygen a peculiar experimental fact is successfully explained by the molecular orbital treatment. Oxygen gas is paramagnetic (see section 14.11), which means that the molecule has electrons with unpaired spins. This is to be

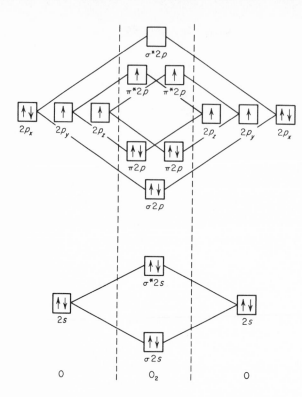

FIG. 14.3. Schematic diagram of occupation of molecular orbitals in O_2.

expected of the two π^*2p electrons, which, because of a mutual repulsion, may be expected to occupy the separate orbitals π^*2p_y and π^*2p_z with parallel spins (Fig. 14.3), giving the molecule a net magnetic moment. Note that this is not to be expected in either nitrogen or fluorine, which are indeed diamagnetic.

EXERCISE 14.3

Write the electron structure of C_2 (observed in flames) according to molecular orbital theory and show that the ground state is expected to be paramagnetic.

14.5 The Heitler-London Treatment of Hydrogen

An alternative to the *L. C.A.O.–M.O.* description of the bonding in hydrogen was provided by W. Heitler and F. London. As a starting point for an understanding of their approach, we shall write down the wave equation for H_2. We shall consider two nuclei, labeled A and B, and two electrons, labeled 1 and 2. The wave function ψ must be differentiated with respect to the coordinates of electron 1, x_1, y_1, z_1, and with respect to those of electron 2, x_2, y_2, z_2. In addition, we must explicitly include all potential energy terms arising from coulombic interactions. That for nucleus A and electron 1 will be of the form $-e^2/r_{A1}$ where r_{A1} is the distance between nucleus A and electron 1; that for nucleus A and electron 2 is $-e^2/r_{A2}$ where r_{A2} is the distance between nucleus A and electron 2 (see Fig. 14.4). The other attractive terms are $-e^2/r_{B1}$ and $-e^2/r_{B2}$. There are in addition two potential energy terms arising from repulsions, $+e^2/r_{12}$ for the interaction between the two electrons, and $+e^2/r_{AB}$ between the two nuclei. The result is the following equation.

FIG. 14.4. Diagram illustrating the potential interactions in H_2.

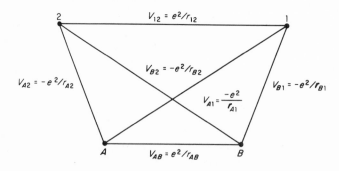

$$\frac{\partial^2 \psi}{\partial x_1^2} + \frac{\partial^2 \psi}{\partial y_1^2} + \frac{\partial^2 \psi}{\partial z_1^2} + \frac{\partial^2 \psi}{\partial x_2^2} + \frac{\partial^2 \psi}{\partial y_2^2} + \frac{\partial^2 \psi}{\partial z_2^2}$$

$$+ \frac{8\pi^2 m}{h^2}\left(E + \frac{e^2}{r_{A1}} + \frac{e^2}{r_{B2}} + \frac{e^2}{r_{A2}} + \frac{e^2}{r_{B1}} - \frac{e^2}{r_{12}} - \frac{e^2}{r_{AB}}\right)\Psi = 0 \qquad (14.1)$$

Equation (14.1) cannot be solved exactly for all possible internuclear distances. However, at large separations the system described by this equation must be two normal hydrogen atoms. We shall now verify by direct substitution into equation (14.1) that at large separations the function $[\psi_A(2)\,\psi_B(1)]$ assigning electron 1 to nucleus B and electron 2 to nucleus A is a solution if the potential energy terms involving r_{A1}, r_{B2}, r_{12}, and r_{AB} are all assumed to be small. These are valid assumptions with this electron assignment at large separations of A and B. Substituting $[\psi_A(2)\,\psi_B(1)]$ into equation (14.1), we have

$$\frac{\partial^2[\psi_A(2)\psi_B(1)]}{\partial x_1^2} + \frac{\partial^2[\psi_A(2)\psi_B(1)]}{\partial y_1^2} + \frac{\partial^2[\psi_A(2)\psi_B(1)]}{\partial z_1^2} + \frac{\partial^2[\psi_A(2)\psi_B(1)]}{\partial x_2^2}$$

$$+ \frac{\partial^2[\psi_A(2)\psi_B(1)]}{\partial y_2^2} + \frac{\partial^2[\psi_A(2)\psi_B(1)]}{\partial z_2^2} + \frac{8\pi^2 m}{h^2}\left(E + \frac{e^2}{r_{A2}} + \frac{e^2}{r_{B1}}\right)\psi_A(2)\psi_B(1) = 0$$

$$(14.2)$$

Recalling that $\psi_A(2)$ contains only the coordinates of electron 2 and is therefore constant with respect to variations in x_1, y_1, and z_1; that the same is true with respect to $\psi_B(1)$ and the coordinates of electron 2; and that E, the total energy of the two-atom system must equal $E_A + E_B$, the sum of the energies of atoms A and B, we rewrite equation (14.2) as

$$\psi_A(2)\left[\frac{\partial^2\psi_B(1)}{\partial x_1^2} + \frac{\partial^2\psi_B(1)}{\partial y_1^2} + \frac{\partial^2\psi_B(1)}{\partial z_1^2} + \frac{8\pi^2 m}{h^2}\left(E_B + \frac{e^2}{r_{B1}}\right)\psi_B(1)\right]$$

$$+ \psi_B(1)\left[\frac{\partial^2\psi_A(2)}{\partial x_2^2} + \frac{\partial^2\psi_A(2)}{\partial y_2^2} + \frac{\partial^2\psi_A(2)}{\partial z_2^2} + \frac{8\pi^2 m}{h^2}\left(E_A + \frac{e^2}{r_{A2}}\right)\psi_A(2)\right] = 0$$

$$(14.3)$$

The terms in brackets are simply wave equations for hydrogen atoms and are, therefore, equal to 0. Thus, we have an identity and $[\psi_A(2)\,\psi_B(1)]$ is indeed a solution of equation (14.1) at large separations.

However, this is not the only solution. An argument similar to that which we have just given shows that $[\psi_A(1)\,\psi_B(2)]$ is also an acceptable solution to equation (14.1) at large separations, and so are the sum function $[\psi_A(2)\,\psi_B(1) + \psi_A(1)\,\psi_B(2)]$ and the difference function $[\psi_A(2)\,\psi_B(1) - \psi_A(1)\,\psi_B(2)]$.

EXERCISE 14.4

Verify that $[\psi_A(1)\,\psi_B(2)]$, $[\psi_A(2)\,\psi_B(1) + \psi_A(1)\,\psi_B(2)]$, and $[\psi_A(2)\,\psi_B(1) - \psi_A(1)\,\psi_B(2)]$ are all solutions of equation (14.1) at large separations.

We now have four exact solutions for the system of two hydrogen atoms at infinite separation $[\psi_A(1)\,\psi_B(2)]$, $[\psi_A(2)\,\psi_B(1)]$, $[\psi_A(2)\psi_B(1) + \psi_A(1)\psi_B(2)]$, and $[\psi_A(2)\,\psi_B(1) - \psi_A(1)\,\psi_B(2)]$. These four functions can be tested as solutions of the wave equation at finite separations. It can be shown [W. Heitler and F. London, *Z. Physik.*, **44**, 455 (1927)] that each of the first three leads to a build-up of electron density in the internuclear region, and to a lowering of potential energy relative to the separated atoms. The first two give bonding energies of only 0.4 e.v., whereas the function $[\psi_A(2)\psi_B(1) + \psi_A(1)\psi_B(2)]$ gives a maximum bonding energy of 3.14 e.v.[1] (Fig. 14.5). The experimental binding energy is 4.75 e.v., and that calculated from the simple molecular orbital approach is 2.68 e.v.

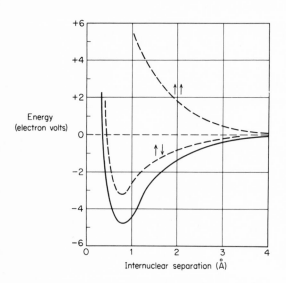

Energy (electron volts)

Internuclear separation (Å)

FIG. 14.5. Binding energy of the hydrogen molecule.

---- theoretical

—— experimental

That the function $[\psi_A(2)\psi_B(1) + \psi_A(1)\psi_B(2)]$ is superior to the functions $[\psi_A(1)\psi_B(2)]$ and $[\psi_A(2)\psi_B(1)]$ is a consequence of the fact that it is the only function of the three which takes into account the basic fact that the two electrons must be indistinguishable, and each must therefore be distributed about both nuclei in the same way. Since in the model which we are considering this was done by the device of exchanging electrons (1) and (2) between nuclei A and B the energy difference, 2.74 e.v., between $[\psi_A(2)\psi_B(1) + \psi_A(1)\psi_B(2)]$ and $[\psi_A(1)\psi_B(2)]$, is often referred to as an *exchange energy*. It should be clear from the discussion that exchange energy is not inherent in nature, but arises in the Heitler-London treatment as a result of the particular method chosen for the synthesis of the approximate wave function. The difference function $[\psi_A(2)\psi_B(1) - \psi_A(1)\psi_B(2)]$ has not yet been considered. This function shows a steady increase in energy as internuclear separation decreases (Fig. 14.5). It therefore represents an unbound state. Finally the question of the electron spins in the two states $[\psi_A(2)\psi_B(1) + \psi_A(1)\psi_B(2)]$ and $[\psi_A(2)\psi_B(1) - \psi_A(1)\psi_B(2)]$, must be considered. As we have mentioned earlier, only two spin states are possible for an electron. We shall designate these as α and β. For a two-electron system two possible combined spin functions are $[\alpha(2)\alpha(1)]$, and $[\beta(2)\beta(1)]$, in which each electron has the same spin function. By analogy to the Heitler-London treatment of wave functions, two other spin functions are

---

[1] The Heitler-London function actually leads to a lowering of kinetic energy in the molecule relative to that of the separated atoms. This contradicts the Virial theorem, and, therefore, must be an incorrect description of the source of the binding energy in H_2. This is not surprising in view of the extreme nature of the basic approximations. See J. W. Linnett, "Wave Mechanics and Valency", Methuen and Co., Ltd., London (1960) for further discussion.

possible of the form $[\alpha(2)\beta(1) + \alpha(1)\beta(2)]$ and $[\alpha(2)\beta(1) - \alpha(1)\beta(2)]$. There are thus four possible spin functions to go with the two wave functions. However, the Pauli postulate eliminates four of the resulting eight possibilities. In its more general form this postulate requires that the total wave function including the spin function, be antisymmetric to the exchange of electrons, that is, the sign of the wave function must change when the electrons are exchanged. If $[\psi_A(2)\psi_B(1) + \psi_A(1)\psi_B(2)]$ is considered, the only spin function with which it can be combined to give a resulting function which is antisymmetric to electron exchange is $[\alpha(2)\beta(1) - \alpha(1)\beta(2)]$. The wave function $[\psi_A(2)\psi_B(1) - \psi_A(1)\psi_B(2)]$ can be combined with any of the other three spin functions. The combined functions with appropriate normalizing constants are shown in Table 14.2.

TABLE 14.2

COMPLETE HEITLER-LONDON WAVE FUNCTION FOR H$_2$.

1. $\left[\dfrac{1}{\sqrt{2}} \psi_A(2)\psi_B(1) + \dfrac{1}{\sqrt{2}} \psi_A(1)\psi_B(2) \right]\left[\dfrac{1}{\sqrt{2}} \alpha(2)\beta(1) - \dfrac{1}{\sqrt{2}} \alpha(1)\beta(2) \right]$

2. $\left[\dfrac{1}{\sqrt{2}} \psi_A(2)\psi_B(1) - \dfrac{1}{\sqrt{2}} \psi_A(1)\psi_B(2) \right]\left[\alpha(2)\alpha(1) \right]$

3. $\left[\dfrac{1}{\sqrt{2}} \psi_A(2)\psi_B(1) - \dfrac{1}{\sqrt{2}} \psi_A(1)\psi_B(2) \right]\left[\beta(2)\beta(1) \right]$

4. $\left[\dfrac{1}{\sqrt{2}} \psi_A(2)\psi_B(1) - \dfrac{1}{\sqrt{2}} \psi_A(1)\psi_B(2) \right]\left[\dfrac{1}{\sqrt{2}} \alpha(2)\beta(1) + \dfrac{1}{\sqrt{2}} \alpha(1)\beta(2) \right]$

The consideration of the spin requirement thus leads to the conclusion that the higher energy function is actually a *triplet*, that is, it is triply degenerate.

The method which we have just outlined can be extended to polyatomic molecules. In this approach chemical bonding is described in terms of the interaction of two atomic orbitals on adjacent nuclei. The relationship to the traditional electron-pair bond of the chemist is clear, and, therefore, this method is known as the *valence bond approach*.

14.6 The Geometry and Bonding of Polyatomic Molecules

The spatial arrangement of atoms in a polyatomic molecule can often be predicted by use of the simple principle that electron pairs will show a coulombic repulsion and at short range an even stronger Pauli repulsion for other electron pairs. (Recall that electrons of the same spin tend to avoid each other.) On the basis of these considerations alone, spatial arrangements will be preferred which place electron pairs as far as possible from each other. For example, consider $CH_3 - Hg - CH_3$. There are two electron pairs about the central mercury atom. These will be as far from each other as possible when the molecule is linear. Therefore, this is the favored arrangement. When there are three electron pairs about a central atom as in BF$_3$ the most favored arrangement should be triangular; for four electron pairs, as in CH$_4$, tetrahedral;

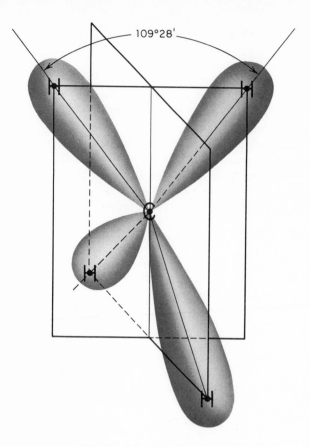

109°28'

FIG. 14.6. Bond orbitals in CH₄.

for six electron pairs, as in SF₆, octahedral, etc. When the number of electron pairs exceeds the number of
bonded groups, variations from these
simple predictions can be observed.
However, even in these situations, electrostatic and Pauli repulsion forces
play major roles in determining the
geometry of molecules.

It is one of the early triumphs of
wave mechanics that it was able to
provide a *description* of the observed
geometry of molecules. Consider, for
example, the methane molecule. All
C — H bonds in this molecule are
equivalent, and, as we have seen, since
there are four electron pairs, the C — H
bonds should be directed to the corners
of a regular tetrahedron with the carbon atom in the center. To meet the
requirement for four covalent bonds
all four of the carbon atom orbitals
must be used in the description of CH₄.
However, the four atomic orbitals cannot be used directly, since they are of
two different classes, 2s and 2p. If
these are used directly, the 2s orbitals lead to a different class of bond than
the 2p orbitals, and the description is unsatisfactory. The solution of this
problem is largely due to Linus Pauling, who proposed that four *hybrid atomic
orbitals* be constructed. Each hybrid orbital is constructed from one s and three
p atomic orbitals (*sp³*). Since there are four atomic orbitals, four equivalent
hybrid orbitals result. These orbitals are directed towards the corners of a regular
tetrahedron (Fig. 14.6). Moreover, they are more concentrated in space than the
atomic orbitals from which they are synthesized. Thus, when the C — H bond
in CH₄ is approximated by the interaction of one of these hybrid orbitals with
an atomic orbital of a hydrogen atom, the result is a function with a high electron
probability density along the C-H axis. This provides a very satisfactory wave
mechanical description of the bonding in methane and analogous compounds.

Ammonia can be treated in a similar way. Experimentally the H — N — H
bond angle is found to be 107 deg. One possible description is in terms of *sp³*
hybridized orbitals. The deviation from the tetrahedral angle of 109 deg. is
attributed to the fact that the lone pair of electrons exhibit a stronger repulsion
on the other electron pairs than do the electrons involved in N — H bonding.
A similar description has been proposed for the water molecule (bond angle
104.5 deg.).

TABLE 14.3

HYBRID ATOMIC ORBITALS

Atomic Orbitals	Configuration	Bond Angles
sp^2	triangular (plane)	120°
sp^3	tetrahedral	109°28′
dsp^2	square (plane)	90°
d^2sp^3	octahedral	90°

Hybrid orbitals can also be made up of combinations of atomic orbitals other than sp^3. Some of these are given in Table 14.3. In addition intermediate descriptions have been proposed. For example, in a given bond s-character might be increased or decreased slightly from that shown in a pure sp^2 bond, with a consequent effect on calculated bond properties.

14.7 Multiple Bonds: Localized and Delocalized

For the description of a double bond such as that of ethylene, two bonding orbitals are required. Since the bond angles in ethylenic type com-

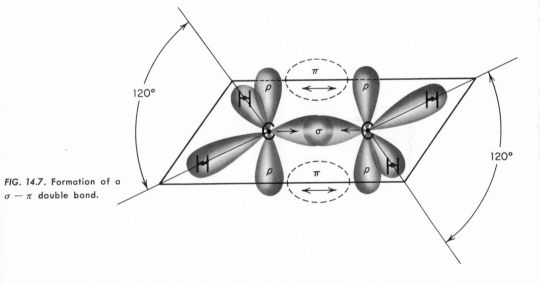

FIG. 14.7. Formation of a $\sigma - \pi$ double bond.

pounds are about 120 deg., one possible description begins with the assignment of sp^2 hybridization to the carbon atoms. This leaves a p orbital projecting at right angles to the plane of the hybridized orbitals. An orbital bonding the two C atoms can then be constructed by combining one sp^2 orbital from each atom. This orbital has σ symmetry, and is therefore referred to as a σ bond. Combination of the two atomic p orbitals leads to a second bond of π-type symmetry (Fig. 14.7).

Although the $\sigma - \pi$ description of the double bond is the more familiar,

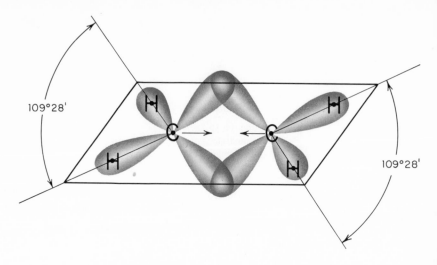

FIG. 14.8. Formation of a double bond from sp^3 hybrids.

there is an alternate description. This involves forming two equivalent orbitals between the carbon atoms by using two sp^3 hybridized orbitals from each atom (Fig. 14.8). Indeed, it can be shown that if a molecular orbital approach is used, this tetrahedral model is mathematically equivalent to the $\sigma - \pi$ model discussed above. Both models can be further refined, and the question of which provides a better approximation of the various properties of ethylene-type multiple bonds is still very much a subject under active discussion.

Let us now turn to the discussion of a different type of multiple bond, that of benzene. That the multiple bonds of benzene are different from those of ethylene is clear, since the two compounds show quite different types of chemical reactivity. Thermochemical evidence supports this conclusion. The heat of formation of the benzene molecule from separated atoms in the gas phase is 1323 kcal./mole. The Kekule structure, 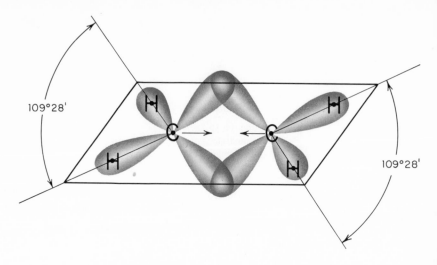 has 6 C—H, 3 C—C, and 3 C = C bonds. The sum of these bond energies is 1286 kcal./mole. Thus, crudely, the benzene molecule is about 37 kcal./mole more stable than the ethylenic-type Kekule structure.

The molecular orbital theory provides the following model for benzene. Since the bond angles are 120 deg., sp^2 hybridization of the carbon atoms is assumed. Using these hybridized atomic orbitals, we can construct localized bonding orbitals to the adjacent carbon atoms, giving the carbon skeleton its characteristic planar hexagonal structure (Fig. 14.9). Each carbon atom has one remaining p orbital projecting normal to the plane of the ring. These six atomic orbitals are combined to form six molecular orbitals, three bonding and three antibonding. Possible representations of the three bonding molecular orbitals are shown in Fig. 14.9. Each of these orbitals extends over more than two nuclei, so they are called *delocalized orbitals*. These orbitals are of differing energies. There is a single bonding orbital of lowest energy. The other two bonding orbitals are somewhat higher in energy and are degenerate. Next in energy are a degenerate antibonding pair of orbitals, and finally a single antibonding orbital.

The molecular orbital treatment provides a very satisfactory model of

408

FIG. 14.9. Schematic representation of trigonal
orbitals and bonding π orbitals in benzene.
  a) Trigonal orbitals (σ bonds). b) π orbitals.

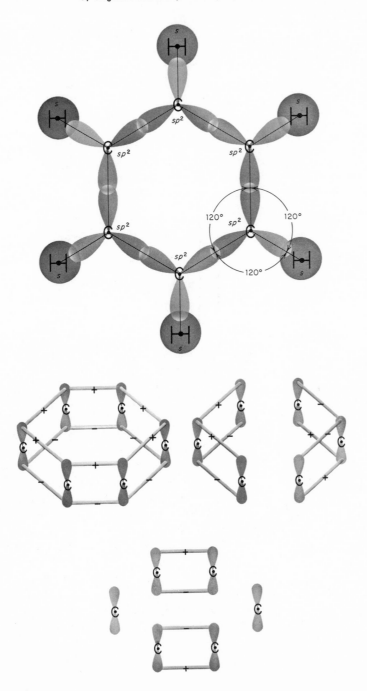

benzene. The delocalized orbitals are lower in energy (more stable) than the localized ethylenic-like orbitals of the Kekule structure, and the energy difference between them is called the *delocalization energy*. The model meets the requirement that all the C — C bonds be equivalent, as evidenced by the fact that they all have the same length, 1.39 Å, intermediate between the C — C bond length in ethane, 1.54 Å, and the C = C bond length in ethylene, 1.30 Å. The general treatment of delocalized electrons represents one of the great successes of the molecular orbital theory.

The valence bond model also provides a treatment of delocalized electron systems through Pauling's very fruitful concept of *resonance*. According to this proposal, if a molecule can be represented by several classical valence bond structures (1) *of roughly the same energy*, (2) *differing only in the position of their electrons*, and (3) *containing the same number of paired and unpaired electrons*, then a wave function ψ describing this molecule can be made up of a linear combination of the wave functions $\psi_1, \psi_2, \psi_3 \ldots$, describing the possible valence bond structures.

$$\psi = c_1\psi_1 + c_2\psi_2 + c_3\psi_3 + \ldots$$

The coefficients, c_1, c_2, c_3, etc., are chosen to minimize the total energy corresponding to the wave function ψ.

Consider benzene from this viewpoint. Two obvious valence bond structures to be considered are the Kekule structures, I and II. (See diagram below.) Other forms, such as the Dewar structures, III, IV, and V, have a higher energy content and, therefore, would have less weight in the final hybrid wave function. Still other structures can be imagined, but they are of even higher energy content and therefore of lesser importance in the final hybrid.

I   II   III   IV   V

The final hybrid wave function constructed from the wave functions for structures I, II, III, IV, and V describes the electrons as being extensively delocalized, since the various structures considered place these electrons between different nuclei. In a qualitative sense, what the molecular orbital treatment seeks to achieve by a combination of atomic wave functions, the resonance treatment seeks to achieve by a combination of "molecular" (valence bond) wave functions. It should be clear from this discussion that the resonance model does not imply that some molecules of benzene have one structure and some another, nor does it imply that at one time the properties of the molecule are those of structure I, at another time those of structure II, etc. Rather, the attempt is to synthesize a single wave function which provides some basis for an understanding of the properties of the benzene molecule as these are revealed by experiment.

14.8 Polar Covalent Bonds

In most of the preceding discussion we have been concerned with chemical bonds of two extreme types. The first is the ionic type, in which one of the bonding atoms has a much stronger attraction for electrons than the other, with the result that the approximation that electrons belong totally to individual nuclei is valid (*i.e.*, Na^+Cl^-). The second is the extreme covalent type, where the attraction of two nuclei for electrons is essentially the same, with the result that the bonding electrons can be considered to be equally shared between them (*i.e.*, H_2). Obviously, a whole range of intermediate types must exist in which electrons are asymmetrically distributed between the two nuclei, but in a less extreme fashion than in Na^+Cl^-. The concept of electron sharing must play an important role in any description of these molecules.

If the bond is thought of as essentially covalent, then it is said to have a certain degree of *ionic character*. The degree of ionic character of a bond is determined by the electronegativity of the atoms involved, that is, their relative electron-attracting powers. The electron affinities and ionization potentials of atoms can be used to develop an electronegativity scale. The ionization potential I measures the energy required to remove an electron from the neutral atom, while the electron affinity A measures the energy evolved on addition of an electron to the neutral atom. Therefore, for the process

$$M + N \longrightarrow M^+ + N^- \qquad \Delta E = I_M - A_N$$

and for the converse process

$$M + N \longrightarrow M^- + N^+ \qquad \Delta E' = I_N - A_M$$

The electronegativity is measured by the difference between ΔE and $\Delta E'$. If

$$\Delta E > \Delta E'$$

$$I_M - A_N > I_N - A_M \tag{14.4}$$

and it is said that element M is more electronegative than element N. By rearrangement of equation (14.4) to

$$I_M + A_M > I_N + A_N \tag{14.5}$$

it is seen that $I + A$ is a measure of electronegativity. Since both I and A increase in going from the beginning to the end of a period, it is evident that the electronegativity will similarly increase.

The normalized relation

$$\frac{I + A}{6.3} \text{ e.v.} \tag{14.6}$$

has been used to estimate electronegativity with I and A expressed in electron volts, and gives values which are comparable to those obtained by the empirical method given below.

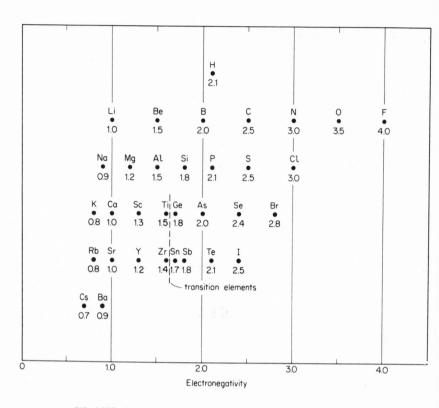

FIG. 14.10. Periodic variation of electronegativity (Pauling).

EXERCISE 14.4

Use the ionization potential (Fig. 13.11) and the electron affinity (Table 14.1) of chlorine to estimate its electronegativity. Compare with Fig. 14.10.

Another frequently used measure of electronegativity differences is based on comparison of the bond dissociation energy, D', expected from purely covalent bonding with the observed value, D. The observed value is higher, because the assumption of pure covalent bonding neglects the lowering of potential energy which can be achieved by increasing the electron probability density at the more electronegative element at the expense of the less electronegative element. In some sense, then, the difference between the pure covalent value and the observed value is related to the electronegativity difference between the elements. Consider HCl as an example. Assume that a purely covalent bond in the molecule HCl would have a bond dissociation energy, D', which is the arithmetic mean of the dissociation energies of the purely covalent H_2 and Cl_2.

$$D'_{HCl} = \tfrac{1}{2}(D_{H_2} + D_{Cl_2}) = \tfrac{1}{2}(4.5 + 2.5) = 3.5 \text{ e.v.}$$

The observed bond dissociation energy of HCl is 4.43 e.v., and the difference

$$D_{HCl} - D'_{HCl} = 4.4 - 3.5 = 0.9 \text{ e.v.} \tag{14.7}$$

is taken as a measure of the ionic character of the bond, and the electronegativity difference between hydrogen and chlorine.

Using an empirical method of computing electronegativity difference, and arbitrarily adjusting the scale so that the elements in the first period range from 2.5 to 4.0, the values indicated in Fig. 14.10 have been obtained by Pauling. Note that electronegativity tends to increase toward the upper right-hand corner of the periodic table.

The electronegativity difference between the atoms of a diatomic molecule is a measure of the degree of ionic character in the bond. Pauling has given an approximate relation, which is shown in Fig. 14.11. From this figure it may be deduced that HI, with an electronegativity difference of 0.4 e.v., has approximately 5 per cent ionic character in its bond, whereas HF, with an electronegativity difference of 1.9 e.v., has 55 per cent ionic character, that is, in HI the shared electron pair is almost equally distributed around the two nuclei, whereas in HF the shared pair strongly favors the fluorine.

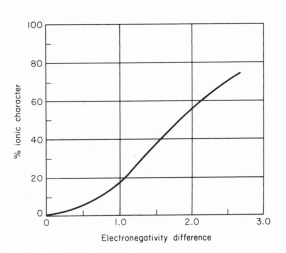

FIG. 14.11. Ionic character vs. electronegativity difference (Pauling).

EXERCISE 14.5

Use the table of electronegativity values and Fig. 14.11 to estimate the per cent ionic character in the O—H bond of water.   *Ans.* 35 per cent.

Under some circumstances it appears that hydrogen is capable of forming two bonds, as in the well-known dimers of the type

$$
\begin{array}{ccc}
& O \cdots H{-}O & \\
R{-}C & & C{-}R \\
& O{-}H \cdots O &
\end{array}
$$

This is called hydrogen bonding and can occur when the hydrogen atom is bonded to an atom of high electronegativity, principally fluorine, oxygen, and nitrogen. In these cases the displacement of the electron cloud away from the proton leaves an exposed, concentrated center of positive charge, which may be bound to other negative centers by what is essentially an electrostatic force. Hydrogen bonding is an important factor in many structures, such as the ice crystal, the semi-regular structure of liquid water near 0°, and the model proposed for the structure of deoxyribonucleic acid (DNA) by J. D. Watson and F. C. H. Crick.

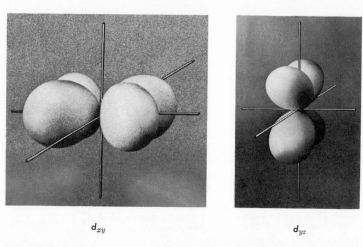

d_{xy} d_{yz}

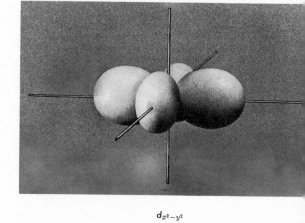

d_{xz} $d_{x^2-y^2}$

d_{z^2}

FIG. 14.12. Representations of the atomic d orbitals for hydrogen [from an article by R. G. Pearson in *Chemical and Engineering News*. Photographs supplied by R. F. Gould].

14.9   Bonding in Complex Ions:
Ligand Field Theory

The formation of a wide variety of complex ions is an intriguing aspect of the chemistry of the transition metals. The simplest description of these compounds is provided by crystal field theory. A fundamental assumption of this theory is that bonding in complexes is primarily electrostatic, either of the ionic or ion-dipolar type. As we have discussed earlier, such an assumption leads immediately to the conclusion that if six groups (called *ligands*) are disposed about a central ion, the favored arrangement will be octahedral; if four groups are disposed about a central ion, the arrangement will be tetrahedral, etc., since these arrangements minimize electrostatic repulsion. These are very commonly observed. However, there is a second factor which must also be considered. The electrons of the central ion exist in a field resulting from the presence of the ligands (*ligand field*). In general, there is an electron configuration for the central ion which minimizes electrostatic repulsions due to interaction with this ligand field.

As an example, consider an octahedral complex of a transition metal ion. Since the ion possesses no outer shell s and p electrons, only interactions between ligands and d orbitals are of interest. Representations of the five d orbitals of the transition metals are given in Fig. 14.12. These orbitals fall into two classes: three of them, d_{xy}, d_{xz}, and d_{yz}, have high electron probability densities in regions *between* the various axes; two of them, $d_{x^2-y^2}$ and d_{z^2} have high electron probability densities *along* the various axes. If the six ligands occupy positions on the x, y, and z axes, then they are in close proximity to these last two orbitals, and any electron in these orbitals will be subjected to a strong electrostatic repulsion. On the other hand, an electron in a d_{xy}, d_{xz}, or d_{yz} orbital is farther removed from the ligands and will suffer a lesser electrostatic repulsion. Obviously, this group is energetically favored. Thus, taking the weighted mean energy of the d orbitals of the ion as a reference point, the d orbitals are split into two groups by the octahedrally disposed ligands. There is a lower-energy group of three, and a higher-energy group of two (Fig. 14.13). The greater the strength of the ligand field, the greater will be the energy separation between these groups.

Spectral observations provide a basis for the evaluation of the energy separation between these groups. It is often possible to excite an electron in the lower group of orbitals into an orbital of the upper group by the use of visible or ultraviolet light. (See section 14.17.) By examining the electronic spectra of a number of compounds, it has proven possible to assign certain observed absorptions to this type of electronic excitation. Thus, there is an experimental method for comparing the degree of separation of the d orbitals caused by various ligands. For a number of common ligands the order of increasing splitting is

$$I^- < Br^- < Cl^- < OH^- < OAc^- < F^- < C_2H_5OH < H_2O < NH_3$$

$$< \text{ethylenediamine} < NO_2^- < CN^-$$

(a) d_{xy}

(b) $d_{x^2-y^2}$

(c) d_{z^2}

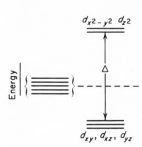

(d) Splitting of the energy levels

FIG. 14.13. Octahedral ligand geometry [from Pearson, *op. cit.*].

This is known as the "spectrochemical series." It is purely empirical. No completely adequate theoretical explanation is known.

We are now prepared to discuss the arrangement of electrons in octahedral complexes. This arrangement will be governed by two factors: (1) Occupation of the low-energy d orbitals by an electron of the central ion is energetically favored over occupation of one of the high-energy orbitals by an amount dependent on the strength of the ligand field. (2) Pairing of electrons in a single orbital is energetically less favorable than allowing them to occupy different

$d_{x^2-y^2}$

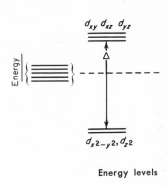

FIG. 14.14a. Effect of tetrahedral geometry on relative
energies of d orbitals [from Pearson, op. cit.].

orbitals. The final electron arrangement represents a balance between these two
factors. Consider a weak ligand field. The splitting Δ between the two sets
of d orbitals is small (Fig. 14.13). As a result, factor (2) above dominates, and
the available electrons are placed in both high- and low-energy d orbitals in
accord with the rule of maximum multiplicity. The result is a "spin-free" complex with a maximum number of unpaired electrons. Such a complex is highly
paramagnetic. An example would be FeF_6^{-3} in which the central Fe^{+3} ion has
five unpaired electrons. If the ligand field is strong, then the splitting Δ between
the two sets of orbitals is great. As a result, factor (1) dominates, and the lower-
energy d orbitals must be filled in accord with the rule of maximum multiplicity
before any electrons are placed in the high-energy orbitals. The result is a
maximum amount of spin pairing for a given number of electrons. Such complexes are called "spin-paired." An example is $Fe(CN)_6^{-3}$, in which the central
Fe^{+3} ion has only one unpaired electron.

EXERCISE 14.6

Predict the number of unpaired electrons for
$$Mn(CN)_6^{-4}, \quad Mn(H_2O)_6^{+2}, \quad Mn(CN)_6^{-3}, \quad Mn(H_2O)^{+3}.$$
Assume that H_2O provides a weak ligand field.   *Ans.* 5,1,4,0.

We shall now turn to an examination of the ligand field effect on the d
orbitals of a central ion which is surrounded by eight ligands at the corners of
a cube. The d_{xy}, d_{xz}, and d_{yz} orbitals are directed towards these corners, and so
are now high-energy orbitals. The $d_{x^2-y^2}$ and d_{z^2} orbitals, however, pierce the
mid-points of walls of the cube and so are more remote from the ligands.

FIG. 14.14b. Effect of square planar geometry on relative energies of d orbitals.

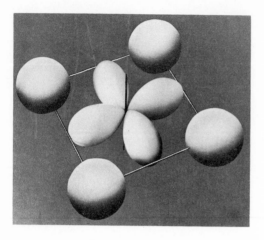

d_{xy}

$d_{x^2-y^2}$

d_{xy}

d_{xz}, d_{yz}

d_{z^2}

Energy

Energy levels

They are now the lower-energy orbitals. Thus, we now have one low-energy group of two orbitals and one high-energy group of three orbitals (Fig. 14.14a). If four alternating ligands are removed from the cube we have discussed above, the result is tetrahedral arrangement. However, the separation of the d orbitals into a low-energy group of two (Fig. 14.14a) and a high-energy group of three still holds.

The other important arrangement of ligands often encountered in complex ions is the square planar arrangement. Despite the fact that this can be derived from the octahedral arrangement by simply removing two ligands, there is no simple way of arriving at the order of the energies of the d orbitals. However, it is clear that one of them (say, the $d_{x^2-y^2}$) will be directed at the ligands and will be a very high-energy orbital. A possible energy ordering is shown in Fig. 14.14b.

FIG. 14.15. Schematic illustration of d-p multiple bonding in a cyano complex.

The original assumption that the bonding in these complex ions is electrostatic cannot be correct. There must be a substantial amount of covalent character. This can be introduced by adopting the idea that the positive charge on the central ion distorts or "polarizes" electron clouds of the ligands towards itself. This introduces to some degree a sharing of electrons. In addition, it is possible for multiple bonding to take place by way of an added interaction between p-type orbitals in the ligand and d orbitals in the central atom (Fig. 14.15). Another way of treating bond-

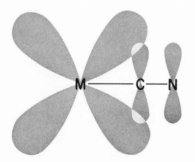

M——C—N

ng in complex ions is by use of the molecular orbital method. This is dis-
ussed in advanced texts.

14.10 Electric Moments

An asymmetric distribution of bonding electrons between atoms in
a molecule gives rise to an electric moment. That is, if the bond orbital is
more dense around one of the atoms of a diatomic molecule, this atom appears
o have an excess of negative charge, while the other has an equal positive
charge. In such a case, the bond constitutes an electric *dipole* which may be
formally represented by charges $+q$ and $-q$ separated by a distance r equal to
he internuclear separation. Since charge transfer is not complete, the formal
magnitude of the charges $+q$ and $-q$ will be somewhat less than the electronic
charge. Two electronic charges ($\pm 4.80 \times 10^{-10}$ e.s.u.) separated by 1 Å (10^{-8}
em.) would have an *electric moment* of 4.80×10^{-18} e.s.u. $\times$ cm. The unit
10^{-18} e.s.u. $\times$ cm. is called the *debye*.

The electric moments of molecules are computed from observations of the
dielectric constant determined as follows: If two parallel metal plates constituting a condenser are connected to a source of electric potential, one plate
acquires a negative charge $-Q$ and the other a positive charge of equal magnitude $+Q$. The charge accumulated is proportional to the potential V applied
to the plates, and the proportionality constant is the capacitance C of the
condenser.

$$Q = CV \qquad C = \frac{Q}{V} \tag{14.8}$$

The capacitance of a parallel-plate condenser is proportional to the area
of the plates and inversely proportional to the distance between them. The
capacitance also depends on the nature of the medium between the plates,
since the electric field causes an orientation of molecular charge as indicated
in Fig. 14.16. The molecular dipoles orient themselves in the field and reduce
its value in the region between the plates, thus permitting a greater accumulation of charge for a given voltage than is observed when the condenser is
evacuated. The ratio of the capacitance C with a given filling to the capacitance
C_0 in a vacuum is called the *dielectric constant* of
the medium ϵ.

$$\frac{C}{C_0} = \epsilon \tag{14.9}$$

All substances have a dielectric constant greater
than unity, whether or not the molecules have a
permanent electric moment. This is due to the fact
that an electric field *induces* an electric moment
even in a completely nonpolar molecule such as

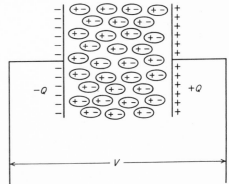

FIG. 14.16. Polarization of a dielectric in a condenser.

H_2. The dielectric constant of the medium is due to both permanent an induced dipoles in the molecule. In order to measure the permanent dipol moment, the effect of the induced moment must be evaluated.

The dipole moment induced by an electric field acting on a molecule i proportional to the field strength and the proportionality constant is called th *distortion polarizability* α_0. In the absence of permanent dipoles, it can b shown that the dielectric constant is related to the distortion polarizability b the Clausius-Mosotti equation

$$\frac{\epsilon - 1}{\epsilon + 2} = \frac{4\pi n \alpha_0}{3} \qquad (14.10$$

where n is the number of molecules per cc. Multiplying both sides of equatio (14.10) by the ratio of molecular weight to density M/ρ yields

$$\frac{\epsilon - 1}{\epsilon + 2} \cdot \frac{M}{\rho} = \frac{4\pi n M \alpha_0}{3\rho} = \frac{4}{3}\pi N \alpha_0 = P_M \qquad (14.11$$

where P_M is the *molar polarization*.

When the medium contains permanent dipoles, these will contribute to th molar polarizability and the expression for P_M must then contain a term whic accounts for this contribution. In contrast to the induced polarization term this term is temperature dependent, decreasing as temperature increases. Thi dependence arises from the fac that the molecules of the medium are in continuous random motion their collisions with other molecule tend to destroy the orientation induced by the electric field. The induced moment, being a distortion of the electron cloud without regard to orientation of the molecule, can quickly adjust to any molecular position. On the other hand, the permanent moment has a definite orientation with respect to the internuclear axis and the increased motion of the molecules at higher temperatures increases the randomness of orientation of this axis.

Debye has developed an equation for the total molar polarization due to the distortion polarizability α_0, and the *permanent dipole moment* μ.

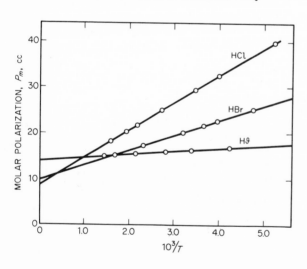

FIG. 14.17. Test of the Debye equation [from W.J. Moore, *Physical Chemistry*, 2d ed., Prentice-Hall, Inc., Englewood Cliffs, N.J., 1956].

$$P_M = \frac{4\pi}{3} N \left(\alpha_0 + \frac{\mu^2}{3kT} \right) \qquad (14.12)$$

Note that the temperature appears in the second term on the right-hand side of equation (14.12). Fig. 14.17 shows a test of this equation for HI, HBr, and HCl, which have permanent dipole moments increasing in that order. The dipole moment is obtained from the slopes of the curves shown. Some values of dipole moments at room temperature are given in Table 14.4.

EXERCISE 14.7

Determine the slope of the line for HCl in Fig. 14.17 and obtain the dipole moment of HCl.

The dipole moment often gives considerable insight into the structure of a molecule. It is a vector property, and in polyatomic molecules the net dipole moment will be the vector sum of the dipoles associated with each bond. For example, the CO_2 molecule seems to have no dipole moment despite the difference in electronegativity between carbon and oxygen. This is consistent with a linear arrangement of the atoms in which the two bond moments cancel. On the other hand, the dipole moment of H_2O is 1.82 debye, indicating a non-linear configuration. From spectroscopic observations (see section 14.16) it is known that the $H - O - H$ bond angle is 105 deg. A simple vector diagram (at right) allows calculation of the electric moment associated with the $O - H$ bond, 1.49 debye.

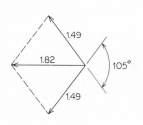 

TABLE 14.4

DIPOLE MOMENTS OF SOME MOLECULES IN THE GAS PHASE*

Compound	Moment (debyes)
HCl	1.07
HBr	0.79
HI	0.38
H_2O	1.82
H_2S	0.95
NH_3	1.47
SO_2	1.61
CO_2	0.0†
CO	0.13

*Taken from A. L. McClellan, *Tables of Experimental Dipole Moments* (W. H. Freeman and Co., San Francisco, 1963).

†Value of C. T. Zahn, *Phys. Rev.*, **27**, 455–9 (1926), and F. G. Keyes and J. G. Kirkwood, *Phys. Rev.*, **36**, 754 (1930).

14.11 Magnetic Moments

According to classical ideas, any system which involves circulation of electrical charges has the potentiality of showing an intrinsic magnetic moment. Molecules and the nuclei which they contain are composed of two such systems, with the unit of magnetic moment for molecules being 1836 times greater than that for nuclei. This potentiality is not always realized, since magnetic moments, like dipole moments, are resultant properties. Thus, for many molecules the intrinsic magnetic moment is zero. However, a magnetic field always induces in all molecules a magnetic moment which opposes it and tends to reduce it, arising from polarization of the molecule by the imposed magnetic field. Substances which have only induced magnetic moments are repelled by an inhomogeneous field and are said to be *diamagnetic*.

Molecules[2] which have a permanent magnetic moment tend to orient parallel to an applied magnetic field and therefore to reinforce it. Such substances are attracted into an inhomogeneous magnetic field and are said to be *paramag netic*. Paramagnetism is often large in magnitude compared to diamagnetism and is temperature-dependent, whereas diamagnetic polarization is temperature independent.

The measure of response to a magnetic field is the *magnetic susceptibility* χ, which is negative for diamagnetic substances and positive for paramagnetic substances. The magnetic susceptibility is measured by suspending a sample partly in the field of a strong electromagnet. A diamagnetic substance tends to be repelled and a paramagnetic substance attracted, and a measurement of the force of attraction or repulsion can be translated into a value of the magnetic susceptibility. An equation which is similar in form to equation (14.12), and which relates the magnetic susceptibility, the magnetic polarizability, α_M, and the permanent magnetic moment μ_M, has been derived on the assumption that each magnetic dipole is completely independent of all others.

$$\chi = N(\alpha_M + \mu_M^2/3kT) \tag{14.13}$$

k is Boltzmann's constant and N is Avogadro's number. Measurement of χ as a function of T permits evaluation of both α_M and μ_M, the first term dealing with the diamagnetic contribution and the second with the paramagnetic contribution.

It is clear from equation (14.13) that the paramagnetic contribution to the total susceptibility, χ_{para}, may be written in the form

$$\chi_{para} = \frac{C}{T}$$

since $\mu_M^2/3k$ is a constant for a given substance. This is called the Curie equation after Pierre Curie. Many solid materials do not obey this law, but instead follow a law of the form

$$\chi_{para} = \frac{C}{T - \Delta},$$

the Curie-Weiss law. Δ is known as the Weiss constant after Pierre Weiss. An equation of this form has been derived on the assumption that the various magnetic dipoles of a substance do actually influence each other, in contrast

---

[2]Although we use the term "molecule" in this discussion, the discussion applies to radicals and atoms as well.

to the assumption on which (14.13) is based. The Weiss constant can thus be thought of as taking into account interactions between species. In some cases, however, this simple interpretation is known to be incorrect and the Curie-Weiss law is inapplicable.

As we mentioned above, classically magnetic moments can be associated with circulating electrical charges. Therefore, it should not be surprising that there is a relationship between the resultant angular momentum of the electrons of an atom or molecule and its magnetic moment. Electrons have both an orbital angular momentum (related to the quantum number l), and a spin angular momentum (related to the quantum number s). Both of these can contribute to the observed magnetic moment, but we shall consider only cases where the spin contribution alone effectively decides the magnetic moment. The magnetic moment associated with one electron spin is 1.73 Bohr magnetons. (The Bohr magneton $= he/4\pi mc$ or 9.273×10^{-21} erg gauss^{-1}.) The resultant magnetic moment for n unpaired electrons which occupy several different orbitals is

$$\mu_M = \sqrt{n(n+2)} \quad \text{Bohr magnetons} \tag{14.14}$$

Thus, the magnetic moment of the FeF_6^{-3} complex to which we referred earlier would be 5.92 Bohr magnetons, corresponding to five unpaired electrons, whereas that of the $Fe(CN)_6^{-3}$ complex should be 1.73 Bohr magnetons corresponding to one unpaired electron. It is this ability to relate paramagnetic properties to electronic structures that makes the measurement of bulk paramagnetism one of the most valuable tools available for the study of transition metal compounds. (Some typical experimental results are given in Table 14.5.)

TABLE 14.5

PARAMAGNETIC MOMENTS OF SOME TRANSITION METAL IONS

Ion	Configuration	No. of unpaired electrons	Calculated moment (spin only)	Observed moment
Sc^{+3}	d^0	0	0	0
Ti^{+2}	d^2	2	2.84	2.76
V^{+2}	d^3	3	3.87	3.86
Cr^{+2}	d^4	4	4.90	4.80
Mn^{+2}	d^5	5	5.92	5.96
Fe^{+2}	d^6	4	4.90	5.0 —5.5
Co^{+2}	d^7	3	3.87	4.4 —5.2
Ni^{+2}	d^8	2	2.84	2.9 —3.4
Cu^{+2}	d^9	1	1.73	1.8 —2.2
Zn^{+2}	d^{10}	0	0	0

In this section only the measurement of bulk paramagnetism has been considered as a means of gaining information about unpaired electrons in molecules. There is also available a newer technique, *electron spin resonance* spectroscopy, which is highly sensitive, and which can often be used to provide a kind of detailed information which is inaccessible through measurement of bulk magnetic properties. We shall defer our brief discussion of this techniqu until after the section on *nuclear magnetic resonance*, since in many respec the two techniques are analogous.

14.12 Nuclear Magnetic Resonance Spectroscopy

Nuclei of many atoms possess a magnetic moment which can b thought of as related to the possession of an angular momentum suggesting a analogy to electrons. A possible model which would account for both of thes properties assumes that the nuclear charge and mass circulate about an axis o the nucleus. In some sense, then, the nucleus may be thought of as "spinning. When a charge moves in a circular path about an axis, a magnetic field alon, that axis is produced. This magnetic field has a definite magnitude and direction and therefore is a vector quantity called the *nuclear magnetic moment*, μ_N.

The angular momentum of a nucleus is described in terms of a spin quantum number I, which is the resultant of the spin quantum numbers of its individua nucleons, that is, neutrons and protons. For both the neutron and the proto $I = \frac{1}{2}$. Thus, for example, the deuterium nucleus can have a spin quantum number of either 1 or 0, depending upon whether the neutron and the proto of its nucleus have parallel or antiparallel spins. Experimentally $I = 1$ fo deuterium in the ground state. No general rule is known for the prediction o the spin quantum numbers of all nuclei, although the nuclear shell model o M. G. Mayer and J. H. D. Jensen successfully treats certain classes of nucle As one example, all nuclei with even atomic number and even mass numbe have zero magnetic moment.

Quantitatively the magnetic moment μ_N of a nucleus is given by the equa tion

$$\mu_N = g \, \mu_n \, I(I + 1)$$

where $\mu_n = 5.050 \times 10^{-24}$ erg gauss^{-1} and is called the *nuclear magneton*, and g is a dimensionless constant characteristic of each nucleus. It can be eithe positive or negative, depending upon whether the magnetic moment and the angular momentum of the nucleus coincide or are opposed. g must be deter mined experimentally. For the proton (hydrogen nucleus) it is 5.585.

The interaction of a nucleus of magnetic moment I with an applied magnetic field is governed by a quantum condition. Only those orientations of the nucleus are allowed which give a component of angular momentum in the direc tion of the applied field equal to $M_I h/2\pi$, where M_I is a quantum number. The angular momentum is thus quantized in units of $h/2\pi$, just as is the electron angular momentum in the Bohr model of the hydrogen atom. The quantum number M_I can have $(2I + 1)$ values ranging from $+I$ to $-I$ and including 0 if I is integral.

The rest of this discussion will consider only the hydrogen nucleus. For the proton, $I = \frac{1}{2}$, and therefore there are two values of M_I, $+\frac{1}{2}$ and $-\frac{1}{2}$. If a magnetic field of strength H_0 is applied at the nucleus, there will be a contribution to the potential energy of that nucleus arising from the interaction of its magnetic moment with the applied field. Since the two degenerate components of the hydrogen nucleus ground state differ in spatial characteristics, they will interact differently with the applied field, and the

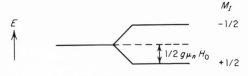

FIG. 14.18. Energy levels in a pure magnetic field for a nucleus of $I = \frac{1}{2}$.

degeneracy of the ground state will be removed. The ground state energy level is thus split into two sublevels of different energy, just as is that of an unpaired electron (Fig. 14.18). The potential energy, E_H, due to the interaction of the nucleus with the magnetic field is given by

$$E_H = -g\mu_n M_I H_0 \tag{14.15}$$

Therefore, the $M = +\frac{1}{2}$ sublevel is lowered in energy by $\frac{1}{2} g\mu_n H_0$, while the $M = -\frac{1}{2}$ sublevel is raised in energy by the same amount (Fig. 14.18). $\mu_n = (e/2m_p c)(h/2\pi)$, where e is the charge on the proton, m_p is the proton mass, c is the velocity of light, and h is Planck's constant. Since g for the proton is a constant, equation (14.15) can be rewritten in the form

$$E_H = -\gamma \left(\frac{h}{2\pi}\right) M_I H_0 \tag{14.16}$$

where γ represents a proportionality constant.

Transitions from the $M = +\frac{1}{2}$ to the $M = -\frac{1}{2}$ sublevel shown in Fig. 14.18 involve a reorientation of the nucleus with respect to the lines of force of the applied magnetic field. The frequency associated with the energy of such transitions can be computed from equation (14.16).

$$\Delta E = E_{H(-1/2)} - E_{H(+1/2)} = h\nu = \frac{\gamma h H_0}{2\pi}$$

and

$$\nu = \frac{\gamma H_0}{2\pi} \tag{14.17}$$

In a field of 10^4 gauss, for the hydrogen nucleus $\nu = 42.57$ Mc. sec.$^{-1}$. Thus, the transition corresponds to a frequency in the short-wave radio band.

If now both radio-frequency energy and a magnetic field are simultaneously applied to the nucleus, transitions from the lower to the higher level should occur when the condition set by equation (14.17) is met. The system is then said to be in *resonance*, hence the name *nuclear magnetic resonance* (n.m.r.). Since the probability of absorption of radiation by nuclei in the lower sublevel is equal to the probability of emission of energy by nuclei in the upper sublevel, the net absorption of energy depends on there being an excess population of nuclei in the lower level. At a field of 10,000 gauss the separation of the two sublevels is only 1.76×10^{-8} e.v. (equivalent to 4.06×10^{-6} kcal. mole^{-1}).

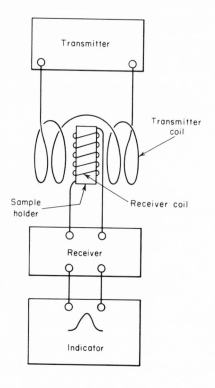

Therefore, at 300°K the two levels ar almost equally populated, the differenc in populations being between 3 to 4 nucle out of every million. (The method fo carrying out a calculation of this type wil be discussed in Chapter 17.)

The absorption of energy from th radio-frequency field tends to equalize th populations of the two energy levels. A a consequence, absorption of energy woulc soon cease if the nuclei could lose energ only to the magnetic field. Fortunately, i most pure liquids and solids rapid mole cular motion produces random magneti fields which interact with the nucleus an provide a path for thermal relaxation. Thi is called *spin-lattice relaxation*. There ar other types of relaxation as well. On example of these is a process in which nucleus in a higher spin state transfer energy to a neighboring nucleus by ex changing spins with it. This is callec *spin-spin relaxation*.

Experimentally the condition of reso nance could be achieved either by varying the radiofrequency ν and holding the applied magnetic field H constant, or by holding ν constant and varying H. The method of variation of the magnetic field is preferred. A constant radio-frequency is applied to the sample through a coil. A detector coil is mounted at right angles to the source coil, and a magnetic field is applied at right angles to both of these coils (Fig. 14.19). The strength of the magnetic field is slowly increased. At the value of the field corresponding to H_0 in the resonance equation (14.17), energy will be absorbed and transitions will occur. These transitions are equivalent to a variation in a magnetic field with the result that an emf is induced in the detector coil. Commonly the experimental information is displayed by showing the variation in magnetic field on the horizontal axis and the variation in the intensity of absorption on the vertical axis (Fig. 14.20). Since γH has the dimensions of a frequency (equation 14.17), the magnetic field variation is often expressed as a frequency, $\omega = \gamma H$.

Our whole discussion up to this point has been in terms of the *magnetic field at the nucleus*. This is not the same as the applied magnetic field, since the nucleus exists in an environment of nuclei and electrons, all of which can affect the local magnetic field to which the nucleus is subjected. Thus, in general, the magnetic field at the nucleus, H_0, will be the sum of the applied magnetic field H and the local magnetic field, $H_{loc.}$.

$$H_0 = H + H_{loc.}$$

One possible source of a local magnetic field at a given nucleus is the proximity of other magnetic nuclei. For example, let us assume perturbing nuclei which can occupy two spin states. The local field due to a perturbing

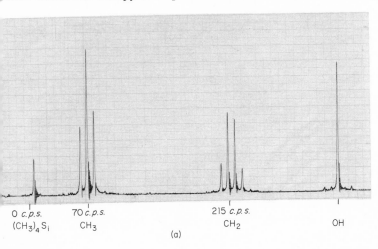

0 c.p.s.   70 c.p.s.   215 c.p.s.
$(CH_3)_4Si$ CH_3 CH_2 OH

(a)

FIG. 14.20. 60 mc. n. m. r. spectra of ethyl alcohol (courtesy of Dr. D. J. Pasto, University of Notre Dame). Peak positions are given relative to the tetramethylsilane standard and are in cps. No value is given for the OH proton since the position of this peak is variable. In (a) (above) a trace of acid was present to catalyze exchange of the hydroxyl hydrogen. Since this exchange is rapid on the n. m. r. time scale, the environment is averaged out for the OH hydrogen, and the OH peak does not show splitting by the CH_2 hydrogens. In (b) no acid is present, the exchange rate is much slower, and the OH peak is a triplet.

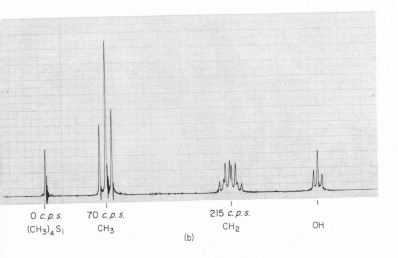

0 c.p.s.   70 c.p.s.   215 c.p.s.
$(CH_3)_4Si$ CH_3 CH_2 OH

(b)

nucleus can either add to or subtract from the applied field, depending upon which of the two spin states the perturbing nucleus occupies. Since the two spin states are quite close in energy, there will be an equal number of nuclei in each of the two possible states. As a result, the resonance due to the nucleus of interest will show two peaks of equal intensity whose field separation, ΔH, is given by the relation $\Delta H = 2 H_{\text{loc.}}$. Proton spectra in solids show this kind of behavior. Characteristically, peaks are broad, ~ 1 gauss wide, since a given nucleus interacts with many other nuclei.

In liquids the frequency of reorientation of molecules due to their natural motions ($\sim 10^{10}$ sec.$^{-1}$) is more than 10^2 times higher than the frequency of nuclear resonance. As a result, a molecule containing a given nucleus can reorient itself many times during a resonance absorption. The local fields due to other magnetic nuclei are thus averaged out, and absorption lines become much sharper, of the order of fractions of a milligauss. The sharpness of these lines allows for precise experimentation, and as a result two very important effects can be observed.

Paired electrons are diamagnetic; that is to say, a magnetic field induces moment in a paired electron system in a direction opposed to its own moment. This induced moment is directly proportional to the strength of the applied field. Thus, both bonding and nonbonding electrons in the vicinity of a nucleus reduce the magnetic field at that nucleus by an amount which depends on their distribution about that nucleus. Since these electrons in turn are influenced by their environment, n.m.r. is a very sensitive probe for distinguishing two or more protons in different locations in a molecule. Thus, ethanol, which contains different kinds of hydrogen atoms, shows three groups of peaks at high resolution (Fig. 14.20). The areas of these groups of peaks are in the ratio 3 to 2 to 1 corresponding to the number of hydrogen atoms at each location. This phenomenon is called the *chemical shift*.

Chemical shifts are reported in terms of a chemical shift parameter δ which is expressed in terms of a reference substance.

$$\delta = \frac{H(\text{sample}) - H(\text{reference})}{H(\text{reference})} \times 10^6 \qquad (14.18)$$

In equation (14.18) H refers to the applied field strength at which a given peak is observed. A common proton reference standard is tetramethylsilane, which is usually mixed with the sample whose spectrum is to be determined.

As Fig. 14.20 shows, groups of peaks rather than single peaks can be observed for each type of H atom. This so-called *splitting* is due to the magnetic moment of the adjacent nuclei in the same molecule. Consider the protons of the CH_2 group, which we shall designate as A and B. There are four possible ways that these protons can align themselves relative to a given proton in the CH_3 group.

(1) Spins of A and B parallel to that of the proton.
(2) Spins of A and B antiparallel to that of the proton.
(3) Spin of A parallel and of B antiparallel to that of the proton.
(4) Spin of A antiparallel and of B parallel to that of the proton.

3) and (4) are energetically equivalent. Therefore, we would expect the CH_3 proton peak to be split into three components, with the middle component, representing (3) plus (4), being twice the height of each of the other two. Figure 4.20 bears this out. In contrast to the chemical shift this *spin-spin* splitting s not dependent on magnetic field strength, at least to a first approximation.

EXERCISE 14.8

Show that the methyl hydrogen atoms will split the CH_2 peak into four components of statistical weights $1:3:3:1$. Why are there eight peaks in Fig. 14.20?

Under some circumstances n.m.r. can be used to investigate the rates of certain rapid chemical reactions. Consider two proton peaks separated by a frequency ω. For these peaks to be distinguished the protons must hold their position for a long time compared to $1/\omega$. As τ, the mean time for exchange of these peaks approaches $1/\omega$ in value, they will gradually fuse into a single peak, with this fusion being completed when the condition $\tau \approx 1/\omega$ is met. For protons $1/\omega$ is of the order of 10^{-2} sec. Therefore, mean lifetimes for exchange of the order of 10^{-2} sec. can be determined by n.m.r.

14.13 Electron Spin Resonance

As noted earlier, in the presence of a magnetic field the spin of an electron can be thought of as oriented in two ways, either with or against the field, corresponding to the existence of two allowed spin states, $s = +\frac{1}{2}$ or $-\frac{1}{2}$. For electrons in a magnetic field there are thus two sublevels differing slightly in energy. The energy separation of these levels is $g\beta H$, where H is the strength of the applied field, β is the Bohr magneton, and g is a "spectroscopic splitting factor" which is a measure of the contribution of the spin and orbital motions of an electron to its total angular momentum. For a free electron where no orbital contribution is possible, $g = 2.00023$.

Transitions from the lower to the upper level should occur when a quantum of applied energy equals the separation of the energy levels.

$$E = h\nu = g\beta H \tag{14.19}$$

This is a condition of resonance. With a magnetic field of 3000 gauss, equation (14.19) indicates that a frequency of 9000 Mc. sec.$^{-1}$ is required for resonance. The corresponding wave length of 3 cm. is in the easily accessible microwave region of the electromagnetic spectrum.

The energy separation of the split levels is quite small. For a 3 cm. wavelength it is only 4.1×10^{-5} e.v. (9.5×10^{-4} kcal. mole^{-1}). Such a small energy can be supplied to the system thermally at ordinary temperatures, so the upper state is already well populated before any electromagnetic radiation is applied. For example, a calculation based on the Maxwell-Boltzmann distribution law (Chapter 17) shows that at 300°K the ratio of the equilibrium populations of the upper and lower states is 0.9984. Thus, the net absorption of radiation and, therefore, the sensitivity of the technique can be improved by working at lower temperatures, where the relative population of the lower state is increased. (The contribution of these unpaired electrons to bulk paramagnetic behavior also depends on the excess population of the lower state, and this is reflected in the temperature dependence of paramagnetism. Recall equation (14.13).

The advantages of electron spin resonance (e.s.r.) are several. It is extremely sensitive, being capable under optimum conditions of detecting less than 10^{12} unpaired electrons per gram. It provides a precise method for the determination of g, and significant variations of g from 2, the spin only value, can be interpreted in terms of contributions from the orbital motion of electrons. In turn, information about orbital motions can be interpreted in terms of orbital populations and hybridizations. As with n.m.r., the magnetic field of nuclei can split e.s.r. lines. The study of such splittings leads to valuable information which can be interpreted in terms of the electron density of the unpaired electron at the magnetic nucleus. As an example of splitting of e.s.r. lines by a nucleus, consider an electron in the field of a proton. The proton can exist in two states, either aligned with the field ($M_I = +\frac{1}{2}$) or aligned against it ($M_I = -\frac{1}{2}$). Therefore, each electron level is split into two components by the protons. Those protons with $M_I = +\frac{1}{2}$ reinforce the effect of the magnetic field, whereas those with $M_I = -\frac{1}{2}$ are opposed to the magnetic field. Thus, four energy levels arise. Since nuclei do not alter their orientation during the short time required for electron transitions, only transitions for which $\Delta M_I = 0$ are allowed, and thus only two lines arise, as illustrated in Fig. 14.21.

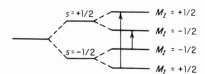

FIG. 14.21. Splitting of electron levels by the magnetic field of a proton.

Slightly more complex spectra, those of the methyl and ethyl free radicals, are shown in Fig. 14.22. For the methyl free radical the four observed peaks in the intensity ratios $1:3:3:1$ can be explained in terms of the proton splitting diagram of Fig. 14.22c and the previously mentioned selection rule. (For the ^{12}C isotope of carbon $I = 0$. See problem 29 for further discussion of the ethyl radical spectrum.) e.s.r. is an invaluable tool for investigating the reaction properties of such radicals.

G. 14.22. e. s. r. spectra. These spectra are presented as the second derivative of the absorp-
on peak. Field increases from left to right [from R. W. Fessenden and R. H. Schuler, *J. Chem.
hys., **39,** 2147 (1963)].

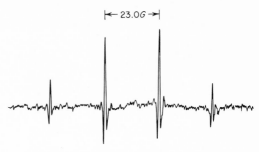

(a) 4 line *e. s. r.* spectrum of the CH_3 radical at $-176°C$.

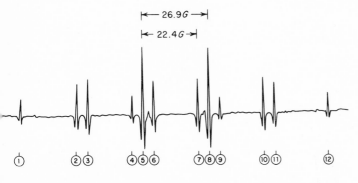

(b) 12 line *e. s. r.* spectrum of the ethyl radical at $-180°C$.

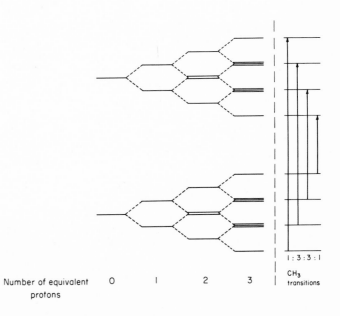

Number of equivalent   0   1   2   3
protons

1 : 3 : 3 : 1

CH_3
transitions

(c) Splitting diagram for one, two, and three equivalent protons

14.14 Mössbauer Spectroscopy

Although the chemist finds nuclear magnetic resonance the mos useful form of nuclear spectroscopy, there is another form of some chemica interest, Mössbauer spectroscopy. This is based on the emission of gamma ray in the decay of certain radioactive nuclei. We shall take the excited nucleu ^{57}Fe as an example. When a gamma ray is emitted by such a nucleus, the lav of conservation of momentum requires that the nucleus achieve a momentur equal in magnitude but opposite in sign to that of the gamma ray. This reco energy R for a free atom is given by the relation

$$R = \frac{E_\gamma^2}{2Mc^2} \tag{14.20}$$

where E_γ is the energy of the emitted gamma ray, M is the mass of the recoilin, nucleus, and c is the velocity of light. For ^{57}Fe, E_γ is 14.4 k.e.v.

If there were no recoil effect, the energy of the gamma ray would be E, th energy corresponding to the full energy difference between the excited and ground states of the nucleus. However, the energy of the gamma ray is reduced to $(E - R)$ by the energy absorbed by the nucleus in the recoil. Now, conside the absorption of a gamma ray by a free ^{57}Fe atom. The energy required fo this is $(E + R)$, since the absorbing atom must recoil in the direction o the gamma ray with an energy R.

The question of the probability of a gamma ray emitted by the nucleus of one ^{57}Fe atom being absorbed by the nucleus of a second ^{57}Fe atom can now be discussed The energy of the gamma ray is distributed about a central energy with a certain spread Γ, as shown in Fig. 14.23. The gamma rays emitted by the first nucleus are distributed about the energy $(E - R)$, while the gamma rays which can be absorbed by the second nucleus are distributed about $(E + R)$. Only if the two distributions overlap (Fig. 14.23) can the gamma rays emitted by the first nucleus be captured by the second in a process called *resonant absorption*. Although the recoil loss R for free atoms is very small, it is large enough to prevent resonant absorption. R. L. Mössbauer (1958) discovered that if the

FIG. 14.23. Illustration of the energy distribution for resonant absorption. (a) represents the energy distribution in the excited state. In (b) are shown the energy distribution of the emitted protons, $(E - R)$, and the energy $(E + R)$ required to both excite a second nucleus and provide it with a recoil energy, R. Resonant absorption can occur only when these overlap.

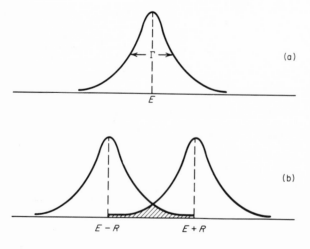

·mitting nucleus were bound into a crystal, for some events M in equation 14.20) is effectively infinite, and the recoil loss is therefore so drastically ·educed that resonant absorption can occur.

The significance of this discovery lies in the following fact. The natural ·ine width Γ of the ^{57}Fe gamma ray is 4.8×10^{-9} e.v. Thus, any change in the ·nvironment of a ^{57}Fe atom which causes a change in the energy of the emitted ·amma ray by $\sim 10^{-7}$ to 10^{-8} e.v. effectively prevents resonant absorption. The Mössbauer effect, therefore, provides an extremely sensitive probe for measure-·nent of very small energy changes. This measurement is accomplished in the ·ollowing way. The energy of a photon can be slightly altered by moving the ·source of the photon with the change in photon energy, ΔE_γ, given by the ·elation

$$\Delta E_\gamma = \frac{E_\gamma v}{c}$$

·where v is the source velocity and c is the velocity of light. A change in gamma ·ray energy of 10^{-7} e.v. corresponds to a velocity of ~ 2 mm. sec.$^{-1}$. Experimentally, ·a movable ^{57}Fe source whose velocity can be continuously varied is provided. The gamma rays from this source are passed through an absorber containing ^{57}Fe nuclei, and then allowed to fall on a detector as shown in Fig. 14.24. The ·source velocity is varied, and a curve of counting rate versus source velocity ·is determined. It is found that at certain source velocities the condition for ·resonant absorption is met, and the counting rate decreases as illustrated in Fig. 14.25.

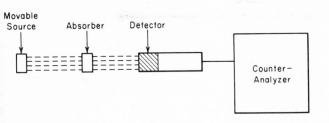

FIG. 14.24. Schematic diagram of a Mössbauer apparatus.

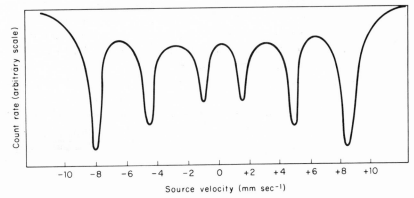

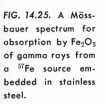

FIG. 14.25. A Mössbauer spectrum for absorption by Fe_2O_3 of gamma rays from a ^{57}Fe source embedded in stainless steel.

The half life of the 14.4 k.e.v. excited state of ^{57}Fe is 10^{-7} sec. Use the uncertainty principle to show that the corresponding line width should be between 10^{-7} and 10^{-8} e.v.

The extreme sensitivity of Mössbauer spectroscopy enables the chemist to detect small changes in the outer electron structure of atoms containing Mössbauer nuclei. We have already seen that s electrons penetrate to the nucleus. The decay of a nucleus is slightly sensitive to the s electron density at that nucleus. This s electron density, in turn, is affected by the distribution of the other electrons of the atom and, therefore, by the chemical environment of the atom. As a very simple specific example, consider $Fe^{+2}(3s^2, 3p^6, 3d^6)$ and Fe^+ $(3s^2, 3p^6, 3d^5)$. The $3s$ electrons in Fe^{+2} are more effectively shielded from the nucleus than are those in Fe^{+3} because of the extra $3d$ electron. Therefore, the two absorb at different source velocities, and can be distinguished by Mössbauer spectroscopy. This effect is called the *isomer shift*, and is the most chemically useful application of Mössbauer spectroscopy.

There are other more complex interactions which also provide valuable information. For example, magnetic fields can cause splitting of Mössbauer lines. Figure 14.25 shows splitting of a ^{57}Fe spectrum by the internal magnetic field of an iron sample. Although Mössbauer spectroscopy is a promising addition to the chemist's tools, it should be pointed out that it is limited by the fact that so far only about twenty-five nuclei are known which possess excited states suitable for such experiments.

14.15 Rotational and Vibrational Energy

The energy content of all particles such as atoms and molecules may be divided into two parts: (1) energy of motion of the center of mass in space called *translational energy*, and (2) *internal energy*. For atoms the potential energy associated with electronic structure falls into the second class. (We disregard nuclear energy, since our subsequent discussions will be confined to processes in which there is no change in intrinsic nuclear properties.) Changes in the internal energy of an atom arising from changes in its electronic structure have been discussed in Chapter 13. Similar changes in the electronic structure of molecules may occur, leading to the absorption or emission of radiation.

A molecule consisting of two or more atoms has two varieties of internal energy not found in atoms. These arise from the fact that each atom in a molecule preserves its identity, at least so far as its inner electronic structure and nucleus are concerned. Therefore, a molecule consists of two or more massive nuclei situated at distances which are large compared to the diameter of the nucleus. These nuclei may execute vibrational motions with respect to each other or may rotate about the center of mass of the molecule. Both of these types of motion are independent of the motion of the center of mass of the molecule in space.

Each of the types of internal energy mentioned above, rotational, vibrational, and electronic, is quantized. The quantum of rotational energy is the smallest, and pure rotational spectra (perturbed only by nuclear effects) have been observed only in the micro-wave region of the spectrum (0.1 to 30 cm.). Next in size is the quantum of vibrational energy which falls into the infra-red region of the spectrum (20,000 to 250,000 Å). Here vibrational absorptions perturbed by rotations are observed. Finally, the relatively large energies required for electronic transitions are available only in the ultraviolet and visible radiation (1000 to 8000 Å). In this region of the spectrum electronic transitions perturbed by both vibrational and rotational effects are observed. The relations between these types of energies are indicated schematically in Fig. 14.26.

The rotational energy of a molecule is given by

$$E_r = \frac{h^2}{8\pi^2 I} J(J+1) \qquad (14.21)$$

where J is the rotational quantum number, which may have only integral values, 0, 1, 2, 3, ... I is the rotational moment of inertia,

$$I = \mu r_e^2 \qquad (14.22)$$

where μ is the reduced mass defined by

$$\mu = \frac{m_1 m_2}{m_1 + m_2} \qquad (14.23)$$

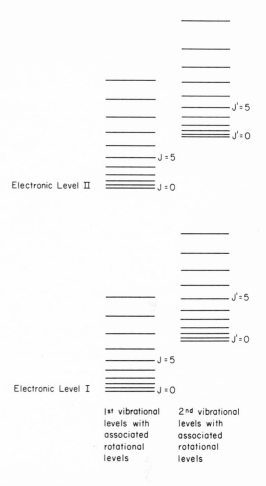

FIG. 14.26. Schematic representation of electronic, vibrational, and rotational energy levels.

and r_e the equilibrium internuclear separation.
(The solution of problem 26, p. 393 is very similar, M^2 being replaced by $J(J+1)$.) Investigations of the spectra of simple gaseous molecules in the microwave region enable one to determine values of I, and from these to compute molecular parameters such as bond angles and bond lengths. These methods provide some of the most precise structural information available.

EXERCISE 14.10

Find the rotational energy corresponding to $J = 1$ for the hydrogen molecule; $r_e = 0.74$ Å.   *Ans.* 0.24×10^{-13} erg.

The vibrational motion of a diatomic molecule may be described as an oscillatory change in the internuclear separation in the fashion of two weights

FIG. 14.27. Harmonic oscillator.

connected by a spring. Such a system is described in Fig. 14.27, where masses m_1 and m_2 oscillate about a mean distance, r_e. Then Δr is the displacement from r_e at any instant. For convenience the position of m_1 is considered as fixed.

As a first approximation we assume that the vibration is a simple harmonic oscillation. That is, the restoring force f is proportional to the displacement Δr.

$$f = -k(\Delta r) \tag{14.24}$$

The proportionality constant is called the *force constant* of the oscillator. The restoring force at any point is the negative of the derivative of the potential energy U_r with respect to Δr at that point.

$$f = \frac{-dU_r}{d(\Delta r)} = -k(\Delta r) \tag{14.25}$$

Integrating equation (14.25) yields the dependence of potential energy on Δr.

$$U_r = \tfrac{1}{2}k(\Delta r)^2 \tag{14.26}$$

This is the equation of a parabola symmetric about $\Delta r = 0$, or $r = r_e$, as shown in Fig. 14.28.

In the classical harmonic oscillator, the potential energy of the system varies from zero when the separation is r_e to a maximum value at $\Delta r_{\text{max.}}$, the maximum amplitude of the oscillation. At the same time the kinetic energy of the system varies in a complementary fashion, being zero at $\Delta r_{\text{max.}}$ and increasing to a maximum at r_e. The total vibrational energy of the system remains constant (unless the oscillation is damped) and is given by

$$E_v = \tfrac{1}{2}k(\Delta r_{\text{max.}})^2 \tag{14.27}$$

One of the fundamental properties of a classical harmonic oscillator is that its frequency of oscillation is independent of amplitude and therefore independent of energy. The frequency ω is related to the force constant by

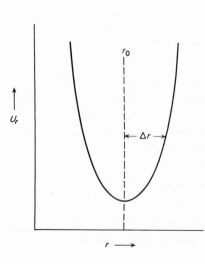

FIG. 14.28. Potential energy of a harmonic oscillator.

$$2\pi\omega = \left(\frac{k}{\mu}\right)^{1/2} \qquad (14.28)$$

where μ is the reduced mass of the system.

That is, the frequency of vibration increases with increasing force constant and decreases with increasing atomic mass.

Of course, the mechanical model that we have just described is inadequate as a model for a diatomic molecule. A more adequate model must be based on wave mechanics, but will contain some of the features of the mechanical model. For example, a potential function such as that of equation (14.26) may be used. When a wave mechanical treatment is carried out, it is found that the energy of the oscillator is quantized. Furthermore, since the wave mechanical oscillator is carrying out to-and-fro motion, the energy of its lowest state cannot be zero, just as was found for the to-and-fro motion of the particle in a box. The permitted energy states for an harmonic oscillator are given by

$$E_v = h\omega(v + \tfrac{1}{2}) \qquad (14.29)$$

where ω is the *fundamental vibrational frequency* of the harmonic oscillator, and v is the vibrational quantum number which can have any integral value, 0, 1, 2, 3, ... The difference in energy between successive energy levels of the harmonic oscillator is thus always $h\omega$. The energy of the lowest vibrational state ($v = 0$) is

$$E_v^0 = \tfrac{1}{2}h\omega \qquad (14.30)$$

This is called the *zero point energy*, and represents the minimum energy which the oscillator must have even when the temperature of the system is so low that all translational motions have ceased.

EXERCISE 14.11

Typical values of the fundamental vibration frequencies of diatomic molecules lie in the region of 5×10^{13} sec.$^{-1}$. Find the corresponding value of the "quantum" of vibrational energy $h\omega$. *Ans.* 3.3×10^{-13} erg.

The very simple model which we have just discussed is, of course, not completely adequate. One difficulty is that the potential function of equation (14.26) and Fig. 14.27 is a poor approximation to the actual molecular potential function at all but the lowest energies, as Fig. 14.5 shows. The actual molecular potential is not a simple parabolic function.

This difference requires that for accurate description of molecular vibrations correction terms must be added to equation (14.29). More important, it causes the permitted vibrational energy states to become more and more closely spaced with increasing v, eventually approaching an energy limit corresponding to dissociation of the molecule, as indicated in Fig. 14.29. In that figure the *bond dissociation energy* D_0 corresponds to the vertical distance between the $v = 0$ vibrational energy state and the energy level corresponding to the separated atoms. This is less than D_e, the dissociation energy from the bottom of the potential energy curve, by E_v^0.

14.16 Vibration-Rotation Spectra

As in the case of the electronic energy states of atoms, the energy states of molecules (vibrational, rotational, and electronic) are observed only by virtue of a transition from one state to another. That is, we observe the absorption or emission of electromagnetic radiation of a frequency related, by the Planck constant, to the change in internal energy of the molecule.

In order for a molecule to absorb electromagnetic energy in vibrational transitions, the vibration in question must be accompanied by an oscillatory change in the dipole moment of the molecule. All homonuclear diatomic molecules, such as H_2, have no dipole moment and are therefore *inactive* with respect to vibration-rotation absorption spectra. On the other hand, molecules such as HBr have a permanent dipole moment which changes in vibration, and consequently they are *active* with respect to absorption of radiation corresponding to changes in vibrational energy.

In the preceding section it was stated that a typical value for the fundamental vibration frequency, ω, for a diatomic molecule is 5×10^{13} sec.$^{-1}$. This is also the frequency, ν, of the radiation corresponding to a change of one unit in the

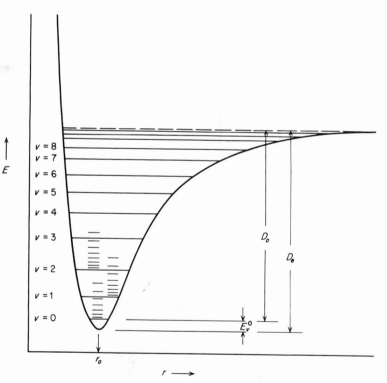

FIG. 14.29. Vibrational and rotational energy states of a diatomic molecule.

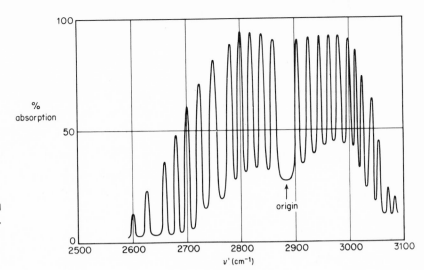

FIG. 14.30. Infrared absorption by $H^{35}Cl$.

vibrational quantum number, since

$$\Delta E = h\nu = E(v = n) - E(v = n - 1)$$

$$= h\omega(n + \tfrac{1}{2}) - h\omega(n - 1 + \tfrac{1}{2}) = h\omega$$

The frequency 5×10^{13} sec.$^{-1}$ corresponds to a wave length of $(3 \times 10^{10}$ cm. sec.$^{-1})/(5 \times 10^{13}$ sec.$^{-1}) = 6 \times 10^{-4}$ cm. $= 60,000$ Å, which is in the infrared region of the spectrum. In the study of such spectra it is more common to characterize the radiation by giving the frequency in wave numbers ν', the reciprocal of wavelength. The region of most vibrational transitions lies between 20,000 and 250,000 Å, that is, between 5000 cm.$^{-1}$ and 400 cm.$^{-1}$.

A vibrational transition may be accompanied by changes in the rotational energy state of the molecule. In Exercise 14.10 the energy of the first rotational state for hydrogen was calculated. All other molecules, having larger masses and larger internuclear separations, have larger rotational moments of inertia and closer spacing of rotational energy states. It is evident that the rotational energy levels are spaced much more closely than are the vibrational levels. In addition, the only transitions observed for diatomic molecules are those for which $\Delta J = \pm 1$. This *selection rule* limits rotational energy changes to a small fraction of the vibrational energy change, causing the spectra to appear as *bands*. Each band corresponds to a definite change in v, the vibrational quantum number, say from $v = 2$ to $v = 3$, or from $v = 3$ to $v = 4$, etc. A *selection rule*, $\Delta v = \pm 1$, also applies to vibrational transitions, but this is a rigid rule only for strictly harmonic vibrations. In the anharmonic vibrations of real molecules, this rule indicates only that $\Delta v = \pm 1$ will be the most probable transition and will, therefore, give rise to the most intense absorption or emission. Each band has a fine structure due to various changes in J, say from $J = 10$ to $J = 11$ or $J = 13$ to $J = 12$, etc.

The principal infrared absorption band of $H^{35}Cl$ is shown in Fig. 14.30. This band arises in transitions from the $v = 0$ level to the $v = 1$ level and is

439

called the *fundamental* (0, 1) band. The *origin* of the band is that frequency corresponding to $\Delta J = 0$, a forbidden transition, and lies at the position of the missing line in the center of the band. To the right of the origin (higher frequencies) lie the successive lines for $\Delta J = +1$, that is, for $J = 0$ in the lower vibrational state to $J = 1$ in the higher vibrational state; $J = 1$ to $J = 2$, $J = 2$ to $J = 3$, etc. To the left of the origin lie the successive lines for $\Delta J = -1$ $J = 1$ to $J = 0$, $J = 2$ to $J = 1$, etc.

Assuming harmonic vibration, equation (14.28) may be used to obtain the force constant of the bond. Since $\omega = c\omega'$ and for the (0, 1) transition $\omega' = 2886$ cm.$^{-1}$, from equation (14.28) we obtain

$$k = 4\pi^2 c^2 \omega'^2 \mu$$

$$= 4\pi^2 2886^2 (3 \times 10^{10})^2 \frac{1 \times 35}{1 + 35} 1.66 \times 10^{-24}$$

$$= 4.8 \times 10^5 \text{ dynes cm.}^{-1}$$

A more precise analysis, taking into account the anharmonicity of the vibration, yields $\omega' = 2989$ cm.$^{-1}$ for the fundamental vibration frequency and 5.15×10^5 dynes cm.$^{-1}$ for the force constant of the bond. Values of these properties for several molecules are given in Table 14.6.

EXERCISE 14.12

At what wave length and frequency will the 0,2 band of $H^{35}Cl$ be found?

Ans. 1.673×10^{-4} cm.; 5978 cm.$^{-1}$.

The rotational structure of the band is due to $\Delta J = \pm 1$ transitions superimposed on the vibrational transition. The general expression for the rotational energy change for $\Delta J = +1$ is

$$\Delta E_r = B(J + 1)(J + 2) - BJ(J + 1)$$

$$= 2B(J + 1) \tag{14.31}$$

where $B = h^2/8\pi^2 I$ and J is the rotational quantum number in the initial state. Since the origin of the band at 2886 cm.$^{-1}$ corresponds to $\Delta J = 0$ (Fig. 14.30, not seen) the position of the successive lines in either branch with respect to the origin should correspond to equation (14.31). For example, in Fig. 14.30 the spacing of the members of each branch is approximately 20 cm.$^{-1}$. From equation (14.31) it is seen that this spacing corresponds to $2B$. That is, increasing J by one unit increases ΔE_r by $2B$. Since

$$\frac{\Delta E_r}{hc} = \Delta v' = \frac{2B}{hc} = \frac{h}{4\pi^2 Ic}$$

substituting for $\Delta v'$ we find

$$I = \frac{6.62 \times 10^{-27}}{4\pi^2 20 (3 \times 10^{10})} = 2.8 \times 10^{-40} \text{ g. cm.}^2$$

and

$$r_e = \left(\frac{I}{\mu}\right)^{1/2} = 1.3 \text{Å}$$

The foregoing analysis of the rotational structure assumes that the molecule
is a perfectly rigid dumbbell rotator. In actual fact, the rotational moment of
inertia increases slightly with increasing J, due to stretching of the bond. Furthermore, the internuclear separation and hence the moment
of inertia also increases with increasing vibrational
energy, since the vibrations are not perfectly harmonic.
A more precise calculation taking these effects into
account yields 1.275 Å for the equilibrium internuclear
separation, r_e, in $H^{35}Cl$. Values for other molecules are
given in Table 14.6.

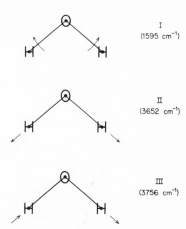

The vibration-rotation spectra of polyatomic molecules increase in complexity with the number of atoms
in the molecule. However, a degree of simplification is
introduced when it is realized that the vibrational displacements of nuclei from their mean positions can be
expressed as sums of a few *normal* or *fundamental*
modes of vibration. These are special vibrations in which
the nuclei move in straight lines and in phase. (By "in
phase" we mean that all nuclei in a molecule must both
pass through their mean positions and reach their turn-
ing points simultaneously.) The number of these normal
modes is equal to the number of vibrational degrees of
freedom of the molecule. For a bent triatomic molecule
there are three such normal modes. These are shown in
Fig. 14.31 for H_2O. They are a bending motion (I), a
concerted compression and stretching of the O-H bonds
(II), and stretching or "distortion" of the O-H bonds
(III). The actual infrared spectrum of H_2O is complex
corresponding to various combinations of those normal
modes, but it has been possible to assign frequencies to
the normal modes, as shown in Fig. 14.31. Note that
the bending motion corresponds to a lower frequency
(lower energy) than the other two vibrations, indicating
that the force constant is smaller in this case.

FIG. 14.31. Vibrations of
the H_2O molecule.

FIG. 14.32. Vibrations of
the CO_2 molecule.

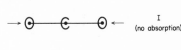

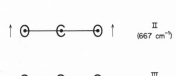

For a linear triatomic molecule there are four normal
modes of vibration. Three of these are shown for CO_2
in Fig. 14.32. The fourth is equivalent to II, but is
executed in the plane normal to the page rather than in the page. Mode I
involves no change in dipole moment and is, therefore, inactive in the infrared.
Again, the bending vibration is assigned to the lower frequency.

The infrared absorption spectra of complex molecules consist of many
bands, but it is often possible to identify the fundamental bands of a particular
type of bond such as C—H or C=O stretching or bending vibrations. Although
the frequency of such vibrations depends to some extent on the constitution
of the remainder of the molecule, the approximate location of the band is usually

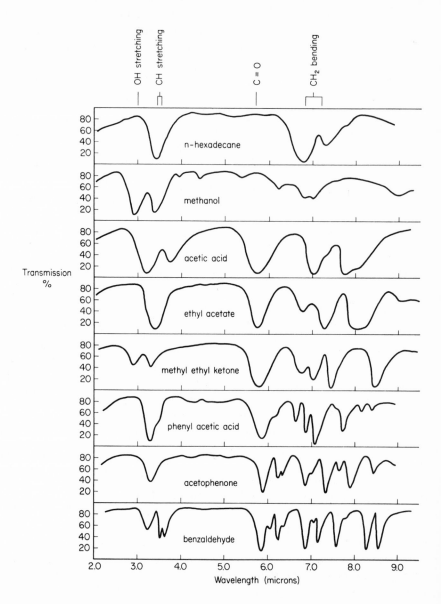

FIG. 14.33. Infrared spectra.

a useful qualitative indication of its nature. Some spectra of complex organic molecules are given in Fig. 14.33 with identification of certain characteristic bands.

14.17 Electronic Spectra

The electronic spectra of molecules arise from transitions between molecular electronic states such as those indicated in Fig. 14.35. It can be seen from that figure that the energy difference of such states is of the order of magnitude of several electron volts. Since 2 e.v. $= 16.2 \times 10^3$ cm.$^{-1} = 6200$ Å, these spectra are usually found in the visible and ultraviolet ranges (1000–8000 Å).

Each attractive (stable) electronic state of a molecule has its set of permitted vibrational energy states and each of these a set of permitted rotational energy states. However, the vibrational force constant and rotational moment of inertia will usually not be the same in the various electronic energy states of a molecule.

In the course of an electronic transition, changes in the rotational and vibrational quantum numbers may also occur, giving rise to a band spectrum such as that shown in Fig. 14.34. All of the bands shown arise from a single electronic transition with various changes in v, the vibrational quantum number, as indicated. The fine structure of each band (not resolved in the photograph) is due to changes in J, the rotational quantum number. The *selection rule* for ΔJ in electronic spectra allows $\Delta J = 0, \pm 1$; there is no selection rule for Δv. The bands in Fig. 14.34 arise from transitions from $v = 0$ in the lower electronic energy state, since at ordinary temperatures this is the most highly populated vibrational energy state.

Electronic emission spectra of molecules originate in transitions from excited electronic states. These excited states can be produced by electron impact, by heating to high temperature, or by light absorption. Emission spectra are more complex than absorption spectra, in the sense that more bands, including those corresponding to transitions to $v = 1, 2, 3$, etc. in the ground electronic state, can be seen. A series of bands such as those in Fig. 14.34, which arise from transitions to or from a single vibrational state, is called a *progression*. A larger variety of band progressions is usually seen in emission spectra.

It is found that a regular change in intensity of absorption occurs in a given progression. That is, the probability for transition from $v = 0$ in the lower electronic state varies with the value of v in the higher state. This phenomenon can be understood with the aid of the *Franck-Condon principle*, which states that *the most probable transitions are those in which separation and kinetic energy of the nuclei do not change*. This arises from the fact that electronic transitions occur in a time much less than the frequency of molecular vibrations, and, therefore, the molecule, upon being excited, must momentarily retain the same nuclear separation and kinetic energy. The Franck-Condon principle may be illustrated by reference to case *a* in Fig. 14.35, which represents, qualitatively,

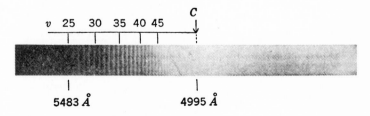

FIG. 14.34. Absorption spectrum of I₂ [from G. Herzberg, *Molecular Spectra and Molecular Structure*, D. Van Nostrand Company, Inc., Princeton, N. J., 1950].

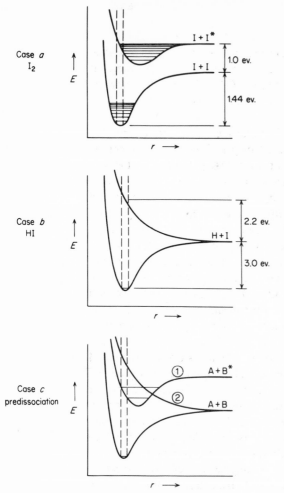

Case *a*
I_2

Case *b*
HI

Case *c*
predissociation

FIG. 14.35. Electronic energy states.

the electronic states involved in absorption by I_2.

Absorption of energy by a molecule in the lower electronic state with $v = 0$ produces an electronically excited molecule with the same internuclear separation. The instantaneous final state, therefore, lies vertically above the initial state in the region enclosed by the dashed lines in the figure. The requirement that the vibrational kinetic energy shall not change discontinuously is met by having the instantaneous final state be one of small vibrational kinetic energy, but large vibrational *potential* energy. That is, the instantaneous final state may be regarded as one in which the nuclei are at an extreme displacement from the new equilibrium internuclear separation r_0'. This is the most probable transition and evidently will give rise to a large value of v in the upper electronic state. Transitions to other vibrational states become less probable as the required change in internuclear separation or vibrational kinetic energy increases.

Absorption of radiation by a molecule in its ground state can lead to dissociation if the potential energy curve for the upper state lies in such a position that vertical displacement gives an energy above the dissociation limit for the upper state as is the case with I_2 at wave lengths below 4995 Å. The absorption spectrum of I_2 is banded at long wave lengths, indicating transitions to quantized vibrational states of the upper electronic energy state. However, at wave lengths less than 4995 Å (2.44 e.v.) the absorption is continuous rather than banded. This behavior is evidence of dissociation into $I + I^*$, where I^* represents an excited iodine atom. The large potential energy of the instantaneous final state becomes relative kinetic energy of the separated atoms. The wave length at which continuous absorption begins corresponds to the energy required for the process

$$I_2 \rightarrow I + I^*$$

It is known that the excitation energy of the iodine atoms is 0.94 e.v.; and therefore, we obtain for the dissociation energy of I_2

$$D_{I_2} = 2.44 - 0.94 = 1.5 \text{ e.v.}$$
$$= 35 \text{ kcal. mole}^{-1}$$

Some bond dissociation energies obtained from analysis of spectra are included in Table 14.6.

For an optical transition to a repulsive electronic state of the molecule, there will be no band structure, but only a continuous absorption leading to dissociation. This is so for HI, illustrated in case *b*, Fig. 14.35. In such instances the Franck-Condon principle indicates that absorption will occur only for energies considerably greater than the bond dissociation energy. The large potential energy of the instantaneous final state becomes relative kinetic energy of the separated atoms. In the case illustrated, the absorption maximum occurs at about 2500 Å (5.2 e.v. per quantum) whereas the bond dissociation energy is only 3.0 e.v. Therefore, at this wavelength, the relative kinetic energy of the H and I atoms will be 2.2 e.v.

In some instances it is observed that a molecule exhibits banded absorption, indicating an attractive upper state, but that in a certain wavelength region the bands become diffuse. That is, the rotational lines are not sharp. This is an indication of the phenomenon of *predissociation* and one of several possible combinations of potential energy curves which can lead to this effect is shown in case *c*, Fig. 14.35. Absorption gives rise to an attractive state (1) at such a vibrational level that dissociation to A + B cannot occur. If the repulsive state (2) "crosses" the state (1) at an energy level corresponding to that formed in the absorption act, an *internal conversion* from state (1) to state (2) may occur and result in dissociation. Such a conversion is governed by the Franck-Condon principle, and the two states must have the same instantaneous nuclear separation and kinetic energy.

TABLE 14.6

PROPERTIES OF MOLECULES OBTAINED FROM SPECTRA*

Molecule	Equilibrium Internuclear separation (r_e) (Å)	Moment of inertia (g. cm.^{2} × 10^{40})	Fundamental vibration frequency (cm.$^{-1}$)	Bond dissociation energy, D_0 (e.v.)
H_2	0.7417	0.460	4395	4.776
D_2	0.7416	0.920	3119	4.554
Cl_2	1.988	114.8	564.9	2.475
I_2	2.667	749	214.6	1.542
N_2	1.094	13.92	2360	9.756
O_2	1.2074	19.36	1580	5.080
$H^{35}Cl$	1.275	2.64	2989	4.430
HBr	1.414	3.30	2650	3.75
H—O—H	0.96	—	3756	—
			3652	—
			1595	—
O=C=O	1.162	—	2349	—
			1340	—
			667	—
O=S=O	1.40	—	1361	—
			1151	—
			524	—

*From G. Herzberg, *Molecular Spectra and Molecular Structure*, Vols. I and II, D. Van Nostrand Co., Princeton, N. J., 1945 and 1950.

Finally there is one other phenomenon which should be considered. When an electron is promoted from an orbital in which it is paired with a second electron, two spin relationships are possible. The promoted electron can have a spin antiparallel or parallel to its original partner. The antiparallel state is a *singlet state* (2s + 1 = 1), whereas the parallel state is triply degenerate (2s + 1 = 3) and therefore is called a *triplet state* (see section 14.5). The triplet state is usually lower in energy than the singlet, in accord with Hund's rule.

In theory electronic transitions are governed by a *spin conservation rule* which states that transitions between states of different multiplicity, for example, singlet to triplet, are "forbidden." In practice such transitions do occur but with a very low probability. In some molecules there is a triplet state close to an excited singlet, and as a result the molecule can cross over into the triplet state. Since de-excitation of the excited triplet to a ground state singlet by emission of radiation is a low-probability event, such excited triplets can have lifetimes of 10^{-3} sec. or longer as compared to the "natural lifetime" for emission of radiation of 10^{-8} to 10^{-9} sec. This type of triplet-singlet emission is called *phosphorescence*. The more rapid emission of radiation in a direct transition from an excited singlet state back to the singlet ground state is called *fluorescence*.

SUMMARY, CHAPTER 14

1. Types of bonds

    Ionic: Between atoms of low ionization potential and atoms of high electron affinity.

    Covalent: Electron pair shared equally in homonuclear molecules.

    Polar covalent: Degree of ionic character increases with increasing electronegativity difference. Electronegativity increases toward upper right of periodic table.

2. Covalent bond

    Necessity for detailed description of electron distribution by use of wave mechanics.

    Molecular orbital theory: Construction of one type of molecular orbital by linear combination of atomic orbitals. Requirement that combination of two atomic orbitals give two molecular orbitals, one bonding and one antibonding. Occurrence of bonding when number of bonding electrons exceeds number of antibonding electrons. Classification of orbitals by symmetry, σ orbitals being cylindrically symmetrical about internuclear axis, in contrast to π orbitals, with node in one plane.

    Valence bond theory: Description of a covalent bond by overlapping of atomic orbitals.

    Construction of hybridized atomic orbitals to describe directional properties of bonds (sp^3 in carbon, for example).

    Construction of a resonance hybrid of valence bond structures to represent the structure of molecules which cannot be described by single valence bond structures.

3. Bonding in complex ions

Electrostatic model based on consideration of effect of geometrical arrangement of perturbing ligands on energies of d orbitals. Necessity for introduction of covalency into model.

4. Electrical and magnetic moment

Measurement of dielectric constant, $\epsilon = C/C_0$, yields molar polarizability, P_M.

$$P_M = \frac{4\pi}{3} N \left(\alpha_0 + \frac{\mu^2}{3kT} \right)$$

Magnetic susceptibility.

$$\chi = N \left(\alpha_M + \frac{\mu_M^2}{3kT} \right)$$

χ is positive for paramagnetic substances. When paramagnetism arises only from unpaired electron spins

$$\mu_M = \sqrt{n(n + 2)} \qquad \text{Bohr magnetons}$$

5. Some types of spectroscopy

Nuclear magnetic resonance (n.m.r.), based on absorption of radio frequency radiation by system of nuclei with magnetic moments which is split in presence of magnetic field.

$$h\nu = g\mu_n H_0$$

Electron spin resonance (e.s.r.) based on absorption of radio-frequency radiation by system of unpaired electrons which is split in presence of magnetic field.

$$h\nu = g\beta H$$

Mössbauer spectroscopy, based on small changes in energy of nuclear levels caused by changes in chemical bond type.

6. Molecular vibration and rotation

Permitted vibrational energy states

$$E_v = h\omega \left(v + \tfrac{1}{2} \right)$$

Permitted rotational energy states

$$E_r = BJ(J + 1)$$

Molecular electronic spectra consists of bands corresponding to transitions between attractive electronic states. Continuous absorption denotes transition to a repulsive electronic state. The Franck-Condon principle states that the most probable transitions are those in which the relative position and vibrational kinetic energy do not change. The spin conservation rule states that transitions between states of different multiplicity are forbidden.

PROBLEMS, CHAPTER 14

1. The equilibrium internuclear separation in gaseous diatomic NaI is 2.90 Å. Find the energy term in the process

$$Na(g) + I(g) \longrightarrow Na^+I^-$$

neglecting the energy of repulsion. *Ans.* 4.97 e.v. molecule^{-1}

2. From the bond dissociation energy of I_2 (page 444) and the electron affinity of I (Table 14.1), find ΔE for the process

$$e + I_2 \longrightarrow I + I^-.$$
Ans. -1.56 e.v.

3. From data in Fig. 13.11 and Table 14.1 estimate the electronegativity of the halogens (*cf.* Exercise 14.4). Compare with the empirical values given in Fig. 14.10.

4. From data in Fig. 13.11 and Table 14.1 show that the process

$$M(g) + X(g) \longrightarrow M^+(g) + X^-(g)$$

is endothermic for all possible combinations of alkali metal and halogen.

5. Use the molecular orbital approach to predict the stability of the diatomic molecules Li_2, Be_2, B_2, and C_2.

6. Use the concept of hybrid bond orbitals to predict the geometry of BH_3. What will the polarity of the B — H bonds be? Will the molecule have a dipole moment?

7. The bond angle in H_2S is 97°. From the dipole moment of the molecule given in Table 14.4 find the S — H bond moment. *Ans.* 0.72 debye.

8. The dipole moments of HCl, HBr, and HI are 1.07, 0.78, and 0.38 debye, respectively. Show that these values are approximately proportional to the electronegativity differences between hydrogen and the respective halogens.

9. The total molar polarization of HCl gas at 200°K is 41 cc. mole^{-1}. Use the dipole moment in Table 14.4 to find the value of the distortion polarizability. Compare with $\mu^2/3kT$. *Ans.* $\alpha = 0.25 \times 10^{-23}$ cm.^{3} molecule^{-1}, $\mu^2/3kT = 1.38 \times 10^{-23}$ cm.^{3} molecule^{-1}.

10. From the dipole moment of HCl given in Table 14.4 and the internuclear separation, 1.275 Å, find the effective charge on each atom in electronic charge units. Compute the % ionic character of the bond.

11. R. P. Bell and I. E. Coop [*Trans. Faraday Soc.*, **34**, 1209 (1938)] have found that the dipole moment of deuterium chloride is greater than that for hydrogen chloride. Explain.

12. The magnetic moments μ of some transition metal complexes are listed. Where possible, use these data as a criterion and show how the d orbitals (Fig. 14.12) are occupied. If it is not possible to reach a decision on the basis of magnetic moments alone, state this and state why this is so.

Complex	μ (Bohr magnetons)
$Co(NO_2)_6^{-4}$	1.9
$Co(NH_3)_6^{+2}$	5.0
CoF_6^{-3}	5.3
$Fe(CN)_6^{-3}$	2.3
$Fe(H_2O)_6^{+2}$	5.3

13. From the following data for the dielectric constant of gaseous HCl as a function of temperature, estimate its dipole moment. The pressure for each measurement was one atmosphere. Assume that the ideal gas law holds.

t (°C)	-75	0	100	200
ϵ	1.0076	1.0042	1.0026	1.0016

14. Sketch the n.m.r. spectrum expected for acetaldehyde, for isopropyl alcohol, and for *t*-butyl alcohol, considering the effects of chemical shifts, spin-spin splitting, and the number of protons of each type.

15. R. A. Ogg [*Discussions of the Faraday Society*, **17**, 215 (1954)] has used n.m.r. to investigate the exchange reaction

$$NH_3 + NH_2^- \longrightarrow NH_2^- + NH_3$$

in liquid NH_3. Sketches of his spectra in the order of increasing concentration of NH_2^- follow.

(a) Explain what is happening.

(b) The separation of these peaks is 46 cycles per second. Compute τ, the mean life for the exchange reaction.   *Ans.* $\tau = 2.2 \times 10^{-2}$ sec.

PROB. FIG. 14.15.

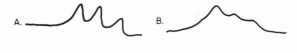

16. Draw sketches showing how the n.m.r. spectrum of ethyl alcohol would be expected to change as temperature is increased.

17. Given the fundamental vibration frequency for $H^{35}Cl = 2886$ cm.$^{-1}$, find the fundamental vibration frequency for (a) $H^{37}Cl$, and (b) $D^{35}Cl$.
                                                          Ans. (a) 2884 cm.$^{-1}$.

18. Pure rotational spectra are observed in the far infrared. Find the frequency in cm.$^{-1}$ corresponding to the changes $J = 0$ to $J = 1$, $J = 1$ to $J = 2$, and $J = 2$ to $J = 3$ for $H^{35}Cl$. (Take I from Table 14.6.)   *Ans.* $J = 0$ to $J = 1$, 21.2 cm.$^{-1}$.

19. The spacing of the rotational lines in the infrared spectrum of CO is approximately 3.86 cm.$^{-1}$. Find the internuclear separation in the molecule.

20. The molecule HI has a force constant of 3.0×10^5 dynes cm.$^{-1}$ and an internuclear separation of 1.60 Å. Calculate

(a) The fundamental vibration frequency of the molecule.

(b) Its zero point energy in calories mole^{-1}.

(c) The position of its first vibrational band in wave numbers.

21. In the near infrared spectrum of CO there is an intense band at 2168 cm.$^{-1}$. Calculate

(a) The fundamental vibrational frequency of CO.

(b) The period of vibration.

(c) The force constant.

(d) The zero point energy of CO in calories per mole.
                                                   Ans. (a) 6.5×10^{13} sec.$^{-1}$,
                                                          (d) 3.10 kcal. mole^{-1}.

22. Construct a graphical representation of the energy of the HBr molecule for $v = 0$, 1, or 2, and for $J = 1,2,3,4$, and 5 in each vibrational state. For $v = 0$ at what value of J will the energy of the system exceed that for $v = 1$ and $J = 0$? Assume harmonic vibration and rigid dumbbell rotation.

23. The kinetic energy of rotation of a homonuclear molecule is $E_r = \frac{1}{2}(Iv^2/R^2)$, where v is the linear velocity of rotation of the molecule at a distance R from the axis of rotation. Find the linear velocity of rotation of the atoms of a hydrogen molecule for $J = 1$.   *Ans.* 2.41×10^5 cm. sec.$^{-1}$.

24. Find the rotational energy corresponding to $J = 1$ for (a) HD, and (b) D_2. Take $r_0 = 0.74$ Å, as in H_2.

25. In the ultraviolet absorption spectrum of oxygen there is a series of bands corresponding to transitions from the ground state to an electronically excited state. These bands converge to the onset of a continuum at 1759 Å. The two atoms formed by dissociation of the excited state are a ground state triplet atom, designated as ^3P, and an excited state singlet atom, designated as ^1D. This is as required by the spin conservation rule. From the spectrum of atomic oxygen it is known that the ^1D state lies 1.97 e.v. above the ^3P state. Calculate in e.v. the energy required to dissociate an oxygen molecule into two ground state (^3P) atoms.

26. The heat of dissociation of Cl_2 in the gas phase is 56,800 calories mole^{-1}. Calculate the work in calories required to separate the two Cl atoms a distance of 0.1 Å from their equilibrium position in the molecule. The equilibrium interatomic distance in the Cl_2 molecule is 1.98 Å, and the fundamental vibrational frequency is 1.603×10^{13} sec.$^{-1}$.

27. The particle in a box treatment provides a very simple model for the electrons in a system of conjugated double bonds, for example CH_3—$(CH{=}CH)_4$—CH_3. Assume that the conjugated double bond system may be approximated as an infinite walled one-dimensional box of effective length, $L = 9.8$ Å, and calculate

(a) The minimum kinetic energy of an electron in this model.

(b) The wavelength of the radiation required to excite an electron to form the first excited state.

(c) The addition of a single $CH{=}CH$ group increases L by 1.4 Å. What is the corresponding increase in the wavelength of the radiation required to reach the first excited state?   *Ans.* (a) 6.27×10^{-13} ergs,
(b) ~ 3520 Å.

28. Sketch a splitting diagram for an unpaired electron interacting with a magnetic nucleus of $I = 1$. How many e.s.r. lines would be expected?

29. The intensity ratios of the peaks in the ethyl radical spectrum shown in Fig. 14.22a are $1:2:3:1:6:3:3:6:1:3:2:1$. Show how such intensity ratios can arise in a radical which has one group of three equivalent protons and a second group of two equivalent protons. In the ethyl radical spectrum, which group of protons causes the greater splitting?

30. The dipole moment of nitrobenzene is 3.93 debye, and the dipole moment of p-nitrotoluene is 4.39 debye (A. L. McClellan, *op. cit.*). Predict the dipole moments of m-nitrotoluene and o-nitrotoluene.   *Ans.* 4.2 and 3.8 debye.

15

SOME PROPERTIES
OF SOLIDS
AND LIQUIDS

5.1 The Crystalline State

Solids can occur in two forms, *crystalline* and *amorphous*. Practically all solids occur as crystals, so we shall concentrate our attention on the crystalline state. Crystals are characterized by the fact that many of their properties are *anisotropic*, that is, are different in nonparallel directions. Examples of the external directional properties of crystals are (1) their symmetry, (2) the constancy of the angles between corresponding faces of different crystals of the same substance, and (3) the production of plane faces on growth. Examples of other directional properties are (1) electrical and magnetic properties, (2) thermal conductivity, (3) behavior when subjected to light. Other important properties of crystals are that of melting sharply at a well-defined melting point and that of possessing a definite heat of fusion.

The macroscopic properties of crystals have been shown to arise from the fact that the atoms, molecules, or ions of which crystals are composed pack together to form an ordered and regular array. Such an array consists of units which repeat themselves periodically in three dimensions in such a way that the environment of each unit is identical to that of any other.

15.2 The Space Lattice

For all types of unit it is convenient to discuss crystals in terms of a geometrical construction, the *space lattice*. The student should understand clearly that the subject of the following discussion is this geometrical abstraction.

A space lattice is simply an infinitely extended regular distribution of points in space. Each point is chosen so that its environment in space is the same as

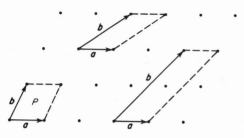

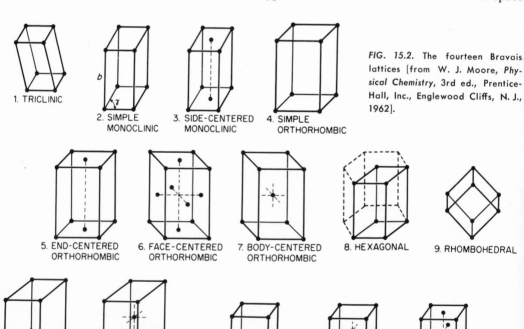

that of any other point. Within this limit choice is free. Two possible choices are a particular atom in a molecule, or the center of symmetry of a molecular unit. An example of a two-dimensional space lattice is shown in Fig. 15.1.

The points in the space lattice can be connected in various ways by vectors. The vector from any lattice point to the next is called a primitive translation. In two-dimensional space two independent primitive translations define a *unit cell*. Three possible unit cells are shown in Fig. 15.1. The whole

FIG. 15.1. A two-dimensional space lattice with possible choices of unit cell outlined. *a* and *b* represent the vectors defining the unit cell. The primitive unit cell is labelled P.

space lattice may be generated by placing these unit cells side by side in space. Usually a particular unit cell is selected, that cell of minimum area which most nearly approaches a rectangle, the *primitive cell*. In Fig. 15.1 the four points of every primitive cell each belong to four other primitive cells. Therefore, each primitive cell may be said to contain one point.

Although for simplicity we have chosen to discuss two-dimensional space lattices, the ideas which we have developed apply equally well to three dimensions. In 1848 A. Bravais showed that all possible three-dimensional space lattices are of fourteen distinct types. Unit cells for the fourteen Bravais space

FIG. 15.2. The fourteen Bravais lattices [from W. J. Moore, *Physical Chemistry*, 3rd ed., Prentice-Hall, Inc., Englewood Cliffs, N. J., 1962].

1. TRICLINIC
2. SIMPLE MONOCLINIC
3. SIDE-CENTERED MONOCLINIC
4. SIMPLE ORTHORHOMBIC
5. END-CENTERED ORTHORHOMBIC
6. FACE-CENTERED ORTHORHOMBIC
7. BODY-CENTERED ORTHORHOMBIC
8. HEXAGONAL
9. RHOMBOHEDRAL
10. SIMPLE TETRAGONAL
11. BODY-CENTERED TETRAGONAL
12. SIMPLE CUBIC
13. BODY-CENTERED CUBIC
14. FACE-CENTERED CUBIC

lattices are shown in Fig. 15.2. To generate a complete space lattice, each of the representations in 15.2 must be repeated in all directions without limit. With three-dimensional lattices, three vectors, usually designated **a, b,** and **c,** are used to establish unit cells. As in the two-dimensional case a primitive cell must contain only one lattice point. Thus, in Fig. 15.2, cells 1, 2, 4, 9, 10, and 12 are primitive cells.

An infinite number of planes can be passed through any space lattice; some of them are shown in the two-dimensional cut of Fig. 15.3. The various lines in this figure may be considered to represent edges of planes. These planes can be defined in terms of the $x, y,$ and z axes using three numbers which represent the simplest whole-number ratio of its intercepts on these axes. This leads to the sets of indices shown in Fig. 15.3. Since all planes shown are parallel to the z axis, the index for this axis is ∞.

Although the indices of Fig. 15.3 can be used to define planes, a more convenient set is usually chosen, the *Miller indices*, which can be derived as follows. Take the reciprocals of the coefficients of **a, b,** and **c** in Fig. 15.3. Clear fractions by multiplying by the lowest common multiple, excluding infinity, and the resulting three numbers are the Miller indices of the plane in question.

The operations are illustrated in Table 15.1, where the Miller indices are represented by the symbols $h, k,$ and l referring to the $x,$ $y,$ and z axes respectively. Each set of three numbers represents an infinite set of parallel planes with a fixed interplanar spacing.

FIG. 15.3. Some possible planes in a cubic lattice. Planes are viewed edge on.

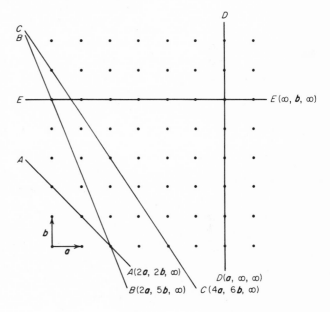

TABLE 15.1

Plane	Intercepts	Reciprocal of multiples			Clear fractions	Miller indices (hkl)
AA	$2a:2b:\infty$	1/2	1/2	1/∞	$\times$ 2	110
BB	$2a:5b:\infty$	1/2	1/5	1/∞	$\times$ 10	520
CC	$4a:6b:\infty$	1/4	1/6	1/∞	$\times$ 12	320
DD	$a:\infty:\infty$	1/1	1/∞	1/∞	$\times$ 1	100
EE	$\infty:\ b:\infty$	1/∞	1/1	1/∞	$\times$ 1	010

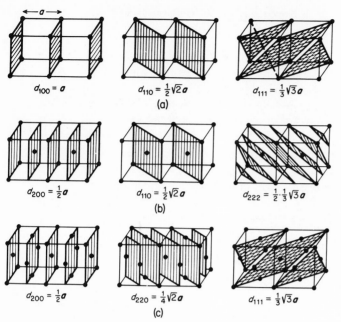

$d_{100} = a$
$d_{110} = \frac{1}{2}\sqrt{2}\,a$
$d_{111} = \frac{1}{3}\sqrt{3}\,a$

(a)

$d_{200} = \frac{1}{2}a$
$d_{110} = \frac{1}{2}\sqrt{2}\,a$
$d_{222} = \frac{1}{2} \cdot \frac{1}{3}\sqrt{3}\,a$

(b)

$d_{200} = \frac{1}{2}a$
$d_{220} = \frac{1}{4}\sqrt{2}\,a$
$d_{111} = \frac{1}{3}\sqrt{3}\,a$

(c)

FIG. 15.4. Spacings in cubic lattices: (a) simple cubic; (b) body-centered cubic; (c) face-centered cubic; [from W. J. Moore. *Physical Chemistry*, 3rd ed., Prentice-Hall, Inc., Englewood Cliffs, N. J., 1956].

The perpendicular distance of separation d between adjacent members of the set of parallel planes represented by the Miller indices h, k, and l can be expressed in terms of the Miller indices. The expression is particularly simple if the axes are at right angles to each other.

$$\frac{1}{d_{hkl}^2} = \frac{h^2}{\mathbf{a}^2} + \frac{k^2}{\mathbf{b}^2} + \frac{l^2}{\mathbf{c}^2} \quad (15.1)$$

For a cubic crystal $\mathbf{a} = \mathbf{b} = \mathbf{c}$, and equation (15.1) becomes

$$d_{hkl} = \frac{\mathbf{a}}{\sqrt{h^2 + k^2 + l^2}} \quad (15.2)$$

Figure 15.4 illustrates spacings between some sets of planes in cubic lattices.

EXERCISE 15.1

For the two-dimensional array of Fig. 15.3 use a geometrical argument to show that the distance of separation of the parallel set of AA planes is given by equation (15.1) with $l = 0$.

EXERCISE 15.2

Show that the distance between 210 planes in the simple cubic lattice is $\mathbf{a}/\sqrt{5}$.

15.3 The Crystal Systems

All crystals can be ordered into six systems: triclinic, monoclinic, orthorhombic, tetragonal, hexagonal, and cubic. (The rhombohedral is now usually considered to belong to the hexagonal class.) The six systems are defined by reference to the shapes of their unit cells. Thus, in all crystals of the cubic class it is possible to choose a unit cell of cubic shape. The vectors defining this cell, $\mathbf{a}$, $\mathbf{b}$, and $\mathbf{c}$, are all equal, and the angles between them are all 90 deg. The angle between $\mathbf{b}$ and $\mathbf{c}$ is called α, that between $\mathbf{c}$ and $\mathbf{a}$ is β, and that between $\mathbf{a}$ and $\mathbf{b}$ is γ. These characteristics of the cubic system together with the characteristics of other crystal systems are summed up in Table 15.2 and in Fig. 15.5. In the table P refers to a primitive cell, C to a cell with points centered in two opposing face, I to a body-centered cell, and F to a cell with points centered in all faces.

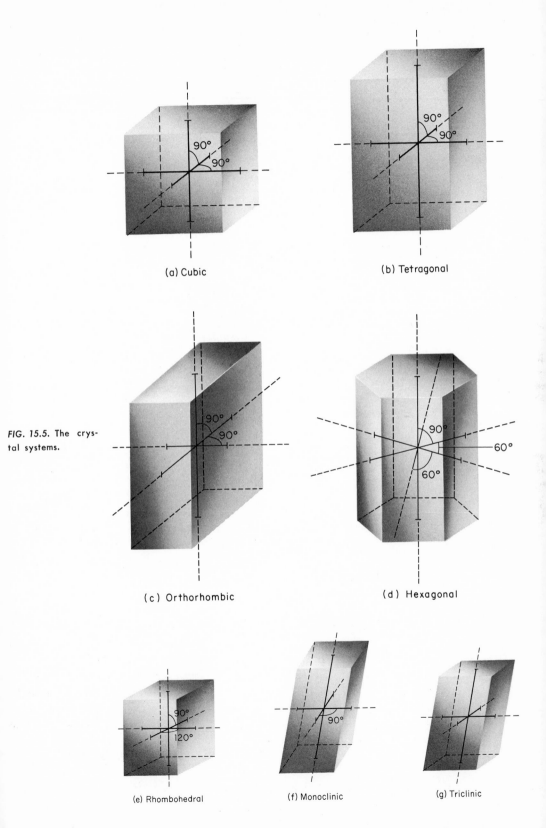

FIG. 15.5. The crystal systems.

(a) Cubic

(b) Tetragonal

(c) Orthorhombic

(d) Hexagonal

(e) Rhombohedral

(f) Monoclinic

(g) Triclinic

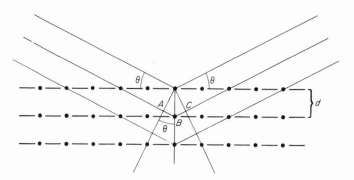

FIG. 15.6. Bragg reflection.

TABLE 15.2

THE CRYSTAL SYSTEMS

System*	Unit cell vectors	Lattice types
Triclinic	$\mathbf{a} \neq \mathbf{b} \neq \mathbf{c}$ $\alpha \neq \beta \neq \gamma \neq 90°$	P
Monoclinic	$\mathbf{a} \neq \mathbf{b} \neq \mathbf{c}$ $\alpha = \gamma = 90° \neq \beta$	P, C
Orthorhombic	$\mathbf{a} \neq \mathbf{b} \neq \mathbf{c}$ $\alpha = \beta = \gamma = 90°$	P, C, I, F
Tetragonal	$\mathbf{a} = \mathbf{b} \neq \mathbf{c}$ $\alpha = \beta = \gamma = 90°$	P, I
Hexagonal	$\mathbf{a} = \mathbf{b} \neq \mathbf{c}$ $\alpha = \beta = 90°, \gamma = 120°$	P
Rhombohedral	$\mathbf{a}' = \mathbf{b}' = \mathbf{c}'$ $\alpha' = \beta' = \gamma' \neq 90°$	P
Cubic	$\mathbf{a} = \mathbf{b} = \mathbf{c}$ $\alpha = \beta = \gamma = 90°$	P, I, F

*Each of these is the highest symmetry class into which a crystal having the properties described in the corresponding entry in column 2 can fall. Occasionally crystals are actually found to be of lower symmetry.

15.4 Diffraction of X rays

X rays are a form of electromagnetic radiation, and as such are capable of interacting with electrons. A model for such an interaction involves excitation of an electron into periodic vibrations by the oscillating electric field of the X rays. This electron can then become a secondary source of electromagnetic waves of the same frequency and wave length as the exciting source. The result will be a new wave front of X rays originating from the electron. The process is called scattering. The scattered waves from the various electrons of an atom can combine to form a single scattered wave.

For the purposes of our present discussion we can treat atoms as point sources of scattered X rays. The X rays scattered from different point sources may reinforce or cancel each other, giving rise to a typical diffraction pattern. The condition for reinforcement may be derived most easily by considering a reflection which has an equivalent effect. As we have already seen, parallel planes defined by sets of Miller indices, h, k, and l, may be passed through these points. Consider Fig. 15.6, which represents a cut through a set of such parallel planes. A ray incident at an angle θ to one of the planes defined by a given row of points can be considered to be reflected at the same angle. A ray reflected from the second plane must travel a distance ABC greater than a ray reflected from the first plane. The increased path length is given by

$$ABC = 2AB = 2d \sin \theta \qquad (15.3)$$

where d is the distance between parallel planes corresponding to a particular set of Miller indices.

If the distance ABC is an integral multiple of the wave length of the incident radiation, then reflections from successive planes will be in phase, and they will reinforce each other. However, if this condition is not met, then the reflections from this set of planes will be out of phase. The result can be shown to be complete cancellation of the scattered waves. Therefore, the condition for maximum intensity of scattered radiation is

$$n\lambda = 2d \sin \theta \qquad (15.4)$$

where n is an integer, and λ is the wave length of the scattered radiation. This is the famous Bragg equation, named for W. L. Bragg, who first developed this approach.

If the angle θ is varied by rotating the crystal, an intense scattering will be observed at values of $\sin \theta$ corresponding to $n = 1, 2, 3$, etc. The reflection with $n = 1$ is referred to as first order, that with $n = 2$ as second order, etc. For second-order reflections the Bragg equation becomes $2\lambda = 2d \sin \theta_2$ where θ_2 refers to the angle at which second-order scattering occurs. This equation may be rewritten as $\lambda = 2(d/2) \sin \theta_2$. Thus, second-order reflection from a set of planes of spacing d is formally equivalent to first-order reflection from a set of planes with spacing $d/2$. As a specific example, if the spacing of the 111 set of planes is d, that of the 222 set of planes is $d/2$. Therefore second-order reflection from the 111 planes and first-order reflection from the 222 planes are equivalent. In general, then, an alternate statement of Bragg's law (equation 15.4) is

$$\lambda = 2d_{hkl} \sin \theta_{hkl} \qquad (15.5)$$

15.5 The Powder Method

For crystals with a simple structure another method of analysis, the powder method, illustrated in Fig. 15.7 is commonly used. A beam of X rays is reflected from a powdered sample. This powder will contain many crystals

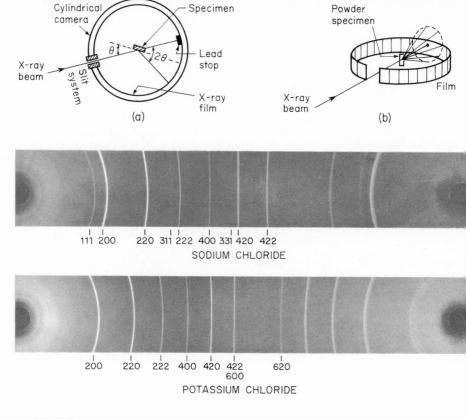

FIG. 15.7. X ray diffraction by NaCl and by KCl powders [from W. J. Moore, *Physical Chemistry*, 3rd ed., Prentice-Hall, Inc., Englewood Cliffs, N.J., 1962; photograph courtesy of Dr Arthur Lessor, IBM Laboratories].

oriented in all conceivable directions. As a result, Bragg reflection is possible from all sets of planes. The scattered X rays are detected by means of an X ray-sensitive film. As is shown in Fig. 15.7, the result is the formation of light areas in the form of arcs (lines) at a varying distance from the incident beam. These distances can be converted into scattering angles. If y is the arc distance along the film from the point of impact of the undeflected beam to a given line corresponding to reflection from a set of Miller planes hkl, and R is the radius of the film then

$$\frac{y_1}{2\pi R} = \frac{2\theta_{hkl}}{360}$$ (15.6)

Using equation (15.6), we can express the data on a powder photograph in terms of Bragg angles. As we shall see below, if we can deduce the appropriate Miller indices for each observed θ, we can then compute the separations of the corresponding Miller planes.

15.6 Cubic Systems

As a first step in seeing how the problems of indexing a set of lines on an X ray photograph might be solved, we shall consider the inverse problem.

Assuming a structure, we shall examine the question of which sets of Miller indices can be expected to give X ray lines, using as examples the simplest systems, cubic lattices.

Combination of equations (15.2) and (15.5) shows that for cubic systems

$$\sin^2 \theta_{hkl} = \frac{\lambda^2}{4a^2} (h^2 + k^2 + l^2) \tag{15.7}$$

$\lambda^2/4a^2$ will, of course, be constant for any given experiment. Let us now consider the simple cubic system with eight identical atoms at the corners of a cube. The smallest allowed value of $(h^2 + k^2 + l^2)$ is 1, corresponding to the 100 plane. Therefore, in the simple cubic system the line with the least deflection from the original X ray beam can be indexed as coming from the 100 plane. For the 110 plane $(h^2 + k^2 + l^2) = 2$, and the next line should correspond to the 110 plane. The general pattern to be expected then is a set of lines corresponding to the equation

$$\sin^2 \theta_{hkl} = \left(\frac{\lambda^2}{4a^2} \right) n$$

where n is an integer equal to $(h^2 + k^2 + l^2)$; that is, the observed values of $\sin^2 \theta_{hkl}$ should progress in even steps. However, there are some important exceptions. For example, $(h^2 + k^2 + l^2)$ cannot equal seven. Thus, the value of $\sin^2 \theta_{hkl}$ for $n = 7$ should be absent (Table 15.3). Similarly, the fifteenth, twenty-third, twenty-eighth, thirty-first, and thirty-ninth lines will be missing. These patterns of absences enable us both to identify a simple cubic crystal and to relate the observed lines to appropriate Miller indices.

TABLE 15.3

SOME ALLOWED VALUES OF $(h^2 + k^2 + l^2)$ FOR A SIMPLE CUBIC CRYSTAL

hkl	100	110	111	200	210	211	220	300 221	310
$(h^2 + k^2 + l^2)$	1	2	3	4	5	6	8	9	10

Other simple crystals of high symmetry can be treated by similar procedures. For a body-centered cubic lattice (Fig. 15.4), the 100 planes are interleaved with a set of 200 spaced so that $d_{200} = d_{100}/2$. When the condition for reinforced scattering from the 100 planes is met, the radiation scattered from the 200 planes will be 180 deg. out of phase with that scattered from the 100 planes. Each 100 plane contains one net atom per unit cell, since each of the four atoms in the 100 plane is shared by four unit cells. There is also one 200 atom per unit cell. Therefore, over the whole crystal the scattering from the 200 planes will completely cancel that from the 100 planes. Similar reasoning based on Fig. 15.4 shows that not only 100 scattering, but so also 111 scattering will be absent. On the other hand, 200, 110, and 222 scatterings will be observed. In general, no scattering will be observed from planes for which $(h + k + l)$ is odd.

For a face-centered cubic crystal (Fig. 15.4) in which all scattering points are equivalent, scattering from the 100 planes will be cancelled by scattering

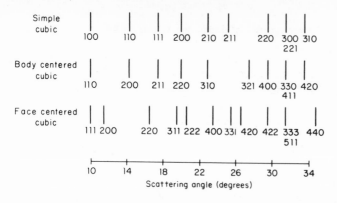

FIG. 15.8. Lines observed with the three cubic lattices as a function of angle. The values of $\lambda^2/4a^2$ are arbitrarily selected so that the first line will fall at 10° for each lattice.

from the 200 planes just as for the body-centered cubic crystal. In addition the 110 planes will be interleaved with a set of 220 planes, with the result that the 110 scattering is also cancelled. In general, it can be shown that reflections are observable only from planes for which the Miller indices are either all even or all odd.

The characteristics of the three basic cubic systems are compared in Fig. 15.8. For all three it is assumed that the first line is at 10 deg., and on this basis the positions of the allowed lines for each system have been calculated by using equation (15.6). The differences in the patterns serve to identify the type of unit cell. (This is an extremely simple example. Patterns are usually more complex, as we shall see below.)

As a concrete example, let us consider the NaCl crystal. It is an easy matter to show that the square of the sines of the scattering angles corresponding to the lines shown in Fig. 15.7 can all be expressed in terms of equation (15.7) and that the crystal is therefore cubic. The value of **a**, the unit cell parameter, is 5.63 Å. The pattern of lines observed shows only all odd or all even values of h, k, and l, indicating that the crystal is face-centered. We have one independent piece of information. The density of crystalline NaCl is 2.163 g. cm.$^{-3}$. The volume occupied by one formula weight is, therefore, $58.45/2.163 = 27.02$ cm.^{3}. The volume per ion pair must then be $27.02/(6.02 \times 10^{23})$ $= 44.9 \times 10^{-24}$ cm.^{3} or 44.9 Å^3. a^3 is $(5.63$ Å$)^3$ or 178.5 Å^3. Therefore, there are $178.5/44.9 = 4$ Na$^+$Cl$^-$ ion pairs per unit cell.

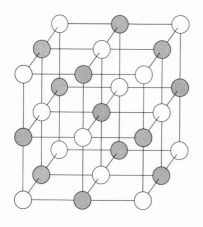

FIG. 15.9. The unit cell for NaCl and KCl.

A unit cell which meets these requirements is shown in Fig. 15.9. This represents two interpenetrating face-centered arrays, one composed only of Na$^+$ ions, the second only of Cl$^-$ ions. If we recall that units at the corners of the cells are shared among eight cells, those on an edge among four cells, and those at the center of a face between two cells, we see that the requirement of four ion pairs per unit cell is met. The scattering centers in this unit cell are not equivalent, since Cl$^-$ has eight more electrons than does Na$^+$. This has an effect on the intensity of the line from the 111 planes. If we assume that the white circles in Fig. 15.9 are Cl$^-$ ions, then we see that there is a set of 111 planes consisting only of Cl$^-$ ions. However, this is interleaved with a set of parallel planes containing only Na^+ ions. If the scattering condition is met for the 111 plane of Cl^- ions, then the Na^+ planes must be scattering radiation out of phase with that from the Cl^- planes, reducing the 111 intensity. Such intensity variations provide powerful clues to the arrangement of the elements of a unit cell.

Figure 15.9 also provides a basis for understanding the powder photograph of KCl. If we assume the same unit cell as for NaCl, then the various planes have the same Miller indices. Again, we expect the 100 and 110 lines to be absent because of interference from the interleaved 200 and 220 planes. However, there will also be no line observed due to scattering by the 111 planes of Cl^- ions. These are now interleaved with planes of K^+ ions. Since K^+ ions and Cl^- ions contain equal numbers of electrons, they are almost equivalent in scattering power. Scattering from the 111 Cl^- planes is thus effectively cancelled by out-of-phase scattering from the interleaved K^+ planes. As Fig. 15.7 shows, this model agrees with the observed powder pattern.

15.7   Structure Determination by X Rays

One of the most important uses of the X ray rotating crystal technique is for the determination of the structure of molecules. We shall indicate how this might be done by considering a simple model. Figure 15.10 represents a two-dimensional array of molecules of the type AB_2. In our treatment of it we shall assume that the dimensions of the unit cell, **a** and **b**, have already been established by methods similar to those discussed earlier.

Now consider the 210 planes of solid atoms shown in Fig. 15.10. The separation of these planes along the x axis is $\mathbf{a}/2$; along the y axis, $\mathbf{b}/1$. Note that 2 and 1 are Miller indices. When the Bragg condition for reinforced scattering by the planes of A atoms is met, their separation along the x axis, $\mathbf{a}/2$, corresponds to a phase difference of 2π.

We shall symbolize the x coordinate of a B atom as x_B. Radiation scattered by the B atoms will interfere with that scattered by the A atoms,

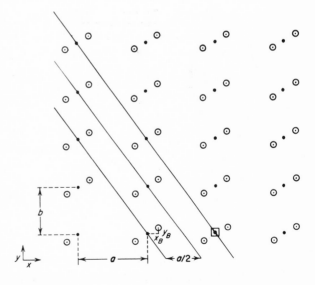

FIG. 15.10. A two-dimensional lattice consisting of AB_2 type units in which scattering from B is out of phase with that from A.

since it is out of phase with that scattered by the A atoms by a phase angle $[x_B/(\mathbf{a}/2)]2\pi$ (Fig. 15.10), which we shall rewrite as $[2x_B/\mathbf{a}]2\pi$. Similarly, along the y axis the phase difference will be $[(1)y_B/\mathbf{b}]2\pi$. This result can be generalized to other planes. For these the phase difference for an atom i along the axis will be $(hx_i/\mathbf{a})2\pi$, along the y axis $(ky_i/\mathbf{b})2\pi$, and along the z axis $(lz_i/\mathbf{c})2\pi$

For simplicity our discussion now will be limited to the x dimension only In Fig. 15.10 we have represented the atoms of the AB_2 molecule as dots. Thi is, of course, unrealistic since the electrons associated with atoms are dis tributed in space in some way. In the x dimension this distribution may be de scribed by a suitable mathematical function of x, which we shall symbolize a $\rho(x)$. It is actually $\rho(x)$ which we are determining, since X rays are scattered by electrons. $\rho(x)$ will vary in some periodic fashion along the x axis, because the structure is periodic along this axis. It will peak where atoms are centered. The electron density in any small element between x and $(x + dx)$ of the one dimensional unit cell will be $\rho(x)\,dx$, and the intensity of the radiation scattered from this element will be proportional to $\rho(x)\,dx$.

We shall now define an origin for the coordinate system. Since our AB_2 system has a center of symmetry, it is convenient to choose as an origin some point in the unit cell which reflects this symmetry. We shall select the black atom inside the square in Fig. 15.10. A ray scattered in the element between x_B and $(x_B + dx)$ will be out of phase with one scattered at the origin by an amount $(hx_B/\mathbf{a})2\pi$. It will superimpose a displacement at the origin propor tional to

$$\rho(x) \cos\left[2\pi\left(\frac{hx_B}{\mathbf{a}}\right)\right] dx$$

FIG. 15.11. Some possible phase rela- tionships between waves scattered from different points in a unit cell.

The phase relations are illustrated in Fig. 15.11, where the solid line represents the wave scattered at the origin, and the dashed line that scattered at x_B. The wave scat tered from x_B has its maximum shifted from the maximum of the wave scattered at the origin. However, the structure shown in Fig. 15.10 is symmetric about the origin. There fore, at the origin there is a contribution from $-x_B$ exactly equal to that from $+x_B$ (the dash-dot line in Fig. 15.11). The com bination of these two contributions should lead to a wave with a maximum at the same place as that scattered from the origin, that is, a wave in phase with that scattered at the origin. There is another possibility. The con

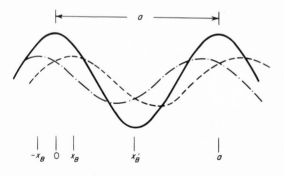

dition that the contribution at the origin from x_B and $-x_B$ be equal could also be met if a point like that labeled x'_B in Fig. 15.11 were at the origin. The two dis placed waves would then combine to give a minimum at the origin, that is, a wave π radians out of phase with that scattered at the origin. We shall return to this problem of the phase shift shortly, and proceed now to compute the scattering over the whole cell, using the assumption of 0 phase shift. This can be done by integrating $\rho(x) \cos 2\pi(hx/\mathbf{a}) \, dx$ over half the cell, and doubling this. The resultant quantity is called the *structure factor*, $F(h)$, where h signifies an appropriate Miller index.

$$F(h) = 2 \int_0^{\mathbf{a}/2} \rho(x) \cos 2\pi \left(\frac{hx}{\mathbf{a}}\right) dx \qquad (15.8)$$

Since $\cos(180° - \theta) = -\cos\theta$, the structure factor is $-F(h)$ when the phase shift is π rather than zero.

We can now begin to see the origin of the central problem in structure determination by the use of X rays. The structure factor $F(h)$ contains the desired information about the structure. However, the experimental information available consists of X ray intensities which for real crystals are proportional to $[F(h)]^2$ and $F(h)$ and $-F(h)$ are therefore experimentally indistinguishable. In other words waves scattered with a phase shift of 0 and a phase shift of π are experimentally equivalent. Thus in the simple example under discussion a given scattered wave could have come from either of two positions in the unit cell. If n scattered waves are observed, then, there are $2n$ possible combinations, only one of which corresponds to the structure of the unit cell. Since this situation arises because the phase shifts of the scattered waves are unknown, this is an example of what is called the *phase problem*. The central strategy of an X ray analysis involves the solution of this phase problem, that is, the deduction of the unobserved phases. Only for simple structures can this be done by a trial and error method, but procedures have been developed which enable the crystallographer to treat many complex situations. These are discussed in more advanced texts.

A more convenient representation of $F(h)$ will now be introduced. $F(h)$ can be expressed in terms of *atomic scattering factors* f. These are functions of the number of electrons in a given species and fall off with increasing Bragg scattering angle. Since they are affected by atomic vibrations, they are temperature-dependent. The integral in equation (15.8) for the 0 phase shift structure factor can be replaced by the equivalent summation in terms of atomic scattering factors. For a unit cell containing n atoms,

$$F(h) = \sum_{i=1}^{i=n} f_i \cos 2\pi \left(\frac{hx_i}{\mathbf{a}}\right)$$

In three dimensions the structure factor corresponding to 0 phase for a centrosymmetric structure is

$$F(hkl) = \sum_{i=1}^{i=n} f_i \cos 2\pi \left(\frac{hx_i}{\mathbf{a}} + \frac{ky_i}{\mathbf{b}} + \frac{lz_i}{\mathbf{c}}\right) \qquad (15.9)$$

We shall now state the relations for more complex systems without proof. In general for both centrosymmetric and noncentrosymmetric structures, two quantities, an amplitude and a phase, must be specified for each coordinate. Since complex numbers contain two components, they provide a convenient means of representation. For example, we can use numbers of the form

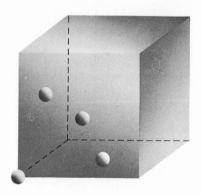

FIG. 15.12. Four atoms which can define a face-centered cubic unit cell.

$\cos 2\pi(hx_i/\mathbf{a}) + i \sin 2\pi(hx_i/\mathbf{a})$, to express both the amplitude and the phase. Since $e^{i\theta} = \cos \theta + i \sin \theta$ (see Appendix 1), a general form of the structure factor is

$$F(hkl) = \sum_{i=1}^{i=n} f_i \exp \left[2\pi i \left(\frac{hx_i}{\mathbf{a}} + \frac{ky_i}{\mathbf{b}} + \frac{lz_i}{\mathbf{c}} \right) \right]$$

Next we shall examine a simple illustration of the computation of a structure factor, that for a face-centered cubic unit cell. Assume that all atoms of the unit cell are similar. The face-centered cubic unit cell contains four atoms, which we shall select as shown in Fig. 15.12. We shall define the lower left corner of the cube as the origin. The coordinates of the four atoms are then $0, 0, 0$; $0, \mathbf{a}/2, \mathbf{a}/2$; $\mathbf{a}/2, 0, \mathbf{a}/2$; $\mathbf{a}/2, \mathbf{a}/2, 0$; where $\mathbf{a}$ is the length of the unit cell, and from equation (15.9)

$$F(hkl) = f\left[\cos 0 + \cos 2\pi \left(\frac{k}{2} + \frac{l}{2} \right) + \cos 2\pi \left(\frac{h}{2} + \frac{l}{2} \right) \right.$$
$$\left. + \cos 2\pi \left(\frac{h}{2} + \frac{k}{2} \right) \right] \qquad (15.10)$$

This equation is consistent with the earlier statement regarding absences in face-centered systems (see problem 10).

A simple approach to a development of a structure will now be presented. Again, we shall consider our simple one-dimensional example. Any function periodic in one dimension can be reproduced by combining a series of harmonic cosine waves, a *Fourier series*. (Consult a suitable mathematics text.) The electron density along the x direction of our simple example then can be written in series form as follows:

$$\rho(x) = 2 \sum_{n=0}^{n=+\infty} \pm C(n) \cos \left(2\pi \frac{nx}{\mathbf{a}} \right) \qquad (15.11)$$

The factor of two appears because terms in $+n$ and $-n$ are combined. Substituting equation (15.11) into equation (15.8) gives

$$F(h) = 2 \int_0^{a/2} \left[2 \sum_{n=0}^{n=\infty} C(n) \cos 2\pi \frac{nx}{a} \right] \cos \left(2\pi \frac{hx}{a} \right) dx$$

The right-hand side of this equation equals 0 for all terms except those for which $n = h$. For these terms it equals $aC(n)$. Therefore, $C(n) = F(h)/a$.[1] This elegant result enables us to replace the coefficients, $C(n)$, in the Fourier series with the corresponding structure factor terms, $F(h)/a$. The equation for electron density in one dimension then becomes

$$\rho(x) = 2 \left(\frac{1}{a} \right) \sum_{h=0}^{h=\infty} F(h) \cos \left(2\pi \frac{hx}{a} \right) \tag{15.12}$$

where any $F(h)$ can be either $+$ or $-$ depending on its phase.

The corresponding general relation which applies to both centrosymmetric and noncentrosymmetric structures in three dimensions is

$$\rho(x, y, z) = \left(\frac{1}{V} \right) \sum_h \sum_k \sum_l F(hkl) \cos 2\pi \left[\frac{hx}{a} + \frac{ky}{b} + \frac{lz}{c} - \alpha(hkl) \right] \tag{15.13}$$

where V is the volume of the unit cell, and $\alpha(hkl)$ is a phase angle.

One general strategy of a structure determination by X ray analysis can now be better appreciated. In the one-dimensional case the absolute magnitudes of structure factors are deduced from the intensity data. Signs (phases) can be either guessed or assumed, clues provided by the data being used. The structure factors thus derived are used to calculate a rough electron density map, which will give some idea of the arrangement of the atoms in the structure. This map is then used as a guide to a more nearly correct assignment of phases. New structure factors are calculated, leading to a new map, giving new positions of the atom, and, therefore, new calculated phases, etc.

For a three-dimensional noncentrosymmetric case considerable ingenuity and much labor is required to establish a structure, since many phase relationships [values of $\alpha(hkl)$] are possible. The systematic procedures devised as aids in establishing phase relationships are discussed in more advanced treatments. An electron density map of glycylglycine is given in Fig. 15.13.

---

[1]This can be seen as follows. By a standard trigonometric identity

$$\cos X \cos Y = \tfrac{1}{2} \cos (X + Y) + \tfrac{1}{2} \cos (X - Y)$$

Therefore, we may rewrite the integral as follows:

$$F(h) = 2 \int_0^{a/2} \left[2 \sum_{n=0}^{n=\infty} \frac{C(n)}{2} \cos 2\pi \frac{x}{a} (n + h) + \frac{C(n)}{2} \cos 2\pi \frac{x}{a} (n - h) \right] dx$$

If $(n + h)$ and $(n - h)$ are any quantity other than 0, corresponding integrals are 0. (The student is invited to test this by carrying out the integration.) Only the terms for which $n = \pm h$ are left. The equation for $F(h)$ becomes

$$F(h) = 2 \left[\int_0^{a/2} \frac{C(n)}{2} dx + \int_0^{a/2} \frac{C(n)}{2} dx \right] \quad \text{and} \quad F(h) = aC(n).$$

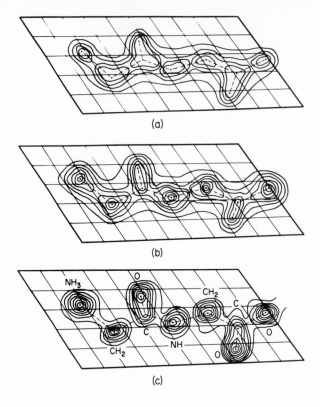

(a)

(b)

NH₃ O CH₂ C O C NH CH₂ O

(c)

FIG. 15.13. A Fourier map of electron density in glycylglycine projected on the base of the unit cell: (a) 40 terms; (b) 100 terms; (c) 160 terms [from W. J. Moore, *Physical Chemistry*, 3rd ed., Prentice-Hall, Inc., Englewood Cliffs, N. J., 1962].

15.8 Close Packing of Spheres

In our discussion of solids up to this point we have not considered the question of why a given array of atoms, molecules, or ions assumes a particular arrangement. In many instances the arrangement assumed is simply that which allows the most efficient use of space, consistent, of course, with stoichiometry in the case of compounds. For uniform spheres there are two simple methods of packing which minimize unoccupied volume, hexagonal close packing (h.c.p.), and cubic close packing (c.c.p.).

These two forms of close packing can be developed as follows. We begin with a layer of particles arranged in an equilateral triangle. (This may also be regarded as six particles arranged in a hexagon around a central sphere.) This first layer of spheres is labeled A in Fig. 15.14. The next layer of particles is formed by placing one particle above the center of every crevice labeled B in the first layer, forming a layer identical with the first, except that it is displaced. There are now two positions in which the spheres of the third layer may be placed. (1) They may be placed directly above particles in the A layer, so that every other layer repeats, AB, AB, etc., and the lattice has hexagonal symmetry (h.c.p.). (2) They may be placed over the positions indicated by C in Fig. 15.14. Then the third layer does not repeat the first layer, but, the fourth will, and an ABC, ABC, ABC packing sequence results. This lattice has cubic symmetry (c.c.p.). In both types of packing the voids amount to about 26 per cent.

The types of packing which we have described here can be observed in many

FIG. 15.14. Close packing of spheres.

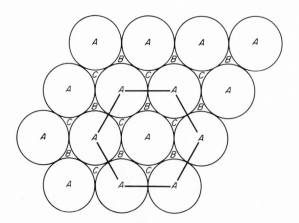

different types of chemical compounds. Many halides, oxides, and sulfides in which the electropositive element is small may be thought of as an array of tightly packed anions with the much smaller cations filling the voids in the close-packed structure. The atoms of many crystalline metals are also arranged in close-packed structures.

15.9 A Classification of Solids According to Bond Type

Until this point in our discussion we have classified solids according to the geometric arrangement of their basic units, atoms, ions, or molecules. This information is experimentally accessible through X ray studies. It is also possible to classify solids as to bond type. As we have seen, real chemical bonds do not always fall neatly into our ideal categories. Despite this, such a classification is useful. The four ideal crystal types which we shall assume are (1) the ionic crystal, (2) the covalent crystal, (3) the molecular crystal, and (4) metallic crystals.

15.10 Ionic Crystals

In the earlier discussions we have implied that one of the factors deciding the arrangement of atoms in an ionic crystal is the ratio of the sizes of the positive and negative ions. By the use of the X ray diffraction technique it is possible to establish the internuclear separation between pairs of ions. These can be thought of as representing the sums of the radii of the individual ions. For example, the sum $r_{K^+} + r_{Cl^-} = 3.14$ Å experimentally. Although K^+ and Cl^- have the same number of electrons, their radii will not be equal. The nuclear charge on K^+ is 19, whereas that on Cl^- is 17. Thus, K^+ should be smaller. When this is considered, and when the shielding effect of the inner electrons is corrected for, it is estimated that $r_{K^+} = 1.33$ Å, and $r_{Cl^-} = 1.81$ Å. By such methods the ionic radii given in Table 15.4 may be derived.

TABLE 15.4

IONIC RADII*

Li+	Be++	B+++	O=	F-
0.60	0.31	0.20	1.40	1.36
Na+	Mg++	Al+++	S=	Cl-
0.95	0.65	0.50	1.84	1.81
K+	Ca++	Sc+++	Se=	Br-
1.33	0.99	0.81	1.98	1.95
Rb+	Sr++	Y+++	Te=	I-
1.48	1.13	0.93	2.21	2.16
Cs+	Ba++	La+++		
1.69	1.35	1.15		

*From L. Pauling, *J. Am. Chem. Soc.* **49**, 765 (1927).

In most instances the internuclear distances obtained by addition of ionic radii agree fairly well with the observed values. An exception is found with lithium salts. For example, the calculated distance in LiBr is $0.59 + 1.95 = 2.54$ Å, whereas the distance observed in X ray diffraction is 2.75 Å. This discrepancy can be understood when it is realized that the cations are so much smaller than the anions that they can fit into the interstices of a face-centered cubic lattice formed by "touching" anions. In such a face-centered cubic lattice this can occur when the ratio of the radius of the cation to that of the anion is less than $(\sqrt{2} - 1)/1$.

EXERCISE 15.3

Show that, when uniform spheres of radius r are arranged in a face-centered cubic lattice (Fig. 15.4) with spheres touching along the diagonals of each face, that there is room, along the edge of the cube, for a sphere with radius $(\sqrt{2} - 1)r$.

At the other extreme, when the cation becomes comparable in size to the anion, as in CsCl, the halide ion lattice may become simple cubic, with a cation at the center of the cube, forming a body-centered cubic lattice. Although the simple cubic lattice of halide ions is not as compact as the face-centered cubic arrangement usually observed, the number of equidistant ions of opposite sign is eight instead of six. Apparently, the increased number of ions compensates for the increase in interionic distance.

In ionic crystals no simple unit consisting of two oppositely charged ions can be recognized. Instead, the whole crystal must be regarded as a single assembly of ions or one giant molecule. Each ion exists in a force field primarily due to its nearest neighbors, but also partially due to more distant ions, both positive and negative.

As a specific example, consider the sodium chloride crystal (Fig. 15.9). Contributions to the coulombic energy of a given Na^+ ion arise from the six neighboring Cl^- ions at an internuclear separation r, twelve nearest Na^+ ions at a distance $r\sqrt{2}$, the eight next nearest Cl^- ions at a distance $r\sqrt{3}$, the six next nearest Na^+ ions at a distance $2r$, the twenty-four next nearest Cl^- ions at a distance $r\sqrt{5}$, etc. When a Na^+ ion is transported from infinity to this lattice site, energy will be released. This energy is simply the sum of the various coulombic interaction energies, and is given by

$$V = \frac{6e^2}{r}(Z_{Na^+}Z_{Cl^-}) + \frac{12e^2}{r\sqrt{2}}(Z_{Na^+})^2 + \frac{8e^2}{r\sqrt{3}}(Z_{Na^+}Z_{Cl^-}) + \frac{6e^2}{2r}(Z_{Na^+})^2 \ldots$$

This can be transformed as follows:

$$V = \frac{-e^2}{r}\left(6 - \frac{12}{\sqrt{2}} + \frac{8}{\sqrt{3}} - \frac{6}{2} + \frac{24}{\sqrt{5}} - \frac{24}{\sqrt{6}} \ldots\right) \quad (15.14)$$

The term in parenthesis is an infinite series which converges at 1.748. It is called the *Madelung constant* for NaCl.

Next we must consider the repulsive forces arising from the proximity of the electron clouds of Na^+ and Cl^-. It was proposed by Born that the repulsive energy arising from this source is inversely proportional to r^n, where r is the internuclear distance. n, the Born exponent, can be determined by experiments on the compressibility of salts containing various ions. When both cation and anion are of the neon configuration it is about 7; for two ions of the argon configuration, about 9; for two krypton-like ions, 10; and for two xenon-like ions, 12. For salts such as NaCl an average value is used, in this case 8. The total potential energy of a Na$^+$ ion in a NaCl lattice is then

$$V = \frac{-Ae^2}{r} + \frac{6be^2}{r^8} \quad (15.15)$$

where A is the Madelung constant, b is a proportionality constant, and 6 is the number of nearest neighbor chloride ions associated with a single sodium ion. The first term represents the potential energy, V_A, arising from attractive forces, and the second term the potential energy, V_R, arising from repulsive forces. These relations are illustrated in Fig. 15.15.

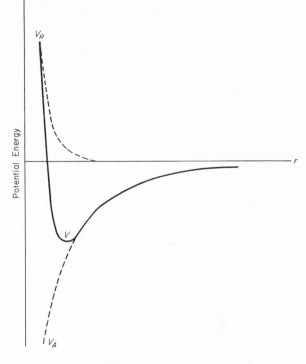

FIG. 15.15. A schematic diagram of the potential energy functions used to describe the ionic bond. r is the distance of separation of two ions. V_A and V_R are the energies arising from attractive and repulsive forces respectively. The resultant energy is V, and the minimum in the V curve corresponds to the separation of the ions at equilibrium.

EXERCISE 15.4

Show that r, the equilibrium interionic distance in NaCl, is given by the relation $r = (48b/A)^{1/7}$. (At the distance r, E is a minimum.) For NaCl r is 2.82 Å. Evaluate the constant b. *Ans. $b = 51.7$ Å^7.*

In order to compute the total energy for a crystal containing Avogadro's number of ion pairs we must now multiply equation (15.15) by N. Using the result of exercise 15.4, and changing sign gives the *crystal lattice energy E_c*, the energy required to separate the crystal into individual Na$^+$ and Cl$^-$ ions.

$$E_c = \frac{7NAe^2}{8r} \quad (15.16)$$

EXERCISE 15.5

Verify equation (15.16), starting with equation (15.15) and using the result of exercise 15.4. Compute the crystal lattice energy for NaCl.

Ans. $E_{NaCl} = 180$ kcal.

469

As Exercise 15.5 shows, the crystal lattice energy computed from equation (15.16) for a formula weight of crystalline NaCl is 180 kcal.

The crystal lattice energy is related to other thermochemical properties through the *Born-Haber cycle*, an application of the first law of thermodynamics. In the case of sodium chloride the cycle is

$$
\begin{array}{c}
\text{NaCl(cryst.)} \xrightarrow{E_c} \text{Na}^+(g) + \text{Cl}^-(g) \\[4pt]
\downarrow{\scriptstyle -Q} \qquad S \qquad\qquad \uparrow{\scriptstyle I} \qquad\qquad \big\uparrow{\scriptstyle -A} \\[2pt]
\text{Na(s)} \xrightarrow{\qquad} \text{Na(g)} \\[2pt]
+ \\[2pt]
\tfrac{1}{2}\text{Cl}_2(g) \xrightarrow{\ \ \frac{1}{2}D\ \ } \text{Cl(g)}
\end{array}
$$

where Q = heat of formation of NaCl (cryst.) = ΔH^0_f.

S = heat of sublimation of Na (s) = ΔH^0_V.

D = heat of dissociation of Cl$_2$ (g) = ΔH^0 (disscn.).

I = ionization potential of Na (g).

A = electron affinity of Cl (g).

By application of Hess' law

$$E_c = -Q + S + \tfrac{1}{2}D + I - A \qquad (15.17)$$

E_c can be computed for the alkali halides since all the quantities on the right-hand side of equation (15.17) can be measured experimentally. Data such as that in Chapter 3 yield $Q = -99$ kcal. mole^{-1} and $S = 26$ kcal. mole^{-1}. Values of I and A are given in Chapters 13 and 14. For sodium, $I = 117$ kcal. mole^{-1}, and for chlorine $A = 84$ kcal. mole^{-1}. A value of $D = 54$ kcal. mole^{-1} is obtained from the molecular spectrum of chlorine, as indicated in Chapter 14. Therefore, by this method

$$E_c = 99 + 26 + \tfrac{1}{2}(54) + 117 - 84 = 185 \text{ kcal. mole}^{-1}$$

in good agreement with the value computed earlier using equation (15.15). Note that the only exothermic step in the cycle is the attachment of an electron to chlorine.

The magnitude of the crystal lattice energy of sodium chloride is typical of ionic crystals and is larger than the bond dissociation energy of most diatomic molecules. That is to say, the lattice structure of an ionic crystal is held together by very strong forces. Consequently, ionic crystals are usually rather hard and have high melting points.

15.11 Covalent and Molecular Crystals

In some crystals the bonding is essentially of the covalent type. A simple example is one of the crystalline forms of carbon, diamond. We can describe the bonding in the diamond crystal in terms of hybrid sp^3 orbitals of carbon with the usual tetrahedral orientation. This leads to the lattice shown in Fig. 15.16 where the atoms marked A correspond to a face-centered cubic lattice, whereas those marked B lie in alternating quadrants of the cube. If this lattice is extended indefinitely, it is found that the B atoms also lie in a face-centered cubic array, interpenetrating that of the A atoms. As shown for the case of the two B atoms in the figure, each atom has disposed about it four others at the corners of a regular tetrahedron, the characteristic arrangement for carbon forming four single bonds. The carbon-carbon bond distance in the lattice is 1.54 Å, identical with that in ethane.

Graphite, which is the more stable form of carbon at ordinary temperatures, has a structure consisting of repeated sheets of carbon atoms. Within each sheet the structure is that of the carbon skeleton of a polynuclear aromatic compound, a connected series of benzene rings, and therefore the bonds in the plane may be described as hybrid sp^2 bonds. The carbon-carbon bond distance in the planes of graphite is 1.34 Å, which is identical with that in anthracene, ⬡⬡⬡ . Bonds between the sheets are attributed to the non-localized π orbitals and are much weaker than those within the sheets. Since the π orbital electrons are in effect delocalized over all the atoms of each single crystal, we have a system very similar to that in metals (see below). This provides an explanation of the high electrical conductivity of graphite. The crystal lattice of graphite is shown in Fig. 15.17.

Covalent bonds are strictly nonpolar only when formed between identical atoms, as in diamond. Therefore, in any covalent crystal which contains two or more kinds of atoms the bonding is, in some degree, ionic. The distinctive feature of the covalent crystal is the important role which directed valence plays in establishing the crystal lattice. For example, it is found that the crystal lattice of zinc blende, ZnS, is identical in form with that of diamond, although the dimensions are of course different. This lattice corresponds to that in Fig. 15.16 when $A =$ Zn and $B =$ S. The bonds in this case may also be described as due to overlap of hybrid sp^3 orbitals, for there are eight valence electrons for each two atoms. If the electron pairs were equally shared by the zinc and sulfur, the formal charges on the atoms would be Zn^{++} and $S^=$, and this gives each atom the possibility of having four unpaired electrons in sp^3 hybrid orbitals. Since sulfur is more electronegative than zinc, the bond is polar and may be said to have a contribution from the ionic form Zn^{++}, $S^=$.

One of the crystal forms of SiO_2, β-cristobalite, also has a lattice closely related to that of diamond, except that in this case oxygen atoms form a bridge between each two silicon atoms, the latter lying at the lattice points indicated in Fig. 15.16. Each silicon atom is bonded to four oxygen atoms, and each oxygen atom to two silicon atoms. In the valence bond model, the bonding orbitals are sp^3 for silicon

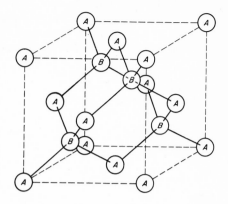

FIG. 15.16. Crystal lattice of diamond.

FIG. 15.17. Crystal lattice of graphite.

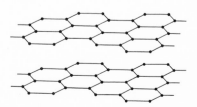

and p^2 for oxygen. However, the bond is quite polar, with a considerable contribution from the ionic form Si^{+4}, $O^=$ and the opening of the $Si-O-Si$ bond to 150 deg. is attributed to ionic repulsion.

Because of the strong three-dimensional forces in these covalent crystals, they are generally very hard and have very high melting points. In these respects they are similar to ionic crystals.

When a covalent substance, because of limitations on the bonding power of its atoms, is not capable of forming a three-dimensional lattice by electron pair bonds, the crystalline form is relatively soft and has a low melting point. These qualities characterize the molecular crystals in which the bonding between units is to be attributed to van der Waals or dipole forces. For example, the diatomic elements such as O_2, Cl_2, etc. and many organic compounds such as CH_4, C_6H_6, etc. form crystals in which the chief determinant of structure is the tendency to efficient packing of the individual molecules. On the other hand, several elements, such as sulfur, are capable of forming two electron-pair bonds which permit the development of chains or rings. Rhombic sulfur consists of S_8 rings bound by electron-pair bonds within the ring, while the attraction between rings in the crystal is due to van der Waals forces.

Crystalline water (ice) is a representative of a special type of molecular crystal. By comparison with the heavier hydrides of its family, H_2S, H_2Te, etc., it has an abnormally high melting point and heat of sublimation. The lattice energy is much higher than could be expected from van der Waals forces and dipole-dipole forces. This is to be attributed to the hydrogen bonds formed between the water molecules (see sections 14.8 and 15.14). The crystal structure is such that each oxygen atom has disposed about it four other oxygen atoms at the corners of a tetrahedron, with hydrogen atoms lying on the line joining each pair of oxygen atoms. Each hydrogen atom is attached to one oxygen atom by an electron pair bond and to another by hydrogen bonding.

FIG. 15.18. Synthesis of energy bands by combination of atomic orbitals.

15.12 The Metals

There are two characteristic properties of metals which any model must take into account. (1) A metal is a conductor of electricity. (2) Metals tend to crystallize in packing arrangements of high coordination number. For a body-centered cubic crystal there are fourteen near neighbors, eight at a distance r, and six at a distance $1.15r$. For a face-centered cubic, or a hexagonal close-packed crystal, the coordination number is twelve. The first of these properties suggests that there are large numbers of *con-*

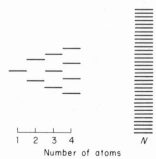

Energy →

1 2 3 4   N
Number of atoms

duction electrons which are not firmly bound to any particular atom, and are, therefore, relatively free to move throughout the crystal. The second suggests a description in terms of delocalized electrons, since the formation of twelve or more localized bonds is unlikely.

A molecular orbital model for the metallic bond can be constructed in much the same way as the molecular orbital description of benzene. As an example, let us consider lithium. We shall assume that the inner $1s$ electrons are so tightly bonded to the nuclei that they are effectively localized. The required delocalized orbitals must then be constructed from the outer orbitals. Two molecular orbitals describing the electron distribution in a system consisting of two lithium atoms designated as A and B, can be constructed from the $2s$ atomic orbitals. They are $\psi_A(2s) + \psi_B(2s)$ and $\psi_A(2s) - \psi_B(2s)$, and they differ in energy. If a third Li atom is to be added to the system, three molecular orbitals may be constructed, and associated with these there will be three energies, grouped about the original energy associated with ψ_A. As each atom is added, a new energy level is added as illustrated in Fig. 15.18. When the number of atoms is very large, there results a band of closely spaced energy levels (Fig. 15.18). The same sort of construction can go on with the $2p$ levels of lithium. If the $2s$ and $2p$ atomic systems are well separated in energy, or if the atoms are well separated in space, then the two bands derived from them will not overlap. Thus we will have two bands separated by an energy gap. This gap may be thought of as a forbidden energy zone. The available electrons will be allocated to the lowest energy levels. Thus if the s and p bands are indeed separated in Li all electrons would be in the band derived from s atomic orbitals.

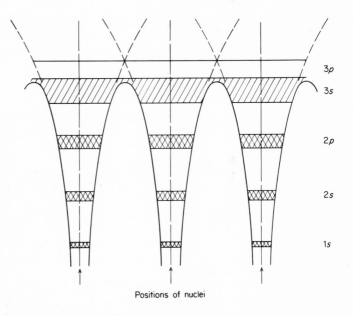

FIG. 15.19. Band model for a one-dimensional metal.

$3p$

$3s$

$2p$

$2s$

$1s$

Positions of nuclei

It is often true that the bands derived from two neighboring atomic states will overlap. Under these circumstances our description will be more complicated. However, the general features which we have pointed out will still be found. The energy levels will be banded, and the electrons will be assigned to the lowest set of energy levels.

Figure 15.19 shows the relationship of the crystal bands and the corresponding atomic orbitals for sodium. The solid lines correspond to the periodic potential field which constrains the electrons in a crystalline solid, and the dashed lines correspond to the field associated with an isolated atom. The $1s$, $2s$, and $2p$ bands are completely filled. The $3s$ and $3p$ bands overlap considerably. These uppermost energy levels are only partly filled and are effectively delocalized. It is these partially filled delocalized levels which account for the phenomenon of metallic conduction. When an external electric field is applied it will tend to make more electrons flow in one direction than in the other.

By contrast consider a nonconductor such as potassium chloride (Fig. 15.20). Since all low-lying atomic orbitals are completely filled, the correspond-

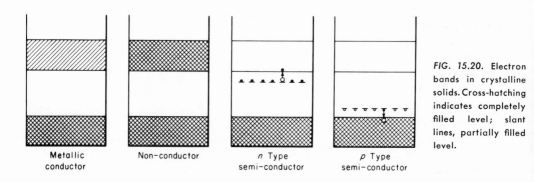

| Metallic conductor | Non-conductor | n Type semi-conductor | p Type semi-conductor |

FIG. 15.20. Electron bands in crystalline solids. Cross-hatching indicates completely filled level; slant lines, partially filled level.

ing crystal bands will be completely filled. There is now no mechanism for a net electron flow in the direction of an applied field. However, if a sufficient amount of energy is supplied to promote electrons into the next empty band, then conduction can take place. Thus, some substances can show *photoconductivity*. Light quanta of appropriate wave length are absorbed, and electrons are thereby promoted to energy levels in the hitherto unoccupied band. Here electron migration in the direction of the field can take place as with any partly occupied band. The contrast between a conductor and a nonconductor is illustrated in Fig. 15.20.

The existence of a conduction band of closely spaced electronic energy levels extending through the solid depends strongly on precise regularity of the arrangement of the atoms, as stated previously. Anything which decreases this regularity tends to increase the resistance to electron migration. Thus, impurities in solids, as in alloys, usually increase resistance. Increasing the temperature, which increases the vibratory motion of the nuclei, also increases the resistance of metallic conductors.

15.13 Semiconductors

There is a third class of solids called *semiconductors*. Characteristically the resistance of semiconductors decreases as temperature increases, and over a range of temperatures they can show a resistance between those of metals and insulators, hence the name. Semiconductors are of two types, *intrinsic semiconductors* and *impurity semiconductors*.

The model for intrinsic semiconductors is similar to that for nonconductors. However, the separation between the filled valence band and the conduction band is quite small, 0.72 e.v. in germanium, for example, and electrons can be thermally excited into the conduction band. The vacancies which are left behind in the upper levels of the valence band are called positive holes. Under an applied electric field both the electrons and the positive holes can migrate, the movement of the positive holes in one direction being equivalent to the movement of electrons in the opposite direction. Conduction band electrons can, of course, return to the valence band. This process represents recombination of an electron and a hole. Thus an equilibrium can exist in which the rate of hole formation by promotion of electrons to the conduction band is equal to the rate of recombination of electrons and holes.

An impurity semconductor can be produced by the systematic introduction of impurities into a material. Impurity semiconductors are of two types, designated as *n* and *p*. An example of an *n*-type semiconductor is germanium into which pentavalent impurity atoms such as As or P have been introduced. The extra electron is very weakly bound to the impurity atom. It can be thought of as occupying a Bohr orbit of high radius around the impurity atom and is, therefore, of relatively high energy and close to a conduction band (Fig. 15.20). Consequently, a small thermal energy input can raise it into the conduction band. Substances which behave in this way are called *n*-type semiconductors, because conduction is due to *n*egative electrons.

In a *p*-type semiconductor conduction is primarily due to *p*ositive holes. An example of such a substance is germanium doped with trivalent atoms such as aluminum. Aluminum has one less outer electron than does germanium. As a result, a set of vacant levels is formed slightly above the valence band. Electrons can be thermally excited into these bound levels from the valence band, leaving behind a positive hole. The migration of these positive holes under the influence of an applied electrical field provides a mechanism for the conduction of an electrical current.

15.14 Structure of Liquids and Glasses

It is often said that the liquid state may be regarded as intermediate between vapor and crystalline solid. As a matter of fact, the liquid state has much more in common with the solid state than with a gas under ordinary circumstances. The densities of liquid and crystalline phases of the same substance are usually only slightly different, and therefore the separation of particles in the two phases is approximately the same. Comparison of the heat of fusion with the heat of vaporization of a given substance invariably shows that the former is much smaller, again indicating the close relation of the liquid and crystalline states.

There is a group of substances which, upon cooling of the liquid phase,

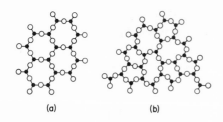

(a)   (b)

FIG. 15.21. Crystal (a) vs. glass (b) [from W. J. Moore, *Physical Chemistry*, 3rd ed., Prentice-Hall, Inc., Englewood Cliffs, N. J., 1962].

become gradually more viscous and rigid without any definite evidence of transformation to another form. These substances, called *glasses*, are best regarded as extremely viscous liquids. As solids, they are distinguished by lack of any crystal form and they soften over a range of temperatures rather than melting at a definite temperature as do crystalline solids.

The distinction between a glass and a crystalline solid may be illustrated by a two-dimensional pattern such as that shown in Fig. 15.21. Note that each atom represented by the filled circles is in both cases bonded to three atoms represented by open circles. In the crystal lattice an ordered arrangement continues indefinitely, and parallel planes of like atoms are evident, which will give rise to a sharp X ray diffraction pattern. In the glass structure, while bond angles and distances are occasionally somewhat distorted, the molecular groupings are preserved. However, the long-range order is destroyed, and parallel planes of like atoms are not observed.

X ray examination of glasses and many liquids reveals a certain degree of order in the arrangement of the elementary particles. Figure 15.7 shows the type of X ray diffraction pattern obtained from a powder consisting of randomly oriented crystallites. With smaller and smaller crystallites, such a pattern would become more and more diffuse, as the regions of ordered arrangement become smaller. The X ray diffraction pattern of liquids and glasses is of the same form, but has rather broad and indefinite maxima and minima, as shown in Fig. 15.22, indicating that the regions of ordered arrangement are very small, but nevertheless do exist.

X ray diffraction data on liquids are usually interpreted by computing, from the diffraction pattern, the *radial distribution function*. This is the probability of finding a second scattering center between a distance r and $r + dr$ irrespective of angle. If all internuclear distances were equally probable, there would be no diffraction maxima, and the radial distribution function would have the form of the dashed line in Fig. 15.22(b). The observed distribution function, shown by the heavy curve, indicates a high probability for the distance between nearest neighbors obtained from X ray diffraction of ice. (X ray scattering by H_2O is due almost exclusively to the O atoms.) The number of nearest neighbors in ice is four, since each oxygen atom forms tetrahedral hydrogen bonds with another oxygen atom. From the areas under the peaks in the radial distribution curve, that is, from the intensity of scattering, it can be estimated that the number of nearest neighbors in liquid water is between four and five.

From the kind of information indicated above, it may be concluded that the structure of water bears considerable resemblance to that of ice. Apparently, melting results in a partial breakdown of the rather open tetrahedral structure. The average internuclear distance increases, but at the same time the average number of nearest neighbors increases. The net effect is the well-known increase

FIG. 15.22. X ray diffraction by liquid water [from J. Morgan and B. E. Warren, *J. Chem. Phys.,* **6**, 666 (1938)].

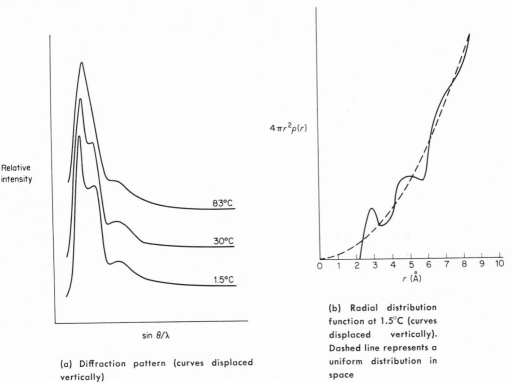

(a) Diffraction pattern (curves displaced vertically)

(b) Radial distribution function at 1.5°C (curves displaced vertically). Dashed line represents a uniform distribution in space

in density upon melting. The average distance to nearest neighbors continues to increase as the temperature of the liquid is increased above 0°, but so also does the average number of nearest neighbors, indicating further breakdown of the tetrahedral structure. This results in a maximum density at 4°. At higher temperatures the increase in thermal agitation and consequent increase in average separation predominates, and the density decreases.

15.15 Interatomic and Intermolecular Forces

At this point it is appropriate to recapitulate by enumerating the various types of forces which bind atoms into molecules and molecules into liquids and solids. In the category of interatomic forces, the most important are the electrostatic forces leading to the chemical bond. As we have seen chemical bonds can be described in terms of two extreme models, the *ionic bond* and the *covalent bond*. The ionic bond approximation is valid when there is a great difference in the attraction of the bound atoms for electrons. In effect, under these circumstances electrons are largely transferred from the less electronegative to the more electronegative element, and the bond can be adequately described in terms of the interaction of two ions. When two like atoms are bound, then the electrons are effectively shared, and a detailed consideration of the electron distribution using wave mechanics is necessary to evaluate the strength of bonding. Most covalent bonds are of an intermediate type in which electrons are unequally shared. There is a net charge separation, so these are called *polar bonds*.

The hydrogen bond constitutes a special case of interatomic force which arises when a hydrogen atom is covalently bound to an atom of high electronegativity such as oxygen or fluorine. In this case the high degree of ionic character of the bond leaves a well-exposed proton whose positive charge may exert a strong attractive force on other nearby electronegative atoms, as in liquid water.

In both ionic and macromolecular crystals we find large three-dimensional structures bound together by coulombic and electron pair bonds, respectively. On the other hand, in molecular crystals and in the corresponding liquids we must look to other sources for the forces which bind the molecules together.

Molecules which have a permanent dipole moment attract each other by electrostatic interaction. In contrast to the energy of interaction between point charges, which varies inversely with the distance between them, the potential energy due to *dipole-dipole force* is given by

$$V = -\frac{2\mu^4}{3r^6}\frac{1}{kT} \tag{15.18}$$

where μ is the dipole moment, r is the distance of separation of the dipoles, and k is Boltzmann's constant. It is evidently a force effective at somewhat shorter distances than simple coulombic attraction. It is this type of force which is largely responsible for the crystal lattice energy of substances like HI, SO_2, etc., and which must be overcome in the vaporization process.

Nonpolar molecules also exert an attractive force on each other, although clearly a weak one. The boiling points of nonpolar substances such as N_2 and O_2 are much lower than those of polar substances of comparable molecular weight. The nature of this force was first explained by F. London. It arises from the fact that a nonpolar atom or molecule is, in effect, an oscillating system of electrical charges and has at any instant a small electric moment which varies with time in such a fashion that the average moment is zero. This moment induces an opposite moment in nearby molecules and results in a small attractive force called a *dispersion force*. The potential energy of attraction due to this force is given by

$$V = -\frac{3h\nu_0}{4}\frac{\alpha^2}{r^6} \tag{15.19}$$

where ν_0 is the frequency of oscillation of the charge cloud and α is the polarizability of the molecule or atom. This force is one of the effects responsible for "van der Waals attraction" in gases. For polar substances the dipole-dipole force is usually of larger magnitude.

At very short distances a repulsive force, due to overlap of electron clouds, sets in between any two atoms, ions or molecules. This force is responsible for the steeply rising portion of the potential energy curve at small distances of separation, as shown in Figs. 14.1 and 14.4. The potential energy of interaction is inversely proportional to some high power of the distance,

$$V = kr^{-n} \tag{15.20}$$

where $n = 9\text{–}12$. Therefore, the net potential energy of interaction of two nonpolar atoms or molecules is given by a function of the form

$$V = -Ar^{-6} + Br^{-n} \tag{15.21}$$

The first term describes an attraction and the second, a repulsion. Since the exponent of the second term is greater than that of the first, there will be a distance of minimum potential energy corresponding to the intermolecular distance in the condensed state.

In order to complete our catalogue, forces between unlike particles must be considered. The first of these is an *ion-dipole* force. The potential energy arising from this type of interaction depends on the relative orientations of the dipole and the ion of charge e_I. For the most stable arrangement it is given by

$$V = -\frac{e_I \mu}{r^2} \tag{15.22}$$

but this arrangement is not ordinarily achieved since it is opposed by thermal motions. Ion-dipole forces are often important in solution, but for this application equation (15.22) must be modified, for example by considering the effective dielectric constant of the medium. The appreciable solubility of many ionic solids in water is due in large part to the fact that the energy resulting from the interaction between the dissolved ions and the dipolar water molecules is comparable to that of the crystal lattice. (A complete analysis must also take the entropy of solvation into account.)

On the other hand the energy of interaction of an ion with a nonpolar molecule, which may be characterized as due to *ion-induced dipole force*, is given by

$$V = -\frac{1}{2} \frac{\alpha e_I^2}{r^4} \tag{15.23}$$

and is a weaker and shorter range attraction. This energy of interaction cannot ordinarily supply the energy requirement for dissolving an ionic substance and consequently such substances are not readily soluble in nonpolar solvents.

An interaction also occurs between dipolar and nonpolar molecules due to the induction of a dipole moment in the latter. This *dipole-induced dipole* force leads to a potential energy of interaction given by

$$V = -\frac{2\alpha\mu^2}{r^6} \tag{15.24}$$

Although this interaction has the same dependence on distance as does the dipole-dipole interaction, it is usually of much smaller magnitude, since α is less than $\mu^2/3kT$ for molecules with an appreciable moment. (See section 14.10.)

It is in part for this reason that polar and nonpolar liquids are often immiscible, for the formation of a mixture requires substitution of the weaker dipole-induced dipole interaction for the stronger dipole-dipole interaction.

SUMMARY, CHAPTER 15

1. Crystal properties
   Crystal systems; cubic, tetragonal, orthorhombic, hexagonal (rhombohedral), monoclinic, triclinic.
   Miller indices (hkl): 100, 010, 001 for the faces of a regular cube.
   Cubic lattices: simple, body-centered, and face-centered.
   Close-packed lattices: hexagonal and face-centered cubic.

2. X ray diffraction
   Bragg reflection

   $$n\lambda = 2d \sin \theta$$

   Cubic crystal

   $$\sin^2 \theta_{hkl} = \frac{\lambda^2}{4a^2}(h^2 + k^2 + l^2)$$

   Structure factor for centrosymmetric crystal (0 phase)

   $$F(hkl) = \sum_i f_i \cos 2\pi \left(\frac{hx_i}{a} + \frac{ky_i}{b} + \frac{lz_i}{c}\right)$$

   Electron density for centrosymmetric crystal [$\alpha\ (hkl) = 0$]

   $$\rho(x, y, z) = \frac{1}{V}\left[\sum_h \sum_k \sum_l F(hkl) \cos 2\pi \left(\frac{hx}{a} + \frac{ky}{b} + \frac{lz}{c}\right)\right]$$

3. Ionic crystals: coulombic forces
   Ionic radii from crystal lattice data.
   Crystal lattice energy, E_c

   $$MX \text{ (cryst.)} = M^+ \text{ (g)} + X^- \text{ (g)}$$

   Born-Haber cycle

   $$E_c = -Q + S + \tfrac{1}{2}D + I - A$$

4. Covalent crystals: electron pair bonds in 3 dimensions
   Diamond: interpenetrating face-centered cubes.
   Graphite: sheets of hexagons.

5. Molecular crystals: van der Waals forces or hydrogen bonds
   Substances such as O_2, CH_4, C_6H_6, S_8.
   High m.p. of water due to hydrogen bonds.

6. Metals: lattice of positive ions, mobile electrons
   Conduction due to partly filled electronic energy bands.
   Nonconductors have only completely filled or empty bands.
   Semiconductors with impurity bands.

7. Liquids: short-range order shown by X ray diffraction

8. Types of interatomic forces
    Coulombic.
    Electron pair sharing.
    Hydrogen bonding.

9. Types of intermolecular forces
    Ion-dipole, $V \propto r^{-2}$.
    Ion-induced dipole, $V \propto r^{-4}$.
    Dipole-dipole, $V \propto r^{-6}$.
    Dipole-induced dipole, $V \propto r^{-6}$.
    Dispersion force, $V \propto r^{-6}$.
    Overlap repulsion, $V \propto r^{-n}$; $9 \leq n \leq 12$.

PROBLEMS

1. A plane intercepts the x, y, and z axes at **3a**, **6b**, and **2c**. What are its Miller indices?   *Ans.* (213).

2. Calculate the longest X ray wave length that may be used to determine a lattice spacing of 1 Å by the Bragg "reflection" method.   *Ans.* 2 Å.

3. Find the wave length of the X radiation which shows a second-order Bragg reflection angle of 14°10′ from the 100 plane of potassium chloride. The density of KCl is 1.984 gm. cm.$^{-3}$, and there are four atoms in the unit cell.

4. Nickel crystallizes in a face-centered cubic lattice of cell parameter 3.52 Å.
    (a) Calculate the separation of the 110 planes and that of the 111 planes.
    (b) Calculate the distance from a nickel atom to its nearest neighbor in the 100, 110, and 111 planes.   *Ans.* (b) 2.47 Å for each.

5. The ΔH of formation of crystalline lithium bromide from the elements is -87.6 kcal. mole^{-1}, and the ΔH of sublimation of lithium metal is 39.0 kcal. mole^{-1}. The ΔH for dissociation of Br$_2$ is 46.2 kcal. mole^{-1}. Use values of the ionization potential from Fig. 13.11 and the electron affinity from Table 14.1 to find the crystal lattice energy of LiBr.

6. The ΔH_f of KCl is -104.4 kcal. per gram formula weight. The heat of sublimation of potassium is 19.8 kcal/g. atom. Use this data, the ionization potential of potassium from Chapter 13, the KCl internuclear distance (3.14 Å), ΔH^0 (dissen.) for Cl$_2$ (p. 470), and compute a value for the electron affinity of the chlorine atom.

7. What are the mutual angles formed by the following pairs of intersecting planes in the cubic system? (a) 100 and 010; (b) 100 and 110; (c) 110 and 101; (d) 100 and 210; (e) 110 and 111.

8. KBr has a lattice which is equivalent to face-centered cubic with a cube edge of 6.54 Å. The unit cell contains four ions of each kind. Calculate the density of the crystal.

9. (a) The edge of the cubic unit cell of lead is 4.92Å. The density of lead is 11.55 gm./cc. What type of cubic lattice does lead exhibit?
    (b) Calculate the smallest angle with respect to the incident beam at which

constructive interference of X rays of wave length 0.708 Å would occur for 110 planes of this crystal.

10. A face-centered unit cell consists entirely of identical atoms of atomic scattering factor f. Calculate the following structure factors: $F(100)$, $F(110)$ $F(111)$, $F(200)$, $F(210)$, $F(211)$, and $F(220)$, all in terms of f. What is the significance of a zero structure factor?

11. Repeat problem 10 for a body-centered unit cell.

12. From the ionic radii given in Table 15.4, find the density of RbBr in the case (a) of a simple cubic lattice and (b) a body-centered cubic lattice, assuming that the ions "touch" along the diagonal of the cube.

13. Cubic close packing of spheres results in the formation of a face-centered cubic unit cell.
(a) Calculate the volume of the unit cell in terms of the radius of a single sphere. *Ans.* (a) $16\sqrt{2}\,r^3$.
(b) How many complete spheres are there in each unit cell? *Ans.* 4
(c) Calculate the percentage of voids in the lattice. *Ans.* 26%

14. Predict the angles of first-order Bragg reflection of 0.586 Å X radiation from the 100, 110, and 111 planes of CsCl. This substance has a density of 3.97 g. cc.$^{-1}$, and a body-centered cubic lattice. Note that the intensity of scattering from the Cs ions will be much greater than from the Cl ions. To what intensity variations will this lead?

15. Calcium oxide crystalizes in a cubic latice. The density of calcium oxide is 3.37 gm./cc. By using Mo X rays ($\lambda = 0.712$ Å) lines are observed at the following angles: 7°23′, 8°30′, 12°6′, 14°12′, 14°51′, 17°30′ and 18°20′.
(a) What type of lattice is this?
(b) How many CaO units are there in one unit cell?
(c) What are the values of d_{100}, d_{110}, and d_{111}?

16. Copper metal shows a cubic crystal habit. X ray diffraction with radiation of wave length 0.586 Å shows maxima at the following angles: 8°5′, 9°19′, 13°15′, 15°35′, 16°18′, 18°55′, and 20°41′.
(a) What type of lattice is this?
(b) Find the dimensions of the unit cell.
(c) Find the density of copper metal.
Ans. (a) Face-centered cubic, (b) 3.62 Å, (c) 8.90 gm./cc.

17. The Copper K_α X ray line ($\lambda = 1.541$ Å) is used to investigate the structure of an iron crystal. Lines are observed at the following scattering angles: 22°23′, 32°35′, 41°16′, 49°37′, and 58°23′. No other lines are observed.
(a) What type of cubic lattice is this?
(b) What is the unit cell dimension?
(c) The density of this phase of iron is 7.86 gm./cc. Estimate Avogadro's number.
(d) Is the copper K_α line the best choice for this analysis?
Ans. (a) Body-centered cubic, (b) 2.86 Å.

18. Referring to Fig. 15.16, find the valence bond angle of carbon in diamond.

19. An X ray powder photograph is taken with the Co K_α X ray ($\lambda = 1.790$ Å).

The first seven lines are found at the following values of $\sin^2 \theta$: 0.0343, 0.0917, 0.1258, 0.1370, 0.1839, 0.2752, 0.3097.

(a) Show that the data correspond to a cubic crystal.

(b) Compute the dimension of the unit cell.

(c) Compute the values of $(h^2 + k^2 + l^2)$ for each observed $\sin^2 \theta$.

(d) Compute the allowed values of $(h^2 + k^2 + l^2)$ for a face-centered cubic lattice for all possible combinations of the integers 0, 1, 2, 3, 4, and compare to (c). What lines are missing?

(e) Could the crystal be face-centered cubic?

(f) Explain the missing lines.

$\qquad$ *Ans.* (b) 8.38 Å; (c) 3, 8, 11, 12, 16, 24, 27; (d) 4, 19, 20; (e) yes.

---

20. The coordination number of a cation in a salt can be related to the relative sizes of cation and anion. Thus, the sodium ion in NaCl shows a coordination number of six, whereas the larger Cs ion in CsCl shows a coordination number of eight.

(a) Draw a cube with eight anions at the corners, and a cation in the center. Assume that the anions just touch and show that for anion-anion contact the maximum value of the ratio of the radius of the cation to that of the anion is 0.732.

(b) Show that for an NaCl type structure anion-anion contact occurs at a radius ratio of 0.414.

21. Verify the following. The Madelung constant for NaCl is the sum of a series of terms of the form

$$\pm \frac{n}{\sqrt{a^2 + b^2 + c^2}}$$

where n, a, b, and c are all integers. When the sum $(a + b + c)$ is even, the term is positive, and when $(a + b + c)$ is odd, it is minus.

22. Neutrons may be used in diffraction experiments since they possess wave properties. A beam of neutrons is allowed to impinge on a diamond crystal. The density of diamond is 3.56 gm./cc., and the unit cell is shown in Fig. 15.16. Reflections are obtained at various angles, the smallest being 10 deg.

(a) Show that the reflection at 10 deg. originates from the 111 rather than from the 100 (or 200) or the 110 (or 220) planes.

(b) What is the wave length of the neutrons?   *Ans.* 0.567 Å.

(c) What is the energy of the neutrons?   *Ans.* 4.1×10^{-13} ergs. per neutron.

23. The common mineral rutile (TiO_2) has a tetragonal unit cell with $\mathbf{a} = 4.49$ Å and $\mathbf{c} = 2.89$ Å. Titanium atoms occupy positions at $(0, 0, 0)$, and $(\frac{1}{2}, \frac{1}{2}, \frac{1}{2})$. Oxygen atoms are at $(0.31, 0.31, 0)$; $(0.81, 0.19, 0.50)$; $(0.69, 0.69, 0)$; and $(0.19, 0.81, 0.50)$. [R. W. G. Wyckoff, *Crystal Structure*, Interscience Publishers, Inc., New York, (1948–   ) Vol. **I**, Chapt. IV.]

(a) Draw a diagram of the unit cell.

(b) Calculate the density of rutile.

(c) Find the average separation of Ti and the six nearest O atoms.

24. For a tetragonal system two axes are equivalent, and

$$\sin^2 \theta_{hkl} = \left(\frac{\lambda^2}{4a^2}\right)(h^2 + k^2) + \frac{\lambda^2 l^2}{4c^2}$$

This relation can be written in the form

$$\sin^2 \theta_{hkl} - \left(\frac{\lambda^2}{4a^2}\right)(h^2 + k^2) = \frac{\lambda^2 l^2}{4c^2}$$

The first nine lines on an X ray powder photograph of $CuAl_2$ have the following values of $\sin^2 \theta_{hkl}$: 0.0440, 0.0882, 0.1449, 0.1767, 0.1811, 0.2204, 0.2245, 0.3117, 0.3554. [See N. F. M. Henry, H. Lipson, and W. A. Wooster, *The Interpretation of X-ray Diffraction Photographs*, Macmillan and Co., Ltd., London (1960).]

(a) Assume that the first line is the 110 line, and compute $\lambda^2/4a^2$.

(b) Compute all possible values of $\sin^2 \theta_{hkl} - (\lambda^2/4a^2)(h^2 + k^2)$ for all values of $(h^2 + k^2)$ less than 16.

(c) What is the value of $\lambda^2 l^2/4c^2$? [This can be recognized as follows. For some lines, one of the allowable values of $\sin^2 \theta_{hkl} - (\lambda^2/4a^2)(h^2 + k^2)$ will be 0. For other lines it will not. For this last class of lines there will be a value of $\sin^2 \theta_{hkl} - (\lambda^2/4a^2)(h^2 + k^2)$ which is C, $(2)^2C$, $(3)^2C$, or $(4)^2C$, where C is $\lambda^2 l^2/4c^2$.

(d) Assign indices to the observed lines.

Ans. (c) 0.0340; (d) 110, 200, 121, 220, 112, 310, 202, 222, 312.

16

PHOTOCHEMISTRY
AND RADIATION
CHEMISTRY

16.1 Photochemistry

Photochemistry is the study of reactions which occur in a system as the result of illumination. In practice such studies have been mainly confined to the visible and ultraviolet regions of the electromagnetic radiation spectrum. Absorption in the infrared imparts too little energy to a molecule to induce chemical change. Absorption in the X ray region leads characteristically to ionization and is conventionally treated as radiation chemistry. In the spectral region most extensively studied, say from 1800 to 6000 Å, the energies imparted to molecules range from 47 to 165 kcal. per mole and result in molecular excitation and dissociation. The absorbed radiant energy provides activation energy for processes which would occur very much more slowly, or not at all, in the dark at the same temperature. Photochemistry is, therefore, first concerned with optical spectroscopy (see Chapter 14) and next with the chemical kinetics of systems containing excited as well as ground state atoms, molecules, and free radicals.

J. von Grotthus proposed in 1818 that *only the light absorbed by a system is effective in producing chemical change.* Later J. W. Draper correlated the rate of photochemical change with the rate of absorption of light. Simple observation shows, however, that absorption of light alone does not necessarily lead to chemical change and the energy simply may be degraded to heat. Furthermore, in some systems, such as mixtures of hydrogen and chlorine, absorption of a small amount of light produces an indefinitely large amount of chemical change (an explosion in the case cited).

Planck's quantum concept (Chapter 13), first enunciated in 1900, did not

485

find immediate application in photochemistry, but somewhat later both J. Stark (1908) and Einstein (1912) proposed that a molecule is led to react by the absorp tion of *one* quantum of light. They later enunciated the *photochemical equivalenc(* *law* which states that *in the primary photochemical process each quantum absorbec* *activates one molecule.* From this principle arises the concept of the *quantum* *yield,* defined as *the number of molecules decomposed or formed per quantum* *absorbed.* For example, in the photolysis of gaseous hydrogen iodide with ligh of 2537 Å it is found that the absorption of 2.36×10^9 ergs of radiant energy causes decomposition of 10^{-3} mole of hydrogen iodide, forming $0.5 \times 10^-$ mole each of hydrogen and iodine. At 2537 Å the energy per quantum is

$$E = h\nu = hc/\lambda$$
$$= \frac{6.62 \times 10^{-27} \times 3.00 \times 10^{10}}{2.537 \times 10^{-5}}$$
$$= 7.84 \times 10^{-12} \text{ erg}$$

An *einstein* is 6.02×10^{23} quanta. In the experiment described the system has absorbed $2.36 \times 10^9/7.84 \times 10^{-12} \times 6.02 \times 10^{23} = 5.0 \times 10^{-4}$ einstein. The quantum yield is given by the number of moles reacting per einstein absorbed Therefore, the quantum yield for decomposition of hydrogen iodide is 2.0, and the quantum yield for formation of molecular iodine and hydrogen is 1.0. The relationship among the quantum yields for decomposition of reactants and formation of products in a photochemical reaction is a consequence of stoich-iometry. It is found that the quantum yield ranges from zero to one million for various reactions. The wide range of values is due to the secondary processes which follow photoexcitation.

The investigation of a photochemical reaction requires first of all some knowledge of the spectroscopy of the light absorbing substances. A continuous absorption spectrum for a gaseous substance indicates dissociation within *ca.* 10^{-13} sec., and quite frequently the products are atoms and free radicals. When the absorption spectrum contains both bands and a continuum, as commonly happens, the primary photochemical process will lead to excitation at some frequencies and dissociation at others.

Because the nature of the primary photochemical process often depends upon the frequency of light absorbed it is usually necessary to use monochromatic light. This is often accomplished by using a mercury arc which has strong lines at 1849, 2537, 3126, 3650, 4047 Å, and at still longer wave lengths. Pyrex glass absorbs radiation at wavelengths less than 3000 Å, Vycor below 2500 Å, and fused silica below 2000 Å. Optical filters are available for isolating several of the mercury arc lines. Prism and grating monochromators yield low intensities of light of high spectral purity.

It is also necessary to know at an early stage how well the substance to be photolyzed absorbs the incident light beam, since this will influence the cell dimensions and pressure or concentration of reactant. The fractional degree of absorption of light in an infinitesimal layer of absorber of thickness *dl* is pro-portional to the concentration of the absorbing substance *c*.

$$\frac{dI}{I} = -kc\,dl \tag{16.1}$$

where I is the intensity of light and k is a constant of proportionality which depends on the nature of the absorbing substance and the wave length of the light. Integrating over a finite thickness of absorber, we obtain the *Lambert-Beer law*,

$$\ln \frac{I}{I_0} = -kcl \tag{16.2}$$

where I_0 and I are the incident and emergent light intensities. When c is molar concentration, k is the molar extinction coefficient for path length l in centimeters.

EXERCISE 16.1

It is found that a substance present at 10^{-3} M absorbs 10% of an incident light beam in a path length of 1 cm. What concentration will be required to absorb 90%?   *Ans.* 0.022 *M*.

A device that measures the energy in a beam of light is called an *actinometer*. Absolute measurement is normally made with a thermopile, which consists of thermoelectric junctions in series. The hot junctions are in contact with black metal light absorbers; the voltage generated, as measured by a galvanometer, is proportional to the light intensity. The thermopile must be calibrated with a standardized lamp. Finally, the reaction cell must be thermostated, although photochemical reactions are usually much less sensitive to temperature than are thermal reactions. A schematic diagram of a typical experimental arrangement is shown in Fig. 16.1.

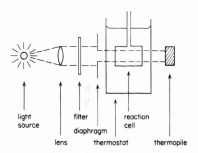

FIG. 16.1. Apparatus for photolysis.

For many studies a photochemical reaction system of known quantum yield can be used as an actinometer. The photolysis of hydrogen iodide, mentioned above, is convenient for gas phase studies. When solutions are to be photolyzed, the uranyl oxalate actinometer

$$H_2C_2O_4 \text{ (in presence of } UO_2^{++}) \rightarrow CO + CO_2 + H_2O$$

is commonly employed. The quantum yield is 0.5–0.6 with light of 2500–4300 Å.

16.2   Absorption of Light by Atoms

It has been shown (Chapter 13) that when an atom absorbs light it exhibits a discrete line spectrum whose well-defined frequencies are associated with the formation of correspondingly well-defined, excited electronic states of the atom. An isolated excited atom will eventually re-emit a quantum of light by *fluorescence* and return to its ground state. In the presence of other gas molecules the excited atom may transfer its energy in a collision. Since the de-excited atom can no longer fluoresce it is said to have been *quenched*.

The rate of formation of excited atoms is directly measured by the rate o$\bullet$ light absorption, I_a.

$$A + h\nu \longrightarrow A^*; \qquad \text{Rate} = I_a \qquad (16.3\bullet$$

The rate of fluorescence of an excited state, in the absence of quenching, i$\bullet$ a unimolecular, first-order process,[1]

$$A^* \longrightarrow A + h\nu \qquad k_f$$

$$-\frac{d(A^*)}{dt} = k_f(A^*) \qquad (16.4\bullet$$

and when the fluorescence is not forbidden by selection rules, $t_{1/2} = 0.693/k\bullet$ is typically $\sim 10^{-8}$ sec.

At moderate gas pressure there is competition between fluorescence an$\bullet$ energy transfer to a quencher, Q

$$A^* + Q \longrightarrow A + Q^* \qquad k_q$$

The total rate of loss of excited atoms is given by

$$-\frac{d(A^*)}{dt} = k_f(A^*) + k_q(A^*)(Q) \qquad (16.5$$

The *fluorescence yield*, or fraction of all excited atoms which fluoresce, is give$\bullet$ by

$$\frac{\text{quanta emitted}}{\text{quanta absorbed}} = \frac{I_f}{I_a} = \frac{k_f(A^*)}{k_f(A^*) + k_q(A^*)(Q)} \qquad (16.6$$

Equation (16.6) rearranges to give the Stern-Volmer equation:

$$\frac{I_f}{I_a} = y_f = \frac{1}{1 + (k_q/k_f)(Q)} \qquad (16.7)$$

The ratio of velocity constants k_q/k_f can be evaluated from measurements o$\bullet$ the fluorescence yield y_f for known concentrations of quencher. When k_f i$\bullet$ known from the measured half life of fluorescence in the absence of quencher then k_q can also be evaluated. Quenching occurs in bimolecular collisions be-tween A* and Q and the rate of such collisions is given by the kinetic theor$\bullet$ of gases (see section 11.10)[2] as

$$Z_{A \cdot Q} = n_A \cdot n_Q \left[\frac{\pi}{4} (d_{A^*} + d_Q)^2 \left(\frac{8kT}{\pi\mu} \right)^{1/2} \right]$$

Identifying the rate constant for quenching with the factor in brackets, we find that the *effective quenching cross section* $\sigma_Q = \dfrac{\pi(d_{A^*} + d_Q)^2}{4}$ is given by

---

[1] The symbol (M) is used for the concentration of species M, c_M.
[2] The factor of $\frac{1}{2}$ in equation (11.52) is eliminated since a collision of the type A→Q can now be distinguished from one of the type Q→A. The diameter d in (11.52) is replaced by the mean molecular diameter, $(d_{A^*} + d_Q)/2$.

$$\sigma_Q = k_q \left(\frac{\pi \mu}{8kT} \right)^{1/2} \tag{16.8}$$

Inefficient energy transfer is indicated by cross sections lower than kinetic theory values. Some typical values of $(d_{A^*} + d_Q)^2/4$, which is defined as the collision cross section in much of the literature, are listed in Table 16.1.

TABLE 16.1

CROSS SECTIONS FOR QUENCHING MERCURY FLUORESCENCE

Gas	$(d_{A^*} + d_Q)^2/4$ (cm^2 × 10^{16})
O_2	13.9
H_2	6.07
CO_2	2.48
CH_4	0.06
C_2H_6	0.11
C_2H_4	1.0
$n\text{-}C_7H_{16}$	24.0

EXERCISE 16.2

Compute k_q at 25° for the quenching of mercury fluorescence by ethylene, using the cross section given in Table 16.1.   *Ans.* 1.6 × 10^{-11} cm.^{3} molecule^{-1} sec.$^{-1}$.

As Table 16.1 shows, the efficiency with which hydrocarbons quench excited mercury atoms is quite high. The mechanisms by which this quenching occurs are not yet well understood, but a common consequence is the rupturing of a bond in the quenched molecule. This should not be surprising, since excited mercury atoms in the $^3P_1$ state have available 112 kcal. per mole of excitation energy.

A chemical reaction induced in one substance by energy transferred from another light-absorbing substance is said to be a *photosensitized* reaction. The uranyl oxalate actinometer, mentioned previously, depends on such a process. Most work has been done with metal vapors, particularly mercury.

Many substances whose free radical reactions would be of interest are not readily photolyzed directly, because they are quite transparent over the easily accessible range of wave lengths. This is the case for paraffin hydrocarbons, which are transparent to wavelengths far below the transmission limit of fused silica, although the bond dissociation energies for C—H and C—C correspond to quantum energies at 2700 Å or longer wave lengths. Therefore photosensitizers are used.

The photosensitizer should be relatively inert chemically and able to absorb light in an effective spectral region. In gaseous systems particularly, mercury is very satisfactory. The vapor strongly absorbs the 2537 Å and 1849 Å (resonance) lines of the mercury spectrum.

$$Hg(^1S_0) + h\nu(2537 \text{ Å}) \longrightarrow Hg(^3P_1)$$

$$Hg(^1S_0) + h\nu(1849 \text{ Å}) \longrightarrow Hg(^1P_1)$$

Photosensitized decompositions of hydrocarbons have been studied extensively (see E. W. R. Steacie, *Atomic and Free Radical Reactions*, 2nd ed., Reinhold,

New York, 1954, pp. 411 ff.) and it appears that the net result of the primary process can be represented as

$$Hg(^3P_1) + RH \longrightarrow Hg(^1S_0) + R + H$$

The mercury sensitized decomposition of ethane yields methane, propane, and butane. The following mechanism has been proposed to account for these facts:

$$Hg(^3P_1) + C_2H_6 \longrightarrow Hg(^1S_0) + C_2H_5 + H$$
$$H + C_2H_6 \longrightarrow C_2H_5 + H_2$$
$$H + C_2H_5 \longrightarrow CH_3 + CH_3$$
$$2\,CH_3 \longrightarrow C_2H_6$$
$$CH_3 + C_2H_5 \longrightarrow C_3H_8$$
$$2\,C_2H_5 \longrightarrow C_4H_{10}$$
$$2\,H \longrightarrow H_2$$

16.3 Absorption of Light by Molecules

The consequences of absorption of light by molecules have been described in Chapter 14 and in the first section of this chapter. We shall be concerned here exclusively with cases in which the primary process is dissociation, which is the process of chief interest for photochemistry.

One of the simplest photochemical reactions is the decomposition of hydrogen iodide. The spectrum of this molecule shows strong structureless absorption extending from 1900Å to above 2800Å, with a peak at 2180Å. This indicates that the final state resulting from absorption of light is unquantized, consisting of the dissociated atoms:[3]

(1) $$HI + h\nu \longrightarrow H + I \qquad Rate = I_a$$

The quantum yield for decomposition of hydrogen iodide is 2.0 over a wide range of conditions. Since the primary act decomposes only one molecule, the other must be accounted for by a secondary reaction. Of the two possibilities

(2) $$H + HI \longrightarrow H_2 + I; \qquad \Delta E = -32 \text{ kcal.}$$

(3) $$I + HI \longrightarrow I_2 + H; \qquad \Delta E = +35 \text{ kcal.}$$

the latter may be eliminated on grounds of endothermicity since $E_a \geq 35$ kcal., while for the former $E_a \geq 0$. (The value of ΔE for such reactions may be obtained from the difference in bond dissociation energies, given in Table 16.2.) The final step in the reaction is

(4) $$I + I + M \longrightarrow I_2 + M$$

where M is any third body. Although it is generally considered that two atoms

---

[3]This assumes that every quantum absorbed results in the decomposition of an HI molecule, that is, that the quantum yield for reaction (1) is one. If this were not so the rate of (1) would be represented by $\phi_1 I_a$, where ϕ_1 is the quantum yield for (1), the ratio of the number of absorbed quanta resulting in (1) to the total number of quanta absorbed. See section 16.7.

or free radicals may combine without activation energy, the diatomic particle formed is quite unstable, since it contains sufficient internal energy for dissociation. Unless relieved of at least part of this energy, as by collision with a third body, it will dissociate within one vibration period, $\sim 10^{-13}$ sec.

A mechanism consisting of steps (1), (2), and (4) accounts for the observed quantum yield of 2.0. It may be asked why steps such as

(5)	$I + H_2 \rightarrow HI + H$;	$\Delta E = +32$ kcal.
(6)	$H + I_2 \rightarrow HI + I$;	$\Delta E = -35$ kcal.
(7)	$H + H + M \rightarrow H_2 + M$	
(8)	$H + I + M \rightarrow HI + M$	

are not also included. Of these, the first is endothermic by a large amount, would have a high value of E_a, and is therefore eliminated. Step (7) is not important, because it must compete with step (2), and their relative rates are

$$\frac{R_2}{R_7} = \frac{k_2(HI)(\cancel{H})}{k_7(H)(M)(\cancel{H})}$$

Bimolecular collision frequencies are much greater than termolecular at a given pressure and, in addition, (H) is quite small under normal experimental conditions. Similarly, step (8) cannot compete with step (2).

EXERCISE 16.3

Suppose that hydrogen atoms react with hydrogen iodide molecules on every collision (process 2). According to the kinetic theory of gases, the value of the bimolecular rate constant for such a process will be *ca.* 10^{10} mole^{-1} l. sec.$^{-1}$. Find the steady-state concentration of hydrogen atoms in hydrogen iodide at 25° and 1 atm. pressure which is absorbing light at the rate of 10^{15} quanta cc.$^{-1}$ sec.$^{-1}$.   *Ans.* 4.1×10^{-15} mole l.$^{-1}$.

Hydrogen atoms will react appreciably with iodine by step (6), unless (I_2) is kept very small. At room temperature, the small equilibrium vapor pressure of iodine satisfies this condition, but at elevated temperatures step (6) must be included in the mechanism.

TABLE 16.2

BOND DISSOCIATION ENERGIES* (kcal. mole^{-1})

	H	CH_3	Cl	Br	I
H	103				
CH_3	101	83			
Cl	102	80	57		
Br	87	67	52	45	
I	71	53	50	42	36

* From T. L. Cottrell, *The Strengths of Chemical Bonds*, 2nd ed., Butterworths Scientific Publications, London, 1958.

The photochemical bromination of hydrogen bears many resemblances to the thermal reaction discussed in Chapter 11. Bromine absorbs in the green region of the spectrum (4500–5500 Å), and the primary process is dissociation into atoms.

(1) $Br_2 + h\nu \longrightarrow 2\ Br$ $Rate = I_a$

The secondary reactions are assumed to be identical with those encountered in the thermal reaction.

(2) $Br +\ H_2 \longrightarrow HBr + H$ k_2

(3) $H\ +\ Br_2 \longrightarrow HBr + Br$ k_3

(4) $H\ + HBr \longrightarrow H_2\ + Br$ k_4

(5) $Br + Br + M \longrightarrow Br_2\ + M$ k_5

Applying the steady-state treatment as in Chapter 11, we find

$$(Br) = \sqrt{\frac{2I_a}{k_5}}$$

$$(H) = \frac{k_2(H_2)(2I_a)^{1/2}k_5^{-1/2}}{k_3(Br_2) + k_4(HBr)}$$

$$\frac{d(HBr)}{dt} = \frac{k_2(H_2)(I_a/2k_5)^{1/2}}{1 + (k_4/k_3)(HBr)/(Br_2)} \tag{16.9}$$

The ratio of rate constants k_4/k_3 also appears in the thermal rate law, has the same value, $\sim$0.1, and shows no temperature dependence. The temperature coefficient of the numerator is found to correspond to an activation energy of 17 kcal./mole, and since k_5 for the recombination of bromine atoms is expected to have zero activation energy, this is identified with the activation energy for step (2) in the mechanism. This agrees satisfactorily with the prediction from the bond dissociation energies of Table 16.2.

$$E_a(2) \geq D_{\text{H–H}} - D_{\text{H–Br}} = 103 - 87 = 16\ \text{kcal. mole}^{-1}$$

Bond dissociation energies are very useful in understanding many reactions involving atoms and free radicals. For example, we may compare the various halogen atom-hydrogen molecule reactions,

$$X + H_2 \longrightarrow HX + H$$

where $X = Cl$ $D_{\text{H–H}} - D_{\text{H–X}} = 1\ \text{kcal. mole}^{-1}$

               $= Br$ $= 16$

               $= I$ $= 32$

In view of these figures it is not surprising to find that the photochemical reaction of chlorine with hydrogen is explosive, while that of bromine occurs at a moderate rate around 200°, and that of iodine has no appreciable rate.

16.4 Hot Atom Reactions

When the energy of the quantum absorbed exceeds the bond dissociation energy of the absorbing molecule, we may expect the excess energy

$$E' = h\nu - D \tag{16.10}$$

to appear as relative kinetic energy of the two fragments. When hydrogen iodide absorbs 2537 Å radiation the excess energy amounts to $112 - 71 = 41$ kcal. mole^{-1} if the iodine atom is formed in its ground electronic state. Since momentum must be conserved between the two fragments

$$m_H v_H = m_I v_I \tag{16.11}$$

and the ratio of kinetic energies is

$$\frac{E'_H}{E'_I} = \frac{\frac{1}{2} m_H v_H^2}{\frac{1}{2} m_I v_I^2} = \frac{m_I}{m_H} = 127 \tag{16.12}$$

Evidently the hydrogen atom acquires most of the energy. It is a *hot atom* and will be shown as H*.

EXERCISE 16.4

Find the kinetic energy of the hydrogen atom produced by photodissociation of hydrogen bromide with light of 2537 Å wave length. Assume the bromine atom is in its ground electronic state.   *Ans.* 25 kcal. mole^{-1}.

According to the considerations of Chapter 11, a hot atom should be abnormally reactive in the sense that it already possesses a large energy and can react upon a single encounter if the energy requirement is the only controlling factor. To test this possibility, it is necessary to be able to distinguish between the reactions of hot atoms and *thermal atoms*, that is, those which obey the Maxwell energy distribution law. A hot atom rapidly loses its excess energy in collisions, and hot atom reactions can occur only in the first few encounters after formation. Therefore, the fate of the majority of the hot atoms will be determined by that component of a mixture which they have the highest probability of meeting in these few encounters. In a two-component system if one component is present in large excess, almost all the hot reactions will occur with it. The fate of a thermal atom, on the other hand, will be determined by the relative activation energies for reaction with the two components as well as by their relative concentrations. A minor component which reacts with the atom by a path of lower activation energy than that for the major component can effectively capture, that is *scavenge*, the bulk of the thermal atoms.

The system deuterium iodide-ethane [R. L. Carter, R. R. Williams, and W. H. Hamill, *J. Am. Chem. Soc.*, **77**, 6457 (1955)] may be used for illustration. The major component of the system is ethane, which is transparent to mercury resonance radiation (2537 Å). This radiation is absorbed by deuterium iodide with the production of hot deuterium atoms. These collide chiefly with ethane and either react according to

(1) $D* + C_2H_6 \rightarrow HD + C_2H_5$

followed by

(2) $C_2H_5 + DI \rightarrow C_2H_5D + I$

or lose their excess energy and become thermal atoms. Of the two possib**l** thermal reactions of deuterium atoms

(3) $$D + C_2H_6 \rightarrow HD + C_2H_5$$

(4) $$D + DI \rightarrow D_2 + I$$

the second has much the smaller activation energy. In this system, the**n** deuterium iodide will act as a scavenger for deuterium atoms. Since deuteriu**m** iodide is a minor component, it cannot often react with hot deuterium atom**s** Thus step (4), the thermal reaction, yields D_2, and step 1, the hot atom reaction yields HD. The observed ratio HD/D_2 is *ca.* 0.25 when C_2H_6 is in large excess

Hot atoms can be produced by nuclear techniques as well. The ^{3}He nucleu**s** reacts with thermalized neutrons to form the radioactive isotope of hydrogen tritium (T or ^{3}H) and a proton, ^{3}He(n, p) ^{3}H. This nuclear reaction is exothermi**c** by 0.78 M.e.v., an enormous energy by chemical standards. This energy i**s** distributed between the proton and the T atom, with the T atom receivin**g** 0.19 M.e.v., as required by momentum conservation. A 0.19 M.e.v. T atom i**s** well above the range (below 100 e.v.) where chemical reactions can occur, an**d** enters this range at an energy inaccessible by other means of activation. As **a** result, it can efficiently enter into new types of reactions. [R. L. Wolfgang "Progress in Reaction Kinetics, Vol. 3.; F. Schmidt-Bleek and F. S. Rowland *Angew. Chem. Intern. Ed. Engl.*, **3**, 769 (1964).] For example, although th**e** characteristic reaction of thermal hydrogen atoms with hydrocarbons is ab-straction (reaction 3 above), these very energetic tritium atoms can displace **a** hydrogen atom.

(5) $$T + CH_4 \rightarrow CH_3T + H$$

The hot atom hypothesis predicts that the yield of the hot atom reaction will be diminished by the addition of large amounts of inert gas, such as helium, since this should "ther-malize" the hot atoms before reactive encounter can oc-cur. This result is indeed obtained.

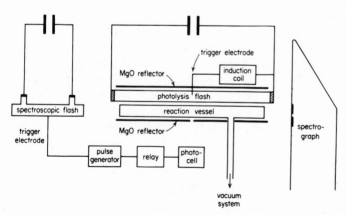

FIG. 16.2. Flash photolysis apparatus [from R.G.W. Norrish and B. A. Thrush, *Quart. Rev.*, **10**, 149 (1956)].

16.5 Flash Photolysis

With ordinary photochemical techniques, the concentrations of atoms and free radicals produced are too small for detection even by the most sensitive methods. A technique has been developed for illumination of reaction systems with extremely intense flashes of light. [See R.G.W. Norrish and B. A. Thrush, *Quarterly Reviews*, **10**, 149 (1956).] The intensity of the flash is typically 2000 joules or more and the duration of the flash about 10^{-4} sec. Absorption of this amount of light energy, 6×10^{-4} einstein, can dissociate more than 50% of the molecules in a small gas sample. By using another flash, set off at a short interval after the first, it is possible to photograph the absorption spectrum of the dissociation products with an arrangement indicated in Fig. 16.2.

Not only have the absorption spectra of several free radical intermediates such as ClO, OH, CH, NH, etc., been obtained, but also by changing the time interval between the dissociation and observation flashes it is possible to follow the concentration-time curve for a free radical intermediate in certain reactions. For example, in the explosion of a mixture of acetylene, 10 mm.; oxygen, 10 mm.; and nitrogen dioxide, 1.5 mm. the radical concentration versus time curves of Fig. 16.3 were obtained.

FIG. 16.3. Radical concentration in flash photolysis of 10 mm. C_2H_2, 10 mm. O_2, 1.5 mm. NO_2 [from R.G.W. Norrish and B. A. Thrush, *Quart. Rev.*, **10**, 149 (1956)].

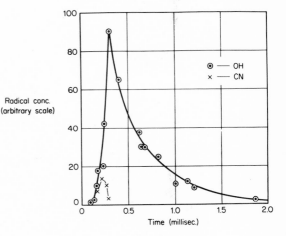

16.6 Dissociation-Recombination in Liquids

When a molecular species is dissociated in the gas phase to produce free radicals, recombination of these particles normally occurs with a high probability at each encounter. It is quite improbable, however, that the two partner radicals of a common parent molecule will ever recombine. When the two radicals have separated by only one mean free path, $\sim 10^3$ molecular diameters at 1 atm., the chance of a re-encounter upon the next collision is much less than 10^{-6} and rapidly diminishes thereafter. This is the normal situation of conventional kinetics and is implicitly assumed in applications of the steady-state method.

The corresponding dissociation process in the liquid state exhibits an important difference in that the two radicals from a given parent molecule are produced with a small initial separation, ~ 1 Å. This is due to a "cage effect" of the neighboring molecules [J. Franck and E. Rabinowitch, *Trans. Far. Soc.*, **30**, 120 (1934)] and may lead to immediate recombination for sufficiently small initial separations. In this case the primary process resembles a vibrational excitation and the incipient bond rupture is reversed within $\sim 10^{-13}$ sec. When the initial separation is greater and the radicals escape from the "cage," *viz.*, by separating by one or more mean free paths, they begin a random jumping or displacement by diffusion. The jump frequency is $\sim 10^{11}$ sec.$^{-1}$; the mean free path for diffusion may be estimated at a few tenths of a molecular diameter.

Diffusion displacements *on the average* tend to separate the initially contiguous pair of radicals, but in their random motion some radical pairs will re-encounter each other while they still lie within a fairly small volume. If we think of the molecules as occupying the positions of a cubic close-packed lattice, and the radicals as occupying two adjacent sites, a single displacement of one relative to the other can move it to any of 12 adjacent sites of which only one is occupied by its former partner. Thus, the probability of recombination after a second displacement is $\frac{1}{12}$. In each succeeding displacement the cumulative probability of recombination is somewhat increased, but this rapidly approaches a finite limit as the most probable displacement from the original partner rapidly increases with time. R. M. Noyes [*J. Chem. Phys.*, **18**, 999 (1950)] has estimated that for dissociation of iodine in hexane solution, the probability of recombination of original partners is 0.4–0.5. This has been called *geminate* recombination to emphasize that the two recombining atoms came from the same original molecule, and is to be distinguished from random recombinations of atoms from different molecules in the system.

In the absence of a scavenger for free radicals, they diffuse in a random way through the solution and eventually combine completely with each other. A scavenger added to the system in small concentration prevents steady-state recombination, but at concentrations less than 10^{-4} mole fraction it cannot be expected to interfere measurably with the geminate recombination. At mole fractions greater than 10^{-3} an efficient scavenger can begin to react with radicals which would otherwise have recombined with the original partner.

A typical photolysis in solution may be represented by

(1) $\quad\quad$ $AB + h\nu \longrightarrow (A + B)$ $\quad$ dissociation

(2) $\quad\quad$ $(A + B) \longrightarrow AB$ $\quad$ geminate recombination

(3) $\quad\quad$ $(A + B) \longrightarrow A + B$ $\quad$ steady state begins

(4) $\quad$ $A \,(\text{or } B) + X \longrightarrow AX \,(\text{or } BX)$ scavenger reaction

(5) $\quad\quad$ $A + B \longrightarrow AB$ $\quad$ steady-state combination

Approximately one-third of all initial processes will be followed by primary recombination, which is not included in the above mechanism since it is of no experimental consequence. Another one-third will undergo geminate recombination unless reaction with a scavenger intervenes. The remaining one-third escape into the steady state, and their behavior is treated in the usual fashion as a competition between steps (4) and (5).

The probability of reaction with scavenger can be represented by a quantum yield; its dependence upon concentration of scavenger is represented approximately in Fig. 16.4. The regions of interference with steady-state reaction and geminate recombination are indicated.

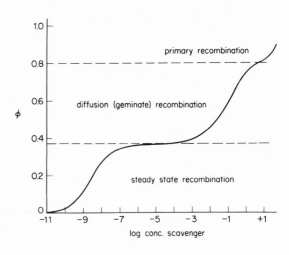

FIG. 16.4. Quantum yield in solution photolysis: effect of scavenger [from R.M. Noyes, J. Am. Chem. Soc., **77**, 2042 (1955)].

16.7 Free Radical Polymerization.

The polymerization of unsaturated monomers may be initiated either thermally or photochemically by a reaction producing a free radical R from an initiator C, such as

$$(1) \qquad C + h\nu \longrightarrow 2\,R$$

The initiator free radicals add to monomer M to form a new radical M_1.

$$(2) \qquad M + R \longrightarrow M_1{-}$$

For example, with ethylene

$$R + CH_2{=}CH_2 \longrightarrow RCH_2{-}CH_2{-}$$

The chain reaction propagates by successive addition of monomer.

$$(3) \qquad M + M_1{-} \qquad \longrightarrow M_2{-}$$

$$(4) \qquad M + M_2{-} \qquad \longrightarrow M_3{-}$$

$$(5) \qquad M + M_n{-} \qquad \longrightarrow M_{n+1}{-}$$

For the case of ethylene, step (5) would be

$$M_n{-} + CH_2{=}CH_2 \longrightarrow M_n{-}CH_2{-}CH_2{-}$$

Chains may terminate by combination of *any* two radicals.

$$(6) \qquad M_m{-} + M_n{-} \qquad \longrightarrow M_{m+n}$$

When a steady state has been established, the rates of initiation R_i and of termination R_t must be equal. The rate of initiation by photochemical dissociation is given by

$$R_i = 2I_a\phi \tag{16.13}$$

where ϕ is the quantum yield[3] for production of free radicals. The rate of termination, step (6), is

$$R_t = 2k_t(M_m{-})\,(M_n{-}) \tag{16.14}$$

The rate of propagation, steps (3), (4), (5), is

$$R_p = k_p(M)(M_n\text{---})$$ (16.1.

Let us postulate that the rate of chain propagation is the same for all M That is, $k_3 = k_4 = k_5 = k_p$. Let us also postulate that the rate of chain te mination is the same for M_m— and M_n—. In the steady state any chain radica is formed by propagation at the same rate that it is removed by propagatio and termination combined. For kinetic purposes, all chain radicals are indi: tinguishable. Recalling that $R_i = R_t$, we find that equations (16.13) and (16.1. combine to give

$$(M_n\text{---}) = \sqrt{\frac{I_a\phi}{k_t}}$$ (16.1.

for photochemical initiation of polymerization.

Combining equations (16.16) and (16.15) gives the rate of propagation c polymerization.

$$R_p = k_p\left(\frac{I_a\phi}{k_t}\right)^{1/2}(M)$$ (16.1.

When the reaction is initiated by a unimolecular thermal decomposition c initiator at concentration (C), R_i is given by

$$R_i = 2k_i(C)$$ (16.18

and

$$(M_n\text{---}) = \left[\frac{k_i(C)}{k_t}\right]^{1/2}$$ (16.1.

TABLE 16.3

POLYMERIZATION OF METHYL METHACRYLATE*

Monomer concentration moles/liter	Initiator concentration $(C) \times 10^4$ moles/liter	Rate of polymerization $R_p \times 10^3$ moles/liter min.	$\dfrac{R_p}{(C)^{1/2}}$	$\dfrac{R_p}{(C)^{1/2}\text{N}}$
	Undiluted monomer at 50°			
	47.00	4.66	0.068	
	115	7.37	.069	
	370	13.31	.069	
	745	18.84	.069	
	1482	26.40	.069	
	2106	31.61	.069	
	In benzene solution at 77°			
9.04	2.35	11.61	0.75	0.084
7.19	2.55	9.92	.62	.086
4.96	3.13	7.31	.41	.083
4.22	2.30	5.20	.34	.081
3.26	2.45	4.29	.27	.084
2.07	2.11	2.49	.17	.083

* L. M. Arnett, *J. Am. Chem. Soc.*, **74**, 2027 (1952).

The corresponding rate of polymerization is

$$R_p = k_p \left(\frac{k_i}{k_t}\right)^{1/2} (C)^{1/2} (M) \qquad (16.20)$$

This equation shows that the rate of polymerization should be proportional to $k_i^{1/2}$ for different initiators. This has been shown for the polymerization of acrylonitrile with three different initiators (azobisnitriles) whose measured values of $k_i^{1/2}$ were in the ratio $1:4.22:10.44$ while the measured values of $R_p/(C)^{1/2}$ were in the ratio $1:4.75:11.3$. When the concentration of monomer is constant, as in polymerizations carried out in pure monomer, equation (16.20) shows that $R_p/(C)^{1/2}$ should remain constant. Results of such a test are shown in Table 16.3. When polymerization is carried out in solution, the concentration of monomer can vary, in which case equation (16.20) shows that $R_p/(C)^{1/2}(M)$ should remain constant. The second series of data in Table 16.3 shows that this is the case.

16.8 Radiation Chemistry : Ionizing Radiations

Radiation chemistry is the study of chemical effects produced by ionizing radiations such as X rays, energetic electrons, and alpha particles. Much of the interest in this field arises from the fact that nuclear reactions, particularly those involved in applications of atomic energy, are accompanied by the emission of such ionizing radiations. However, the initiation of chemical reactions in such fashion is by no means inevitably associated with nuclear radiations.

X rays and gamma rays are electromagnetic radiations of short wave lengths. A wave length of 1 Å corresponds to an energy of 12,500 electron volts per quantum. Since this energy is more than sufficient to ionize atoms and molecules, absorption of these radiations is characterized by ejection of electrons from the atoms of absorbing materials. Such *secondary electrons*, with kinetic energies of a few hundred electron volts, cause further ionization near the original ion. If the primary radiation is energetic electrons or positive ions, collisions with atoms of the absorbing material likewise produce ions and secondary electrons. In all cases, the number of ionizations caused by secondary electrons is much greater than the number due to direct action of the original radiation. Therefore, the primary process in radiation chemistry, regardless of the nature of the radiation used, can be regarded as the collision of a low-energy electron, say 100 e.v., with a molecule.

Fig. 16.5 shows a much expanded representation of the track of a high-energy electron. The ions formed by collisions of the energetic electron are far apart, but those formed by the secondary electrons lie close to the ion from which they originated. These groups of ions are called *spurs*, and this phenomenon has important kinetic consequences in irradiation of liquids, as will be shown in a later section.

FIG. 16.5. Track of a high-energy electron.

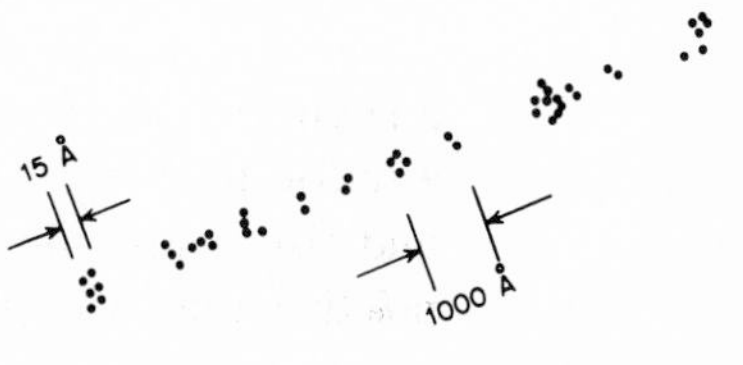

The collision of an electron with kinetic energy ~ 100 e.v. with the electronic structure of an atom or molecule produces excited electronic states and, when an electron is completely ejected from the atom, a positive ion. It has

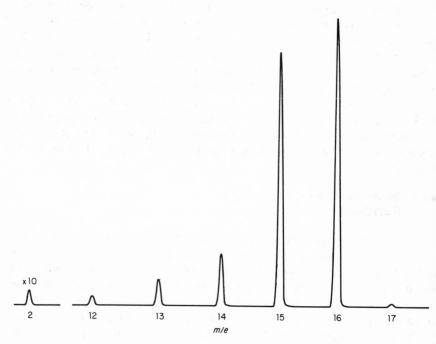

FIG. 16.6. Mass spectrum of methane.

been estimated (but not demonstrated) that ionization and excitation events occur in approximately equal numbers, but it is ionization rather than excitation which receives the greater attention in radiation chemistry, because it is characteristic and also more susceptible to measurement. Radiation-induced reactions in the gas phase can be described conveniently in terms of the *ion pair yield, M/N*, where M is the measured number of molecules produced or decomposed during an irradiation in which N ion pairs (positive ion and electron) were formed. In the liquid phase it has become the practice to report yields in terms of the number of molecules produced or consumed per 100 e.v. of energy absorbed by the system, and this is called the G value.

16.9 Electron Impact Processes

The mass spectrometer (see section 13.6) is not only a very useful analytical instrument but it is also a powerful tool for the examination of electron impact processes. It measures both the energy of the ionizing electron and also, within limits, the identity of the ionic reaction product. Actually, the positive ions are characterized by their mass-to-charge ratio, but since the charge is almost always unity, the result is referred to as a mass spectrum. For example, methane under 70 v. electron bombardment yields ions of masses 16, 15, 14, 13, 12, and 2 as indicated in Fig. 16.6. The small peak at mass 17 is due to the natural abundance of ^{13}C, the heavy stable isotope of carbon, which yields $^{13}CH_4^+$, mass 17.

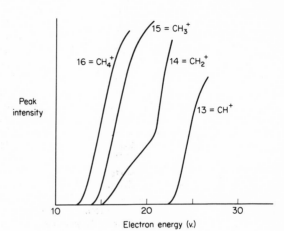

FIG. 16.7. Appearance potential curves for methane.

The intensities of the various mass peaks in the methane spectrum depend on the kinetic energy of the bombarding electrons as indicated in Fig. 16.7. For each ionic species there is a characteristic minimum electron energy, called the appearance potential AP, which is required to produce the given species. For CH_4, $AP(16) = 13.12$ e.v. When the parent molecule ion so formed is in its lowest energy state, the appearance potential is the same as the ionization potential. For the general case of producing an ionic fragment in its lowest state,

$$R_1R_2 + e = R_1^+ + R_2 + 2e$$

the appearance potential $AP(R_1^+)$, bond dissociation energy $D(R_1 - R_2)$ and ionization potential $I(R_1)$ of the radical R_1 are related by

$$AP(R_1^+) = I(R_1) + D(R_1 - R_2) \qquad (16.21)$$

Appearance potentials of ions have been used to evaluate bond strengths. For methane, $AP(CH_3^+) = 14.4$ e.v. Similarly, with the use of special techniques, the appearance potential of CH_3^+ from CH_3 radicals (equivalent to the ionization potential of CH_3) has been measured. $I(CH_3) = 9.96$ e.v. Substitution in equation (16.21) yields a value for the bond dissociation energy.

$$D(CH_3 - H) = AP - I = 4.4 \text{ e.v.} = 101 \text{ kcal./mole}$$

Energy measurements from appearance potentials are not yet so precise as spectroscopic or calorimetric measurements, but they are providing much information not otherwise available. Table 16.4 contains some data obtained by these methods.

TABLE 16.4

IONIZATION POTENTIALS AND HEATS OF FORMATION OF THE CORRESPONDING
GASEOUS IONS FROM ELECTRON IMPACT MEASUREMENTS‡

	I. (e.v.)	ΔH_f (kcal. mole^{-1})
H	13.62	365
H_2	15.44	356
CH_2	11.9	333
CH_3	9.96	262
CH_4	13.12	285
C_2H_2	11.42	317
C_2H_3	8.69	280
C_2H_4	10.56	255
C_2H_5	8.72	224
C_2H_6	11.65	249
C_3H_6	9.80	231
$s\text{-}C_3H_7$	7.90	190
C_3H_8	11.21	234
C_4H_8	9.24	209
$t\text{-}C_4H_9$	6.90	166
$n\text{-}C_4H_{10}$	10.80	219

‡ From F. H. Field and J. L. Franklin, *Electron Impact Phenomena*, Academic Press Inc., New York, 1957.

EXERCISE 16.5

The appearance potential for CH_3^+ from methane is 14.4 e.v. and from ethane 13.95 e.v. Use these data together with the CH_3—H bond dissociation energy from Table 16.2 to find the CH_3—CH_3 bond dissociation energy in ethane.

Ans. 3.9 e.v.; 90 kcal. mole$^-$

Figure 16.8 summarizes some important features of the mass spectra of several simple hydrocarbons. It should be observed that each component of the spectrum, although known only by its charge-to-mass ratio, can often be plausibly identified with a particular fragment of the parent molecule. Thus mass 44 from propane is necessarily $C_3H_8^+$, but mass 43 may correspond either to an *n*-propyl or to an *i*-propyl carbonium ion. With this limitation it is possible to account for almost all masses by assuming simple fragmentation of the parent molecule. Some notable exceptions, such as the 29 peak from neopentane, must result from internal rearrangements during the fragmentation.

It is not, of course, possible positively to identify the neutral fragments, but it is an interesting fact that for very many hydrocarbons the more abundant ions are of such masses that the residual masses of the uncharged fragment or fragments correspond to molecules or particularly stable radicals. For example, the most abundant ion in the mass spectrum of ethane is $C_2H_4^+$, mass 28, corresponding to the loss of H_2; in the mass spectra of higher hydrocarbons the ion peak corresponding to loss of CH_3 is usually large, i.e., the $C_3H_7^+$ peak is large in the butane spectrum, the $C_4H_9^+$ peak is large in the pentane spectrum, etc. This and other evidence suggest that such ion decompositions behave as unimolecular thermal reactions. That is, the process of ionization appears to

FIG. 16.8. Mass spectra of simple hydrocarbons.

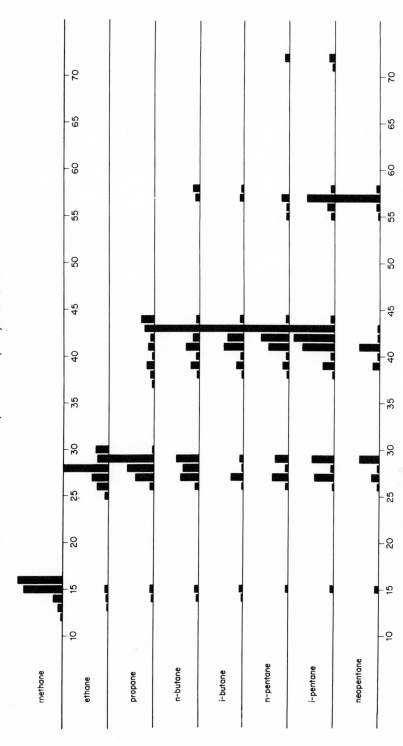

be accompanied by extensive vibrational excitation and the resulting fragments correspond largely to ruptures at the weakest bonds.

16.10 The Study of Ion-Molecule Reactions in a Mass Spectrometer

Gaseous ions are extremely reactive species as evidenced by the fact that reactions between ions and molecules proceed with a much higher efficiency than do even reactions between radicals. A few typical ion-molecule reactions are

(1) $CH_4^+ + CH_4 \rightarrow CH_5^+ + CH_3$

(2) $CH_3^+ + CH_4 \rightarrow C_2H_5^+ + H_2$

(3) $H_2^+ + H_2 \quad \rightarrow H_3^+ + H$

(4) $Ar^+ + CH_4 \quad \rightarrow CH_3^+ + Ar + H$

(5) $Ar^+ + H_2 \quad \rightarrow ArH^+ + H$

The products of such reactions can be observed in a mass spectrometer at a pressure of one micron or higher in the source region, a pressure which favors multiple collisions and is greatly in excess of that suitable for analysis. Mass spectrometric peaks arising from reactions (1) through (5) are small. They can be distinguished from peaks arising from the existence of small impurities in the sample in part by the fact that they are formed in bimolecular processes and, therefore, show a dependence on the square of the sample pressure, as shown in Fig. 16.9.

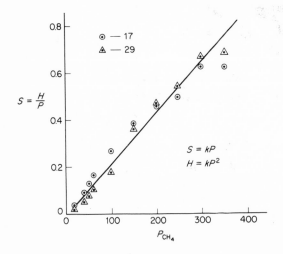

FIG. 16.9. Ion-molecule reactions in methane. H = peak intensity, P = inlet pressure.

The rates of ion-molecule reactions can be described by methods resembling those of simple collision theory, but modified to allow for the fact that attractive ion-induced dipolar forces (section 15.15) enhance the probability of collision. We shall begin with an order of magnitude calculation of the collision radius. A collision can be defined as occurring whenever the particles are at a distance at which the attractive ion-dipolar force can overcome the centrifugal force due to the ion's motion. This can be approximated as the radius of the closed circular orbit in which these forces balance. (Recall the Bohr hydrogen atom.) From equation (15.23) the force of attraction, dV/dr, is

$$dV/dr = 2e^2\alpha/r^5$$

The centrifugal force is $\mu v^2/r$, μ being the reduced mass and v the relative velocity of the particles. Equating these and solving for r_c, the radius of the largest closed orbit

$$r_c = (2e^2\alpha/\mu v^2)^{1/4}$$

This result is surprisingly close to that of a more rigorous calculation of s_o, the maximum distance of separation at which collision occurs between an ion and molecule.

$$s_o = (4e^2\alpha/\mu v^2)^{1/4} \tag{16.22}$$

The collision cross section, σ, is defined as the area swept out by a circle of radius s_o. (See Fig. 11.15.)

$$\sigma = \pi s_o^2 = (4e^2\alpha/\mu v^2)^{1/2} \tag{16.23}$$

[G. Gioumousis and D. P. Stevenson, *J. Chem. Phys.*, **29**, 294 (1958)]

For measurements in a mass spectrometer the molecule may be considered at rest relative to the accelerated ion, and v is essentially the velocity acquired by the primary ion in the electric field of the source. Since molecular polarizabilities are of the order of 10^{-24} to 10^{-23} cm^3, σ can be greater than 100 Å^2, and is often more than 10 times kinetic theory cross sections.

In order to establish empirical cross sections, analysis of mass spectrometric data is necessary. Let i_p be the current due to primary ions passing through a source of path length l at an average speed, v. Let i_s be the current arising from secondary ions formed by ion-molecule reactions with molecules of concentration c. Clearly, if only a small fraction of the primary ions reacts, then i_s will be directly proportional to i_p, to c, and to the path length l.

$$i_s = \sigma_e \, i_p \, l \, c \tag{16.24}$$

The proportionality constant, σ_e, with dimensions of cm.^{2} is called the phenomenological cross section. Thus, measurement of the ratio i_s/i_p allows evaluation of σ_e. It is amazing that the calculated *collision* cross sections and the experimental *reaction* cross sections are often almost equal. It must, therefore, be concluded that in these instances reaction occurs at every collision, and that the rate of the chemical process is dominated by the physical situation.

Although the expression of these data in terms of cross sections is instructive, expression in terms of rate constants which are independent of instrumental parameters is more meaningful. For a beam of monoenergetic ions of mass m_i and charge e accelerated by a potential field E over a distance l this can be done as follows. v, the velocity of the incident ions, is given by $v = (2Eel/m_i)^{1/2}$. Assuming that the mean residence time of an ion in the reaction zone is given by l/v, the steady-state charge density in the source is $i_p l(m_i/2Eel)^{1/2}$, and this is also a measure of the primary ion concentration, c_p. The rate of production of secondary ions, (dS/dt), which is equal to the current i_s (rate of charge flow) is

$$dS/dt = kc_p c = ki_p l(m_i/2Eel)^{1/2}c = i_s \tag{16.25}$$

where c is the concentration of molecules. Comparing (16.25) to (16.24)

$$k = \sigma_e(2Eel/m_i)^{1/2}.$$

The situation in a mass spectrometer is more complex, but analysis of the problem for Maxwellian distributions of ions and reactants gives a similar result.

$$k = \sigma_e (Eel/2m_i)^{1/2} \tag{16.26}$$

EXERCISE 16.6

In an experiment $E = 10.3$ volts cm.$^{-1}$, and $l = 0.27$ cm. σ_e for Ar$^+$ + H$_2 \rightarrow$ ArH$^+$ + H is 82×10^{-16} cm.^{2} Compute k. (Keep units consistent.)

Ans. $k = 1.5 \times 10^{-9}$ cm.^{3} molecule^{-1} sec.$^{-1}$

As mentioned earlier, high energy radiation characteristically produces high concentrations of ions. Since reactions of ions are highly efficient, they must play an important role in radiation chemistry. We shall return to this topic again in section 16.13.

The fate of the electrons produced in the ionization processes must also be considered. When no substance of significant electron affinity is present in the system, as in irradiation of a hydrocarbon, electron-positive ion recombination occurs rapidly. Such neutralization processes are the inverse of ionization and are therefore invariably highly exothermic. This energy undoubtedly causes bond rupture, producing atoms and radicals.

$$AB^+ + e \longrightarrow AB^* \longrightarrow A + B$$

When a substance with appreciable electron affinity is present, electron attachment may precede neutralization. In numerous instances the electron attachment process is sufficiently exothermic to produce bond rupture. For example, the electron affinity of iodine is 3.1 e.v., whereas the bond dissociation energy of hydrogen iodide is 3.0 e.v. Therefore, the process

$$HI + e \longrightarrow H + I^-$$

is exothermic by 0.1 e.v. Furthermore, this kind of event may strongly affect the subsequent neutralization process. For example, whereas electron neutralization of a carbonium ion

$$RH^+ + e \longrightarrow RH^* \longrightarrow R + H$$

is exothermic by 6–8 e.v., the neutralization process

$$RH^+ + I^- \longrightarrow RH + I$$

is less exothermic by 3.1 e.v., the electron affinity of iodine, and, therefore, may not result in bond rupture.

16.11 Radiolysis of Hydrogen Bromide

The radiolysis of hydrogen-bromine-hydrogen bromide systems was studied experimentally by S. C. Lind and R. Livingston [*J. Am. Chem. Soc.* **58**, 612 (1936)], who used radon as an internal source of radiation. From the measured rate of reaction and the calculated ionization rate of the alpha radiations from radon, they were able to compute the ion pair yield M/N for the reaction. Some typical results are given in Table 16.5.

Up to this time, no satisfactory detailed mechanism for a radiation-induced reaction had appeared. In what is now a classic paper in this field, H. Eyring, J. O. Hirschfelder and H. S. Taylor [*J.Chem. Phys.*, **4**, 570 (1936)] were able to propose a detailed mechanism for this reaction. The various steps proposed illustrate many of the primary and secondary reactions mentioned in the preceding sections, and the relationship to the thermal and photochemical reactions in the hydrogen-bromine system is clarified.

It is known that the principal ionization process for hydrogen is

(1) $H_2 \longrightarrow\!\!\!\sim\!\!\!\sim\!\!\!\sim\!\!\! H_2^+ + e$

where the symbol $\longrightarrow\!\!\!\sim\!\!\!\sim\!\!\!\sim\!\!\!$ means "acted upon by ionizing radiation." Excitation without ionization may also occur, but for the purposes of subsequent reaction only dissociative excitation is considered.

(2) $H_2 \longrightarrow\!\!\!\sim\!\!\!\sim\!\!\!\sim\!\!\! H_2^* \rightarrow 2\,H$

An efficient ion-molecule reaction probably occurs, namely,

(3) $H_2^+ + H_2 \rightarrow H_3^+ + H$

When H_3^+ is neutralized by either an electron or a negative ion, three H atoms are produced.

(4) $H_3^+ + e(\text{or } Br^-) \rightarrow 3\,H$

In a mixture of gases, the number of ion pairs formed by any component such as hydrogen, N_{H_2}, can be calculated with some confidence from the known stopping power, specific ionization and partial pressure. Then the number of H atoms per ion pair produced by the action of radiation on hydrogen is aN_{H_2}, where $a \geq 4$. (a exceeds 4 insofar as process 2 contributes to H atom formation.)

In the case of hydrogen bromide, the ionization process is principally

(5) $HBr \longrightarrow\!\!\!\sim\!\!\!\sim\!\!\!\sim\!\!\! HBr^+ + e$

and dissociative excitation may also be important.

(6) $HBr \longrightarrow\!\!\!\sim\!\!\!\sim\!\!\!\sim\!\!\! HBr^* \rightarrow H + Br$

An efficient ion-molecule reaction probably occurs, namely,

(7) $HBr^+ + HBr \rightarrow H_2Br^+ + Br$

and the H_2Br^+ ion, on neutralization, will produce two hydrogen atoms.

(8) $H_2Br^+ + e(\text{or } Br^-) \rightarrow 2\,H + Br$

The number of H atoms formed by action of radiation on HBr in a mixture is bN_{HBr}, where $b \geq 2$. (b exceeds 2 insofar as process 6 contributes to H atom formation.)

Ionization of bromine probably produces Br_2^+ and, on subsequent neutralization, Br atoms. However, these do not contribute to the reaction, since the rate of the process $Br + H_2 \rightarrow HBr + H$ is negligible at room temperature.

Both bromine and hydrogen bromide can attach electrons and for each ion pair originally formed, $N = N_{HBr} + N_{H_2} + N_{Br_2}$, an electron will be captured by one of the two processes

(9) $HBr + e \longrightarrow H + Br^-$

(10) $Br_2 + e \longrightarrow Br + Br^-$

The ratio of rates of these two processes is not known, and the quantity A, the chance that the electron will be captured by HBr,

$$A = \frac{1}{1 + \dfrac{k_{10}}{k_9}\dfrac{P_{Br_2}}{P_{HBr}}}$$

must be left as an unknown parameter. (The experimental results indicate that $A = 1$.) Process (9) will yield AN hydrogen atoms per ion pair.

After the ionic reactions have taken place, hydrogen atoms will react with hydrogen and bromine in a ratio known from photochemical and thermal studies.

(11) $H + Br_2 \longrightarrow HBr + Br$

(12) $H + HBr \longrightarrow H_2 + Br$

The chance B that a hydrogen atom will react with bromine to form hydrogen bromide is

$$B = \frac{k_{11}(H)(Br_2)}{k_{11}(H)(Br_2) + k_{12}(H)(HBr)} = \frac{1}{1 + 0.12 \times P_{HBr}/P_{Br_2}}$$

An expression for the dependence of the ion pair yield on composition was formulated by Eyring, Hirschfelder, and Taylor as follows: The total number of H atoms per ion pair is

$$aN_{H_2} + bN_{HBr} + AN \qquad (16.27)$$

The number of HBr molecules decomposed directly is

$$bN_{HBr} + AN \qquad (16.28)$$

Since each H atom has the chance B to form HBr (process 11) and the chance $1 - B$ to decompose HBr (process 12), we obtain for the yield of HBr per ion pair

$$\frac{M}{N} = [B - (1 - B)]\left[a\frac{N_{H_2}}{N} + b\frac{N_{HBr}}{N} + A \right] - b\frac{N_{HBr}}{N} - A \qquad (16.29)$$

B, N_{H_2}, N_{HBr} and N are known for any experiment. A, a, and b are not known and are chosen for best fit with the experimental data. The best values are found to be

$$a = 6.0, \quad b = 2.0, \quad A = 1$$

The calculated values of M/N are compared with experimental values in Table 16.5. Considering the range of conditions covered, the agreement is fairly good. The value of a indicates that dissociation of hydrogen by excitation must be a significant process, whereas it is apparently not important in hydrogen bromide.

TABLE 16.5

RADIOLYSIS OF THE HYDROGEN-BROMINE SYSTEM

P_{HBr} (mm. Hg)	P_{Br_2} (mm. Hg)	P_{H_2} (mm. Hg)	$(M/N)_{obs.}$ §	$(M/N)_{calc.}$ §
1.2	127.8	84.9	0.24	0.24
2.4	95.5	250.4	0.88	0.84
5.4	56.6	411.3	1.90	1.79
3.8	26.4	424.6	2.76	2.83
162.3	4.5	4.5	−3.98	−4.70
148.3	10.6	10.6	−3.57	−3.44
84.5	1.3	571.1	−5.07	−5.74

§ Negative values of M/N signify decomposition of HBr.

16.12 Radiolysis of Water

Water is decomposed by ionizing radiations to give H_2 and H_2O_2. In the absence of solutes, the latter decomposes further to yield oxygen gas. In very pure water the yields from electron or gamma ray bombardment are very small, while that from alpha particle bombardment is substantial. This suggests that the density of ionization, which is much greater for alpha particles, has an important role in the mechanism. With small amounts of added solutes the yields for electron and gamma ray bombardment are greatly increased, indicating that the low yields in their absence are not due to failure of the primary process, but rather to reverse reactions.

The primary molecular process in the radiation decomposition of water is

(1) $H_2O \longrightarrow\mathord{\sim\!\sim\!\sim}\rightarrow H_2O^+ + e$

According to one interpretation [A. H. Samuel and J. L. Magee, *J. Chem. Phys.*, **21**, 1080 (1953)] the low-energy electron produced in the ionization act quickly loses its energy to the medium and is not likely to escape from the field of its parent ion. It is recaptured within 10^{-13} sec., causing dissociation.

(2) $H_2O^+ + e \rightarrow H_2O^* \rightarrow H + OH$

It is an important consequence of this view that the charged particles, as such, do not contribute to the chemistry. The only effect of the ionizing radiation is to produce radical pairs and all chemical effects are attributed to them.

As suggested above, the spatial distribution of primary events is of considerable importance in the radiolysis of water and, presumably, other liquid systems. According to Samuel and Magee, a *spur* (see Fig. 16.5) in water typically contains three atom-radical pairs in a volume of $2\text{–}4 \times (10)^{-21}$ cc., or a local concentration of approximately 1 M. The average distance between spurs in water is estimated to be 10^4 Å (as compared to a "diameter" of *ca.* 10 Å). The high local concentration of H and OH radicals in the spurs results in the radical combination reactions (3) and (4) being extremely rapid.

(3) $H + H \rightarrow H_2$

(4) $OH + OH \rightarrow H_2O_2$

In addition, the process

(5) $H + OH \rightarrow H_2O$

must occur, but this has no directly measurable experimental consequences.

Reactions (3) and (4) in spurs are similar to the geminate recombination processes discussed in section 16.6, and like these cannot be affected by low concentrations of radical scavengers. The unscavengable yield of H_2 and H_2O_2 per 100 e.v. of absorbed energy is called the molecular yield, and is symbolized by G_M. However, at ordinary radiation intensities, only a fraction of the H atoms and OH radicals undergo such geminate diffusion-recombination and the remainder diffuse away from the spurs and become more or less homogeneously distributed through the system at a net concentration of 10^{-8} M. In this case, the chance of radical-atom encounters is negligible in comparison with the chance of reaction with a solute present in concentrations even as low as 10^{-6} M.

When the system contains solutes which react efficiently with atoms and radicals, the extent of such a reaction can be used to measure the radical yield G_R, that is, the number of radical pairs which escape from the spur per 100 e.v. of energy absorbed. In aerated water containing ferrous sulfate and 0.8 N sulfuric acid, the following sequence of reactions occurs:

$$H + O_2 \rightarrow HO_2$$
$$OH + Fe^{+2} \rightarrow Fe^{+3} + OH^-$$
$$Fe^{+2} + HO_2 \rightarrow Fe^{+3} + HO_2^-$$
$$HO_2^- + H^+ \rightarrow H_2O_2$$
$$Fe^{+2} + H_2O_2 \rightarrow Fe^{+3} + OH^- + OH$$

This amounts to oxidation of four ferrous ions by each radical pair. In addition, each H_2O_2 molecule produced in the spur will oxidize two Fe^{+2}, and therefore

$$G_{Fe^{+3}} = 4G_R + 2G_M \qquad (16.30)$$

The measured value of $G_{Fe^{+3}}$ is 15.5, and this system can be used as a *dosimeter* for measurement of unknown radiation intensities in a manner analogous to the use of an actinometer in photochemistry.

The value of G_M is measured by the hydrogen yield in the ferrous sulfate system.

$$G_{H_2} = G_M = 0.45 \qquad (16.31)$$

Combining equations (16.30) and (16.31) yields

$$G_R = \frac{(15.5 - 0.90)}{4} = 3.7$$

In the absence of solute, the radicals escaping from the spur react with any products present via the chain

(6) $H + H_2O_2 \rightarrow H_2O + OH$

(7) $OH + H_2 \rightarrow H_2O + H$

and thus prevent the accumulation of appreciable amounts of H_2 and H_2O_2. This accounts for the low yields in electron irradiation of very pure water. Alpha particle bombardment, in contrast, produces spurs which are very close together so that they overlap to form a cylinder in which the local concentration of atoms and radicals is very high. This enhances G_M and diminishes G_R, making the net yield of products in pure water much higher.

Although the values of G_M and G_R depend only on the character of the radiation in dilute solutions, it has been shown by H. A. Schwarz [*J. Am. Chem. Soc.*, **77**, 4960 (1955)] that, with increasing concentrations of various solutes, the value of G_M diminishes. This is attributed to intrusion of the solute into the region of geminate diffusion-recombination. Although the efficiencies of the various solutes differ, it is remarkable that the shapes of the G_M vs. concentration curves are the same, as shown in Fig. 16.10. Here the concentration of

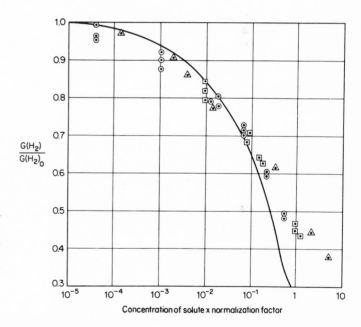

FIG. 16.10 Effect of solutes on hydrogen yield in aqueous solutions : solid curve is theoretical [from Schwartz, *loc. cit.*]. ⊙ NO_2^- in KNO_2 solution ; ⊡ Cu^{2+} in $CuSO_4$ solution ; △ H_2O_2 solutions.

Concentration of solute × normalization factor

each solute has been multiplied by a normalization constant chosen so that points for all solutes fall on essentially the same curve. Reasoning that the shape of this curve is governed by the diffusion controlled recombination process, Schwarz has developed a theoretical treatment which yields the curve of Fig. 16.10.

The preceding discussion of radiation-induced processes occuring in aqueous solution has been based on inferences drawn from the study of product yields and the effect of variation of experimental parameters on these yields. Recently techniques have been developed for a more direct examination of radiolytic reactions. One such technique, pulse radiolysis, [M. S. Matheson and L. M. Dorfman, *J. Chem. Phys.*, **32**, 1870 (1960).], is related to flash photolysis, which was discussed in section 16.5. A sample is irradiated with an intense pulse of 15 M.e.v. electrons and analyzed spectroscopically for short-lived transients. When a number of aqueous solutions are examined in this way, a transient absorption band peaking near 7000 Å is found in each. The similarity of this band to that of the solvated electron in solutions of alkali metals in liquid ammonia, its short lifetime, and its sensitivity to electron scavengers (section

TABLE 16.6

RATE CONSTANTS FOR SOME REACTIONS OF THE HYDRATED ELECTRON[a]

Reaction	Rate constant[b]
$e_{aq.} + H_3O^+ \longrightarrow H + H_2O$	2.36×10^{10}
$e_{aq.} + H_2O_2 \longrightarrow OH^-_{aq.} + OH$	1.23×10^{10}
$e_{aq.} + O_2 \longrightarrow O^-_{2aq.}$	1.88×10^{10}
$e_{aq.} + Cu^{++}_{aq.} \longrightarrow Cu^+_{aq.}$	3.3×10^{10}
$e_{aq.} + Fe(CN)^{-3}_{6aq.} \longrightarrow Fe(CN)^{-4}_{6aq.}$	0.30×10^{10}
$e_{aq.} + H_2O \longrightarrow H + OH^-_{aq.}$	$<4 \times 10^4$

[a] Taken from S. Gordon, E. J. Hart, M. S. Matheson, J. Rabani, and J. K. Thomas, *J. Am. Chem. Soc.*, **85**, 1375 (1963).
[b] Rate constant is in units of liters moles^{-1} sec.$^{-1}$. Temperature is 21–23°C.

16.10) have lead to its assignment as the spectrum of the hydrated electron. [E. J. Hart and J. W. Boag, *J. Am. Chem. Soc.*, **84**, 4090 (1962). See also E. J. Hart, *Science*, **146**, 19 (1964).] It has proven possible to measure the rate constants for various reactions of the hydrated electron. Some values are summarized in Table 16.6.

16.13 Radiolysis of Organic Systems

Both ionic and radical processes occur in the radiolysis of organic systems. Investigation of radical processes involves the use of a scavenger, a reagent which reacts efficiently with a radical intermediate to convert it uniquely into a readily identifiable product. Clearly it is desirable that the scavenger should not perturb the system in any other way. In experiments involving ionizing radiation, this means that it should not react with ions or electrons. Iodine labeled with the radioactive isotope, ^{131}I, has often been used as a scavenger, since it apparently reacts very efficiently with many organic free radicals [L. H. Gevantman and R. R. Williams, *J. Phys. Chem.*, **56**, 569 (1952)]. Although iodine also reacts readily with electrons, the lifetime of electrons in low dielectric liquids is much shorter than the lifetime of free radicals, and thus if quite small concentrations of iodine are used, it should react only with free radicals and not with electrons or ions.

Another useful reagent for radicals is ethylene labeled with radioactive ^{14}C, since it should not interfere with ionic processes in liquid hydrocarbons. Ethylene-^{14}C reacts efficiently with H atoms to form ethyl radicals, which in turn react with radicals R to give products of the type $^{14}CH_3{}^{12}CH_2$ R. The yields in G units of primary radicals formed in liquid n-hexane at $10°C$ are illustrative.

CH$_3$	C$_2$H$_5$	n-C$_3$H$_7$	n-C$_4$H$_9$	n-C$_5$H$_{11}$	1-Methylpentyl +1-Ethylbutyl	n-C$_6$H$_{13}$
0.06	0.33	0.32	0.28	0.06	3.58	0.99

These results are consistent with the interpretation that the reactions occuring are simple $C - H$ and $C - C$ bond ruptures [R. A. Holroyd and G. W. Klein, *J. Am. Chem. Soc.*, **84**, 4000 (1962)]. In the absence of ethylene scavenger, the primary radicals react by random combination, or by *disproportionation*, a reaction in which a hydrogen atom is transferred from one radical to another to give two stable molecules; for example,

$$(1) \quad C_2H_5 + C_2H_5 \longrightarrow C_2H_4 + C_2H_6$$

Much current effort in radiation chemistry is devoted to the important class of ionic reactions. Indeed, one of the great advantages of radiation chemistry relative to photochemistry lies in the ease with which a mass spectrometer can be used to observe ionic intermediates. By the use of a specially designed instrument operated at very high pressures ($\sim$0.2 mm.), it has been possible to observe sequences of ion-molecule reactions initiated by a given primary ion in gaseous methane [S. Wexler and N. Jesse, *J. Am. Chem. Soc.*, **84**, 3425 (1962)]. The results, summarized in Table 16.7, clearly demonstrate that there are several sequences of ion-molecule reactions corresponding to

TABLE 16.7

CONSECUTIVE ION-MOLECULE REACTIONS IN METHANE

Primary Ion	Intermediate Ions
CH$_4^+$	CH$_5^+$, C$_2$H$_6^+$, C$_3$H$_8^+$, C$_4$H$_8^+$, C$_4$H$_9^+$
CH$_3^+$	C$_2$H$_4^+$, C$_2$H$_5^+$, C$_2$H$_7^+$, C$_4$H$_7^+$, C$_5$H$_9^+$, C$_5$H$_{11}^+$
CH$_2^+$	C$_2$H$_3^+$, C$_3$H$_5^+$, C$_3$H$_6^+$
CH$^+$	C$_2$H$_2^+$, C$_3$H$_3^+$, C$_3$H$_4^+$

initiation by different primary ions. However, so complex is the radiation chemistry of methane that it is not yet well understood, despite such detailed results. Evidence of this complexity is the fact that alkane and alkene products up to C$_6$ have been observed. Also, the role of ion-electron recombination is not yet established, since products of such reactions have not yet been measured and cannot be predicted.

The occurrence of ionic processes in organic liquids and solids exposed to high energy radiation has long been assumed, but has only recently been

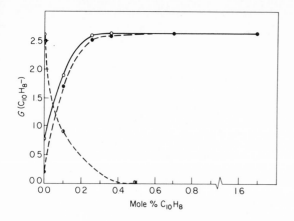

FIG. 16.11 Electron attachment in solid situations of napthalene in 2-Methyltetrahydrofuran at 77°K. ● $G(C_{10}H_8^-)$ vs. mole % $C_{10}H_8$; ○ $G(C_{10}H_8^-)$ vs. mole % $C_{10}H_8$ after bleaching solvated electrons; ◐ G (solvated electrons) vs. mole % $C_{10}H_8$ [from M.R. Ronayne, J.P. Guarino, and W. H. Hamill, J. Am. Chem. Soc., **84**, 4230 (1962)].

demonstrated. Naphthalene and other aromatic hydrocarbons can be reduced by sodium in appropriate solvents (*e.g.*, ethers) to yield solutions of mono-negative anions which have very characteristic optical spectra and such large extinction coefficients that very small amounts can be measured easily by optical absorption spectroscopy. When a dilute solution of naphthalene in 2-methyl tetrahydrofuran is cooled to 77°K, it forms a transparent glassy solid which, when irradiated with gamma rays, exhibits the characteristic spectrum of $C_{10}H_8^-$. This result suggests that the major effect of irradiation is the generation of electrons from the solvent, and that these electrons then diffuse through the matrix and become attached to the solute. In addition to the spectrum of $C_{10}H_8^-$, there is an absorption in the near infrared region which is easily removed by optical bleaching with a simultaneous increase in absorption due to $C_{10}H_8^-$ (see Fig. 16.11). Apparently, some electrons have been trapped by the solvent, are detached by optical excitation, and finally migrate to the solute. When sufficiently high concentrations of naphthalene are used, a constant limiting yield of approximately 2.5 for $G(C_{10}H_8^-)$ is found, as shown in Fig. 16.11.

Processes of dissociative electron attachment

$$RX + e \rightarrow R + X^-$$

are well-known in mass spectrometry, and may be expected in radiation chemistry. When a glassy solution containing both naphthalene and benzyl acetate is irradiated, the yield of $C_{10}H_8^-$ is strongly suppressed, indicating reaction of benzyl acetate with electrons. Also, the well-known spectrum of the benzyl radical appears. Finally, when the solution is thawed and analyzed, CO_2 is recovered as a product. The neutralization product of $CH_3CO_2^-$ is the acetoxy radical, which is known to decompose very rapidly to CH_3 and CO_2. The results, therefore, strongly suggest that dissociative electron attachment is an efficient process in condensed media. These and other related effects demonstrate the importance of the ionic processes which characterize radiation chemistry [J. P. Guarino and W. H. Hamill, J. Am. Chem. Soc., **86**, 777 (1964)].

SUMMARY, CHAPTER 16

1. Fundamental laws of photochemistry

   Grotthus-Draper law: Only the light absorbed by a system is effective in producing chemical change.

Stark-Einstein law: In the primary process each quantum absorbed activates one molecule.

Quantum yield: number of molecules decomposed or formed per quantum absorbed.

Lambert-Beer law

$$\ln \frac{I}{I_0} = -kcl$$

2. Consequences of light absorption

Fluorescence

$$A + h\nu \longrightarrow A^*$$

$$A^* \longrightarrow A + h\nu$$

Quenching

$$A^* + Q \longrightarrow A + Q^*$$

Photosensitization

$$A^* + RH \longrightarrow A + R + H$$

Dissociation

$$AB + h\nu \longrightarrow A + B; \quad E(h\nu) \geq D(A - B)$$

Photochemical hot atoms

$$K.E. = E(h\nu) - D(A - B)$$

Geminate recombination in liquids

$$AB + h\nu \longrightarrow (A + B)$$

$$(A + B) \longrightarrow AB$$

Initiation of polymerization

$$C + h\nu \longrightarrow 2 R$$

$$R + CH_2{=}CH_2 \longrightarrow RCH_2{-}CH_2{-}$$

3. Elementary reactions of radiation chemistry

Electron impact

Excitation

$$M + e \longrightarrow M^* + e$$

Ionization

$$M + e \longrightarrow M^+ + 2e$$

Dissociation

$$AB + e \longrightarrow A^+ + B + 2e$$

Ion-molecule reactions

$$AB^+ + CD \longrightarrow ABC^+ + D$$

Electron capture

$$AB + e \longrightarrow A + B^-$$

Charge neutralization

$$CD^+ + e \longrightarrow C + D$$

or

$$CD^+ + B^- \rightarrow C + D + B$$

Reactions in spurs (water)

$$H + H \rightarrow H_2$$
$$OH + OH \rightarrow H_2O_2$$

PROBLEMS, CHAPTER 16

1. A 2mm. thickness of Vycor glass is found to have a transmission of 70 for light of 2537 Å. What will be the transmission of a 0.55 mm. thickness of the glass?

Ans. 90.7%

2. Iodine is to be determined in solution by optical transmission measurement. In carbon tetrachloride the absorption coefficient defined by $k = [\log_{10} (I_0/I)]/$ is 900 l. mole^{-1} cm.$^{-1}$ at 5100 Å. Find the concentration which will correspond to 50% absorption in a 1 cm. cell.

Ans. 3.35×10^{-4} moles liter^{-}

3. Gaseous hydrogen iodide serves as a simple convenient actinometer for mercury resonance radiation (2537 Å). In a given experiment, the radiation from a monochromatic light source of constant intensity, in the form of a short capillary, passes through a diaphragm 0.5 cm. $\times$ 0.5 cm. at a distance of 10 cm. and entirely absorbed in a cell filled with hydrogen iodide. After 10 hr. illumination the cell is cooled in liquid air, and the noncondensable gas (hydrogen) is collected and found to amount to 2 cc. at 27° and 20 mm. Hg pressure. What is the total output of the lamp in quanta per second?

Ans. 1.08×10^{18} quanta sec.$^{-}$

4. Apply the steady-state treatment to the following mechanism for the photolysis of hydrogen iodide:

$$HI + h\nu \rightarrow H + I \quad \text{Rate} = I_a$$
$$H + HI \rightarrow H_2 + I \quad k_2$$
$$H + I_2 \rightarrow HI + I \quad k_3$$
$$I + I \rightarrow I_2$$

and show that the differential rate law obtained is

$$\frac{d(H_2)}{dt} = \frac{d(I_2)}{dt} = \frac{I_a}{1 + k_3(I_2)/k_2(HI)}$$

5. Determine whether the time dependence of the concentration of free radicals in Fig. 16.3 follows a second-order or a first-order rate law.

6. According to an approximation due to Hirschfelder, the value of the activation energy for

$$A + BC \rightarrow AB + C$$

(A is an atom, BC a diatomic molecule) is $E_a = 0.055 \, D_{B-C}$ when the reaction is written in the exothermic direction. Use data in Table 16.2 to estimate activation energies for

(a) $Cl + I_2 \rightarrow ICl + I$

(b) $Cl + H_2 \rightarrow HCl + H$

(c) $H + Br_2 \rightarrow HBr + Br$

(d) $Br + H_2 \rightarrow HBr + H$

Ans. (a) 2.0 kcal. mole^{-}

7. If an energetic electron collides elastically with a helium atom, what is the maximum fractional energy loss by the electron? *Ans.* 1.4×10^{-4}.

8. From equation 16.29 and the values of the parameters given below that equation, predict the initial ion pair yield for radiation decomposition of pure hydrogen bromide. *Ans.* 6.0.

9. The photoionization potentials of many different gaseous molecular species have been measured [K. Watanabe *J. Chem. Phys.*, **26**, 542 (1957)]. The longest wave length which can produce photoionization in CO is 885 Å. Calculate the ionization potential of CO. *Ans.* 14.0 e.v.

10. Given $D_{\text{H}-\text{H}} = 103$ kcal. mole^{-1} and the ionization potential of H = 13.60 e.v., find the appearance potential of H$^+$ from H$_2$. *Ans.* 18.08 e.v.

11. Use the electron affinity of Cl from Table 14.1 together with data from Tables 16.2 and 16.4 to find the energy term for the process

$$CH_4^+ + Cl^- \longrightarrow CH_3 + H + Cl \qquad\qquad Ans.\ 5.1\ \text{e.v.}$$

12. From the fact that $\Delta H \leq 0$ for the process

$$CH_4^+ + CH_4 \longrightarrow CH_5^+ + CH_3$$

find the minimum heat of reaction for

$$CH_4 + H^+ \longrightarrow CH_5^+$$

Use values of ionization potentials from Table 16.4 and bond dissociation energies from Table 16.2. *Ans.* ≤ -4.88 e.v.

13. Using ionization potentials from Table 16.4, evaluate the difference in the energy change for reactions of the type

(1) $R—CH_3^+ \longrightarrow R^+ + CH_3$

as opposed to

(2) $R—CH_3^+ \longrightarrow R + CH_3^+$

for the following:

(a) $C_3H_8^+$.

(b) $C_4H_{10}^+$.

Ans. (a) -1.24 e.v.

14. Using values of ΔH_f of gaseous ions in Table 16.4, evaluate ΔH for the following reactions:

(a) $n\text{-}C_4H_{10}^+ \longrightarrow t\text{-}C_4H_9^+ + H$.

(b) $n\text{-}C_4H_{10}^+ \longrightarrow s\text{-}C_3H_7^+ + CH_3$.

(c) $n\text{-}C_4H_{10}^+ \longrightarrow C_2H_5^+ + C_2H_5$.

(d) $n\text{-}C_4H_{10}^+ \longrightarrow C_4H_8^+ + H_2$.

(e) $n\text{-}C_4H_{10}^+ \longrightarrow C_3H_6^+ + CH_4$.

(f) $n\text{-}C_4H_{10}^+ \longrightarrow C_2H_4^+ + C_2H_6$.

$\Delta H_f(\text{H}) = 51.5$, $\Delta H_f(\text{CH}_3) = 31$, $\Delta H_f(\text{C}_2\text{H}_5) = 24$ kcal. mole^{-1}.

Ans. (a) -1.5 kcal. mole^{-1}.

15. Use data from Table 16.4 to show that for ions listed there the general type of ion-molecule reaction

$$CH_3^+ + C_nH_{2n+2} \longrightarrow C_{n+1}H_{2n+3}^+ + H_2$$

will be exothermic. Find ΔH for the ion-molecule reaction

$$C_2H_5^+ + CH_4 \longrightarrow C_3H_7^+ + H_2$$

---

16. When a mixture of chlorine and carbon monoxide is irradiated, phosgene is formed.

$$CO + Cl_2 \longrightarrow COCl_2$$

The rate law for this reaction is $d(COCl_2)/dt = kI_a^{1/2}\,(CO)^{1/2}(Cl_2)$. Devise a mechanism which fits this rate law.

17. Photolysis of HBr at 1849 Å has been used to produce hot H atoms [R. M. Martin and J. E. Willard, *J. Chem. Phys.*, **40**, 3007 (1964)].

(a) The bonding energy of HBr is 87 kcal. mole^{-1}. Compute the translational energy of an H atom produced in this way.

(b) Compute the translational energy of a D atom produced from DBr in this way.

18. It has been reported that with a potential field of 2.3 v. cm.$^{-1}$, the quantity $(i_s/i_p\,m)$ is 3.65×10^{-15} molecules^{-1} cm.^{3} for the reaction $Ar^+ + H_2 \rightarrow ArH^+ + H$ in a mass spectrometer of source path length $l = 0.24$ cm.

(a) Compute σ_e for this reaction and compare it to the collision cross section σ.

(b) Calculate k, the specific rate constant.

19. B. deB. Darwent [*J. Chem. Phys.*, **18**, 1532 (1950)] has studied the quenching of excited $Hg(^3P_1)$ atoms by hydrocarbons. He has expressed his results in terms of a parameter, τZ_Q, the number of collisions undergone by the excited mercury atom during its lifetime τ. τ for mercury is 1.0×10^{-7} sec. Some of his data follow.

All experiments were at 20°C.

Molecule	Pressure (mm.)	τZ_Q
Neopentane	3.72	0.192
Propane	0.55	0.027
n-butane	1.53	0.166

(a) Use this data to calculate a quenching diameter for each of the three molecules.

(b) Assume that a simple additivity rule relates molecular diameter and the quenching efficiency of a molecule and estimate the quenching diameter of the CH_2 group. Which is a more efficient quencher, the CH_2 group or the CH_3 group?

(c) Compute k_q, the quenching rate constant for the neopentane reaction in units of liters moles^{-1} sec.$^{-1}$.

20. Calculate the cross section for the reaction $Ar^+ + H_2 \rightarrow ArH^+ + H$ for ions accelerated by a field of 1.28 volts cm.$^{-1}$ over a distance of 0.27 cm. α for H_2 is 0.789×10^{-24} cm.^{3} Compare this to the experimental cross section of 254×10^{-16} cm^2. [D. P. Stevenson and D. O. Schissler, *J. Chem. Phys.* **29**, 282 (1958).]

17

CHEMICAL
STATISTICS

17.1 Introduction

A word of caution to the student is in order at this point. The subject matter of this chapter is largely chemical thermodynamics, but the treatment is quite different from that previously employed. In classical thermodynamics the data used describe the properties of matter in bulk, and no assumptions are made about the structure of matter. In the present chapter the data required describe the properties of matter in the atomic and molecular states, using quantum concepts. This, in turn, requires an entirely different and more sustained mathematical treatment. However, the procedures will be within the grasp of students who have had two years of college mathematics. It is not our intention to teach the student the details of calculating useful quantities, but rather to acquaint him with the basic postulates, to give an appreciation of the nature of the methods and to indicate the possibilities of practical applications.

17.2 Equipartition of Energy

We know that classical thermodynamics is inherently incapable of explaining the facts which are the raw material upon which it operates. Our intuition tells us that understanding will be increased by attempting to take the structure of matter into account, by using a model. The heat capacities of gases are suitable for illustration, and the elementary kinetic theory of gases provides an appropriate transition. (See section 11.9.)

The average kinetic energy of translation per molecule of an ideal gas is

$$E_t = \tfrac{1}{2}m(\overline{c_x^2} + \overline{c_y^2} + \overline{c_z^2}) = \tfrac{1}{2}m\overline{c^2} \tag{17.1}$$

519

where $\overline{c^2} = \overline{c_x^2} + \overline{c_y^2} + \overline{c_z^2}$. According to equation (11.46) for 1 mole

$$\tfrac{1}{2}nm\overline{c^2} = \tfrac{3}{2}RT \tag{17.2}$$

and, therefore,

$$E_t = \tfrac{3}{2}RT \text{ per mole} \tag{17.3}$$

Note that equation (17.1) describes the translational energy in terms of three square coordinates, c_x^2, c_y^2, and c_z^2, and that corresponding to each of these square terms there is a contribution of $\tfrac{1}{2}RT$ to equation (17.3). (The choice of coordinates is immaterial and could, for example, be polar coordinates. There would again be three square terms.)

If the ideal gas molecule is assumed to possess only translational energy, E_t represents its thermodynamic internal energy. On this assumption C_v for the gas can be computed from equation (2.22).

$$\left(\frac{\partial E}{\partial T}\right)_V = C_V = \tfrac{3}{2}R \tag{17.4}$$

Therefore, according to the simple kinetic theory of gases C_V for an ideal gas should be 2.98 cal. deg.$^{-1}$ mole^{-1}. Table 17.1 shows that this expectation is realized for monatomic gases, but that polyatomic gases have consistently higher values of C_V. Evidently, these more complex molecules possess energy in forms other than translational. These other forms of energy are, of course, vibrational and rotational, as discussed in Chapter 14.

Vibrational and rotational motions can be treated by the methods of classical mechanics. Both types of motion are found to depend on square terms, with the actual number of such terms depending on the structure of the molecule. Further-more, it can be shown that there is a contribution of $\tfrac{1}{2}RT$ to the total energy of a system of 6.02×10^{23} molecules for each square term, whether translational, vibrational, or rotational, as will be discussed later in this chapter. This classical result is summed up in the *principal of equipartition of energy*, which states that *each square term contributes an equal amount, $\tfrac{1}{2}RT$ per mole, to the internal energy of a system of molecules*. The three square terms for translational energy give, of course, $\tfrac{3}{2}RT$ per mole for the internal energy of monatomic gases, as shown by equation (17.3).

Applying the principle of equipartition first to rotational contributions to the internal energy, we observe that only two coordinates are required to describe the rotational motions of a diatomic molecule (noting that rotation about the internuclear axis is of no consequence). That is, there are two square terms for the rotational energy, and the contribution to the internal energy should be $E_r = RT$ per mole. For linear polyatomic molecules two coordinates again suffice, and in this case, also, the contribution to the internal energy should be $E_r = RT$ per mole. On the other hand, nonlinear polyatomic molecules have no such symmetry, and the rotational energy expression will accordingly contain three square terms. This will lead to a rotational contribution of $E_r = \tfrac{3}{2}RT$ per mole to the internal energy.

The vibrational energy of a simple diatomic harmonic oscillator was discussed in section 14.15, where it was shown that two kinds of energy, potential and kinetic, are involved. Each of these gives rise to one square term, and, therefore, a diatomic molecule should have a contribution of $E_v = RT$ per mole to the total internal energy. In a polyatomic molecule there are many possible vibrational motions, and it can be shown that for a molecule of n atoms the number of vibrational modes is $3n - 5$ for linear molecules and $3n - 6$ for nonlinear molecules.

The foregoing analysis can now be compared with experiment, taking

$$E_{\text{tot.}} = E_t + E_r + E_v \qquad (17.5)$$

Monatomic gases should have $C_V = \frac{3}{2}R \cong 3$ cal. deg.$^{-1}$ mole^{-1}, and this is indeed the case, as shown in Table 17.1. Diatomic molecules should have

$$C_V = \frac{3}{2}R + R + R \cong 7 \text{ cal. deg.}^{-1} \text{ mole}^{-1}$$

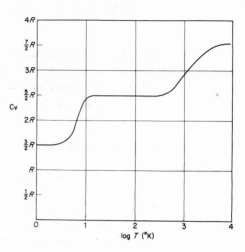

FIG. 17.1. Heat capacity of nitrogen (excluding nuclear spin effects) [from H.L. Johnston and C.O. Davis, J. Am. Chem. Soc., **56**, 271 (1934)].

TABLE 17.1

HEAT CAPACITIES OF GASES

C_V in cal. deg.$^{-1}$ mole^{-1}

Gas	Temperature (°C)		
	0°	100°	400°
He	3.0	3.0	3.0
Ar	3.0	3.0	3.0
Hg	3.0	3.0	3.0
H_2	4.9	5.0	5.0
N_2	5.0	5.0	5.3
CO	5.0	5.0	5.2
CO_2	6.7	7.7	8.5
H_2O	—	6.4	6.7
CH_4	8.6	10.5	16.3

but this is clearly not the case, at least near room temperature, where values of ~ 5 cal. deg.$^{-1}$ mole^{-1} are most common for diatomic molecules. The observed values of C_V for polyatomic molecules are also lower than expected. Evidently the classical equipartition principle does not fully explain these facts.

If C_V is examined over a wide range of temperature, as shown for nitrogen in Fig. 17.1, the nature of the discrepancy becomes clearer. It appears that at low temperatures $C_V \cong \frac{3}{2}R$; that is, there is evidently no vibrational or rotational contribution to the internal energy. At intermediate temperatures values of C_V around $\frac{5}{2}R$ are observed for several diatomic molecules and at still higher temperatures $C_V \cong \frac{7}{2}R$. It will be shown that the first increase in C_V is due to the appearance of the rotational contribution to the internal energy, whereas the second at higher temperatures is due to the vibrational contribution.

Similar variations in heat capacity with temperature are observed for all diatomic and polyatomic molecules. Although classical mechanics correctly predicts the high-temperature limiting value of the heat capacity and explains its origin, the temperature dependence is completely foreign to such a model. The explanation is to be found in the quantum concept of energy, as will be shown in the next section.

17.3 Quantum Effects

Classical theory successfully accounts for the translational component of heat capacity but can give only the high-temperature limiting contributions from rotation and vibration. It will be seen that interpretations based upon quantum theory succeed for all three components. The difference depends upon the relative size of quanta involved in changes of translational, rotational, or vibrational energy. A transition from one quantum state to another by absorption of heat proves to be less likely the larger the quantum.

Quanta of translational energy are defined by equation (13.65) which describes the quantum levels for the particle in a box. For simplicity we shall consider a cubical box of dimension a. Then from equation (13.65),

$$E_t = \frac{h^2}{8ma^2} (n_x^2 + n_y^2 + n_z^2) \tag{17.6}$$

For given m and a the value of E_t depends only upon the quantum numbers. The unit of translational energy is given by $h^2/8ma^2$ and approximates 10^{-31} erg for a molecule of nitrogen in a 1 cm.^{3} box. This value should be compared with $kT \cong 5 \times 10^{-14}$ ergs at 300°K.

The energy of rotation for a rigid linear molecule in the rotational state of quantum number J is given by equation (14.21) as

$$E_r = \frac{J(J+1)h^2}{8\pi^2 I} \tag{17.7}$$

where $I = \mu r_0^2$ is the moment of inertia. The degeneracy of rotational energy states is $2J + 1$. That is, there are $2J + 1$ states of identical energy for each value of J.

Taking the rotational moment of inertia of nitrogen from Table 14.6 and using equation (17.7), we find that the rotational energy for $J = 1$ is 7.9×10^{-16} erg per molecule, much smaller than kT at 300°K. (Note also Exercise 14.10, which shows that for hydrogen, with exceptionally small I, E_r is comparable with kT for $J = 1$.)

From equation (14.29) the quantum of vibrational energy for a harmonic oscillator is

$$\Delta E_v = h\omega \tag{17.8}$$

where ω is the characteristic or fundamental frequency. From Table 14.6, the fundamental vibration frequency of nitrogen is 2360 cm.$^{-1}$, and therefore the quantum of vibrational energy is 4.69×10^{-13} erg per molecule, somewhat larger than kT at 300°K.

A qualitative and intuitive explanation of the temperature dependence of the heat capacity is now evident. Clearly, at all except the very lowest temperatures the quantum of translational energy is very small compared to kT, which is a measure of the average translational energy. On the other hand, the vibrational quantum is somewhat larger than the average translational energy at room temperature and below. This suggests that vibrational energy changes cannot contribute to the internal energy and heat capacity. Rotational energy is intermediate, kT being larger than the rotational quantum at room temperature for most molecules, but at low temperatures the situation is reversed. On this basis the assignment of contributions to the heat capacity shown in Fig. 17.4 may be made.

17.4 Energy Distribution

Let us now consider how the quantization of energy affects a system of molecules at constant energy. It is a convenient device in such considerations to replace the actual system (of molecules) by an idealized system whose behavior is well understood. In the present case it will be expedient to choose a system of distinguishable harmonic oscillators which have the convenient property of equally spaced energy levels. For numerical simplicity, take 100 oscillators (molecules) with a fixed total energy of five equal quanta. We shall assume that a molecule can be assigned to any one of the six energy states identified by the energies 5q, 4q, 3q, 2q, q, and 0, where q represents the value of the quantum. We shall designate these as states 5, 4, 3, 2, 1, and 0. We shall further postulate that these quanta are randomly distributed; that is, at constant energy any one arrangement of quanta is as probable as any other. This extremely important postulate is fundamental to the statistical approach to the treatment of matter. We shall regard it as justified by the success of the structure erected upon it.

A possible arrangement or statistical state of the system, designated as state a, corresponds to one molecule with 5 quanta ($n_5 = 1$) and 99 with none ($n_0 = 99$). There are 100 different ways to realize this arrangement, the various ways corresponding to the assignment of the five quanta to each one of the hundred molecules. Therefore, we shall say that the thermodynamic probability of this arrangement, W_a, is 100, as given by the expression

$$W_a = \frac{n!}{n_0!\,n_5!} = \frac{100!}{99!\,1!} = 100.$$

Another possible state of the system (designated as g) consists of five molecules with one quantum of energy ($n_1 = 5$). This arrangement can be achieved in $100 \times 99 \times 98 \times 97 \times 96$ or $100!/95!$ different ways. However there are 5! permutations which do not change the identity of the five particles to which the single quantum of energy is assigned, but merely alter the order in which they are selected. Therefore the number of significant arrangements is a factor $(1/5!)$

lower than the total number of arrangements, and we have

$$W_g = \frac{100!}{95! \, 5!}$$

In general, when a total of n molecules are arranged with n_0 in the lowest energy group, n_1 in the next, etc., the number of arrangements at constant total energy is given by

$$W = \frac{n!}{n_0! \, n_1! \, n_2! \ldots n_i! \ldots} \tag{17.9}$$

This expression is now used to determine the relative probability W for all distributions of 100 molecules among five energy levels at a constant total energy of five equal quanta. The results of these calculations in Table 17.2 can be understood in the following sense. When the system reaches thermal equilibrium, it changes at random from one distribution to another. The two distributions a and b have relative probabilities $W_a = 100$ and $W_b = 9900$, so the latter will occur 99 times as frequently as the former. In general, the frequency of occurrence of any distribution k will be given by the ratio of W_k to the sum of all possible values of W, ΣW_i. It is notable that one of these distributions occurs with a much greater frequency than any other.

EXERCISE 17.1

Use equation (17.9) to evaluate W_b and W_d in Table 17.2.

In systems containing very large numbers of molecules (e.g., 6×10^{23}) it can be shown that the relative probability of the most probable statistical distribution $W_{max.}$ is very much greater than the probability of occurrence of a slightly different state which is denoted by $W_{max.} + \Delta W$. As an illustration of exaggerated simplicity, consider the probability that $2n$ molecules are divided $n + \Delta n$ and $n - \Delta n$ between connected containers of equal volume at the same temperature as a result of random fluctuation.

TABLE 17.2

THE DISTRIBUTION OF EQUAL QUANTA AMONG MOLECULES

Entry	Number quanta	n_5	n_4	n_3	n_2	n_1	n_0	log W	log $\Sigma W/W$	$W/\Sigma W$ (%)
a	5	1	0	0	0	0	99	2.000	5.964	0.00
b	5	0	1	0	0	1	98	3.996	3.968	0.01
c	5	0	0	1	1	0	98	3.996	3.968	0.01
d	5	0	0	1	0	2	97	5.686	2.278	0.53
e	5	0	0	0	2	1	97	5.686	2.278	0.53
f	5	0	0	0	1	3	96	7.196	0.768	17.1
g	5	0	0	0	0	5	95	7.877	0.084	81.9
h	6	0	0	2	0	0	98	3.695	5.517	0.00
i	6	0	0	1	1	1	97	5.987	3.225	0.06
j	6	0	0	1	0	3	96	7.196	2.016	1.0

It can be shown[1] that the probability for unequal distribution, $W_{max.} + \Delta W$, is related to that for equal distribution, $W_{max.}$, by

$$\ln \frac{W_{max.} + \Delta W}{W_{max.}} \cong -\frac{(\Delta n)^2}{n}$$

For $n = 10^{20}$ and $\Delta n/n = 10^{-6}$ the probability of even this small deviation is only e^{-10^8}. It is not possible to detect such small statistical fluctuations in density. For fewer particles, as in some measurements with colloids, the fluctuations may be observable.

EXERCISE 17.2

During what fraction of time would an aerosol of 2×10^6 identical particles distributed randomly between two equal volumes show a 1% fluctuation from uniform distribution?   *Ans.* $10^{-86.8}$.

It is pertinent to ask how the population of any particular energy level is affected by the total available energy. To illustrate, choose 100 molecules with six equal quanta and consider only arrangements containing at least one molecule with three quanta. The results appear as entries h, i, j, in Table 17.2. Values of W for this group cannot be compared with the preceding group a–g, because the ΣW are not the same. The quantities to be compared are the normalized ratios $W/\Sigma W$ for entries c, d, and h, i, j. The former comprise 0.54% of available distributions, the latter 1.06%. This shows that increasing the energy of a molecular system increases the fraction of states with high energy.

17.5 The Boltzmann Distribution Law

The preceding considerations need not be restricted to one kind of energy nor to small samples. To generalize the treatment, let us consider n similar, indistinguishable molecules which are *localized* in space and which are *independent* of each other. The requirement that the molecules be localized means that the average position of each molecule is fixed, but allows vibrations about this average position. Crystals in which molecules are at fixed lattice points obviously meet this requirement. By the requirement that the molecules be independent, we mean that at any given instant all properties of one molecule must be independent of the properties of every other molecule.

Now we shall consider the energy of the various molecules. Each molecule may exist in any of its allowed quantum states. The energies of these states must be specified relative to that of the lowest state. The energy, ϵ_i, in excess of this lowest energy is characteristic of the ith quantum state and is, of course, zero for the lowest state. The energy, ϵ_i, can include contributions from translational, rotational, vibrational, and electronic states. There are, on a time average, n_i

---

[1] M. Dole, *Introduction to Statistical Thermodynamics* (Prentice-Hall, Inc., Englewood Cliffs, N. J. 1954), p. 44.

molecules of energy ϵ_i, although the population of the ith state is made up of different molecules at each instant of time as energy is transferred from molecule to molecule.

The total number of molecules, n, must remain constant, and is the sum of the numbers of molecules in each of the available s quantum states. That is,

$$n_0 + n_1 + n_2 + \ldots + n_i + \ldots + n_s = n \tag{17.10}$$

The summation equation 17.10 is conveniently represented by $\sum_{i=0}^{i=s} n_i$ or, more simply, by Σn_i. Summations of other quantities will be represented similarly. It is to be understood that such summations are to be carried out over all quantum states.

Representing the lowest possible energy of the system by E_0 (the zero point energy) and the constant total energy by E, we may write

$$n_0 \epsilon_0 + n_1 \epsilon_1 + n_2 \epsilon_2 + \ldots + n_i \epsilon_i + \ldots = \Sigma n_i \epsilon_i = E - E_0 \tag{17.11}$$

There are a great many ways to distribute the energy $E - E_0$ among n molecules. Another distribution is

$$n_0' \epsilon_0 + n_1' \epsilon_1 + n_2' \epsilon_2 + \ldots + n_i' \epsilon_i + \ldots = \Sigma n_i' \epsilon_i = E - E_0$$

Terms in ϵ_0 equal zero but have been included for the sake of completeness.

The total number of ways to distribute the fixed, available energy is W, the number of possible arrangements of n distinguishable objects among s groups, or

$$W = \frac{n!}{n_0! n_1! n_2! \ldots n_i! \ldots n_s!} \tag{17.12}$$

In other words, this is the number of ways to arrange n molecules to give n_0 with energy ϵ_0, n_1 with energy ϵ_1, n_2 with energy ϵ_2, etc.

Using our previous numerical example as a guide, we *identify the equilibrium state of the system with the most probable state* for which $W = W_{\text{max.}}$. Following the usual procedure for maximizing the value of a function, let $dW = 0$. An equivalent and more convenient choice is to let $d \ln W = 0$.

Taking the logarithm of W, we have

$$\ln W = \ln n! - \ln n_0! - \ln n_1! - \ln n_2! - \ldots - \ln n_i! - \ldots$$

$$\ln W = \ln n! - \Sigma \ln n_i! \tag{17.13}$$

The second term can be simplified by using Stirling's approximation for large numbers, $\ln n! = n \ln n - n$, yielding[2]

$$\ln W = \ln n! - \Sigma(n_i \ln n_i - n_i) \tag{17.14}$$

Differentiating $\ln W$, remembering that n is a constant, yields

$$d \ln W = -\Sigma d(n_i \ln n_i - n_i) = 0 \tag{17.15}$$

---

[2]This is demonstrated in Appendix 1.

for the condition of maximum probability. This can be simplified as follows:

$$\Sigma[n_i(dn_i/n_i) + \ln n_i dn_i - dn_i] = 0$$
$$\Sigma \ln n_i dn_i = 0 \tag{17.16}$$

There are two additional conditions to be satisfied, namely

$$\Sigma dn_i = dn = 0 \tag{17.17}$$

$$\Sigma \epsilon_i dn_i = dE = 0 \tag{17.18}$$

That is, the number of particles and the total energy of the system are both fixed. In order to satisfy these conditions simultaneously, it is necessary to multiply two of the equations by arbitrary constants[3] α and β and combine the resulting equations to give

$$\Sigma(\ln n_i + \alpha + \beta \epsilon_i)dn_i = 0 \tag{17.19}$$

The variables in equation (17.19) are independent of each other for each term of the summation. That is, for this equation to remain valid for every possible variation in dn_i it must be that each coefficient of dn_i individually equals zero. That is,

$$\ln n_i + \alpha + \beta \epsilon_i = 0$$

or

$$n_i = e^{-\alpha}e^{-\beta \epsilon_i} \tag{17.20}$$

The factor $e^{-\alpha}$ can be evaluated from the summation of n_i over all states.

$$\Sigma n_i = n = e^{-\alpha}\Sigma e^{-\beta \epsilon_i} \tag{17.21}$$

These two equations are then combined to give the fraction of molecules in a given state.

$$\frac{n_i}{n} = \frac{e^{-\beta \epsilon_i}}{\Sigma e^{-\beta \epsilon_i}} \tag{17.22}$$

The numerical example in the preceding section showed that increasing the energy content of a system increased the number n_i of molecules having energy ϵ_i in excess of ϵ_0. It is well known that in molecular systems the total energy content of a given number of molecules is greater, the greater the temperature. For equation (17.22) correctly to describe this behavior, β must decrease with increasing temperature. Accordingly, we *define* a temperature scale by equation (17.22) and the relation $\beta = 1/kT$, where k is a proportionality constant. Without proof, the constant k is identified with Boltzmann's constant[4], which is related to the molar gas constant R and Avogadro's number N by $R = Nk$. The equation of energy distribution (17.22) is now written in its final form

$$\frac{n_i}{n} = \frac{e^{-\epsilon_i/kT}}{\Sigma e^{-\epsilon_i/kT}} \tag{17.23}$$

---

[3]This is Lagrange's method of undetermined multipliers which is explained in K. S. Pitzer, *Quantum Chemistry* (Prentice-Hall, Inc., Englewood Cliffs, N. J., 1953), p. 102.
[4]See K. S. Pitzer, *op. cit.*, p. 110.

This is the Boltzmann law. Although we have derived it on the assumption of localized molecules, as we shall see below, it can easily be extended to non-localized systems such as those consisting of ideal gas molecules.

EXERCISE 17.3

Show that when $\epsilon_i = 5kT$ or more for the first state above ϵ_0, with other states correspondingly higher, Boltzmann's law may be written $n_i/n = e^{-\epsilon_i/kT}$ as an adequate approximation.

17.6 The Partition Function

The summation $\Sigma e^{-\epsilon_i/kT}$ in equation (17.23) is to be performed over all *quantum states*. If two or more quantum states, as p, q, have the same or nearly the same energy, $\epsilon_p = \epsilon_q$, a term for each must be included. In general, if there are g_i such degenerate states with a common energy ϵ_i, they may for convenience be grouped together, since they contain equal numbers of molecules, as $g_i e^{-\epsilon_i/kT}$. The factor g_i is the *degeneracy* or the *statistical weight*.

The denominator of equation (17.23) is the *partition function Q*. That is,

$$Q = \Sigma g_i e^{-\epsilon_i/kT} = g_0 e^{-\epsilon_0/kT} + g_1 e^{-\epsilon_1/kT} + \ldots + g_i e^{-\epsilon_i/kT} + \ldots \quad (17.24)$$

EXERCISE 17.4

Remembering that energies are measured with reference to the ground state and referring to equation 17.11, show that Q approaches unity as its minimum value if $g_0 = 1$. Show that its value is greater, the more closely the sequence of energy states are spaced. Use the energy sequences (a) $\epsilon_1 = 5kT$, $\epsilon_2 = 10kT$, ... ; (b) $\epsilon_1 = kT$, $\epsilon_2 = 2kT$, ... ; (c) $\epsilon_1 = 0.5kT$, $\epsilon_2 = 1.0kT$, ... ; etc.

The relative population of any two quantum states p and q is given by the ratio n_p/n_q obtained by application of equation (17.23).

$$\frac{n_p}{n_q} = \frac{ne^{-\epsilon_p/kT}/\Sigma e^{-\epsilon_i/kT}}{ne^{-\epsilon_q/kT}/\Sigma e^{-\epsilon_i/kT}}$$
$$= e^{-(\epsilon_p - \epsilon_q)/kT} \quad (17.25)$$

If these two states are degenerate, that is, if $\epsilon_p = \epsilon_q$, it follows that they are equally populated. If $\epsilon_p > \epsilon_q$, then $n_p < n_q$. Note that as long as $\epsilon_p - \epsilon_q < kT$ the populations will be of the same order of magnitude. Furthermore, if there are many low-lying states of energy substantially lower than kT, they all will be well populated relative to the ground state. A further consequence of such uniform distribution is that no one state is heavily populated. Such distributions correspond to large values of Q. In contrast, widely spaced energy levels result in very uneven distributions of molecules among states and values of Q approaching unity. These situations are illustrated in Table 17.3 and Fig. 17.2. Equal energy intervals have been taken for convenience but are not essential to the argument. The Boltzmann distributions in the figure and table illustrate that molecules are largely confined to their lowest energy levels when $\epsilon \gg kT$. Conversely, small energy gradations from level to level result in more nearly uniform distributions of molecules among the available states.

TABLE 17.3
EFFECT OF QUANTUM SIZE UPON POPULATIONS OF STATES

State	ϵ_i/kT	$e^{-\epsilon_i/kT}$	n_i/n	ϵ_j/kT	$e^{-\epsilon_j/kT}$	n_j/n	ϵ_k/kT	$e^{-\epsilon_k/kT}$	n_k/n
0	0	1.0000	0.9932	0	1.0000	0.6317	0.0	1.0000	0.0952
1	5	0.0067	0.0066	1	0.3679	0.2324	0.1	0.9048	0.0861
2	10	0.0000	0.0000	2	0.1353	0.0855	0.2	0.8187	0.0779
3	15	0.0000	0.0000	3	0.0498	0.0315	0.3	0.7408	0.0705
4	20			4	0.0183	0.0116	0.4	0.6703	0.0638
5	25			5	0.0067	0.0042	0.5	0.6065	0.0577
6	30			6	0.0025	0.0016	0.6	0.5488	0.0522
7	35			7	0.0009	0.0006	0.7	0.4966	0.0473
8	40			8	0.0003	0.0002	0.8	0.4493	0.0428
9	45			9	0.0001	0.0001	0.9	0.4066	0.0387
10	50			10	0.0000	0.0000	1.0	0.3679	0.0350
	$Q = 1.0068$			$Q = 1.583$			$Q = 10.508$		

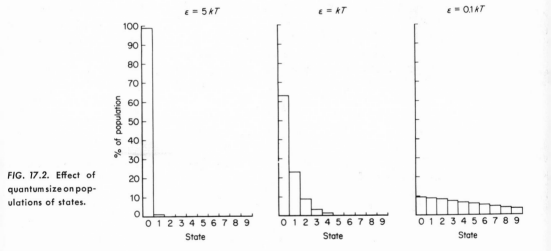

FIG. 17.2. Effect of quantum size on populations of states.

The energy term ϵ in the preceding equations represents the total energy of the molecule. It includes contributions ϵ_t for translation, ϵ_r for rotation, ϵ_v for vibration, and ϵ_e for electronic excitation. It may be expressed

$$\epsilon = \epsilon_t + \epsilon_r + \epsilon_v + \epsilon_e \qquad (17.26)$$

By limiting our considerations to moderate temperatures, it can be assumed that there is no interaction between the various degrees of freedom. It is readily seen that the amount of internal energy should not affect the translational energy. On the other hand, electronic excitation may appreciably affect force constants and, therefore, the vibrational energy. Also, in higher vibrational states the internuclear separation differs from that in the ground state. This

affects the moment of inertia and therefore the rotational energy. Except a
relatively high temperatures the assumed freedom of interaction does not lea
to serious error. It is then possible to write

$$e^{-\epsilon/kT} = e^{-(\epsilon_t + \epsilon_r + \epsilon_v + \epsilon_e)/kT}$$

$$= e^{-\epsilon_t/kT} \times e^{-\epsilon_r/kT} \times e^{-\epsilon_v/kT} \times e^{-\epsilon_e/kT}$$

Correspondingly, the partition function can be factored.

$$\Sigma e^{-\epsilon/kT} = \Sigma e^{-\epsilon_t/kT} \times \Sigma e^{-\epsilon_r/kT} \times \Sigma e^{-\epsilon_v/kT} \times \Sigma e^{-\epsilon_e/kT} \qquad (17.27$$

Each of the factors on the right-hand side of equation (17.27) is a partia
partition function and will be represented by q with appropriate subscript. I
abbreviated notation this becomes

$$Q = q_t \times q_r \times q_v \times q_e \qquad (17.28$$

17.7 Thermodynamic Properties

The preceding discussion has shown that in principle the Boltzman
equation can describe the energy content and its temperature dependence fo
a system of localized, independent molecules, i.e., a crystal. In other words, i
can be used to "predict" heat capacities. The usual thermodynamic definitio
of heat capacity $C_V = (\partial E/\partial T)_V$ provides a convenient starting point an
suggests that we first obtain an expression for the internal energy. By equation
(17.11), (17.23), and (17.24) for a system of n molecules

$$E - E_0 = n_0 \epsilon_0 + n_1 \epsilon_1 + n_2 \epsilon_2 + \ldots + n_i \epsilon_i + \ldots$$

and

$$n_i = \frac{n}{Q} g_i e^{-\epsilon_i/kT}$$

By simple combination of these two equations, there follows an expression fo
the energy of the system.

$$E - E_0 = \frac{\epsilon_0 n}{Q} g_0 e^{-\epsilon_0/kT} + \frac{\epsilon_1 n}{Q} g_1 e^{-\epsilon_1/kT} + \ldots$$
$$+ \frac{\epsilon_i n}{Q} g_i e^{-\epsilon_i/kT} + \ldots \qquad (17.29$$

This equation can be written in alternative form, since it follows from equation
(17.24) that

$$\left(\frac{\partial Q}{\partial T}\right)_V = \frac{g_0 \epsilon_0 e^{-\epsilon_0/kT}}{kT^2} + \frac{g_1 \epsilon_1 e^{-\epsilon_1/kT}}{kT^2} + \ldots + \frac{g_i \epsilon_i e^{-\epsilon_i/kT}}{kT^2} + \ldots \qquad (17.30$$

The differentiation is carried out at constant volume, because the energies of
the various states, ϵ_0, ϵ_1, ϵ_2, etc., may be volume dependent. Multiplying each
term in equation (17.30) by kT^2/Q yields

$$\frac{kT^2}{Q}\left(\frac{\partial Q}{\partial T}\right)_V = \frac{g_0 \epsilon_0 e^{-\epsilon_0/kT}}{Q} + \frac{g_1 \epsilon_1 e^{-\epsilon_1/kT}}{Q} + \ldots + \frac{g_i \epsilon_i e^{-\epsilon_i/kT}}{Q} + \ldots \qquad (17.31$$

The internal energy of the system can now be expressed in terms of the partition
function of the system by combining equations (17.29) and (17.31).

$$E - E_0 = \frac{nkT^2}{Q} \left(\frac{\partial Q}{\partial T}\right)_V = nkT^2 \left(\frac{\partial \ln Q}{\partial T}\right)_V \qquad (17.32)$$

For an Avogadro's number N of molecules, replace Nk by R to give

$$E - E_0 = RT^2 \left(\frac{\partial \ln Q}{\partial T}\right)_V \qquad (17.33)$$

It follows at once that the molar heat capacity of a system whose energy distribution is described by the Boltzmann law is given by

$$C_V = \left(\frac{\partial E}{\partial T}\right)_V = \left[\frac{\partial}{\partial T}\left(\frac{RT^2 \, \partial \ln Q}{\partial T}\right)\right]_V \qquad (17.34)$$

EXERCISE 17.5

Use the data of Table 17.3 and equations (17.11) and (17.23) to evaluate $E - E_0$ for 1 mole of gas when $\epsilon/kT = 5$, 10, 15, etc., and compare with $\epsilon/kT = 1, 2, 3$, etc.

The total energy of a system can be conveniently resolved into its separate contributions from translation, rotation, vibration, and electronic excitation because the partition function can be correspondingly factored. Expressing equation (17.28) as

$$\ln Q = \ln q_t + \ln q_r + \ln q_v + \ln q_e$$

and substituting into equation (17.33) gives

$$E - E_0 = RT^2 \left(\frac{\partial \ln q_t}{\partial T}\right)_V + RT^2 \left(\frac{\partial \ln q_r}{\partial T}\right)_V + RT^2 \left(\frac{\partial \ln q_v}{\partial T}\right)_V + RT^2 \left(\frac{\partial \ln q_e}{\partial T}\right)_V$$
$$(17.35)$$

By comparing equations (17.34) and (17.35), we see that the heat capacity can be simply expressed as the sum of separate contributions from each of the various types of internal energy.

$$C_V = C_t + C_r + C_v + C_e \qquad (17.36)$$

The experimental evidence for this equation was discussed above. The separate contributions will be examined presently term by term, but let us first relate some of the other thermodynamic properties of a system to the partition function. We shall begin with entropy.

The Boltzmann relationship between entropy and probability

$$S = k \ln W \qquad (17.37)$$

was originally postulated in section 6.7 on the basis of the similarity between equations describing entropy of mixing and the probability of achieving a specified mixture. Equation (17.37) makes the reasonable but unproven assumption that since in the equilibrium state both entropy and probability have their maximum values, they can be related. As we have said earlier, on this basis an increase in the entropy of a closed system is a consequence of the natural tendency of a system to go from a less probable state to a more probable state. As is true of all such postulates, equation (17.37) must be justified by its consequences. Expressions for the computation of entropy changes must be developed, and the computed entropy changes compared to experimental values. As a first step toward this goal, we shall develop expressions for the entropy of localized systems such as ideal crystals in terms of partition functions.

From equation (17.14) for localized systems and from equation (6.63), Stirling's approximation,[2] we see that

$$\ln W = n \ln n - n - \Sigma(n_i \ln n_i - n_i)$$

Since $\Sigma n_i = n$, this equation becomes

$$\ln W = n \ln n - \Sigma n_i \ln n_i$$

Using equations (17.29) and (17.11), and considering Avogadro's number of molecules,

$$\ln W = N \ln Q + \frac{1}{kT}(E - E_0)$$

or

$$W = Q^N e^{(E-E_0)/kT} \tag{17.38}$$

EXERCISE 17.6

Derive (17.38) from the expression starting with (17.14) and using the method outlined in the text.

Substitution of this result into equation (17.37) and using (17.33) gives

$$S = R \ln Q + \frac{E - E_0}{T}$$
$$= R \ln Q + RT \left(\frac{\partial \ln Q}{\partial T}\right)_v \tag{17.39}$$

By equations (17.24) and (17.30) at the absolute zero of temperature, equation (17.39) becomes $S_0 = R \ln g_0$. If $g_0 = 1$, as it will for perfect crystals if nuclear effects are neglected, S_0 will be zero, and we arrive at a statement of the third law of thermodynamics. However, if at absolute zero molecules can be randomly distributed between two different states, then $g_0 = 2$, and there will be a residual entropy of $R \ln 2$. (Recall the discussion in section 6.7.)

We have now developed equations for both E and S in terms of partition functions. Since all thermodynamic functions can be expressed in terms of E and S, all thermodynamic functions can be expressed in terms of partition functions.

As we have already mentioned, the preceding set of equations relating thermodynamic quantities and the partition function were all developed on the assumption of independent localized molecules, such as are found in a crystal. These molecules possess vibrational energy, but possess neither rotational nor translational energy. The situation is quite different with an ideal gas, in which all three types of energy are possible. In particular, the fact that the gas molecules possess translational energy and, therefore, cannot be considered as localized requires some modification of the treatment. We shall now attempt to explain why this is so. A crystal is essentially an array of distinguishable lattice points which can be occupied by molecules. Thus, we can assign two quanta of energy to lattice point A, and one quantum of energy to lattice point B, each point being occupied by a molecule. This assignment is physically distinguishable from that which assigns one quantum of energy to A and two quanta to B, since *the two lattice points are physically distinguishable*. This is indicated schematically in Fig. 17.3. Indeed, in our previous discussion we arrived at the expression for W by assuming these to be different arrangements.

FIG. 17.3. Schematic illustration of (a) distinguishable permutations in a localized system; (b) indistinguishable permutations in a non-localized system.

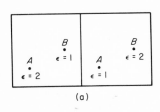

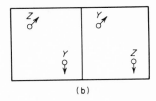

(a)

(b)

Now consider an ideal gas, the molecules of which possess translational energy. Since the gas molecules are not localized, it is convenient to label them for counting purposes in terms of their positions and velocities. In one possible arrangement molecule Y is in location 1, and possesses velocity v, while molecule Z is in location 2 and possesses a different velocity, v' (Fig. 17.3). In another arrangement molecule Z is in location 1 with velocity v, while molecule Y is in location 2 with velocity v'. However, although lattice points A and B are distinguishable, molecules Y and Z are not. Therefore, the two arrangements which we have just discussed are indistinguishable, and if we count both, we overcount by the number of permutations of the labels Z and Y, 2!. Suppose that there are three such indistinguishable molecules. The possible number of permutations of the labels is 3!, and, therefore, we must reduce W as computed from equation (17.38) by a factor of 1/3!. For N such molecules the number of permutations is $N!$. Therefore, for an ideal gas the probability of a given arrangement is reduced from that of the ideal crystal by a factor of $1/N!$. Applying this factor to equation (17.38), we find that the probability for the equilibrium distribution in the ideal gas W_g, is given by

$$W_g = \left(\frac{Q^N}{N^N}\right) e^N e^{(E-E_0)/kT} \tag{17.40}$$

where Stirling's approximation has been used to substitute for $N!$. Substituting equation (17.40) into equation (17.37), the Boltzmann relation, we find that for the ideal gas

$$S = Nk \ln Q - Nk \ln N + Nk + \frac{(E - E_0)}{T}$$

or

$$S = R \ln \left(\frac{Q}{N}\right) + R + \frac{(E - E_0)}{T} \tag{17.41}$$

Although the entropy expressions differ for the nonlocalized system as exemplified by the ideal gas, and for the localized system as exemplified by the perfect crystal, the internal energy, E, of both is given by equation (17.33). (See exercise 17.7.)

EXERCISE 17.7

Use equation (17.40) and show that the Boltzmann distribution law, equation (17.23), which was developed for a crystal, is also valid for an ideal gas, and that therefore equation (17.33), which is based on (17.23), gives E for an ideal gas.

The free energy of one mole of a perfect gas is

$$F = E + RT - TS$$

Substituting for S from equation (17.41) gives

$$F = E + RT - RT \ln \left(\frac{Q}{N} \right) - E + E_0 - RT = E_0 - RT \ln \left(\frac{Q}{N} \right) \quad (17.42)$$

The change in free energy for a thermodynamic change in state is then

$$\Delta F = \Delta E_0 - RT \Delta \ln \left(\frac{Q}{N} \right)$$

For a chemical change involving reactants and products in their standard states

$$\Delta F^\circ = \Delta E_0^\circ - RT \Delta \ln \left(\frac{Q^\circ}{N} \right)$$

The related expression for the equilibrium constant is

$$\ln K = - \frac{\Delta F^\circ}{RT} = \Delta \ln \left(\frac{Q^\circ}{N} \right) - \frac{\Delta E_0^\circ}{RT} \quad (17.43)$$

The equilibrium constant for any change in state

$$aA + bB + \ldots = mM + nN + \ldots$$

is also conveniently expressed

$$K = \frac{(Q_M^\circ/N)^m (Q_N^\circ/N)^n \ldots}{(Q_A^\circ/N)^a (Q_B^\circ/N)^b \ldots} e^{-\Delta E_0^\circ/RT} \quad (17.44)$$

It is both interesting and important that equation (17.44) can be used to evaluate equilibrium constants. The data required are the calorimetrically measured heat of reaction ΔE_0° and other information from spectroscopy, which will be examined next.

Equation (17.44) clearly reveals that the position of an equilibrium is the result of two effects, an energy effect and an entropy effect. Products are favored by an exothermic energy term, and also by the products having a greater number of readily accessible quantum states than do the reactants, resulting in a favorable entropy term.

EXERCISE 17.8

Show that the pre-exponential factor in equation (17.44) depends upon the entropy change of the reaction.

17.8 Evaluation of Partition Functions

The partition function for translation is the same for all perfect gases. Since it is a factor of the total partition function, it is an advantage to determine it once for all. The increment of energy between adjacent energy levels of translation is so small [see equation (17.6)] that the partition function can be evaluated by integration over all quantum states. In other words, the function is effectively continuous.

For one degree of translational freedom, say along the x-axis, let $h^2/8ma_x^2$ of equation (17.6) be represented by ϵ_x. Then, by the definition of the partition function and considering that $n_x \geq 1$, we have

$$q_x = \sum_0^\infty e^{-\epsilon_t/kT} = \sum_{n_x=1}^\infty e^{-(n_x^2-1)\epsilon_x/kT}$$

Recalling that $\epsilon_x \ll kT$, we see that it is permissible to replace $n_x^2 - 1$ by n_x^2 and to replace summation by integration. Then[5]

$$q_x = \int_0^\infty e^{-n_x^2\epsilon_x/kT}\, dn_x = \frac{1}{2}\left(\frac{\pi kT}{\epsilon_x}\right)^{1/2} \tag{17.45}$$

Substituting for ϵ_x gives the important relation

$$q_x = \frac{(2\pi mkT)^{1/2}}{h}\, a_x \tag{17.46}$$

Since the components of translational energy along the x, y, and z axes are independent and separable, it follows that the partition function for translation in three dimensions can be factored into its one-dimensional components. Considering that q_x, q_y, and q_z are similar, we can write at once

$$q_t = q_x q_y q_z = \frac{(2\pi mkT)^{3/2}V}{h^3} \tag{17.47}$$

where $V = a_x a_y a_z =$ the volume of the container.

For rotational states degeneracy must be considered explicitly. A linear molecule possesses two rotational degrees of freedom. For J quanta there are $(2J + 1)$ possible quantum states for a given energy level. That is, there are $2J + 1$ terms of the type $e^{-\epsilon_J/kT}$ for each energy level ϵ_J. The rotational partition function q_r for linear molecules, by equations (17.7) and (17.24), is

$$q_r = \sum_J (2J + 1)e^{-J(J+1)h^2/8\pi^2 IkT} \tag{17.48}$$

Rotational energy levels are sufficiently closely spaced that it is again possible,

---

[5]Equation (17.45) is a standard integral

$$\int_0^\infty e^{-c^2z^2}\, dz = \pi^{1/2}/2c$$

where $c^2 = h^2/8mkTa_x^2$
see Appendix 1.

in almost all cases, to replace summation by integration from $J = 0$ to $J = \infty$, giving

$$q_r = \frac{8\pi^2 IkT}{h^2} \tag{17.49}$$

EXERCISE 17.9

Integrate equation (17.48) by substituting $c = h^2/8\pi^2 IkT$ and $J(J + 1) = z$. Observe that $dz = (2J + 1)\, dJ$.

The spectra of symmetric linear molecules such as H—H, O=O, N≡N, O=C=O, H—C≡C—H, etc., show that only half of the J values are actually possible for any given molecule. In some cases it is the even values of J and in other cases the odd values of J that occur. This effect reduces q_r to one-half the value in equation (17.49). It is customary to introduce a symmetry number σ, which is the number of equivalent or indistinguishable molecular orientations. Then the rotational partition function for linear molecules becomes

$$q_r = \frac{8\pi^2 IkT}{h^2 \sigma} \tag{17.50}$$

and $\sigma = 2$ for symmetrical linear molecules since end-for-end rotation yields an equivalent orientation. On the other hand $\sigma = 1$ for unsymmetrical linear molecules such as H—Cl, O=C=S, etc.

For the nonlinear polyatomic molecule the appropriate partition function is

$$q_r = \frac{8\pi^2 (8\pi^3 ABC)^{1/2}(kT)^{3/2}}{\sigma h^3} \tag{17.51}$$

where A, B, and C are the moments of inertia about the three principal axes.

The vibrational partition function is

$$q_v = \Sigma e^{-\epsilon_v/kT}$$

where ϵ_v is the vibrational energy as measured from the lowest state ($v = 0$). Substituting for ϵ_v by equation (14.29) gives

$$q_v = \Sigma e^{-vh\omega/kT} \tag{17.52}$$

where ω is the fundamental vibration frequency. Vibrational states are nondegenerate, and the quantum numbers v constitute a simple arithmetic progression, $v = 0, 1, 2, \ldots$. Representing $h\omega/kT$ by U the preceding summation becomes

$$\Sigma e^{-vU} = 1 + e^{-U} + e^{-2U} + \ldots + e^{-vU} + \ldots$$

which is the familiar series $(1 - e^{-U})^{-1}$. Correspondingly, the vibrational partition function in terms of energy measured above the zero-point level is

$$q_v = \frac{1}{(1 - e^{-h\omega/kT})} \tag{17.53}$$

For most diatomic molecules at ordinary temperature the value of q_v is nearly unity because $h\omega$ is appreciably greater than kT. This is illustrated by considering HCl for which the energy difference between the states $v = 1$ and $v = 0$ is 5.75×10^{-13} erg, and at 298°K the value of $h\omega/kT$ is 14.0. The relative populations of these two states are

$$\frac{n_1}{n_0} = e^{-\Delta\epsilon/kT} = e^{-14.0}$$

Still higher states will have still smaller populations, and we conclude that at 298°K practically all molecules of HCl are in the ground vibrational state and that q_v is 1.000001.

Weak valence bonds and heavy atoms make for low fundamental frequencies and for vibrational excitation at lower temperatures. The fundamental frequency for I_2 is $\omega' = 214.57$ cm.$^{-1}$, where $\omega' = \omega/c$. If we replace $\hbar\omega/kT$ by $hc\omega'/kT = 1.035$, the distribution between the ground and first excited vibrational levels becomes, at 298°K,

$$\frac{n_1}{n_0} = e^{-hc\omega'/kT} = e^{-1.035} = 0.355$$

Similarly, for state $v = 2$,

$$\frac{n_2}{n_0} = e^{-2hc\omega'/kT} = e^{-2.07} = 0.126$$

The corresponding value of q_v is given by equation (17.53) as 1.55.

EXERCISE 17.10

Evaluate q_v for N_2 at 300°K and at 1000°K.

Ans. At 300°K, $q_v = 1.00001$; at 1000°K, $q_v = 1.035$.

Diatomic molecules are almost always in their electronic ground states at ordinary temperature. Even for oxygen, with an exceptionally low-lying first excited state, the electronic partition function only begins to increase at very high temperature. The value of the electronic partition function q_e nevertheless may exceed unity because of degeneracy. For example, the ground electronic state of O_2 has two unpaired electrons (see Chapter 14) and is triply degenerate, giving $q_e = 3e^{-0/kT} = 3$. For atoms and molecules with one unpaired electron, the electron spin degeneracy is 2, and q_e will equal 2 unless there is orbital degeneracy also. In general, for an atomic state, the degeneracy is $g = 2J + 1$, where J is the total angular momentum. J values are denoted by spectral term symbols as $S_{1/2}$, $P_{1/2}$, $P_{3/2}$ where the subscript equals J.

The methods outlined in the preceding paragraphs permit evaluation of the complete partition function of any molecule for which the molecular properties are known in adequate detail. The partition function can then be used in turn to evaluate the usual thermodynamic properties, including the equilibrium constant in chemical reactions, as by equation (17.44). Even for diatomic molecules, the precise evaluation of the partition function may be a tedious process, but in some simple classes of reactions this need not be carried out in detail. The reaction

$$^{35}Cl + H^{127}I = H^{35}Cl + {}^{127}I$$

provides a simple numerical illustration of the preceding equations. By equation (17.44)

$$K = \frac{Q_{HCl} \times Q_I}{Q_{HI} \times Q_{Cl}} e^{-\Delta E_0^0/RT}$$

Referring to equations (17.46) and (17.50) we can write

$$q_t = A_t M^{3/2}$$

and

$$q_r = \frac{A_r I}{\sigma}$$

where the A's represent collected constants. For both HCl and HI, as with many diatomic molecules, the vibrational quanta are sufficiently large so that at ordinary temperatures $q_v = 1$. The electronic partition functions for I and Cl are the same.

Because of the symmetric nature of the reaction all factors in A_t and A_r and the electronic factors will cancel to give

$$K = \frac{M_{HCl}^{3/2} \times M_I^{3/2} \times I_{HCl}}{M_{HI}^{3/2} \times M_{Cl}^{3/2} \times I_{HI}} e^{-\Delta E_0^0/RT}$$

The moments of inertia for HCl and HI are 2.71×10^{-40} g. cm.^{2} and 4.31×10^{-40} g. cm.^{2}, respectively. From Table 16.2 the bond dissociation energies give $\Delta E_0^0 = D_{H-I} - D_{H-Cl} = -31$ kcal./mole. The final expression is

$$K = 0.648 \, \exp. \left(\frac{31000}{RT} \right)$$

EXERCISE 17.11

Use the preceding data to verify the expression for the equilibrium constant and evaluate K at 600°K. *Ans.* 1.3×10^{11}.

17.9 Heat Capacity

We are now in a position to return to the problem of the heat capacities of polyatomic gases which was presented at the beginning of this chapter. First, consider the translational contribution to the heat capacity. By equations (17.34) and (17.47)

$$\ln q_t = \tfrac{3}{2} \ln T + \text{const.}$$

$$C_t = \left[\frac{\partial}{\partial T} \left(RT^2 \frac{\partial \ln q_t}{\partial T} \right) \right]_V = \left[\frac{\partial}{\partial T} \left(RT^2 \times \frac{3}{2T} \right) \right]_V = \tfrac{3}{2} R \qquad (17.54)$$

The translational contribution to heat capacity is the same for all gases, without regard to molecular complexity, and is independent of temperature.

The rotational contribution to heat capacity for linear molecules follows from equations (17.34) and (17.49) (except at very low temperature).

$$\ln q_r = \ln T + \text{const.}$$

$$C_r = \left[\frac{\partial}{\partial T} \left(RT^2 \frac{\partial \ln q_r}{\partial T} \right) \right]_V = \left[\frac{\partial}{\partial T} \left(RT^2 \times \frac{1}{T} \right) \right]_V = R \qquad (17.55)$$

Similarly, for nonlinear molecules, by equations (17.34) and (17.51)

$$\ln q_r = \tfrac{3}{2} \ln T + \text{const.}$$

$$C_r = \left[\frac{\partial}{\partial T} \left(RT^2 \frac{\partial \ln q_r}{\partial T} \right) \right]_v = \left[\frac{\partial}{\partial T} \left(RT^2 \times \frac{3}{2T} \right) \right]_v = \tfrac{3}{2} R \qquad (17.56)$$

That is, the rotational contribution to heat capacity may be either $\tfrac{2}{2} R$ or $\tfrac{3}{2} R$, according to whether one has diatomic and linear polyatomic molecules on the one hand or nonlinear polyatomic molecules on the other hand.

The vibrational heat capacity can be obtained from equations (17.34) and (17.53). Again, let $U = h\omega/kT = hc\omega'/kT = 1.439\omega'/T$, where hc/k has the value 1.439 deg. cm. and ω' is in cm.$^{-1}$. From equation (17.53)

$$\frac{\partial \ln q_v}{\partial T} = \frac{Ue^{-U}}{T(1 - e^{-U})}$$

it follows that

$$C_v = \left\{ \frac{\partial}{\partial T} \left[RT^2 \frac{Ue^{-U}}{T(1 - e^{-U})} \right] \right\}_v = R \frac{U^2 e^U}{(e^U - 1)^2} \qquad (17.57)$$

To determine the numerical contribution to heat capacity from vibrational excitation, it is necessary only to have values of the fundamental frequency from spectroscopic measurements. Some useful values are given in Table 14.6. Calculations of C_v are simplified by using tables of values of the function $U^2 e^U / (e^U - 1)^2$ (M. Dole, *op. cit.*).

EXERCISE 17.12

Find the vibrational heat capacity for $H^{35}Cl$ at 1000°K.   *Ans.* 0.26R.

For most diatomic molecules at ordinary temperatures we may write

$$C_V = C_t + C_r + C_v = \tfrac{5}{2} R + C_v$$

The molar heat capacities at constant volume for N_2, Cl_2, and I_2 have been calculated by the preceding equations and represented in Fig. 17.4 over a range of temperature. All values refer to the ideal gaseous state, even at low temperature. The approximate temperature at which the vibrational energy begins to contribute to C_V is clearly higher, the higher the characteristic frequency. Unless the absolute temperature is at least one-fifth as great as $hc\omega'/k$, the value of q_v is nearly unity. Thus, over a range of temperature, its temperature derivative is almost zero, and the vibrational heat capacity is effectively zero. At such low temperatures the vibrational degree of freedom is said to be "frozen in."

Polyatomic molecules have bond-stretching frequencies similar to those of diatomic molecules. Correspondingly, they contribute little to heat ca-

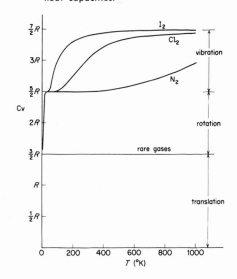

FIG. 17.4. Calculated heat capacities.

pacity unless very heavy atoms are present or the temperature is high. On the other hand, large molecules also have bending or deformation frequencies which are smaller and may contribute significantly at ordinary temperature. Internal rotations often involve potential barriers so that motion is "restricted" and tends to be oscillatory, resembling loose vibrations.

When there are several vibrational modes in the molecule each with its own characteristic frequency $\omega_1', \omega_2', \omega_3', \ldots$, the vibrational partition function becomes $q_{v, \text{tot.}} = (q_v)_1 \times (q_v)_2 \times (q_v)_3 \times \ldots$. Each of these terms makes a corresponding contribution to the vibrational heat capacity which may be expressed

$$C = (C_v)_1 + (C_v)_2 + (C_v)_3 + \ldots$$

At sufficiently high temperature, for each degree of vibrational freedom, the value of $U = hc\omega'/kT$ finally becomes rather small and the component (partial) partition function approaches its classical limit. Expanding at small U gives

$$q_v = (1 - e^{-U})^{-1} = (U - U^2 + \ldots)^{-1} = U^{-1} = (hc\omega'/kT)^{-1} \quad (17.58)$$

The vibrational heat capacity correspondingly approaches its classical limit and applying equations (17.34) and (17.58) leads to $C_v = 2 \times \frac{1}{2} R$ for each degree of freedom.

17.10 Maxwell-Boltzmann Distribution

In attempting to explain the origin of activation energy in chemical kinetics, we stated, without proof, the law governing distribution of molecular velocities. This relation can now be derived by using the methods developed in this chapter. The problem is to find the number of molecules dn with velocities (say in the x-direction) between v_x and $v_x + dv_x$. It is actually more convenient to restate the problem thus: find the number of molecules dn with momenta in the x-direction between p_x and $p_x + dp_x$. This is equivalent to finding the number of quantum states within this interval, but the quantum condition must be restated.

Translational quanta are very small by usual standards, but their size is limited by the uncertainty principle, which states that the combined uncertainties in momentum Δp and in coordinate Δx are related by $\Delta p \Delta x = h$, where h is Planck's constant. In other words, the size of a "cell" which contains one quantum state cannot be smaller than h. The momentum-coordinate cell of interest has a size $dx\,dp_x$ and it therefore contains $dx\,dp_x/h$ quantum states. Within these limits the energy levels are not distinguishable and the number of such levels is identified with the degeneracy, $g = dx\,dp_x/h$.

According to Boltzmann's equation (17.23), the fraction of molecules dn/n in a g-fold degenerate energy level ϵ is

$$\frac{dn}{n} = \frac{g e^{-\epsilon/kT}}{q_x} = \frac{e^{-\epsilon/kT} dx\,dp_x}{hq_x} \quad (17.59)$$

The energy is $\frac{1}{2}mv_x^2$ or, in terms of momentum, $\epsilon = p_x^2/2m$, where m is the mass of a molecule. The preceding equation becomes

$$\frac{dn}{n} = \frac{e^{-p_x^2/2mkT}}{hq_x} \, dx \, dp_x \qquad (17.60)$$

The partition function q_x is to be evaluated over the ranges $0 < x < l_x$ and $-\infty < p_x < +\infty$. From equation (17.24) and the condition $g = dx \, dp_x/h$ we obtain

$$q_x = \Sigma \, ge^{-\epsilon/kT} = \int_{x=0}^{x=l_x} \int_{p_x=-\infty}^{p_x=\infty} e^{-p_x^2/2mkT} \frac{dx \, dp_x}{h} \qquad (17.61)$$

Since we wish to know the number of molecules dn within the interval dp_x at all x, the numerator of equation (17.60) is to be integrated over the range $0 < x < l_x$, or

$$\text{numerator} = \int_{x=0}^{x=l_x} e^{-p_x^2/2mkT} \, dp_x \, dx$$

Combining numerator and denominator gives

$$\frac{dn}{n} = \frac{e^{-p_x^2/2mkT} \, dp_x}{\int_{-\infty}^{\infty} e^{-p_x^2/2mkT} \, dp_x} \qquad (17.62)$$

The denominator of equation (17.62) is a standard integral of the type $\int_{-\infty}^{\infty} e^{-a^2x^2} \, dx = \pi^{1/2}/a$, whose value is $(2\pi mkT)^{1/2}$. Consequently,

$$\frac{dn}{n} = \frac{e^{-p_x^2/2mkT}}{(2\pi mkT)^{1/2}} \, dp_x \qquad (17.63)$$

In terms of velocity, since $p_x = mv_x$

$$\frac{dn}{n} = \frac{e^{-mv_x^2/2kT}}{(2\pi kT/m)^{1/2}} \, dv_x \qquad (17.64)$$

Equation (17.64) is a statement of the Maxwell-Boltzmann distribution law for molecular velocities in one dimension. The fraction of molecules within the velocity interval from v_x to $v_x + dv_x$ is very small. Accordingly, the fraction per unit velocity interval dv_x, viz., (dn/n) $(1/dv_x)$, is chosen in Fig. 17.5 to represent the distribution as a function of the energy. The choice of $(mv_x^2/2kT)^{1/2}$ as the independent variable is convenient since otherwise a separate numerical relation would apply for each molecular weight and each temperature.

The distribution of velocities in three dimensions follows in the preceding pattern. Letting $p^2 = p_x^2 + p_y^2 + p_z^2$, we find that the fraction of molecules with momenta in the interval $dp_x \, dp_y \, dp_z$ is

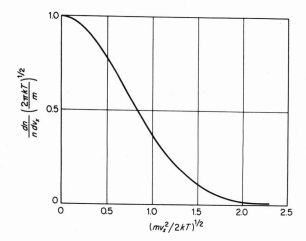

FIG. 17.5. Maxwell-Boltzmann distribution in one dimension.

$$\frac{dn}{n} = \frac{e^{-p^2/2mkT}\,dp_x\,dp_y\,dp_z}{\int_{-\infty}^{\infty} e^{-p_x^2/2mkT}\,dp_x \int_{-\infty}^{\infty} e^{-p_y^2/2mkT}\,dp_y \int_{-\infty}^{\infty} e^{-p_z^2/2mkT}\,dp_z} \qquad (17.65)$$

Each of these integrals is completely analogous to that in equation (17.62), so the denominator is simply $(2\pi mkT)^{3/2}$. Accordingly,

$$\frac{dn}{n} = (2\pi mkT)^{-3/2} e^{-p^2/2mkT}\,dp_x\,dp_y\,dp_z \qquad (17.66)$$

Direction in space is not important in this problem, so that in terms of molecular speed c we have $c = m^{-1}(p_x^2 + p_y^2 + p_z^2)^{1/2}$. The velocity distribution is the same in all directions, and the set of vectors representing magnitudes of the momentum $mc = p$ within the interval $dp_x\,dp_y\,dp_z$ would terminate in a differential spherical annulus or shell whose volume is $d(\frac{4}{3}\pi m^3 c^3) = 4\pi m^3 c^2\,dc$. After this substitution is made, the preceding equation becomes

$$\frac{dn}{n} = \frac{4\pi e^{-mc^2/2kT} c^2\,dc}{(2\pi kT/m)^{3/2}} \qquad (17.67)$$

Equation (17.67), which represents the distribution of molecular speeds, has been illustrated in Fig. 11.14. It shows a maximum at some value of c other than 0, in contrast to the one-dimensional velocity distribution function of equation (17.64).

The corresponding distribution in terms of molecular energy $\epsilon = \frac{1}{2}mc^2$ follows directly from equation (17.67), since $d\epsilon = mc\,dc$.

$$\frac{dn_\epsilon}{n} = \frac{2\epsilon^{1/2} e^{-\epsilon/kT}}{\pi^{1/2}(kT)^{3/2}}\,d\epsilon \qquad (17.68)$$

Integrating over the energy range from ϵ to ∞ gives the fraction of molecules having a kinetic energy in excess of a chosen value ϵ. For large values of ϵ

$$\frac{n_\epsilon}{n} = \int_\epsilon^\infty \frac{2\epsilon^{1/2} e^{-\epsilon/kT}}{\pi^{1/2}(kT)^{3/2}}\,d\epsilon = 2\pi^{-1/2}\left(\frac{\epsilon}{kT}\right)^{1/2} e^{-\epsilon/kT}$$

EXERCISE 17.13

By analogy with the preceding equations, show that the fraction of molecules with energy in two dimensions equal to or greater than ϵ is given by $n_\epsilon/n = \exp.(-\epsilon/kT)$. This is the relation used in simple collision theory of reaction rates (Chapter 11).

Average values of the molecular speed and energy are frequently required in applications of the Maxwell-Boltzmann distribution law. In general, the average value $\bar{r}$ of a property r is obtained by

$$\bar{r} = \frac{\Sigma n_i r_i}{\Sigma n_i} = \frac{1}{n}\Sigma n_i r_i$$

where n_i is the number of particles having each particular value of the property, r_i. When n is a continuously varying function of r, the summations are replaced by integrals, so in the case of the molecular speed we have

$$\bar{c} = \frac{1}{n} \int_0^\infty c\, dn$$

Substituting for dn by equation (17.67) yields

$$\bar{c} = 4\pi \left(\frac{m}{2\pi kT}\right)^{3/2} \int_0^\infty c^3 e^{-mc^2/2kT}\, dc \qquad (17.69)$$

This integral is of the form

$$\int_0^\infty x^3 e^{-ax^2}\, dx = \frac{1}{2a^2}$$

and, therefore,

$$\bar{c} = \left(\frac{8kT}{\pi m}\right)^{1/2} \qquad (17.70)$$

This result was given previously (equation 11.49) without proof.

EXERCISE 17.14

Use the procedure described above to verify equation (11.48).

$$(\overline{c^2})^{1/2} = \left(\frac{3kT}{m}\right)^{1/2}$$

The average molecular velocity in one coordinate, $|\bar{v}|$, will be required for application in the next section. In all of the foregoing discussion it has been implicitly assumed that the system as a whole is at rest and therefore $\bar{v} = 0$ along any coordinate. We shall, therefore, take the average without regard to sign. Applying the procedure described above, we have

$$|\bar{v}| = \frac{1}{n} \int_0^\infty v\, dn$$

Substituting by equation (17.64) yields

$$|\bar{v}| = \left(\frac{m}{2\pi kT}\right)^{1/2} \int_0^\infty v e^{-mv^2/2kT}\, dv$$

This integral is of the form

$$\int_0^\infty x e^{-ax^2}\, dx = \frac{1}{2a}$$

and, therefore,

$$|\bar{v}| = \left(\frac{kT}{2\pi m}\right)^{1/2} \qquad (17.71)$$

The average kinetic energy may be obtained in analogous fashion.

$$\bar{\epsilon} = \frac{1}{n} \int_0^\infty \epsilon\, dn_\epsilon$$

Substitution by equation (17.68) yields

$$\bar{\epsilon} = \frac{2}{\pi^{1/2}(kT)^{3/2}} \int_0^\infty \epsilon^{3/2} e^{-\epsilon/kT}\, d\epsilon$$

Changing the variable to $x^2 = \epsilon$ yields an integral of the form

$$\int_0^\infty x^4 e^{-ax^2} dx = \frac{3}{8} \sqrt{\frac{\pi}{a^5}}$$

and, therefore,

$$\bar{\epsilon} = \tfrac{3}{2}kT \tag{17.72}$$

It is notable that for three forms of energy, translation, rotation, and vibration, there is a common limiting behavior. When the energy levels are separated by approximately kT or less, the average kinetic energy amounts to $\tfrac{1}{2}kT$ for each degree of freedom. This common result is a consequence of the type of integral involved. Any form of energy which depends upon a square term of its coordinate or momentum will lead to an average energy of $\tfrac{1}{2}kT$ for each such term, i.e., for each degree of freedom. This is the principle of the equipartition of energy which was stated, without proof, at the beginning of this chapter.

17.11 Transition State Theory of Reaction Rates[6]

Statistical methods may be used to examine in further detail the consequences of the assumption (Chapter 11) that there is an equilibrium between gaseous reactants A, B and a transition state complex X^+.

$$A + B \rightleftharpoons X^+ \longrightarrow Y + Z$$

It may be assumed here that the equilibrium is not significantly influenced by decomposition of the complex to form reaction products and that products are not formed by any other path. Then $(X^+) = K^+(A)(B)$, where K^+ is a true equilibrium constant and the rate of reaction is

$$\text{rate} = k(X^+) = kK^+(A)(B)$$

By equation (17.44) for 1 molecule per cc. the expression for K^+ is

$$K^+ = \frac{Q_{X^*}}{Q_A Q_B} e^{-E_a/RT} = \frac{(X^+)}{(A)(B)} \tag{17.73}$$

where the activation energy E_a has been identified with the energy difference ΔE_0^0 between reactants A, B and complex X^+, all in their respective ground states.

The problem of describing the rate of reaction now becomes the problem of describing the rate of unimolecular decomposition of the critical complex. A plausible assumption would be that the rate of this decomposition is the rate of breaking of some one valence bond in the complex and that in all other respects X^+ is an ordinary molecule. From the preceding considerations we have found that the greater the energy required in any degree of freedom, the less probable the event. We shall, therefore, assume that the rate-controlling bond breaking does not produce product molecules with large relative translational energy. Some energy must be specified in order to proceed, and it

---

[6]See S. Glasstone, K. J. Laidler, and H. Eyring, *The Theory of Rate Processes*, McGraw-Hill Book Company, New York, 1941.

seems plausible to suppose that the product molecules Y, Z are formed by an act which converts their relative vibrational motion into relative average translational motion. The coordinate describing this motion is called the reaction coordinate. The average velocity of displacement is further assumed to be described by equation (17.71), $|\bar{v}| = (kT/2\pi m)^{1/2}$.

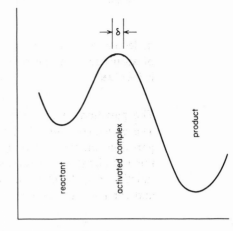

FIG. 17.6. Potential energy along the reaction coordinate.

The potential energy function which describes the reaction, shown in Fig. 17.6, may be compared to a barrier whose width at the top, along the reaction coordinate, is δ. The complex surmounts the top of the barrier in a time given by

$$\frac{\delta}{|\bar{v}|} = \delta \left(\frac{2\pi m}{kT} \right)^{1/2} \tag{17.74}$$

which we take to be the mean lifetime of the complex. Dividing the number of complexes by the mean lifetime of a complex gives the rate of reaction. That is,

$$\text{rate} = \frac{(X^{\ddagger})}{\delta/|\bar{v}|} = \frac{(X^{\ddagger})}{\delta} \left(\frac{kT}{2\pi m} \right)^{1/2} = \frac{K^{\ddagger}}{\delta} (A)(B) \left(\frac{kT}{2\pi m} \right)^{1/2} \tag{17.75}$$

The partition function for the activated complex can be resolved into partial partition functions. The partial function for the translation leading to decomposition corresponds to a displacement of magnitude δ in one dimension. By equation (17.46), setting $a_x = \delta$ gives

$$q_\delta = \frac{(2\pi mkT)^{1/2}\delta}{h} \tag{17.76}$$

The total partition function for the complex is factored to remove q_δ, $Q = Q'_{X^{\ddagger}} \cdot q_\delta$, and equation (17.73) becomes

$$K^{\ddagger} = \frac{Q'_{X^{\ddagger}} q_\delta}{Q_A Q_B} e^{-E_a/RT} \tag{17.77}$$

The rate equation follows from equations (17.75), (17.76), (17.77) as

$$\text{rate} = \frac{Q'_{X^{\ddagger}}(2\pi mkT)^{1/2}\delta}{Q_A Q_B h} \cdot \frac{(kT/2\pi m)^{1/2}(A)(B)}{\delta} e^{-E_a/RT} \tag{17.78}$$

The factor of the concentrations is the specific rate constant, which is simplified to give

$$\text{rate } k = \frac{kT}{h} \cdot \frac{Q'_{X^{\ddagger}}}{Q_A Q_B} e^{-E_a/RT} \tag{17.79}$$

The factor kT/h is common to all reactions at a given temperature.

The partition functions Q_A and Q_B refer to ordinary molecules and methods previously used apply. The activated complex, by definition, is not an ordinary molecule, and the necessary data can only be estimated. The simple reaction of atom-atom combination will be chosen as an example, since little guessing is involved.

$$A + B \longrightarrow AB$$

The partition functions of atoms A and B are simply those for translation. The activated complex AB is a diatomic molecule for which the vibrational partition function has been replaced by a translational partition function, and this has already been factored out in equation (17.79). The partial partition function Q'_X, therefore, includes only factors for three degrees of translation and for two of rotation. Consequently, from equation (17.79)

$$rate \ k = \frac{[2\pi(m_A + m_B)kT]^{3/2}h^{-3}8\pi^2 I_{AB}kTh^{-2}}{(2\pi m_A kT)^{3/2}h^{-3}(2\pi m_B kT)^{3/2}h^{-3}} \ \frac{kT}{h} \ e^{-E_a/RT} \qquad (17.80)$$

The numerator of equation (17.80) is $q_t \times q_r$ for the complex. Now replace I_{AB} by μr^2_{AB}, where $\mu = m_A m_B/(m_A + m_B)$ and r_{AB} is the internuclear separation. This gives, after simplifying

$$rate \ k = \left(\frac{8\pi kT}{\mu_{AB}}\right)^{1/2} r^2_{AB} e^{-E_a/RT} \qquad (17.81)$$

In the case of the combination of two atoms, the result obtained from the activated complex theory must, of course, agree with the simpler collision theory. The latter theory gives, for the rate of collision of two unlike species having collision radii r_A and r_B,

$$Z_{AB} = \sqrt{2} \ \pi (r_A + r_B)^2 \ \bar{v}_{AB} \qquad (17.82)$$

where $\bar{v}_{AB}$ is the average relative velocity of the two particles. This is related to the individual molecular speeds by

$$\bar{v}_{AB} = \left(\frac{\bar{c}^2_A + \bar{c}^2_B}{2}\right)^{1/2}$$

Substituting by equation (17.70) yields

$$\bar{v}_{AB} = \left(\frac{4kT}{\pi\mu}\right)^{1/2}$$

The collision rate is, therefore,

$$Z_{AB} = (r_A + r_B)^2 \left(\frac{8\pi kT}{\mu}\right)^{1/2}$$

and the specific rate of reaction is

$$rate \ k = (r_A + r_B)^2 \left(\frac{8\pi kT}{\mu}\right)^{1/2} e^{-E_a/RT} \qquad (17.83)$$

Equations (17.81) and (17.83) are in agreement if we may assume that the internuclear separation r_{AB} which determines the moment of inertia in the activated complex is equal to the internuclear separation during a collision.

The good agreement of the activated complex theory and the collision theory does not extend to reactions between diatomic or larger molecules because simple collision theory neglects the internal degrees of freedom.

SUMMARY, CHAPTER 17

1. Equipartition principle

Each square term can contribute $\frac{1}{2}RT$ to E and $\frac{1}{2}R$ to C_V.

Translational Energy: $\frac{3}{2}RT$

Rotational Energy: linear, RT; nonlinear, $\frac{3}{2}RT$

Vibrational Energy: linear, $(3n - 5)RT$; nonlinear, $(3n - 6)RT$

2. The Boltzmann law

$$\frac{n_i}{n} = \frac{g_i e^{-\epsilon_i/kT}}{\Sigma g_i e^{-\epsilon_i/kT}}$$

The partition function

$$Q = \Sigma g_i e^{-\epsilon_i/kT}$$

$$Q = q_t q_r q_v q_e$$

$$q_t = \frac{(2\pi mkT)^{3/2} V}{h^3}$$

$$q_r = \frac{8\pi^2 IkT}{\sigma h^2} \quad \text{(linear molecules)}.$$

$$q_v = \frac{1}{(1 - e^{-\hbar\omega/kT})}$$

3. Thermodynamic properties of an ideal gas

$$E - E_0 = RT^2 \left(\frac{\partial \ln Q}{\partial T}\right)_V$$

$$C_V = \left[\frac{\partial}{\partial T}\left(RT^2 \frac{\partial \ln Q}{\partial T}\right)\right]_V$$

$$S = R \ln\left(\frac{Q}{N}\right) + \frac{E - E_0}{T} + R$$

$$\Delta F^o = \Delta E_0^o - RT \Delta \ln\left(\frac{Q^0}{N}\right)$$

$$K = \frac{(Q_M^0/N)^m (Q_N^0/N)^n}{(Q_A^0/N)^a (Q_B^0/N)^b} e^{-\Delta E_0^o/RT}$$

4. Maxwell-Boltzmann distribution

Velocity in one dimension

$$\frac{dn}{n} = \frac{e^{-mv_x^2/2kT}}{(2\pi kT/m)^{1/2}} dv_x$$

Speed in three dimensions

$$\frac{dn}{n} = \frac{4\pi e^{-mc^2/2kT}}{(2\pi kT/m)^{3/2}} c^2 dc$$

Average speed

$$\bar{c} = \left(\frac{8kT}{\pi m}\right)^{1/2}$$

Average kinetic energy

$$\bar{\epsilon} = \tfrac{3}{2}kT$$

5. Transition state theory
   Reaction rate constant

$$rate\ k = \frac{kT}{h}\frac{Q'_{X^*}}{Q_A Q_B}e^{-E_a/RT}$$

PROBLEMS, CHAPTER 17

1. Estimate the high-temperature limiting value of C_V (neglecting electronic contributions) for each of the following molecules: (a) CO_2 (linear), (b) H_2O (nonlinear), (c) CH_4.

2. Consider a localized system of n particles which are to be distributed among three levels of energy 0, ϵ, and 2ϵ. The partition function for the system is

$$q = 1 + e^{-\theta/T} + e^{-2\theta/T}$$

where $\theta = \epsilon/k$ is called the "characteristic temperature."
   (a) Write the expressions for n_0, n_1, and n_2.
   (b) Derive the expression for the fraction of particles in each energy level in the limit when $\theta \gg T$. In the limit when $T \gg \theta$, show that n_0/n, n_1/n, and n_2/n all approach $\tfrac{1}{3}$. Note that the temperature T is "high" or "low" only in terms of its relation to the characteristic termperature, θ.
   (c) Derive expressions for S and E. Show that at low temperatures S approaches 0 and E approaches 0, whereas at high temperatures E approaches $n\epsilon$ and S approaches $R \ln 3$.

3. Find the ratio of hydrogen molecules between states with $J = 0$ and $J = 1$ at (a) $100°K$, (b) $300°K$, (c) $600°K$. (See Exercise 14.10.)   *Ans.* (a) $1.0/0.176$

4. Enumerate some of the possible distributions of 11 equal quanta among 15 molecules. For simplicity you may confine your attention to those distributions in which no one molecule has more than 3 quanta and the number of molecules with n quanta never exceeds the number with $n - 1$ quanta. Show that the highest probability is obtained for $n_0 = 8$, $n_1 = 4$, $n_2 = 2$, $n_3 = 1$.

5. Given

$$Cl\ (^2P_{3/2}) = Cl\ (^2P_{1/2});\qquad \Delta E = 2.5\ \text{kcal. mole}^{-1}$$

Find the distribution of chlorine atoms between these two states at $300°K$.

6. In the reactions of hydrocarbons with oxygen in flames abnormally large numbers of OH radicals are produced in high rotational states. Analysis of the spectrum indicates that $\epsilon_r = kT$ at $J = 16$. The rotational moment of inertia of OH is 1.48×10^{-40} g. cm.^{2}. Find the effective rotational "temperature."
     Ans. $7.4 \times 10^3 K$

7. The heat capacity of HCl at $1000°K$ is $C_V = 5.579$ cal. mole.$^{-1}$
   (a) Find the vibrational contribution to C_V.
   (b) Referring to tables of the function $C_V/R = U^2 e^U (e^U - 1)^{-2}$ (M. Dole, *op. cit.*) find the corresponding value of $U = hc\omega'/kT$.
   (c) What value of ω' is consistent with this result? [Data from H. M. Spencer and J. L. Justice, *J. Am. Chem. Soc.*, **56**, 2311 (1934).]

8. Find the translational energy in one dimension of an H atom trapped in a crystal lattice with $a_x = 2 \times 10^{-8}$ cm. and $n_x = 1$.

Ans. 8.20×10^{-15} erg molecule^{-1}

9. Assuming that the force constant and bond length of the H—X bond are not altered by isotopic substitution, find ω' and I for (a) $D^{35}Cl$ and (b) $D^{80}Br$ from the data in Table 14.6.

Ans. (a) $\omega' = 2143$ cm.$^{-1}$, $I = 5.14 \times 10^{-40}$ gm. cm.^{2}.

10. Find the difference in zero point energies for $D^{35}Cl$ versus $H^{35}Cl$ and $D^{80}Br$ versus $H^{80}Br$. Combine these values to obtain ΔE_0^o for the process

$$H^{35}Cl + D^{80}Br = D^{35}Cl + H^{80}Br$$

Use the methods of statistical mechanics to predict the equilibrium constant for this process at 300°K, assuming $q_e = q_v = 1$ for all molecules involved.

Ans. K = 1.21

11. Find the vibrational heat capacity of (a) H_2 and (b) D_2 at 1000°K.

12. Calculate the entropy of one mole of argon gas at one atmosphere and 298.15°K. The measured value is 36.95 cal. deg.$^{-1}$ mole^{-1}.

13. Thallium forms a monatomic vapor. It has a low-lying electronic state 0.96 e.v. above the ground state. The degeneracy of the ground state is 2, and that of the first excited state is 4. All other excited electronic states lie much higher.

   (a) Write expressions for the electronic partition function at 100°K, 1000°K, and 10,000°K.

   (b) What fraction of the atoms are in the first excited state at 10,000°K?

   (c) Compute the electronic contributions to E, S, and C_V at 10,000°K. (In equation (17.41) the factor N in the first term and the second term are assigned to the translational partition function. Why?)

14. The moment of inertia of H_2 is 0.460×10^{-40} gm. cm.^{2}, and the frequency of the fundamental vibration is 4395 cm.$^{-1}$. Estimate the spectroscopic entropy of one mole of H_2 gas at 25°C and one atmosphere pressure. The calorimetric entropy is 29.64 cal. deg.$^{-1}$ mole^{-1} [W. F. Giauque, *J. Am. Chem. Soc.*, **52**, 4823 (1930)]. The difference is largely due to the fact that hydrogen molecules exist in two forms called *ortho* and *para* hydrogen, in one of which the nuclear spins are parallel, whereas in the other they are antiparallel. (For further discussion see M. Dole, *Introduction to Statistical Thermodynamics*, p. 183, Prentice-Hall, Inc., Englewood Cliffs, N. J., 1954.)

15. From spectroscopic data the moment of inertia of CO is 14.48×10^{-40} gm. cm.^{2}, and the frequency of the fundamental vibration is 2168 cm.$^{-1}$. Use this data to calculate the spectroscopic entropy of one mole of CO at 25°C and one atmosphere pressure. The calculated calorimetric entropy is 45.93 cal. deg.$^{-1}$ mole^{-1} [J. O. Clayton and W. F. Giauque, *J. Am. Chem. Soc.*, **54**, 2610 (1932)]. What is the significance of this difference?   *Ans.* 47.30 cal. deg.$^{-1}$ mole^{-1}

16. The fundamental frequency of vibration of Na_2 is 159.23 cm.$^{-1}$, and the internuclear separation is 3.078 Å. For the reaction

$$Na_2 = 2\,Na$$

the dissociation energy is 0.73 e.v. Compute the equilibrium constant for this reaction at 10^3 °K. Treat all substances as ideal gases; recall that $P = 1$ atm. for the standard state, and keep units consistent.

APPENDIXES

APPENDIX 1

PARTIAL DIFFERENTIATION

Consider a continuous function, z, of two real, independent variables, x and y.

$$[z = f(x, y)]$$

Just as a function, y, of a real, independent variable, x, $[y = f(x)]$ can be represented graphically by a curve in the xy plane, the function z can be thought of as a surface in three-dimensional space. (See App. Fig. 1.1.)

Consider y_0, a fixed value of y, and allow x to vary giving the curve CD in the figure. Then $z = f(x, y_0)$ represents the equation of CD. The equation for the slope of this curve can be obtained by taking the derivative of z with respect to x, treating y as a constant. This function is represented by $(\partial z/\partial x)_y$, and is called a partial differential. As an example consider the function $z = x^2 + 2xy + y^2$. $(\partial z/\partial x)_y = (2x + 2)$. In an analogous way we can arrive at a function $(\partial z/\partial y)_x$, which also has a simple geometrical interpretation, for example, the slope of a curve such as AB in App. Fig. 1.1.

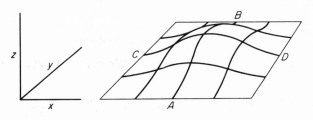

APP. FIG. 1.1.

In the case of function of one variable, $y = f(x)$, the differential of y is

$$dy = f'(x)dx = \left(\frac{dy}{dx}\right)dx$$

With the function $z = f(x, y)$, a total differential can be defined in a similar way,

$$dz = \left(\frac{\partial z}{\partial x}\right)_y dx + \left(\frac{\partial z}{\partial y}\right)_x dy$$

We have considered here only a two-variable function which is simply interpretable in geometrical terms. However, the treatment can be extended to include functions of more than two variables, even though they cannot be represented in three-dimensional space.

EXPANSION IN SERIES

Consider a function, $f(x)$, which has a continuous nth derivative throughout an interval (a, b). The nth derivative, $f^n(x)$, can then be integrated n successive times between the limits a and x, where x is a point in the interval (a, b).

$$\int_a^x f^n(x)\,dx = f^{(n-1)}(x)\Big|_a^x = f^{(n-1)}(x) - f^{(n-1)}(a) ;$$

$$\int_a^x \int_a^x f^n(x)(dx)^2 = \int_a^x f^{(n-1)}(x)\,dx - \int_a^x f^{(n-1)}(a)\,dx$$

$$= f^{(n-2)}(x) - f^{(n-2)}(a) - (x-a)f^{(n-1)}(a)$$

$$\int_a^x \int_a^x \int_a^x f^n(x)(dx)^3 = f^{(n-3)}(x) - f^{(n-3)}(a)$$

$$- (x-a)f^{(n-2)}(a) - \frac{(x-a)^2}{2!}f^{(n-1)}(a)$$

If the process is carried out n times

$$\int_a^x \cdots \int_a^x f^n(dx)^n = f(x) - f(a) - (x-a)f'(a)$$

$$- \frac{(x-a)^2}{2!}f''(a) \cdots - \frac{(x-a)^{(n-1)}}{(n-1)!}f^{(n-1)}(a)$$

Solving for $f(x)$

$$f(x) = f(a) + (x-a)f'(a)$$

$$+ \frac{(x-a)^2}{2!}f''(a) + \cdots + \frac{(x-a)^{(n-1)}}{(n-1)!}f^{(n-1)}(a) + R_n$$

where

$$R_n = \int_a^x \cdots \int_a^x f^n(x)(dx)^n$$

This is Taylor's formula with remainder. When $a = 0$, Maclaurin's formula results.

$$f(x) = f(0) + f'(0)x + f''(0)\frac{x^2}{2!} + \cdots + f^{(n-1)}(0)\frac{x^{(n-1)}}{(n-1)!} + R_n$$

If such a series converges to a limit, R_n is small, and $f(x)$ can be evaluated by a power series expansion. Such an expansion is particularly useful when values of x are small, that is, near $x = 0$, since then only a small number of terms need be evaluated to establish the value of $f(x)$.

RELATIONSHIP OF e^{ix}, e^{-ix}, $\sin x$, and $\cos x$

Use Maclaurin's series to expand, e^{ix}, e^{-ix}, $\sin x$, and $\cos x$.

$$e^{ix} = 1 + (ix) - \frac{x^2}{2!} - \frac{ix^3}{3!} + \frac{x^4}{4!} + \frac{ix^5}{5!} \cdots$$

$$e^{-ix} = 1 - (ix) - \frac{x^2}{2!} + \frac{ix^3}{3!} + \frac{x^4}{4!} - \frac{ix^5}{5!} \cdots$$

$$\sin x = (x) - \frac{x^3}{3!} + \frac{x^5}{5!} - \frac{x^7}{7!} \cdots$$

$$\cos x = 1 - \frac{x^2}{2!} + \frac{x^4}{4!} - \frac{x^6}{6!} \cdots$$

By comparing series we see that

$$e^{ix} + e^{-ix} = 2 \cos x$$

$$e^{ix} - e^{-ix} = 2i \sin x.$$

Adding these relations gives

$$e^{ix} = \cos x + i \sin x$$

and subtracting them gives

$$e^{-ix} = \cos x - i \sin x.$$

Thus a function $y = C_1 e^{ix} + C_2 e^{-ix}$ can also be written

$$y = C_1(\cos x + i \sin x) + C_2(\cos x - i \sin x) = A \cos x + B \sin x.$$

where

$$A = (C_1 + C_2), \quad \text{and} \quad B = (C_1 - C_2)i$$

SOLUTION OF $(1/\psi)(d^2\psi/dx^2) = -k$

This equation is of the same form as $(1/y)(dy/dx) = -k$, the solution of which is $\ln y = -kx$, or $y = e^{-kx}$. Assume a solution of the same form, $\psi = e^{cx}$. Upon substitution into the original differential equation

$$\frac{1}{e^{-cx}} c^2 e^{-cx} = -k, \quad \text{and} \quad c = \pm ik^{1/2}$$

Therefore there are two solutions,

$$\psi_1 = C_1 e^{ik^{1/2}x}, \quad \text{and} \quad \psi_2 = C_2 e^{-ik^{1/2}x}$$

where C_1 and C_2 are constants. The sum of these solutions is also a solution and is known as the general solution.

$$\psi = C_1 e^{ik^{1/2}x} + C_2 e^{-ik^{1/2}x}$$

An equivalent form is

$$\psi = A \cos k^{1/2}x + B \sin k^{1/2}x$$

(See above.)

STIRLING'S APPROXIMATION

$$\ln(x!) = \ln 2 + \ln 3 + \ldots + \ln x$$

This is exactly equal to the area under the step curve shown by the dotted line in App. Fig. 1.2. This area can be approximated by the integral

$$\ln(x!) = \int_1^x \ln x \, dx$$

Integration by parts gives

$$\ln(x!) = x \ln x - x - 1$$

For large x, 1 may be neglected, giving

$$\ln(x!) = x \ln x - x$$

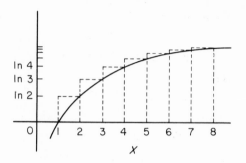

APP. FIG. 1.2.

EVALUATION OF $\displaystyle\int_{-\infty}^{+\infty} e^{-x^2}dx$

Integrals such as this and $\displaystyle\int_{-\infty}^{+\infty} e^{-x^2}x^2dx$ can be evaluated easily if they are transformed into polar coordinates. Since the function is symmetric, about 0,

$$\int_{-\infty}^{+\infty} e^{-x^2}dx = 2\int_{0}^{\infty} e^{-x^2}dx = I$$

Consider a second integral of the same form, $\displaystyle\int_{0}^{\infty} e^{-y^2}dy.$

$$I^2 = 4\int_{0}^{\infty} e^{-x^2}dx \int_{0}^{\infty} e^{-y^2}dy = 4\int_{0}^{\infty}\int_{0}^{\infty} e^{-(x^2+y^2)}\,dxdy$$

In polar coordinates

$$x = r\sin\theta$$
$$y = r\cos\theta,\quad \text{and}$$
$$r^2 = x^2 + y^2$$

since $\sin^2\theta + \cos^2\theta = 1$. The appropriate element of area is $rdrd\theta$, where θ is expressed in radians. (See App. Fig. 1.3.)

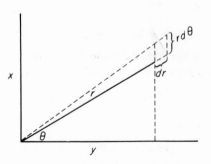

APP. FIG. 1.3.

Since this area is to be determined from $x = 0$ to $x = \infty$, the corresponding limits for θ are 0 to $\pi/2$, and for r, 0 to ∞. Therefore

$$I^2 = 4 \int_0^{\frac{\pi}{2}} \int_0^\infty e^{-r^2} r\, d\theta\, dr$$

Since

$$\int_0^\infty e^{-r^2} r\, dr = -\frac{1}{2} e^{-r^2} \Big|_0^\infty = \frac{1}{2},$$

$$I^2 = 2 \int_0^{\frac{\pi}{2}} d\theta = \pi, \quad \text{and}$$

$$I = (\pi)^{1/2}$$

APPENDIX 2

VALUES OF FUNDAMENTAL CONSTANTS*

Name	Symbol	Value		Unit
Velocity of light	c	2.997925	$\times 10^{10}$	cm. sec.$^{-1}$
Planck constant	h	6.6256	$\times 10^{-27}$	erg sec. molecule^{-1}
Avogadro constant	N	6.02252	$\times 10^{23}$	molecules mole^{-1}
Faraday constant	$\mathscr{F}$	9.64870	$\times 10^{4}$	coulombs equivalent^{-1}
Absolute temperature of the ice point		273.15		$°K$
Boltzmann constant	$k = R/N$	1.38054	$\times 10^{-16}$	erg deg.$^{-1}$ molecule^{-1}
Electronic charge	$e = \mathscr{F}/N$	1.60210	$\times 10^{-19}$	coulomb
		4.80298	$\times 10^{-10}$	e.s.u.
Gas constant	R	8.3143	$\times 10^{7}$	erg deg.$^{-1}$ mole^{-1}
		8.2056	$\times 10^{-2}$	liter atm. deg.$^{-1}$ mole^{-1}
Electron mass	m_e	9.1091	$\times 10^{-28}$	gram
Proton mass	m_p	1.67252	$\times 10^{-24}$	gram

*Constants are based on the atomic weight $^{12}C = 12.0000$. From the report of the committee on fundamental constants of the National Academy of Sciences-National Research Council.

APPENDIX 3

TABLE OF MASS-ENERGY CONVERSION FACTORS

ergs molecule^{-1}	electron volts molecule^{-1}	cm.$^{-1}$ molecule^{-1}	l. atm. mole^{-1}	joule mole^{-1}	cal. mole^{-1}	gram	atomic mass units
1	6.242×10^{11}	5.035×10^{15}	5.944×10^{14}	6.023×10^{16}	1.439×10^{16}	1.113×10^{-21}	6.701×10^{2}
1.602×10^{-12}	1	8.066×10^{3}	9.523×10^{2}	9.649×10^{4}	2.306×10^{4}	1.783×10^{-33}	1.074×10^{-9}
1.986×10^{-16}	1.240×10^{-4}	1	1.181×10^{-1}	1.196×10^{1}	2.859	2.210×10^{-37}	1.331×10^{-13}
1.682×10^{-15}	1.050×10^{-3}	8.470	1	1.013×10^{2}	2.421×10^{1}	1.872×10^{-36}	1.127×10^{-12}
1.660×10^{-17}	1.036×10^{-5}	8.359×10^{-2}	9.869×10^{-3}	1	2.390×10^{-1}	1.847×10^{-38}	1.113×10^{-14}
6.947×10^{-17}	4.336×10^{-5}	3.498×10^{-1}	4.129×10^{-2}	4.184	1	7.730×10^{-38}	4.656×10^{-14}
8.988×10^{20}	5.610×10^{32}	4.525×10^{36}	5.342×10^{35}	5.413×10^{37}	1.294×10^{37}	1	6.023×10^{23}
1.492×10^{-3}	9.315×10^{8}	7.513×10^{12}	8.869×10^{11}	8.987×10^{13}	2.148×10^{13}	1.660×10^{-24}	1

APPENDIX 4

TABLE OF LOGARITHMS TO BASE 10

N	0	1	2	3	4	5	6	7	8	9	1	2	P. P. 3	4	5
10	0000	0043	0086	0128	0170	0212	0253	0294	0334	0374	4	8	12	17	21
11	0414	0453	0492	0531	0569	0607	0645	0682	0719	0755	4	8	11	15	19
12	0792	0828	0864	0899	0934	0969	1004	1038	1072	1106	3	7	10	14	17
13	1139	1173	1206	1239	1271	1303	1335	1367	1399	1430	3	6	10	13	16
14	1461	1492	1523	1553	1584	1614	1644	1673	1703	1732	3	6	9	12	15
15	1761	1790	1818	1847	1875	1903	1931	1959	1987	2014	3	6	8	11	14
16	2041	2068	2095	2122	2148	2175	2201	2227	2253	2279	3	5	8	11	13
17	2304	2330	2355	2380	2405	2430	2455	2480	2504	2529	2	5	7	10	12
18	2553	2577	2601	2625	2648	2672	2695	2718	2742	2765	2	5	7	9	12
19	2788	2810	2833	2856	2878	2900	2923	2945	2967	2989	2	4	7	9	11
20	3010	3032	3054	3075	3096	3118	3139	3160	3181	3201	2	4	6	8	11
21	3222	3243	3263	3284	3304	3324	3345	3365	3385	3404	2	4	6	8	10
22	3424	3444	3464	3483	3502	3522	3541	3560	3579	3598	2	4	6	8	10
23	3617	3636	3655	3674	3692	3711	3729	3747	3766	3784	2	4	5	7	9
24	3802	3820	3838	3856	3874	3892	3909	3927	3945	3962	2	4	5	7	9
25	3979	3997	4014	4031	4048	4065	4082	4099	4116	4133	2	3	5	7	9
26	4150	4166	4183	4200	4216	4232	4249	4265	4281	4298	2	3	5	7	8
27	4314	4330	4346	4362	4378	4393	4409	4425	4440	4456	2	3	5	6	8
28	4472	4487	4502	4518	4533	4548	4564	4579	4594	4609	2	3	5	6	8
29	4624	4639	4654	4669	4683	4698	4713	4728	4742	4757	1	3	4	6	7
30	4771	4786	4800	4814	4829	4843	4857	4871	4886	4900	1	3	4	6	7
31	4914	4928	4942	4955	4969	4983	4997	5011	5024	5038	1	3	4	6	7
32	5051	5065	5079	5092	5105	5119	5132	5145	5159	5172	1	3	4	5	7
33	5185	5198	5211	5224	5237	5250	5263	5276	5289	5302	1	3	4	5	6
34	5315	5328	5340	5353	5366	5378	5391	5403	5416	5428	1	3	4	5	6
35	5441	5453	5465	5478	5490	5502	5514	5527	5539	5551	1	2	4	5	6
36	5563	5575	5587	5599	5611	5623	5635	5647	5658	5670	1	2	4	5	6
37	5682	5694	5705	5717	5729	5740	5752	5763	5775	5786	1	2	3	5	6
38	5798	5809	5821	5832	5843	5855	5866	5877	5888	5899	1	2	3	5	6
39	5911	5922	5933	5944	5955	5966	5977	5988	5999	6010	1	2	3	4	6
40	6021	6031	6042	6053	6064	6075	6085	6096	6107	6117	1	2	3	4	5
41	6128	6138	6149	6160	6170	6180	6191	6201	6212	6222	1	2	3	4	5
42	6232	6243	6253	6263	6274	6284	6294	6304	6314	6325	1	2	3	4	5
43	6335	6345	6355	6365	6375	6385	6395	6405	6415	6425	1	2	3	4	5
44	6435	6444	6454	6464	6474	6484	6493	6503	6513	6522	1	2	3	4	5
45	6532	6542	6551	6561	6571	6580	6590	6599	6609	6618	1	2	3	4	5
46	6628	6637	6646	6656	6665	6675	6684	6693	6702	6712	1	2	3	4	5
47	6721	6730	6739	6749	6758	6767	6776	6785	6794	6803	1	2	3	4	5
48	6812	6821	6830	6839	6848	6857	6866	6875	6884	6893	1	2	3	4	4
49	6902	6911	6920	6928	6937	6946	6955	6964	6972	6981	1	2	3	4	4
50	6990	6998	7007	7016	7024	7033	7042	7050	7059	7067	1	2	3	3	4
51	7076	7084	7093	7101	7110	7118	7126	7135	7143	7152	1	2	3	3	4
52	7160	7168	7177	7185	7193	7202	7210	7218	7226	7235	1	2	2	3	4
53	7243	7251	7259	7267	7275	7284	7292	7300	7308	7316	1	2	2	3	4
54	7324	7332	7340	7348	7356	7364	7372	7380	7388	7396	1	2	2	3	4

NOTE: $\log_e N = \log_e 10 \log_{10} N = 2.3026 \log_{10} N$

$\log_{10} e^x = x \log_{10} e = 0.43429x$

N	0	1	2	3	4	5	6	7	8	9	1	2	3	4	5
55	7404	7412	7419	7427	7435	7443	7451	7459	7466	7474	1	2	2	3	4
56	7482	7490	7497	7505	7513	7520	7528	7536	7543	7551	1	2	2	3	4
57	7559	7566	7574	7582	7589	7597	7604	7612	7619	7627	1	2	2	3	4
58	7634	7642	7649	7657	7664	7672	7679	7686	7694	7701	1	1	2	3	4
59	7709	7716	7723	7731	7738	7745	7752	7760	7767	7774	1	1	2	3	4
60	7782	7789	7796	7803	7810	7818	7825	7832	7839	7846	1	1	2	3	4
61	7853	7860	7868	7875	7882	7889	7896	7903	7910	7917	1	1	2	3	4
62	7924	7931	7938	7945	7952	7959	7966	7973	7980	7987	1	1	2	3	3
63	7993	8000	8007	8014	8021	8028	8035	8041	8048	8055	1	1	2	3	3
64	8062	8069	8075	8082	8089	8096	8102	8109	8116	8122	1	1	2	3	3
65	8129	8136	8142	8149	8156	8162	8169	8176	8182	8189	1	1	2	3	3
66	8195	8202	8209	8215	8222	8228	8235	8241	8248	8254	1	1	2	3	3
67	8261	8267	8274	8280	8287	8293	8299	8306	8312	8319	1	1	2	3	3
68	8325	8331	8338	8344	8351	8357	8363	8370	8376	8382	1	1	2	3	3
69	8388	8395	8401	8407	8414	8420	8426	8432	8439	8445	1	1	2	3	3
70	8451	8457	8463	8470	8476	8482	8488	8494	8500	8506	1	1	2	2	3
71	8513	8519	8525	8531	8537	8543	8549	8555	8561	8567	1	1	2	2	3
72	8573	8579	8585	8591	8597	8603	8609	8615	8621	8627	1	1	2	2	3
73	8633	8639	8645	8651	8657	8663	8669	8675	8681	8686	1	1	2	2	3
74	8692	8698	8704	8710	8716	8722	8727	8733	8739	8745	1	1	2	2	3
75	8751	8756	8762	8768	8774	8779	8785	8791	8797	8802	1	1	2	2	3
76	8808	8814	8820	8825	8831	8837	8842	8848	8854	8859	1	1	2	2	3
77	8865	8871	8876	8882	8887	8893	8899	8904	8910	8915	1	1	2	2	3
78	8921	8927	8932	8938	8943	8949	8954	8960	8965	8971	1	1	2	2	3
79	8976	8982	8987	8993	8998	9004	9009	9015	9020	9025	1	1	2	2	3
80	9031	9036	9042	9047	9053	9058	9063	9069	9074	9079	1	1	2	2	3
81	9085	9090	9096	9101	9106	9112	9117	9122	9128	9133	1	1	2	2	3
82	9138	9143	9149	9154	9159	9165	9170	9175	9180	9186	1	1	2	2	3
83	9191	9196	9201	9206	9212	9217	9222	9227	9232	9238	1	1	2	2	3
84	9243	9248	9253	9258	9263	9269	9274	9279	9284	9289	1	1	2	2	3
85	9294	9299	9304	9309	9315	9320	9325	9330	9335	9340	1	1	2	2	3
86	9345	9350	9355	9360	9365	9370	9375	9380	9385	9390	1	1	2	2	3
87	9395	9400	9405	9410	9415	9420	9425	9430	9435	9440	0	1	1	2	2
88	9445	9450	9455	9460	9465	9469	9474	9479	9484	9489	0	1	1	2	2
89	9494	9499	9504	9509	9513	9518	9523	9528	9533	9538	0	1	1	2	2
90	9542	9547	9552	9557	9562	9566	9571	9576	9581	9586	0	1	1	2	2
91	9590	9595	9600	9605	9609	9614	9619	9624	9628	9633	0	1	1	2	2
92	9638	9643	9647	9652	9657	9661	9666	9671	9675	9680	0	1	1	2	2
93	9685	9689	9694	9699	9703	9708	9713	9717	9722	9727	0	1	1	2	2
94	9731	9736	9741	9745	9750	9754	9759	9763	9768	9773	0	1	1	2	2
95	9777	9782	9786	9791	9795	9800	9805	9809	9814	9818	0	1	1	2	2
96	9823	9827	9832	9836	9841	9845	9850	9854	9859	9863	0	1	1	2	2
97	9868	9872	9877	9881	9886	9890	9894	9899	9903	9908	0	1	1	2	2
98	9912	9917	9921	9926	9930	9934	9939	9943	9948	9952	0	1	1	2	2
99	9956	9961	9965	9969	9974	9978	9983	9987	9991	9996	0	1	1	2	2

APPENDIX 5

SUPPLEMENTARY READING LIST

1. *General Physical Chemistry*

Glasstone, S., *Textbook of Physical Chemistry*, Van Nostrand, Princeton, N.J., 1946.

Hinshelwood, C. N., *The Structure of Physical Chemistry*, Oxford Press, London, 1951.

Moelwyn-Hughes, E. A, *Physical Chemistry*, 2nd ed., Pergamon, New York, 1964.

Moore, W. J., *Physical Chemistry*, 3rd ed., Prentice-Hall, Englewood Cliffs, N.J., 1962.

Noyes, A.A. and M.S. Sherrill, *A Course of Study in Chemical Principles*, Macmillan, New York, 1938.

Partington, J. R., *An Advanced Treatise on Physical Chemistry*, Vols. 1–5, David McKay, New York, 1949–55.

Rutgers, A. J., *Physical Chemistry*, Interscience, New York, 1954.

Taylor, H.S. and S. Glasstone, eds., *A Treatise on Physical Chemistry*, Vols. 1 and 2, Van Nostrand, Princeton, N. J., 1942, 1951.

2. *General Physical Chemistry—Mathematical Treatment*

Daniels, F., *Mathematical Preparation for Physical Chemistry*, McGraw-Hill, New York, 1928.

Guggenheim, E. A. and J. E. Prue, *Physicochemical Calculations*, Interscience, New York, 1955.

Margenau, H. and G. M. Murphy, 2nd ed., *The Mathematics of Physics and Chemistry*, Van Nostrand, Princeton, N.J., 1964.

Sillen, L. G., P. W. Lange, and C. O. Gabrielson, *Problems in Physical Chemistry*, Prentice-Hall, Englewood Cliffs, N.J., 1952.

Wolfenden, J. H., *Numerical Problems in Advanced Physical Chemistry*, Oxford Press, London, 1938.

3. *Thermodynamics*

Dole, M., *Introduction to Statistical Thermodynamics*, Prentice-Hall, Englewood Cliffs, N.J., 1954.

Fitts, D. D., *Nonequilibrium Thermodynamics*, McGraw-Hill, New York, 1962.

Klotz, I. M., *Chemical Thermodynamics*, W. A. Benjamin, New York, 1964.

Lewis, G. N. and M. Randall, *Thermodynamics and the Free Energy of Chemical Substances*, McGraw-Hill, New York, 1923. Revised by K. S. Pitzer and L. Brewer, 1961.

Rossini, F. D., *Chemical Thermodynamics*, Wiley, New York, 1950.

Rushbrooke, G. S., *Introduction to Statistical Mechanics*, Oxford Press, 1949.

Sears, F. W., *Thermodynamics, the Kinetic Theory of Gases, and Statistical Mechanics*, 2nd ed., Addison-Wesley, Reading, Mass., 1953.

Steiner, L. E., *Introduction to Chemical Thermodynamics*, McGraw-Hill, New York, 1941.

Wall, F. T., *Chemical Thermodynamics*, 2nd ed., Freeman, San Francisco, 1965.

4. *Phase Equilibria*

Carney, T. P., *Laboratory Fractional Distillation*, Macmillan, New York, 1948.

Findlay, A., A. N. Campbell, and N. O. Smith, *The Phase Rule and Its Applications*, 2nd ed., Dover, New York, 1951.

Hildebrand, J. H., and Scott, R. L., *The Solubility of Non-Electrolytes*, Reinhold, New York, 1950.

Ricci, J. E., *The Phase Rule and Heterogeneous Equilibrium*, Van Nostrand, Princeton, N.J., 1951.

5. *Electrochemistry and Electrolyte Solutions*

Glasstone, S., *An Introduction to Electrochemistry*, Van Nostrand, Princeton, N.J., 1942.

Harned, H. S. and B. B. Owen, *The Physical Chemistry of Electrolytic Solutions*, Reinhold, New York, 1943.

Latimer, W. M., *Oxidation Potentials*, 2nd ed., Prentice-Hall, Englewood Cliffs, N.J., 1952.

MacInnes, D. A., *The Principles of Electrochemistry*, Reinhold, New York, 1939.

6. *Surface and Colloid Chemistry*

Adam, N. K., *The Physics and Chemistry of Surfaces*, Oxford Press, London, 1941.

Adamson, A. W., *The Physical Chemistry of Surfaces*, Wiley, New York, 1960.

Alexander, A. E. and P. Johnson, *Colloid Science*, Oxford Press, London, 1949.

Dean, R. B., *Modern Colloids*, Van Nostrand, Princeton, N.J., 1948.

Mysels, K. S., *Introduction to Colloid Chemistry*, Wiley, New York, 1959.

Weiser, H. B., *A Textbook of Colloid Chemistry*, Wiley, New York, 1949.

7. *Chemical Kinetics*

Amis, E. S., *Kinetics of Chemical Change in Solution*, Macmillan, New York, 1949.

Benson, S. W., *Foundations of Chemical Kinetics*, McGraw-Hill, New York, 1960.

Caldin, E. F., *Fast Reactions in Solution*, Wiley, New York, 1964.

Frost, A. A. and R. G. Pearson, *Kinetics and Mechanism*, 2nd ed., Wiley, New York, 1961.

Glasstone, S., K. J. Laidler, and H. Eyring, *The Theory of Rate Processes*, McGraw-Hill, New York, 1941.

Laidler, K. J., *Chemical Kinetics*, 2nd ed., McGraw-Hill, New York, 1965.

Noyes, W. A. and P. A. Leighton, *The Photochemistry of Gases*, Reinhold, New York, 1941.

Rollefson, G. K. and M. Burton, *Photochemistry and the Mechanism of Chemical Reactions*, Prentice-Hall, Englewood Cliffs, N.J., 1939.

Steacie, E. W. R., *Free Radical Mechanisms*, Reinhold, New York, 1946.

Trotman-Dickinson, A. F., *Gas Kinetics*, Academic Press, New York, 1955.

8. *Atomic Structure*

Herzberg, G., *Atomic Spectra and Atomic Structure*, Dover, New York, 1941.
Richtmeyer, F. K. and E. A. Kennard, *Introduction to Modern Physics*, McGraw-Hill, New York, 1947.

Semat, H., *Introduction to Atomic and Nuclear Physics*, Holt, Rhinehart, & Winston, New York, 1962.

Sherwin, C. W., *Introduction to Quantum Mechanics*, Holt, Rhinehart, & Winston, New York, 1959.

Stranathan, J. D., *The Particles of Modern Physics*, Blakiston, Philadelphia, 1954.

9. *Molecular Structure*

Barrow, G. M., *Introduction to Molecular Spectroscopy*, McGraw-Hill, New York, 1962.

Brand, J. C. D. and J. C. Speakman, *Molecular Structure*, St. Martin's Press, New York, 1960.

Cartmell, E. and G. W. A. Fowles, *Valency and Molecular Structure*, Butterworth & Co., London, 1956.

Coulson, C. A., *Valence*, 2nd ed., Oxford Press, London, 1960.

Glasstone, S., *Theoretical Chemistry*, Van Nostrand, Princeton, N.J., 1944.

Herzberg, G., *Molecular Spectra and Molecular Structure*, 2 vols., Prentice-Hall, Englewood Cliffs, N.J., 1939.

Kauzmann, W. H., *Quantum Chemistry*, Academic Press, New York, 1957.

Linnett, J. W., *Wave Mechanics and Valency*, Methuen, London, 1960.

Orgel, L., *Transition Metal Chemistry*, Methuen, London, 1960.

Pauling, L., *The Nature of the Chemical Bond*, 3rd ed., Cornell University Press, Ithaca, N.Y., 1960.

Pauling, L. and E. B. Wilson, *Introduction to Quantum Mechanics*, McGraw-Hill, New York, 1935.

Pitzer, K. S., *Quantum Chemistry*, Prentice-Hall, Englewood Cliffs, N.J., 1954.

Reid, C. E., *Excited States in Chemistry and Biology*, Butterworth & Co., London, 1957.

Rice, O. K., *Electronic Structure and Chemical Binding*, McGraw-Hill, New York, 1940.

Rice, F. O. and E. Teller, *The Structure of Matter*, Wiley, New York, 1949.

Seitz, F., *Modern Theory of Solids*, McGraw-Hill, New York, 1940.

Wheatley, P. J., *The Determination of Molecular Structure*, Oxford Press, London, 1959.

Index